AF (Ret.)

)

First In, Last Out: Stories by The Wild Weasels

By

The Society Of Wild Weasels

authorHOUSE™
1663 Liberty Drive, Suite 200
Bloomington, Indiana 47403
(800) 839-8640
www.AuthorHouse.com

First published by AuthorHouse 02/10/05

ISBN: 1-4208-1620-9 (sc)
ISBN: 1-4208-1621-7 (dj)

Library of Congress Control Number: 2004099254

Printed in the United States of America
Bloomington, Indiana

This book is printed on acid-free paper.

Cover design by
Colonel (Ret.) Edward T. Rock

Photos Arranged by
Colonel (Ret.) Edward T. Rock

Stories by Wild Weasels and their Associates themselves.

First In, Last Out: Stories by the Wild Weasels

First Person Stories By Wild Weasel Pilots, EWOs and Their Associates

Lincoln 3, Medal of Honor Mission 10 March 1967
Merle Dethlefsen and Mike Gilroy
Painting by Joe Kline
Courtesy of Joe Kline(Atrist) and Mike Gilroy (Owner)

Edited by
Colonel Edward T. Rock, USAF (Ret.)

Mostly First Person Stories of the Wild Weasel Aircrews and Associates

By the Pilots, Electronic Warfare Officers, Maintenance Personnel and Others

Edited by
Colonel (Ret.) Edward T. Rock, Wild Weasel #185

For information contact:

rockjo19@ix.netcom.com

Acknowledgements

This book would not have happened at all without the active support of the Wild Weasel Board of Directors and particularly, George Acree the Chief Wild Weasels at the time we first proposed this effort (now Chief Wild Weasel Emeritus) and later Edward Ballanco, Chief Wild Weasel. It would not have been possible without the active participation and contributions made by Wild Weasel Aircrews and their associates. There are many that did not make contributions for whatever reason, some are no longer with us and their stories are, unfortunately, lost forever. Others may have their stories told in future Wild Weasel publications. For those that took the time and effort to tell your stories we thank you. Stories that are written down and published can last forever, or at least long after we are gone. To those that flew with us, maintained our aircraft, and supported us you made this book possible just as much as those that actually flew the missions…we thank you very much. It was an honor to have served with you. God bless you and your families.

Thanks are also due to the proofreaders and assistant editors whose help greatly enhanced the content and presentation of this publication, particularly Dr. John Grigsby and Colonel Dr. Phil (Quack Bear) Steeves. We thank several that sent in photos from their personal collections including Joe Telford, Robert E. (Bob) Dorrough, John Revack, Phil Steeves, John Grigsby, Billy Sparks, Allen Lamb, Stan Goldstein, Mike Gilroy, Bob King, George Shamblee and Jim Howard. We also thank Howard Plunket who supplied important historical information. Special thanks go to Joe Kline and Keith Ferris for granting permission to use their paintings on the covers of this book and to Dick Jonas for letting us use his poem "Will There Be A Tomorrow?"

Wild Weasel Crews

Dedication

To all Wild Weasels, and their families, past and present:
Especially to those that were killed in combat and also to the wives who remained true to their husbands while they were off gallivanting around the world in defense of their country and way of life.

LIFE IS A PROMISE; FULFILL IT.
Mother Theresa

LIFE IS NOT A JOURNEY TO THE GRAVE WITH THE INTENTION OF ARRIVING SAFELY IN A PRETTY AND WELL PRESERVED BODY, BUT RATHER TO SKID IN BROADSIDE, THOROUGHLY USED UP, TOTALLY WORN OUT, AND LOUDLY PROCLAIMING: WOW…. WHAT A RIDE!!!
Author: Unknown

Will There Be a Tomorrow?

For more than 58,000 who gave their all in Southeast Asia, there is no tomorrow — only eternity. Especially during 1965, 66, 67 and 68 and again in 1972, American fighter pilots, mostly F-105 aircrews, were paying the ultimate price. I know that on many days I surely wondered if there would be a tomorrow for me. When you were being scheduled to go to RP VI on every mission and you had been told that only 50% would survive, you often wondered if there would be a tomorrow. Many were killed in action and hundreds of others had their tomorrows interrupted by being taken a prisoner of war.

Edward T. Rock

Will There Be a Tomorrow?

by Dick Jonas

Can you say, will the sun rise tomorrow
Will there be any time left to borrow
Will the poet make a rhyme, will there be any time
Can you say will there be a tomorrow
Seems to me I have been here forever
Will this war ever end, maybe never
Will the dawn still arrive, will I still be alive
Or will I sleep alone here forever
There's someone who I'm sure, loves me only
She's the one on my mind, when I'm lonely
Does she know, can she see, is she still true to me
Does she know what it's like to be lonely
From the sea comes the sun, dawn is breaking
Soon the fight of my life, I'll be making

If I die over here, will they know, will they care
Will there be joy or hearts that are breaking
Can you say, will the sun rise tomorrow
Will there be any time left to borrow
Will the poet make a rhyme, will there be any time
Can you say will there be a tomorrow

Will There By A Tomorrow, by Dick Jonas is reprinted here courtesy of the author.

Table of Contents

Forward

We endeavored to obtain first person stories from a cross section of Wild Weasels and their associates from all eras including the F-100, Wild Weasel One, the F-105F/G, Wild Weasel Three, The F-4C/G, Wild Weasel Four and the F-16 Wild Weasel. We were successful in obtaining numerous stories from all eras except the F-16.

These stories are mostly from Wild Weasel pilots, and Electronic Warfare Officers (EWOs), and also from some of their associates including a Flight Surgeon, Chaplain, Maintance Officer and Technicians, Contractor, Strike pilots, Test and Evaluation Personal, and the wife of a pilot killed in action. All of the facts may not be totally accurate. Some kept copious records and photos of their experiences while many others are writing only from memory. It is, nonetheless, a true history of many Wild Weasel experiences in peace and war as recalled from the records and memories of the authors.

The Wild Weasels

Introduction

"Wild Weasel" was the code name for a group of intrepid warriors first deployed to Southeast Asia in 1965 during the Vietnam War. The mission of the Wild Weasels was to attack and destroy radar-directed antiaircraft systems, primarily the Fan Song (NATO code name for the Soviet designed, manufactured and often Soviet operated Surface-to-Air Missile system) radar and the SA-2 Guideline surface-to-air missile (SAM). The missions they flew were code named "Iron Hand". They normally preceded the strike force into the target area to suppress or destroy enemy defenses and they stayed until the strike force withdrew and then followed them out. They were "First In, Last Out" of the target area. The Wild Weasel mission continues to this day with newer aircraft, tactics and weapons.

SAM sites were first detected in North Vietnam on 5 April 1965. However, they were prohibited from attack by American forces. Washington apparently believed that they would not be used against American aircraft because it would be viewed by the United States as an unjustified escalation of the air war upon the part of the North Vietnamese and their Soviet Union and Communist Chinese backer and could result in a dramatic retaliation by American forces. Furthermore Washington believed that the US could very effectively deal with the SAM threat using traditional tactics, weapons and techniques, if required. The Soviets, on the other hand, and their North Vietnamese comrades believed that the SAM would be decisive in the air war and make it to costly for the Americans to operate in any area defended by their SA-2 surface to air missile system. Regardless, on 24 July 1965, the U.S. lost its first plane to a Soviet-built SAM (Surface-to-Air Missile). Washington had been completely wrong in their assessment of Communist intentions to use these then new weapons against US forces. The next month a U.S. Navy plane was lost to a SAM, and the U.S. began a series of special missions code named Iron Hand against the rapidly expanding missile sites. Most SAM sites were then located near the Hanoi/Haiphong area, but unbelievably Washington had exempted these from air attack. However, sites in other areas were fair game. By the end of 1965 a total of 56 SAM sites had been located by U.S.

reconnaissance aircraft. Although 56 sites were identified, only about 31 were ever occupied by active SA-2 missile systems at any one time.

The crucial component of this array of hardware was the **Fan Song** (NATO code name) radar, which detected airborne targets and guided Soviet **SA-2 Guideline** (NATO code name) SAMs to their objective. With a 195-kg (430lb) high-explosive warhead, a slant range of about 20 nautical miles and a maximum speed in excess of Mach 3, the SA-2 proved to be accurate and, without real time warning, difficult to detect and evade. Its liquid-fueled sustainer rocket motor left a long tongue of fire and a visible smoke trail easily detected by pilots in clear weather if they knew where to look for the missile in flight. In bad weather or when visibility was significantly reduced the missile was often difficult or impossible to detect until it was too late to take evasive action

When the SAM sites were first authorized for attack, traditional methods were employed to neutralize this new threat. Electronic and optical reconnaissance as well as pilot reports were used to identify occupied SAM sites. Once an occupied site was identified, an operations order would be sent out and some fighter Wing(s) would be tasked to strike the target. However, in nearly every instance, the sites were empty by the time the fighters arrived or they were occupied by dummy equipment made to appear as though they were in use by enemy forces. These dummy sites often served simply as flak traps for attacking aircraft. Regardless of how hard American forces tried, the enemy was often able to defeat our efforts to attack and destroy occupied SAM sites in North Vietnam when we used our traditional methods and tactics. What was needed was some means to identify active, occupied SAM sites in real time for immediate attack before they could be moved to a new location. Thus the Wild Weasel was born.

Ed Rock WW # 185

Chapter One

How It All Started

Story by Edward T. Rock WW # 185

In the Beginning

How it all Began

The North Vietnamese, with assistance from the Soviet Union, were first observed building surface-to-air missiles (SAM) sites near Hanoi in the spring of 1965. In fact US intelligence speculated that Soviet made SAMs, SAM operators and other technicians might be deployed in North Vietnam as early as February 65. A very high altitude U-2 reconnaissance aircraft finally photographed SAM installations actually under construction in April 65 and by July the sites formed a defensive perimeter around Hanoi, the capital of North Vietnam. Also, about 15 July 65 an RB-66 electronic reconnaissance aircraft then assigned to Takhli Royal Thai Air Base (RTAFB), Thailand detected an SA-2 Spoon Rest (NATO Code Name) SAM target acquisition radar. Then on 23 July 65 they detected a Soviet made SA-2 track-while-scan Fan Song (NATO Code Name) SAM radar. American political leaders decided that these sites could not be attacked for three primary reasons 1) Intelligence "experts" believed that Ho Chi Minh, the North Vietnamese leader, would not permit use of the SA-2 except in the case of extreme provocation, such as an invasion of North Vietnam. 2) Fear of killing Soviet SAM operators and other Soviet technicians that were helping the North Vietnamese to build, maintain and operate the SA-2 SAM System and 3) It was believed that the US could easily attack and destroy these SAM sites using traditional weapons and tactics. Soon we would be attacking many of these sites and yes, we did kill at least some Soviet technicians and no we were not successful using traditional weapons and tactics. US intelligence was, as all too often, wrong on nearly all counts.

An F-105 strike force was tasked to attack ground targets in North Vietnam on 24 July 65. They were escorted by two fights, eight aircraft, of F-4C MiG CAP (Combat Air Patrol) aircraft. The call signs of the F-4 MiG CAP were Leopard and Panther. They planned to cover the ingress and egress of the F-105 strike force and would engage any MiGs that might rise to challenge the strike force. They had intended that their route of flight would avoid all known SAM threats. They would enter North

Vietnam air space at an altitude of 23,000 feet well above the effective range of most anti-aircraft artillery (AAA) and few MiGs had been seen to date in the war. A "Milk Run" was anticipated.

The "Milk Run" belief was altered when the radio call "Bluebells Ringing, Bluebells Ringing," (some sources indicate the radio call was "Bluebells Singing") was broadcast from an RB-66 when they detected an SA-2 Fan Song SAM guidance radar! No SAMs were observed in flight at this time. However, about five minutes later the same RB-66 again broadcast, "Bluebells Ringing, Bluebells Ringing". Leopard flight was in the clouds and they were not monitoring the SAM warning frequency when the second warning was broadcast. All of a sudden Leopard 4 saw a long white missile trailing a bright orange/red flame climbing steeply toward the opposite side of his formation. The missile detonated almost immediately after it was first sighted. The force of the explosion flipped Leopard 2 upside down; the crew ejected shortly before the aircraft fell to pieces and the remainder of Leopard flight took evasive action and escaped destruction but suffered damage from other SAMs.

Leopard 2 was flown by Capt. Roscoe H. Fobar, pilot (KIA) and Capt. Richard P. Keirn, pilot systems operator (POW). They were assigned to the 47th TFS, 15 TFW and were flying out of Ubon RTAFB. Both Fobar and Keirn appeared to have ejected safely from their aircraft but only Keirn was released by the NVN on 12 Feb 73. The NVN reported that Fobar had died in captivity but refused to disclose the date or circumstances.

The Soviet designed, developed and manufactured SA-2 was first identified by NATO intelligence in 1953. Some predicted that this threat would be the end of the flying air force! A SAM had shot down Francis Gary Powers who was flying a U-2 very high altitude reconnaissance aircraft in 1960 and Major Rudolph Anderson, flying another U-2 was also shot down by an SA-2 during the Cuban Missile crisis in 1962. Clearly the SA-2 was a real threat to US aircraft but Tactical Air Forces took little notice and relied on low-level penetration and attack to gain protection against this then new threat.

In retaliation of the shooting down of Leopard 2 on 24 July 65, the SA-2 SAM sites came off the restricted list except for the still restricted "Golden Circles" around Hanoi and Haiphong. 27 July 65 saw the first Air Force strike attempted against the SA-2 and it turned out to be a complete disaster. 48 F-105s using low altitude tactics and weapons including napalm, CBU-2 bomblets and high drag bombs, attacked two SAM sites generally in the area 30 miles west of Hanoi, North Vietnam and not far from the banks of the Black River. During the attack six F-105 were lost and the targeted SAM sites turned out to be dummies or unoccupied. It was a flack trap. The enemy appeared to have been warned and were ready and waiting for the attack by American aircraft.

Wild Weasel One (WW 1)

The SAM was now obviously a serious threat to tactical forces, and traditional methods of attack were not working well, to say the least. Although the Soviet SAM threat was first identified by NATO intelligence 13 years before the first aircraft was lost over North Vietnam, little had been done by tactical forces to counter this then new threat. This was a clear failure in tactical thinking. In general it was thought that the SAM could be defeated or degraded to a great extent simply by flying at low altitude. The aircraft flying at low altitude would be lost in radar ground clutter and therefore could not be detected and tracked, or so it was thought. Low altitude penetration and weapons delivery were taught in all the Air Force fighter and bomber training courses, practiced religiously in operational units, prescribed in every major war plan and evaluated during operational readiness inspections (ORIs). Most weapons and aircraft (Bombers, Attack aircraft and Fighter Bombers) were designed around low altitude, high speed, penetration and weapons delivery concepts as the best defense against the SAM. In addition the routes of flight were planned to avoid known AAA and SAM threats to the maximum extent practical. Unfortunately, in North Vietnam, it became all too apparent that: 1) we did not know (or if intelligence sources knew they weren't telling operational units) where active SAM sites were located because they were often expertly camouflaged, rapidly relocated, and could not normally be found and attacked in a timely manner using traditional tactics and methods and 2) low altitude penetration and weapons delivery was a disaster because when you reached the target, terminal defenses could not be avoided and at low altitude you were in range of every weapon at the enemy's disposal including AAA, automatic weapons, aircraft, and barrage balloons, not to mention rifles, pistols and sticks and stones. In addition, intelligence estimates of SAM low altitude capabilities were completely wrong as indicated by the countless and constant pilot reports of SAMs tracking their aircraft when they were flying at low and very low altitudes.

In fact the Air Force had turned down a Bendix proposal submitted in early 1965 for the installation of Radar Homing and Warning (RHAW) equipment on the F-100F because "there was no requirement for it". But then on 13 August 1965, less than three weeks after the first Air force F-4 was shot down by a SAM, the Air Force formed a special anti-SAM task force (The Air Staff Task Force on Surface-to-Air Missiles in Southeast Asia) headed by then Brigadier General K. C. Dempster to study this "new" threat and to recommend ways to counteract it. In a period of 3 weeks, this special task force considered nearly 200 proposals!

The task force made several recommendations:

1. Modify a small number of fighters with electronic equipment to enable them to find active SAM sites. These aircraft would mark the active sites for destruction by accompanying strike aircraft.

2. Develop a missile that could be fired from a fighter and home on a radar emitter.

3. Develop jamming equipment [Electronic Countermeasures (ECM)] for carriage on fighter aircraft to counter the SAM radars

4. A radar homing and warning (RHAW) capability was needed immediately—a capability that would provide warning to the aircrews that a SAM radar was looking at them and provide some clue to its location.

In addition it is important to note that not long afterward the commanders of the Tactical Air Force (TAC), Pacific Air Force (PACAF), and United States Air Force Europe (USAFE) met in one of their periodic "Tri-Commanders" conferences and established a requirement for 25% of tactical fighters to be Wild Weasel configured.

To help meet this requirement Applied Technology Incorporated (ATI) was selected to provide the electronics that would constitute the initial Wild Weasel Radar Homing and Warning system as well as the tactical fighter Radar Warning Receiver (RWR). (See story "A Contractor's View," by Dr. John Grigsby also found in this book.) **Editor's Note**: The ATI APR-25/26 radar warning receivers would eventually be installed in all

INFO. COPY

CUSTOMER SALES ORDER

Change
Verbal
TWX
Confirm

Customer Project # 10105 Proposal # Proj. Engr. R. Johnson
Shop Order # Responsibility: Engineering

Customer: USAF
Address: Andrews AFB, Maryland
Buyer: Miss Jean Ryder
Tel. No. 202-981-2225 Ext.

CUSTOMER ORDER DATA
P.O. No. AF 18(600) 2879
Type of P.O. Fixed Price
Change No.
Verbal P. O. Received On
Conf. P. O. Expected On
Conf. P. O. Dated
Order Received By J. Reid

EQUIPMENT

Item No.	Qty.	Description	Delivery	Unit Price	Total Price
		First Vector-IR order First IR-133 order			
1.	2	Vector/IR-100 Systems as defined by discussions with contractor Work Statement to be supplied to ATI.	1 ea by 9/28/65 and second by 10/13/65		TBE (Order of magnitude $80,000)

DELIVERY INSTRUCTIONS
Ship to: TBE
Via
f.o.b.

BILLING
Bill to: TBE
No. of copies
Terms
Commission Due to
Commission Percent Amt.
ATI-20 (Rev 8/60)

MISCELLANEOUS
Q C Level
Inspection TBE
Packing TBE
D. O. Rating TBE
Proposal/P. O. compared for:
Price
Delivery
T & C
Copy of Proposal to: Admin.
Engrg.
Mfg.
Acctg.
Delivery follow-up Required XX
Expenditure Report Required Eng.
See attached special instructions
Prepared By D. F. Lacers Date 8/30/65
Approved By Date 8/31/65

First Air Force order for Wild Weasel Vector warning receiver and IR-133, panoramic receiver for F-100F, WW I aircraft. Note that delivery date for first system is less than one month from date of order and the cost was $80,000. Courtesy of Dr. John Grigsby

The F-100F was selected for the first "Wild Weasel" aircraft and was configured with the ATI Vector Homing and Warning System, which included the IR-133 Panoramic Scan Receiver and the WR-300 Receiver. A highly experienced and well-qualified F-100 pilot would fly the F-100F, and the RHAW system would be operated primarily by an experienced and highly qualified Electronic Warfare Officer (EWO) located in the rear cockpit of the F-100F. The operation was designated Wild Weasel 1 (WW 1). The operation was first going to be code-named "Mongoose" but when it was found that this name was already taken, the code name Wild Weasel was chosen. The WW 1 aircrews were pilots: Gary Willard, Commander, Robert Swartz, Operations Officer, Maurice Firckie, George "Shep" Kerr, Allen Lamb, Leslie Lindenmuth, John Pitchford, and Ed White. The EWOs were: John (Jack) Donovan, Truman (Walt) Lifsey, Don Madden, Ed Sandelius and Bob Trier.

The Vector system provided 360° warning by threat frequency band. An S band threat was displayed as a solid line, a C band signal was displayed as a dotted line, and an X band threat was displayed as a dashed line. The signals were displayed on a small 3" azimuth warning scope [cathode ray tube (CRT)] and the direction of the strobe indicated the direction of the threat. The length of the strobe gave some indication of threat range and level of threat. A long strobe indicated a near threat along with a high probability that you were the target. A short strobe indicated either that the threat was probably out of range or that you were not in the main beam of the enemy radar and therefore not the intended target. Until very late in 1972 or early 1973 all AAA and SAM threats in SEA operated in the S band. Additionally the Vector System contained a warning panel which had a group of warning lights that indicated whether the displayed signals were from a SAM, AAA, or Airborne Interceptor (AI). If both SAM and AAA radars were on the air at the same time, there was no way to differentiate between the various S band strobes displayed on the azimuth warning scope until a SAM missile was actually launched. If a SAM was launched, then the azimuth strobe associated with the threat was supposed to blink at 3 cycles per second. I can say that I probably had more than 100 SAM missiles launched at my aircraft and never, not even once, saw the strobe blinking. Probably busy with more important things like saving my life.

The IR-133 was located in the rear cockpit of the aircraft and operated by the EWO. All signals in S band, which included AAA, SAM and some Ground Controlled Intercept (GCI)/Early Warning (EW) radars, could be analyzed by frequency which helped tell the crew if the signal was from a SAM, AAA or some other type of emitter. The EWO could also determine if the SAM signal was in a search, track, missile launch or missile guidance mode. In addition the EWO could compare the signal strength on each side of the aircraft and tell the pilot to turn left or right to even out the signal strength and home on the target emitter. Unfortunately there was no way to obtain accurate range to the emitter and this problem plagued the Wild Weasels throughout the war in SEA.

The WR-300 provided SAM launch warning by monitoring the SA-2 guidance and control frequency. When the receiver detected a missile launch it illuminated a bright red LAUNCH warning light on the same warning panel that indicated whether the threat was from a SAM, AAA, or AI radar.

The equipment was installed in the F-100F primarily because the aircraft was immediately available. This turned out to be a mistake because the F-100 was not compatible with the F-105 (then the primary Air Force strike aircraft used in SEA) in speed or range. The F-100F Wild Weasel configuration was designated Modification 1778. The electronic equipment would be installed and operated primarily by the EWO in the rear cockpit. Under this concept the EWO would concentrate on the identification and location of threat radars, especially the SA-2 SAM system. The pilot would concentrate on flying the aircraft, navigation, searching visually for the SAM sites, marking the sites for follow-on attack by strike aircraft and taking evasive action against threats as necessary. Initial F-100F aircraft conversion to the Wild Weasel configuration took place at Long Beach International Airport. Initial flight-testing and aircrew training was conducted principally at Eglin AFB, FL and was successfully completed on 19 November 65.

On 20 November 1965 the test team departed Eglin AFB for Korat RTAFB, Thailand just less than 100 days after Leopard 2 had been shot down by an SA-2 over North Vietnam. This was a truly extraordinary accomplishment by any measure.

The Wild Weasel 1 operational test and evaluation (OT & E) continued at Korat RTAFB, Thailand, from 28 November 65 until 26 January 66. The general purpose was to evaluate the Wild Weasel 1 equipment and tactics in a combat environment.

The stated objectives were:

1.) "To determine the warning capability of RHAW equipment installed in the Wild Weasel F-100F."

2.) "To investigate the effect of jamming, by friendly aircraft, on Vector and IR-133 equipment."

3.) "To determine the homing accuracy of the RHAW equipment and the capability of the crew to place the aircraft within visual range of the target."

4.) "To develop tactics for employing the Wild Weasel aircraft against SAM defense systems."

5.) "To determine maintenance requirements and reliability of RHAW equipment."

6.) "To determine the organization and manning requirements for Wild Weasel operations."

7.) "To determine training requirements for flight crews and RHAW maintenance personnel."

8.) "To test any additional equipment which may be made available for this system during the period of the operational test and evaluation."

The first Wild Weasel 1 missions in SEA were orientation missions flown along with RB/B-66 aircraft when they were performing their regularly scheduled electronic countermeasures (ECM) and ELINT missions. The objectives of these missions included area orientation, observation of the Wild Weasel equipment in a real world jamming environment, and verification of capabilities of the RHAW gear as determined during the Eglin test phase.

In general the Wild Weasel gear operated essentially the same as it had at Eglin and the electronic countermeasures jamming from the RB/B-

66C had no significant effect on the Wild Weasel equipment in a typical operational scenario.

Accuracy of the system when attempting to home on a radar emitter was very difficult to accurately assess in an SEA combat environment. During Eglin OT & E an average accuracy of 77 feet had been measured when the F-100F over-flew the target radar emitter. During combat it was found that due to the expert use of heavy and very effective camouflage, enemy SAM sites were extremely difficult to find even when electronic equipment indicated that the emitter had been over-flown. This very effective use of enemy camouflage was unexpected. On at least two missions the site could not be identified even after the Wild Weasel equipment indicated that the emitter location had been directly over-flown. On another occasion the F-100F pilot saw the missiles in the SA-2 radar complex under thatched roofs and fired 2.75-inch rockets to mark the target area. However, his wingman never did identify the SAM site but fired his rockets into the marked target area just the same. In practice the SAM site was very often not found until after it had fired its first salvo of missiles when the dust and debris from the projectile launch highlighted the occupied site.

Wild Weasel 1 Iron Hand missions were of two general types. First, the Wild Weasels would accompany the strike force with the objective of destroying or neutralizing any SA-2 threats to the strike force. However, the Wild Weasels were also permitted to strike targets of opportunity going to or from the primary target area. Second, were "search and destroy missions" where Wild Weasels were directed to search particular geographic areas and to home on and destroy any occupied SAM sites found in that area. These missions were often conducted in coordination with a missions carrying out strikes in the same general target area, the objective being to get the enemy to turn on his radar so that it could be detected and homed on, attacked and destroyed by Wild Weasel lead forces.

Edward T. Rock, WW # 185

Story By Billy Sparks (Once Charlie Foxtrot Three), WW # 330

Iron Hand One – How To Become Disillusioned

A little background is probably required before I present my cautionary tale about the first attack ever against Surface-To-Air Missile (SAM) sites, Iron Hand One. I was born near Hardyville in central Kentucky 7 Dec 1934, grew up in Louisville, graduated from Indiana University in 1957, and upon graduation was commissioned as a Second Lieutenant, USAF. I received my Wings in November 1958 at Webb AFB, Texas and went to Luke AFB, Arizona for F-100 training. After completing F-100 training at Nellis AFB, Nevada, I was assigned to the 8th Squadron, 49th Tactical Fighter Wing at Spangdahlem for four years. We were equipped with the F-105 in '61. My next assignment was to McConnell AFB, Kansas where I was assigned to the 563rd Squadron, 23rd Tactical Fighter Wing. By 1965, I had over 1300 hours in Fighters, had been an Instructor Pilot in F-105's for 3 years, had been on Test Pilot orders for both the F-100 and F-105, had been my squadron's Weapons officer for over 4 years in both the 8th Squadron and the 563rd. I do not imply that my excrement was not odorous, rather to suggest that I did have a reasonable amount of expertise in Fighter Tactics and Weapons employment. I did finish first in my class at the USAF Fighter Weapons a year later. I celebrated my 30th birthday on Pearl Harbor Day, 1964.

The 563rd was put on alert for a deployment to Takhli Royal Thai Air Force Base, Thailand in March 1965. Our new Squadron Commander was Major Jack Brown who had completed two combat tours in Europe during WWII and had also flown a combat tour in Korea. Major Brown had been one of the Top Guns at Nellis for several years. Our Operations Officer, Major Everett Wayne Harris, was very competent and ran Operations extremely well. Our Flight Commanders were less grounded in Tactics since they had only recently been assigned to Tactical Fighters, but took excellent care of their flights. About 50% of our pilots had come from Tactical Fighters and four of us had between 600 and 1,000 hours in the F-105. We were about average in experience for Tactical Air Command (TAC) at that time. The entire Squadron, 20 F-105Ds, left for Takhli on 13

Apr 65. We all arrived at Takhli after one night in Hawaii and two nights in Guam on 17 Apr since the dateline ate a day. We had 18 F-105Ds when we arrived and 24 squadron pilots total. Two spares went from Guam to Yakota as replacements for their wing.

Takhli had been occupied by only about 50 USAF personnel to maintain the 'USAF' side of the base. The Yokota Wing had kept one squadron at Takhli for over six months. They had, I think, the 36th there when we arrived. The first night we slept on the floor of the small Officers Club while we waited for the barracks to be completed. Takhli had no Operations people assigned and there were no personnel to man a command section. Jack Brown and the Yokota Squadron commander worked out a plan for a pseudo Operations section. The 563rd would run Ops on odd numbered days and the Yakota squadron would run Ops on even numbered days. It worked very well for the four months we were there. The Yakota Squadrons rotated every 30 days from Japan to Takhli and back. We flew with almost everyone from there and had zero friction. We had no Command Headquarters at Takhli until much later in '65.

Four of us from the 563rd flew on the second day we were there. I flew my first combat mission as number two on the wing of the 36th Tactical Fighter Squadron Commander. We had four people 'checked out' that day and the next day we four again flew with the 36th as element leads with a 563rd pilot as our wingman. We had all of our flight leaders checked out in three days and were on our own.

We lost our first pilot on day three; a Captain with over 2,000 hours of TAC time flew into the ground on a Rocket pass in Laos. It was the start of a very interesting tour. We flew between 12 and 24 sorties almost every day depending on the assignments from 2nd Air Division (2AD) who had Operational Control of all USAF aircraft in Southeast Asia (SEA) until 7th Air Force (7AF) was established late in '65. We were starting to relearn the lessons from WWII and Korea.

In early May, Al Logan landed from a mission near Hanoi and reported that A SAM SITE was being built about 25 miles south of Hanoi! My reply was that "We get all the technology and they get all the Elephants. They're cheating." Russ Violette and I both flew to the area that afternoon and somebody was indeed building a SAM site. We went to our boss, Major Brown, and reported our concerns. Jack took a flight to the same area early the next morning and found the site. He called all of us together and told us to get a plan ready to kill the site and left the next day for Saigon. He returned two days later with his tail between his legs, carrying a message to not fly with-in five miles of ANY SAM site. The word was not to 'disturb' any activity because it might anger the Russians who were doing the construction. A few days later, a directive came down from 2AD ordering everyone to not over-fly or disturb any SAM activity in North Vietnam (NVN). The penalty for noncompliance would be courts-martial.

Takhli received a squadron of EB-66 aircraft in May who had the mission to track all electronic activity in the North. The EB-66 had four Electronic Warfare Officers (EWOs) in each bomb bay with downward ejection seats. It was an under-powered, old, creaky aircraft, but they did a hell of a job that has never been properly recognized. Our B-66 friends kept track of the SAM activity and reported daily the progress in building missile sites in the North. We continued to receive directives not to bother the Russians. The number and activity of the SAMs continued to increase.

My Flight Commander, an Edwards Test Pilot type with almost no operational time, was killed on a mission in Laos. His replacement was Captain Paul Craw, AKA Charlie Chicken Expletive-deleted, one of the very best, most aggressive, natural Fighter Jocks ever born. Paul was a firm believer in flying with the same people every mission. He was mean enough and strong enough to make it happen. D-Flight became 'Charlie Foxtrot' Flight and flew 39 consecutive missions together. Paul Craw was lead, Kyle Berg was Two, I was Three, and Marty Case flew as Four. We grew to be very competent, totally confident in each other, and were sure that Charlie Foxtrot Flight was the meanest SOB in the valley.

The reports from the B-66 EWOs continued to convince us that the SAMs were ready to shoot at any time. By the first week of July '65, the EWOs announced that all of the SAM component systems were operating, had been checked out, and were fully operational. At that time 2AD issued a code phrase to be used when a SAM was being launched, 'Bluebells are Singing'. They also reiterated the ban on any attempt to take out the threat. To say that we were nervous is an understatement.

On July 24, Paul was leading the Charlie Foxtrots south of Hanoi after having hit a target nearby. I heard a B-66, on guard channel, saying,

"Bluebells are Singing, repeat, Bluebells are Singing, south of Hanoi." I was on Paul's left wing looking north and saw a Guideline Missile, followed by a second, lift off and climb into the clouds at about 5,000 feet. The Russians had finished the checkout of their systems. The target for the SAMs was a flight of F-4C aircraft from Ubon that were in close formation penetrating the weather. The F-4 flight had switched off guard channel and were hit with no warning. One aircraft was blown away and the other three were badly damaged. The damaged birds managed to make it back to Udorn and land. It is amazing that all were not lost. The missile is 20 feet long, smokes along at almost MACH 3, and has a 500-pound warhead.

The restrictions on hitting SAMs remained in effect and we were restricted from flying within 40 miles of Hanoi. This was a totally stupid reaction that deserves to be questioned by anyone with any knowledge of the use of force. Two days later Paul brought a clipping from the Bangkok paper quoting McNamara. The main point was that "We can take out the Surface-to-Air threats at any time we desire." The quote also contained the coordinates of two sites that had fired. In the same article Dr Strange stated that we had too many fighter pilots and that we should reduce the number. Paul commented on the article in rather foul language and pointed out that a good way to reduce the number of fighter pilots was to print where they were going. We also couldn't understand why TWO sites when only one had fired.

I was told that a message was delivered to the South Vietnamese Headquarters by DOD directive on July 25 that listed, in detail, two SAM sites to be attacked, date and times, route of flight to and from each target, ordnance, speeds, and altitudes that would be flown. Since anything given to the South Vietnamese would be in Hanoi in hours, I am convinced that any such directive constitutes at least Dereliction of Duty, if not Treason since 2AD, and everyone else in Saigon, knew of the leaks from the South Vietnamese HQ.

About 0600 on 27 July 1955, I had a hand shake me awake and tell me that I didn't need to get up for my scheduled mission brief since I was now on Iron Hand One, the first SAM raid. I pretended to be asleep for as long as possible to be cool and then went to the CRUB for a breakfast martini with Paul. We left for INTELL as soon as we could and found the mission order. It was the absolute most incredible bunch of crap imaginable. The 563rd was to hit a SAM site, the one that had fired three days earlier, using three flights of four F-105Ds in trail with only one-mile spacing between flights. The ordnance listed was rear-dispensed bomblets (CBU-2) dropped from 50 feet and at 360 knots. My Grandmother knew more about targeting than that! The next two flights were ordered to carry Napalm and also drop from 50 feet and 360 knots. The idiocy of DOD was now apparent to all. If you tell anyone that you are going to hit him and then give him almost a week's notice, any half-wit can figure out that the place will be empty and/or well defended. To over-fly an extremely well defended complex at 50 feet and 360 knots is a suicide order. The Japanese had better sense when they sent out their Kamikaze. To exacerbate an already insane order, have all aircraft fly at the same altitude, airspeed and attack from the same direction, with close intervals. I may have been a Slick Wing Captain, but I certainly knew better that that. HQ USAF, HQ PACAF, and 2AD all passed this load of excrement down without demur. I had been taught that you were supposed to, or at least try to, keep some of your troops alive.

We truly bitched, whined and moaned. Major Brown got on the horn and tried to talk to Saigon at least three times. The Yakota Squadron Commander also gave it his best shot, all to no avail. What we asked was to change the ingress and egress, change the altitudes, and drop at atleast 500 knots. At no time did we ever request not to hit the site. We were ordered to go as directed WITH ZERO CHANGES! The 563rd was ordered to have 12 aircraft hit the SAM site and 12 aircraft from the Yakota squadron were to hit the 'Supporting Barracks'. Korat had the same order for a SAM site less than 10 miles from ours. The Time-on-Target (TOT) for both sites were the same and the directed routes to and from insured that we would be almost head on with the Korat aircraft. It appeared that DOD also tried to schedule a mid-air collision.

We realized that we could comply with the order or mutiny, so we went to the squadron and briefed this insanity. Major Brown led the first flight, Major Harris led the second, and Paul was leader of the last flight, Hudson. All of the wingmen were volunteers. Paul never spent much time on routine details and this day his briefing was very brief. He said, "Well, we're going to takeoff with four. I wonder how many will land? Let's look at the photography and figure out what the hell we might be able to salvage." Jack Brown stuck his head in and told us to screw the airspeed restriction and to hold 540 knots from our letdown point to the target. We completed what little we could do and suited up for the debacle.

Takhli was most fortunate to have an outstanding Chaplain, Father Frank McMullen. Father Mac started the Takhli tradition of blessing, complete with sprinkling, every aircraft that took off anytime day or night. This day Father Mac, who often attended our briefings and flew with the B-66 guys, came to the line and blessed each pilot before takeoff. He climbed up the ladder of my Thud just before start engine time and gave me absolution along with his blessing. I was raised as a Methodist and was definitely not used to a guy wearing a shawl to either bless or absolve me. I decided that I needed all the help I could get and was truly thankful for the gesture. We launched on time and headed north.

We flew into central Laos at 28,000 feet and then let down to 50', held 540 knots, and headed for our Initial Point (IP), Yen Bai, on the Red River. In July '65, Yen Bai had more guns than Hanoi, yet, it was a mandatory checkpoint in the tasking message. DOD strikes again. Paul did not over-fly Yen Bai since he is at least as smart as a chicken and we hit the Red River at 50 feet and started for the target two miles behind the second flight.

Almost immediately we started to have 37MM flak burst directly over our flight path. 37MM guns do not have a fuse that will detonate on proximity, ergo, all of the rounds had to have been manually set to detonate at a fixed time that corresponded with the range from gun to target. It was absolutely obvious that they knew we were coming and at what route. The reason that the 37MM rounds were high was that the guns could not be depressed any more. We flew either down the Red River or over its edges for about 40 miles, always with 37MM bursting over us. When we hit the confluence of the Red and Black Rivers, we left the river and flew over rice paddies for the next 25 miles to the SAM site. A B-66 took a picture looking down on one of our flights and they were leaving rooster tails in the paddies. We started to take hits from small arms and 50-caliber equivalent Automatic Weapons as soon as we left the river. I was hit 12 times between the IP and target, all small caliber. As we neared the SAM site, we came under fire from the 37MM and 57MM weapons that had been brought in to protect the site. We counted over 250 37mm and 57MM guns and a horde of Automatic Weapons around each site when we finally got the post-strike photography. Korat's experience was similar to ours. We underwhelmed them a ton. I saw what looked like a Missile propped up against a pole and a couple of huts in the cleared area of the site when we were about a mile out. There were no vans or other service equipment normal to a SA-2 site. Surprise, Surprise, it was a dummy site! It was hard to see much since Jack Brown's flight had hit the area with eight CBU-2s with all 19 tubes dispensing bomblets. Major Harris' flight had dropped 24 Napalm cans. We dropped 24 more cans into the mess. As our first flight hit the target, Walt Kosko, flying TWO was hit and only made it back to the Black River before he had to punch out. As I dropped, I saw Kyle Berg's aircraft on fire from in front of the inlets past the 'burners. The aircraft slowly pulled up, rolled right and went in. Marty Case, who had gone through Cadets with Kyle, called "Bailout, Bailout" and then "No way, he went in!" Paul started to pull up through a hail of bursting flak to cover Kyle and both Marty and I yelled at him to stay down and get the hell out of Dodge. Paul stayed on the deck, accelerated to 600 and wheeled for the Black. We passed Major Jack Brown as he was trying to CAP Walt's 'chute in the water. He ordered both Paul and Major Harris to go home. He stayed to see if Walt could be found, solo for 30 minutes, went out to a tanker, and returned for another 30 minutes, still all alone. Walt was never recovered.

We stayed low past the Black and then climbed to 35,000 feet and flew back to Takhli. For the first time in my life, I completely lost all control of myself. I bawled, raved, beat the canopy, and totally acted like a fool. I have never been so very angry. Luckily, I could put the Thud on Autopilot and indulge my childish behavior. I finally got myself under control about the time we crossed back into Thailand. In the meantime, I heard various radio calls indicating that Korat had lost four F-105s. We had lost at least two Thuds. We actually lost six aircraft in less than three minutes, all for dummy targets that had been listed in the New York Times a week earlier. I was so damned angry, I was spluttering. I am still almost as angry now as I was then.

Kosko, Farr, and Barthelmas were all killed. Berg and Purcell were alive, captured, and spent an eternity in Prison. A Rescue helicopter picked up Tullo from East of the Black River and took him to Laos. I'm not sure what happened to the RECCE drivers. To drive the spike in a bit further, Kyle told me in '73, after he was released, that I had rolled some Napalm under him before he hit the ground. I had a major problem with the Thud losses that day. The F-105 community was small and we knew most of the drivers or knew someone who knew them. Jack Farr had been in the 8th Squadron with me for nearly three years. Kyle and Walt were also at Spangdahlem the same time. Purcell was from Louisville and Black Matt and I had been friends for over two years. It was a very bad day at Black Rock.

Paul landed at Takhli with three Charlie Foxtrots and we counted holes. Of the twelve 563rd aircraft that went on the mission, two were shot down, nine had multiple holes and only one was not hit. My aircraft, 169, had 12 holes and was one of only four flyable aircraft the squadron had the next day. When I parked my bird, the first one up the ladder was Father Mac. He handed me a French 75, slightly warm, blessed me again and kissed my forehead. I told him that if he ever came up my ladder again, I would jump off and abort. He laughed and said, "It worked, didn't it? Be thankful!"

I joined Paul and Marty for an INTELL debriefing and noticed that the Intelligence folk seemed to be afraid of us. We were on a short fuse and irked at everyone. We grabbed a jug of 'Old Overshoes', mission whiskey, away from the poor Lieutenant and waded through the debriefing. We then went to the squadron and covered the mission taking the Old Overshoes.

Paul said that he would never again allow anyone to dictate such a stupid set of rules. Marty and I agreed. I promised myself that I would never, ever allow anyone, regardless of rank, to waste so many folk. I owed it to the people I flew with to take better care of them than that. Every one of us would have volunteered to go on a mission to whack SAMs. To be thrown away by idiots is another thing. I flew my second tour as a Wild Weasel and never allowed anyone to put my flight in that kind of a bind. Rank or position can not excuse incompetence. I decided that being promoted mattered much less than caring for my troops. What was anyone going to do to me, make me fly to Hanoi?

I just noticed that today, 26 July 2004, as I compose this cautionary piece, is 39 years, to the day, since I flew on Iron Hand One and became disillusioned with my own service (It was 26 July in the US). I have tried for all this time to determine what went wrong. It has become commonplace for Senior Officers, from all services, to blame everything on Robert Strange. That is the cheap way out. Iron Hand One came down from DOD as a package. McNamara's band planned it by using a book that listed the probabilities of each weapon to kill a SAM complex. All they looked at were the estimated probability of kill for a SAM site for a long list of weapons. They chose the ordnance that gave the best probability of kill. It computed to be 99.999999% for the numbers and types they selected. Zero thought went into routes, altitudes, vulnerabilities and all of the things that even a Captain must consider before planning a trip to the head. I am not apologizing for McNamara, he was a conceited ass; however, where were the USAF Staff people when they received that mess? Not one person ever fell on his sword, not one Flag Rank ever acknowledged that they didn't question the order for Iron Hand One, and no one ever paid any penalty for those names that went on the wall. My own service showed that they cared more for themselves than for the troops in the field. The actions of the General Staff and the Flag Ranks below the Pentagon with Command Authority were derelict in their duty to us. They continued to act the same way for the next 10 years. I hold the majority of my own service's Senior Officers from that era in contempt. They did nothing to help the combat aircrew. The seeds of the change in the way the USAF operates today all started with Iron Hand One.

I do not include all Senior Officers in that indictment. In '67, for example, Takhli had Colonel John Giraudo, Colonel Larry Pickett, and Colonel Bob White as the Command Section and they were all devoted to their men. Colonel Robin Olds at Ubon had a Command Section equally as good. I doubt that there could be any better examples any time. Seventh Air Force in Saigon was a whole different kettle of fish. As far as I know, very few there ever tried to understand the world we lived in. Until Colonel White went down to run the 'Out of Country' shop, there had been no one in that shop that had ever been to North Vietnam.

Two of my best friends, Al Logan and Russ Violett, both graduated from the USAF with Two Buttons and both worked their rears off to make a difference. Korat had some outstanding folk as interested as anyone in making changes. Captain Chuck Horner flew on Iron Hand One and later did his second tour as a Wild Weasel at Korat. I cannot speak for General Horner, but I remember Captain Horner and Major Horner being as adamant as I am about the duty owed to your troops. The Gulf under Lieutenant General Horner was a far cry from Korat and Takhli under 2AD in '65 or 7AF in '67. Some other flag officers were not at all like Chuck Horner.

I am sure that the deep-seated feelings of any single officer matters little; however, I am speaking for a significant part of a whole generation of officers that distrusted their Senior Commanders. We had some very good Leaders. Most were Commanders and Managers rather than leaders. The workers in the squadrons distrusted most of them. Very few had the stature of Robin Olds at Ubon. My generation provided the nucleus of dedicated Officers that led to the Gulf and today's totally different Air Force. It does matter to have the Jocks trust their seniors. In '66, McConnell had over 30% of our troops leave the USAF after their first tour in SEA. Why? The men were very tired of duplicity, lack of support, and cover-up of munition and fuse problems. The biggest problem there was lack of leadership at the squadron level. The squadron that replaced the 563rd had 15 of the 18 pilots that made it back tender their resignations for that very reason.

It has been 39 years and I still am saddened and disillusioned by the first SAM raid. I only hope that enough people will remember that debacle and work to eliminate the self-serving mind set that caused it to happen.

Bill Sparks, Once Charlie Foxtrot Three, WW # 330

Story by Michael P. Cooper, Thud Driver

Navy/Air Force Joint Iron Hand

(One of The First Destructions of a NVN SAM site by USAF Forces!)

This narrative relates to the circumstances of a joint Air Force and Navy effort to suppress North Vietnam's surface-to-air missile threat for a specific U.S. Navy air strike on/near Kep Air Field on 31 October 1965.

I was an experienced combat flight leader assigned to the 334th Tac Ftr Sq, TDY to Takhli RTAFB, Thailand and flying the F-105D at that time. We had yet to have any radar homing and warning gear (RHAW) installed in any of the three F-105 squadrons at Takhli.

The plan was for a U.S. Navy A-4E, with RHAW gear, to act as a pathfinder to locate and mark one or more SA-2 missile sites for destruction by eight USAF F-105s in coordination with the Navy's Kep strike force.

Lt Cmdr Dick Power, XO, VA-164, off the USS Oriskany, led two A-4E aircraft to Takhli on the previous day. We had the pleasure to share an informal social hour and meal that evening. This brave warrior conveyed an air of confident professionalism then and throughout the entire episode. He had a higher level of experience and knowledge of his radar homing gear than most of his contemporaries.

A standard "last meal" steak and egg breakfast was had early the next morning. I never liked that deal. Somebody got shot down every time I ate that meal. Sometimes more than one.

Capt Dale Williams, 562nd Tac Ftr Sq and I were selected to lead individual flights of four F-105Ds in support of this mission. Our loads were 8 X 750 pound, M-117 bombs plus 2 X 450 gallon drop tanks each. Commander Power's A-4 was max loaded with Mk-82, 500 pound "Snakeye", high drag bombs. His call sign was "Magic Stone". Our flight call signs were cars, as were all Takhli F-105s in those days (i.e., Dodge, Ford, Chevy, Cadillac…). I have long forgotten which car we were.

One of the scheduled KC-135 tankers was configured with a drogue to facilitate the A-4's, probe only, refueling system. Cmdr. Power had never refueled from the KC-135. I don't think he had ever refueled to max gross weight either; however, he had no problem with in-flight refueling. He was briefed on the possibility of needing to call for descent (Toboggan) to maintain tanker contact, but that never occurred. We extended his northbound tanker track somewhat north of the Plaine de Jares because he agreed to carry higher than his normal speeds for better compatibility, hence higher fuel burn.

We all agreed on our ingress route which was to be medium altitude to the Red River, Northwest of Yen Bai, descent to low level in the mountains, eastbound to a prominent check point north of the Thai-Nguyen steel mill. We all felt that staying low in the mountains, as long as possible, was the best way to go. As we turned south toward the plains and our designated SA-2 trolling area, cloud ceilings deteriorated to a point where we were now an A-4 leading eight heavy, slow (420 knots) F-105s, in very loose trail, through the mountain passes, in the soup. Very scary indeed! What a relief to break out into the clear plains merely to get shot at. No sweat!

Our valiant leader called RHAW activity and turned eastward toward Kep airfield and the attack. My flight was trailing, so when we broke out in the flats, I stayed southbound long enough and made a large outside eastward turn to get to our pop-up velocity of nearly 600 knots which was our combat speed comfort zone.

We didn't have to wait long. As luck would have it, an SA-2 site that the leader and his other flight members had just passed fired two missiles harmlessly westward, clearly marking their position. Since it was Halloween, I thought it was appropriate when my number three, John Stell, called, "There rises the Great Pumpkin". We immediately popped up to 8000 feet for our standard, random heading, dive bomb attack. Our bombs were on target. I broke back hard down to the deck for egress as briefed. As our attack was terminating, Dale Williams and the 562nd were attacking a second SAM site marked by Dick Power. Sadly, someone in that flight was also calling that the A-4 was going down on fire.

Commander Powers was seen to begin his attack on the SAM site at an altitude of about 150 feet, to release his high drag "Snakeye" bombs on the target, and mark the site for attack by the F-105s. During the bomb run, AAA hit him and his aircraft burst into flames. The aircraft was observed to climb for a short distance, but then it banked suddenly and Powers ejected at an altitude of about 200 feet. He was observed safely on the ground and waved to others in his flight to indicate he was OK. Radio contact was not made and further search and rescue efforts were not attempted due to the location of the shoot down. In spite of the fact that he had been seen alive and well on the ground, no further word was ever heard about Powers' fate from the NVN until May 1987 when some remains were handed over to the US and later identified to include those of Powers. He was posthumously awarded the Navy Cross for his actions on this mission.

Our pre-planned egress was "feet wet" north of Haiphong, then south to home, Da Nang, or whatever conditions dictated. Stell was badly shot up, but no fire. He lost utility hydraulics, "PC #1", and other stuff. Jim Butler, #2, and Lee Adams (RIP), #4, were also hit, but not so badly. I had dodged a few bullets one more time! The element recovered at Da Nang, and Butler and I went home. We had the sad duty to inform the young Navy Lieutenant of the loss of his remarkable leader. He returned alone to the Oriskany, broken hearted.

The next day, Dale Williams and I flew down to Saigon to debrief the "wheels" and to give a press brief. At that time, there was yet no photographic BDA (bomb damage assessment) from our strike. We were informed that the undamaged equipment and other materials from both sites had been moved and relocated.

This was the first successful joint USN/USAF destruction of North Vietnamese SAM sites by American forces during the Vietnam War.

Michael P. Cooper, Lt. Col., USAF Ret.

Story by Dr. John L. Grigsby WW# 231

A Contractor's View

Preface

The morning of January 4, 1964, a Saturday, dawned clear and bright. This was to be the big day for the move of Applied Technology, Inc., from the "garages" of Industrial Avenue in Palo Alto, CA, to our brand-new building in the Stanford Industrial Park. We were moving from 15,600 square-feet of space to 31,000 square-feet on two floors. In mid-1963, we had signed a 51-years-lease for 5 acres from Stanford for $25,000 an acre. The lease cost and the building construction resulted in an acquisition cost of approximately $660,000, a rather princely sum for small company in those days.

We had spent the two days after New Years day packing all of the boxes with the contents of desk drawers; packing up piece parts and engineering - and manufacturing - drawings; disconnecting all of the electrically powered machines; and, of course, labeling all of the items as to their destinations in the new building.

It all went like clockwork, and we were back in operation in a matter of a couple of days. It took a little longer to get everything completely sorted out, but by the time the following week was over almost everything was in order.

Simultaneously with the planning and the physical move, we were in the throes of an Initial Public Offering. The Company was founded on April 8, 1959, by Dr. Bill (William Emerson) Ayer (WW#200-deceased) after leaving his position as Vice President and Director of Engineering for Granger Associates. So, we were just four and one-half years old, but we were profitable by the end of year one and had grown to where we had 120 employees and sales were at a rate of $3-million per year. In those days, unlike today, if a founder or an employee wanted to own a piece of the company you put a five-dollar bill on the barrel head and got one share of stock. Today, founders get millions of shares of penny (or less) stock and bodacious numbers of stock options. The Prospectus for ATI was dated

December 30, 1963, and the grand total of 54,200 shares were sold to the public at a price of $9.00 per share. The total number of shares outstanding after the offering was 619,280 shares after giving effect to a 20:1 stock split to $0.25 per share from the initial value of $5.00 per share.

The business of the company at that time was about 50% in active countermeasures systems all of which were repeater jammers at S-band and X-band called BSTRs and ATIRs, respectively. They incorporated, primarily, techniques for breaking-lock on conical-scan radars. Some were mounted inboard on some airplanes and others were mounted in tip tanks on the left and right sides of multi-engined airplanes all of which were flown by folks with a lot of derring-do. Many of the installations had a rudimentary threat warning system with a cathode-ray-tube-display and a Vector-Sector Control Panel for the ECM operator to switch from one horn antenna to another as the threat signal moved relative to the aircraft heading. This enabled the operator to get the most effective radiated power in the direction of the target radar for the best jamming effectiveness. In one type of airplane, a more sophisticated warning receiver was used in order for the pilot to be able to distinguish one type of threat from another and when and if he should enable the countermeasures system.

About 30% of the business was Receiving Preamplifiers and Multicouplers for monitoring, both from the ground and from the air, communications signals, telemetry signals, and command and control signals. In some cases, the airplanes would have up to 10 receiver operating positions on board. The units covered broadband frequency ranges of 30 to 260 megacycles per second (the U.S. hadn't yet adopted the Hertz as the standard for frequency), 250 to 500 mc/s, and 500 to 1,100 mc/s. All of these subsystems were designed with vacuum tubes since hf, vhf, and uhf transistors did not yet exist.

The remaining 20% of the business was in Reconnaissance and Surveillance Receiving Systems and Special Radar Warning Systems. The Reconn and Surveillance receivers spanned the range from 30 mc/s on up to 40,000 mc/s. The K-band receivers covered 10 to 20 and 20 to 40 kmc/s simultaneously using one local oscillator. The ground based version (RMK-1) had a rotating splash plate above a circular horn in order to get an azimuthally scanning receiving beam. One airborne version (RAK-3) had two sets of horn antennas pointed out the left and right sides of the airplane so that it was possible to fly up one side of an area, reverse course and fly down the same side of the area for a second look at what was on the air. For that particular time, these were the most advanced systems available to the US.

The Special Warning Receivers had microwave filters to restrict the received signals to the threat bands of interest in order to eliminate as much clutter and false alarms as was consistent without losing any signals of interest. They also incorporated some relatively sophisticated signal processing to try to identify only those signals which might pose a realistic threat to the aircraft.

In the summer of 1964 we had a visit from an Air Force captain who wanted to give us a briefing on some areas of the electronic defense business that the Requirements people in the Pentagon were studying and asking industry to help. I think that he was steered to ATI by one of our men in our Falls Church, VA, office, Mike Smith. Mike had been a "Busy Major" in the Pentagon prior to his retirement and coming to work for ATI. He described a Busy Major's job as that of a go-fer, a General's briefer, preparer of briefings for the Generals, and any other odd jobs necessary to run the office. (As a side-light, Mike and I may have met in World War 2 on the island of Ie Shima just off Okinawa. He was the Officer in Charge of an SCR-584 radar controlled AAA battery and I was a radar mechanic in the 6th Emergency Rescue Squadron. A couple of times I visited the battery to get a better idea of their radar as compared to ours. Our squadron had eight PBY-5A amphibians and twelve B-17's with 34 foot-long boats slung under their bellies to drop to downed air crews flying from the Marianas to Japan and back.)

Anyway, the USAF captain arrives with secret clearance approved, and guess who he is? Pierre (Irving Joel) Levy (WW#2-deceased)! Pierre wasn't always the most coherent speaker, but we got the idea that what we were doing with our limited Internal Research and Development money was headed in the right direction as far as Air Force perceived requirements were concerned. We couldn't brief Pierre on everything that we were doing because a large percentage of the work was compartmented and he wasn't "read into" the programs as far as we knew. However, even the compartmentalized work could be talked about in terms of techniques employed as long as we didn't get into customer references and specific performance parameters. All in all, it was a good afternoon and the start of a four-decades-long friendship with Pierre and Miriam, his wife.

As the year wore on, we ran into some new orders delays and found ourselves in the position of running out of production work at the same time we were hiring engineers to do the IR&D and new development jobs. We beat the bushes for assembly work and Hewlett Packard and IBM came through with some r-f and computer cable work for us to enable us to hold on to most of our experienced assembly ladies. It was rather menial work, but it provided revenue for the company and paychecks for the women. It was almost a case of "any old port in a storm": do what you have to do as long as it's legal, moral, and non-fattening.

So, we got through the year with still larger sales and earnings compared to the year before. The stock had taken a drop from its initial public offering price and we had some not too happy outside shareholders, but it wasn't too bad.

In the Beginning

The start of 1965 brought with it a request from our marketing department to the management of the company to spend some IR&D funds on a warning receiver to replace the AN/APS-54 Tail Warning Receiver used in the B-52. I think the idea came from Mike T. Smith (WW# 220) or Ed (Edwin K.) Chapman (WW# 195) in our Falls Church office subsequent to their talks with folks in the Pentagon. (Ed was a graduate of the U.S. Naval Academy, but had transferred to the Air Force and had become a B-52 Electronic Warfare Officer prior to joining ATI.) Their idea had been presented to management at the company by Larry (Lawrence) Thielen of our in-house marketing department. (Larry would later leave ATI and be the founder of Avantek, Inc.)

We didn't have a lot of information about the APS-54, but allowed as how we could come up with something a lot better if we could get approval to use the techniques from one of our special warning receivers. So, we contacted our sponsor and got permission from them to use the technology as long as we didn't use the same form factor for the boxes or have any other identification from whence the design had come. We allowed as how we could handle those restrictions. So, we approved an IR&D budget of $12,500 and assigned Bob (Robert R., frequently known as R-squared) Johnson (WW#218) as the project engineer with technician support from Bob Bobrink and drafting support from George Sakoi. So, it was late January or early February when the project got under way.

Well, we knew the size of the processor box for the APS-54 and, since this new system was to be a replacement for the old system, it was paramount to minimize the installation costs to the Air Force. So, the processor box for the VECTOR-4 was to be the same size as that of the -54. Our warning systems typically had four antennas with 90-degrees patterns with circular polarization, four Amplifier-Detector boxes with band separation filters to cover appropriate regions of S, C, and X bands. The S-band was to cover the GCI, Firecan, Firewheel, and the Fan Song frequencies as best we knew them. The C-band didn't really have any known-to-us threat at that time, but usage was predicted for the future. The X-band was to cover the airborne-interceptor frequency range so as not to get surprised by MiGs and Sukois. The display would be a repeat of the three-inches-diameter CRT that we had used in other applications for presentation of relative bearing to the target radar and we would include a Threat Display with lights and operational control switches on it. Initially, both of these functions were on the single control unit of the VECTOR-IV. Of course, the Amp-Detectors were to be reasonably small so that they, hopefully, could be mounted close by the antennas.

We selected flat spiral antennas from AEL Industries (Dr. Leon Riebman's company). These antennas were about 3-inches in diameter, had nearly the patterns that we wanted all the way from S- through X-band, and had circularly polarized flat spirals as their active elements. In theory, if the beam shapes were exactly circular power patterns, the antennas were mounted exactly 90-degrees apart around the aircraft, and the detectors were truly square-law devices then there would be an exact one-to-one correlation between the relative bearing to the radar and the angular deflection on the CRT. Well, it is all good in theory, but practice is often something different as we all learned over and over with each aircraft installation.

The development of the system proceeded with no particular problems and it was completed through in-house bench testing in July. We took the system on a "road show" to the folks at Wright-Patterson AFB and the US Navy. Everywhere our people went they were told essentially, "go away boys, we've got our own programs". Luckily, Mike Smith and Ed Chapman had talked with Pierre Levy about what we were doing on R&D dollars, so he was aware of our activity.

Coincidentally, on July 10,1965, an unarmed RF-4C was shot down in North Vietnam by a Surface-to-Air Missile. That, evidently, was the straw that broke the camel's back with respect to the Air Force attitude about flying into North Vietnam.

An Air Staff Task Force on Surface-to-Air Missiles in Southeast Asia was established, headed by Brigadier General KC (Kenneth C.) Dempster (WW#1-deceased), with its inaugural meeting being held on August 3rd. KC was Deputy Director of Operational Requirements at the time. The purpose of the first meeting was to lay out a plan for determining what might soon be available to help to solve this missile threat to our aircraft. As it turns out, Pierre had told about our development program. So, ATI was invited to make a presentation and demonstration of the VECTOR-IV. The demonstration of the system was made on August 5th to the assembled multitude, which included Col. Willie (William B.) Williamson (WW# 3-deceased) as well as KC, Pierre, and other USAF personnel including, I think, Maj. Dick Haggren (WW# 239) and Maj. Marty Selmanovitz. The presentation went well and our folks packed up the equipment and left. (Note: In a letter dated September 29, over KC's signature, we learned that nearly 200 proposals from industrial, scientific, and military communities had been considered in a period of three weeks.)

With Mike Smith and Ed Chapman keeping their ears to the ground, we began to get the feeling that this might be the start of something big. So, due to interest shown by the Air Force, on August 20th the Company management decided that we should build five VECTOR-IV systems on Company money under an inventory account. We figured that if the Task Force didn't come up with anything better than what we had, we might be the likely candidates to supply Radar Warning Systems. If we started early on our own risk, we could be "Johnny at the rat hole" when a decision was taken by the Air Staff.

At about 5:30 pm on August 27th, a Friday, my office phone rang as I was cleaning things up to go home for supper. On the line was Pierre; he was working late in the Pentagon, which wasn't particularly unusual. He said, "John, you know that IR-100 Receiver that your company has been advertising?" I said, "Yes." He went on the say that he needed two of them and he had \$40,000 in his account. I told him that they were \$40,000 each, so in my book he would need \$80,000. His reply was that he only had one-half of that amount. So, we went back and forth for a few minutes with Pierre eventually saying, "I don't think you'll be hurt in the long run if you do this for us. If the program goes, you'll be in a good position." I asked him to hold the phone and said that I'd go see Bill Ayer about our conversation. When I told Bill about what was going on, he wasn't exactly wild about the idea. I finally said that I thought we ought to do it; Bill gritted his teeth and told me to tell Pierre that he had better be right.

So, I went back to my office and told Pierre that he had a deal. We then went on to discuss what the receiver characteristics should be. We had to cover S-band; it should have a sensitivity of -70 dbm to -80 dbm, should be able to handle 0.3-microsecond-wide pulses, should have both automatic scanning and manual tuning, should have a panoramic display on a 1" by 3" CRT, the main box could be a B-1D size case, the indicator would be mounted in the instrument panel of a fighter airplane so it needed to be relatively small, etc.

All of that seemed reasonable enough, then he dropped the bombshell: you have to deliver the first one in 30 days and the second one 15 days later. I said, "Pierre, these things don't exist; they are paper-ware, advertising flyers used to try to stir up some interest in the reconnaissance and surveillance community." His reply was to the effect that well, we're not that community, but you did stir up some interest, didn't you? He went on to say that the contract would be ready early the next week at AFSC Headquarters at Andrews AFB in the office of a Col. Packard. The effective date of contract would be August 30, the following Monday. The contract was to have a priority of DX-A9 if we needed it to get parts or manpower priority from other customers. The conversation closed with the admonition from Pierre: Don't be late!

Rather than heading for home, I hot footed it up to the engineering floor and got Bob Johnson, Tony (Noah W.) Taussig (WW# 199), and Chuck Wilcox (WW# 226) together and told them what we needed to do. I asked them to think about it overnight and asked that we get together again in the morning, Saturday, to lay out a plan of action. Both Bob and I came up with block diagrams overnight and discussed them in the morning with Tony and Chuck. Bob was assigned as the Project Engineer with support from the two other men; they were individually very capable and worked together very well, I knew from past experience.

They began to check with our vendors as to what was available off-the-shelf for YIG (yttrium-iron-garnet) filters, TWT's (traveling-wave tubes), S-band circulators, CRTs, and all kinds of less exotic parts. The receivers were to be of the tuned-radio-frequency type with one YIG filter before the TWT and one YIG behind the TWT, this would afford good signal resolution and signal sensitivity. This design type had been used many times in previous systems by ATI. So, the project was under way in short order and the detailed design began. In order to ensure enough manpower to do the job, we temporarily shut down an ECM Trainer Project and an Army All-Band Receiver Study Project.

The next Monday, I flew to Washington in order to attend a meeting scheduled for Tuesday afternoon with another customer. During the morning, Ed Chapman took me out to Andrews Air Force Base and we went to the contracts office. There we were met by a little old lady who said, "I've never seen anything happen so fast in all of my life." She had typed up the contract and the technical specifications for the IR-133, with multiple carbon copies, on Monday so that they were ready for signing on Tuesday morning. Remember that this is in the days of carbon copies, and Ditto- and Mimeograph-machines, not xerographic copiers. The specifications took a grand total of one and one-third pages and essentially said build us a couple of S-band radios to the numbers Pierre and I had discussed on the telephone the previous Friday evening. So contract AF18(600)-2879 was issued for two VECTOR-IV and two IR-133 Systems at an "order of magnitude" Firm Fixed Price of $80,000 with delivery dates of 9/28/65 for the first system and 10/13/65 for the second system plus some undefined field/installation support. The in-house project number assigned was 10105. Thusly, we had a "home" for the first two VECTOR systems that we were building for inventory.

At essentially the same time, the USAF had initiated a contract with The Space and Information Division of NAA (North American Aviation), which was then headed by Col. (Ret.) John Paup (WW# 19) who had been the main honcho for ECM and Reconnaissance and Surveillance under Gen. Curtis LeMay, the Head of the Strategic Air Command. John and I had met several times when he came to the Stanford Electronics Laboratories to review development programs which were being conducted in my Systems Techniques Group during the mid- to late-1950's. The plan was to install the warning system in the NAA-owned F-100F so that there would be a fighter pilot in the front seat and an EWO in the back seat to operate all of the dedicated electronics and to tell the pilot what was going on in the electronic environment.

The IR&D model of the VECTOR was taken to the NAA facility at the Long Beach Airport so that the NAA people could see what needed to be done in the way of stringing wires and cables, installing antennas and black boxes, and moving instruments out of the backseat panel to accommodate the indicators that we would be supplying. The initial VECTOR-IV had a single box for the CRT and the Threat Display lights; this was to be mounted in the rear instrument panel. The IR-133 was still in development, but we knew the sizes of the receiver box (B-1D) and the panoramic display indicator so the NAA could do their installation planning. We advised on types of cables to use, where the antennas should be located, and general installation requirements. NAA had a man there who knew that airplane mechanically up one side and down the other. His name was Kay (Cyril K.) Bullock (WW# 21-deceased) and was a great man with whom to work. If there was something in the way to prevent a box of ours from being mounted where we wanted it, he would either get the offending item moved or would suggest an alternative location for our gear. As I recall, the receiver box wound up in the "turtle-deck", the hump behind the second seat in the airplane.

On September 9th, KC arrived at ATI and for the first time we really found out the plans that had been laid out at the Air Staff. The idea was to outfit a number of airplanes with the warning systems and to go looking for SAMs with the purpose of destroying them so that the strike force could then fly into the area with less risk of being shot down. If any AAAs were found along the way, they could be taken out, too. This became the SEAD (Suppression of Enemy Air Defenses) Mission. KC let us know that the program was of the utmost importance to the Air Force and that the air crews would be laying their lives on the line, so don't screw up!

KC was accompanied to this meeting by a Col. Shaeffer, a Col. Lindberg, Maj. Jim (James R.) Odom (WW# 246) and Col. (ret) John Paup. During the meeting presentations were made as to the engineering status of the VECTOR-IV and the IR-133 System, Program Management, and Preliminary Production Plans. We had had an inkling that there were really going to be quite a few systems purchased if the F-100F program was successful, so we had done some planning in advance of getting a formal Request For Proposal from the Air Force.

In addition, on September 9th, we received a contract from NAA for $67,865 for in-plant support, laboratory support, field support, redesign of the VECTOR Amp-Detectors, test simulators, and spare parts.

The first VECTOR System was delivered to NAA on September 12th, and the airplane first flew on September 16th with a NAA pilot and back seater. The system performed as advertised, but the "observer" allowed as how there was some angular error on the display when they were trying to track to or from the station so that homing in on a target might be a bit difficult. So, what to do? We came up with the idea of putting a flat-spiral antenna flush-mounted on both the left and right sides of the nose. We would then use a microwave switch to flip back and forth between the two antennas and deflect a vertical trace on the IR-133 indicator to the left when connected to the left antenna and to deflect the beam to the right when connected to the right antenna. It was the old World War Two trick of pip matching that was used on the SCR-729 radar flown in our PBY-5As of the 6th Emergency Rescue Squadron. The two antenna beams would cross over in front of the airplane and the system should have a great sensitivity to any change in relative bearing. Fly the heading that kept the left- and right- pips the same length, and you would be heading directly to the station. This meant boring more holes in the airplane and stringing more wires and cables, but it was done in short order.

At about this same time (Sept.9), Bill (William C.) Doyle (WW# 217), Director of Systems Engineering for ATI, was visiting a U.S. Government Office and came across a rather peculiar piece of data. It was not corroborated by any other source data, so it was not to be considered an official position by that Office. However, on the airplane on the way back home, Bill sketched out the block diagram of a possible new receiver which, if it worked the way he hoped, would give the air crews a few seconds warning prior to a missile coming off the rails of the Guideline launcher-transporter vehicle.

As was usual for a Saturday morning, Bill Ayer and a goodly portion of the engineering staff were at the office for at least a half-day of work. So, Bill Ayer, Bill Doyle, a couple of design engineers and I gathered together to hear Doyle's ideas for this new receiver. It looked promising enough that we decided then and there to get in touch with KC and to give him a briefing over the telephone as to what we had in mind and what it might do for air crew survivability. KC, in his usual fashion, said why don't you get started on your own nickel and if it's worth really pursuing we will cover you. We decided to proceed immediately with the design of the new receiver and that Bill Ayer would send a letter to KC the next week detailing what we thought about the technical data and what we were doing in engineering. Bill sent the letter to KC dated September 17th and the company began the official design of the WR-300 on September 23rd with a notation that we expected to receive contractual coverage for two Detection and Warning Systems in two weeks at an anticipated value of $18,800, the contract was to be Firm Fixed Price; with a FFP contract we didn't have to worry about whether or not pre-contractual costs would be allowed by the government auditors. John R. Arnold (WW# 211) was assigned as the Project Engineer.

One of the features of the WR-300 was that if the receiver "saw" the anticipated signal anomaly, a light would be lighted on the instrument panel. This little light got the infamous name of the "Oh, Shit!" light, meaning that a Guideline Missile was on its way. Believe it or not, but there was actually some discussion about if that light came on it would simultaneously initiate the seat ejection system of the airplane! It never got out of the "Boy, is that a dumb idea" stage.

As convenience to the Air Force, the official contract actually came through NAA. The delivery dates were to be November 8 for the first receiver and November 9th for the second—45 days from the start with only an idea in mind to actual delivery of hardware.

Things were going pretty well with the development of the IR-133 and we were in the habit of keeping NAA personnel up-to-date as to our progress. On Saturday, September 25, Terry Bibbens (WW# 209) got a call from Joe Ferrari and Jim Keegan, both of them from NAA, stating that they would visit us the following Monday for first article inspection and acceptance and, if things went well, they would like to take delivery of the system and take it back to Long Beach that night. So, things went pretty well and we delivered the first IR-133 on September 28, twenty-nine days after starting the design with blank pieces of paper and no parts! North American then had in hand all the pieces necessary to complete the installation in their company-owned F-100F. The third VECTOR-IV and the second IR-133 were delivered to NAA on October 12th.

Neither my memory nor my notes tell me exactly when the program got its name WILD WEASEL. It initially was to be called Project MONGOOSE, a name picked, I believe, by North American. However, this name had previously been chosen for another program so it couldn't be used again. I do know that ATI used the name Project FAKIR for the original program with NAA, and that FAKIR and MONGOOSE would have a certain kinship—think of the Indian Snake Charmer with his wooden flute and the wicker basket with the hooded cobra swaying back and forth to the music. At any rate, the F-100F program became known as WILD WEASEL and the name stuck.

We were beginning to get rumbles that there might be some requirements coming down from the Sacramento Air Materiel Area (SMAMA) at McClellan Air Force Base for the F-105 fleet. So, I got checked out in a Cherokee-235 at Nystrom Aviation at the Palo Alto Airport, which was only about 15 minutes by car from our building in the Stanford Industrial Park. Sure enough, we got a call for us to go to McClellan and demonstrate the VECTOR-IV to their engineering department in the Modification Center. Terry Bibbens and I flew up there on October 13th, Col. JT (James Troy) Johnson (WW# 4) having got us a clearance from Base Ops to land at MCC which, in general, is pretty unusual; but then, this whole program had been pretty unusual so far.

Now JT and several hundred other people of all types of professions had been transferred from Mobile Air Materiel Area to SMAMA to support both the F-100s and the F-105s. JT was a fighter pilot of World War Two who had flown Close Air Support against Rommel in North Africa in P-40s, gone to Sicily, then to Italy, then up to France where his squadron switched to P-47s. Checkout in the P-47s was: read the book, sit in the cockpit to identify all of the switches and instruments, crank up the 2,000-HP engine, take-off, fly, and land. After three or four hours of flight time they took the planes into combat; it was a reasonably sporty proposition. JT was the last Squadron Commander of the 316th Fighter Squadron of the 324th Fighter Group. We have now been good friends for nearly forty years.

We gave the briefing, showed them the hardware and talked about where various boxes might be mounted, what kind of A-Kit Might be necessary, etc. After the briefing and demonstration, Terry and I flew back to Palo Alto. The next day, October 14, JT got a call from Col. "Willie" Williamson in the Pentagon asking him how the briefing and demonstration had gone. The upshot of that phone call was that JT's crew was turned on to proceed with the installation and to conduct a flight test of the VECTOR-IV in the F-105. We delivered the VECTOR to them on October 16 out of our inventory account of the first five systems to be built.

On October 21, the NAA contract was modified to add two more WR-300s to the order at a price of $12,000 for the two of them with delivery dates of one on November 9 and the second one on November 10th. That really translated to four non-existing receivers to be delivered over a period of three days starting 45 days after the first order. We must have been crazy to agree to that schedule! (Note: They were delivered on time.) Bob Johnson, Jim (James R.) Reid (WW# 23), and I provided technical support to the installation crew at McClellan. The questions arose as to where, specifically, to mount the nose and tail antennas. The nose antennas were pretty simple: they could mount in a fairing under the radome, aft of the radar dish, and forward of the hinge line. The Amp-Detectors could then be easily mounted just aft of the forward bulkhead on the right-hand side of the fuselage with short r-f cables to connect them to the antennas to minimize the microwave losses.

The tail antennas were another matter. We wanted them to be mounted in a short-stubby fairing with the antennas directly mounted to the flat, 45-degrees-offset faces. This fairing would then be attached to the vertical stabilizer "flag". Tony Aratoli, the Republic Aviation Representative, wanted to build a long, skinny fairing with the antennas about 12-inches away from the flat 45-degrees-offset faces. I explained to JT that with all that separation from the antenna faces to the fairing faces we would have reflections that would really tear up the patterns something fierce. Tony kept arguing for the long fairing as being more aerodynamically appropriate. JT finally said, "Doc, how do we resolve this argument". My reply was that we would maintain symmetry about the longitudinal axis of the fuselage so there shouldn't be any reason to expect any tail flutter, but the only way to really know would be to build it and try it. Equally importantly, the stubby fairing would result in the better antenna patterns which would give the best warning from the rear. So, JT said, "Are you sure?" The reply was, "As sure as I can be." Hell, I'm no aerodynamicist, but I do know that Mother Nature does LOVE symmetry! So, he told his folks to proceed with the short-design of the fairing.

The "mod squad" had "our" F-105 in one bay of the hangar and right next to it was another F-105 being modified to take the so-called "MAX-DIX" radar-warning system. This was a joint venture of Maxson and Bendix and was to become the AN/APS-107, if I remember properly. The installation on the F-105 was completed the morning of October 21st, and was taken on its first flight a little before noon. Bob Johnson an I were having a "brown-bag" lunch in my office in Palo Alto when the telephone rang about 12:20 pm. Jim Reid was on the other end and he sounded as though he was in a semi-panic mode. He told us that no matter what heading the pilot flew relative to the test radar, the strobe on the scope pointed toward the rear of the airplane. It would swing back and forth and was totally useless. There wasn't any heading that would get the strobe to point towards the nose. So, we told Jim to relax and that we would be there as quickly as we could be.

Bob started rounding up an oscilloscope, a volt-ohm meter, a couple of Hewlett Packard signal generators and anything else he thought that he would need to trouble-shoot the system. I called Nystrom Aviation and rented a Piper Cherokee-180 and phoned the tail number and the ETA up to JT so that we could get a clearance to land at McClellan. Bob had the bright idea of calling "Bud" (Warren F.) Arnold at Point Mugu Naval Air Station to see if there was any chance of getting the "beach" conscan tracking radars turned on for us. He told Bob to give him a call when we got to MCC and he would let us know whether or not he had been able to arrange the radar turn-ons for us.

So, we land at McClellan with a "Follow Me" truck awaiting our arrival to guide us to the F-105 parking area. After shutting everything down and climbing out of the little bird, Bob found the problem in about 10-seconds flat. It seems that someone with due diligence had put a placard on the radome access panel that said: "DISCONNECT ECM ANTENNAS BEFORE OPENING RADOME". What it did not say was: "RECONNECT ECM ANTENNAS AFTER CLOSING RADOME". When Bob opened the access panel, the two cables for the front Amp-Detectors dangled out of the opening. Bob went to work re-attaching the antenna cables and going through a general checkout of the system with the "walk around" test sets that we had brought with us from Palo Alto.

While Bob was busy at the airplane, I went to the Ops Office and called Bud Arnold to find out the status of our request. Bud told me that both "beach" tracking radars would be on as well as the search radar on the hill inland from Pt. Mugu. We should have "our guy" call Erskine Control on 2xx.x frequency at Angels 18 over Anacapa Island and Erskine would tell him what to do. I read back the clearance and the conversation ended with me thanking Bud for his efforts. A couple of minutes later this big, strapping Major comes striding in and asks the Ops Officer what he is suppose to do with the F-105. The Ops guy says, pointing to me, "Ask him". So, I rattled off what Bud had told me. The pilot asked, "Is this for real?" The Ops Officer replies: "I guess you do what the man says."

We went out to the airplane where Bob had finished all of his tests and he said that the system had checked out OK and was ready to go. The F-105 departed in a matter of a few minutes and was back at its spot on the ramp in about an hour and forty-five minutes, I would guess. After shutting down, the pilot climbed out and wouldn't say a thing except let's go to the briefing room and I'll tell you all about it. So, about thirty of us civilians and Air Force types trudged to the briefing room where the Major walks up to the podium. He slowly looked around at his audience and, at last, said: "IT WORKED." He then went on to tell us that Erskine Control had vectored him around the Pt. Mugu area in a manner that would allow him to test all relative bearing angles from both the "beach" radars and the search radar on the hill. As I recall, he said there were only a minor relative-bearing angle-errors when tracking directly towards and directly away from the radars. As best he could tell, when he was abeam the radars the strobes pointed appropriately to the left or to the right. So, he was pretty happy with how the VECTOR responded.

Just think, three civilians, Bud Arnold, Grigsby, and Bob Johnson, arrange for a United States Air Force F-105 to test-fly on a United States Navy radar range and the total time from start to finish is from Jim Reid's call at 12:20 to about 5:00 pm when the aircraft lands back at McClellan. Just how long do you think it would have taken for the USAF to go through Channels to the USN, gotten approval, and have the answer get back to Sacramento? My guess that the elapsed time would have been measured in days if not weeks. It really pays sometimes to have friends who know how to get things done in a short period of time and who are willing to stick their necks out just a little bit for you.

I think it was somewhere around October 25th, when Terry and I had again flown up to MCC, that we were out on the flight line checking something or another and an RF-101 taxied up to the ramp. This Colonel (Wilkerson?) gets out of the plane and says he is there to talk to SMAMA folks about getting some kind of a Warning System put in that type of airplane. As we headed into the office to talk with JT and his engineering staff, I asked him how his flight had been from Hill AFB at Ogden to Sacramento. He allowed as how it was a nice flight, but that he couldn't use his radar. So, I piped up and said maybe we can get JT to put someone on the job while we are talking about the Warning System. He replied that there really wasn't anything wrong with the radar as far as he knew, but that he had his golf clubs stashed in the radome so he couldn't let the antenna scan or it would be damaged! It's always nice to know where your priorities are, isn't it?

The flight tests at SMAMA were completed on October 26th flying against whatever radars were available such as Air Traffic Control and tracking radars in the area. Since we were now talking about F-100Fs, F-105s and RF-101s, ATI took the decision to build another 20 VECTOR-IVs on Company money.

One day in late October or early November as I recall, a whole gaggle of folks gathered in the ATI Conference Room to discuss the program to date and what it forebode for the future. I think, but I'm not sure, that our visitors included Major Pierre Levy, Major Gary A. Willard (WW# 5), Walt (Truman W.) Lifsey (WW# 8), Jack (John E.) Donovan (WW# 15), and a number of folks from SMAMA engineering-, procurement-, and production-offices. Joe (Joseph W.) Telford (WW# 258) from Eglin AFB APGC was there, too. It may have been at this meeting where Jack Donovan asked his famous question "You want me to ride in the back of a two-seat fighter airplane with a teenage killer in the front seat? You Gotta Be Shitting Me!" This may have been the start of the Wild Weasel slogan: YGBSM!

At any rate, the systems were briefed to the government people, and price and production schedules were discussed in some detail for an order of 500 Vector systems. Now, you should know that ATI had never had an order for more than a dozen of any kind of equipment that it had developed. To think of an order for 500 was almost mind-boggling. The folks from Sacramento were very helpful. They kept asking if we had put enough production and test equipment in our proposal to be sure that we had enough of everything so that there would be no excuse for getting behind schedule. So, we wound up by putting somewhere in excess of $300,000 of manufacturing and test hardware into the bid; since the bid was going to be for a Firm Fixed Price Contract, all of that gear would become ATI property.

As different items were discussed, quantities were written, along with their prices, on the blackboard at the end of the conference room. When the list had been completed and negotiated, it was totaled to a value of about $6.7 million. Then Bill Ayer said, "OK, Pierre, get up there and sign it." So, Pierre did. Then Bill signed it and we took a picture of the blackboard with a Polaroid camera. That photograph became the basis for the official contract. Unfortunately, that picture has disappeared; it would be nice to have it for the archives, wouldn't it? This one order was to be greater than the previous fiscal year sales of the company by 25 percent.

On November 1, the installation of the VECTOR-IV and the WR-300 in both the RF-4C and the RF-101 began at OAMA (Ogden Air Materiel Area). My recollection is that the RF-4C was to be Wild Weasel-IV-C. There was, nearly simultaneously, the installation of the AN/APS-107 (The MAX-DIX System) into the F-4C with the designation of Wild Weasel-II; this installation would also include the Sanders AN/ALQ-51 Repeater Jammer that was based on a design we had made at Stanford in the mid-1950s. Flight tests of this configuration were to begin at Eglin AFB on January 4, 1966. The ATI equipment installations in the RF-4C and the RF-101 were completed at OAMA on November 12th. At any rate, the installation of the ATI equipment in the RF-4C, the RF-101, and the F-105 was the Air Force "Mod 1805" according to a memo resulting from a meeting of Mike Smith and L/Col. Marty Selmanovitz on January 5, 1966.

On November 7th we got word via Col. Bally (exec) that KC Dempster had visited Eglin AFB and that he was pleased with what he saw there in terms of the preparation for the deployment of Wild Weasel-1 that was to have Major Gary A. Willard, Jr., as the Commander. ATI had both Jim Reid and Joe (Joseph P.) Day (WW# 22) at Eglin for the squadron support with Jim getting prepared to go to Southeast Asia to be our man in-theater. His job would be to assist in the maintenance of the hardware and to report back to ATI as to what was good and what were the shortcomings of the system as seen from a "pilot-in-combat" view of the world.

Things continued to proceed rapidly and on November 10 we got a call from Lt. Stan Bevens at Wright-Patterson AFB telling us that the nomenclature AN/APR-25 (V) had been assigned to the VECTOR-IV and that he was working on a set of MIL-SPECS for the system. Up to now all of ATI's work had been "best commercial practices" with a special emphasis on the part of engineering to ensure performance and reliability. We knew that almost all of our systems were for use in aircraft of one sort or another and that the air crews depended upon excellent performance and reliable operation to protect them from harm in so far as was possible. Given this news about the assigned nomenclature for the VECTOR-IV, we decided to build fifteen WR-300s on our own nickel, too.

We received the formal contract from SMAMA for 500 AN/APR-25 (V) and WR-300 systems on November 19th. On the 24th, we delivered the first five of these systems to Sacramento from our inventory account.

JT Johnson and I had become good friends over the past 30 days, so we had each other's home telephone numbers so that the best coordination could be accomplished when problems arose during the outfitting of the F-105s. Thanksgiving Eve, November 24, JT called me to let me know that the "our" F-105 was going to fly to Eglin on Thanksgiving Day via Tinker AFB for a refueling stop. My wife, children, and I were sitting in church Thanksgiving day and I kept thinking about the airplane arriving at Eglin and came to the decision that I should leave that day to be at the base for the checkout and first flight tests against the Eglin Radar Range. So, I got myself a ticket and flew to Eglin.

The next day we met with Jim Odom's folks to lay out a plan for the upcoming flight tests. I think that Joe Day was our man at Eglin for Field Support. During a break in the planning process, I asked the pilot how his flight had been from McClellan to Eglin. He allowed as how it had been good, but when he landed at Tinker he found that the nose wheel was canted about 15-degrees off axis when the rudder pedals were neutral. So, I asked him if he had been able to get someone to fix it there at Tinker on Thanksgiving Day. He said, "No. I just took off and flew on to Eglin." My reply was, "Do you know how much trouble you would have been in if you had bent that airplane? It is the only one in the world outfitted like this." His response was with the true humility of a fighter pilot: "No, but I didn't, did I?" Enough said.

Coincidentally, on Thanksgiving Day, the first four F-100F Wild Weasel airplanes arrived in Thailand under Major Gary Willard's command. These four aircraft were equipped with the VECTOR-IV, the WR-300, and the IR-133. This was just 83 days from the beginning of the program when only an IR&D model of the VECTOR existed. Not a bad track record!

Well, the other F-105 (with the MAX-DIX system) which had been in the adjacent modification bay at SMAMA showed up at Eglin a few days after the ATI equipped airplane. During its flight tests it seemed to have more problems than our airplane was having and the engineers had a tougher time getting Eglin maintenance folks to help them. I think that there was some sort of a personality/cultural clash, but I didn't want to get into that sort of a discussion. When we needed help, it was forthcoming very quickly. If memory serves me correctly, both the ATI and the MAX-DIX F-105s were D models.

Joe Telford was the designer of the flight tests for the two airplanes and he tells an interesting story about the KC Dempster visit to Eglin to see how the training and testing program of the F-100Fs was going prior to deployment. Joe says that he and KC were at Hangar 68 chatting when two Majors walk up after having just landed from a flight test of the MAX-DIX system. One of them interrupts KC saying that the system was hard to operate and that on a low altitude inbound run he was concentrating on the electronics so much that he didn't notice that he had rolled inverted. Of course, he recovered; but he told KC and Joe that he would never again fly that system and give it his full attention. Evidently, he wasn't the only pilot who felt that way. Sometime later, we heard via the grapevine that the APS-107 Program had several "get well" contract mods, but that it never was well accepted by the air crews.

According to my notes, the first Iron Hand Wild Weasel F-100F mission was flown on December 1, 1965, out of Korat Royal Thailand Air Force Base. Then, sadly, on December 20th, John Pitchford (WW# 103) and Bob (Robert D.) Trier (WW# 107) were shot down. They parachuted into enemy territory where Bob decided to try to fight his way out, but was killed. John surrendered, but they shot him anyway, and he spent many years imprisoned in North Vietnam. It was a sad time for all of us. Like most of us at that time, they had families. So, it was doubly devastating.

Two days after John and Bob were shot down, on December 22nd, Allen Lamb (WW# 16) and Jack Donovan got the first SAM kill. The VECTOR and the WR-300 had done their jobs! Allen and Jack also got the next two SAM-site kills.

Sometime in roughly mid-December, A VECTOR system in one of the F-100Fs intercepted a C-band Track-While-Scan radar, a new version of the Fan Song! When we got the news in Palo Alto, we once again decided to build, on our own money, a receiver that would be of use to the Wild Weasel Program. We started the development of what we called the ER-142. This was a two-band tuned-radio-frequency receiver of exactly the same type of design as was used in the IR-133. Since we started this on our own initiative, we felt we had a little more time for the development, so quite a bit of effort was expended to contain both receivers in the same size box as the one-band IR-133. We knew from our work to date that there was essentially no spare room inside either the F-100F or the F-105, so it was mandatory to fit the two-band version in the same volume as we had been allotted before.

Now you may recall that this whole VECTOR business started out as an Internal Research and Development (IR&D) Project to replace the AN/APS-54 Tail Warning System in the B-52. Well, guess what? On December 27th in a meeting at Wright-Patterson AFB the decision was taken to install the system in a B-52D during the time frame of January 11,1966, through January 14th at Amarillo, Texas. Winton E. Cass (WW# 197) would be our field man to assist in the installation and to observe the flight tests which were scheduled to take place starting January 17th and terminating on January 28th after six flights. The test report was to be sent by SAC to USAF Headquarters on February 8th. As a result, a number of B-52s were outfitted with the warning system. The airframe for which we had designed the VECTOR-IV was finally getting its new system.

The Program Matures...

After all of these initial installations, we were looking at putting production quantities of systems into a half a dozen different air frames for the Air Force since there was now talk about putting the warning receivers into the Lockheed F-104 Star Fighter airplane. The production of hardware for all of the different aircraft types was ramped up and eventually reached 225 systems per month, counting spares. Additional buildings had to be rented, assembly- and test-workers hired and trained, and materials procured. All of this was accomplished with no missed delivery dates. It was a strain on a lot of people, but they all were briefed on the importance of the program and that air crews would be flying into regions of great danger and would be staking their lives on the equipment; a high degree of reliability of the receivers was a must. We heard subsequently that the "availability" and reliability of the systems was in the neighborhood of 96% to 98%. We were justifiably proud of this performance.

When information began flowing into the company from both the Air Force and Jim Reid about the peculiarities of the electronic environment in SEA, Bill Doyle came up with the idea of putting a tape recorder on board one of the airplanes to record the actual signal environment seen in combat. Who could be closer to the real emitters than the Wild Weasels? So, we talked AstroSciences into lending us a 7-track tape recorder that was worth about $14,000. We told them that if we broke it we would pay for it, otherwise it was just a piece of rental equipment. (Actually, we would insure it so that if anything went wrong we would be covered.) Well, the folks at Air Staff thought this was a pretty good idea, so we prepared a proposal to deliver two systems for installation in two F-100Fs. The recorders would only be used on special missions: they would not be carried on every Wild Weasel flight made by these two special airplanes. The interfaces were designed and built and the airplanes deployed to the theater of operation. The systems did record good data and gave us much greater insight into types of signals, their anomalies, and the density of the environment. It was a good experiment.

During one visit to McClellan, Col. Johnson got to talking about how nice it would be to have a homing system on the airplanes that would permit the pilot to visually find the target radar even if it were heavily camouflaged. Recall the JT had spent several years in World War Two as a Close Air Support pilot from North Africa to Germany. Ultimately, JT thought it would be even better if such a system would enable blind-bombing through an undercast. It turns out that the Wild Weasel pilots didn't think that that was such a good idea since it didn't give them time to locate and to maneuver away from an SA-2 missile popping out of the clouds.

At any rate, ATI began the development of an Azimuth-Elevation System as an adjunct to the IR-133. Our plan was to place four antennas just in front of the metal mounting-ring of the radome on the F-105F. These antennas would then be sequentially sampled and the output of the IR-133 would be fed to a resolving network to establish up, down, left, and right output signals. Bud Sahlberg developed a small, planar log periodic broadband antenna, which would be mounted in small housings at 45-, 135-. 225-, and 315-degrees around the radome. These positions were chosen because the antennas were linearly polarized and we needed to receive both vertical- and horizontal- polarizations as well as circular polarization.

In order to develop the interface between the AE-100 and the Heads-Up-Display of the F-105F, JT "bailed" us the all of the boxes that made up the display electronics of the HUD as well as the display itself. The idea was that we would put a "pipper" dot on the gunsight reticle that the pilot could use to identify the target radar. The pilot would not have to divert his eyesight from looking through the combining glass and the windshield to look at another display somewhere on the instrument panel. If everything worked out the way we wanted it to, the pipper would stay on the target even with some maneuvering including inverted flight.

The F-105F was flown to Eglin somewhere around mid-April of 1966. Bob (Robert L.) Tidwell (WW# 259) flew a number of sorties with the AZ-EL System trying to evaluate its capabilities. After every flight he would brief us on his findings and we would make whatever adjustments seemed to be needed. There was an anomaly that really puzzled Bob and us. It seems that as he would fly from over the water to over the land, the pipper would initially "ping" low into the water rather than on the radar site. Then, after the airplane transitioned to the land environment and the range to the target was reduced, the pipper would "walk up" to where it was actually pinging on the radar site. I thought that I had Bob talked into letting me ride in the back seat to get first hand notes on what he was seeing on the HUD. The next day he said if anything went wrong, not that it would, mind you, his career in the Air Force would be down the tubes. So, the ride never happened, much to my disappointment; but I understood his concern, so it was okay.

The action of the pipper, pinging low and then walking up to the target radar, seemed quite strange, but I thought maybe it had something to do with a change in the refractive index of the atmosphere at the water/land interface. I knew that the folks at the Pacific Missile Range at Pt. Mugu had an airplane outfitted with a refractometer. They flew that airplane everyday that there was to be a missile shot from PMR out to the west. They were investigating the "ducting" phenomena for telemetry purposes—they had to keep a viable radio link with the birds as they were in flight. They were testing Regulus and Bomarc vehicles at the time as I recall. Anyway, my suggestion was to call Pt. Mugu and see if they wouldn't fly their airplane to Eglin and run some refraction flights for us to see if we could solve the problem of the wayward pipper. The suggestion was never acted upon with the explanation that there wasn't time for that and that the airplanes would go "as is". So much for that idea.

The AZ-EL System did get some use "in theater" with a lot of tender loving care, but it never performed the way we wished that it would. Sometime in late-1966, Don Ayer (WW# 219), one of our Field Representatives, Bill Doyle and Jim Reid hand-carried a mod-kit to SEA to try to correct what was thought Might be a temperature problem with the AE-100; unfortunately, this did not solve the problem, either.

At the same time as the AZ-EL tests were being performed, the WILD WEASEL-3-1 aircrews were forming and going through training. Major Bob (Robert B.) Brinckman (WW# 79) was to be the senior officer with Captain Vince (Vincent A.) Scungio (WW# 99) as his EWO. One day Bob invited a rather large group of us to have a barbecue after work at his home on a lake in Ft. Walton Beach. He had a speed boat and water skis so we all took turns skiing around the lake. Now, in 1966 I was a little thinner than I am now; so when I was being pulled around on the skis Bob hollered out, "Grigsby, you look like a tall, scrawny chicken out there on those skis." Of course, everyone who lived around the lake could hear what he had yelled. Only slightly embarrassing, eh, what?

It must have been mid-May of 1966 that the Wild Weasel 3-1 air crews arrived at McClellan to pick up their airplanes to deploy to South East Asia. We had a big meeting and a little celebration in the offices of Col. Johnson where we wished the crews happy hunting and a safe return after their tour of duty. That evening several of us from ATI took the crews to dinner in San Francisco. Afterwards, some of us wound up at a North

Beach "Topless" bar. It was an amateur night and some of the talent was reasonably good looking. After a few displays of feminine pulchritude, a sixty-plus-year-old woman came out to dance with everything visible sagging greatly. It was not a beautiful sight. After that, we called it a night and dispersed.

Sadly, Bob And Vince were shot down by a AAA and killed in action on November 4, 1966, which was about six months from the time they deployed to South East Asia. Bob evidently didn't "break" when they got the warning from the system that they were being tracked by a radar. Their F-105F caught on fire and the airplane crashed in hostile territory. No parachutes were observed. They, too, were married with children: wives who would have to manage without a husband and children who would have to grow up without a father. Tough times for all concerned!

It must have been about late spring or early summer of 1966 when Captain Bob (Robert A.) Klimek, Jr. (WW# 255) came to ATI after having been in SEA to observe the happenings and to see how the equipment was doing. We met in the "tank" conference room and Bob proceeded to tell us of his idea for an additional receiver which might help the air crews to know when they were in the center of the scanning beams of the SA-2. The enemy radar used a Track-While-Scan (TWS) technique that enabled a field of view of multiple tens of degrees both in azimuth and elevation. It was not necessary for the radar to be pointing directly at the aircraft being tracked: multiple targets could be entered into the tracking system and be appropriately accounted for as long as they were within the scanning area of the horizontal- and vertical-scanning beams. However, it appeared to be pretty standard practice for the operators of the radar to aim the center of the scan at the particular target at which they intended to shoot a missile.

Bob's idea was to have the EWO lock onto the scanning pattern of the radar and to adjust a sweep circuit so that the receiver scan-pattern was synchronized to the radar. That way, you could observe whether, or not, you were in the center of the scan. If so, you were undoubtedly the target of primary interest to the radar operator. Well, the radar operator does not have to have you in the center of his beam to track you—that is the beauty of a TWS system. So, it is possible, if not probable, that your aircraft will not be centered in the scanning pattern, but you may still be the primary target.

At any rate, the systems engineers, who reported into the Plans and Programs Department of ATI, convinced themselves and some people in management, that the proposed technique would not always work to give a sure-fire warning that you were about to be shot at. Consequently, ATI did not follow up on Bob's idea even though he said that he could get money to put into a development program. That was a BIG MISTAKE! Bob took his idea to Loral and they developed the AN/ALR-31, SEESAM. We had pulled a huge marketing blunder and let another defense electronics company into the Wild Weasel program.

Despite this terrible marketing fiasco, overall the business was really going quite well, and our marketing intelligence was letting us know that if the B-52 tests went well that there might be orders for up to 600 systems, counting spares. Furthermore, other USAF Programs, including more Wild Weasels, might result in an additional several thousand systems in new orders over a period of a couple of years. Based upon these estimates, about April of 1966, the Board of Director's of ATI approved the expenditure of approximately $5,000,000 for the placement of orders for 1,000 sets of parts of long-lead items for the anticipated new contracts.

Due to the growth of the company, related almost entirely to the Radar Homing And Warning business, a Program Office was established in Sunnyvale with H.E."Tony" Ethier (WW# 214) as the Program Manager reporting directly to Bill Ayer. To ensure the most rapid response possible to customer needs, an engineering department was established to directly respond to Program Requirements. This office was headed by John D. Adkins (WW# 215) who had hired a number of engineers from Lockheed, Sunnyvale, whom he knew from his prior employment there. With reports coming in from the field, this group of engineers initially designed and introduced into production those modifications that were approved by the engineering and contracts people at SMAMA. One of their activities included the Mil Spec qualification of the WR-300 to become the AN/APR-26. The support of this Development Engineering Group to the manufacturing department resulted in ATI shipping the 500th warning system of the "blackboard" contract in September, 1966, two months ahead of the contractual requirement.

Coming in dribs and drabs and a couple of big orders, surely enough we were able to consume all of the parts that we had on order. In December of

1966 we were up to 1,000 employees with thirteen Field Representatives overseas in support of the Wild Weasel Program.

January of 1967 saw us leasing an office building and a very large hangar at the former Strategic Air Command AFB at Lincoln, Nebraska. It would be here that we would enter into Inspect and Repair As Necessary (IRAN) contracts for Army helicopters, USAF T-39s and, eventually, the F-4Es.

This book is really about the Wild Weasel Program of the Air Force, but you might be wondering what the U. S. Navy was doing during this same period of time. The Navy had a program with Melpar to build the AN/APR-23 that was updated to the -23B, and then was redesigned to become the AN/APR-24. These were the radar warning systems that were used in, I believe, the A-4 SkyHawk and A-7 Corsair. Somewhere along the line, Rear Admiral Julian S. Lake was briefed on the Wild Weasel Program. He decided that he would like to try out an APR-25 in one of the F-4Bs, the Navy Phantom built by McDonnell Aircraft, and compare it with the Melpar systems. So, we got an APR-25 down to Miramar (San Diego) and assisted in the installation. However, the Navy was not interested in the WR-300/APR-26; they let a contract to Magnavox to develop the AN/ALR-50 for their missile-warning receiver.

As a result of the APR-25 flight test success, the Navy ultimately decided to procure a number of systems via the MIPR process (Multi-service Inter Procurement Regulations) from the Air Force to outfit a squadron of A-7s for an aircraft carrier deployment to South East Asia. If my memory serves me correctly, the Naval Air Repair Facility (NARF) in Philadelphia was assigned the installation work for the Corsairs. One day we got a phone call from the EW shop at Point Mugu informing us that a couple of A-7s would be there the next day and asking if we would like to come down and see the installation. We allowed as how we would certainly like to do that. So, the next day about half a dozen of us drove down to Pt. Mugu and got there early afternoon and found that the aircraft had already arrived.

We started looking over the airplanes and began to find a lot of discrepancies. Antennas were mounted with only two to three of the four required screws; where there should have been coaxial cables from the Amp-Detector boxes to the processor there were just lossy, shielded wires;

cable harnesses were not well supported; and so on. After about an hour of poking around and seeing the problems, I decided to call Julian who was in Washington, D.C. When I told him about our findings, he said he would be there the next day to see for himself.

Sure enough, the next morning he hops in his A-4 and flies out to Pt. Mugu. He took a look at the airplanes on the ramp and was more than mildly ticked-off. It seems these airplanes were due to be flown aboard the carrier two days from then while the carrier was steaming to Hawaii on its way to Vietnam. He borrowed an office and a telephone in the EW shop and called the NARF and chewed someone out rather soundly. We could hear his elevated voice through the door. Even though we couldn't understand the words, we knew that he was not a happy camper. The ultimate arrangement was that the airplane installations would be reworked here on the west coast, either at Miramar or Alameda Naval Air Station (Oakland), with ATI assistance and the birds would be flown to Hawaii to catch up with the carrier. When I asked Julian why don't you just delay the sailing date of the ship, the response was that a carrier never sails late!

In March, 1967, we got a Navy contract for a number of systems which were to be nomenclatured the AN/APR-25 (N). These systems would be modified from the Air Force systems to accommodate threat logic that covered Russian ship threat radars as well as the land-based SA-2 and AAA, and MiG interceptors/fighters. This was to be the Navy standard for a short time, but more about that later.

Julian, having been briefed by KC Dempster on the Wild Weasel activities, thought it would be great if the Navy had a similar program. However, his bosses told him not to pursue that idea and to leave the SAM and Triple A SEAD role to the Air Force as they were currently engaged.

One of the most memorable gatherings that I have ever attended was the first Society of Wild Weasels meeting held on April 22,1967, at Nellis Air Force Base, Las Vega, Nevada. There were thirteen of us from ATI including Bill Ayer, Bill Doyle, Tony Ethier, Bob Johnson, and Tony Taussig; Gen. K. C. Dempster, Lt. Col. Gary Willard, Capt. Jack Donovan, and a host of other USAF pilots and EWOs; people from NAA and Republic Aircraft; and a gaggle of folks from SMAMA. Some of us had brought our wives, at the invitation of KC, because he wanted us non-military folks to get a better feeling of what the air crews and their families were up against.

I know that my wife, Virginia, was really affected when meeting Pat Trier and Mrs. John Pitchford and she realized that Pat's husband was dead and Mrs. Pitchford's husband was a North Vietnamese prisoner. Virginia said later that evening that "Now I understand why you spend all of that time at the plant and even bring work home to do in the evening".

It was also April of 1967, on my birthday to be exact, when we shook hands with the Board of Directors of ITEK Corporation in an agreement of merger, with ITEK to be the surviving entity, and ATI to be a Division of the company. Bill Ayer had been getting a bit concerned about our huge success in the RHAW business almost to the exclusion of everything else—about 80% RHAW and 20% other business. So, we had talked to Henry Singleton of Teledyne, a number of people from Magnavox (which, incidentally, developed the AN/ALR-50 Missile Warning Receiver for the Navy), and a couple of other companies that seemed far less compatible in life style to ATI. The ITEK folk were pleasant and reasonable; the company had a National Asset in their Optical Systems Division; and it had commercial businesses as well; so we thought that we would have a better merger with them than with any of the other companies with whom we had talked. With all of the "due diligence" meetings and the drafting of the terms of the merger, the marriage did not take place until September 1967.

During this period of investigation, ATI began the work on what was to be our new administration, marketing, and finance building at 3412 Hillview Avenue. This was another 5-acres site and adjacent to the original building into which we had moved in January 1964. Now it turns out that the Mexican Company, SYNTEX, moved part of their research operations to across the street from us. They were deeply into hormonal research, initially for cattle. However, they had some geniuses who were pursuing human hormone studies. Out of some of their research came the "PILL". Thusly, Hillview Avenue became known as Countermeasures Row with ATI on one side and SYNTEX on the other.

Somewhere along here in time, we were awarded a contract from the Air Force to upgrade the APR-25 and APR -26 to the AN/APR-36 and AN/APR-37, respectively. This would initially be a lot of work for the Sunnyvale engineering development group since updated logic was to be provided, more modern parts were to be used, and the systems were to be full Mil-Spec'd from the outset. This was great for the engineering group, but manufacturing was beginning to feel a pinch in that production orders were on the shy side. As a result, we had a layoff of about 20% company wide with normal attrition taking care of several percent more people. This reduction in force lasted through to the spring of 1968.

Also, in 1967, we began the development of the ER-151 that was based upon an IR&D program of the company that resulted in the PR-500 multi-band, electronically-tuned- superheterodyne receiver. The ER-151 was a tri-band receiver which was to give additional capabilities as compared to the IR-133 and the ER-142 tuned r-f type receivers. We envisioned this receiver as going into an updated F-105F that would eventually be named the F-105G. After being nomenclatured by the Air Force, the system would be known as the AN/APR-35. This gave us the unusual position of having three AN numbers in a row: AN/APR-35, -36, and -37.

In November of 1967, the USAF asked ATI to make a tour of Belgium, Denmark, Germany, The Hague, The Netherlands, Norway, and Great Britain to tell them of the success that the US was having with Radar Warning Receivers, to brief them on the technology, and to show them via a simulator how the systems worked. So, Ed Chapman, Jim Reid, and I made a seven-country tour in ten days under the sponsorship of both the Air Force and NATO. We had a Lt. Col. from NATO Headquarters assigned to us to ease us through customs at each airport since our data and simulator were classified. He was really a big help. We would get to a customs area and he would show a badge and we were on our way through the gate in no time flat. Also, he was well versed in European travel whereas the three of us were in Europe for the first time. So, he made all of the travel and hotel arrangements in real time since we never knew how long we might be in any one location. The briefings were well received by the Ministry of Defense of each of the countries, but it would be a couple of years before any RWR systems would begin to be introduced into their aircraft and ships.

Then, in June 1968, all hell began to break loose. 1) The Navy awarded us a contract for $4.6 million for 400 RHAW systems. 2) A contract was signed with the USAF for $2.8 million for installation of "improved" RHAW equipment in the F-4E airplanes at our Lincoln, Nebraska, facility. The contract was negotiated and signed by Col. Frank Witry, Jr., for the Air Force and by me for the company. This contract would eventually total 500 F-4Es modified at Lincoln. 3) A USAF contract for $2.9 million were awarded a $1.15 million contract for T-39 IRAN work at Lincoln. 5) The Microwave Lab received an order from Westinghouse for 150 additional solid-state oscillators for use in their airborne radars at a value of $400K. 6) A $114K contract was received from the Army for modification and installation of a RHAW system in the SP-2 aircraft. 7) A USAF contact for $374K was received for the start of design and production of 25 new RHAW systems. 8) A $1.9 million contract was awarded by the Air Force for airborne recorders for the F-105F/G airplanes. That was one helluva month for new orders!

The contract for the airborne recorders was for a system that we called the ARRS-100 (Airborne Receiver Recorder System-100) The idea was that we would install these recorders in the F-105Gs and have the aircrews record pertinent aircraft data such as airspeed, altitude, attitude, heading, and all audio chatter cockpit-to-cockpit and air-to-air from the aircraft internal systems along with the video outputs from the AN/APR-35, -36, and -37. This way an entire mission could be played back on the ground with a system, the GRPS-75 (Ground Receiver Playback System-75), including all of the appropriate instruments that the pilot and the EWO would have in the cockpits of the airplane. It was our plan that a mission could be played back in its entirety for "post-mortems" of the aircrew actions and for training of new crews prior to their going into combat.

In September, 1968, we moved into our new building at 3412 Hillview Avenue, Palo Alto, CA. Almost as though it were to celebrate the completion of this beautiful new structure by the company, we were awarded $26 million in new orders by the Air Force. The largest of these was for $14 million to manufacture APR-36s and -37s that were to be installed in F-4Es at our Lincoln Aerospace Center in Nebraska. Another $6.5 million was for advanced airborne ECM equipment including $1.5 million for spare parts. Finally, a $6 million contract was signed with the Air Force for the benefit of the U.S. Navy for more RHAW equipment plus spare parts.

In October, the first two AN/APR-35s were delivered, five-and-one-half months after the contract had been signed on April 15, 1968. Systems number 3 and 4 were coming along right behind the first two systems under the contract which called for the delivery of 25 of these sophisticated receiver systems.

I remember one incident that I thought was rather humorous at the time. A system was in test in the manufacturing department and the test folks were having trouble getting a CRT indicator for the APR-35 to pass its acceptance tests. So, Joe Russell, who was leading the manufacturing effort, called me at home about 1 o'clock that Saturday afternoon and said that we had a problem. I went down to the plant, but I had had nothing to do with the design of the unit under test so I wasn't of a lot of use. So, I called Frank A. Wilshusen (WW # 956) and asked him to come down and to give us a hand. Frank solved the problem in short order and, as he headed back home, he said: "John, I want you to know that we bachelors have private lives, too." Frank was dating his wife-to-be, Doreen, at that time and they had serious plans for the weekend and I had interrupted whatever it was that they had planned. At any rate, the Indicator then passed its required tests and was sold off to the AF inspectors.

There was another incident with respect to Indicators, only this one was for the 3"-diameter CRTs used in the Warning Receivers. We used about two CRTs for every system shipped, counting spares, and we were shipping about 225 systems per month, equivalent. Corning Glass was the producer of the glass "bottles" for the tubes and we were using up a significant proportion of their production of these envelopes. We got the word somehow or another that they were planning a plant shutdown for summer vacations for their people. That meant there would not be any tubes produced for about two weeks; that could put a real glitch into the shipping schedule. I don't remember exactly how it came about, but Dick (Richard A.) Haggren (WW # 239) was at the Air Staff at the time, so he got something like a DX-A2 Priority Rating from the Secretary of the Air Force and got Corning to keep their production line open so that the supply of CRTs would not be interrupted. I think that Dick would have gotten a DX-A9 or maybe even a "BrickBat" rating if Corning had put up an argument. It was a big help to us and for the people at the AMAs installing hardware in airplanes.

As you might imagine, running a business is not always a lot of fun and "sweetness and light". A situation arose where the Director of Development Engineering in Sunnyvale got "crosswise-in-the-slot" with Tony (H.E.) Ethier (WW # 214) who was Director of the RHAW Program Office and who reported directly to Bill Ayer. The Engineering Director, in turn, reported directly to Tony. Well, he did something or other that caused Tony to summarily fire him. Very shortly after that, we were served with a lawsuit alleging "unlawful termination". He had gotten a Labor Relations attorney to file a suit claiming that since the Director's last annual performance review stated that his salary would be such and such on an annual basis, he was at least entitled to termination pay in one lump sum equivalent to his anticipated salary for a full year.

The company attorneys suggested that the ex-Director might actually win since this was a civil action and you don't need a "beyond a reasonable doubt" unanimous jury decision in such a case. So, we settled out of court to get rid of the hassle and to spend our efforts on the programs that were so very important to us. However, problems such as this often have further ramifications. In our case, the lawsuit resulted in the immediate adoption of hourly pay rates for everyone from the President on down. All offers of employment would also be stated in hourly pay rates. There were no more annual salaries within the company.

Incidentally, this man was the same person who had earlier caused a "palace revolution" within the engineering department when it all reported to me. We had hired him from Lockheed Missiles and Space Company (LMSC) in Sunnyvale to report directly to me with the job of running the engineering department on a day-to-day basis. After a few months of his management, I got a phone call one evening from one of the engineers, Tim Murphy, who asked me to come to a meeting at his house. So, I agreed and went there after supper to learn what was going on. Well, there were several of the top engineers of the company meeting in Tim's garage workshop. The issue was that if something wasn't done about this new Director, they were all going to quit! These were the men who had been the prime movers in the development of the Wild Weasel equipment up to this point in time. We couldn't afford to lose them!

It seems that this fellow's management style was to totally restrict the contact of engineers with upper management unless he gave his specific approval and knew exactly what was to be discussed. Preferably, he would be in the meeting, as well. Now, these were the men who had rubbed elbows with Bill Ayer and me while we jointly designed, built, and trouble-shot all the new systems when we were small. So, they were used to walking into Bill's or my office whenever they felt like it, whenever our doors were open. This new regime was not at all to their liking and they weren't going to put up with this martinet telling them how they were going to live. The solution to the problem was to establish the Development Engineering Group in Sunnyvale with the Director's own hand-chosen folks from LMSC who were used to his particular style of leading.

November 1968 ushered in the halt of bombing of North Vietnam as ordered by President Lyndon Johnson. The Wild Weasels had to "stand down". As is typical in such situations, the U.S. tends to forget that equipment needs to be maintained and refurbished regardless of whether or not you are using it every day or have it in reserve for future use. During this bombing-halt period of time, the RWRs were allowed to deteriorate to the point where it took the Field Service Personnel and the Military Personnel a number of weeks to get ready when the whistle blew again for North Vietnam bombing. This, of course, happened in April 1972.

A Change in Management...

In early January 1969, Bill Ayer announced his resignation as President of the Applied Technology Division of the ITEK Corporation, although he would stay on the Board of Directors of ITEK. He, therefore, would no longer be involved in the day-to-day operation of the company that he had founded in April of 1959, nearly ten years earlier.

The Directors asked me if I would like to take the job, but I declined explaining that I felt quite strongly that the President should have both a flair for—and a love of—marketing. I could do marketing work, but it was a struggle for me; my love was more for the engineering and management of new product development. So, I recommended that they appoint George W. Deskin (WW # 216) to be the new President since he wanted that position very badly and I thought that he had the requisite marketing skills to do the job. The Board accepted my recommendation and that came to pass—George took over the Presidency of ATI. He had joined ATI in 1964 from Sylvania Electric in Mountain View, CA, where he had been worked in the Reconnaissance Systems Laboratory that did work primarily for the Army and the Navy. He was a degreed electrical engineer from University of California at Berkeley and had spent some time in the Navy as an enlisted seaman prior to his university work. The only thing that I should have remembered at the time was that he was in charge of the Systems Engineering Group that turned down Bob Klimek's idea for SEESAM in early 1966, ATI's first significant marketing blunder. Oops!

The Division had it pretty well "made in the shade" when George took over as the President since we had received beaucoup new orders in the last half of 1968—something over $40 million. Also, during mid-1968 we had initiated a study of the Navy requirements for their radar warning needs. We studied the Elint tables and identified the Soviet sea systems which the Navy might one day have to fight as well as the land-based threats with which the Marines would have to contend. This in-house study was followed in mid-1969 by an unsolicited proposal to the Navy to replace their AN/APR-25s with a new system. The Navy, in January of 1970, issued ATI a contract for the development and delivery of four service test models of the AN/ALR-45 that would become the new standard for Navy RWRs.

The Signal Processor in the ALR-45 was really different from the previous processors that we had designed for the radar warning systems. The company had established a micro-electronics facility that could dramatically increase the component density by assembling "unmounted" electronic components into one-inch square packages. This meant that more signal processing could be accomplished in the same size box as all of the other warning systems. Not only that, but the technical architecture of the processor was such that it used quartz-crystal clocks for the establishment of the timing during the signal processing. It was, in fact, a digital processor, albeit that it was hardware programmable, not software programmable. That meant that to update the processing for new threat data it was necessary to use long-nosed pliers, a soldering iron, and wire-wrap tools to physically move wires from one terminal to another. Also, it was possible that a new micro-electronic circuit would need to be developed to handle a new, complex signal. This was really the state of the art at that point in time—there were no small airborne software-programmable digital computers available.

The USAF in 1970 issued contracts in the amount of $4.8 million for AN/APR-35s and $1.4 million for the GRPS-75 ground playback systems for the F-105Gs in addition to more orders for the APR-36 and -37. The Navy, in December, awarded a production contract for ALR-45s in the amount of $6.6 million with delivery of the first system scheduled for March, 1971.

In 1971 we delivered six LRU (Line Replaceable Unit) Testers for the APR-35s for Field- and Depot-test and repair of the removable boxes of the receiver system. This would immensely reduce the trouble shooting and repair cycle time of the hardware when there was a problem. The QRC-535 Program was initiated for the updating of the APR-26 and –37 missile warning receivers, and the Air Force and the Navy awarded the company another $17.6 million for -36, -37, and -45s in three contracts during the year.

One of our big breaks came when Bill Rambo, who was on old friend and boss of both Bill Ayer and me during our Stanford days, and also was a Director of ATI at its formation, told us about a young, brilliant graduate student who was just finishing his Ph.D. This young man was a rather independent soul and was supposed to have an interview at Hewlett Packard; however, the personnel department at HP kept him cooling his heels for upwards of an hour without paying any attention to him. So, he walked out the door and gave us a call. We interviewed him and immediately hired him. What a lucky break for us and a real loss for HP, but they never knew it. The gentleman was Dr. Eckhard Schulz who was born in Germany, was fluent in several languages and could get by in half a dozen others. He was to become a kingpin in our International business and in the development of our in-house computer; but more about that later.

This same year saw the delivery of the AN/ALR-53 for the Air Force and the AN/ALR-54 for the Navy; both systems were adaptations of the APR-36 and -37. The ALR-54 was to be mounted in helicopters that would, typically, land on helipads on smaller naval vessels. One story about the -54 is that one day a helo returned to its ship and landed as usual. While the pilot was in the process of shutting down and cleaning up the cockpit another crew member looked at the display of the -54 and asked “what’s that?” The answer was that the display was showing a missile approaching the ship from the rear where the helicopter had landed. Countermeasures were employed and the missile missed. After that, it was standard practice on that ship to leave the -54 on all the time and have someone monitor the display.

The year 1972 brought our first direct international order: Denmark bought the AN/ALR-45 for their aircraft. The -45 was a better fit for them than the -36/-37 due to its programming for Naval radars. Also, we delivered our first light-weight warning system, the AN/APR-41, to the U.S. Army for helicopter installations. The program really never did go much of anywhere because Dalmo Victor had its AN/APR-39 Warning System which was being sold into Army programs. They also had the AN/APS-109 Warning Receiver, so DV and ATI were competitors in the RWR business, but we had bought antenna systems from them in the early days of ATI for our ground based Dual-band 10-20 GHz and 20-40 GHz superheterodyne direction finding receivers for an unnamed agency of the U.S. Government.

A very significant event also occurred in 1972. The Request for Proposal for the Radar Warning Receiver for the F-15 Eagle was issued in late 1971 with a deadline for submittal right after the first of the next year. Of course, this meant that all of the proposal teams would have to work like mad over the Christmas and New Year Holiday period. It wasn't easy, but the proposal was completed on time and was hand-delivered to the appropriate office at Wright-Patterson AFB at Dayton, Ohio. It was anticipated that this system would be the next Wild Weasel for the Air Force. After a short period for the USAF and McDonnell to review the proposals submitted by industry, we were requested to be at WPAFB in early February to defend our proposal and to potentially negotiate a contract for the development of this new system.

The weather in Dayton had been very snowy in the weeks prior to the meeting. The streets, parking lots, and sidewalks were covered with ice making it exceedingly difficult to drive or even to walk. Besides that, it was colder than the dickens.

Well, we were not the only ones invited to the soiree. My recollection is that three contractors showed up: Applied Technology, Loral, and Sylvania, Buffalo, NY. The three contractors were duly quizzed in parallel by three teams of McDonnell people since they were the airplane prime contractor: they would be the decision makers with Air Force concurrence. All three companies negotiated prices and specifications with the McD folks. Then a representative of each company who had the authorization to contractually bind the company was asked to sign a Model Contract, which we all did. The three teams of inquisitors and negotiators then proceeded to evaluate and compare their respective quotes. At the end of the third day, the decision had been made: Loral was the winner! This receiver system then became the AN/ALR-56. The F-15 was the only Tactical Fighter in the entire Air Force that ATI would not be a supplier of radar warning equipment. I have always felt that if ATI had taken Bob Klimek up on his

SEESAM idea, Loral would have never gotten into the Wild Weasel or radar warning business. It was a tough one to lose.

As it turned out, even though there was a lot of talk several times about making the two-seat F-15 into a Wild Weasel bird, it never came to pass.

I don't remember when it actually occurred, but it must have been around this time that a new Request for Proposal was issued for the new RHAW system for the F-4F. McDonnell was again to be the prime contractor for the electronics since they were the airframe prime, as well. In order to try to get the latest information, I visited Walt (Truman W.) Lifsey (WW# 8) in the Pentagon. Walt was on the Air Staff and was heavily involved in the requirements definition of the new hardware. The meeting was cordial, but no new useful information was obtained to help us in the proposal writing. The proposals were submitted on time by us and the other potential contractors. McDonnell then chose the winning team, which included IBM for software, Loral for receivers, and Texas Instruments for digital computers, if I remember correctly. Once again, ATI was on the outside looking in. This was not good!

Then, to top things off, we had another marketing disaster, a result of a senior management goof. Adm. Julian Lake visited ATI with the idea of having a digital processor at the heart of Navy warning systems. He wanted it to be software programmable and, hopefully, to be able to walk up to an airplane with a plastic card in hand, plug it into a slot in the side of the airplane and thereby reprogram the processor for the very latest threat table. A great idea that all the Military Services would love to have implemented.

Recall, now, that ATI was building lots of ALR-45s for the Navy and that the processor was digital, but it was hardware programmable only. Julian wanted a software programmable processor. The President of ATI, now George Deskin, kept telling Julian that he didn't need a S/W programmable processor, that ATI would keep updating the -45 as needed and that would satisfy the Navy perceived requirements. Julian kept coming back with I WANT A SOFTWARE PROGRAMMABLE DIGITAL PROCESSOR. George would then try to sell more -45s. Finally, Julian gave up. What did he do? He took his $1.6 million, got another $1.4 million from the Air Force, and drove fifteen miles up the road to Belmont to Dalmo Victor, our competitor, and gave them a contract to do what he wanted. Talking about someone having a flair for marketing—this was giant mistake number two! If it had been my call, I would have taken his money and did what he wanted. This fiasco darn near sank ATI because DV wound up with "our" processor business and caused the creation of the AN/ALR-46. That left us with the Antennas, Amp-Detectors, CRT Indicators and the Threat Display Unit. We then had about half the system value and DV had the other half.

What did DV do? Well, it turns out that the ROLM Corporation in Sunnyvale had a license from Data General (computers) to militarize one of their digital computers. ROLM was successful at that redesign and had their new computer put through environmental tests so that it could be used for whatever necessary military purposes including airborne applications. So, DV got into a business relationship with ROLM where DV would buy their computer circuit cards and put them into a processor box the same size as that of all of the warning systems that ATI had built and was building: it was the de facto standard size for all RWR processor boxes. DV worked closely with the engineering folks at Warner Robin Air Logistics Center, Georgia, (WRALC) and developed the software that would control the processor and perform the signal processing. The engineering people at WRALC whom I remember were Joe Black (WW # 2011) and John Lavecchia (WW # 2047), in particular.

In order to gain better control of our fate, we decided to develop our own airborne computer, one that would be designed specifically to best handle the signal processing required in a dense electromagnetic environment. We launched the development of the ATAC (APPLIED TECHNOLOGY ADVANCED COMPUTER). The program was under the overall direction of Bill Doyle with Ed Radkowski as the Project Manager and Dr. Eckhard Schulz as the technical lead. Strangely enough, Texas Instruments allowed us to use their emulator to design our computer. We hooked up via telephone line to their computer in Texas and paid them by the minute of CPU time consumed by our requests for design time. It turned out to be terribly beneficial to us: we wouldn't have been able to accomplish the design without that assistance. Why TI ever allowed that has always puzzled me. It was allowing someone to get at the family jewels. It turns out that it was the last time they let anyone use their emulator. Anyhow, the ATAC was completed in early 1973.

With this new specialized EW computer in hand, we designed the VECTOR V under our IR&D program to be our answer to new system requirements. Although it wouldn't displace the DV processor with the ROLM computer boards, it gave us a leg up on International sales because our computer was not AN nomenclatured and the government did not have any of their money in the computer development—it was all ours. Of course, we had to jump through the hoops of The State Department, The Commerce Department, and the Military Review Boards for the suitability of technology transfer. We got licenses to talk to Germany, Denmark, and Norway, among others.

The APR-37 was updated to the APR-37(M) via the QRC-535 Program. This saw its way into the VECTOR V system and subsequently, with certain modifications, became the APR-37D for Denmark to go with their ALR-45D that had a different Threat Table than the US Navy. Also, the APR-37C was adapted for sale to Canada along with the ALR-45C with still a different Threat Table defined by Canada. These two units considered as a system were then nomenclatured the AN/ALR-501C and were installed in all of Canada's F-104Cs, both domestic and overseas.

As Dalmo Victor proceeded with their manufacture of the first production quantity of ROLM-based processors, George Deskin, ATI's President, was keeping in touch with the Colonel in charge of procurement at Warner Robins (WRALC). That was good on George's part—good marketing, right? George was sure that he had an agreement with the Colonel that when the next production quantity was defined, an RFP would be issued to industry to bid on—one that could include the incumbent, DV, and ATI, TI, IBM, and any other qualified bidder. Guess what? The next thing we knew was that DV had been awarded a sole-source contract for the next production lot of Processors!

George was really P-O'd! He called the Colonel at WRALC and read him the riot act, told him he thought we had a deal about competitive procurement and that if the order to DV wasn't rescinded that he would sue the Air Force. That latter part was not too swift—another super marketing blunder. The Air Force did NOT rescind the procurement, but the blue-suiters locked arms from the Pentagon to Warner Robins making an almost impenetrable wall for ATI. The US Air Force does not take lightly to the threat of a law suit from a disgruntled contractor. Anyway, a few weeks later I had to go to Washington as an emissary of the Company.

I was, at the time, the Executive Vice President of ATI with absolutely no one reporting to me, not even a secretary—a result of one of the many management shuffles performed by George in his experimentation of how to run a company. I guess you might think of my position as an Ambassador Without Portfolio. Anyhow, Joe Russell, who was ATI's VP of Manufacturing, and I had an appointment with Lt. Col. Leon Huffman in the Pentagon.

Lt. Col. Huffman had a nicely appointed office and there were several other officers with him. I made our spiel about how we thought that the company had had an agreement with the WRALC Colonel with respect to a competitive procurement and that we would really like to be able to participate in the Processor Program even if it had to be as a second source. Leon and his cohorts were polite, but cool, listened to us, and said that there was nothing that they could do about the sole-source procurement, that was in the domain of WRALC to decide. If we wanted to pursue a second source position that was okay with him, but it would be up to DV to make that decision if they wanted to split up their order and share it with us, and oh, by the by, of course we would have to become a "qualified" supplier. They also let it be known, without directly saying so, that suing the Air Force would not win ATI any brownie points for future work which would include follow-on orders for the Antennas, Amp-Detectors, CRT Indicators, TDUs, and Walk-Around Test Sets for the ALR-46. Now, that was something to ponder!

Upon returning to Sunnyvale, I told George that he had better formally back off of the threat of the lawsuit or that ATI would likely lose the half of the system that we still retained. He was not really wild about that idea because he thought there was an implied contract, as a result of his telephone conversations with the Colonel, for the Air Force to hold a competitive procurement. Of course, DV was not interested in the least of splitting up their order for the Processors to have us be a second source. Their having the whole thing to themselves was far more to their liking, as you might imagine.

In August of 1973, a group of us from ATI were invited to the First Real Reunion of the Red River Valley Fighter Pilots Association in Las Vegas, Nevada. Our group consisted of Jim Brennan, Marketing; Bill Doyle, acting V.P. of Engineering; Pierre Levy, Marketing; Dave McBride, Field Service; Jerry Stone, Field Service; and me. Those of us who were married took our wives, as well. There were over 2,600 people in attendance at the reunion, so the banquet was held in the Convention Center of Las Vegas. Virginia and I were honored to be seated at the table with Major General Bill Chairsell and his wife, H. Ross Perot and Margo, Tech Sgt. Don Rander, and Lt. Col. "Doc"Cataldo. Sgt. Rander had been a POW since about 1965 and had been located at the Son Tay prison. "Doc" Cataldo was the Army Chief Flight Surgeon and he had participated in the Son Tay raid in 1970. You may recall that the raid was not successful in rescuing the prisoners because the North Vietnamese had taken the prisoners out of that prison and moved them elsewhere just a few days prior to the raid.

Each of the major casinos donated an act for entertainment at the banquet in honor of all of the returned POW's in addition to honoring all the rest of the River Rat Community and the Wild Weasels. There was Foster Brooks (The Drunk), the B. B. King Group, Tony Martin, Wayne Newton, Patti Page, Connie Stevens, and other acts. The brightest moment during the entertainment came when Patti Page sang the song "Tie a Yellow Ribbon 'Round the Old Oak Tree. Two men tied dozens of pieces of the yellow table linen together and began to festoon them across the girders of the dome of the banquet hall. They continued onto the stage where Miss Page was singing and began to wrap her in the "yellow ribbon". It really brought the house down!

The most poignant moment of the reunion came when it was time to install the clapper in the Freedom Bell. The bell had been cast in 1967 in South Vietnam with the resolve that it would not be rung until all of the prisoners had been released. As I recall, the idea of the bell originated with members of the 388th Tactical Fighter Wing which was based in Thailand. A crack was molded into the bell to simulate The Liberty Bell in Philadelphia. On the top of the "Pagoda" supporting the bell was a box with a pair of untied sneakers of the type that had been used on the Son Tay raid. "Doc" Cataldo and Tech. Sgt. Rander were invited to go to the table holding the display and to tie the shoes for the first time while the bell was being rung and rung and rung for its first time. There were a lot of moist eyes in the banquet room, as you might well imagine.

During the reunion, I was told two stories which I have never forgotten. One story was told by Jim (James W.) O'Neill (WW # 72). Jim said that after he had finished his one hundred missions in Wild Weasel 3-1, he had returned stateside and had then volunteered to return for another tour of duty in the Wild Weasel program. One day, on his fifth mission of this second tour, leading a flight of four F-105Ds, his warning system told them that there was a Fan Song on the air. Soon his "OS" light came on meaning that a missile was likely headed in his direction. He said that "I've done this so many times, that I just kept motoring along, but I told the squadron to "break". Then I looked out to the side of the airplane and there was this big telephone pole and it went 'BANG'." The airplane was hit by shrapnel, caught on fire and he and his EWO ejected. As a result of this miscalculation, he spent about six months in the "Hanoi Hilton". Fortunately, he survived his ordeal at the hands of his captors.

The other story was told to me by EWO Mike (Kevin A.) Gilroy (WW # 174). He said that numerous times he flew over the harbor at Haiphong and could see crated Guideline missiles on the docks, but they were refused permission to bomb them. As a result, the aircrews had to take the missiles on one at a time in the air, in combat! What a helluva way to run a war! Of course, the politicians in Washington had their reasons, but it doesn't make a man in combat feel too good about the proposition when he is being shot at.

One day we had a visit at ATI from General Abrhamson who was the Director of the F-16 Special Project Office for this brand new fighter airplane. He told us of the overall plans for the airplane that it might evolve into a two-seat airplane, and potentially could become a Wild Weasel type platform. It would need a Radar Warning System on board in the strictly fighter version, that there would be a whole lot of them, and that the airplanes were to cost no more than $6.3 million each in then-year dollars. Also, he went on to say that in order to get Belgium, The Netherlands, Denmark, and Norway to buy the F-16, the Memorandum of Understanding between the US and the foreign community stated that, in the aggregate, we, the US, would guarantee those four countries an offset of 115% of the value of the airplanes that they purchased from us. That meant, for example, if they bought a billion dollars worth of airplanes produced in the US, that we, in turn, would give them 1.15 billion dollars of work, somehow or another. This "offset" problem didn't appear to be of any concern of ours at the time, but it would come into play a little later.

As time passed and we kept producing our part of the warning systems, we got the word that the Air Force, through WRALC, had let a contract to ARINC to "reverse engineer" our proprietary Radar Warning

System. This was not good at all because it meant that Warner Robins would be able to go to industry for competitive bids for our portion of the ALR-46; however, it would leave DV in a sole-source position for the processor using the ROLM computer cards. Did the Air Force take this position because George had threatened the lawsuit? Were they going to show ATI that it was not in the driver's seat with its proprietary position in the Warning Receiver business, or what? I tend to think, but I'll never know, that the USAF was upset enough about the threatened lawsuit that they were going to become independent of ATI even though if another company won a competitive bid that the Air Force would have either another single-source supplier, or a group of suppliers who would provide the individual portions which made up the system. It would also mean a learning curve as the new contractors came up to speed in piece-parts procurement, manufacturing techniques, individual box and system test, and got their parts of the system passed through the MIL-SPEC process. It seemed to me that it was almost a case of "cutting one's nose off to spite one's face." Nevertheless, ARINC was doing the job that they were hired to do. We didn't know their schedule or their contractual delivery date, and it seemed that there wasn't anyone about to tell us. It sounded as though we might be in terrible straits in the not too distant future.

Meanwhile, McDonnell had a need for a Special Warning Receiver (SWR) to be developed for the AN/APR-38 to go into the F-4Fs. We bid the job and won it: this would put us into the Advanced Wild Weasel System. That was wonderful. However, the design and development turned out to be a real bear. Bill Doyle and the engineers really had their hands full. The design was especially difficult because the box had to be fairly small for the functions which the receiver had to perform. It was a lot of electronics for a small box.

ANOTHER CHANGE IN MANAGEMENT...

Well, along about this same time, George and Bob Henderson, who was the President of ITEK Corp. and to whom George reported, went on an International trip so that Bob could meet some of the higher-ups in the various countries where ATI was doing business either on a Foreign Military Sales (FMS) basis as in Iran for their F-4E fleet, or direct sales to countries such as Germany for the MRCA Tornado. Something went terribly wrong on the trip and when they returned to the U.S., Bob transferred George to the Corporate payroll and asked me to take over the Division. This time I said "Yes!" This took me from the Ambassador Without Portfolio role to being the Division President.

So, in June of 1975, I became the President of the Applied Technology Division of ITEK Corporation reporting to Sal Macera who, in turn, reported to Bob Henderson. I told Bob that my wife and I were about to have our twenty-fifth wedding anniversary and that we had tickets for a ten-days cruise of the Caribbean to take place in mid-July. As luck would have it, the SWR development was in fairly deep trouble so that McDonnell put an engineer and a quality inspector in our plant in Sunnyvale so that the St. Louis folks would have someone with whom to talk everyday. They wanted "tight coupling" so that they would know exactly what progress was occurring with the design. The delivery date was getting close and we still had a lot of work to do. I was willing to delay our "second honeymoon" trip, but Bob told me to go ahead with our plans, that I wasn't involved in the design and it was up to the engineering department to get the problems solved. So, Virginia and I went on our cruise and had a wonderful time. I put Joe Russell, the head of manufacturing and a Senior Vice President of ATI, in charge while I was to be gone. No one, but no one, tried to get in touch with me to indicate that things were going from bad to worse.

When I returned to the plant after having had a wonderful vacation, I immediately learned that we had a real-life lawsuit on our hands. Joe had been talking to Col. (Ret.) Jake Pompan who, at WRALC, had been a lawyer in the contracts department. Jake evidently told Joe that since the company was having a tremendous amount of trouble getting the SWR designed and running, ATI could take the position that it was "Commercially Infeasible" and that the contract should be called null and void. So, he filed a lawsuit against McDonnell without Joe calling me or ITEK Headquarters. Now it turns out that McDonnell had been talking about penalties on the contract since the company was late with delivery of the first SWR. So, I guess, Joe figured he would get the jump on McDonnell and starts a suit against them before they filed a suit against us. This was not an auspicious beginning to my tour of duty as President of ATI.

ITEK Headquarters got their own lawyers involved now that the suit was under way. I went to St. Louis hoping that I could get an agreement with them to call off the suit and ATI would negotiate a settlement in good faith. They let me know in no uncertain terms that there had been some unpleasantness between their folks and ours and that we had started this and they would finish it on their terms. Ouch! So, depositions were taken from me, some of our engineers, and Joe Russell as well as folks from McDonnell and someone from Wright-Patterson AFB. Recognize that the SWR contract was between two commercial organizations, not between the government and a company. That put the contract under the Uniform Commercial Code as opposed to Government Procurement Regulations.

McDonnell was pushing for repayment of all the monies they had paid us to date plus Reprocurement costs. That latter item could be a "break your company" deal because you would have absolutely no control over the new company doing the development. We broached the subject of an out of court settlement asking what would it cost to get this lawsuit settled. The response was return all of the money they had paid to date, about $1.3 million, plus $1.0 million for their internal expenses and a cushion for the reprocurement. So, right off the bat, I've got a $2.3 million loss on my hands, no contract for the SWR (so once again we are out of the Advanced Wild Weasel program), and another black mark on our escutcheon. Damnation! When would things start going right?

As this whole fiasco was winding down, we had a visit from a Colonel assigned to WPAFB. He was from the F-4F SPO and was very interested in getting the APR-38 ready for flight test with an SWR as part of the system. He was looking for information from us as to what the major problems had been with our design and why we were having so much trouble. We gave him a thorough briefing and after it was all over, just before he left the plant, he pulled me aside and said, "John, you could have shipped us a box with sand in it and you would have met the delivery date". He went on to say that if ATI had worked with the Air Force we jointly could have solved all of the problems, but with that lawsuit, it just got out of hand and the USAF could do nothing to help us. I thanked him and let him know that I was really sorry that it had gotten to this state of affairs. So, that was that.

In November of 1975 we bid to the Navy on a new warning system for them, which would be nomenclatured the AN/ALR-67. This would be the system for the F-14 and the F-18 fleets—it would be the system of the future for the Navy. Our bid had our Applied Technology Advanced Computer (ATAC) at its heart for all of the system control and signal processing. It was quite a complex system which the Navy wanted and we felt that we knew the overall technology better than any other company. So, we bid $2.238 million and won the job that year.

Well, the funding for doing the work was pretty crazy. We initially got something like $300,000 on the Cost Plus Fixed Fee (CPFF) contract. When we were getting near the end of those funds, we contacted the Program Manager in the Navy and told him that we needed more money by such and such a date. Well, we got, maybe, another $50K. This sort of operation kept going on and on; sometimes we had more money invested in the program than the Navy did. We felt it was best to keep the program going on our money from time to time than to have it shut down and restart. We had the concurrence of the Administrative Contracting Officer (ACO) of the government, who resided in our facility, that our costs would be recognized as legitimate as long as the Navy kept coming through with additional funds. If the Navy canceled the contract on us while we were burning our own money, we would have to take that amount of money as a loss on our books: the government would have no responsibility for paying us from any account! It was risky, but it was the right thing to do.

I later found out from R. Adm. Julian Lake that the program manager, a Navy Captain, had "bootlegged" the whole thing. He was supposed to have his funding for the contract all lined up prior to the Navy signing the contract. He didn't, so he had to scrounge around his buddies in other program offices and scrape up left over dollars from their programs. That is why we kept getting dribs and drabs of money with large gaps of time involved from time to time. By the time the development was successfully concluded and the system was headed for production, ATI had accepted a ceiling-price on the contract and we had somewhere over $6 million invested in the program compared to the Navy's $5 million. Yes, there were some overruns due to the complexity of the development job, but it turned out to be a wonderful system for the Navy, and the company made back its investment during the multi-year production phase of the program.

In late-1975, Roger W. Anderson, our ALR-46 Program Manager, and I took a trip to WRALC to explain to the procurement and engineering offices that ATI was running out of contractually covered business and if we didn't get some additional orders in the very near future, we would have to reduce our manufacturing and assembly areas from multiple hundreds of people to a grand total of thirteen folks within three to four months. Not only that, but if they continued with their idea of a competitive procurement using the ARINC drawing package, one of the bidders might possibly undercut our price. If that were the case, the new contract would go to a company that had never built these systems. They would have to become qualified suppliers, and the systems passed through MIL-SPEC testing. This new "sole-source" supplier would need at least a year to come up to speed and it might take two years. What would the Air Force do for new installations and for spare parts in this scenario? They listened to us, but they didn't commit to anything that would help us out.

So here we were at the beginning of 1976 licking our wounds from the SWR fiasco, occasionally funding the Navy ALR-67 CPFF program, and using up our backlog of orders as we shipped the manufactured items on the various contracts with the Air Force. Lo and behold! We received the RFP from WRALC for the competitive procurement of another production quantity of warning systems. The package of drawings that arrived with the RFP were the ARINC Reverse Engineering documents for our proprietary system and the drawings were simultaneously sent to several other companies who were deemed by the government to be qualified vendors for such a procurement. Well, you can bet your bottom dollar that those drawings were reviewed by a group of eagle-eyed ATI people.

Again, guess what? One of our folks in Configuration Management was studying one of the ARINC drawings and found something very curious. He went back to our VECTOR IV drawings of 1965 and checked the same specific circuit area that he had been studying on the ARINC drawing. They were exactly the same. Well, you might say, ARINC was paid to reverse engineer our system, so it should be exactly the same. There is just one little problem. It turns out that the 1965 drawing had an error in it that was never corrected. The systems were not wired exactly as our old drawing showed: they were wired so that the particular circuit would work! Hence, the ARINC drawing had the 1965 ATI error in it and, therefore, ARINC could not possibly have taken a good, working unit, disassembled it, and determined the schematic diagram of that good unit and have this new schematic have the 1965 error in it. Someone had to have cut a corner and copied our erroneous drawing rather than spend the time in actual reverse engineering. OOPS!

So, after discovering this anomaly, Joe (Joseph F.) Lee (WW # 1008), whom I had appointed to be V.P. of Manufacturing, and I made an appointment with the new Colonel who was now the head of procurement at WRALC. We went to Warner Robins and met with the Colonel and his Deputy, who was a civilian. We explained to our audience that the procurement was flawed and that we felt like the procurement should be canceled and that all of the ARINC drawings and any and all copies thereof should be returned to WRALC forthwith. We showed them the old ATI drawing, the new ARINC drawing, and an ATI drawing that represented present production. The difference between the current ATI drawing and the ARINC drawing was obvious as was the similarity of the old ATI drawing and the ARINC version. The discussion was held in low-key with no histrionics and no threats of a lawsuit: It was just a matter-of-fact presentation that explained that we felt we had been done wrong and that we were relying on the government to make it right. Well, after a little while, when the enormity of the situation had had a chance to sink in, the Col. said, "Well, I guess we got caught with our hand in the cookie jar." That was the beginning of a wonderful relationship between the Col. and his Deputy and us. We became good business—as well as personal—friends. What did they do? They canceled the procurement, ordered all the ARINC drawings and any and all copies to be certified as being returned to WRALC. Finally, things were starting to go right for my term as president of ATI.

During all of this difficulty on the US programs, the German Advanced Radar Warning System was progressing through its development with the ATAC computer. A system was taken to the Dynamic Electromagnetic Environmental Simulator (DEES) simulator at WPAFB to prove to us, the Germans, and the US Government that we had a workable system for export to the Federal Republic of Germany (FRG). After the completion of the tests, the system was nomenclatured the AN/ALR-68, the next number after our AN/ALR-67 for the US Navy.

Returning now to the MOU of the US Government with the Four Consortium Countries who were buying the F-16, Joe Lee and I made another trip to Warner Robins to talk about additional production quantities of the Amp-Detectors of the ALR-46. I stayed up half the night in the motel trying to figure out the correct prices to quote for a large lot of Amp-Detectors. Well, the next day during a late morning meeting, I presented my thoughts as to how we should jointly proceed. Our hosts said that wasn't exactly what they had in mind and would we go to lunch with them at the "O"-Club? They said they would buy. What? That was essentially unheard of in my experience. So, we went as their guests.

What they had in mind was the fact that Norway was on the short end of the stick with respect to the 115% offset agreement in the F-16 MOU. That shortcoming had to be corrected and they could only think of one way to do it—would we help? Help with what? It was the natural response. They proceeded to lay out a plan. Norway wanted their fair share of business and they wanted it to be fairly high-tech. The processor being built by DV for the ALR-46 was off limits due to US restrictions on transfer of computer and software data as established by the Department of State, the Commerce Department, and the Military. However, the Amp-Detectors of the -46 were high-tech due to the triplexer-filter-detector and they had high dollar value per unit. The proposition presented to us was to put NERA of Bergen, Norway, into the Amp-Detector manufacturing business. Warner Robins contracts people would entertain a CPFF proposal from us to train NERA engineers, manufacturing people, and quality assurance inspectors in the vagaries of the production of the front ends of the warning system. How many Amp-Detectors would NERA get to build was our question back to them? They were prepared for that question: the number was tossed back to us as 4,528.

Holy smokes! NERA would get the equivalent of roughly a thousand F-16s plus spares since there are four units per RWR. What was in it for us, other than the CPFF contract if we agreed to help the F-16 SPO out of its offset problem? They were prepared for that question, too. The response shot back immediately was that there are estimated to be 12,000 Amp-Detectors required by the USAF and if we could see our way clear to help solve the "offset" problem ATI would have essentially a sole-source-lock on all of the US units. Now that sounded interesting. So, Joe and I looked at each other and asked to be excused for a couple of minutes.

We headed to a quiet spot and each expressed to the other a sense of amazement. Roughly, the 4,528 Amp-Detectors to be built by Norway represented somewhere in the neighborhood of $15-million of business potentially lost to ATI, but the prospect of 12,000 units essentially guaranteed for us represented about $40-million of business. Then, too, the CPFF contract to put NERA into the business would be in the millions of dollars and we would further cement a good and growing relationship with our prime source of domestic business. What really did we have to lose, we asked each other? The advantages seemed to be overwhelmingly in the favor of doing what WRALC wanted. We went back to the table and told our hosts that we would be glad to cooperate with them, but we had one question to which we needed to have answered. What would happen to the units built by NERA? Would they be solely for the Consortium F-16s, or would we see some of them going into U.S. airplanes. The answer was that they would be strictly for the Consortium planes, they would not be installed in our aircraft. So, we shook hands on a great cooperative effort.

The contracts people went on to lay down a proposed schedule of our supplying the proposal to the Warner Robins contracts department, getting the NERA folks trained in all aspects of manufacturing the Amp-Detectors, and getting NERA into full scale production. They felt that NERA could be up and running in a year, but we felt that it would really take two years for them to get into qualified production. Manufacturing those units with all of the precision machining necessary for the triplexer-filters was not like falling off a log. Joe and I headed back to Sunnyvale and a proposal was duly sent to WRALC for a two-years' program providing for training in our plant for their machinists, test technicians, and lead assembly folks. We would supply several people in the Bergen facility to monitor the progress of their development and to oversee the quality of the units from our standpoint. The government would task the European arm of the Defense Contract Administration Services Region (DCASR) to approve and to monitor the NERA Quality Assurance Program and would also task the Defense Contracts Audit Agency (DCAA) to oversee the financial aspects of the contract between Warner Robins and NERA. Our contract for our support to the program came to $5.7-million on a CPFF basis with a two-years' duration. If it didn't take that long, the government would experience less cost. If the WRALC estimate of one year being sufficient to get NERA up and running was achieved the reduction in cost would be very significant and we would be willing to renegotiate the fee that was based upon the two-years effort.

In reality, the NERA machinists initially let us know in no uncertain terms that they really knew their business and they didn't exactly cotton to the idea that we would need to teach them anything. Over a period of several months of producing filters that came nowhere near to passing the specifications, the machinists agreed to being shown how to do it and they began to be successful. All in all, it did take two years to get production quantities of Amp-Detectors coming off their assembly line. So, we had a happy co-producer of Amp-Detectors and a very happy F-16 SPO and Warner Robins contracting office. It really pays to work with the customer and not try to tell them what they want, nor how to do it. Another nicety that came about was that Col. Huffman, who had been so cool toward ATI when he was in the Pentagon, was now at Warner Robins and he treated us almost as long-lost friends. What a difference cooperation can make!

In 1978 the Navy decided that while they were waiting for the AN/ALR-67 to get into production, they should update all of the AN/ALR-45s in the fleet. A program named Colt 45 was initiated whereby we would supply update and modification crews at both Miramar, California, and Oceana Naval Air Station, Virginia. This work went on for a full year as black boxes were recycled from all over the world to be repaired and to be updated with the then present threat tables.

In this same general time frame, the folks at WRALC awarded us a contract for the Frequency Selective Receiver System (FSRS). This receiver, coupled with the AN/ALR-46 (still using the DV processor), would become nomenclatured the AN/ALR-69. This gave us, then, the –67 for the Navy, the -68 for the FRG, and the -69 for the USAF. It wasn't part of the Wild Weasel Program, per se, but it was certainly a very solid Radar Warning System for our F-16s. The development was a tough job, but it got done essentially on time. There was a catch, though. Warner Robins wanted a production quote before we had really completed all of the design and testing. We developed a quote, but it had to be approved by ITEK Corporate Headquarters before it could be submitted to WRALC. The proposal could not have a lot of fat built into it for protection of the company; WRALC didn't have an open pocketbook. The presentation was made to the Corporate people and it was recognized that the number of receivers and the amount of money we were talking about could be a "break your company" if we were wrong and the production turned out to be much more difficult than we thought. On the other hand, however, if this contract should wind up somewhere else, then ATI would be in dire straits for business for the next several years. We convinced the ITEK folks that we were sure that we knew what we were doing and they allowed us to submit the proposal. Whew! The production phase turned out to be essentially as we had estimated; we were happy with the program.

It must have been about 1979 when we got a surprise from the contracts people at Warner Robins. We were invited to meet with them and the engineering management people to discuss a new Radar Warning System for the Air Force. This was to upgrade essentially every tactical airplane in the USAF fleet except the F-4F and F-4G Wild Weasel birds and, perhaps, the F-15. Loral still had a solid lock on that airplane. We were granted a sole-source $52.8-million contract to develop this new system, the AN/ALR-74. It would have our ATAC computer as its brains, would cover all of the threat bands, and would have growth capability into the future. It was a wonderful concept. It was also tougher than the dickens.

After about a year-and-a-half into the development phase, the engineering manager for the software announced in a project review that we had a slight problem. He told us that the 53,000 manhours that had been spent on the software project would have to be written off as a loss because the software wouldn't work. In essence, we would have to start from scratch and take a different path in the redevelopment. Wages were a lot lower then than they are now, of course; but, even so, that meant we would have to write off something in the region of $2.3-million counting plant overhead and general and administrative expenses. As you might imagine, this was quite a shock for it also probably meant a delay in getting the first unit completed and into systems test. There wasn't anything to do but to bite the bullet and to tell Corporate and the Warner Robins people about the circumstances. They both took the news fairly calmly and let it be known that they wanted frequent updates in the future. The development was eventually completed successfully, but I wasn't around any longer when it happened.

As additional examples of getting back into the good graces of our USAF customer, I was invited to the Change of Command Ceremony at Warner Robins Air Logistics Center where Maj. Gen. John R. Spalding, Jr., turned over command to Maj. Gen. John R. Paulk on January 31, 1980. I was also invited to the "catfish fry" when Col. James C. Dever departed WRALC procurement for his next command. Last, but not least, I was honored to be invited to the "Dining In" "Commemorating the Active Duty Career of the F-105 Thunderchief." This was the "THUD SAWADEE" held on July 12, 1980. Dr. Kartveli of Republic Aviation was an honored guest: he had designed the P-47 of World War 2 as well as the F-105 Thunderchief. The two Wild Weasel F-105 Medal of Honor recipients were also in attendance: Merle Dethlefsen and Leo Thorsness.

Epilogue...........

In November of 1982, Bob Henderson, the President of ITEK, and I and a group of other ATI management people were serving Thanksgiving Dinner to the employees at the Bold Knight Restaurant in Sunnyvale. I needed to leave to go to a dental appointment, so I headed out the back door to the parking lot towards my car. A waitress came running after me calling my name and letting me know that my secretary was on the phone. So, I went back into the restaurant and got to the appointed phone. Fran told me that there was a Mr. Fred O'Green trying to get in touch with Mr. Henderson and requesting that I please pass the phone number on to him. So, I gave Bob the number and he said he would make the call after he finished serving lunch.

For me, this was the beginning of the end of my employment at ATI, although I didn't know it at the time. The phone call between O'Green and Henderson was the beginning of merger talks between Litton Industries, Inc., and ITEK Corporation. Litton was to be the surviving corporation. The merger process went through the "due diligence" investigations covering contracts in process, projections for the future, financial status of ITEK, its Optical Systems Division, Graphics Products, and, particularly, ATI. In March or April of 1983 the merger was completed. Litton apparently had bought ITEK specifically to obtain ATI at what I judged to be the desires of Charlie Fink who was a Litton Corporate V.P. and the head of the Litton Amecom Division. Amecom had developed the TEREC reconnaissance system that was being flown in some of the McDonnell F-4s in Europe, but we got the impression from our German friends that not all was well in the relationship.

We had met with Charlie a couple of times in the past when he was trying to get us to make Amecom a partner in one of our development and production contracts, the FSRS. We didn't see that Amecom brought anything to the table and giving them some of ATI's business would only reduce our work. So, we never did business together.

A few years prior to the merger with Litton, ITEK had purchased Antekna, Inc., a company that had "spun" out of ATI shortly after our merger with ITEK in 1967. Antekna was in the radar simulator business and it looked like a good adjunct to ATI's business in the "walk around test" simulators that had been developed for the Wild Weasel program.

As a result of this acquisition we established the Defense Electronics Operations of ITEK with me as a Corporate V.P. of ITEK and Joe Lee appointed by the V.P. and General Manager of ATI reporting directly to me. After the merger, things started going to pot at high speed as far as I was concerned. Joe Caligiuri of Litton told me that I would not report to him as I had thought, but that I would be a Staff Consultant who would be available as a resource throughout the entire Defense Electronics business of Litton. Joe went on to say that they wanted me to stay with Litton until I was ready to retire. So, once again I was an Ambassador Without Portfolio. My phone never rang, even when Litton bought International Laser Systems in Orlando, Florida, about six months later.

Joe Lee stayed as the General Manager of ATI, Antekna having been folded into Applied Technology some time before the merger due to problems that existed with some of the Antekna management and their lack of business. So, I now nominally reported to Joe. After about eight months of really having nothing to do and being bored stiff, I asked for a meeting with Joe Caligiuri, Charlie Fink, and Joe Lee during a "break" at a Program Review in December, 1983. At that meeting I expressed my disappointment in my role, no one reporting to me except for my secretary and, even worse, no responsibility for anything. Over the next two months we amicably negotiated an agreement for my departure from the company that was scheduled for February 15, 1984.

A short time before my departure, Joe Lee made a trip to Washington, D.C., to make a Progress report to Charlie and his staff. He was to return on the Friday evening flight from Dulles to San Francisco. Before he left Dulles, he gave me a call and reported that all apparently had gone well with his presentation of the status of ATI and that Charlie seemed pleased with the progress. About four in the afternoon of that Friday, I got a call from Joe Kearney who had been a friend for about 30 years. Joe was working for Northrop in San Diego and he called to ask me: "What's going on at ATI?" I said that I didn't know, tell me. He went on to say that there was scuttlebutt within Northrop that ATI was going to have a new General Manager starting the next Monday. I told Kearney that that was news to me since nothing had been said from anywhere in Litton to anyone associated with ITEK and ATI. I thanked him and told him that I would get back to him when I learned something.

The next day, Saturday, I went to the office figuring that Joe Lee would come in, too. Surely enough, he had arrived shortly before I did and so had Roger Anderson who had also been in Washington on Friday. Roger was in the process of telling Joe that he had heard from some Navy people that ATI was going to get a new General Manager, that it was to happen on Monday, and that the rumor was the person would be from Northrop. Then I told about my phone call on Friday with Joe Kearney. So, the two inputs matched. There was to be a new GM on Monday and that he was coming from Northrop, most likely Chicago.

It was Joe Lee who had a bright idea. He said that Charlie Fink always stayed at the Great America Marriott Hotel in Santa Clara so let's call there and see if he has a reservation. What do you know? The operator told us that yes there was a reservation for a Mr. Fink from Litton and another man by the name of Battaglia was with him. The scuttlebutt was correct. There was nothing for us to do but to wait until Monday morning and see what would transpire.

That following Monday morning, about nine o'clock, Charlie arrived and had a private meeting with Joe. It was a short meeting, the upshot of which was that Charlie wanted Joe to be packed up and to be out of his office by noon because his replacement would be sitting in his chair at one o'clock. What a shock to Joe and to all the rest of us! Who was to be Joe's replacement? It was Vincent Battaglia from Northrop, Chicago. This seemed so odd to be told on a Friday afternoon that your progress at the Division was good and then find out less than seventy-two hours later that you've been fired and that the plans had been in progress for weeks to months.

So, I left ATI shortly thereafter and didn't hear much about the company for a couple of years. One day I was talking to one of the men in the contracts department and just happened to ask how the ALR-74 contract with Warner Robins was doing. I got an earful! I was told that ATI had been asked to quote on a large production lot of -74's and the General Manager and some others had taken the proposal personally down to WRALC. My source went on to say that the quote was for about $105-million, but Warner Robins folks said that they only had $100-million for the program. The bargaining kept going back and forth and got into fairly loud voices from ATI. As the story goes, the General Manager eventually said one hundred and five million, take it or leave it. The government representatives said: "We'll leave it".

So the ALR-74 business, which had been ATI's sole-source, evidently went almost to zero. If it had been Joe Lee and me negotiating with them we would have kept our voices down, we would have figured out that the government negotiators were serious about their money (we knew them pretty well), and we would have settled for the $100-million. We, in all likelihood, would have been back in six months or so, in a new fiscal year, with an ECP (Engineering Change Proposal) to get some of the missing $5-million back, and I'll bet a dollar to a doughnut that they would have expected it from us. As it was, several hundred million dollars of -74 work dried up for ATI due to a poor personal relationship with the customer. This was yet another marketing booboo performed by a General Manager.

Sometime later I was again talking to someone at ATI and asked how the ALR-67 program was going with the Navy. All of the OPEVAL Tests had been completed and the system had been released to production. This person told me that the Navy folks had gotten ticked off with ATI's management style and was in the process of finding other suppliers for the system. Hughes Electronics in Los Angeles won a proposal in competition with ATI's electro-optics receiver for the -67. Competitive procurements were held and Raytheon won a lot of the business. The last I heard was that Raytheon had taken over almost all of the system and that ATI had practically nothing left of that Navy program after we had worked so long and hard and made such a huge investment. It pays to treat your customer with respect, dignity, and a sense of being cooperative; the converse puts one in a position of watching the business go elsewhere, sometimes rather rapidly.

Well, the Air Force was still in need of updating their Radar Warning Systems and the ALR-74 was to have done just that, but it was in limbo due to ATI's recalcitrance. So, sometime in 1988 the Air Force ran a competition that pitted Loral and its AN/ALR-56M (there had been updates since the original F-15 contract for the ALR-56 in 1972) against ATI/Litton and its ALR-74. In December, 1988, the contract award was made to Loral by the Air Force. ATI was once again on the outside looking in due to a marketing mistake.

However, ATI filed a protest with the government saying that the procurement was tainted in that Loral had obtained ATI proprietary data with respect to the competitive bid. According to various magazines and industry papers, Loral used a consultant who was also later hired by ATI (that wasn't too smart in my view). This man was paid somewhere between $448,000 and $578,000 (it depends on which report you read) to provide a series of reports which were intended to mask his role in obtaining and passing to Loral both government-private and company-proprietary information regarding the procurement. The trade journals said that a man in the office of the Air Force's Assistant Secretary for Acquisition was involved in the conspiracy. This series of events got wrapped into the Justice Department's Project "ILL WIND" (FBI) which was investigating government contracting fraud. The Air Force took the position that it would set their RWR updating back several years and cost an additional $300-400 million if they had to go through the procurement process again. So the award to Loral was allowed to stand notwithstanding the position of the GAO that the contract should be rescinded and the fact that "Loral Corp. has pleaded guilty to conspiracy to defraud the government in its ALR-56M radar warning receiver program." (AVIATION WEEK & SPACE TECHNOLOGY/December 18, 1989). The settlement of the criminal suit resulted in about $6-million in fines and penalties, reduction of profit on the first two production lots of ALR-56Ms, and share 35% of Lot 3 with second sources of which Litton would get three of the five Line Replaceable Units (LRUs), and delete the fourth production Lot of 319 units from the contract. So, ATI got a fair amount of business in the form of "build-to-print" work, but it wasn't the ALR-74 that the company had developed for the Air Force.

In my view, this whole fiasco could have been avoided by merely negotiating with the Warner Robins people in a gentlemanly and understanding manner. That way, ATI would have had the whole system to itself and, if second-sourcing had been subsequently required, would have been in the position of assisting in the establishment of the second sources just as we had done with NERA for the Amp-Detectors for the ALR-46 many years earlier. Once the bridge is burned, however, it is very difficult or impossible to get back to your initial position.

The Litton Division management style also grated badly on our friends in the German Ministry of Defense. A close friend in the MOD once told me that they had been abused in the winding-up of the Amecom Field Support to the TEREC program and that as far as he was concerned that was the end of doing business with them. Then I heard much later that the ALR-68 Program for the Tornado was in trouble as a result of personal relationships. How is it that a couple of people can screw up so badly from a marketing standpoint?

To complete this saga it should be noted that Litton decided (ca. 1998) to combine Amecom and ATI into one organization called Litton Advanced Systems. So, having done this, Applied Technology ceased to exist as a name to be promoted in the industry. Subsequently, Northrop Grumman bought Litton Industries, and even the Advanced Systems name evidently has succumbed to this latest merger in a dwindling industry.

As for me personally, I had a wonderful twenty-four years with ATI: old badge #13 was a pretty lucky number. I had the privilege of working with many wonderful, dedicated, and talented people in industry, the government, and the military. Many of them I still count as very good friends even though we rarely, or even never, see each other anymore. The memories are there and I have no doubt that if we were to cross paths tomorrow, we could pick up again where we left off many years ago.

I SALUTE YOU ALL!

Dr. John L Grigsby, WW # 231

Chapter Two

Wild Weasel One
The First Wild Weasels – F-100F Era

Story by Allen Lamb, "The Worlds Greatest Fighter Pilot" WW Charter # 16

The First Wild Weasel and The First Wild Weasel SAM Kill

Editors Note: Allen had the words "**Worlds Greatest Fighter Pilot**" written in reverse on his helmet sun visor so it would read correct in the mirror.

I was stationed at Myrtle Beach AFB, SC and on 24 August 1965 I received a phone call from Lt. Col. Charlie Joseph who was then assigned to Headquarters Tactical Air Command, Langley AFB, VA. I had known Col. Joseph since we were stationed together at Misawa Air Base, Japan a few years before, and I thought a lot of him. Charlie said he was flying down to Myrtle Beach the next day and wanted me to pick him up at his aircraft when he landed and we would have lunch together. I picked him up at Base Operations the next day, 25 Aug. 66. During lunch he told me that Major General Walter B. "Benny" Putnam had asked for me personally to volunteer for a program down at Eglin AFB, FL. He could not, and would not, tell me what the program was until after I had volunteered! Sitting in the parking lot at the Myrtle Beach Officers Club, I said, "Yes, I volunteer." He then preceded to hand me a set of temporary duty (TDY) travel orders with variations in itinerary authorized (These orders would carry me all the way through our assignment to Korat) In addition to the travel orders there was a commercial airline ticket for me to use for a flight the next day from Myrtle Beach to Ft. Walton Beach Fl. After lunch and on the way back to Base Operations he told me that I would be hunting and killing SAM sites in North Vietnam! I looked down at the orders he had given me and he said, "I knew you would volunteer so I brought them with me!" He told me not to discuss this with anyone and not to sign out when I left the base! I would just disappear form Myrtle Beach AFB. This was extremely unusual. He said that I should just get my gear and catch the flight the next morning, 26 Aug. 65, to Fort Walton. He also briefed me that the program was TOP SECRET and could not be discussed with others except on a strict "need to know" basis. I was not to discuss this assignment with anyone at Myrtle Beach. When I got to Fort Walton he told me to go to Eglin AFB and report to Gen. Putnam's office at the

Tactical Air Warfare Center (TAWC) where I would be briefed in more detail on the program. As I found out at Eglin, Col. Joseph was the TAC project officer for the Wild Weasel (code name) anti-SAM program. After reporting in at the TAWC I had an all-afternoon briefing by Major Jim Odom who was the TAWC project officer for the Wild Weasel program and the primary person we would be working with at Eglin.

In the original plan there were two Wild Weasel configured F-100Fs and three crews. The original pilots were Capt. Allen Lamb, Capt. Maurice "Maury" Fircke and a pilot from Homestead AFB, FL. I was the senior officer.

We were cautioned to be very security conscious and to be extremely careful about who we discussed the mission with and when, where, and how we planned to perform that mission. This came to a head the second week in September 1965. The Capt. from Homestead had driven a government staff car to the "Beach Club" and was overheard talking to a nurse during Friday night Happy Hour telling her that he was going to Vietnam and was hitting on her. We had security watching us but did not know it.

The next morning, Saturday, we were all rounded up in the hanger and addressed by Gen. Putnam. This included support civilian technical representatives and all military personal associated with the program. The General had at us! He said that the Capt. from Homestead was gone and so was his Air Force career. We would be isolated from the rest of the base personnel for the duration of our stay at Eglin and that we had damn will better keep our mouths shut to any outsiders. We were then moved to quarters in the backwoods and had the lower floor blocked off with round the clock security for the rest of our stay. We are still bleeding from the chewing we received by Gen. Putnam.

Capt. Ed White replaced the pilot from Homestead. The original Electronic Warfare Officers (EWOs) were Capt. John "Jack" Donovan and Capt. Truman "Walt" Lifsey, both from the Strategic Air Command (SAC) and Capt. Edward Sandelius from Headquarters 12th Air Force. The original crew parings were: Allen Lamb, pilot and Jack Donovan, EWO; Maury Fricke, pilot and Walt Lifsey, EWO; and Ed White, pilot, and Ed Sandelius, EWO.

A little later, probably about 15 October 65, it was decided to add two more aircraft and two more aircrews. These new crews were: Capt. Leslie Lindenmuth, pilot and Capt. Robert Trier, EWO; and Capt. George "Shep" Kerr, pilot and Capt. Don Madden, EWO. Lt. Col. John Kropenick was originally assigned at the Wild Weasel Commander but was relieved of his command by Gen. Putnam after only a short time. Kropenick was replaced by Major Garry Willard as the Wild Weasel Commander and Major Bob Swartz was brought in to serve as Wild Weasel Operations Officer. A little later Capt. John Pitchford came down to Eglin as the Tactical Air Command (TAC) evaluation officer along with Major Ted Lyons from Air Force Logistics Command (AFLC).

There was no training program in the traditional sense. It was cut and paste and try to see if this or that will work. If it works then good, and if it doesn't work then try something new and different. No one had ever done this before. Considering the capabilities and limitations of our equipments and the weapons available our options were definitely limited. Each Wild Weasel pilot and EWO had their way of thinking how we were going to do the job. To the anguish and consternation of my EWO, Jack Donavan, I said, "The only way to get these guys is to go right down their throat and take them out! At the very least we will see the SAM launch if we can't find them any other way." Jack said, "I'm going to fly with you and we are going to shoot a SAM site before it shoots us? YOU GOT TO BE SHITTING ME?" Thus the famous expression "Wild Weasel, YGBSM" was born!

We flew, studied the new Wild Weasel equipment and the SAM and worked to understand and learn as much as we could about this new threat and our new equipment. We learned how the SAM operated, its capabilities and limitations, its technical characteristics and so forth. We were learning a lot that we never knew before. We wondered why fighter pilots had never been exposed to this information until now. We learned how the threat would be displayed on our new equipment and what the bells and whistles meet. We learned when to be concerned and when to be terrified. We learned about main beams, side and back lobes. We learned that our Wild Weasel system did not have the ability to give us accurate range to the target but that we could get some idea of what the range was by looking at the length of the threat strobe. A short strobe meant that the threat was out of range or that we were in a side or back lobe of the radar.

A long strobe meant that we were probably the target and also that we were probably in range for a successful Anti-Radiation Missile (ARM) launch. Of course we didn't have any ARMs at that time but that would come a little later. We learned to try to correlate the threat azimuth strobe displayed on our small round cathode ray tube (CRT) with the threat light warning panel. We learned that the tactical air forces had neglected this threat for to long.

One other interesting bit of history is that we operated out of the same hanger at Eglin once used by Doolittle's Tokyo Raiders!

I was also working on the actual aircraft deployment to Thailand. I brought in two bright young Captains who worked for me at Myrtle Beach and who just happened to be at Eglin on temporary duty for another project. They were Captains Earl Fowler and Dennis Biggs and they helped me work up the navigation and flight data for the deployment. They knew we were deploying to Southeast Asia but were not privy to any other details.

Col. (Later Brigadier General) Robin Olds from Headquarters 9th Air Force came down to TAWC to review our deployment briefing and provide TAC approval for the plan. Maj. Willard started the presentation with a brief overview and then I presented the details of the deployment plan to Col. Olds including navigation, refueling, no return points, abort bases and so forth. I had done this many times at Myrtle Beach for our deployments to Italy and Turkey.

Around 14 November 65 our advanced party left for Southeast Asia on a C-130 transport. They were charged with getting everything set up for our arrival at Korat RTAFB. If everything went as planned we would arrive at Korat on 23 November 65. There were about 42 people in this group including aircrews Pitchford, Lifsey, Lyons, Swartz, White and Sandelius as will as maintenance personal, all tech reps and special equipment, etc.

Secretary of the Air Force Harold Brown and the Vice Chief of Staff United States Air Force came down to Eglin and gave us a send off on the Friday before our departure. Brown explained how important the mission was and how much was depending on our being successful in our mission. Someone asked where the Air Force Chief of Stall was? I said, "He's in church praying for us and the success of our mission." I was joking, but it was true. Bob Trier turned to me and said, "He's talking like some of us aren't going to return." Bob didn't realize how right he was.

When we were all strapped in and ready to go General Putnam came up the ladder on every aircraft and wished us good hunting and success with the mission. He said that a lot was depending on our success. Being rather macho, I said, "General, I'll get you one by Christmas." The flight line up was: Flight leader, Willard/Frickie, number 2, Lindenmuth/Trier, number 3, Lamb/Donovan and number 4, Kerr/Madden.

We took off at 1000 hours on Sunday 21 November 65 on the first leg of our flight from Eglin AFB to Hickam AFB, Honolulu, Hawaii. We rendezvoused with three aerial refueling tankers that were there just for us, over St. Louis, MO. We did this in radio silence. We had cancelled our normal flight plan with air traffic control, switched to a special frequency just for the tankers and us, and went to a new call sign that would take us to Korat. We were trailing the 421st TFS, which was deploying from McConnell AFB, KS to Korat at the same time and along the same route of flight we were using. This was so that we would have air sea rescue support and etc., while crossing the pond between California and Korat. They were on different radio frequencies and they never knew we were there. We also did not use our radios unless absolutely necessary. We knew when we needed fuel and we just slid into position behind the tanker and took fuel as needed. Capt. Earl Flower was in the lead tanker as F-100 tech support. We were probe and drogue configured and had a spare tanker just in case one or the primary tankers aborted. We topped off our fuel load about 300 miles out from Hickam, pushed the throttles up, and left the tankers for landing in Honolulu. When we landed word was out not to ask who we were and we were meet by a "Follow-Me" truck and lead to a guarded and isolated location on the base. I had a 5th of Beefeaters along with a little vermouth in the gin in the F-100 gun bay. We were going to war, so we had a toast after we landed. The gin was super cooled by being in a space on the aircraft that was not air conditioned and had been exposed to the extremely cold temperatures found at high altitude for several hours. It. had a quick effect especially on the EWOs. They had never been there before.

We were to leave the next morning 22 November 65 for Anderson AFB, Guam. However, our departure was postponed one day because of bad weather in the first refueling area. The weather was even worse the next day 23 November 65 but we had a release even before we briefed for the mission. They wanted those Wild Weasel birds at Korat really bad. As forecast, the weather was really bad. The ceiling at takeoff was about 800 feet. The takeoff was very unusual. The lead tanker rolled then Wild Weasel 1 & 2. Then the second tanker blocked the taxiway and then rolled. Next, I, Wild Weasel 3 and Kerr, Wild Weasel 4, never stopped to run up we just rolled right behind tanker 2, checked the engine instruments on the roll, and joined up with our tanker with our tanker under the weather. Tanker 3, the spare, came after us. . In the first refueling area we had turbulence that made it very difficult to get hooked up with the refueling basket on the tanker. The basket was bouncing up, down and sideways and out of synchronization with our movements. In addition we were icing up in the clouds but nonetheless we finally got hooked up and took on our fuel. After the long leg to Guam we landed and were again isolated. The next morning, 24 November 65, Thanksgiving Day, we took of for Korat and landed there around 1430 hours local time. By the time we got to the Club all of the turkey was gone.

The F-105 pilots at Takhli and Korat were briefed on what we were trying to do. We would fly a 5-ship formation. The Wild Weasel would take over the lead at a briefed point in the mission. Tactics were "just get it done somehow." We just planned for the Wild Weasel to take out the radar van and the other four Thuds to give the Coup De Grace to the entire site. We would try our best to kill the SAM radar operators if we could. Every Wild Weasel crew had their own idea of what their tactics would be. There were no regular tactics or standards. It was see if we can find what works and then do it. On a Rolling Thunder strike mission we were always "First In, and Last Out" which has always been the Wild Weasel motto from Vietnam until the present day.

First SAM Kill Mission

The first SAM kill by a Wild Weasel occurred on 22 December 65. You may recall that I had promised Gen. Putnam that I would get one for him before Christmas and we did. The flight call sign for our mission was "Spruce". The F-105 aircraft and pilots were all from the 421st TFS, Spruce #1 was Don Langwell, #2 was Van Heywood, #3 was Bob Bush and #4 was Art Brattkus (Spruce #3, was later shot down on 24 March 66 near Dong Hoi NVN and KIA. His remains were returned in December 1988 and positively identified in September 89. He is buried at Arlington

National Cemetery.) We were configured with two pods of 2.75" High Velocity Aerial Rockets (HVAR) and our two internal 20mm cannons. The F-105s were configured with four pods of 2.75" HVARs each and their internal 20mm M-61 gun. Each rocket pod contained 19 rockets and each M-61gun had just over 1000 rounds of ammunition.

Spruce flight taxied out for take off on 22 December 65 as the Bob Hope show was getting off of an Air Force C-141 transport. We waved to them.

After refueling and at the pre-briefed point the Wild Weasel, Spruce 5, Allen Lamb and Jack Donovan, took the lead. We then changed to the strike frequency and checked in 5, 1, 2, 3, and 4. Our call sign "Spruce" was not used. After initial check in we maintained radio silence. Soon Jack picked up a SAM in low PRF (Pulse Repetition Frequency). In low PRF the SAM radar had a longer range but he had to go to high PRF to shoot.

We estimated that we were about 95 miles away from the site at the time we initially detected his radar signal. I pushed the power up and locked the throttle in position. This gave us 595 knots, just 5 knots under the maximum allowable speed restriction of 600 knots for the rocket pods. After about 5 or 6 minutes he went to high PRF. I knew he was looking right at us and getting ready to shoot. I called "Tally Ho". It was the only thing I said but we were off and running. Since we were going at a speed of almost 600 knots this meant that we were traveling a distance of 10 nautical miles every minute or one mile every 6 seconds. If we picked him up at 95 miles range as estimate then we were now at a range to target of between 35 and 45 nautical miles and we would be within range of his missiles within about two minutes. I had two Thuds on each wing and I would dip down into the valleys and try to keep a hill between us and the radar site that was looking for us. I also tried to keep the SAM site at between the1030 and 1100 o'clock position so that he would not think we were running at him. I broke out of the hills and into the river valley and turned north directly into him. I had him at 1200 o'clock and the strobes were at the outer edge of the cathode ray tube (CRT) and starting to curve or waterfall back. I knew I was right on top of him and I started to climb. I pulled up and rolled inverted trying to get a visual on the site. I saw the site when I was at an altitude of about 4,000 feet and rolled in at a steep dive angle. I was way too steep and pulled out way to low. Spruce #4, Art Brattkus, said he thought for a minute that I was going to mark the target with my aircraft. My rockets hit short but as I was pulling off there was a bright flash. I must have hit the oxidizers tank used for SAM fueling. The site was next to the Red River dike and the enemy had AAA guns all along the dike.

I was pulling up from my rocket pass and I called out the site. Don Lnagwell, Spruce #1, and the Thud leader said, "I got it. I got it." Spruce #1 and #2 were in on the SAM site like two dogs on a bone. Later Don Langwell said that when he first spotted the site it was covered to look like part of a village. In the middle of his first pass he saw a few wheels under what appeared to be brush huts. He then fired 76 High Explosive Armor Piercing (HEAP) head 2.75" rockets, which were probably the best armament available for that type of target at the time. The vans, missile transporters and other structures appeared to jump up in the air a small amount when the load of rockets hit. We didn't get and noticeable ground fire until the second pass. I heard Spruce #3, Bob Bush call out the guns and saw him hitting them. I called Spruce #4, and told him I was coming around for a second pass on the site and that I was between him and the target. I finally saw the radar van and strafed it. At the same time as the cannon shells hit the radar he went off the air. Another SAM site came up then but we had no armament left to go after it but we really blew this site away. We later learned, thru intelligence channels, that we had really cleaned their clock. We then exited the target are, rejoined, post strike refueled and retuned to Korat.

Allen Lamb and Jack Donovan Wild Weasel Crew of Spruce 5 during First SAM Kill 22 December 1965. Courtesy Allen Lamb

With the F-100F Wild Weasel leading, we made a five ships, "V" formation, fly by over the Bob Hope USO show, which was in progress. After the post flight debriefing we went to the officers club and the party was on. Jack Donovan, my EWO, was drinking martinis and holding them by the rim with his thumb and one finger. He was dropping them and the club was raising hell because they were running out of glasses. We got some tape and taped the glass to Jacks hand.

We went down to 7th Air Force headquarters in Saigon the next day, 23 December 65. TV and radio interviewed the Thud drivers but not Jack and I. It was not disclosed how we had found the site but only that it had been destroyed.

Jack Donovan and I flew together for 12 more missions before he was transferred to Nellis AFB in February 66 to begin planning for and development of the Wild Weasel training program. Jack and I were a very strong team. We worked well together. We often knew what the other was thinking even before we said anything. We lived together, partied together, flew together and were really closer to one another than some married couples. Jack and his wonderful wife Joyce named their fourth son after me.

Second SAM Kill

We attacked our second SAM site in mid February 66. Major Bob Krone, 469th TFS was the F-105 flight leader. I had Captain Rick Morgan, who was a new replacement EWO with the follow-on F-100 Wild Weasels, in my back seat. I had started flying with the new EWOs since Jack Donovan had returned to the states in early February. This was Ricks first mission into Route Package VI since the completion of his orientation flights. We had been trolling for SAMs for almost 40 minutes with no luck. Everyone in the flight had reached Bingo fuel and we were on our way out of the area when the SAM came on the air. As it turned out he was almost on our egress route of flight and we were able to quickly home in on his emissions, spot him, and attack. He was located just south of Yen Bai, which was always heavily defended by AAA. Since we were all low on fuel and couldn't hang around we hit him with just one pass each.

Third SAM Kill

I will never forget the date of the third kill. It was on my Mothers birthday 4 March. Captain Frank O'Donnell was my back seater that day. He was another of the follow-on Wild Weasel EWOs. This was also his first mission in Route Package VI. We were on an Iron Hand mission supporting a Rolling Thunder strike in the Hanoi area. Our F-105, Thud, leader had aborted just after completing air refueling and we were a flight of four, one F-100F Wild Weasel and three F-105Ds. We were trolling just outside Hanoi near the Black river. It was a hazy day with the bottom of the haze layer at about 2500 feet. I homed in on the site and fired two pods, 38 rockets, but missed the radar van. Visibility was around three miles. Not a good day to be there. The three Thuds dropped some new "funny" bombs, a cross between napalm and white phosphorous. They also missed the radar van. The SAM radar stayed on the air after we started to exit the target area one at a time. Since he stayed on the air I turned back and homed in on the radar using my APR-25/26. I kind of just pushed over and when I broke out of the haze he was at 12 o'clock and I strafed the radar van. He went off the air as the cannon shells hit the target. This time he stayed off. The site was located just 17 miles from Hanoi, was a training site for the North Vietnamese, and operated by our friends from the Soviet

Union. (Editors Note: In Saigon, at Hq. 7th Air Force, I was tolled we had indeed killed some Soviet advisors in our Wild Weasel attacks on SAM sites in NVN.)

After the attack Frank O'Donnell said, "There has to be a better way! If I get back from this I am going to find it." You might say that I was the motivator for the Standard ARM and later the High Speed Anti-Radiation Missile (HARM) programs. Frank is one of the Daddy Rabbits for both of these programs.

F-4C Wild Weasel

I left Korat a few days later, mid March 66, and returned to Myrtle Beach. Garry Willard remained at Korat with the follow-on F-100F Wild Weasels. All others from the first group had returned to the states in February 66 and most were heading to Nellis to set up the Wild Weasel School House. When I arrived back at Myrtle Beach I found that I had permanent change of station (PCS) orders waiting for me to be transferred to Nellis too. I tried to get out of the assignment but was told that I was going to Nellis and was going to be in the F-4 Wild Weasel IV test program. First, I went on temporary duty to Davis Monthan Air Force Base, Tucson, AZ to attend a Mobile Training Detachment (MTD) short course on the F-4. Then I went back to Myrtle Beach. I was finally transferred to Nellis and assigned to the Fighter Weapons School test and evaluation section in April 66. I set up shop and waited for the first Wild Weasel IV to arrive from McDonnell Aircraft (McAir) in St. Louis, MO.

In the interim I checked out in the F-4 and flew the F-4D models assigned to the Fighter Weapons School (FWS). I got a total of 10 sorties in the F-4D including standardization, evaluation, and instrument flight checks.

The first Wild Weasel F-4C delivered to Nellis also came in June 66 and was flown from St. Louis to Nellis AFB by a McAir test pilot. I joined up with the Wild Weasel configured F-4C on his way to Nellis. I had Captain Rodger Peden (RIP) in my back seat. Rodger was one of two EWOs assigned to the F-4C Wild Weasel program at the time and Captain Eddie Adcock was the other. As part of the acceptance of the Wild Weasel IV aircraft from McAir I had to certify that the test pilot did a 7 G maneuver and the pod containing the Wild Weasel equipment stayed on the aircraft. The Wild Weasel gear in the F-4C was mounted in a pod and the pod was installed on the left inboard pylon. There were six F-4C Wild Weasel crews assigned on PCS orders to the program. These were two pilot crews. In addition we had the two EWOs, Eddie Adcock and Roger Peden as mentioned earlier. In the past all Wild Weasel crews had been made up of one pilot and one EWO. For the F-4C Wile Weasel the crew would be made up of two pilots! I was assigned on temporary duty orders to deploy to Ubon RTAFB, Thailand with the Wild Weasel F-4Cs and I was to do an evaluation to see how the pilot/pilot crew compared to the pilot/EWO crews. At Nellis I flew with the different GIBs/EWOs. One of the pilots, I forget his name, was a former EWO. The six crews were: Merkling/Lafferty, Park/Milligan, Raspberry/Gullick, Pasco/Wells, Friesel/Barrett and Badeker/Murray. Major Dick Merkling was the Commander.

The Wild Weasel gear in the F-4C would not operate properly in a typical combat environment. If you flew around at medium altitude and at cruse speed it operated great. When you pushed the speed up to combat velocity and increased G forces the pod with the Weasel equipment vibrated so bad that the equipment was for all practical purposes worthless. Nonetheless we finally thought McAir engineers had it fixed and I, Peden and a Sgt. we went over together as the Advanced Party. We left the states on 4 Sept 66 and arrived in Bangkok as scheduled then took a C-130 to Ubon RTAFB. The F-4Cs never made it to Thailand until 1972 when they participated in Linebacker I and II. The aircrews finally showed up and were assigned to the 555th TFS. I flew strike missions in the 555th mostly with pilots in my back seat and also about 15-20 missions with Rodger Peden who had completed a short course at Nellis to learn how to use the radar in the F-4. I returned to Nellis on 23 December 66 and Roger and Eddie were transferred to B-66s at Takhli to finish their first SEA tours. Both Roger and Eddie returned to SEA in 1972 with the 561st TFS and flew about 70 Wild Weasel combat missions in the F-105G.

F-4D Wild Weasel

In January 67 I took F-4D tail number 65-660 into the hanger at Nellis. We abandoned the idea of mounting the equipment in a pod and went to an internal aircraft equipment installation. With the help of ATI engineers we ripped out the left forward missile well and made a platform that could be raised and lowered and we mounted the Wild Weasel equipment on the platform. With the equipment installed on the platform it would be raised into the space originally intended for the AIM-7 missile and the bottom covered over with an equipment access door. At the same time we mounted the APR-35/36 RHAW scope on the left side of the pilots instruments panel. The EWOs panoramic signal analysis receiver scope was mounted in the rear cockpit without losing any of the original rear cockpit capability.

I flew this aircraft from January to September 67 with EWOs Frank O'Donnell and Rick Morgan who were with me on SAM site kills number 2 and 3. Captain Clyde Hayman, who had just finished 100 missions in the F-105F Wild Weasel, was also assigned to work and fly with me. Clyde probably had more sorties with me in 660 than any other EWO. He always joked that I taxied with 4 Gs on the aircraft. Jack Donovan and several EWOs also flew with me to help evaluate the F-4D as a Wild Weasel. We flew it every way possible and on all types of sorties. Then we got the first hick-up! We started getting "grass" (interference) on the EWOs panoramic receiver scope when we were at high Mach (about Mach 1 or higher) and also at low speed with the gear up and/or down. The engineers were dumbfounded. However, they decided on a bunch of potential fixed to try. I flew 11 sorties in one day with EWOs Frank O'Donnell, Rick Morgan, and Clyde Hayman. No matter what was tried the grass on the EWOs scope would just come and go away at different times. Everybody just threw up their hands!

The next day Sgt. Stephen Sopko who had been with us on WW I came to me and said, "Major Lamb, lets take 660 out to the run up pad and see if we can't duplicate the problem on the ground." which we did. We put screens over the engine intakes and he got an antenna with an extended cable tied to where the antenna was on the aircraft. I had one of my EWOs in the back and I would go to full military on an engine and kick it into and out of afterburner. This went on for a few minutes and then guess what? He got to the front of the aircraft and we started picking up grass that the EWO could see on his panoramic signal analysis receiver. We narrowed it down and I shut down the engines. We came down out of the cockpit and cut off the communications ground plug on the nose strut. We cut it open and one of the female plugs had corroded and broken off. It would vibrate together and give us the grass or interference on the scope. We flew it for 30-40 more sorties and we never had grass again. According to the EWOs it was as good as or better than any of the other Wild Weasel aircraft.

Capt. Hayman was later an F-4C Wild Weasel EWO and his pilot was Lt., now General, Richard Meyers, Chairman Joint Chiefs of Staff. I left Nellis in August 67 and was assigned to Fort Bragg, NC as WVIII Airborne Corp. Air Liaison Officer (ALO).

F-4D 65-660 was still going strong when I left and served as the prototype for the successful installation of Wild Weasel equipment in the F-4C and served as a teat bed for the Bendix APS-107 RHAW gear.

Allen Lamb, Charter Member, WW # 16

Story by Joe W. Telford, WW # 258

MEMORIES OF INTERESTING EVENTS DURING MY ASSOCIATION WITH THE TESTING AND TRAINING OF THE WILD WEASEL 1 PROGRAM AT EGLIN AIR FORCE BASE, FLORICA OCTOBER – NOVEMBER 1965

1. BACKGROUND

Major James "Jim" R. Odom of the United States Air Force (USAF) Tactical Air Warfare Center (TAWC) of the Tactical Air Command (TAC) and myself, Captain Joe W. Telford of the Air Proving Ground Center (APGC) of the Air Force Systems Command (AFSC), were joint Test Project Officers (TPO) for our respective units at Eglin Air Force Base (AFB) for the initial Wild Weasel-I (F-100F) training and Operational Test and Evaluation (OT&E) program.

These Wild Weasel-I aircraft (4) and crews belonged to TAC. At this time, the latter part of 1965, TAWC was spearheading the effort in TAC to develop the capability to counter the Russian SA-2 Fan Song radar surface-to-air missile (SAM) sites and threat in North Vietnam. So naturally, in this joint training and testing of the Weasel program, Jim Odom, and TAWC, had the lead in dealing with such matters as aircrews, aircraft maintenance, deployment, briefing the program progress to TAC Headquarters and other organizations and dignitaries, and the ultimate writing and printing of the joint test plan and report, with APGC's approval.

Since the Wild Weasel-I OT&E and training were to be conducted requiring APGC resources such as ranges and range support; mission scheduling; mission command and control (call sign Wolf Call); threat radars and signals; time, space, position, information (TSPI) for aircraft; mission reduced data; and the APGC test documents providing the guidance for all of this, I had the lead in these matters. In addition, I had a major input to the design of the joint test plan and the final joint test report produced by TAWC.

There was probably never before an Air Force program of this magnitude so new and different in concept and tactics that was conceived, contracted for, equipped and installed, manned, trained, tested, deployed, and successful in combat in such a short period of time. Success initially started with the destruction of the first SAM site on 22 December 1965 by pilot Captain Allen Lamb and his back seat electronic warfare officer (EWO) Captain Jack Donovan in their F-100F, and four accompanying F-105D aircraft, all from Korat Royal Thai Air Base, (RTAB), Thailand. The estimates of how much time all this required ranges from about 90 days to 120 days, depending mainly on when one considers USAF Brigadier General Kenneth C. Dempster's study phase on possible concepts to defeat the SAM threat in North Vietnam (NVN) to have been initiated. As such, I readily acknowledge up front this testing and training program for the initial Wild Weasel-I crews and F-100F aircraft was the least sophisticated of all the following Wild Weasel testing and training programs – and it was also the "wildest" of all the Wild Weasels.

For a person to understand and appreciate most of the activities I am about to reiterate here you must understand and feel the pressure this program and the associated personnel were training, testing, and working under. At the time these activities occurred they were not humorous to me at all, in fact, there were several occasions when I just knew my career in the Air Force was finished. In retrospect, since the program was a success, I now view these activities and incidents in an entirely different light, and some are even very humorous to me now. As such, I pass them all on to you, your children, and your grandchildren for enlightenment and enjoyment.

2.
TESTING AT EGLIN AND TEST ORGANIZATONS RELATIOINSHIP

At this time, 1965, there were two major test organizations in APGC; the Deputy for Test Operations (PGO), and a new one spun up about 1962, the Deputy for Effectiveness Test (PGT). The Deputy for Test Operations was the older by far and also the larger by far of the two organizations, and it owned all the test aircraft belonging to APGC. Most of the testing conducted at APGC, before the start of the Southeast Asian War, could be considered engineering testing, and the land and water ranges were accordingly heavily instrumented to accomplish this type of testing. At this time Eglin was probably the best military instrumented large water and land range site in the US, possessing 724 square miles in land ranges and over 133,000 square miles in Eastern Gulf of Mexico water ranges. Of course the instrumentation (ground radars, photo, and other) were limited in their coverage when it came to the water ranges. Because of Eglin's instrumentation capabilities and its engineering testing mission, the Deputy for Test Operations was not happy when in the early starting years of the Southeast Asian War tenant operational testing organizations arrived, often with higher testing priories and increasingly utilized the Eglin ranges for operational testing. This situation almost "bit" me during Wild Weasel-I.

In about 1962, when the Deputy for Effectiveness Test was organized in APGC, the Deputy for Test Operations was even unhappier. While the Deputy for Effectiveness Test often utilized much of the engineering instrumentation on the Eglin ranges, most of its testing was considered to lean toward being operational testing.

About 1964 TAWC was spun up at Eglin, with very high priories for its mostly operational testing associated with the Southeast Asian War. For about the first six months of TAWC's existence it had no, or very few, test officers knowledgeable of the APGC rules and requirements for requesting missions and all the different kinds of mission support, or the writing of the documentation that preceded and accompanied all this testing. As such, during these six months test officers in the Deputy for Effectiveness Test temporarily conducted a significant number of TAWC's tests.

As a result of the above situation, by the time the Wild Weasel-I effort showed up on the Eglin scene testing was an around the clock activity. If a test required day light hours, but did not have a high priority, it was just almost a lost cause, certainly a long lasting cause at best. However, if a test could be conducted in the not so prim time test hours, especially at night, and/or it had over time money available for support, then it would have a good chance of being conducted in a reasonable amount of time.

THE EGLIN TEST MISSION REQUEST AND THE SUPPORT SCHEDULING "GAME"

Before any action could occur on a test at Eglin a detailed test plan had to be written and approved by the test organization, this included tenet organizations with their higher commands such as TAWC with Wild Weasel-I. Then, after the approved test plan had been distributed to the appropriate APGC support organizations and reviewed, the TPO would convene a meeting with the support representatives to develop a formal APGC Project Directive (PD). Nothing, but nothing, was accomplished at Eglin in the way of testing, by any organization at this time, without a detailed written and distributed PD. Among other things, the PD provided the test's priority, authorization, funding information, a brief test description that included methods and objectives, and the kinds of support required from the support organizations, and when and how, and etc. The different types of test missions to be conducted were described in detail and their required support, and, some type of unclassified support requirements numbering identification assigned to each type of mission to be conducted.

Also, there was a mission profile page attached for every different type of mission that might be flown during the test. A mission profile identified the required ranges and altitudes, speeds, and the track the test aircraft were going to fly. There were usually approximately six to eight Eglin offices required to review, approve, and sigh off on a profile page, depending on what was being tested. Some of these offices were usually the base operations officer, the APGC ground range safety officer, the APGC air safety officer, range control (Wolf Call), and etc. Woe be to the TPO, and aircrew, that had an aircraft major incident or accident and they had committed a deviation in their approved flight profile, or the TPO had failed to acquire all of the necessary approval signatures on the involved mission profile.

At this time the requesting and scheduling of test missions and support at Eglin was not automated, it was strictly a manual and labor intensified effort. On about a Wednesday or Thursday, before test missions were to be conducted the following week, that is Monday through Sunday, a PTO had to fill out and submit a mission request form for each of those days he desired to test and submit these forms to the APGC Mission Scheduling organization.

A Mission Scheduling individual, at this time usually M/Sgt Hall, would convene a scheduling meeting about Thursday where representatives from all the support organizations would be present, usually consisting of at least 20 people. First, they would line up the missions by the highest priority to lowest and assign the requested ranges and support to these missions by their rank order, and then deconflict occasions where the same ranges and support were requested simultaneously.

Often the situation would occur where two conflicting tests possessed the same test priority but were being conducted by different test organizations. When this occurred Mission Scheduling would have to call in representatives from the two organizations and some type of compromise worked out.

The scheduling activity for a day would last until all the APGC range normal contracted support time had been utilized. At this time the VITRO Corporation had the APGC Range support contract. Requested test missions that did not make the "cut" would have to wait and see if they would be scheduled for a future day. As stated earlier, if a low priority test had range support overtime authorized in its budget sometimes this was as good as a high test priority, unless there were a large number of competing low priority tests that all had overtime too.

On about Friday, Mission Scheduling would have combined all the next weeks scheduled missions, by day, with all the support information needed to conduct the missions and an unclassified document published. This unclassified document of a week's worth of missions to be run was known as, I think, the Test Mission Schedule. The reason this document could be unclassified when it addressed the conduct of many classified tests was because of the unclassified mission support codes that were defined in detail in the classified APGC PD, which was available to all the applicable support agencies and sites.

Once testing commenced there were few tests and their activities that remained perfectly predictable and consistent; something was always changing day to day just by the very nature of testing. PTOs would call in these changes to their scheduled missions as printed in the Test Mission Schedule. In order to accommodate this type of situation, Mission Scheduling held a "daily noon time mission run down" for the following day's missions. Again, at least 20 support represents were present and would pencil in last minute support changes on their previously printed Test Mission Schedule for that day, after the new support requirements had been deconflicted. This effort compensated for, hopefully, all the last minute support changes and allowed the support organizations to be ready to go by mission time the next day.

Or, in an even more extreme emergency, if the mission changed the day of the mission, like only hours ahead of time, the TPO could get on the phone to the different support sites and just call out the required unclassified support identification codes in the classified PD that applied to the mission. This procedure would only be successful if some other mission had not been previously scheduled to utilize the desired support. This situation, but even more complicated, turned out to be the norm for the Wild Weasel-I OT&E.

I LEARN THE APGC MISSION SCHEDULING AND SUPPORT "GAME" IN DETAIL

For six months prior to being assigned to the Wild Weasel-I OT&E effort I was assigned to a job that provided me invaluable knowledge and experience for future Weasel testing. In my opinion, this assignment was providential.

I have explained in the above paragraphs how the organization I was in, Deputy for Effectiveness Test, at Eglin was conducing many high priority tests, so many that it was getting far more than its share of the ranges, support, and mission time each day. However, Mission Scheduling was having a critical problem with this situation. Sometimes as many as four different PTOs in the Deputy for Effectiveness Test would be submitting a weeks worth of mission request forms for the same ranges, support, and times – and each test would have the same high testing priority. Mission Scheduling was in a state of perplexity with this situation; they did not know enough about each of the test programs to determine an equable and proper solution. As a result, the commander of Mission Scheduling was continuously calling up Col. Marshall R. Peterson, the commander for the Deputy for Effectiveness Test, and requesting an in house resolution. In turn, Col. Peterson viewed this situation as an indication of his own lack of in house management in his organization, and an embarrassment.

Col. Peterson's solution was to create an internal scheduling office within his deputy. All the mission request forms would be submitted by his PTOs to this office first, deconflicted, and then submitted to Mission Scheduling. This meant the people manning this office had to have a good under standing of all the tests the Deputy for Effectiveness Test was conducting. In addition, the personnel in this office would have to know a certain amount concerning the capabilities of all the support units on Eglin and how they all conducted their tasks. As a simple example, how much time did each radar site require for data collection after a mission was completed, and how much set up time did it require before it would be ready to support the next mission?

I had only been in the Deputy for Effectiveness Test for a year but I, and a staff sergeant, were chosen to man this in house scheduling office. I had assisted in conducting two tests during this year but still had much to learn about testing and the mission support and request "game" at Eglin. Needless to say – of necessity, I learned enough quickly in order to survive in this new duty. More important, looking forward to Wild Weasel-I, I got to know just about everyone personally in the Eglin scheduling and support arena, and they got to know me. This situation, and having the highest test priority on Eglin, turned out to be invaluable in conducting Wild Weasel-I and follow-on Wild Weasel OT&E tests.

As would be expected, most PTOs in the deputy viewed their test as probably the most important in the organization. So, when the sergeant and I would schedule some PTO's test to occur at maybe not the most optimum time of the day, or something similar like that, I often would experience the displeasure and wrath of a PTO. A couple of names of tests being conducted by the deputy are indicative of the wide range of subjects that were under going testing at this time: the OT&E of the Gatling Gun Pod for the F-4 conducted by Capt. Jim Mehserle; and Major John Boyd's ("Forty-Second Boyd") fledgling and struggling Energy-Maneuverability (E-M) Theory Test. When Major Boyd thought his test mission requests were not being given their due and proper scheduling consideration, he was capable of dispensing much grief and consternation.

3.
THE FAMOUS MEETING AND POLAROID CAMERA PICTURES CONTRACT AT APPLIED TECHNOLIGILY INCORPORATED (ATI)

About the 25th of September 1965 the number two man in the Deputy for Effectiveness Test, Howard L. Dimmig, and probably a GS-15 at that time, called me into his office. He very briefly informed me I was being assigned to a joint test program with TAWC and I would be the APGC TPO. He further stated the name of the program was Wild Weasel-I, it was highly classified, and would have the highest testing priority of all the tests being conducted on the Eglin ranges at that time. I guess, the reason he, or Col. Petterson, selected me as the TPO was because Wild Weasel-I encompassed electronic warfare and aircraft, which was part of my experience and background. This was about the sum total of knowledge of the program he imparted to me at that time. And, one last thing, I was to go TDY on Friday, 30 September 1965, to the North American Aviation "secret skunk works" facility located at Long Beach International Airport, California, where I would learn more about the Wild Weasel program and met my TAWC counter part, Major Jim R. Odom. Then, that evening I would fly to Palo Alto, California and attend a meeting at ATI on Saturday and return to Eglin AFB on Sunday. This – was my introduction and spin up to the Wild Weasel-I program.

At the North American Aviation facilities I did met Major Odom and a Lt. Col. Charles Joseph who was the Hqs TAC/DORQ program officer. Also I met three, and possible a fourth, Wild Weasel-I EWOs. I definitely remember Captains Jack Donovan, Truman Walter "Walt" Lifsey, and Edward "Ed" Sandelius. We, and others from different involved organizations, were shown several of the first four Wild Weasel-I F-100Fs that were being equipped with the ATI radar warning and homing equipment. The APR-25/26 was installed in both the front and rear instrument panels while the IR-133 was only in the rear. We were also briefed on the results of the limited testing of the equipment North American had been able to accomplish in the short time allocated to it in this early phase of the program. Fuzzy ideas of what this program was about and possible tactics were starting to grow in our minds. Late that afternoon those of us who were scheduled to attend the meeting the next day at ATI flew up to Palo Alto and obtained rooms at a motel.

I had forgotten to bring a travel alarm clock on this trip so I asked the motel clerk to give me an early wake up call in the morning. The clerk failed to give me the call and by the time I was up and hurriedly dressed I just was able to catch a ride with the last car in our group headed for ATI, and I missed breakfast. Now, missing breakfast may not be a big deal for most people but it was a catastrophe of major proportions for me. Back then my body especially required a good breakfast soon after I was up, and later, lunch and dinner in order to keep functioning properly during the day. If I failed to have breakfast my whole day was soon in a nosedive.

We arrived at ATI and were ushered into, and seated, in a room that looked very similar to a school classroom with black boards on two sides and no windows. Of course there were numerous ATI people in attendance; the most notable were the company president, Dr. William E. Ayer, and a Dr. John Grigsby. And, the most notable non-ATI person present was a Lt. Colonel Irwin "Pierre" Joel Levy from Hqs USAF, from Brig. Gen. Dempster's office that was managing this new and high priority Wild Weasel program.

The Air Force was negotiating at this meeting the buying of ATI APR-25/26 and IR-133 equipments, support equipment, spare parts, contractor support, and a time schedule. However, it has never been clear to me if this contract also included the equipment that was currently being installed by North American in the first four F-100Fs, or just follow-on equipments.

Nevertheless, the unusual thing was Lt. Col. Levy had sole authority to approve a contract with ATI for equipment and support right there on the spot, in that room – a done deal! Each phase of the contract was developed and constructed by writing it on the blackboards. As soon as a particular phase was developed and documented on the blackboards, which involved very lengthy discussions and negotiations, the proper ATI company officials would sign their names and titles and date, along with Lt. Col. Levy. Then a Polaroid picture would be taken of that portion of the blackboard contract, judged for adequate quality, and then the negotiations would proceed to the next phase of the contract, and subsequent signing of signatures and picture taking, and so forth until it was all completed.

This procedure and process took the entire day, until about 6 pm. The contracting "action" was so hot and heavy there was no thought given to lunch. Not only was there no break for lunch, there was not even a word uttered by ATI that addressed lunch. It was "throttle to the wall" with the contract negotiations! I never have been a coffee drinker but by early noon I was drinking, with lots of sugar, as were the rest of us who were involved more in the testing and operations and not so deeply concerned with the contract. By mid afternoon ATI had run out of coffee and I was reduced to eating sugar cubes, until they too were all soon consumed by myself and others. I was starting to feel like I was having an out of body experience.

As the afternoon wore on and I was watching and listening to Lt. Col. Levy I begin to release I had seen and heard this man someplace before. However, at first I thought maybe I was hallucinating from hunger, but no, I was sure I had seen and heard him before - and then I remembered. It was in the late summer of 1958 at the Brize-Norton Air Base near Oxford, England where I had interfaced with Levy. I was a 1st Lt. EWO on a six-man crew of an electronic intelligence (ELINT) reconnaissance RB-47H aircraft belonging to the 38th Strategic Reconnaissance Squadron (SRS) of the 55th Strategic Reconnaissance Wing (SRW). We were flying ELINT missions that summer against Russia and other countries of the Warsaw Pack.

The Russian SA-2 system was not yet operational at this time but there were, supposedly, a number of them at selected locations around Russia under going testing. One of our crew's top priorities was to try and intercept, record, and locate an SA-2 signal and site. Early on in this tour our crew had entered the Baltic Sea from the south by international waters between southern Sweden and northern Germany and had traversed the Baltic Sea to the north and back down and out to the south. On the leg back to the south a MiG had tried to slip into our 6 o'clock position from high and to the east of us. Fortunately, our alert co-pilot had seen the MiG's contrails in time for us to take evasive action and remain out of harms way.

Later, a special mission tasking was asked of our crew. We were to fly into the Barents Sea by international waters to north of the area where Norway and Russia join. Then we were to make a mad dash to the south, over the tip of Russia and then Finland, and into the northern part of the Baltic Sea and on out to the south. It was believed there was one of these early SA-2 test sites in this area, and we would be "chumming" and hopefully cause every type of radar site in the area to radiate.

The USAF intelligence officer who was briefing our crew on this effort and coordinating it was none other than Capt. Pierre Levy. At our last briefing on the morning of 3 September 1958, just before the mission was to be flown, Levy announced the mission had been cancelled. Unknown to most of the world that morning, the day before a Russian MiG had shot down a USAF C-130 communications intelligence (COMINT) aircraft when it had been lured across the eastern Turkish boarder into the Russian Armenian Republic by a deceptive navigational system on the Russian side. All 17 of the USAF aircrew had been killed. Capt. Levy stated something like, "Considering the Russian shoot down yesterday of one of our COMINT C-130 aircraft, the time does not seem right today to twist the Russian bear's tail." And, all of us on the crew allowed how that sounded like a good idea to us too.

As I recalled all of the above during the ATI meeting I thought, "How many and how often does this Pierre Levy get involved in things like this, and is it always around the September to October time frame of the year?" The obvious tactics for the Wild Weasel mission were starting to come into even sharper focus for all of us by now.

During the year 2002 I was talking to Levy on the phone and I reminded him of his briefing my RB-47H crew for the above mission in 1958 in England. He quickly recalled it and then proceeded to tell me even more details of the situation that I, nor the others on our crew, had ever been informed about.

I also asked Levy what ever became of the ATI Polaroid camera pictures contract. He stated they had been in his files at the Pentagon, and even though he had made an exhaustive search for them before he retired, they were never found.

A CLARIFICATION OF THE "NO LUNCH" SITUATION AT THE ATI MEETING

My above comments concerning the no lunch situation during the ATI contract meeting were not stated to cast any type of a negative reflection on ATI, such as, all ATI was interested in was Air Force money. ATI's relationship and attitude toward the Wild Weasel program was just the opposite! My experience with ATI and its employees from October 1965 thru October 1966, which included being the joint APGC TPO with TAWC on the OT&E of Wild Weasel-I (F-100F), IA (F-105D), III (F-105F), and IV (F-4C), and included the installation and test of ATI's equipment on other none Weasel jet fighter/reconnaissance type aircraft, was - ATI and its people provided outstanding support. They consistently went the none-contracted for second, and even third, mile. Wild Weasel-I would have never happened in the time frame it did without ATI's "can do" attitude and actions. I especially remember the outstanding support I received from ATI's technical representative Melvin "Mel" F. Klemmick.

THE CITY BUS RIDE WITH JACK DONOVAN FROM THE SAN FRANCISCO AIRPORT TO DOWNTOWN

After the meeting at ATI all of us, especially us Air Force captains, quickly went to dinner. I can't recall now what I ordered but I am sure it tasted like the best meal I had ever eaten. The Wild Weasel EWOs decided they would not return this Saturday night, nor early the next morning, to each of their local bases, or where ever they were now located. They decided instead to book a couple of hotel rooms downtown and live it up in San Francisco this Saturday night. Someway, somehow, Jack Donovan was chosen to get a ride with an ATI person to the airport and get everyone's tickets changed, and then ride a city bus back into town to the hotel. Ed Sandelius did not make the trip to ATI, but Walt Lifsey did, and I think at least one other person who I can't remember now.

I was ticketed to depart the San Francisco airport about noon, or early afternoon, the next day, Sunday. However, as the ATI meeting wore on and I was developing a better understanding of the program, the tremendous amount of testing and training never heretofore attempted that would have to be thought out and accomplished in such a short time – I started to panic. I instinctively knew I would never have the required time I would need to write an adequate detailed Wild Weasel-I Eglin APGC Project Directive (PD), much less other required documentation. The first rule at APGC was – nothing, but nothing, was accomplished on the Eglin ranges without a detailed PD. The PD might be classified and close hold to only those with the need to know, but, it would be detail and encompassing. I thought, "I need to catch the red eye flight tonight out of San Francisco so I can hit the street running at Eglin early tomorrow, Sunday morning." So, I too caught a ride with Jack to the airport to change my tickets to the red eye flight late that night.

A person really had to know Jack Donovan to fully appreciate the following. As we both rode to the airport with the ATI person it was obvious Jack's mind had also been working in overdrive during all the past two days activities concerning the Weasel mission, and future tactics were also coming into better focus for him with each passing hour. This was true for all the Weasel aircrews, but only Jack Donovan could express it so – completely, or simply, or profoundly. Actually, he was by now audibly carrying on a conversation with himself, and it really did not matter if I listened or answered him.

We arrived at the airport, got the tickets exchanged, and waited a short time for the bus, a rather large, nice, cruise type bus. We were occupying the first two seats on the right side, first ones past the front entrance door. All the way into downtown Jack was having this louder and louder conversation with himself, and occasionally looking at me as if I was expected to comment, which I did several times at first, until I realized that he was not hearing a word I was saying. Part of his conversation with himself was going over and over what a Weasel mission was going to be like, and what the obvious tactics were going to be – roll into a SA-2 site and destroy it at close range, while riding in the back seat of a two seat F-100F, with everybody and his brother on the ground shooting at you!

I was also fearful that someone would over hear Jack talking about the Wild Weasel mission and maybe be able to put together more than they should. I tried several times to get him to lower his voice, but to no avail.

Close to the end of the bus ride Jack reiterated again all that had been going through his mind, and he paused, and pronounced in a very profound manner his famous statement, "You have got to be shitting me!" For me, this was the first time I had ever heard him make that statement. Maybe he had made it earlier with the other Weasel crewmen, but it was the first time I had ever heard it, and he seemed to have just worked up to it during the bus ride and capped his total bus conversation off with it.

4.
WILD WEASEL – I

SUNDAY, BACK AT EGLIN AFB

I arrived back at Eglin about 7 am Sunday the 3rd of October 1965. I quickly drove to my on base quarters and first, before I took the time to clean up, I called Capt. Robert "Bob" Klimek, Jr. who was also in my organization and who I had been working with on one of his Westinghouse jamming pod tests. I don't think Bob was all that happy to hear me that early on a Sunday morning. I told him I really needed to talk to him and could he meet me at his office in one hour. This is the same Robert Klimek who, along with a Civil Service employee, Elias A. "Mac" McCormac, later thought up the technology for the SEE-SAMS radar detection equipment, which was later produced by North American Aviation. McCormac was in charge of an APGC organization at that time which was located in the basement of building 11 on Eglin. I referred to the organization during those days as, "McCormac's electronics skunk works."

When I met Klimek at his office he started off by telling me what I had to say had better be good to get him out of bed that early on a Sunday morning! I told him what all had happened during the past two days and we then brain stormed about how, and what was required, in order to test and train with the Weasel equipment and crews. However, when I told Klimek how little time I had to produce the paper work that would accompany and define the support required for this test, and the limited time I had to run the test, he just could not grasp it and surely thought I was somehow confused. The Wild Weasel-I test started on 11 October and was completed on 18 November 1965, and the four F-100F aircraft departed Eglin AFB on 21 November and arrived in SEA on 25 November 1965.

Klimek and I worked together again in 1967-1968 when I was on my second long temporary duty (TDY) assignment in Southeast Asia (SEA) and he was at the Electronic Warfare shop at Hqs 7th AF, Tan Son Nhut Air Base, Saigon, South Vietnam. I was the 388th Tactical Fighter Wing (TFW) Electronic Warfare Advisor, so to speak, at the Korat Royal Thai Air Base (RTAB), Thailand. Actually, by this time I was officially assigned to TAWC and was a member of their Anti-SAM Combat Assistance Team (ASCAT) which was trained and managed at TAWC by Lt. Col. Milton E. "Jim" Allen.

WORKING WITH TAWC – TEST PLANNING

On Monday, the 4th of October 1965, I walked out of my office in building 1 and half a block down the street to meet with Major Odom and the TAWC Operations Analysts (OA) people who were going to assist us in designing the Wild Weasel I testing and training. There were two TAWC OAs present who were to assist us, plus other personnel, but I can now only remember the names of the OAs. One was a 1Lt. Hugh Curtis and a Civil Service employee, Joe Naughton, a USAF Reserve captian C-130 pilot at Duke Field on Eglin. Joe was the type person who needed to have everything identified, designed, and fashioned in an orderly manner with no loose strings, or he would become agitated. As the meeting progressed and there were so many unknowns with the program, and unbelievable short time frames and limits – Naughton became highly agitated and just got up and walked out of the meeting. So, those of us who remained pressed on with the test planning without him. In several days Joe rejoined our group and he continued with us this time until the effort was completed. About a year after this meeting Hugh Curtis completed his Air Force military obligation and continued his TAWC OA career, and association with Weasel activities, as a Civil Service employee until his retirement.

At this time the TAWC commander was Major General Walter B. Putnam. Colonel Ross L. Blachly was the TAWC DCS for Fighter Systems, which at this time had the responsibility for conducing the Wild Weasel I testing and training program, and I think Lt. Col. Richard "Dick" F. Bailey was the Project Director. However, it was not but a short time later that TAWC had a major reorganization and formed a new DCS for Anti-Sam, which pretty much included the above personnel and not only specialized in countering the SA-2 but also provided electronic warfare assistance in general (the above referenced ASCAT Teams) to the tactical wings in Southeast Asia that were flying jet fighter/bomber and reconnaissance type aircraft over North Vietnam.

In the joint TAWC/APGC Wild Weasel-I Test Plan and the APGC Wild Weasel-I PD (project no. 0510T1) documentation there would be three major areas that had to be addressed for Weasel training and testing: accuracy of the ATI equipment; the crews ability to locate and home in on a SA-2 radar signal; and development of tactics. The Weasel test plan was really required to be developed, or substantially developed, first before I would know the combination of what, how, when, and where APGC support was required in order to be correctly identified in the APGC PD – but the test plan was not developed in time. Had I known all the mission support requirements in time they would have been translated into the unclassified identification codes I wrote about earlier, which would have allowed flexibility in scheduling missions and changing support requirements.

Anyway, as I had anticipated, because of the lack of time in which to prepare for the Wild Weasel-I OT&E, I was unable to write a comprehensible APGC PD, and I paid dearly for it. With mission requirements changing as the OT&E progressed, I often, literally, found myself sitting at my office, or an office at TAWC, or at Site A-20 (at that time mission control), talking on as many as four phones at the same time to four different sets of people trying to reconfigure the support for an imminent mission. Since Wild Weasel-I had the highest test priority on the Eglin ranges, when I requested a mission – it was scheduled and supported! Or, mission support was attempted to the best of everyone's knowledge, even when there was confusion. Had Wild Weasel I had a lesser priority, and the same problems, I am sure Wolf Call would have cancelled a large number of the missions without giving me the opportunity to "salvage" them on the phones. As I pointed out earlier, it was most fortunate at this time that I had a good working relationship with all the personnel in Mission Scheduling and Wolf Call, and other support units.

Admittedly, not knowing all the requirements far enough in advance, I sometimes ended up requesting too much air space on a Wild Weasel-I PD profile for a particular type of test or training mission. In this situation the high priority for Wild Weasel sometimes worked against me. When I asked for a range, and its airspace, it was mine, totally. Often, just before the start of a mission, or during the conduct, Wolf Call would call me up and state that they were observing that the Weasel mission in progress was not using all of a requested range or altitude and if I could continue to keep the Weasel crews away from that part, another test could use it and conduct their mission. I always tried to accommodate other TPO's and their tests and Wolf Call in these situations. However, several times I almost regretted my good intentions when the distances between two high-speed aircraft, of two different tests being controlled at two different locations, suddenly narrowed.

To the best of my memory, the officer in charge of running Wolf Call at this point in time was a Capt. Stevens. He was a very energetic person, which he needed to be in order to keep up with and bring some semblance of order concerning all the aircraft flying on the Eglin ranges at this time.

THE APGC WILD WEASEL ONE PROJECT DIRECTIVE (PD) PLANING MEETING

My Wild Weasel-I testing notes indicate I conducted the PD planning meeting on 8 October 1965, six days after returning from the TDY to ATI, and five days after the start of defining and writing the Wild Weasel-I test plan at TAWC, and, the first test mission was flown on 11 October. Prior to the APGC PD planning meeting I had written a brief, classified, description of the Wild Weasel-I OT&E and sent it to various support organizations. In addition, I requested representatives from all these Eglin organizations that thought they would be required to provide support for this test to have representatives in attendance at the planning meeting, and ask questions concerning their support. Shortly after the planning meeting these support organizations sent me a written description of how they planned to support the Wild Weasel-I OT&E, as best as they understood the test. Then, with this information I wrote the classified PD (such as it was with the limited understanding I too had at this time), got it approved, and distributed it.

My notes identify the following people representing their organization attended the Wild Weasel-I PD meeting:

Capt. J. C. Buehug	PGVSF
G. H. James	PGVSF
Lt. Col. L. R. Perkins	TAWC-FT
C. P. Helms	PGUP
D. T. Hails	PGVE
D. D. Brown	VITRO
L. D. Fowles	PGVEP-3
R. M. Higgins	PGVP
CM/Sgt. E. W. Williamson	PGLOC-2
W. L. Daniels	PGL
Robert S. Laws	PGML

NAMES OF OTHER PEOPLE, AND THEIR ORGANIZATIONS, PROVIDING SUPPORT FOR WW-I, IA, AND III

According to my notes, which are not all inclusive or absolutely correct, the following people and organizations also provided support for Wild Weasel training and testing efforts at Eglin AFB at one time or another.

North American Aviation:

Cyril Knowles Ballock
Francis L. Bertolino
Joseph Salvador Ferrari
Robert William Fero
Robert Lyon
Wallace Stanley Opheim
Robert William Schonle
J. Swicert

John B. Travers
Donald George Whitman

Applied Technology Incorporated:

Joseph Day
Robert Ross Johnson
Earl Ray Malone
Mel F. Klemmick

Maxson Electronics Division:

Arnold Rosen
John Bruno

Bendix Corporation:

Dick Handlen

Republic Aviation:

Salvatore Fucci
George Kearin
Peter R. Zuzolo

APGC/PGOOF – Test Operations:

Capt. Robert S. Beale
Capt. Oscar M. Dardeau
Capt. Hardy
Major Robert L. Jondahl

APGC/PGVMD – Mission Control:

Fred Tillman

APGC/PGVEL – C Band Beacon:

Mr. Wealsh
Donald L. Oglesby

APGC/PGLP Plans:

John Killingsworth

TAWC Test Operations Maintenance Officer:

1Lt. Martancik

TAWC Test Operations:

Major Wade
Sgt. Falk

THE TAWC COMANDER, MAJ. GEN. WALTER B. PUTNAM, EXPECTS WILD WEASEL ONE MILITARY AND CONTRACTORS TO ADHERE TO REGULATIONS AND HIGH STANDARDS

I believe the following incident occurred even before all the Wild Weasel-I crews had arrived and the commencement of testing, and if not, then soon after.

One of the early pilot arrivals was a tall slim captain from Homestead AFB. One night soon after his arrival he had a date with a base nurse and took her to a local bar in an AF staff car, which he parked in a location where it could be observed. Two Eglin Air Police rode past the bar and spotted the staff car. They stopped and investigated and found out who had driven the staff car to the bar.

The next day, Gen. Walter B. Putnam had all personnel, military (TAWC and others, including myself), and all the support contractors to met in a large room where he addressed the captain's use of an official AF car to take a date to a bar. At the time of this meeting I believe the subject captain was already on a plane and on his way back home, and, I don't know what else was planned or did occur to the captain. Anyway, Gen. Putnam's ideas and expectations for professional conduct were made very clear to everyone. I don't know if Gen. Putnam knew about it, but at this time his unofficial nickname by the troops was, "Benny the Bang-Bang," which I don't believe requires an explanation.

I don't remember Gen. Putnam stating the following, but Allen Lamb says he remembers and considering the overall situation and the Wild Weasel mission, Allen is probably correct. Gen. Putnam also dismissed the subject captain because he was talking and telling too much openly about the Wild Weasel mission at the bar, which at this time during the program was highly classified.

Approximately one and a half years after this incident I ran into this subject captain in the Officer's Club at the Udorn RTAB, Thailand. He was a Sandy (A1-E) rescue pilot. It would have been ironic if during his Sandy tour he had helped rescue a downed Wild Weasel crew.

Continue to hold on to this security subject, for it will appear again, and I will be involved this time.

SUMMARY OF WILD WEASEL ONE OT&E TESTING AT EGLIN

The following information was copied verbatim from a TAWC declassified summary report for the Wild Weasel-I OT&E, dated 4 January 1966:

PROJECT NUMBER: 0510T1 (TAC Test Order 65-85

TITLE: Wild Weasel-I

PROJECT OFFICER: Major James R. Odom, Jr.

DESCRIPTON OF PROJECT: The items to be tested are installed internally in four F-100F aircraft with the operation controls and displays located in the rear cockpit for use by an Electronic Warfare Officer (EWO). The equipment consists of: (a) An Applied Technology Incorporated Vector Homing and Warning System; and (b) An IR-133 Panoramic Scan Receiver. The Vector System is designed to provide homing and warning of C, S, or X Band signals and instantaneous bearing to the station. The IR-133 receiver is designed to receive and analyze the S band signals from victim radars.

TEST OBJECTIVES: To test and evaluate equipment and tactics, and train aircrews specifically for detection, location, neutralization and/or destruction of SA-2 missile systems. This evaluation will include flights in the combat theater against actual SA-2 missile sites.

TEST METHODOLOGY: Approximately 100 sorties were flown at various altitudes using different profiles against ground S Band transmitters simulating the FAN SONG radar. Runs were made at varying aspect angles to determine 360 degree warning capability and homing accuracy. Usable ranges were determined for the main beam, side lobes, and back lobes of the target radar. Various attack maneuvers were developed and tested. Sorties were also flown to determine the capability of the equipment to operate in an ECM environment, to verify the capability to home on C-band TWS radars, and to detect and warn of illumination by X-band air-to-air radar. The aircraft have been deployed to Southeast Asia to employ the tactics and techniques developed during the Eglin phase of this test and for combat evaluation.

ESTABLISHED MILESTONES:

11 Oct 65 – First F-100F aircraft began physical testing.

20 Oct 65 – Second F-100F aircraft began physical testing.

29 Oct 65 – Equipment capability tests completed for two F-100F A/C.

1 Nov 65 – Tactics/training phase began.

2 Nov 65 – Third F-100F aircraft began physical testing.

8 Nov 65 – Fourth F-100F began physical testing.

18 Nov 65 – Physical testing complete.

17 Nov 65 – Interim TWX test report submitted.

21 Nov 65 – Aircraft and personnel departed for SEA.

25 Nov 65 – Aircraft arrived in SEA.

15 Dec 65 – Final report published on Eglin phase.

23 Feb 66 – SEA evaluation complete.

31 Mar 66 – Final report due on SEA operation.

STATUS:

a. Total F-100F sorties flown: 105

b. Total F-100F sorties productive: 99

c. Productive sorties flown for North American equipment tests: 13

d. Productive sorties flown for data collection: 34

e. Productive sorties flown for tactics and training: 52

In addition to the above sorties 4 F-105 aircraft flew 21 sorties in support of the tactics phase.

Preliminary test results are contained in teletype interim report USAFTAWC-FTE 08285 17 November 1965.

Final test results are contained in Wild Weasel-I Final Report (Eglin Phase), Eglin AF Base, Florida, December 1965.

A BAD FIRST WEEK FOR WILD WEASEL ONE OT&E RESULTS

I believe we started off by flying missions in the morning that tested the homing ability of the crews to use the ATI equipment to home in on signals, especially the simulated SA-2 signal from the SADS-I radar at Site A-7. The crews flew a south to north racetrack profile with the north bound leg being the homing leg as they approached the Okaloosa Island on which Site A-7 was located. The crews flew homing missions at 100, 300, 500, 1,500, 5,000, and 10,00 feet against the SADS-I radar system. Also, a significant number of test missions were flown against the SADS-I radar using the IR-133 to determine at what range it could detect the SADS-I back lobe.

Then, in the afternoon, we flew missions that would test the threat strobes at varying aspect angles to determine the 360 degrees warning capability of the equipment and the signal strobe accuracy. For these missions I would schedule a large block of air space south of Okaloosa Island and just about all the radar sites located on the island.

Before each mission's scheduled range time I would go to Hanger 68 (the Weasel hanger) and brief the Weasel commander and the crews on what was required. If I remember correctly I was able to be at Site A-20 for the morning Site A-7 signal homing flights, but was not able to be there for the afternoon signals aspect angles missions. However, I had briefed my VITRO controller at Site A-20 and he knew what was required. I was not able to make it to the site for the afternoon missions this first week due to resolving, by phone, last minute problems with mission support requirements for these first missions due to the Weasel APGC "weak" PD.

This first week I relied on the VITRO currier system to collect all the mission data from the radar sites, such as the radar TSPI plots providing the track of the aircraft(s), and delivering them to my office, which took three to four days. I would usually collect the logs of the crews at Hanger 68 some time after they landed the day they flew a mission.

At the end of the first week I finally had all the data from the radars and the crew's logs and was able to fit them together to get a quick idea of what we had before I took it all over to the TAWC OA people. When I got all the information together it did not take much of an examination to determine I had garbage for the afternoon tests of the signal strobe aspect accuracy! I guess the situation of having all those radars up in the afternoon was just too much of a temptation for the crews to play around with trying to develop tactics.

Considering all the pressure that was on this OT&E, my first thoughts were, should I go up stairs and inform my management of the situation? But then Jim Odom and the others at the working level in TAWC would be blind sided if and when the news went across at my top level to TAWC, and then back down to Odom and the others. On the other hand, if I told Odom at the working level in TAWC, and they panicked, and informed their upper management, would they give me time to get back to my upper management and inform them before TAWC management called and blind sided them? I did not yet really know these TAWC people I was working with - how level headed were they?

I decided the right thing to do, regardless, was to take a chance with the TAWC people before I first talked to my people. I called up Odom and stated I was coming over with the fist week's data and I needed to talk to him, and the others, because we had big problems - the Weasel commander was not following and/or enforcing my instructions. After Odom, and the others at his level, looked at the data they asked me, "Joe, can you hold off just two more days before you inform your management of what has happened? You may not need to tell anyone after tomorrow because Gen. Putnam is going to fire the Weasel commander tomorrow." It seemed he had not been doing some things the general had request he accomplish, either. So, that is how Major Gary Willard became the Wild Weasel I commander about one to two weeks after the OT&E started at Eglin. And, from then on I had no problems with the crews flying and obtaining the data I requested.

I never told my management about this loss of data, and I don't think Odom did his management either, and we were able to make up the lost time in the long run. Also, from then on I no longer utilized the VITRO currier system to collect the mission data and information from the radar sites utilized on a mission. I, or someone else in my organization, would drive to each site and collect their logs and records after a mission had ended. This, and many other activities, resulted in long days for me since I was the only person in my organization that was actually dedicated to the Wild Weasel-I OT&E. I kept a record of my work hours during this OT&E and I averaged working, 7 days a week, in excess of 80 hours a week for approximately 7 weeks.

As I previously stated, during this time frame at APGC the Deputy for Test Operations was the largest test organization and primarily conducted engineering tests. It's Electronic Systems Test Directorate, commanded by Col. Joe Gillespie, was responsible for electronic warfare equipment engineering testing, and other types of electronic equipments too. In my opinion, Col. Gillespie had mixed emotions about the Deputy of Effectiveness Test being chosen to conduct the high priority Wild Weasel-I OT&E. Probably his most intense emotion was frustration at Wild Weasel-I OT&E having the highest test priority and preventing many of his tests from being conducted quickly. Second, he was frustrated because the Wild Weasel-I OT&E utilized Eglin's highly instrumented ranges for operational testing, instead for engineering testing. And third, in a way, if he did recognize this situation, he may have been kind of secretly relieved his organization was not conducting the Weasel testing. For lack of a better definition and explanation, engineering testing is so much more structured and methodical than the "kick the tires and light the fire – right now" first ever Wild Weasel OT&E. Now, speaking from the position of wisdom learned from hindsight, personally, I have my doubts if Col. Gillespie's organization and people would have been flexible enough to have worked with TAWC, and at the same time, conduct the OT&E testing with all its unknowns and time constraints.

Nevertheless, Col. Gillespie was frustrated, and rightfully so. So, it was shortly after this first bad week of Weasel testing, he escorted his boss, Col. Joe Davis, the Deputy for Test Operations (the equivalent now of the Test Wing), to Hanger 68 and preceded to point out and inform Col. Davis how this Wild Weasel test was running amuck and the people conducting it did not know what in the world they were doing. Apparently Col. Davis was not too overly concerned because I never received any negative feedback that he might have passed over to my chain of command as a result of his visit. Or, if there was negative feedback, someone above me prevented it from flowing on down to me.

DETERMING THE ACCURACY OF THE HOMING STROB AND THE WEASEL CREWS ABILITY TO HOME IN ON THE SITE A-7 SIMULATED SA-2 SIGNAL

Probably the most dangerous and scary test missions, for me, were training and testing the crew's ability to use the ATI equipment to home in on the Site A-7 signal. What made these flights so dangerous were their location and the surrounding air traffic. As previously stated, we first started off homing in on the signal of the SA-2 simulated radar of the SADS-I located at Site A-7 on Okaloosa Island. To my knowledge this was the first major threat simulated SA-2 radar at Eglin; and the only one during Wild Weasel-I OT&E. While I could schedule the water range and air space starting to the immediate south of Okaloosa Island solely for Weasel testing, I could not control the low narrow air corridor running parallel to the island just on shore where any civilian small light aircraft could fly along the coast line.

Also, once a Weasel aircraft was over the shoreline, and if turning to the west to go back south into the Gulf to make another homing run, it also had to content with the Hurlburt Field air traffic. As stated before, some of these south to north homing tracks were flown as low as 100 feet. When flying these type missions most of the time I had a VITRO man at

Site A-20 on the phone in constant contact with the Hurlburt Field tower personnel and warning them when we had an incoming Weasel aircraft.

The Site A-7 radar antenna was housed in a very large, white, rubber type bubble. The reasons for this cover were to protect the equipment from the salt air and other weather elements, and to prevent observations of it by Russian satellites. Needless to say, the Weasel crews could easily see this structure from a long distance, which could be either good or bad, depending on the type mission being flown.

A VITRO male employee who worked at Site A-7 related the following incident to me, and he swore he was telling the truth, and he probably was. Various VITRO personnel working at Site A-7, or VITRO personnel working at other close sites, often stood on the shore between the bubble and the water to get a gun sight view of the low homing runs over the Site A-7 bubble. On this occasion the individual was alone on the shore.

It seems the Weasel crew made a much lower homing run than 100 feet on Site A-7. In fact, it was so low the VITRO individual claimed there was a very high "rooster's tail" of water being sucked up into the air behind the F-100F as it approached the site. And, in order not to hit the bubble, the pilot had to pull up at the last second to clear the top of the bubble. The VITRO individual claimed he was hit and soaked by the "rooster's tail" as it came ashore, plus, his eardrums were damaged by the low jet aircraft's very loud engine noise. At the time he was telling me about this incident he stated he was seriously considering the possibility of initiating an injurious lawsuit against the Air Force. It he did, I never heard about it; and if he had I am sure I would have been involved.

During all this Wild Weasel-I testing Odom pretty much remained at the Hqs. TAWC building handling TAC matters and I was constantly, by word of mouth, keeping Odom informed of the latest daily test activities and results. In most intendances and for most subjects, I would express myself with words like, "It looks like such and such is the situation, but we need to wait a little longer and collect more data to be certain."

Jim Odom was one of the most accomplished briefers I ever witnessed. He had always been an Air Force pilot during his career and of course could speak and relate in an exceptional manner on flying subjects to this group. However, someway and somehow, during his career he had also acquired a good knowledge of electronics and electronic warfare. He just had the knack of getting this subject across to his listeners, especially senior pilot commanders, in a very brief and simple manor. During the Southeast Asian War many of these senior commanders had suddenly found themselves thrust into a war of electrons and many were ill prepared and very much ill at ease and Odom's briefing skills had a great appeal to them.

On this particular occasion, about half way through the Wild Weasel-I OT&E program, I visited Odom's office unannounced. He was not in his office but I was told by others he was about to give a briefing in the TAWC briefing room and I could just slip in and sit at the back of the briefing room and catch him when the briefing was completed. I have now forgotten who the visiting general, or generals were, but they were given a progress briefing of the Wild Weasel-I OT&E by Odom. To my surprise, and horror, Odom was briefing all of my "maybes" and "looks like" and "lets wait and see" statements to the visitors as absolutes and the way it had turned out. And actually, that was the way most of them did turn out, after the testing was completed and the data was analyzed.

I learned that every since the Weasel program had started Odom had been giving progress briefings like this to visiting dignitaries at TAWC. I my opinion, I contribute my preliminary estimates being briefed by Odom as factual, and then turning out to be actually true, as providential. All during my association with Jim Odom I consistently witnessed his great briefing skills, both in the US and in Southeast Asia.

ENTER THE ELECTRONIC SECURITY COMMAND (ESC) AND THE WILD WEASEL SECURITY ISSUE

While flying ELINT missions in the RB-47H aircraft from selected bases around the world I had always hear rumors about how ESC personnel were tapping our phone lines and listening. I knew for a fact the AF Office of Special Investigation (OSI) had their people listening in on, and recording, our conversions in the officer clubs, trying to catch someone talking about something classified. In fact, the rumors concerning ESC went so far as to state ESC was not beyond using entrapment methods to catch someone in a phone security violation. As far as I was concerned, from the rumors I had always heard, ESC personnel were not to be taken at face value at anytime or anyplace – even though I had never knowingly had any experience with any of them.

At about this time during the Wild Weasel-I OT&E, about the second to third week, I was in my office with other people I shared it with when this captain entered, by himself. He was a tall friendly looking fellow and well spoken. He stated he wanted to speak with Capt. Telford, and I replied that would be me.

He then stated something that went like, "I am Capt. Wayne Noster of the Electronic Security Command and my job, with my team, is to perform intercept and analysis of radio traffic to determine the degree of revealing critical and classified operations information. My team is setting up our listening site and equipment on Okaloosa Island in order to intercept and record radio conversations, both ground and air, of the tests being conducted at Eglin. My airmen know nothing about the tests being conducted but we want to see what they can determine about the Eglin tests when we let them combine the unclassified Eglin Test Mission Schedule for the missions to be conducted with the radio traffic we intercept and record. And, I want to know if you are Capt. Joe Telford who is the APGC TPO for the Wild Weasel-I OT&E because I need to know what this Wild Weasel-I OT&E is about?"

When the captain paused and was waiting for my answer, my brain was going at about mach 5 and the adrenalin was being pumped into my blood stream with every heart beat, in very large doses! Nobody had informed me about this Capt. Noster and his mission here at Eglin. Immediately I thought – ESC entrapment!

I looked Capt. Noster in the eye, and tried to sound firm and unruffled when I replied, "I am Capt. Telford, and that is all I have to say!" I would not even say the words "Wild Weasel." I shared my office with several other officers who were conducting other tests and none of them were saying a word by now, they did not even move, they just froze, and all eyes were on us two captains.

To make about 15 minutes worth of conversation exchanges brief I will just summarize by saying I did not answer any of Capt. Noster's questions concerning Wild Weasel. I just refused to address the subject at all. Capt. Noster was no longer the cool individual who had entered my office just a few minutes previously. He was visibly and audibly unset by my answers that failed to acknowledge that I even knew a Wild Weasel-I

OT&E existed, much less any of its details. In utter exasperation Capt. Noster turned on his heels and quickly exited my office.

I went back to working on whatever it was I was doing before Capt. Noster entered my office. In about 15 minutes my phone rang and it was John Killingsworth, a long time Civil Service APGC employee who was in electronic warfare requirements upstairs. John stated, "Joe, I want to first apologize to you. I forgot to tell you I had requested ESC to provide us one of their evaluation teams down here to try and determine what, if any, sensitive information our unclassified Test Mission Schedule, and testing, and radio traffic at Eglin are giving away to the Russian intelligence trawlers just off our coast in the Gulf. Would you please cooperate with Capt. Noster and his team?"

The bottom line of Capt. Noster's team's work and analysis reveled they did obtain a pretty good idea of what Wild Weasel-I was trying to accomplish, even though we were using codes, most of the time, for information being passed by radios. Actually, the team judged the Weasel capability was far more than it was capable of accomplishing. Oddly enough, several months after the deployment of the first Wild Weasel-I crews the magazine, Aviation Week, came out with an article on the Weasel testing at Eglin and what it would accomplish in Southeast Asia. And it too over estimated the capability of the Weasels at that time.

As for Capt. Noster, he survived his encounter with the Wild Weasels very well, and after serving his Air Force active duty obligation time became a GS-15 in the upper levels of management in ESC.

A DIFFERENT BALL GAME - HOMING IN ON A HIDDEN THREAT SIGNAL

Early on in our thinking about and trying to plan the Wild Weasel-I OT&E, I recognized the crews homing in on Site A-7 and its big white bubble was good to start with, and good to determine the threat strobe's accuracy, and the strobes reaction as a crew flew toward and over the threat. However, once the above objectives were well in hand, how were we to train the crews to locate a hidden SA-2 signal source, and determine how effectively they could accomplish this feat? Even the radars on the Elgin land ranges, without a big white bubble, stood out like the preverbal sore thumb because they were always located in a cleared area so there would be no obstruction of their radar beam.

My early thoughts, and actions, on this was to request Mac "McCormac's electronic skunk works" to build several small easily transportable S band transmitting devices that could be hidden on the ranges. Every other day they could be moved and rehidden by VITRO range people and the Weasel crews would always have a new challenge every day of finding and homing in on them.

Mac and his people first built a prototype model using some type of S band transmitter and high gain antenna, and some kind of battery for power. The device did work, but unfortunately it just did not have the power to provide enough signal range. By the time this experiment was completed and proven impractical we had run out of lead-time, the first Weasel crews were ready to practice locating a hidden threat signal.

My fall back position was to request VITRO to put one of their mobile S band tracking radars, and its 5 man crew, on an AF blue flat bed truck and hide it on the ranges. However, there were two problems with this solution. The radar dish and the equipment cab were white, making it easier to be seen; and, the radar beam was a pencil beam, making it difficult to intercept. However, this was the best I could quickly come up with, with time running out.

I asked Major Odom if he could assign someone in TAWC to be in charge of relocating this truck and radar to a new location about every other day. Odom assigned Capt. Author "Art" Oken, an EWO, to this duty. I briefed Oken on what was needed and this was one less problem I had to concern myself with and I pretty much concentrated on other pressing problems.

After about a week had gone by and I was in my office working on other problems when my phone rang. When I answered the phone the person on the other end stated, in a very strong and formal voice, "Capt. Telford, this is Maj. Van Liere, the Eglin Range Safety Officer." Now, no TPO wanted to run afoul of the Eglin Range Safety Officer so immediately he had my full attention. Also, Maj. Van Liere lived only three or four houses down the street from me, and while we were certainly not friends, we did speak to each other on occasions – so, why all the formality? I sensed trouble.

Continuing on in his very commanding and formal voice he asked, "Capt. Telford, you are the TPO for the Wild Weasel-I OT&E, are you not?" I knew he knew that, so why is he asking me this question? I replied, "Yes sir, I am."

He continued, "Well Capt. Telford, according to APGC directivities, as the TPO would you then say you are responsible for everything concerning the conduct of the Wild Weasel-I OT&E?" I did not know, yet, where this phone conversation was going, but I was growing more uncomfortable with each question. I replied, "Yes sir, I am."

I did not know if Maj. Van Liere knew or not, but this thing of the TPO being absolutely and solely responsible for everything concerning his test was a "big thing" with Col. Petterson, my big boss! With a TPO having to rely on so many support units and people to help him with his test, sometimes it was an easy out to blame lack of planning, effort, meeting schedules, and results on others. Col Petterson constantly hammered home the concept that "the buck stopped with the TPO!"

Maj. Van Liere continued, "You have an AF flat bed truck with a mobile radar on it that you move around on the ranges, do you not?" And I replied, "Yes sir, I do."

Maj. Van Liere, "Well then, Capt. Telford, can you tell me where it is right now?"

I thought, "Hot dog, I see an out from where ever this conversation is going." So I replied, "Well sir, I don't really know where it is because you see, Capt. Oken, in TAWC, is in charge of locating it and you need to contact him to find out the answer to that question."

Before I could really get the last words out of my mouth for this reply, Maj. Van Liere jumped right in and stated, "Oh no, Capt. Telford! You just told me a second ago that as the Wild Weasel-I TPO you are responsible for every thing concerning your test! Is this not true?"

With the knowledge that I had been had, I replied in a resigned voice, "Yes sir, I am responsible, for everything."

Then, Maj. Van Liere literally shouted into the phone, "Well then - I will tell where your radar is located, where it has been for the last five days, with its five man VITRO crew – it is in the woods in the off limits ricochet area of the Cluster Bomb Unit bombing range. Get it out of there!" And with that, he slammed down his phone without giving me a chance to reply, which at that moment I really did not want to do anyway.

Needless to say, the truck, the radar, and the crew were moved in short order to a new location, and to a new location about every other day after that. In trying to determine how close the Weasels were flying over this hidden radar I would station several people, at set distances, on either side of the radar, looking in the direction we anticipated the approach of the Weasel aircraft. These "observers" would look up and estimate how far off the Weasel aircraft missed the radar. Yes, crude, but it was very flexible, which was what was required.

DEVELOPMENT OF WEASEL TACTICS

For the missions for the development of Wild Weasel-I tactics I just pretty much scheduled the ranges, water or land, or both, and the radars to be used as threats, if required, and let the crews be on their own and do their thing. I just always tried to schedule enough, and maybe even more, airspace and altitude to cover any thing they were going to try.

THE WILD WEASEL ONE CREWS GET A SECRETARY OF THE AIR FORCE HAROLD BROWN SEND OFF

Just a few days before the Weasel crews deployed to Korat RTAB, Secretary of the Air Force Harold Brown, and a bus load of AF generals, descended upon Hanger 68 where the Weasel F-100Fs were parked and Brown gave the crews a send off speech. Also, the aircraft had maintenance ladders and platforms around them and the generals were able to climb up and observe the cockpits and equipment. Also, I think selected crews were standing by to answer the general's questions.

I remember I was standing by this two star general while he was viewing the APR-25 and he remarked that an earlier and similar model of this equipment had been installed in the U-2s for several years. I was unaware this ATI equipment had been around for that long, I was under the impression its first use was in the Weasel program. I also believe the AF had prior experience with ATI's IR-133 equipment.

In my opinion, this bit of information explained to me why later when I conducted OT&Es on other company's radar warning equipment there were always more problems at first than with the ATI equipment. ATI's APR-25 equipment was more tried and seasoned. This was most fortunate for the AF because for had it not been that way, Wild Weasel I would have never deployed as quickly as it did. It affirms for me that Gen. Dempster and his people did their homework.

5.
WILD WEASEL - IA TEST

Most people associated with any of the Weasel programs probably never heard about the Wild Weasel-IA Test. I only knew about the testing of two of the four systems, which I think were involved. I can't remember now if it was even called an OT&E, since the testing I was involved in was so unstructured. I know TAWC was to issue an interim test report on 17 December 1965 and a final report on 17 January 1966.

I only remember I was told Gen. Dempster had requested a very, very quick test be conducted on ATI, Bendix-Maxson, Melpar, and Loral radar warning equipments. The test results would be compared and large quantities of equipment would be quickly bought from the preferred company, above and beyond the already procured Wild Weasel-I systems. I had no involvement with the testing of the Melpar or Loral equipment. They were probably at this time undergoing some type of engineering testing by the Eglin APGC Electronic System Test Directorate (PGOY), of the Deputy of Test Operations (PGO), and installed in their test aircraft.

Toward the end of Wild Weasel-I OT&E two F-105Ds arrived at Eglin AFB for testing. One aircraft, I think tail number 24291, had ATI's APR-25 installed and the other aircraft, I think tail number 10138, had a very early Bendix – Maxsonm prototype model of the APS –107 (DPN-61) warning equipment installed. Later, Bendix was the sole developer of this system. But, in this prototype model of the APS-107, there were several black boxes installed on top of the cockpit instrument shield and positioned from one side of the shield to the other, that required observation and probably switch action too. It is difficult to remember all the details now.

The names of the two TDY pilots who were sent here to fly the test missions were a Maj. D. E. "Doug" Whatley and a Maj. H. P. "Hap" Maree.

They may have not only flown the two TDY F-105D aircraft for me, but also maybe the PGOY aircraft that had the Melpar and Loral systems installed, if they were in F-105s?

As for these two F-105D aircraft and testing that I was involved with, to the best of my memory, there was no APGC or TAWC test documentation generated. These test missions utilized the Wild Weasel I documentation to acquire support, but with a lesser priority. The missions required no radar data or tracking. To the best of my memory I just scheduled the SADS-I radar at Site A-7 and maybe some other radars in the C and X band as threat signal sources, and I believe I only scheduled water ranges. I believe the test data was just the opinion of these two majors after they had flown several missions with the ATI and Bendix equipments. As I stated earlier, I know nothing about the testing of the other two systems. There probably was some one in TAWC who was taking and recording these two pilot's comments, and any other involved pilots. I only remember briefing my two pilots concerning the ranges and radar threat signal support.

Toward the end of this test, and unknown to me, Gen. Dempster was visiting Eglin and was at the Wild Weasel hanger. I was coming around one end of the hanger, outside, when I ran into Watley and Maree right after they each had just flown a mission in the F-105Ds. I believe these two majors just previously to this test had completed a combat tour in Southeast Asia in strike F-105Ds, before the advent of radar warning equipment or Weasels. I don't know if they flew long enough in Southeast Asia to fly 100 missions, but I do know they were not young, they were physically tired, and were irritable, and I think especially Whatley who was also very outspoken.

I think it was Whatley who immediately jumped on my case. At this time in my life my hair was still red and Whatley growled at me, "Red, this was the last mission with that APS-107 where I am going to give you test people my undivided attention of looking from one side of that cockpit to the other in order to operate it! I was homing in on Site A-7, not far off shore, at about 200 feet and I suddenly realized the aircraft had inverted itself without me doing a thing to the controls." And, he continued to chew on me.

Right in the middle of this conversation, around the corner of the hanger walks Gen. Dempster. I am sure he already knew both of these pilots. Immediately he picks up on the subject and commences to ask the two pilots questions concerning the equipment and their experiences with it, which took the pressure off of me.

As I stated earlier, based on the test results of Wild Weasel-IA Gen. Dempster, and possibly along with Lt. Col. Levy, made the decision to buy and install ATI's APR-25/26, in large numbers, as the first radar homing and warning equipment in strike aircraft flying in Southeast Asia. Given the short time fuse, the equipments in being, and the urgency of the situation, in my opinion Gen. Dempster made the correct choice.

Joe W. Telford, WW # 258

Story by Keith Ferris, WW # 2021

How I Became a Wild Weasel and Painted "First In,..."

My first awareness of the Wild Weasels was the appearance of strange little animal footprints leading into the front door of the old officers club at Nellis in the late 1960s.

I was on one of my frequent visits to Nellis over the years, while participating in the Air Force Art Program at the invitation of the Secretary of the Air Force. My mission was to learn as much as possible about the tactical employment of fighter aircraft by flying with each of the weapons schools and the 422 OT&E Squadron. This knowledge has served me well in documenting the mission of the Air Force through art for now 44 years.

Shortly after that Nellis visit, I deployed to Korat with Eglin's 40th TFS as a civilian GIB with the first F-4Es to replace F-105Ds in Southeast Asia, becoming the 469 TFS.

Not long after drying off (out?) from our very wet reception at Korat we all went out to the end of the runway to welcome the return of John Revak and Stan Goldstein from their 100th mission over North Vietnam. More water and then to the club to celebrate the occasion and to get to know John and Stan, the beginning of our long friendship.

My painting "Big Brass Ones" celebrates the Wild Weasel mission and crews through John Revak, Stan Goldstein, and their F-105F 62-4424 "Crown Seven".

On my last day at Korat, after earlier chasing an F-4E strike flight in the F-4E, I had the privilege of flying in 44th TFS F-105F 62- 4446 "Mostes" with George Connolly. We chased an F-105 strike flight until they dropped off the tanker and then checked out all the bases in Thailand. I was unfortunately forbidden to participate in F-4E or F-105 combat flights over Laos or North Vietnam. I guess they did not want to lose a non-combatant civilian in either of those places. But that did not prevent me from a mission dropping 108 500-pound bombs on the Mu Gia Pass early the next day as I made my way home from Thailand in a B-52D from U Tapao.

When we recovered at Anderson, it occurred to me that I am probably the only person

ever to have actually flown all three aircraft, the F-4E, the F-105F and the B-52D within the same 24 hour time period.

On my next visits to Nellis, in continuation of my education about the Weasel mission, I was able to visit Wimpy Peake's SAM Sites up at Caliente in F-105Fs of the 66th FWS.

I was to put my Thud experiences to good use with a series of F-105 paintings. In addition to "Big Brass Ones", created for the Air Force Art Collection, there was "Thud Ridge", created for a Chandler Evans Control Systems Aviation Week ad. Republic commissioned three paintings: "Rolling Thunder" depicts George Avila, the last Thud pilot in the 469th TFS, taxiing out of Korat's Spot 28 in his F-105D 61-0093 "Honey Babe". "Wild Weasel" shows Robby Robinson and Pete Tsouprake engaged with a SAM site north of Hanoi on their Air Force Cross mission of 5 July 1967, while "Doumer Bridge" depicts the 11 August 1967 F-105 strike on Hanoi's Paul Doumer Bridge by the 355th and 388th Tactical Fighter Wings.

All but one of the above paintings are permanent parts of the Air Force Art Collection.

I was surprised and honored to be invited to speak to the 8 November 1969 Reunion in Las Vegas and to accept Honorary Membership in the Society of Wild Weasels. My membership has been a very much valued association for the past quarter century.

In December of 2000, I was contacted by old friend and then Chief Weasel George Acree concerning the possibility of commissioning a Ferris painting depicting the first SAM kill by a Wild Weasel team. This was the 22 December 1965 mission with Allan Lamb, pilot, and Jack Donovan, EWO (Bear) as crew of the Weasel F-100F with four F-105D strikers from Korat.

An agreement was reached to create the painting "First In" when Allan Lamb and George Acree visited our home and studio 11-12 February 2001.

We debriefed the mission in front of my drawing board as I sketched the approach, pop-up and roll-in of the Lamb/Donovan Weasel F-100F and the tracks of the four Korat

F-105D strikers. We discussed the appearance of the SAM Site itself, the terrain and defenses along the Red River, the attack sequence and defensive reaction involved.

We located the approximate position of the site on a chart and laid out the ingress and egress tracks. I quizzed Allen about altitudes involved, ordnance loads, and results of the strike while proceeding to do some rough sketches of possible approaches to the painting.

I decided to place the viewer at about 3000 feet AGL, about 12,000feet west of the site, as Allan and Jack were turning back in for their second pass. The F-100 is seen from a position almost 100 feet in front, 40 feet to its right and 30 feet below, as created from three-view drawings by *perspective projection by descriptive geometry*. The painting becomes a "window" on the scene. If one scans *left and right* and *up and down* from the viewing position to the extremities of the art, the *visual angle* created can be extended to the ground surface in top and side views in scale. This creates a "footprint" on the surface, allowing precise positioning and scale of the SAM site, river, village, buildings, rice patties and other details of the background.

Study of strike photos of that area of North Vietnam, photos of villages, rice paddies, SAM sites and defensive gun sites, plus Allen's verbal, and surviving striker's written descriptions and memories, filled out the story. The painting shows the SAM site under a cloud of smoke and debris as the site's oxidizer tank exploded and other explosions are created by the rockets fired by the F-100F and F-105s in the first pass.

I was pleased to relate the process of creating this painting at the 2003 Wild Weasel Convention, Symposium and Family Reunion at Disney World in November 2003.

The original painting: "First In" was donated to the Air Force Art Collection by the Wild Weasel Foundation, LLC. A limited edition of 1000 signed and numbered fine art reproductions of "First In" was created and these are available for $150.00 each, plus $10.00 for shipping and handling, from The Wild Weasel Foundation, LLC, P.O. Box 7637, Lumberton, NC 28359, or call: Allen Lamb at (910) 739-3181 or George Acree at (410) 647-9511.

Keith Ferris

Story by Ed White, WW Charter # 15

A COUPLE OF DECADES OF BUMPING INTO WEASEL STUFF

It was October 1965 and Captain Ed White was happy, as life was good. Bombing along in his fire engine red Porsche 356SC, he reflected on the good leave time with his family in Connecticut as well as getting to play Pinehurst #2 on the way back to his base. Long trips leave lots of thinking time and reflections on his military life were included. Experience in overseas deployments to Turkey, two temporary duty tours to Southeast Asia (with combat time on both), graduation from the USAF Fighter Weapons School as Top Gun in the class and Instructor Pilot status were pretty good qualifications. Returning to the 615th Tactical Fighter Squadron at England Air Force Base was looking good for lots of quality flying. Little did he know that the next week would mark a departure from this life into what would become a couple decades of gaining proficiency in the F-100F, F-105F/G and F-4G Wild Weasels.

Two days later the young Captain (in a clean flying suit) was lurking around the scheduling desk in the squadron, hopeful that his sniveling would bring him a flight that day. While catching up on the latest news from those walking by, he noticed that his friend Maury Fricke was not on the schedule and nowhere to be seen. A bit later the Squadron Commander walked by and the question was posed. Major Jim Minish said to follow him into his office. He closed the door and said that the conversation would remain inside his door. Maury Fricke had volunteered for a special project and already gone to Eglin Air Force Base. It had something to do with developing some sort of a communications platform in the F-100F for use in Southeast Asia. He offered that it was a "good deal" and asked Captain Ed if he would like to volunteer also. Curiosity as to his friend's activities and the "good deal" label from his Commander resulted in a thoughtful but fairly quick "yes". Major Minish said he would see what he could do.

The next day Captain White was asked into Major Minish's office and the door was closed. The Commander said there was a pilot vacancy at the project; Captain White had been accepted and this move had received approval from the local Wing Headquarters. His instructions were to go get packed, departure was to be the next day, plan on a 90 day temporary duty and that his orders (verbal orders of the Commander) would suffice until the more formal paper orders were done. (The paper orders to "Participate in Project Wild Weasel" were finally issued on 22 October 1965). The trip began as instructed after putting a few flying suits, boots, shoes and some civvies into a parachute bag which got tossed into the Porsche. The short trip to Florida found the young aviator wondering what was really going on.

After a few inquiries at Eglin "about the F-100 project" had received blank stares, a visit to the Housing Office finally revealed where Friend Maury Fricke was staying. Going to the identified set of quarters and that room was successful. A buzz of conversation from a nearby room was the clue to the whereabouts of the team. After being introduced around, it sank in to the "new guy" that some of the people in flying suits had different wings on their nametags. The obvious question brought the answer they were for an Electronic Warfare Officer (EWO). The newly arrived aviator searched through the memory banks for a connection between the F-100 and EWOs and came up dry. The obvious question brought the answer "we can't tell you here", and as the beer was already purchased, business would wait till the next day.

Captain Ed Sandelius (Sandy naturally) was an EWO and without a pilot. His front seater, for whatever reasons, had returned to his home unit. It was right then that Sandy and Ed became a crew. (How to best mate up pilots and EWOs to make a compatible team would be a matter for lots of discussion in the months to come.) In the course of the evening Ed got to know of Sandy's B-66 (electronic) background and his stint as Drill Instructor in the Marines, as well as the backgrounds of the rest of the team.

The next day was orientation for the newcomer. Observation showed that on the hangared F-100, there were some extra pieces sticking out on the nose and tail. Meeting with project officers from Eglin revealed the nature of the test. The civilians constantly roaming around the aircraft was different from the flight line activity at England AFB for sure. These civilians showed themselves to be, first, masters of their trade, both metal-bending and electronic; and second, they were imbued with a can-do spirit different from any previously observed by the young Captain. They could literally rebuild and change components between closely scheduled flights. The more senior industry representatives reinforced this attitude.

Flying soon morphed into a pretty predictable pattern. After takeoff, all electronic signals were interesting as picking them up and determining what they were was part of the challenge. A regular part of most missions was heading out over the Gulf of Mexico and homing in on the simulated threat signal on the coast. Passing over the site, or offset to the left or right, was duly recorded by the test staff standing on the beach. The aircrews noted that as you passed the site, there was a waterfall sort of effect on the APR-25, important information to know as it was "now you are there". These memories would cause a feeling of deja-vu a couple of months later when White/Sandelius got the waterfall, dumped the tanks and fired rockets and cannon to show the SAM site location to the accompanying F-105s.

Changes in leadership ended when Major Garry Willard was selected to be the commander. Major Willard was an experienced, articulate fighter pilot, and his leadership technique of caring about his troops while providing excellent interfacing with Superiors and outside agencies would prove to be key elements to the success of the Project. As the new Commander struggled to get his arms around his responsibilities, the crews continued to do mostly test duties and hardly any tactics development in the air, although there was lots of "how we gonna do this?" on the ground. On the other hand, the experienced fighter pilots were supposed to have brought their ordnance delivery skills with them.

This "test phase" came to an end in late November 1965. Air Force Secretary Harold Brown and other senior Officers stopped at the little hangar on 19 November to become personally acquainted with the project and to pass on their best wishes. Two days later, Major Willard led the 4 F-100s from Eglin, to Hickam, Guam and then to Korat in Thailand. The advance party had begun liaison with the Wing starting on Thanksgiving 1965. An experienced fighter pilot, Colonel Monroe S. Sams, was the Wing Commander and he assigned the Wild Weasels to the 6234th Tactical Fighter Wing (Wild Weasel Detachment).

After lots of get-acquainted briefings with 388th Wing personnel, orientation flights began on 28 November. A Wild Weasel or two would meet up with a EB-66 and fly along the North Vietnam border for geographic orientation as well as electronic orientation, sort of "I see this; what do you see?" On 1 December Willard/Lifsey and White/Sandelius flew the first sorties (accompanied by F-105s) that were to be called "Iron Hand".

Napalm and 2.75 inch rockets were tried on the F-100 Wild Weasels and both were just OK. (The AGM-45 Shrike would be tried by the second group of F-100 Wild Weasels.) Captain White and Captain Sandelius homed into a SAM signal, observed the waterfall, dumped the tanks and fired their ordnance where they thought the site to be. At delivery, the flak got fairly intense and after a couple of F-105s had released, discretion took over and they all egressed. These somewhat tentative steps ended on 20 December when Captain Jack Pitchford and Captain Bob Trier were shot down in a high threat area northwest of Hanoi. Bob shot it out with the ground forces (he had competed in the USAF pistol championships) and was killed. Captain Pitchford evaded into a culvert, was found and shot before he was captured, spending over 7 years in the "Hilton".

Two days later, Captain Al Lamb and Captain Jack Donovan masked their aircraft behind a mountain ridge and with their F-105s , shot up a SAM site for the first authenticated kill of a surface-to-air missile site. This was the proof of the pudding and put the stamp of success on the Wild Weasel program. Toward the end of the tour for these first Wild Weasels, Brigadier General (Speedy Pete) Everest visited Korat to become more acquainted with the Wild Weasel Operation. During a discussion of where this concept is going, some of the crews mentioned the need for a training operation, perhaps located at Nellis in the Fighter Weapons School. This discussion and probably lots of other factors caused this to happen. In February the first group welcomed the second, and last, F-100 group to Korat.

Captain White returned to his home station at England AFB, believing that a school would probably start at Nellis AFB in Las Vegas. Sure enough, on 24 March 1966, orders were issued which transferred the Captain to the Fighter Weapons School. Going on a permanent change of station was simple for this bachelor, get the movers to pack a few things, throw immediately needed things into the Porsche and hit the road. Arrival in the "Magic City" was a bit like coming home as there had been a lot of hard work (and fun) in his two previous training sessions at Nellis.

Getting started at the Weapons School was like stepping into a whirlwind. Room was made in the F-105 Weapons School building for the Wild Weasels. The highly trained F-105 and F-4 instructors were cast into another regimen, that of getting some F-100 pilots into the new platforms. Major Willard issued orders like "you go fly that" and again "you go fly that." The pilots found the appropriate dash-ones (the aircraft bible), studied quickly and got assigned to an Instructor for the checkout. Captain White's records show the first flight in the F-105 to be an orientation flight in the front seat. Two days later he got credit for a backseat landing, a requirement for being an Instructor pilot. The next day was a F-105D (single seat) flight, encompassing a few low approaches at unoccupied Caliente and a full stop at Nellis. Instructor Pilot orders were then cut, with the young pilot having less than 6 hours in the aircraft. This made for some goofy situations like being the leader and Instructor Pilot of a 4 ship F-105 Wild Weasel flight where the other 3 pilots each had over 1,500 hours in the airplane. It was amazing but it worked. All the F-100 pilots were highly experienced as far as maneuvering through the air and it would just take some time to become proficient in the aircraft systems. Of course, the overriding need was to get the combat experienced pilots into the airframes (F-105 and F-4) that were to become the next Wild Weasels.

Starting a training operation is a front loaded task. There was no course length established for the school, no training objectives, no lesson plans, no radar systems identified to practice upon and no equipped aircraft to practice with. And yet, these were dealt with. The early classes brought the aircraft with them and deployed with them. Course materials were written and a semblance of order was slowly achieved. In hindsight, some of the early classes didn't get very good training. What they got was all that was available from the only people that were available. Daily inputs from the Wild Weasels flying combat from Korat, codifying the first group's (many of whom were at Nellis) experiences and the daily feedback from Korat into training materials as well as the personal thrash of getting checked out in new airframes were some of the "have to do right now" items which contributed to the hectic environment. Many of the personnel worked 7 days a week for over three months, just to get things somewhat organized.

One of the challenges was to match up pilots and EWOs early so they could learn and fly together. This matching up process had been discussed a lot by the first group and all strongly felt that Instructors/Management/Personnel was NOT the way to do it. It had to be a natural selection process (whatever that meant) done by the aircrews themselves. This was complicated by the need for urgency. The syllabus was intensive from the first day and the process of matching up crews should be done, ideally, before it started. The idea adopted was based on the idea that after a few drinks, people became more open and really showed themselves. Therefore, a stag bar was scheduled on the day of reporting in. The entering crews were informed of the challenge and they responded. It worked! Personalities matched and meshed. Captain White was so proud of this process that he invited one of his F-100 Weapons School Instructors (Major John Boyd) to come to the stag bar and watch the process. He watched for a while, then returned to his energy maneuverability calculations and ate the 2 pound box of peanut brittle he had brought. Nonetheless, the process was very successful and there were hardly any (any?) instances of crews needing to re-crew. In fact, this process prompted Major Ed Malone (Class III-7) to take quill in hand and compose this poem, titled:

WEASEL WORDED
or
HOW THE CROW OUTFOXED THE TIGER-NELLIS FABLES

It's inconceivable, I know,
To mate tiger and crow,
And perhaps biologically unsound.
But, it happened one day
In a very odd way
And this is the word goin' round.

Thus, the scene had been set
To begin to beget
When the question immediately
arose
About who had the gender
Enabling the sender
To transmit the life-sparking dose.

All tigers are known
For solo hours they've flown
Plus their nocturnal habit of prowling.
And, the thought of a crow
Being part on their show
Results in an outbreak of growling.

In addition to that,
Agreed both bird and cat,
As each could clearly perceive;
Despite the transmission
There'd be no fission
If the other couldn't receive.

Now, the crows as we know,
Once let in on a show,
Eye the whole bit as their own dominion.
Making loud raucous caws
And displaying their claws,

Then a factor called pride
Joined up for the ride
Injecting a note that appalled.
Should there be such a thing
As a bird/cat offspring,

They'll attempt to assert their opinion. What should the bastard be called?

An odd pairing you see
But the word from D. C.
Was that this combination would fly.
So, the fur and the feather
Were suited together
Determined to do or to die.

Now the tiger and crow
Were both in the know
As they worked as artist on easel.
Neither shafted the other
No — No mother,
And the combo-resultant was
Weasel.

And it was wild!

There were many other humorous times despite the stress. The aircrews wanted to include the crew-matching stag bar session in the formal course syllabus, attesting to its importance to the training program. Naturally this was shot down by cooler heads, but to the workers it was a no-brainer. Each experienced Wild Weasel crewmember had his unique instructional style, and the standouts usually received the point of the spear. One instructor was focused upon, in the poem titled:

ZIRCON IN THE ROUGH

In Weasel-land a legend lives
That will be difficult to equal,
A troop so bad and foul-mouthed
There can never be a sequel.

He really knows the game he's in
That no one can dispute,
But his briefings sound like SOP's
For a house of ill repute.

We won't describe this EWO,
Or his name denote'
But his favorite phrase is just one word——
That word is simply "GOAT"……

Some of the fun was more focused on the aircrews going through the school. They knew where they were going and that it was tough. News like a class losing all its airplanes within weeks of arrival and another class that was 100% shot down were downers. It is mental health for those who are following to make light of the situation. An example of this self -depreciating humor (credited to "any mouse") is a poem titled:

THE WEASELS' LAMENT

High above Nevada's desert fly the Weaseleers,
Chasing queer electrons daily–nightly drinking beers.

Frequencies and Shrikes confuse us–not to mention noise,
Dauntlessly we do our duty in Willard's school for boys.

Black containers give the answers which the birdmen lack,
But with luck and much aborting we'll never see the flak.

SA-2s are not so bad, Lifsey said in class,
But tell us more about the ones that whistle up your ass.

Pilot's quaking, EWO's barfing, off we go to war,
Can we hack it–we don't think so–we're cowards to the core.

If we see a puff of flak, or an SA-2,
We may form a Weasel squadron at Dien Bien Phu.....

The F-4 Wild Weasel was being readied at Nellis, but ran into seemingly never-ending problems. (McDonnell did a great job on the F-4G.) This prompted someone to write a poem titled:

WILD WEASEL IVC

Are the Phantom Weasels really phinks or is this just a phable?
Can the 5's hack the job, while the F-4 is unable?

Thud crews file through the course so fast you hardly see 'em,
Phantom Phylers file too—but only for per diem.

Can ATI repair the damage McDonnell seems to wreak?
Or are the Phantom Weasels condemned to fly a phreak?

It climbs up nice and goes real phast in blue Nevada sky,
But Phantom crews can't win a war at Nellis TDY.

If they are to earn their combat pay, Garry Willard's been heard to sigh,
Uncle Ho must send some gunners to Hawthorne TDY.

The getting older White (now a Major) maintained his Instructor status with the Wild Weasel Squadron while moving to the Doctrine Shop at the Tactical Fighter Weapons Center. He was still in the Wild Weasel loop as he ran the Southeast Asia liaison program, where aviators rotated to Vietnam and Thailand to fly combat with the units. Their first hand and timely reports gave good credibility to the Wild Weasel training in particular as the learning curve remained steep. Major White took two of these tours, flying both Strike and Wild Weasel at Korat and Takhli in 1967 and 1968. But alas, the good times ended with a tour in the Pentagon.

Ed White

Chapter Three

Wild Weasel III
F-105 Wild Weasel Era

Story by Clyde Hayman, WW # 82

Being One of The First

Editors Note: Clyde was a member of Wild Weasel III-1, the first F-105F Wild Weasels. When he left the states his orders said he was assigned to Takhli RTAFB and he accordingly reported for duty as directed. However, when he got to Takhli he learned that he should have been assigned to Korat RTAFB. When the next group of Wild Weasels (Wild Weasel III-2) departed to Thailand they had orders to report to Korat but when they arrived at Korat they discovered that they should have been ordered to Takhli.

Another story about the initial deployment of the F105 Wild Weasels to SEA happened to me. Six of us had to go by commercial air since there were more crews than F-105F Wild Weasel configured aircraft. I was one of the 4 EWOs to go by Pan Am. I took two weeks leave to settle my family in my hometown and left from there to go directly to Thailand.

When I got to Takhli, I reported into to Base Personnel at 0900 as directed. There I joined a group of pilots, navigators, and EWOs. A young three stripe Airman got our attention and then announced all F105 pilots were to follow a two striper and off they went. He then announced that all the B66 Navs and EWOs were to follow another airman and off they went leaving me standing there alone.

He walked up to me and seeing my navigator wings told me that I was to go to with the B66 people. I told him "No, that I flew in a F105 and I was a Wild Weasel." I didn't know that I was one of first two Wild Weasels backseaters to report in and he had never heard of Wild Weasel.

He explained to me that an F105 had only one seat and that I was to go to the B66. I replied that there were two seat 105s on the flight line and that I was a Wild Weasel. I again didn't know that there were no two seat 105s since the deployment had been delayed and they were still in the states.

Since the Airman had never seen a two seat F105, he was beginning to wonder, who is this crazy EWO who wants to fly in a 105 and claims to be a "Wild Weasel." He again tried to explain to no avail that I belonged in the B66 group. Thank goodness that MASH had not been made or he would have thought I was a Klinger.

After a few more minutes of neither of us making their point, a lieutenant came over and asks what was the matter. The airman politely explained that this EWO doesn't want to go to the B66s, and to stress that he thought that I was crazy stated "...and he keeps saying he's a Wild Weasel."

Fortunately for me, the Lieutenant told the Airman that he would take care of it. The airman walked away shaking his head and the Lieutenant then told me that I was the second EWO this week that said he was a Wild Weasel and that I was to go to see Col Bowman the Wing DO. Then in an even lower voice he asked what Wild Weasel was.

I then realized that because Wild Weasel was Top Secret almost no one knew about us and I was damn lucky not to be spending my first few nights in Thailand in a padded cell.

Clyde Hayman

Story by Kevin A. "Mike" Gilroy WW# 174

First in...Wrong Way Out

Then Captain Mike Gilroy
Photo Courtesy of Mike Gilroy

Editor's Note: This story was first published in the October 1999, Journal of Electronic Defense. Mike has graciously consented for the publication again as part of this collection of first person stories. Mike retired from the USAF with the rank of Colonel and returned to his home in Gilroy, CA where he served as a member of the City Council and Mayor. He is now retired and lives in Florida.

Takhli Royal Thai Air Force Base, at 5 AM on 7 August 1966. Today's target is a railroad-marshaling yard on the Northeast Railroad, the major rail link between Hanoi and southern China. I haven't been much of anywhere in this air war yet.

This is my 11th mission, and I don't as yet know the Northeast railway from any other section of North Vietnam. But the older heads are quiet during the mission briefing. That's about as much emotion as anyone shows, but it's enough to let me know that the mission is going to be tough. The briefing is boring, but briefings have probably been boring since man began to fly. I sit smoking a cigarette and nursing a cup of black coffee while the weather man does his best to give a professional presentation regarding expected weather en route, during air refueling and in the target area. He knows from experience that his forecast information is hours old and probably only about 50 percent accurate. He says that visibility is likely to be poor in the target area.

A first-lieutenant intelligence officer, too arrogant to realize that his information is probably only around 10 percent accurate, gives a run down on expected anti-aircraft artillery (AAA) and surface-to-air missiles (SAMs) protecting the target area. He speaks with a slight quaver in his voice, as if he is the one who is going to fly the mission and face those defenses. He is not well liked.

He came into the Stag Bar the other night with his hat on. The Stag Bar is where most of us hang out between missions. Unlike the "proper" officers' club bar, the patrons here are rowdy, the attire is flight suits, the songs are profane, the jukebox is loud and the colonels seldom show their faces. There is one simple rule: don't wear your hat in the bar. If you come into the bar with your hat on and someone rings the bell before you get it off, you buy a round of drinks. When the lieutenant walked in with his hat on, one of the pilots rang the bell. The lieutenant pleaded ignorance and scurried out the side door, to the jeers of the crowd. The crews don't understand anyone not complying with the rule, especially as drinks are only 25 cents each. Everyone thinks he's a real jerk.

"OUR THING"

The Mission Commander today is the Operations Officer from the 354th Squadron. Like most old heads, he is cool and professional. He doesn't try to pump smoke up anyone's butt with a lot of Rah-Rah! stuff. It is a tough and well-defended target that the fighters haven't been allowed to hit with enough regularity to soften up. Some guys are not going to come back. He doesn't have a lot to say.

Our wing, the 355th Tac Fighter Wing, is going in first, with the other F-105 wing from Korat Air Base going in about 30 minutes later. He will be leading the flak-suppression flight and will try to have the anti-aircraft guns in the immediate target area out of commission by the time the strike aircraft start their dive-bomb attacks. He doesn't have any special words for the Wild Weasels. We are just supposed to go in and "do our thing."

The Wild Weasels have only been at Takhli for about five weeks, and none of the strike crews have figured out yet what we are supposed to add to their war-fighting effort.

The concept behind the Wild Weasel program seems to be a good one — kill SAM sites. To do this, the two-seat version of the F-105 (the F-105F) has been modified with equipment to detect and home in on the radars associated with the SA-2 SAM system. Our aircraft is equipped with AN/APR-25 Vector scope, which gives a coded strobe indicating the bearings and relative strength of SAM, AAA or airborne-interceptor radars; the AN/APR-26, which alerts of activity of a SAM site's missile-guidance radar; and the IR-133, a panoramic receiver of very high sensitivity, with which I can observe the activities of most early-warning, height-finder, GCI, AAA and SAM radars.

OUR EDUCATION

The pilot/electronic warfare officer teams have practiced this concept during six weeks of training at Nellis Air Force Base, north of Las Vegas, NV. It seems to work well when flying from Nellis to the training sites at St. George, UT, and at Walker Lake, NV. But the sites at those locations aren't camouflaged, don't move between missions and, more importantly, don't shoot back.

We arrived at Takhli Royal Thai Air Force Base, on 4 July 1966. A few days later, two crews from Korat Air Base, our sister F-105 base 100 mi. to the south, came to give us a checkout in what they knew about flying the Wild Weasel mission when people shoot back. The weather had turned sour, however, and the only missions flown were easy ones in the southern part of North Vietnam. At that time there were no SAM sites in that area. It became immediately obvious that the guys from Korat, who were supposed to check us out, didn't know much more about our mission than we did. They had only been in the theater for around a month longer than us. So, after 10 days of an abortive checkout program, the Korat crews declared to our wing commander that the checkout program was complete and that we were ready to go to war.

Since the checkout crews left Takhli, the Wild Weasels had gone up north into the heavily defended areas several times. Most of those missions had been ineffective. Missiles and flak had claimed one of the planes and its crew. One other Wild Weasel bird with a wounded pilot managed to recover, but had severe battle damage and was sent to the repair facility on Taiwan to be rebuilt. Of the five planes we arrived with on the Fourth of July, only three are left. Two are scheduled on today's mission. Ed Larson and I will be in the first airplane. Bob Sandvick and Tom Pyle are in the second, 15 min. behind us. Each of us has an F-105D single seater as our wingman, whose job is to help destroy the SAM sites after we locate them with our equipment and mark them with our ordnance. It's time to see how the concept works in the real world.

We go from the wing briefing room to the squadron, to conduct our individual flight briefings. The flight briefing is pretty innocuous. Our wingman is Pete Pitman, a buddy of Ed Larson's from Nellis, and a "good stick." Ed does his thing during the briefing, spelling out tactics learned at Nellis. Pete listens attentively as a good wingmen should, but is probably thinking, "How in hell did I get myself scheduled into hunting for SAM sites with these turkeys, when they have never seen one and have never even been shot at before?"

KICKING THE TIRES

It's close to take-off time and we suit up with G-suit, survival vest and .38 Combat Masterpiece. Everything but dog tags, ID card and Geneva Convention card is left behind. We grab our helmets and parachutes, pile into the squadron van and are taken to our airplanes. The sun hasn't risen yet, but there is enough light to allow us to preflight the aircraft without resorting to flashlights or the noisy, powerful portable lights the maintenance people use getting our planes ready.

The walk-around inspection reveals no problems with the bird. Ordnance load consists of two AGM-45 Shrike antiradiation missiles, two pods of 2.75 inch rockets and 1028 rounds of 20mm ammunition for our Gatling gun. We also have a 650-gallon centerline fuel tank. The Shrikes are to damage and mark the site from a distance of 7-10 miles then the rockets, our wingman's six 500-lb bombs and our Gatling guns are to put the SAM site out of business. The fuel tank is to give us the extra range we need, as well as to absorb some of the flak that might come our way.

Photo Courtesy of Mike Gilroy

Time to climb in and start the engines and warm up the Wild Weasel gear to see if it is operating properly. Everything looks good, and, shortly thereafter, the Crew Chief waves us out of our parking slot and gives us a sharp salute.

LIGHTING THE FIRES

The flight line is a roar of activity now as the 20 F-105s and four spare aircraft start up and taxi toward the end of the runway where they will receive a final maintenance check and where the safety pins will be pulled from the ordnance. As we pull into the arming area, the Catholic chaplain walks past each aircraft giving his blessing to the crews. Not too many of the guys are deeply religious or Catholic, but most are superstitious enough not to want to piss off anyone's God. So, we all smile and wave politely at the chaplain as he walks by.

The armorers step out to the front of our aircraft showing the red streamers and safety pins they have removed from our airplane. This indicates that the mechanical links preventing landing-gear retraction, bomb release and missile firing have been removed. We wait until our wingman's check is complete, close our canopies and taxi into position for take off.

We take the near side of the runway and Pete pulls into position on our left and slightly behind. Ed sets the brakes and twirls his finger in the air. Both aircraft are run up to full power and all engine gauges are checked. Pete gives us a thumbs up. Ed calls the tower: "Kingfish flight ready for takeoff." As clearance is received, Ed nods to signal brake release, afterburner light-off and water-injection activation. 26,500 lb. of thrust push the world's fastest tricycle down the runway. At 140 knots, we are airborne and climbing, on our way to rendezvous with our refueling tanker, 500 miles away.

We are at cruising altitude with our wingman comfortably around 10 ft. off our right wing tip. I fly and Ed snoozes. Life is good! The tanker track today is out over the water, paralleling the coast of Vietnam. The plan is for the strike force to enter North Vietnam from north of Haiphong Harbor, attack the target from northeast to southwest, pull off the target to the left and exit toward the safety of the water. The Wild Weasels are to place themselves between the strike force and the SAM sites, and keep the missiles away from the strike force long enough for them to bomb their targets.

Ed bitches to me over the intercom. We are sharing our tanker with two EB-66 electronic warfare aircraft, which means that our KC-135 tanker aircraft is equipped for "probe and drogue" air-to-air refueling. Usually they are equipped with a flying boom — a solid pipe extending from the rear of the tanker. Booms are stable and easy to hook up to. But EB-66s are only equipped for the "probe and drogue." The probe and drogue is a basket on the end of a flexible hose into which the pilot must insert a probe. It is anything but stable, and F-105s have been known to tear the drogues off tankers and return home with the basket and a length of hose dangling ignominiously from the aircraft. Ed manages the refueling with no problem, as I knew he would.

FIRST ENGAGEMENT

We drop off the tanker with full fuel tanks, and switch our radios over to the strike frequency all aircraft will use in the target area. As we will be the first into the target area, all is quiet for a few minutes. I pick up a AAA radar on my equipment and tell Ed "Guns at ten o'clock," indicating a radar that provides tracking information to 37 mm, 57 mm, 85 mm, 100 mm or 120 mm anti-aircraft guns off our left side. Ed relays that information over the radio, and says to me, "Let's go get him," and turns toward the radar. Ed flies directly toward the gun-controlling radar by following the heading corrections I give him. The azimuth information which the equipment gives us is pretty good, but range information is at best an educated guess on my part.

Ed and I continue to home in on our AAA site. The weather is pretty crappy — about 50 percent of the area obscured by towering cumulus clouds whose tops are around 30,000 ft. I think to myself that this is not great weather for hunting SAM sites or for visually acquiring missiles launched at you.

The Wild Weasel gear is indicating more activity in our area, and I tell Ed that we now have a SAM site dead ahead, apparently in the same vicinity as the AAA radar we have been chasing. A bit more trouble than the AAA radar, whose guns only have a range of a few miles. The SAM has a firing range of around 19 mi. to our Shrike missile's 10 miles Ed arms one of the Shrike missiles and gets ready to launch it. "Do you think we are close enough?" he asks. I really don't have a clue, but tell him, "Yeah, I think so."

Ed pulls up the nose of the airplane to pitch the Shrike missile at our SAM site. The Shrike roars off our wing. I watch the signal on the scope to see if the Shrike finds its target. Fifteen seconds elapse. The Shrike should be impacting about now. The signal abruptly goes off the air. Bingo! "It looks like we got him," I yell to Ed. An emergency beeper shatters the relative calm. Someone has been hit and bailed out. It's not any of the guys from our air base, as they are not over land yet. The beeper is distracting, but we've got our own war to fight, and our own problems.

SECOND SHOT

Since we launched our Shrike, another Sam site has started tracking us. "SAM at two o'clock," I yell to Ed, "really strong." "Roger that," he answers and brings the plane right 20 degrees to line us up with this new threat. "I'm going to throw a Shrike at him," Ed calls. The second Shrike roars off the wing as the yellow and red lights on my equipment light up, accompanied by the shrill howl over the intercom that indicates the SAM site has launched at us.

Ed relays my "Launch!" call out over the air, followed by "Kingfish flight, take it down." We light the afterburner to get more airspeed, put the SAM radar signal off our left wing and start a descent, hoping to see the missiles and dodge them before they get us. "I've got the missile in sight!" Ed says in a tight voice. He pulls the nose of the airplane up sharply and turns into the missile. The missile roars underneath us and explodes harmlessly behind us. The maneuver has bled off a lot of airspeed. I hear Ed shout "Christ!" as a second missile roars out of the clouds, and explodes just in front of the airplane.

The aircraft is rocked, hard. Seconds later, the cockpit fills with black smoke and the bitter smell and taste of burned cordite. The gun drum, which holds the ammunition for our 20 mm Gatling gun, has blown up. I can see nothing but flames and the red fire-warning light glaring at me through the smoke. The plane is rocking from side to side, but at least it hasn't exploded or gone completely out of control. I'm having serious trouble breathing. My oxygen mask is not sealed tight and I'm choking on the smoke. There is a handle on my left-hand side panel that will blow the canopy off and get me some air. I try to reach it before I black out completely. I can't find it and am about to lose consciousness. The only other way to get the canopy off is to initiate the firing sequence for the ejection seat. No decision. Better to march in their damn prisoner-of-war parade than to asphyxiate sitting in the seat. I reach for the ejection-seat levers and rotate the handles. I've got to get out of this damn airplane before I die of oxygen starvation or it blows up.

The canopy blows off with a roar, and I stop the ejection sequence and fill my lungs with beautiful clean air. Incongruously, I think what a beautiful day it is. The towering cumulus clouds are as pretty and white as any I have ever seen in the States, and I see a few patches of clear blue sky. The Wild Weasel equipment is quiet. The antennas have probably been blown away, and the radios are out, so we aren't hearing the radar signals, the emergency beepers or the frantic radio calls any more. I hope the old saying is true: "What you don't know won't hurt you."

Ed calls from the front seat, "Mike, are you still there?" "Yes, Ed." I answer, "How about you?" He chuckles. "I couldn't find the auxiliary canopy jettison handle and had to raise the ejection handles to get rid of my canopy," he says. Well that makes me feel a little bit better. "Me too," I answer. "We'll head out over the coast. How bad is the damage back there?"

I strain around in my seat trying to check the damage to the wings and vertical stabilizer, staying out of the wind stream. The left wing has a big hole in the leading edge — around 3 ft. in diameter. The top of the vertical stabilizer is gone. The nose of the aircraft is gone. Other than that we're in great shape in our 500-mph, open-cockpit airplane.

The fire warning and master-caution lights have gone out and the plane seems controllable, so maybe we got lucky and the fires have blown themselves out. No sign of our wingman, since we started the SAM evasive maneuver. Without our radios, we don't know if he has just gotten separated, or if he has been hit too. Ed says, "I've got the coast in sight. Just a little farther."

I keep a lookout below and behind us. MiGs haven't been much of a threat during the war, but there's no point in getting careless and letting one hammer us now. Unknown to either Ed or me, we are exiting right over the Cam Pha iron mines, the home of one of the North Vietnamese gunnery schools and several batteries of 57mm and 85 mm anti-aircraft guns.

THIRD TIME'S THE CHARM

As I'm looking back over my left shoulder, I see the first evidence that the defenses haven't forgotten us — a circular ring of black puffs bursting around 1000 ft. to the left and behind us. I call to Ed, "They're shooting at us." "Rog!" he says, and then adds, "Here comes our wingman." More flak is coming our way. The second ring of bursts is about 500 ft. behind us. About 10 sec. later, the third burst goes off right under the aircraft and jolts us hard. Pete, our wingman, overshoots us and slides underneath our aircraft and out to the right. For some reason, the North Vietnamese gunners start shooting at him, giving us some time to get out of range.

ABANDON SHIP

We're over the beach and soon cross over the small rocky islands just off the coast. The hit from the flak seems to have severed our hydraulic lines. Ed calls, "The controls are going, Mike. We'd better get out of here." Just then the plane starts into a 20 degree left bank heading north. There's nothing up there but Red China — no place to spend a vacation. "Okay, Ed. Good luck. See you in the water."

I check the tightness of my seat belt and shoulder harness for the tenth time and finish the ejection sequence I started 15 min. earlier. The jolt in the butt from the ejection seat is pretty hairy. An instantaneous 18 Gs, I'm told later. Quite a ride — better than you can get at any amusement park. The seat separates cleanly from the aircraft, and, a few seconds later, I separate cleanly from the seat and find myself swinging under my parachute. I can see Ed's chute about a half mile north of me. Our plane is in a shallow dive and explodes seconds later. There must have been a fire going on in there after all.

It looks like I am about 6,000 ft. in the air and have a good bit of time before hitting the water. I follow the routine I had learned in Survival School. Check the parachute for any line-overs or torn panels. I don't really remember what I'm supposed to do if I have either. All I know is that something would have to be pretty bad before I'd screw with an open parachute. I release the survival kit and life raft from the seat kit so that it dangles at the end of its 15-ft. cord. I save the survival kit handle, putting it into the pocket of my G-suit. It'll make a good souvenir, if I get out of this. I pull one of the two survival radios from my survival vest and switch it on. This is the first time in twenty minutes that I can hear what is going on with the war. I hear my own parachute beeper wailing away and reach up on the parachute riser for the switch that turns it off. Our wingman is calling geographic coordinates to Crown Alfa, the rescue coordinator. They tell him help is on the way and ask how much fuel he has and can he stay in the area performing rescue combat air patrol (RESCAP) duty for a while. Pete responds that he is good for another 15 minutes or so, anyway. Two other aircraft call in that they are in the area and can help. The sound of circling fighters is reassuring, and there is no doubt in my mind that this is going to turn out all right.

Crown Alfa asks Pete if he has been able to contact either of the pilots. I try to answer, but am less than eloquent and am sort of glad when my transmission doesn't seem to be picked up. The water is getting pretty close, now. It's time to put the survival radio away, and get ready for the next phase. I try to remember the drill.

Pull the protective covers off the parachute-canopy releases.

Let the life raft touch the water, then turn your body to face the wind.

Release your risers as your feet hit the water. That way the canopy will blow clear of you, and you won't drown under it.

Seems simple enough, except that all this must happen within a few seconds. I manage to pull it all off, but something isn't right. I'm under water, sinking fast. I've forgotten to inflate my life vest! Holding my breath, I try to find the inflation pull-tabs that dangle under each armpit. I can't find the damn things, and for the second time today, I'm about to die from lack of air. I feel for the nylon cord that has me attached to the life raft, and in desperation, pull myself hand over hand up to the surface. With a good strong kick, I land on my back in the raft. A lot of things not done by the book, but, what the hell, I'm alive!

BE PREPARED

Time to take stock of things. I look around for Ed but there are slight sea swells that limit line of sight to a pretty short distance. The nearest island look to be about 1,000 yards away. I sure hope it's unoccupied. I open the survival kit to see what's there. There should be concentrated food bars, water, fishing stuff, shark repellent, sea dye marker, emergency flares and all sorts of stuff necessary to make this a pleasant stay. To my chagrin, the kit contains nothing but two pairs of wool socks. Not a good start. Like most of the guys who fly out of Takhli, however, I've brought my own stuff. Our personal equipment NCO, Tech Sergeant Joe Perry, has rigged our survival vests with most of the necessities. I've got two blue plastic baby bottles full of water, two survival radios, a packet of sea-dye marker, a day/night signaling flare, my .38 Combat Masterpiece, extra ammunition and my trusty Buck General knife. I drink one of the baby bottles of water, reflecting that two of the best things in the world are good fresh air to breathe and cool water to drink.

In the back of my mind, I remember hearing that the South China Sea is one of the worst places in the world for poisonous sea snakes and sharks. I don't know whether sharks like yellow rubber life rafts. "Yummy Yellow" is probably their favorite color. I quickly put that thought out of my mind. Maybe if I don't go looking for them, they won't come looking for me.

I get the radio out again, to see how the rescue operation is coming along. Everything seems to be going OK. Crown Alfa, one of the rescue planes, is asking our wingman if he has us spotted in the water. Ed is obviously listening too, as, a few seconds later, Pete says "I see one sea-dye marker, but don't have the other pilot in sight." I consider putting out my own sea dye marker, or popping my flare, but decide against it. As long as they can see Ed, the rescue forces will come and then it'll be time enough to let everyone know where I am. No telling how long we'll have to wait.

COMPLICATIONS

"There's a ship coming out of the harbor," Pete calls. Another of the circling fighters calls, "I'm going to jettison my bombs — armed. Maybe that will make them turn back." Minutes later, a string of six 750-lb. bombs explodes in the water about a mile from us and about a half mile from the ship. It appears to do the trick. "They've turned back," I hear Pete say. We've got nine airplanes flying cover for us now. Crown Alfa calls now for a direction finding (DF) steer to the rescue area and says that they are about 10 minutes out. Pete reports that all is well , but that he still has only one pilot in sight. I have spotted Ed's raft in the meantime, about 300 yards to the north of me, and pass that message over the survival radio to the general public. No answer. Well, no sweat, there's still time enough to sort it out.

I hear the wail of another parachute beeper on the radio, followed seconds later by a second beeper. I wonder if somehow our beepers have started transmitting again. Beepers are probably the most pathetic sounds on earth. A few minutes later, I hear Duke 2 relay on Guard channel that "Duke lead has been shot down in the target area. There were two good parachutes." Duke 2 is Bob Sandvick and my good friend, Tom Pyle, the other Wild Weasel crew that was flying today.

A new complication arises. "I see what looks like mortar fire coming from one of the islands. It looks like they're trying to hit them in their rafts," one of the orbiting pilots calls out. I neither see nor hear the mortar fire, but the bursts would have to be pretty close for me to see them. Anyway , I'd just as soon not see them. Pitman rolls in and strafes the island. Minutes later comes the announcement —"That appears to have quieted them down."

This latest bit of news has gotten Crown Alfa's attention. "Is the rescue area hot?" a tense, high-pitched voice asks. I think to myself, "What the hell! Are you going to call off the rescue just because someone is shooting? It's war, they're supposed to shoot." It must have been some staff weenie on the radio, for a second later, a calmer voice, probably the pilot's, calls for another DF steer, asks for the location of the downed pilots in relation to some landmark and announces they're on their way in. Ed lets loose with his orange smoke, which Crown Alfa spots almost immediately. Minutes later, a beautiful sight passes overhead. A Grumman HU-16 Albatross seaplane, probably built 25 years ago, is looking the situation over. It banks around and settles down on the water and I see them taxiing toward Ed. Crown Alfa announces, "The pilot seems to be all right, he's waving at us."

I give them a few minutes to get Ed into the airplane, and then hear the rescue pilot asking "Where is the other pilot in relation to our position?" Time to pop my smoke. I pull the tab that ignites the flare, and it spews out its bright orange smoke. A few seconds later, I hear the call I've been waiting for: "I've got smoke in sight." Simultaneously comes the call from the rescue aircraft and one of the RESCAP planes. The HU-16 taxies over and positions itself between my raft and the nearest island. No markings on the aircraft at all. A young oriental in a black wet suit, appears in the door of the aircraft, and shouts, "Don't shoot. I'm Hawaiian," and dives into the water. I feel that I need to do something to help. "Just stay still, I'll take care of everything," he says calmly, as if this was just routine business for him. I gladly do what I've been told and minutes later I'm being lifted into the side door of the Albatross.

MORE COMPLICATIONS

The HU-16 crew seem elated that they've got us, but not nearly as elated as Ed and I feel — although we're in a bit of shock right now. I'll save my celebrating until I get onto dry land. "The other pilot has hurt his back," the pararescueman tells me. Then, "You didn't inflate your Mae West, did you?" "Thanks," I say sarcastically. That's all I need, is to get my chain pulled by some rescue puke. I go up to check on Ed. He is wrapped up in a blanket, his back messed up from the ejection. The plane taxies forward, as I shake the hand of everyone I can get to. I give a big thanks to the pilot — "Red" Angstadt, from San Antonio. "Better take a seat," he says, while we see if we can get the hell out of here." That's when

I find out that the HU-16 has a sick engine, apparently bad enough that they had considered aborting the mission and leaving the rescue to another plane. I'm sure glad that they didn't.

The guys on the island are shooting at the plane, and mortar shells hit the water, about 100 ft. off our right wing. Red taxies out of range of the mortars but must make his takeoff run into the wind, which takes him back toward the islands. He uses the good engine to get up as much speed as possible, then brings the sick engine up to full power, hoping to get us airborne before the sick engine blows up. Twice we can't get up enough airspeed and turn around within firing range of the islands.

The third time is the charm, and we get off the water, seemingly by hitting the tops of the swells until we are bounced high enough to remain airborne. The old aircraft has taken a lot of punishment, but everything seems OK as we get some altitude beneath us. "Where are we going?" I ask. "We're out of Da Nang," says the navigator. "We'll take you back there, and then your unit will send a plane to pick you up."

AFTERMATH

Ed and I are quiet. His back is hurting — a compression fracture from the ejection seat that will keep him out of jet fighters for the rest of his Air Force career. Seven planes altogether have been shot down today, ensuring that Ed and I make the front pages of The Washington Post and The New York Times.

I'm depressed. My first mission of any consequence, and the score is North Vietnamese 1, Mike Gilroy 0. Not a great start to my career as a warrior. But then, there's no way for things to go but up.

Kevin A. "Mike" Gilroy WW# 174

Story by Kevin A. "Mike" Gilroy, WW # 174

Single Ship Iron Hand

Glenn Davis and I paired up as a Wild Weasel crew about a month ago. Glenn's Electronic Warfare Officer returned to the states because of medical and family problems, and my first pilot Ed Larson is in a hospital in the states. Ed suffered a severe compression fracture when we ejected from our fatally damaged F-105, following an unsuccessful duel with a SAM site and several AAA batteries. The other pilots jokingly refer to us as Mutt and Jeff. Glenn is built like a fire plug, around 5'6" tall and weighs around 175#. On the other hand, I'm 6'5" tall and weigh the same 175#. Glenn is one of the smartest people I have ever met, especially as relates to the F-105 Thunderchief. So far, we have flown twenty missions together, and have quickly developed that special rapport typical of the very best Weasel crews. It starts with mutual respect for each other's unique skills in an airplane, develops into strong friendships and results in formidable SAM killing crews. When dueling with the surface to air missile sites, we communicate easily and succinctly, seemingly in tune with each other's thoughts, and seek out, attack and kill as a unit. We are both low-key people. We do our job and don't talk a lot about it. The strike pilots seem to be very comfortable flying with us. So far, we have never lost a wingmen and more importantly, never had a strike pilot shot down by a SAM when we were flying cover for them. To paraphrase the verse from Proverbs: "Yea though we walk through the valley of the shadow of death we shall fear no evil, for we are the meanest sons of bitches in the valley."

Today, our call sign is "Avenger", which has a good sound to it. I have a feeling it is going to be a good mission. Our primary target, a military barracks area just west of Hanoi, is forecast to be below a 3000 foot overcast, making visual dive-bombing impossible. Therefore the strike force is to go to its secondary target, which is in the northwest section of North Vietnam. That area might have been tough when the French were beaten at Dien Bien Phu, but as air missions go, it's a piece of cake. All of the missions into North Vietnam count toward the 100 Missions needed to go home. This one is going to be what we call an "easy counter".

Weasels are allowed a little more flexibility in doing their mission than the strike force. That doesn't mean we are restriction free, as everyone from the president down to our Wing Commander has put some limits on our fighting ability, limits that make no sense at all. We can drop our bombs on a road or bridge, but not on a power plant, fuel or oil storage area, unless specifically tasked to do so. Military airfields are off limits. We can attack and destroy an individual SAM site, but not the storage area at 21-07N/105-51E, where hundreds of SAMs are stored out in the open in canisters. Unless tasked against a specific target, we cannot fly within 30 miles of Hanoi or 15 miles of Haiphong. If we fly past an airfield and see enemy aircraft taking off to intercept us, we cannot fire upon them until their landing gear has been fully raised, and their wheels are in the wheel well. Whoever thinks of these restrictions has probably never put his life on the line in battle. Whoever enforces them is guilty of moral cowardice.

As Weasels, we are allowed to go where we want in order to hunt down and kill SAM sites. The only exceptions are the restricted areas around Hanoi or Haiphong. And, of course, we usually try to stay out of the Navy's areas. Our plan today is to accompany the strike force to the area of Dien Bien Phu, make a quick sweep of the area to ensure the North Vietnamese haven't moved any new defenses into the area, then head east, over the flatlands south and west of Hanoi. That's where the heavy SAM defenses are. We'll see if we can stir up a little action.

Our wingman today is a captain from the 333rd squadron. He has been at Takhli for approximately two months and, although he may have flown Weasel missions before, has never flown with Glenn and me. He has obviously been looking forward to an easy mission, one where no one is going to shoot at him. When he hears of our plan, he wastes no time letting us know he thinks it to be some sort of lunacy.

"You're going to Route Pack VI, when you don't have to? You guys are out of your minds!" Followed in a whiney voice by, "Don't you have to go where the rest of the strike force goes?"

This type of questioning doesn't sit too well with either Glenn or me. But it goes to show you that even among F-105 pilots there exists an occasional candy ass. His questioning is almost a slur on our manhood. Doesn't he know that we are bulletproof? He doesn't win any points by questioning our plan, but at least has enough sense to drop his questions and keep his mouth shut.

It is six o'clock in the morning when we finally get into the crew van and head out to our airplanes. Everyone is pretty relaxed. Unlike the primary targets where the defenses are always heavy and always waiting for us, and where we lose usually three or four aircraft and crews, everyone should get back from this one.

Arrival at our airplane shows that we don't have a full ordnance load. Normally the weasels carry two AGM-45 Shrike anti-radiation missiles and either CBU-24s (Cluster bomb units) or two pods of 2.75 inch rockets. We have the two Shrikes but the two inboard pylons, which should be loaded with CBUs or rockets, are empty. I look at the F-105s parked nearby and see that they also have partial bomb loads. This is just another one of the many things about this air war that isn't right. You risk your life going against the toughest defenses in the world with only a partial weapon load to deliver on the target. Our main source of information, the Pacific edition of the Stars and Stripes recently had a front page article regarding a supposed bomb shortage. The conclusion of the article was a statement from Secretary of Defense McNamara that we had no shortage of bombs. That man and our president have a major lack of credibility with the aircrews. It's a good thing we're not going to our primary target.

"Sarge, did they download some of our ordnance, when the target was changed, or is this all we were going to get?" I asked the crew chief. "That's all they were going to give you, Sir", he answered. He was embarrassed, as if somehow he should have been able to get a full ordnance load for his airplane. I really appreciated his attitude, but that didn't help load bombs on the airplane. Damn, this sure is a screwed up way to fight a war.

The walk around inspection shows the airplane to be in good shape. Thank God for that. Easy missions like this one don't occur very often. It is no time to have a maintenance abort. Completion of one hundred missions, easy or hard, into North Vietnam is the price of a ticket home. Someone passed the news around the stag bar the other evening that at the current loss rate, everyone would be shot down three times before they finish their 100 missions. Well, I've only got two times to go. We don't dwell on statistics or the poor odds of living long enough to complete a combat tour. We are here doing the best job we can. Most of us think that we are bullet proof anyway, and enjoy pitting our skills against those of the North Vietnamese, their Russian-made weapons and their Russian advisors. All that aside, it's nice to get an easy mission every once in awhile.

We get in, crank up the engine, check out the aircraft and systems and taxi out to the arming area. Everything is looking good. The weather is hot and humid, like Florida in the summertime, and it's a good day to be alive. With this piece of cake mission ahead of us, we might just return to enjoy the rest of it. It's a beautiful day at Takhli Royal Thai Air Force Base, I'm flying with someone I respect and trust, we've got a good airplane, a full load of gas, some missiles and a cannon, and we're going to go kill some SAM sites. Life doesn't get any better than this!

Our wingman still seems to be a little pissed off, for he makes an obscene gesture to the Catholic Chaplain who is walking by blessing the aircraft and crews. The Chaplain smiles and shakes his head as he sees the gesture. He's a pretty nice guy, but the severe losses of pilots seems to be bothering him. The past couple of weeks he has really been putting away the booze at the Stag bar. He is taking the losses personally. Most of the aircrews shy away from him. We don't get maudlin about the losses and don't feel comfortable with those that do. But, I guess that's something you can say about the support people here at Takhli, they really care.

We are next in line for takeoff as the preceding flight of F-105s light their afterburners and roll down the runway. I've been taxiing the aircraft out and taxi it into position for takeoff. Glenn takes over to conduct his takeoff checklist items.

"Do you want to make the takeoff, Mike?" he asks. "Sure", I answer, not knowing if I'm capable of seeing well enough from the back seat to do so, (the forward visibility of the Weasel F-105F is pretty poor.) I've never made a take off before, but there shouldn't be too much to it. Just go real fast and pull back on the stick. Glenn tells our wingman that we will be making single ship takeoffs, and calls the tower for our clearance. This received, we are ready to go. I push the throttle to the stops, let it stabilize a few seconds, release the brakes and move the throttle outboard to light the afterburner. With a kick in the butt and a satisfying roar, we are rolling. Glenn switches on the water injection, which adds extra thrust and we are now really moving. I'm having a hell of a time keeping the aircraft centered on the runway. It seems to want to go from one side to the other, almost as if the nose wheel steering is still engaged. I cycle the nose wheel steering switch on and off and the aircraft settles down and smoothly tracks the centerline of the runway. Must be a malfunction in the switch. Glenn chooses that moment to tactfully say that he probably should continue the takeoff. Well, I really messed that up. I should have recognized and corrected that switch malfunction quicker. It's a little embarrassing, but no big deal, I'll get over it, and it won't happen again.

We're airborne and climbing toward the rendezvous with our tanker. Our wingman is about 10 feet off our right wing and I'm checking out my equipment. Everything seems to be operating great. We will rendezvous with our tanker over Laos today. It will take us about 45 minutes to get there. I kill the time by flying the airplane. Glenn occupies himself by looking around, and enjoying the scenery. He switches the flight over to the tanker frequency, and gives a call to the KC-135 that will be our tanker for today. Red Anchor responds immediately and gives us his position. We are first on the tanker, will both refuel once, and then top off our tanks when we get to the north end of the tanker track.

Our flight of two aircraft is refueled and heading north now. Four other flights of four F-105s are visible off to our left and right. Glenn calls to our wingman to switch to the strike frequency, the radio frequency that all of us will use for the duration of the air strike.

I tune through the frequency bands on my Weasel equipment, and pick up the first sign of North Vietnamese radar activity, a Soviet made Barlock radar. The strong signal means that the enemy knows that we are coming and that our altitude, heading, and the number of aircraft in the raid are being passed to the air defenses. It is easy to imagine the frenzied activity taking place on the ground with sirens wailing, and crews rushing to man their airplanes, gun positions and missile sites. My APR-25 Vector scope displays the first of the precision tracking radars. It's a Firecan radar, another Soviet designed, built and possibly manned radar, this one usually associated with one or several batteries of 57 or 85 millimeter anti-aircraft guns.

"Guns at 11 o'clock," I call to Glenn. He repeats my call over the radio to the strike force. The signal is pretty weak. He's probably the gun battery at Yen Bai, which is about 60 miles ahead of us. The F-105s from both Takhli and Korat normally cross the Red River in the vicinity of Yen Bai, in order to attack the targets in the Hanoi area from the North, where the more mountainous terrain offers some protection. The North Vietnamese (NVN) moved that Firecan radar and its associated guns into position several months ago. It's more of a nuisance than a threat. The guns always shoot, but have been particularly lousy in their aim. The precision tracking of that particular radar though has passed vital information of our timing, intentions and strike force size to the rest of the NVN defenses. Its presence has been a thorn in the side of the Weasels. Most of the Weasel crews have tried, at one time or another, to knock it out with Shrike missiles. All have missed. We have all speculated that the radar was probably very well revetted, thus making it particularly hard to damage with anything but a direct hit.

A few days ago on another easy mission like today, Jerry Hoblit and Tom Wilson tried something different. Notice that I said different, not necessarily tactically sound or intelligent. Back at Weasel School, we had practiced a technique that we called "Station Passage". The idea was, if you keep correcting your heading as you approach a radar site so as to keep the radar signal directly off your nose, you will eventually fly over the radar. The equipment will tell you when you fly over the site, as the signal will switch quickly from your nose to your 6 O'clock position. Well, Jerry and Tom went through that drill with the Yen Bai Firecan. When they got station passage, Jerry lit the afterburner and pulled up into an Immelmann maneuver. Their idea was to fire their Shrike missile when their nose was pointed straight up. The missile should then continue on up for a bit then reverse itself and head straight down onto the radar. Theoretically, it was a sound plan, and couldn't miss. It was really neat to watch from a safe orbit nearby. It's always neat to sit safely by and watch your friends do dumb things. Up went the airplane. Off went the Shrike. Down came the airplane. Down came the Shrike. Up came an intense barrage of flak. By some miracle, Jerry and Tom are able to fly out of there unscathed. The Shrike missed its target and the radar kept on transmitting. After that miss, we sort of left that Firecan alone. The guy wasn't very accurate. If we killed him, they would probably have replaced him with someone who could shoot better. Might as well leave well enough alone.

Back to today's mission. We head west-northwest toward Son La and Dien Bien Phu. It is a short hop over there. Only about 15 minutes pass until we are in the area, and looking things over . "Nothing on the scope,

Glenn. They must know that we are going to secondary targets today, as there isn't much activity over towards Hanoi, either."

"Well", Glenn calls back, "Let's go over there and see what we can stir up." "Avenger, is leaving the area", Glenn calls to the strike force over the radio. With that, he pulls the nose of the plane around, pushes up the power and takes up a heading of 120 degrees towards the flats south and west of Hanoi.

There still are very few radars on the air, just a few distant Firecans probably looking toward some Navy planes coming in over the Gulf of Tonkin. I turn up the sensitivity of my receiver and detect a very weak SAM radar from amidst the electronic noise. It isn't strong enough for me to determine its exact direction, but common sense tells us that it is directly ahead. That's good, just stay on the air a littler longer. The SAM signal gradually grows stronger as we close the gap between ourselves and Hanoi at a rate of eight miles a minute. The signal is now growing strong enough for me to get a reasonable indication of its location. "Weak SAM at our 11 o'clock position, Glenn."

"Roger. It is probably that site just south of Hoa Binh. That's the one that hammered those guys from Korat, yesterday. Let's go pay him as visit ."

Glenn keeps the Sam site slightly off the left of our nose, as we close the distance. My job now is to give him heading corrections as to where the site is, until we can get close enough to launch one of our anti-radiation missiles. We must also make sure we don't get surprised by anything else while we are doing it.

The North Vietnamese radar network has apparently told the site that there are two aircraft heading toward it from the west. The radar signal now increases significantly in strength, indicating it is now looking our way. I work with my IR-133 Receiver, synchronize the receiver scan with that of the radar, and determine that we are almost directly in the middle of the SAM's azimuth beam. I move to the elevation beam and get the same result.

"He's tracking us", I tell Glenn

"I think we're close enough to put a Shrike on this guy," Glenn says. Seconds later the Shrike comes off the left wing, leaving a trail of smoke behind as it roars toward the SAM radar. Moments later, the red "Launch" lights illuminate in our cockpits and the shrill screech in our headsets indicates that the site has launched missiles at us.

"Valid launch off the nose", I tell Glenn.

"Avenger flight has a valid launch. Take it down, Avenger." Glenn calmly announces to the world. He lowers the nose, pushes up the power and heads for the site. It's now a matter of us visually acquiring the missiles and dodging them, while hoping that our Shrike finds its way to the radar and puts it out of commission. The Weasels have the edge in this battle. We can dodge. SAM sites can't. Of course, we have only a semi-dumb, short-range missile with a 50-pound warhead. The enemy has a fairly sophisticated weapon system operated by a four men crew, with information fed to it from several other radars. The SAM usually has another SAM site providing him overlapping coverage, as well as dozens of anti -aircraft guns of various calibers, in the vicinity. He also has six missiles that can go twice as far and twice as fast as our Shrikes and which have 300-pound warheads. Still, we feel we have the advantage as long as we don't screw up, like loosing sight of the missiles, getting too slow or too stupid .

We've got the missiles in sight. Glenn has maneuvered the aircraft so the missiles are coming at us from our 2 o'clock position. They're easier to dodge when they are coming at you from the side. We can see two coming our way, although a third one may have been launched. Soviet launch doctrine, which the North Vietnamese use is Shoot, Shoot, Look, Shoot.

"I see the smoke from the launch site", Glenn says, It's near the bend in the river." Glenn decides the first missiles is close enough and pulls up sharply and turns into the missile. Both missiles pass harmlessly below us and detonate in the distance. He rolls the wings level to look for the probable third missile, when another site at our nine o'clock position launches at us.

"Launch at nine o'clock!" I call to Glenn .

"Roger", he says and turns hard to the left toward that site, temporarily forgetting about the first site. I quickly look at my scope. It looks like the radar signal from the first site has gone off the air, indicating a possible hit from our Shrike. It's hard to tell now as we are now the center of attraction for several SAM and AAA sites, and the scope is cluttered with signals.

" I see smoke from our Shrike at the first site." Glenn confirms my suspicion. At least the radar is disabled. We can go in and destroy the vans and missiles as soon as we can stop dodging missiles.

"I've got two missiles in sight", Glenn calls. We now descend to about 50 feet above the ground, doing around 700 Knots. Too close to the deck to dodge missiles , but they won't be able to track us at this altitude. Seconds later the first missile roars overhead. followed shortly thereafter by another. They are at least 500 feet away, but look a lot closer.

"I'm going to climb a little and see if I can put a Shrike into this guy from point blank range.", Glenn calmly says .

"Go to it ." I tell him . As we leave the sanctuary of 50 feet above the ground and climb up to 4000 feet to give the Shrike a better look at its target, two more SAM sites start tracking us strongly.

"SAM sites looking at us at 4 and 8 o'clock", I call to Glenn . "Roger" he answers. "I'll just be a bit longer."

"Missile Launch", I call, "It's the one at our four o'clock!" "Avenger flight, Missile Launch." Glenn calls out on the radio. He hangs on a few seconds longer, and sends the Shrike on its way . We're now diving back to the relative safety of the ground. Down where the radars of the SAMS will have trouble picking our aircraft out of the ground clutter. "Where the hell is Avenger Two, Mike?"

"We lost him in the first SAM break!" I answer Glenn.

"Avenger Two where are you?" Glenn calls out over the radio. "I lost you during the SAM break", Two answers. "I'm over on Thud Ridge." Christ, Thud Ridge is 30 miles away. How the hell did he get over there so fast? What a major candy ass…

"Well, head on home," Glenn directs him. "We've got some business here yet." Surprisingly, neither Glenn nor I give much thought to being in Route Package VI, hunting SAM sites by ourselves. Instead, we both wonder how our candy ass wingman is going to explain returning to Takhli as a single ship and how he managed to lose his flight leader.

Neither of us can see the missiles from the third site, and assume that we are too low for them to track us. We are now heading back on our original heading, where we were first fired upon. We are going back to destroy the first site that fired on us. Glenn arms the 20-millimeter gatling gun—the best SAM killing weapon ever devised. We are still about 50 feet off the ground, but have slowed down to around 600 knots. Forward visibility is not too great, as our speed and the high moisture content in the air combine to make our own little fog bank on each side of the nose. Glenn climbs to around 2000 feet in order to get a better look at the SAM site which is to be our target. Little red balls are rising up to meet us. They are harmless looking, but they are quite deadly. They are tracers associated with some pretty fast shooting guns, and they are all around us. What doesn't show are the multiple non-tracers which are in between each tracer. We can hear the rounds hitting the aircraft. We seem to be surrounded by about a half-mile square of anti-aircraft projectiles. Glenn moves the airplane around seeming to spoil their aim.

"I see the site." says Glenn. We've got time, gas and inclination for just one pass. We make good use of it. Our 20-millimeter rounds start through one missile launcher, across the site through the radar van and control van and out the other side through another missile launcher. We break hard right. The explosions shake the airplane and tell tale orange SAM smoke and fire is reaching hundreds of feet in the air.

"Good shooting , Glenn".

"Thank you sir", he answers cheerfully. "Now let's get the hell out of here." We descend back down to 50 feet and stay on the deck for another thirty miles, until we get out of the heavily defended areas. Twice on the way out Glenn strafes gun positions, which pop up in front of us.

Finally, we are able to climb back up to safety, take our oxygen masks away from our faces, and have a cigarette . We're both on an adrenalin high. It had been an exciting 20 minutes.

"Boy, we really stirred up a hornets' nest there", Glenn chuckles . Yes, we really had. We had killed a SAM site, and shot up several anti-aircraft gun positions, dodged six missiles and hundreds of anti-aircraft shells, and had been the sole focus of the Hanoi defensive network for 20 minutes. Just another routine Weasel mission, a lot of fun and worth 1/10th of an Air Medal.

"Did you hear that joke that Norm Frith told in the bar last night?" I asked Glenn.

"No", he said , "tell me."

"Well it goes like this "Do you know the definition of the world's greatest optimist? It's a Weasel who quits smoking, because he's afraid that he will die of lung cancer."

, OBTW, that night at the Stag Bar, the Ops Officer for the 333TFS brings his drink over, sits down with me and asks what had happened that day. His manner is non-confrontational. He just wants to know. He says that the captain, our lost wingman, had complained that we had flown someplace where we were not supposed to. I explain to him the rules of engagement that the Weasels operate under, that we were supposed to protect the strike force from SAMs and also to kill SAM sites. In order to do that, we went where the SAM sites lived. I also add what I think about his candy ass captain, and his lack of guts and flying skill. Neither Glenn nor I make an issue of the Captain's conduct or flying ability, feeling it best to just let the matter go. Six months later, I again flew with this guy in my flight. At that time, I'm flying with another and much different pilot, and the mission results are significantly different. But, that is another story.

Mike Gilroy

Story by Billy R. Sparks (AKA Barracuda), WW # 330

A Very Long Day In Pack Six

My memory never was very good; however, some things seem to stick in my head. This particular mission in RP-6 is as vivid as though it happened yesterday. Nothing much happened exciting, but it was unique since everything was off the cuff and really unplanned.

I think this was either late July or early August '67 during one of those truly Dog-Squeeze water routes using Brown Anchor that every one hated due to the length of the mission. There were two over water refueling areas that were parallel, Brown and Tan. Both ran from just north of the DMZ to a drop off point about even with Than Hoa with Brown being closer to the coast of North Vietnam. For some reason we only seemed to be assigned those Anchors for afternoon missions so the gunners didn't have to squint into the sun. We flew from Takhli about due east to the coast out just near Hue, and then northeast to the Brown track. We would refuel up track and then drop off and head north of Haiphong well out from land and turn into the coast just north of the Kam Pha mines. The routes then normally went from there into the Northeast Railroad, Kep Airfield, Bac Giang, or some other choice area. RTB (return to base) was the reverse. A round trip was almost 6 hours.

The mission for this day was a small bridge that was west of Bac Giang and, as usual, surrounded by guns and covered by about 4 or 5 SAM sites. Our Force Commander was Col. Bob White, Shark Lead, leading 16 F-105D aircraft with 6 M117 bombs each. I was leading 4 F-105F Wild Weasels, Barracuda, loaded with 2 AGM-45 Shrike anti radiation missiles, 2 CBU-24 bombs, and a 650-gallon centerline tank, each. We had 4 F-4D MiG CAP, Olds, from the 8th Wing. Ubon had call signs that were cars. Strangely enough, Col. Robin Olds always seemed to have 'Olds' as his call sign. The Korat force was 15 minutes ahead of us with a target within 10 miles or so of our area. They also consisted of 16 F-105D, 4 Wild Weasels, and a 4 ship MiG CAP from Ubon.

Carlo Lombardo, my EWO, and I were doing our usual routine grousing about long over water, 6-hour missions. As we approached Ubon, I heard a call on Guard that said, "Sparky, Sparky, come up 1234". This was repeated 3 or 4 times and I asked Carlo who had the call sign 'Sparky' when I heard "Damn it Sparky, I can't remember your call sign, come up 1234". I switched to that frequency and checked in. Baldwin was the Korat Force Commander and had a problem. All of his Wild Weasels had aborted and he flat did not want to head in North of Haiphong with no Wild Weasels. He wanted to know if I could cover them for their mission. I told him that I was only a Captain and I had better get Bob White on frequency. I went back and brought Shark Lead up and Shark and Baldwin discussed WTFO (What the f— over). I told both that it wasn't a very hard thing to do and Barracuda could cut it easy. White was worried about MiGs and said he would approve if Barracuda could have Korat's MiG CAP. Baldy's answer was "Hell, they can have my wife, I want some Weasels!" I went back and brought Barracuda to the Korat channel, briefed a couple of changes, and cut about a 45 left. We went between Vinh and Than Hoa to where I thought the Korat force would be. We coasted out and the whole string of tankers was smack in front of us. I joined with the lead low KC-135 (normal position for the Wild Weasel Tanker) and filled up. We hit the drop point on time and headed for the mines.

Barracuda went in about 20 miles or so in front of the strike force with the Korat MiG CAP at our 6 o'clock, normal spacing, and only had a few sporadic SAM signals along with the normal bunch of Firecan gun layer, height finders and early warning radars. I briefed my flight to drop the 650-gallon centerline tank as soon as it went dry to allow as much time as possible in the Pack. Sam Adams was Barracuda 3 for the mission and was about as good as anyone I ever met. We did our usual 5-mile or so split into a semi-trail and had some SAMs come up fairly seriously near the target. Sam and I lined them up with our wingman neatly line abreast, fairly close in and both wingmen shot an AGM-45 Shrike. The SAMs went down and Korat hit the target bang on. We fell in trail with the Korat birds and came out behind them with few problems except for another SAM that we smacked with 2 AGM-45 Shrikes on the way out.

When we hit the coast, I picked up Shark Force about 5 miles out and we fell in front of them and went to Takhli Strike Frequency. We led Shark back in to the target area using the same set of tactics. Two more SAMs came up and we knocked them down with Shrikes. Shark had nothing but guns around their bridge and smacked it into the water. We headed out behind Shark and hit a 57mm gun emplacement near the Northeast Railroad on the way back to use up our CBU-24 bombs since the SAMs would not play long enough to find the sites. As we neared the coast the second time, Robin Olds, Olds Lead, asked if we could make another swing back through the area due to some MiG calls from Red Crown. At that time Sam Adams and I had one Shrike each, no bombs or centerline tank and #2 and #4 had no ordnance except the gun. I waggled my wings and hand signaled Sam for a fuel check. He had enough for about 10 minutes more before we really had to scoot. I had a couple hundred pounds less. I told Olds we could cover him and sent #2 and #4 to the tanker and home with the Force. Sam and I went back to the Northeast Railroad in front of Olds. The F-4s worked the area until #2 called Bingo. We followed them out. When we hit the coast, Sam and I had been in Route Pack 6 for 43 consecutive minutes and had enough fuel remaining to make Da Nang straight in with 600 pounds of fuel remaining. Piece of cake!

At this point I screwed the pooch. I was sightseeing and allowed Olds to get to the Tanker first. Very dumb thing to do when you are skoshi for petrol. No problem, Sam had 600 pounds to play with and I had a bit less. Olds 2 was a brand new Lt. on his very first Pack 6 mission. He forgot how to refuel and was really rocking and rolling behind the KC-135 filling station. It did not help to have both Robin Olds and, I think, Bill Kirk give him flying lessons while he made a fool of himself. Sam and I were starting to sweat a bit and Carlo began to gripe about his belief that my parents had not been legally wed and other less charming comments. After a subjectively long time, I called Olds and the following conversation ensued.

"Olds, Cuda, we are hurting"

"Barracuda, Bad?"

"Tres Bad Boss"

"Olds 2 get off the boom"

"Lead I'm Bingo"

"Olds 2 get off the damned boom now!"

"Olds 2 is bingo minus 500!"

"I don't care if you F****** die! Get off the boom NOW!"

Olds 2 moved off and I had Sam slide in with me very close on his wing. He had about 300 pounds straight in to Da Nang and I had 200. Sam took about 3500 pounds and I did the same. We departed the tanker just north of Vinh and headed a straight line for Takhli. As we started our turn to RTB, I thanked Robin for the gas. He said "No sweat, Barracuda, thanks for the cover. OK #2 let's see you make a fool of yourself one more time!". Sam and I left the freq and headed for home.

Sam and I joined our flight at the INTEL debriefing and then had a separate debrief with Col. White. Everyone was happy and we wrote it all up in the Tactics book in case we had to do it again. At least I never had to do that again and I'm not sure anyone else did either. As a footnote, as I was leaving the Wing Headquarters for the bar, I was told I had a call on the RED PHONE in the command center. It was Col. Olds calling from Ubon to say Hello. He talked about the mission a bit and never asked how low on fuel we were. As he ended his chat, I asked if his nugget ever got any gas. "The damned fool finally took fuel. Don't worry about that ass, he's going on the night mission and will never fly with me again!". I asked him a couple of years ago at Steamboat if he remembered that and he told me "Hell, yes! That jerk never did fly with me again." I finished with well over 100 missions in RP-6 and 43 minutes is still my max for time in an aircraft inside the Pack. I later had about 2½ consecutive hours in Pack 6; but that was on the ground waiting for a helicopter.

Billy R. Sparks (AKA Barracuda), WW # 330

Story by Robert E. (Bob) Dorrough WW # 349

MiG Bait

Even though AAA had hit me the day before near Hanoi, my 84th mission on 20 December 1967, proved to be pretty exciting, too. The MiGs had been pretty quiet lately, but our intelligence thought they wanted some action. So why not give them some? The plan was to make a strike north of Hanoi using only one Wild Weasel flight and no F-4 MiG CAP. The surprise was that the twelve-ship strike-force was not F-105s, but F-4Ds! The F-4s were much better against the MiGs than the less maneuverable Thud, and the Phantoms would have a great chance for some MiG kills. I got together with the F-4 Commander the night before via telephone. I don't remember if he was flying out of Ubon or Udorn, the two F-4 bases in Thailand. We planned our route for minimum SAM exposure, giving the MiGs more room to attack. The F-4s would fly in the standard Thud jamming pod formation, at a speed of .9 Mach, so that the North Vietnamese early warning radar would think it was a typical F-105 strike mission. (Note: The F-4s usually liked to fly inbound to the target a little bit slower than the F-105s for better fuel economy.) The Phantoms carried a light bomb load in case they made it to the target before the MiGs came up to play, but the main objective was to get some MiGs. Of course, the Phantoms carried their normal air-to-air missile load, but no external gun pods since they did not work too well against the MiGs and added drag (F-4Ds did not have internally mounted guns). For this mission my Wild Weasel flight had 450 gallon drop tanks on the inboard wing pylons and a Shrike (SAM radar homing missile) on one outboard wing station and two air-to-air heat seeking Sidewinder missiles on the other wing, but carried no bombs. We also had our 20mm Gatling cannon, but the Thud's gun-sight system was not very good for air-to-air combat. Although I had three other dogfights with MiGs during my 100-mission tour, only one other time did I carry Sidewinders. This was because my primary objective was the SAM (SA-2 ground-to-air radar controlled missile) sites, and I needed to carry more Shrikes, but not today.

My flight, Dallas, met the F-4s and the KC-135 refueling tankers over Laos. Everything was normal as we refueled, dropped off the tankers, joined up, and sped north to our hopeful rendezvous with the MiGs. Inbound, we used fuel from our wing drop tanks first. This was to save our internal fuel because we would jettison our tanks to reduce weight and drag if attacked by MiGs. Over enemy territory, my Wild Weasel flight spread out almost line abreast (number two on my left and three and four on the right) at 12,000 feet, sprinted ahead of the F-4s, and began looking for SAMs and MiGs. We knew there was a good chance the MiGs would hit us first since the loss of SAM protection would make the strike force very vulnerable. As we swung north of Thud Ridge, my bear, Major Bud Summers, called out several SA-2 sites painting us with their Fan Song radars, but we were out of their launch range. The weather was ideal for a MiG attack, a solid undercast for them to hide in until they made their move. I made sure all my flight had armed their Sidewinders, and the trap was set.

As we neared the target, Dallas two called out two MiG-17s climbing out of the clouds at our seven o'clock position. At the same time, number four spotted two more -17s coming up from five o'clock. I called for everyone to jettison their drop tanks and told Dallas three and four to make a defensive split to the right while myself and number two selected afterburner and split left. Bad news. When I hit the jettison button only the right tank left the aircraft, and at 0.9 Mach there was a tremendous yaw to the left caused by the drag of the remaining tank. Regaining control, I continued a diving left turn toward the MiGs, causing them to make a climbing overshoot. I reversed and pulled as many G's as I could without causing a high-speed stall. My Sidewinder started to make a faint growling sound in my earphones, indicating it was almost in firing parameters, as I tried to keep up with the tight turning MiGs. Just then my trusty wingman called out two MiG-21s coming up from our four o'clock position. It was obvious the North Vietnamese (with "technical help" from other Communist nations) had planned their attack well. I wanted to get that -17 so bad, but knew the noose was tightening on us, too. It was time to make an exit, so I broke down into the -21s. As they flashed past, I made a few jinks to spoil the -17s aim if they had reversed on me and headed for the low cloud cover at the speed of heat. Where were those ##**%!!! F-4s when I need them? We hit the clouds at 1.2 Mach, left the MiGs in our dust since they were no match for our speed, leaving the F-4s to tangle with any MiGs who hung around. A few minutes later we climbed up to 20,000 to keep the radar controlled 85mm guns at Yen Bai from getting too good a bead on us. Sure enough, flak bursts began appearing at our six o'clock, tracking toward us. We pushed the speed up, did a little jinking, and avoided the last threat of the day. Dallas three and four met us at the tanker after a short skirmish with their two MiGs, but no one got a shot off on either side.

The F-4s did not have the turkey shoot they had hoped for. They did engage some MiGs, but I do not know if they were the same ones we encountered. The Phantoms may have gotten one of the agile enemy fighters, but I am not sure. I was looking forward to listening to my audiotape of the dogfight when we debriefed (all Thud Wild Weasels carried tape recorders), but pulled so many Gs I broke the recorder! This was the closest I came to getting a MiG, and I was very disappointed it did not happen. Oh, well, the MiG was a superior air-to-air fighter and they had my flight outnumbered and in a box, but never got a shot at us, so I guess we came out okay. I thought I had a milk run on my next mission, a night B-52 support to Pack One. However, a radar-controlled 85mm at Dong Hoi just about ruined my night, but that is another story.

Robert E. (Bob) Dorrough WW # 349

Story by Robert E. (Bob) Dorrough WW # 349

Info On My Vietnam Tour

In the winter of 1966-67, DoD said that all F-105 pilots were frozen on active duty until they flew a 100 mission tour over North Vietnam. High time fighter pilots, but not necessarily in the Thud, were selected by name to fly Wild Weasels. The EWOs were all volunteers. Now that took some Big Brass Ones, since most were coming from SAC and had never been in a fighter. We got so low on qualified F-105 pilots that the Pentagon took B-52 guys, gave them a minimum time checkout, and sent them over to be Ablue four@. Of course the odds were much greater that the number four wingman would be the most likely to get hit. If the ex-SAC guys did make their 100 missions, most were shipped back to bombers, whether they wanted to go or not.

Some statistics during my tour (29 June 1967 – 24 January 1968):

- Our very first mission was to support a strike near the MiG base at Kep airfield. Some combat checkout. Bud and I flew a total of 23 Route Pack Six missions.

- The dawn, a big gaggle, strike briefed about 0245. Roscoe, the Wing's mascot dog, always made the big briefings and he had his special spot on the front row. If he snoozed, we knew it would be an easy mission. However, everyone got pretty nervous if Roscoe was restless.

- During my seven months in Thailand, the two Thud bases had 58 combat losses (six Wild Weasel aircraft) and 15 non-combat losses (4 Wild Weasels). The two worst combat months were October 1967, when 16 F-105s were shot down (2 Wild Weasels) and November with 14 losses (3 Wild Weasels).

- From 27 October 1967 to 3 January 1968, the 388th Tactical Fighter Wing at Korat lost two Wing D.O.s and a Wing commander. The first two, Cols Flynn and Bean, survived as POWs. However, Col. Burdett, our Wing Commander, perished. I am proud to say that he was my wingman on a mission only eight days before he was shot down and he was a fine pilot. Korat also lost two more F-105Ds and a Wild Weasel crew on the same mission that Col. Burdett was hit. It was a very somber debriefing after losing 20% of your aircraft and crews on one trip to Pack Six. Then on 21 January 1968, our new Wing Commander, Col. Graham, died of a heart attack. Just think, four O-6s lost in less than three months, and most, if not all, had flown in World War II and Korea!

When I first got to Korat, B/Gen. Chairsell was the Wing Commander. He was also the Commander when I was at Spangdahlem AB, Germany, and was always known for taking care of his troops. One of his goals at Korat was getting a swimming pool built next to the Officers Club, and he wanted to go swimming in it before he completed his tour. Finally, the pool was dug and the concrete poured the week before General Chairsell was leaving. Two days before his departure the pool was filled. It looked beautiful. A big party was planned for the next day, but something went wrong with the Thai engineering. It seems like this was the first pool they had ever built, and the next morning a 3-inch crack had appeared all the way across the pool and the water was gone! We all thought it was very funny, except for General Chairsell. Eventually the pool was repaired, and Bud and I got to be tossed in after our 100th mission parade.

The radar jamming pods we used on the Thuds were still having problems when Bud and I arrived at Korat. To test modifications, Wild Weasels like us would take a modified pod on a mission to see how it worked. Can you spell guinea pig? We would wait until a SAM was fired at us and then turn on the jammer. If the SA-2 stopped tracking us, we knew the jammer was working; if not, we would avoid the missile and have a little debriefing with the tech reps after we landed. My pilot words did not compute with the electrical engineers, but Bud was in his element. He would make notes as we flew back to base, and then he would disappear with the engineers, talking about PRFs, sine waves, etc., etc. I just wanted a beer.

Korat was the home of the Royal Thai Air Force Flight School. They were located on one side of the base, and the 388th TFW on the other. Of course, they were doing flight training while we were launching and recovering from combat missions. The Thais used British-built, single engine propeller-driven Chipmunks for basic training, and T-33 jets for their advanced students. We did not have any problems with the T-33s, but the Chipmunks were something else since they did not have radios!! When we got ready to launch or recover a strike, mobile control would fire several red flares warning the Chipmunks to clear the area. They would putt-putt over the horizon as we would blast off or turn initial approach at 300 knots. After the last F-105 took off or landed, green flares were fired, and from over the trees you would see little Chipmunks fluttering back to shoot more touch and go's.

Other notes of interest:

- The Korat Officers Club had the longest bar in SEA: 84 feet long.

- Every Sunday was Malaria pill day.

- Our average Wild Weasel mission was three hours long.

- All Thud drivers were on duty for 25 days, then off seven. We were required to take our R&R off base each month. A good idea to get away for a little bit.

- While on R&R in Hong Kong, we caught a Pan American flight back to Bangkok for $86.50.

Robert E. (Bob) Dorrough, WW # 349

Story by Billy R. Sparks (AKA Barracuda) WW # 330

Carlo's Best Day

Billy Sparks, Pilot and Carlo Lombardo, EWO
Photo Courtesy of Billy Sparks

Carlo Lombardo's best mission was in late July or early August 1967. Carlo and I were scheduled to lead the Wild Weasel Flight, Barracuda, once again to RP-6. Col Bob White, 355TFW/DO was the Force Commander for Shark Force consisting of four flights of four each F-105Ds. We had the normal Alpha Strike setup consisting of two flights from the 357TFS (strike force scheduled lead) and one each from the 333rd and 354th.The assignment for each Alpha Strike lead rotated through the three squadrons of the 355TFW at Takhli Thailand. The Target for this mission was downtown Hanoi at, or near, the Thermal Power Plant. The F-105D Birds were configured with two 450 gallon fuel tanks on the inboard stations, a Jamming Pod outboard and a Multiple-Ejector-Rack (MER) centerline. Shark was carrying six CBU-24 bombs on each MER for flak suppression and the other three strike flights had six M117 750-pound bombs on their MERs. The four F-105F Weasels had our standard configuration consisting of a single CBU-24 on each inboard, a Shrike Anti-Radiation-Missile (ARM) on each outboard and a 650 gallon centerline tank. That load was best for us since it allowed us to kill SAMs, keep our Mach up, and have the endurance to stay in RP-6 for at least thirty minutes. The four ship MiGCAP flight of F-4C aircraft was from the 8TFW at Ubon and had a standard load of AIM-9 and AIM-7 missiles, Jammers, and fuel tanks. Since we were the early morning launch, we planned the mission the afternoon before with Col White and a few guys from the 357TFS. SAM activity had been very low for a couple of weeks and I hadn't seen a Guideline Missile in the air for about 10 days. When the SAM activity dropped off like that, the situation normally shifted to a sharp increase in Missile firings a few days later. The bad guys operating the SAMs would get scared after we killed a site or two and they would pull in their horns. Their bosses would then get on their cases and the SAM drivers would come out shooting for a while until we would smack them another serious lick. Carlo and I had decided that this day might be a busy one and we had better be ready to dodge at a great rate if it looked like it would be a "SAM Day." We discussed this with Col. White and came up with as good a plan for a SAM day as we could. If the SAMs were really up and roaring, there would normally be few, if any MiGs in the area since the NVN would shoot and sort them out on the ground.

We had three really good, highly experienced crews scheduled to fly with us. Lead and #2 were from the 357TFS, #3 from the 354th. and #4 from the 333rd. Everyone was Wild Weasel flight lead qualified, the low time jock had over 2000 hours of fighter time, all four EWOs were aggressive, and everyone had been to RP-6 a lot more than they wanted to. This set of four crews had also flown together as a flight several times before and we expected a smooth, very disciplined flight. Disciplined it was; however, it was to be very rough rather than smooth.

Shark Force, all twenty crews, briefed at 0-dark-30, did the usual individual flight briefings, normal pre-flight stuff, and the whole Gorilla (20 ship strike package) taxied on time for a pre-dawn takeoff in the very black Thai night. Everything was a piece of cake through the refueling on Green Anchor Extend in northern Laos and I had moved the Wild Weasels out to about five to ten minutes in front of Shark Force. Carlo was doing his standard bit of trying to figure out the Radar Order of Battle for the day. He would start while we were still in Northern Laos and used every piece of gear in the aircraft. He would have me turn up the Audio on the Shrike Missile and slowly move the nose around to see what he could hear in that spectrum. He would have the Shrike audio turned back down and would use the ER-142 in all of its modes, creating all sorts of strange squeaks and squawks. He'd diddle with the APR35/36 by pressing the Press-To-Test buttons. That defeated the logic in the system and allowed him to get a raw feed from each band. All of these strange noises made little sense to me; however, they made a bunch of sense to Carlo. He was especially interested in the fairly high pitched EEK-EEK made by height-finder Radars and the much lower pitched, more slowly spaced UNKs from the BARLOCK (GCI) Radars. If there were no BARLOCKS and only one or two height finders, we could expect very little trouble from the MiGs. We never saw an MiG-21 without a BARLOCK and two or more height finders up and operating. Carlo then started checking out the number of FIRECAN Gun Layer Radars that were up. They gave out the normal modulated sizzling sound that always seemed to be in the background. Carlo had figured out a month or so back that since they could not see us at ranges of 75 miles or greater, they were being used to track the blob of jamming put out by the 16 ship Strike force and the trailing MiGCAP. The Radars were denied range; however, by using several FIRECANs, they could get line-of-sight bearings to the jamming blob and they could then track our course. The idea seemed logical and, according to Carlo, since I was only a nose gunner and not very bright, he would tell me what was really happening and to shut up and listen. I seldom argued with Grouchy Bear and never won for three reasons: First, he was older than God; second, he was downright mean when crossed; and third, he was always right. Carlo had joined the US Army two weeks before I started in the 1st Grade in '41 and had been in one of the first classes of Old Crows. He had more Electronic Warfare experience than anyone I ever met and was a very good EWO indeed. I was extremely fortunate to have him in my "Pit." Carlo was 49 and earned his nickname, Grouchy Bear.

On this day we had more FIRECANs than anyone in the flight had ever seen as we crossed into NVN from Laos. The FIRECANs were all operating from a great distance watching our track in-bound to the Red River. We could find only one BARLOCK GCI Radar and no height finders, which meant that we should expect few, if any, enemy fighters. It was looking like a SAM day. As we kept heading for the Red River crossing about 10 miles downstream from Yen Bai, the count of FIRECANs increased until the ER-142 was almost solid in that band width. The scope on Carlo's gear was very small, two inches or so wide, and was a bear to read. Carlo estimated over thirty Gun Layers up at one time. We started to pick up the rattlesnake noise of a couple of SAM Radars along with the associated blinking strobes on the APR-35 as we passed the Black River and the count started up. This was earlier than normal for the NVN. All of the Radar activity was much higher than we were used to. Carlo had been right and it was going to be a real SAM day.

By the time we had crossed the Red River and headed towards Hanoi along Thud Ridge, we had more SA-2 Radars up than I had ever encountered before. Carlo counted a total of eighteen different SAM Radars by the time we were about to enter the outer missile range of the first one in the Hanoi outer defense ring. Our best Intelligence estimate was that they only had 21 in the whole country. Carlo always kept a steady stream of commentary going that covered all of the threats we were about to meet and as much additional information that he thought I could handle. He could hit peaks of 10,000 words a minute on a good day. As we passed the middle of the ridge, maybe 30 miles out from the valley, he told me he was dropping all guns because he couldn't break them out and would only call 3-Ring SAMs. This meant that I was to look out for the 10,000+ guns in the valley since he was too busy with the SAMs to help, very reassuring. I had never heard him do that before and figured that we were in deep trouble...and hadn't even gotten into the Hanoi area yet.

For those of you who haven't been there, the Hanoi area is about the size of the Las Vegas Valley. There is a ridge of fairly tall mountains (Thud Ridge) that runs from the Northwest toward Hanoi. We preferred to come down the ridge towards the city since there were no guns on the ridge, it was easy to see, and it gave us a place to play hide and seek with the Radars in the flats. The valley floor was as level as a pool table with no place to hide and it extends all the way to the Gulf of Tonkin south of

Haiphong. What we had were eighteen SA-2 sites in an area about 30 miles in diameter. We had no fewer than sixteen at any one time, up and operating simultaneously, for the next 28 minutes. We were headed for a very busy day.

I had split Barracuda Flight into two elements, very normal, in a staggered trail about five miles apart. Every time either element would head for a site to take it down, it would stay up and three or more others would challenge us. Normally, when you headed directly towards a SAM site, it would drop off the air and another would come up and try to catch you from a blind spot. Not this day, they came up, stayed up, and kept shooting missiles. The APR-35 scope had three concentric rings etched on it from the center dot to the case. Any signal strobe that extended from the center to 2 ½ rings or more was considered to valid threat, in range, and ready to fire a missile with a good chance of a kill. A "Four-Ringer" (out to the edge of the case) was really close and a "Waterfall" (bouncing off the case) was cause for browning of the shorts. Needless to say, we had almost continuous "Four-Ringers" and numerous "Waterfalls" for what seemed forever. A phenomenon of stress is that time becomes elastic and seconds seem like minutes or, in other words, time flies when you're having fun. I never, before or after, saw so many SAM Radars up or so many SA-2 Missiles in the air. We came up with a count of approximately 72 launches during the debriefing. I really don't know how many there were. Carlo called every launch to include the bearing and approximate distance. He called them by saying they were targeted at us (lead and #2), the element (Barracuda 3 and 4), or the Force. I had to dance with 12 separate firings that day alone. When a SAM is being directed at you, first you visually acquire it, turn to place it at 2 or 10-o'clock, push up the power and lower your nose for extra airspeed, and then wait until it is about to hit you. When you can't stand it any longer, you pull up and into the missile with at least 4"G". This will cause the missile to miss, break apart, or go ballistic. You have just been forced to dance with a very ugly partner. Barracuda 3 and 4 had about the same number to jig with as my lead element. I would line up a site and try to fire, or have my wingman fire a Shrike. If we were lucky, we could get the Shrike off before we had to waltz with another incoming SA-2 Guideline smoking along at a bit over Mach 2+. Sometime during the fray, I had the flight jettison the 650-gallon centerline tanks to give us a bit more maneuverability. After about 15 minutes of this extreme amount of fun, the element had to join up with me. The element lead joined up because both his EWO and the EWO in #4 had lost the electronic picture of the fight and all four heads were now out of their cockpits looking for supersonic telephone poles. My wingman's EWO also had to go head-out for the same reason. This left Carlo as the only EWO with his head down, watching the scopes, deciding what all eighteen SAM sites were doing, and calling the shots for Barracuda flight. We basically were just rolling with the punches and absorbing missiles to cover the Strike Force.

Shark came down Thud Ridge, located the target, and hit it while a hail of missiles was being fired at the Weasels. Less than half the missiles headed anywhere near the strike force and, of those that were fired in their direction, all were very wide misses. Shark made it to target and through rejoin without having anyone hit or having to really dodge a single missile. During all this time, Barracuda Flight spent over 26 minutes consecutive minutes inside the overlapping missile envelopes of sixteen or more SAM sites. Carlo called every shot and kept up a running commentary on "What's Happening." If he had hiccuped, even once, we would have been history. The NVN were after the Weasels for sure and pulled out all the stops to get us. They failed. My shorts were very brown, and I suspect the rest of Barracuda flight had the same problem. We all made it.

We still had our CBU-24's as we finally followed Shark and the MiGCAP out of the valley because we just flat couldn't pick out a site and hit it due to the activity all around us. I would have lost at least one or more wingmen had I tried. We found a 57MM gun site near Thud Ridge and killed it with our CBUs on egress. I don't have the foggiest idea whether we hit any emitters with our shrikes. We were a bit too busy to really determine if we hit or not. We tried to determine what, if anything, we hit during debriefing and decided we hit an emitter with more than four and less than all eight. I still don't care. We did as well as we could.

Shortly after we crossed the Red River, Carlo called "Cold Mike" (no transmissions) and went dead silent. He stayed cold mike until I turned on initial at Takhli almost an hour later. I could smell the cigarette smoke all the way to Takhli (450+ miles) while he decompressed. I checked our fuel and decided that we did not need any gas from our post-strike tanker and went directly home at over 30,000 and landed ahead of Shark Force. I think all of us were too beat to really care.

As usual after an interesting mission, I got the whips and jangles as I wound down. We were way too busy to be nervous while we were in the barrel. Going home was as good a time to calm down, decide what happened, and how to do better next time. I decided that we had done about as well as we could and that Carlo was the key to what we did right. To this day, I have never seen anyone function as well, or even nearly as well, as he did that day. Grouchy Bear was the very best, at least that day. The only person who knew how truly afraid I became was my laundress and I slipped her enough extra coin to keep her silent.

We had a very lengthy debriefing with INTEL, with Carlo conducting most of it. Grouchy Bear was never at his best in debriefings and had a habit of really jumping down the necks of the young INTEL debriefers. He did a masterful job of recreating the mission, including which site shot which missile and from where. Col White came by our table and listened for a while and tapped me on the shoulder for a chat. I walked away with him and he said that this had been a very good mission. I replied that it was a very bad mission from our viewpoint. He smiled and reminded me that we were supposed to be 'First In and Last Out' and to 'Protect The Force.' He said that that was what he had seen and to shut up. I normally agree with Colonels, especially those I like and respect. He asked if Carlo had a good day. I assured him it would be impossible for any EWO to have a better. He suggested that he should get an award. I agreed and he recommended a Silver Star. I agreed and he asked "What about the nose gunner?" I told him that I had earned at most a tenth of an Air Medal (an Air Medal for every ten missions in RP-6 was standard). His reply was "Sounds about right to me". Carlo later received that Silver Star to go along with his two others, and I got another tenth of an Air Medal. It still seems about right to me and I am convinced that we did about as good as is possible protecting the Force, given the circumstances.

Charles A. Lombardo was the bravest man I ever met. At the risk of having Bear Wilson, Mike Gilroy, and/or several other EWOs call me collect at 0300 some weekend for a sense of humor check, he was also the best EWO ever. He kept me alive on 49 trips downtown Hanoi, the majority as the lead Weasel. That alone makes him very damned good. It is an honor to have been a part of something that demanded total dedication and competence. To watch anyone perform at such an extreme level of excellence day after day is almost worth the heightened pulse rate and the subsequent whips and jangles. Carlo's day-to-day performance was uniformly outstanding. The Grouchy Bear just flat didn't make mistakes. Carlo, I want to thank you for making us a hell of a team. I also thank your family for lending you to me in order to allow you to keep Kathleen Sparks' only child alive.

Bill Sparks, Once known as Barracuda

Story by Eddie Adcock, WW # 100

What To Do?

12 April 72, 30 Miles West of Bulls eye (Hanoi), 18,000 ft. 520 kts.06:00 hrs.

A flight of two F-105Gs (call sign - Flapper) is in front of the strike force looking for any SAM activity. In the lead are Dick Moser and Eddie Adcock. Number two is Jim Caldwell and Steve Figun.

It had been a routine mission so far. No SAMs were transmitting and only a few squeaks from a Firecan or two. The weather had been forecast to be clear, but it was undercast and hazy at our altitude which would prove to be a problem.

We pressed on planning to do a 180 at the Black River. But then the weather went sour. The haze at our altitude got thicker. Just as we started turning, a SAM site came on the Radar Warning Receiver. And immediately the Missile Launch light illuminated. Dick rolled level and the radar was at our 3 o'clock position. He pushed the nose over and we started down. Number 2 was hanging with us off the right wing.

Dick and I were both straining to see the missile(s). But with the haze and undercast, we had no visual contact, not even with the ground. The way I describe the weather condition is, it was like being inside an empty milk bottle.

The F-105G was equipped with the ALQ-105 jammer. It was attached to the fuselage in two flarings on the belly of the aircraft. It normally was never used because of the interference it caused to the electronic receivers.

We were on the defensive end of this engagement. Neither us nor number 2 had any joy on the SAM missile(s). So, I at least remembered to switched on the jammer to the noise mode. It was very soon after turning on the jammer that the Launch light went off and number 2 called that he had taken a hit.

By this time, we were down to 5,000 ft. and in the clear. We joined on number 2 and headed west. Jim and Steve (no. 2) were leaking fuel from the right wing. The SAM missile had apparently exploded above them. When we met later, Steve said that just at the last moment, he had caught sight of the missile, but there wasn't any time to take evasive action.

We flew on no. 2's wing as he jettisoned his armament for an emergency at Udorn Royal Thai Air Base. At Udorn, Jim declared an emergency and made an uneventful straight-in landing. Dick and I RTB'd to Korat.

In retrospect, we screwed up. We never should have pressed on with the weather going down hill. And it is still a mystery of how the SAM site knew our position to immediately launch missiles after only being in transmit mode for a few seconds. As to the effectiveness of the jammer, will never know except no. 2 did not turn their jammer on and the SAM missile detonated near to them.

Eddie Adcock

Story by Michael B. O'Brien, WW # 847

ATTACK!

Editor's Note: This article appeared in the June 1974 issue of The Navigator magazine, AFRP 50-3 Vol. XXI, Number 2. It is based on a transcript of an in-flight mission recording entitled "Two Plus Two and We Blew Their Shit Away". It is reprinted here with the consent of the author, Colonel Michael B O'Brien, USAF (Ret.).

The G model of the F-105 Thunderchief (or Thud as it is affectionately named) is appropriately called the Wild Weasel and, because of the role it plays, the Wild Weasel emphatically denotes ***attack***. The Wild Weasel crew is made up of two crewmembers: the Pilot and the Bear, or backseater. The Bear is really a triple threat: navigator, electronic warfare officer and weapon system officer.

Enemy defenses, particularly Surface-to-Air Missile (SAM) sites, are our objective. We're first in the target area with the strike force, and the last out. And, in between, we encounter all the excitement and satisfaction that any crew can handle.

"First in" starts early on 6 October 1972; the target is a few miles southwest of Hanoi. You've got to know where SAM is; what he's going to do. My Pilot is going over the strike force route while I update my maps. SAM hasn't been in the flats southwest of the city, but it's time for him to move in... Two hours before brief time, four before sunrise, we start mission planning and putting it together.

Major Ed Cleveland and I have been "married" for eight months now. He's a Thud driver from way back, now on his second tour, and one of the best in the business. "When the strike force crosses the Black River, we'll want to be slightly to the south...." We trace the path, look at the defenses, getting a feel for how it'll be. You've got to know what SAM is going to do, how you're going to find him. Some call it instinct, but it's really only detailed preparation. You think of all the possibilities, you run through how you're going to handle it. Then when it happens, you don't have to think about it or decide; you've been there before.

After the formal briefing, we get together for a flight briefing. Today, we're going as a "Hunter-Killer" unit—a Hunter element of two F-105Gs in the lead which locates the SAM sites and suppresses them with Anti-Radiation Missiles (ARMs), while the Killer element of two F-4E Phantoms rolls in with bombs to destroy them. We review our plan and incorporate F-4 tactical considerations. Each player is finely tuned for his part in the "concerto".

The sun is now high in the east. Prestrike refueling is 20 minutes behind; the radar warning receivers are turned on. The nervous anticipation has given way to the details of the moment. The F-4 element, to the right and line abreast, is always a comforting sight. *I'll never forget the day Major Luke Lucas took that MiG-19 off our tail...* I cross check the Doppler, then come back to keep the strike force in visual contact while scanning for MiGs. A SAM guidance signal shrieks. "They're warming up their radars; it looks like a SAM day." Time to go to work.

Ed selects the AGM-78 Standard ARM; another SAM guidance signal comes up. A final Doppler check is made. As we come up on Hoa Binh, we receive the first indication of a SAM radar, but he's out of range. Activity picks up with numerous indications of anti-aircraft (AAA) radars, then another SAM radar. The sounds of the electronic environment continue to increase.

So far, it's just been an indicator. Three minutes after the first intercept of a ground radar, we get a persistent SAM guidance signal. When this site to the north of us turns on his radar, we're ready for him. I've got the "78" set for Ed, and he fires. Then excitement reaches a peak as an adversary lets us know he cares. "Valid launch from 10 o'clock!" Our venerable Thud is already moving fast, and Ed pushes the nose over to gain additional speed. Another SAM site to the east comes up as Ed visually acquires the SAM fired from the north. He calls it to the flight, and that engagement terminates with the drastic tug of the G-suit as we out-maneuver the SAM.

The site to the east is still up, and another site comes up to the southeast. Ed has switched to the other "78"; I set it up and he fires. On the way, the site to the southeast also gives us a SAM to think about. "Condor 1, SAM at two o'clock!" Ed calls on the radio. He starts modifying the jink pattern to cause an effective left turn to the north. The G-suit tugs again, the southeast site is down. Throughout this second engagement, the east site has been up and down, up and down, a few seconds at a time. "Another SAM at five o'clock!" I call to Ed. "Condor 3 SAM at five o'clock" is Ed's warning to the second element. The receivers are quiet for a few seconds as our Phantoms go through their SAM avoidance maneuver. AAA radars now become the highest threat as we continue our turn to the left. The F-4s spot the east site on the ground, and the Thud element takes up a protective weave as the Killers roll in. "Condor 3 is in," followed by "Condor 3 off to the northeast." Ed, keeping the element in sight, remarks on the results. "They won't bother anyone for a while."

The first five minute pattern has been interesting. The activity continues. "Signal to the north…North of the Red, no threat." For the next three minutes, this and another site north of the Red River play with us. Up and down, up and down… a little SAM radar, a little SAM guidance signal, a little of both… another site across the Red and to the west joins the staccato.

We complete the second pattern at Hoa Binh and turn east. The F-4 element to the right continues their lookout for MiGs, scanning the skies while looking through us towards the SAM threat area. "Signal at eight o'clock!", I call to Ed. It's the site in the flats, the one that's never there. We turn left to say "hello," then the indication, "Valid Launch! Condor 1, SAMs at 11 o'clock." As the SAMs travel our way, it appears they'll cross in front of us. "Condor 4's got 'em, they're on me." Condor 4 takes his turn at evading the SAMs as Condor 3 visually acquires the site.

The Thuds again provide cover as the Killers do their work. "Signal to the north" are the words as the western site across the Red gets our attention. During our turn to the north, the signal goes down. Meanwhile, the F-4 element's path "down the slide" is bracketed by very heavy AAA. They really keep their birds moving, yet ordnance is right on target. Good work…

The F-4s join up and we turn east again. But, "Condor 3 is bingo." As we begin our turn outbound, another site to the east and across the Red from the previously struck east site tickles our fancy. "Signal at five o'clock, across the Red." Ed reverses, pulls up and fires our last missile, the AGM-45 Shrike. Condor 2 on the wing also fires his Shrikes. "Valid launch, 12 o'clock", confirms we're the item of interest. But fortunately, no SAMs have been fired and we turn outbound safely.

We're about a minute behind the strike force as we pass Hoa Binh on the way home. I update the Doppler, set in the tanker coordinates, and keep a lookout for MiGs. Even during the trip to the tanker, the electronic environment is active. We get indications ranging from SAM radars to valid launches for the next nine minutes. There's a SAM site out of range to the southwest who just loves to bother us. He's no threat now, but maybe someday we'll meet him.

The action is over, all of 15 minutes in the target area. Post-strike refueling, then recovery, and a most welcome sight—the Crew Chief, smiling as he sees us taxi in, all our ordnance expended. His efforts make the mission possible. "A good day, chief." The missile lanyard, which remains with the aircraft after an ARM is fired, is a coveted prize, and he accepts it with pride.

Of course, the job isn't done until the paperwork has been completed. So for the next two hours, we reconstruct the mission with Intelligence. Lieutenant Lloyd Tucker is our debriefer and, as usual, he understands how difficult it is to write down all the signal parameters, aircraft parameters, and missile firing parameters at the same time we're trying to attack and survive. By using my tape recorder, it's just a matter of picking the parameters from the tape and the navigation parameters from a map. Tomorrow's mission has already begun as we update the Intelligence Order of Battle. And so, 6 October 1972 is over in the early afternoon.

This one day in Wild Weasel history characterizes the mission: a dedication to the strike force. The strike force can deliver ordnance more accurately if it's not evading SAMs, so when the Wild Weasels do their job properly, the danger to the heavies and other strike aircraft is significantly reduced.

For real job satisfaction, it's hard to match the feeling that you were a determining factor in the strike force returning home from such a heavily defended area without a loss.

So, there's an overview of what it's like to be a Wild Weasel. It's much more, of course. It's nice to be able to see outside your aircraft, to be entrusted with the decision-making process on an equal basis, to be able to evaluate your efforts in real time. Little things maybe…but also, consider the camaraderie with your fellow Wild Weasels, with the Strike pilots and air-to-air guys who rely on you so heavily—call it, if you will, a dedication to people.

Col. Michael B. O'Brien, USAF Ret., WW # 847

Story by Edward Rock, WW # 185

Joseph D. Howard and George L. Shamblee Two More Wild Weasel Hero's

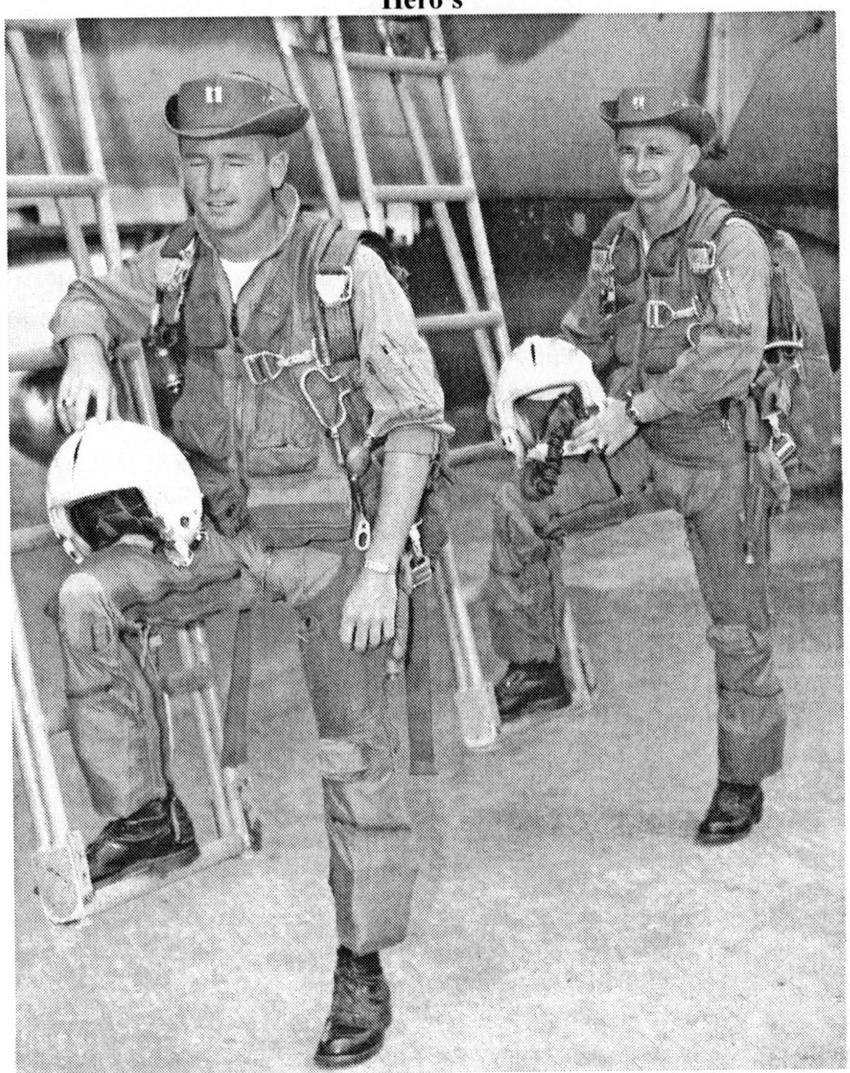

Joe Howard, left and George Shamblee, right
USAF photo courtesy of George Shamblee

Editor's Note: This is written in honor of Joe Howard (Deceased) and George Shamblee. I knew Joe before his untimely death, and George was assigned to the 561st TFW when I was commander. They deserve to be honored and it is my hope that this short article will help honor them and preserve their memory and some of the contributions they made.

Joe Howard, WW # 350, pilot and George Shamblee, WW # 348, EWO were in Wild Weasel Class Number 67WWIII-11 flying the F-105F. They graduated from training on 1 June 67 and were subsequently assigned to the 388th TFW, 13th TFS, Korat RTAFB, Thailand.

They were flying F-105F 63-8330 when they were shot down by fire from 85MM AAA and a missile from a MiG-21 on 7 October 67. Howard and Shamblee were on an Iron Hand mission supporting a strike force of F-105Ds from the 388th TFW. The strike force had been tasked to bomb a railway-marshaling yard near Kep Air Base, North Vietnam. The Wild Weasels were first in, ahead of the strike force, and performing their SAM hunting mission and also a weather reconnaissance for the strike force when six MiG-21 enemy fighter aircraft bounced them. During the ensuing engagement one of the MiG-21s fired a heat-seeking missile that impacted their aircraft in the tail section. Subsequently they were hit by fire from an 85MM anti-aircraft artillery (AAA) weapon and very badly damaged with a large hole, about three feet in diameter, in the left wing of their F-105. Neither the missile nor the 85MM hit was immediately catastrophic and they were able to continue to the east and out to the Gulf of Tonkin. However, the aircraft was on fire, they had lost all oil pressure, their engine could freeze at any movement and the engine had developed compressor stalls. They headed south over the Gulf in an attempt to make it to Da Nang, South Vietnam for an emergency landing with their badly damaged aircraft. The fire went out but they were losing fuel at a great rate and were concerned that they would run out of fuel before reaching Da Nang. A SAC refueling tanker became aware of their predicament and headed north to effect a rendezvous before they flamed out from fuel starvation. A successful emergency refueling took place; however, with more fuel the fire started again and finally the controls went out and a bailout was the only alternative. They were in a shallow dive and at about 10,000 feet altitude and 510 Knots indicated when they ejected somewhere over the Gulf of Tonkin, probably about 70 NM North of Da Nang. Neither Joe nor George was wearing leg restrainers at the time and both suffered broken legs in the bail out. George Shamblee suffered two broken legs and Joe Howard one. Shamblee said that he could hear the bones in his legs grinding together as he floated in the Gulf awaiting rescue. He did not realize that he had broken his legs until he attempted to get into his one-man life raft and his legs would not react as wanted. Very soon after they landed in the water a helicopter from the U. S. Marine amphibious assault ship Tripoli arrived on the scene and proceed to pick up Joe Howard, the pilot. Joe tried to tell the helicopter crew that his EWO was still in the water about 2 miles away and that they should pick him up immediately. The helicopter crew thought that Joe was in shock and delirious because the F-105s were single seat aircraft, weren't they? They proceeded to the hospital ship USS Sanctuary (AH-17) where they turned Joe over to the hospital personal. In the mean time George Shamblee was still in the Gulf of Tonkin wondering what happened! He eventually got out his survival radio, activated the emergency beacon and finally noticed some F-105s from the strike force circling overhead. Finally after about two hours in the water another helicopter showed up, he was picked up, and flown to the hospital ship Sanctuary to be reunited with Joe Howard.

George Shamblee spent 16 months in a body cast. When they removed his cast he was three inches shorter than he was before the bail out. He was discharged from the hospital in 1969 and eventually returned to flying status in 1970. He was assigned to the 561st TFS when it was deployed to Korat RTAFB in April 1972 where he yet again served in combat as a Wild Weasel EWO. A true American Hero of the Vietnam War.

Joe Howard went on to become a member of the famed United States Air Force Flight Demonstration Team, the Thunderbirds. Joe was the number four man in the Thunderbirds formation and flew the slot position behind the leader and between the two wingmen. He was killed in the summer of 1972 when his F-4 crashed at Dulles International airport near Washington DC during a Thunderbird demonstration flight. The horizontal slab became disconnected and he had to eject form his crippled F-4 at low altitude. His last words over the air were "I have to go!" He came down beside the fireball of the F-4 crash impact and his parachute was shucked into the fire and collapsed. He is buried at Ahoskie N.C.

Joe was North Carolina man of the year, the first military person ever accorded this honor.

Story By Al Siebecke (Dancing Bear, WW # 2513

Those Air Force F-4 Drivers Need a Vision Test

Editor's Note: All Siebecke is a retired Commander, USN.

Will try to make the bio simple: Enlisted in Army at 16 and served in the AAF with 13th Air Force in B29s in the PI, then with the 20th Air Force on Guam, again with the B29s. I saw the light and went into the Navy in 1949 and did Korea in ADs and F4U 5N night fighters. Was crewman in TBMs, ADs, and F3Ds. Made CPO in 1956, was commissioned in 1960, and was a B/N in A3Ds until the A6 came to the fleet, then made three tours in Vietnam with VA 52 flying A6A and A6B STD ARM from the USS Coral SEA and two cruises on the USS Kitty Hawk. I was Wing MO for EA6B at Whidbey Island until retirement in 1977. My awards include seven DFC's and twenty seven Air medals, three are individual awards.

I would like to tell a story that took place over Laos in 1972 while flying an A6B mission up the Ho Chi Min trail and probing into the pass area where the trail came into Laos from North Vietnam trying to see if a SAM site would come up so we could engage it. My pilot was LCDR Dick Klemm, one super stick. We had left Yankee station and the USS Kitty Hawk that morning as a single aircraft on a beautiful day, WX CAVU, coasted into South Vietnam and onto Laos and checked in with the various controllers and set the IFF as required. We were about FL 230 and doing a mild jinking being well above any AAA envelope, things were going smoothly. With no SAM activity in the pass we started back down the trail heading for the ship. We approached Chapone when we started getting painted with X band radar which was indicated on the ECM gear. This was not an unusual event as other aircraft could be in the area. Then it happened. A large explosion shook our aircraft and when we rolled and looked behind us a large black cloud of smoke was close by. The X band indications were then taking on a new meaning like, OH SHIT, the world's largest AAA or someone is on our ass. We started a high g turn when again we were shaken by another explosion and cloud of smoke. Looking behind, I saw two aircraft trying to get a shot at us. We pulled high g turns, they did a yo-yo, and we kept getting pushed to the ground, which was not a good place to be, as the AAA was coming our way in addition to the aircraft that were attacking from above. We had some serious ACM going with two F-4's that fired two Sparrow missiles and emptied their guns at us before they got close enough to read US Navy on our aircraft. Sure would like to find out just what flight surgeon signed off on those Air Force F-4 driver's vision test.

Al Siebecke (Dancing Bear), WW # 2513

Story by Larry LeMieux, Wild Weasel Bear, WW # 453

Homestead Story

In the early 1970's, I was stationed at Nellis AFB as an Instructor Bear in the Wild Weasel squadron. The war was still going on in Vietnam and there was a steady flow of classes through the squadron. However, the squadrons in Thailand wanted more crews in order to meet their sortie rate. As a result, they were augmented by the squadrons from McConnell AFB, Kansas. The McConnell squadrons were the stateside operational squadrons and the Nellis squadrons were training squadrons. Because of that, the Wild Weasels at McConnell were called upon for all the stateside operational requirements until they went to Thailand to help out.

As the war continued, the rest of the world kept rolling along and stateside requirements kept coming up. The Nellis Wild Weasels deployed to Seymour Johnson AFB to participate in an exercise and then the Organization of American States (OAS) decided to have their annual conference at Homestead AFB just outside of Miami, Florida. The Air Force wanted to put on a really big show for the delegates from all the member states. The Air Force wasn't going to settle for a standard static display of Air Force might, they were going to have a Dynamic Display! And, they were going to have a fire power demonstration with real simulated bombing attacks. I know, the first question that comes to mind is "what is a Dynamic Display?" and the second question is "what are real simulated bombing attacks?" Well, I'm coming to that.

What the Air Force wanted for their display was a ramp full of Air Force fighting birds all tricked out ready to go to war, sort of. They wanted all these airplanes to have electrical power supplied and have all the gee whiz stuff working so the OAS delegates could see what the Air Force could really do. They had an F-4 with the TISEO (Target Identification System, Electro-Optical) system, an F-111, and, of course, an F-105 (Thud) Wild Weasel, among others. Since the McConnell squadrons who usually supported the conferences were in Thailand, Nellis was asked to provide the Wild Weasel. By the way, getting back to the second question, the one about "real simulated bombing attacks." What they were going to do was set charges on the ground and have aircraft fly dry passes over them as they were set off to make it look like the aircraft were dropping bombs.

Tom Coady and I were selected to take the F-105 from Nellis to Homestead for what we thought would be a week's vacation. The trip to Homestead was to be the usual uneventful stateside cross-country. Tom had a friend in Tampa, so we decided to stay overnight there and fly on to Homestead on the second day. If you fly a Thud from Nellis to MacDill AFB at Tampa over land you have to stop twice for gas. However, if you fly over the gulf from Nellis to Texas to MacDill, you only have to stop once. So in the interest of saving time and gas, yeah right, we decided to fly over the gulf. After a little flight planning, we took off for Carswell AFB and gas and then off we went out over the gulf. As any Fighter Pilot will tell you, as soon as we were out of sight of land, our single engine started to sound funny and appeared to be running a little rough. In spite of that we made it to MacDill as planned. I guess Tom enjoyed the evening with his friend and I made sure the BOQ (Bachelor Officer Quarters) was fit to sleep in.

The next morning we took off for Homestead. I forgot to mention that the maintenance troops at Nellis had done their best to make the Thud look good. She had a fresh coat of paint and the drop tanks only had a few dents in their noses. After all, if you run into things, even as small as raindrops, at 400 to 600 knots you're going to acquire a few dents to say nothing of what happens when large solid objects on the ground run into you. The flight to Homestead was uneventful right up until we turned final from an overhead pattern. Yep, you guessed it, there it was, a rain squall right off the approach end of the runway. We had nowhere to go except through it, and there went all our shiny new paint from the leading edge surfaces of the airplane. We landed and taxied into our spot in the Dynamic Display lineup. Another thing, the Thud is notorious for spitting oil and hydraulic fluid on the sides of the airplane during flight. We climbed out of the airplane and started to make friends with the Homestead people. We talked a little while we got our gear out of the airplane and then headed for the BOQ.

Tactical Air Command (TAC) had a C-130 that brought all the maintenance equipment and crews to Homestead to work on the TAC birds. It arrived late on the night we arrived. It turns out that the senior ranking NCO (Non-Commissioned Officer) on a C-130 is designated to supervise the unloading of the equipment. Our Crew Chief was a Chief Master Sergeant and a supervisor in maintenance at Nellis. He had elected himself Crew Chief for our airplane in order to get a free ride to Florida so he could go fishing with his brother in the Keys after we were done at Homestead. He was the senior ranking NCO on the C-130 and spent most of the night supervising the equipment unloading. From there he went directly to the NCOQ Non-Commissioned Officers Quarters) to get some sleep. None of us had touched the Thud since we had parked it.

When Tom and I landed, we were met by two local officers who were to brief us on what was planned. They described how the Dynamic Display was going to be set up and asked what we would need to show off our equipment. Then they told us how the fire power demonstration was going to work with the charges and dry passes. We then made our first friends at Homestead by explaining how we did fire power demonstrations at Nellis. Nellis has several hundred square miles of bombing ranges in the southern part of Nevada. From Las Vegas and the base, it's a short drive to arrive on a live bombing range. So, our response to the description of the fire power demonstration was "At Nellis, we use live ordnance for our fire power demonstrations." The conversation ended shortly after that and we were left to find our own way to the BOQ.

Bright and early the next morning, well before any self-respecting Fighter Pilot on TDY would normally be awake, Tom gets a call at the BOQ. The Base Commander was out inspecting his Dynamic Display aircraft and there is our Thud in all her glory. The paint is pealed off the leading edges, the tanks are dented, and oil and hydraulic fluid has streamed down her sides. The Base Commander is beside himself and demands that Tom, the Crew Chief, and I get down to the aircraft ASAP. When we get to the airplane, the Base Commander demands that we take the airplane back to Nellis and that Nellis send a replacement. Tom, ever the diplomat, explained that this bird was the best at Nellis and any replacement would look worse. The Base Commander sputtered for a while and then ordered the three of us to get the airplane cleaned up. There we were: a Major, a Captain, and a Chief Master Sergeant wiping oil smears from one of the biggest fighters in the US inventory. While we were there, a crew of Homestead painters showed up at the airplane to repaint it. Score another one for Nellis Fighter Pilot diplomacy. Our Thud is now show ready, except for the dents and the fact that the flaps are still down. The ECM shop came out with three signal generators that would put signals on the EW (Electronic Warfare) receiver equipment in the back seat. We were now ready for the Dynamic Display scheduled for the next day.

That afternoon we were at the Q with nothing to do, so we decided to go to the BX. We called for base transportation and were told that they could only provide transportation to and from the flight line. Since the BX (Base Exchange) was on the way to Base Ops we said, "Send the car, we need to go to Base Ops." Soon the car arrived; we jumped in and started off for Base Ops. When the driver stopped at the intersection by the BX for a stop sign, we told him, "We're getting out here, if you want to go to Base Ops, go right ahead." He laughed and took off, later he came back to the BX and gave us a ride back to the Q.

The next morning we got all dressed up and went down to the flight line for the Dynamic Display. I climbed into the cockpit and started turning on the equipment. When we checked out the equipment and signal generators the day before, our airplane was the only one with power on it and everything worked as it should. This day, all the aircraft in the display area had power. As my equipment came on there were so many electrons flying around the ramp that all I could see on the scopes was grass. Normally, the grass (interference) on the scopes was barely visible. That day it covered about half the scope and it totally covered the signals from the signal generators. My first thought was, "Well, so much for any equipment demonstration!" Tom was standing by the wing tip and as people walked up, he would tell them about the mission, the airplane, and the armament. Then he'd send them up the stairs to me in the rear cockpit. I'd wave my hands at the scopes and give the people a song and dance about what they were supposed to look like without the grass. Then, depending on which way they came to our airplane, we would send them either to the F-111 on our right side (where it was busy swinging its wings back and forth) or to the F-4 TISEO on our left. They had an airplane orbiting about 20 miles south of Homestead and the TISEO was tracking it. They also had an LGB loaded on the F-4's wing. And that leads me to our next adventure.

Remember the Base Commander that had apoplexy when he first saw our airplane on the ramp? Well, he arrived at the F-4 with an entourage of OAS VIPs. As luck would have it no one was at our airplane. I was sitting in the cockpit and Tom was standing by the wing waiting for someone to show up. Since I was 12 feet off the ground, I could see the whole display area clearly and watched the Base Commander and his group walk up to the F-4. They talked to the F-4 driver for a few minutes and then the entire group got very interested in the LGB. They stood around it for a long time and all the while, no one came to our aircraft. Finally, a junior Canadian officer that was wandering around on his own walked over to Tom and asked him a question. As soon as the Canadian stopped in front of Tom, the Base Commander gathered his entourage and almost sprinted past our Thud. He led them by about 20 feet in front of the airplane, and as he went by, he waved a hand in our direction while saying something to the group. The whole transit from the F-4 to the F-111 couldn't have taken more than 30 seconds. As the group started by us I saw what he was doing, so I stood up in the cockpit, pointed to them, and yelled at Tom so he could see what they were doing. It was obvious that the Base Commander didn't want anyone anywhere near us and what he thought was the worst looking airplane on the ramp. It took me a while to stop laughing. Score yet again for Nellis Fighter Pilot diplomacy.

With the conference over the next day, it was time for us to get back to Nellis..We did a quick preflight, jumped in, and started up. One of the first things you have to do is call the tower for the clearance. It turns out that the UHF radio in the Thud is cooled by ram air. The problem is, you don't have ram air when you're on the ground and not moving. However, the designers thoughtfully provided a ground blower motor to cool the radio when on the ground. The next problem is, when you're in Miami, Florida, in the summer and the blower motor doesn't work, the radio doesn't stay on very long. When the radio gets hot, it shuts down. So, guess what? Our blower motor didn't work. We'd call the tower and ask for our clearance and they'd start to read it to us. The guy would get about half way through it and the radio would time out. So much for the clearance. We'd wait for the radio to cool down and call them again. The first time we called back, we asked for the clearance again. The guy started to read it, got to exactly the same place and the radio timed out. The next time we called, we told him we had the first part of the clearance and to just read us the last half. So, he started from the beginning and the radio timed out at the same place. So, now we had the first part of the clearance three times and none of the last part. After a couple of more tries, we finally got the entire clearance and were able to take off and headed back to Tampa so Tom could see his friend. When we left Homestead, the sky was clear and it was a beautiful day. But, there was a line of severe thunderstorms just south of the Florida panhandle and it was moving south. Sure enough, both we and the thunderstorms got to MacDill at the same time. There we were, on final with visibility at less than a quarter mile in driving rain. The blower motor didn't work, so we were sure the radio would time out after we landed and the tower wouldn't be able to see us on the end of the runway. Remember the Senior Master Sergeant Crew Chief we had? The one that hadn't worked on the flight line for many, many years. Well, he installed our drag chute for us, and you guessed it, it didn't come out when Tom pulled the handle. So, now we're rolling out on the runway at MacDill at 150+ knots, no drag chute, can't see the tower so they can't see us, the radio is about to time out, and Tampa Bay is fast approaching. We talked about dropping the hook and taking the barrier and then sitting on the end of the runway in the barrier with no radio where no one can see us. Then how we would feel if someone else landed not knowing we were sitting there. We figured it might ruin our whole day. As it turned out, nothing bad happened. Tom got the airplane stopped without the hook or going into Tampa Bay. The rain storm cooled the air enough so the radio didn't time out. We cleared the runway, called tower, and taxied in to the parking spot.

We headed for home the next day. We picked a nice Training Command base in Texas to refuel because they had the required barrier on their runway. When we got there, half the base showed up as we taxied up to Base Ops. There hadn't been a 105 in there in … forever, maybe. One of the transient maintenance crewmembers had had a tour in Thailand working on Thuds and crawled all over the airplane while we were there. We had to be especially careful on the preflight to make sure he hadn't left any panels open when he was done refueling and installing a drag chute. Finally, we left Texas and made our way back to Nellis, a successful mission to show the Wild Weasel flag to the masses. And, we made a lot of friends along the way, especially the Base Commander at Homestead.

Larry LeMieux, Wild Weasel Bear, WW # 453

Story by Carol Reitmann Sumner Wife of Capt. Thomas E. Reitmann

An American Tragedy

Editor's Note: Carol wrote this story in 1995. Tom Reitmann, her husband, an F-105 pilot, was shot down and probably (no remains have ever been recovered) KIA by AAA on 1 December 1965 while attacking a railway bridge on the northeast railway about 50 miles from Hanoi, North Vietnam. He was officially declared MIA at that time. The enemy AAA guns were manned by troops from the Peoples Republic of China. We were stationed together at George AFB, CA, and Itazuke AB, Japan. I am Godfather to one of their children. I first read this story in 1999 when we visited with Carol in Hawaii. I am including it here because I think it typifies the love, faith, courage, strength and determination of many military wives whose husbands were lost in combat. She was told to vacate base housing three months after her husband was declared MIA. (So much for the Air Force taking care of its own.) She doesn't say it here but when she arrived at what was to be her new home, she had about $400 to her name, four very young children, and a very uncertain future. She overcame all adversities and eventually established her own business, which was a resounding success. Carol is a former airline stewardess, from that time when stewardesses (not "flight attendants") were young and beautiful, and her husband Tom was tall, and handsome. They were a great couple.

Carol's Story

The Vietnam War (or Armed Conflict) has had lasting effects on more than just the men and women who did the fighting. The wives, children, parents, and other relatives that were left behind have also had to cope with a lot. Many wonder why we were there in the first place and why our government made so many mistakes. Have we learned anything from this terrible mess or will we do it again and again?

The story of the effects of the war on one American woman begins in the early evening in the second week of December 1965. The young woman is standing in a Christmas tree lot gazing at all the trees. She holds a five month baby girl in her arms while her other three small children stand around her. Tears are running down her cheeks. An attendant runs over to her and says kindly, "Don't cry lady, I'll help you find a tree." She can't bring herself to tell him that she's not crying about finding a tree.

As she stands there, her thoughts flash back two weeks earlier to December 1st. She remembers she was rushing to get the baby to the sitter after her other three children had left for school. She was going to the Officers' Wives Club Christmas Coffee, the one big highlight of her month. She knew Christmas would be lonely with her husband in Southeast Asia.

After the coffee, she and her best friend, Connie, decided to go Christmas shopping. They would leave her car at the Club and take Connie's. They had a great time shopping, but after almost two hours decided they should get back.

As they drove into the Club parking lot, Connie slammed on the brakes and clutching the wheel stared at the entrance of the Club. As she followed Connie's gaze she saw the Wing Commander, his wife, the base doctor and the Catholic Chaplain. Connie said that something must have happened to Harry. Harry, Connie's husband was also in Southeast Asia. She told Connie to calm down. She was sure that nothing had happened. She said goodbye and went over to her own car. After getting in and starting it she looked up and saw the group of four walking toward her. No, no, don't come over here, she thought. Quickly she locked the car door. She decided that if they couldn't tell her anything, then nothing had happened.

They came up to the car and tried to open the driver's door. Finding it locked, they asked her to open it. She just sat there, tears in her eves and a look of disbelief on her face. They knocked on the door, and then pounded. She ignored them. Finally, after what seemed like an eternity to all of them, she unlocked the door. They asked her to move over so they could drive her home. On the way no one said a word. They really didn't have to. She already knew.

They all sat in the living room of her quarters. "He's dead, isn't he?" she said. They told her they weren't sure, but it didn't look good. He had been on a bombing raid of a railroad bridge north of Hanoi and his plane had been hit by ground fire. His wingman in the formation had followed him down as far as possible, but hadn't seen a chute. They would know more in the next couple of days, as search and rescue teams were looking for him. That was all they could tell her. It didn't matter as she was in a state of shock. She began crying hysterically. She remembered later that the doctor had given her some pills, obviously to calm her down. The others in the group tried to comfort her to no avail.

After they left, she was vaguely aware of many of the other squadron wives including Connie, coming to talk to her. Someone gave her a glass of wine. They didn't realize she had been given tranquilizers. About two in the morning she finally came to her senses enough to ask where her children were. Thankfully, they were spending the night at the next-door neighbors.

The next thing she knew, the sun was up. She asked Connie to please tell all the other wives to go home. Then she knew she must face the task of telling her children. But, what would she tell those three small kids? They adored their Daddy and missed him terribly in the four months since he had been gone. She guessed the truth would be best, but she dreaded it.

When they came in, she knew they were aware of something being wrong. The six-year-old girl said, "What's happened to Daddy?" After explaining as gently as possible she was amazed at the response. The four and five year old boys told her that they were sure Daddy would be O.K. and ran off to play. The girl was devastated. She sat there in tears. Then she hugged her mother and asked what she could do to help. Thankfully, the baby slept through it all.

Suddenly, she was back to reality and still in the middle of all the Christmas trees. The attendant had been calling her and tapping on her shoulder. He had been worried when it had taken her so long to respond. Now he smiled with relief and showed her one of the most beautiful trees she had ever seen. After it was paid for and tied to her car she thanked him for his kindness. She and the children piled into the car, and wishing him a Merry Christmas she drove off.

On the way home the baby slept through the incessant chattering of the boys. The girl was quiet, as she had been for much of the last two weeks. How was this mother of four going to be able to make this a good Christmas for them? They need her so much now. She had to straighten up and be strong. That wasn't going to be easy for a twenty-eight year old who most probably was a widow.

She made it through Christmas. Then came the January homecoming of the squadron. Three of the pilots wouldn't be coming back with them. She had been born and raised in a military family and had always been told that a good military wife had to carry on as normally as possible in these situations. Still in shock, she decided that she must be at the flight line to welcome the pilots back. The other two wives, whose husbands were also missing, had the good sense not to put themselves through that. To this day she doesn't know how she managed to get through the homecoming without breaking down and crying. Of course when she got home she fell apart.

The next day the pilot that had followed her husband's plane down after it had been hit came to visit her. He let her listen to the tape recording of the flight radio chatter. She heard the plane being hit and a voice frantically yelling at him to eject. There was no answer. She was told that there really was no hope that her husband could have survived. However, U.S. policy was to list him as missing in action until further notice.

In March two officers from the base housing office came to inform her that her family must move out of base quarters. They needed the unit for active duty personnel. Of course, the government would pay to send them anywhere the wanted to go. They would even send her furniture and car. How magnanimous, she thought. The possibility of having to move had never entered her mind. She was still receiving all of her husbands' benefits including flight and combat pay. Officially anyway he was still alive and Missing in Action. She had just assumed they would be allowed to live on base indefinitely. Now her she was in Goldsboro, North Carolina with no idea of where to go.

While a military dependent, she had never lived in any one place for more than two years. Her parents were in Dallas, Texas and she didn't want to go there. The thought of staying in Goldsboro didn't appeal to her either. Their previous duty station had been in Japan. On their way back to the States they had spent two fabulous weeks in Hawaii. That, she decided, was where they would go. Looking back, she realizes that it was God answering her prayers and not her decision at all.

The years came and went. As wonderful as Hawaii was, she felt she was virtually a prisoner of war. She was married to a dead man. When she inquired as to how long this would go on, she was told there was no special time limit. Her husband's status would be changed only when concrete evidence of his death was discovered. It dawned on her that if his plane had blown up on impact they might never find any concrete evidence. So, would she be a prisoner forever?

In 1973, North Vietnam released our P.O.W.'s. She watched television knowing that her husband would not be among those prisoners getting off the pane. But deep in her heart she really hoped that by some miracle she would see him walk down those steps.

Two months later she received a call from the Joint Casualty Division in San Antonio, Texas. The conversation was incredible. She was told that all of the P.O.W.s had been debriefed and that none of them had seen or heard of her husband. Then she was asked what she thought. She wanted to respond with, "What do you mean, what do I think?" However, she calmly said that she thought her husband had been killed when his plane went down. She was then told that they would be in touch. She wondered what in the world that was all about.

Six weeks after the call from San Antonio, two officers from Hickam Air Force Base, Hawaii came to her home and notified her that her husband had been declared dead but unaccounted-for. So much for concrete evidence.

The final traumatic event, or so she thought, would be the memorial service. The Air Force provided an honor guard. As the seven young men and women stood at attention during the eulogy, she noticed one young serviceman had tears running down his cheeks. Outside the church after the service there was the military salute. With each crack of the rifles she felt like the bullets were piercing her heart. Then came taps and the Hawaiian Air National Guard flew overhead in the missing man formation. She thought of the poem "High flight" that he had loved so much. One line stuck in her mind. "He reached out his hand and touched the face of God." Then she remembered a letter she had received from the chaplain in Southeast Asia years before. The letter ended with "He is with God and God is with Him." She was sure that was true.

Almost thirty years have passed since that terrible December day. She has remarried and the children are all in their thirties. Her oldest daughter has taken over the reins of primary next of kin. Sometimes people ask her how long it took her to get over the loss. Her answer is "I'll let you know when I have." On December 1, 1995 Tom's status will undoubtedly still be the same. While she will never forget him, she has decided that at the thirty-year date there must be some kind of closure. The last Sunday in November she will have the altar flowers at Blessed Sacrament church in Honolulu dedicated to the memory of a loving husband and father. May he rest in peace. And may those of us left behind be at peace.

This is the story of part of my life. Thomas E. Reitmann, Capt., USAF (he was promoted to major while in the missing status) was my husband and the father my four children. We had seven years and four months of a wonderful marriage. His name is one of the 58, 213 on "The Wall". He has a marker at Punchbowl and at Hickam AFB near the Officers' Club. This story was written for an English Composition course I took in 1995. Tom is still in the KIA but unaccounted-for status. The Joint Casualty Division is still searching for his remains.

Carol Reitmann Sumner

Story by A. L. "Mike" Michael WW # 328

An Unforgettable Character

In late February 1967 I checked in at the BOQ at Nellis AFB with orders to begin training at the "Wild Weasel" school. I was excited at the prospect of meeting the fighter pilots that were reported to be the "cream of the crop" in the tactical forces. My flying experience had been restricted to flying as an Electronic Warfare Officer (EWO) in the Strategic Air Command (SAC) bombers. Although I was proud of my 1500 hours in the B-52 G/H it was mind numbing to sit seven-day ground alert, and fly 24-hour airborne alert in a continuous expectation of an unthinkable mission. I was anxious to get away from the checklists and constant standardization.

A young Captain in the room next door knocked and entered demanding an adult beverage. As I unpacked the Jim Beam he introduced himself as Sparky and told me he was here for Weasel training. He had been stationed at Nellis and had recently sent his wife, "old what's her name", home while he was in SEA. It was immediately determined that we would be in the same class along with seven other pilots and EWO's starting Monday. Sparky was full of information about the recently formed school and the work of the Weasels. He had flown the F-105D while TDY in 1966 from the base at Takhli in Thailand and had volunteered to go back. We spent the weekend visiting with friends of Sparky, telling war stories, drinking copious amounts of adult beverages and getting me used to the fighter pilot persona. I was impressed and in awe of my coming adventure.

On Monday the schools Commander, Lt. Col. Gary Willard, briefed us. He told us that the first two weeks we would be flying with each pilot primarily to familiarize the EWOs with high performance tactical aircraft and allow each student to get to know the others. At the end of two weeks we would decide the crew make up and then complete the training as teams. Our success as "Wild Weasels" depended on how well the pilot and EW worked together. In addition to Sparky (Capt. Billy Sparks), the pilots included such notables as Major Jim Hartney (the White Fang), Capt Chuck Homer and five high time F-105 drivers. The EWOs, nearly all volunteers, were from ADC, SAC Reconnaissance and various multiple engine aircraft crew positions. With obvious glee the pilots proceeded to make us ill with the gamut of maneuvering, low level passes, split-S and pitch-out.

It was a new world for me flying fast and being able to see where I was going. I was too busy keeping up with the airplane to get sick. Each evening we would critique at the bar or at one of Sparky's buddies talking of Pack Six strikes, MiG attacks and the dreaded SAMs. One evening we were a little late and I had to rush to keep a date with a lady that worked on the top floor of the Mint Casino. I was at an apartment, which was almost downtown. Being somewhat dazzled by the war stories and a little "confused" by the libations I decided to meet the lady at the Top of the Mint and we could continue to the "O" club as planned. I was in my dirty, sweaty flight suit but not deterred. The next day I was asked to report to the Commanding Officer along with the class ranking EWO, Major Carlos Lombardo. After seeing the error in my behavior I was dismissed along with instructions for Major Lombardo to see to it that I would "Go and sin no more". As Carlo and I were walking away from Colonel Willard's office he looked, rather sternly at me and said "Mike, can I use your car tonight?" I said "sure Carlo", and that was the end of it. I later learned that it was a standard briefing to subsequent classes to "Never go to the Top of the Mint in your flight suit"

I flew with Sparky a couple of times and confirmed that he was a superb pilot. He got my attention flying so low over the desert that the sand billowed behind us. At the end of two weeks our class met at the bar and announced our agreed crew make up. I had made the decision I would train and fly with Captain Jim Mirehouse who had agreed we would try for an assignment at Korat RTAFB. The Wing at Korat had a separate squadron of "Wild Weasel" crews where as the Wing at Takhli had crews assigned to the individual squadrons. This approach appealed to my concept of the mission. Sparky ended up with Carlo Lombardo as his EWO.

After the "marriage" I went back to my BOQ room. Shortly after, the door to my room opened and Sparky strode in and poured himself a drink of Jim Beam without saying a word. After he finished his drink he departed, slamming the door behind him. A moment later Sparky stuck his head in the door and said "damn Mike I thought we were going to fly together" Somewhat stunned, I replied "Sparky, I didn't tell you we would crew up, you told me you wanted to go back to Takhli, and I want to fly out of the 13th at Korat." He took another drink and said, "shit, I was going to teach you to play the banjo", and left without another word.

It might have been a mistake on my part. As soon as I arrived at Korat I was sent to Yokota, Japan to train for night low level bombing as a "Ryan's Raider" crew. My plans to fly as a Weasel in an all "Wild Weasel" squadron were dashed. Sparky became notorious as a Weasel leader. He and his "Bear", Carlo did great work together. Sometime later Sparky was shot down flying an extra counter in an F-105D. His rescue was the first pick up of a pilot across the Red river. When I finally got a phone call to him about midnight I found him at the club. After he understood who was calling in the midst of one hell of a party, he started blubbering, "Damn Mike the bastards grounded me".

The next time I saw Sparky was at the first state side practice reunion in Wichita. He was in his mustard Serria Hotel party suit with his banjo strung across his back.

Mike Michaels

"RYAN'S RAIDERS"

After Wild Weasel training at Nellis AFB and a rush movement to Korat RTAFB in May 1967, Jim Mirehouse, the Worlds Greatest Fighter Pilot (WGFP), and I found ourselves waiting to begin our first combat mission. It seems the pipeline was full and it would be a month before Brigadier General Chairsell, the 388th FFW Commander, had enough crews finish their "100" before he could let us start. Little did we know that Headquarters Pacific Air forces (PACAF) had other plans for us. Mysterious orders had arrived assigning five Weasel crews to additional training as night low-level penetrators in the little known and often misunderstood "Commando Nail" program. We had been selected to replace the dual pilot crews currently flying a modified two seat F-105F on night, single ship, low level missions into route package five and six. The concept was to match the US Navy's around-the-clock, all weather bombing efforts in the Air Forces' area of responsibility. General Ryan's staff at PACAF reasoned that rated navigators might be more familiar with radar directed bombing than the disgruntled fighter pilots who had been relegated to the back seat as bomb aimers. This was a stopgap measure by PACAF until the new F-111A, "Harvest Reaper" could join the fracas in early 1968.

Wrong —— The ex SAC Electronic Warfare Officers on the Weasel crews had little experience navigating aircraft much less radar bombing. However, "ours is not to reason why ——". After a few daylight training sorties at Yokota, Japan, we promptly dubbed ourselves "Ryan's Raider", started wearing a shoulder patch showing a large screw protruding through a caricature F-105, and began flying missions in mid July, 1967. Once around Mu Gia pass and Ron ferry made us think we were ready to go north.

On 19 July, Jim and I were fragged into a suspected staging area a few miles south of Yen Bai airfield in pack five. The plan was to cross the Red River at 1000 feet MEA, line up on the target by radar, and then fly constant airspeed and altitude to allow the toss bomb computer (TBC) to automatically release six 750's. We calculated it would take one minute and forty five seconds on the bomb run after we had identified the target and started the TBC with a "freeze" switch installed in the back cockpit. Jim and I had meticulously planned to reverse course after release using time and distance to work our way south through the mountains until we were clear of the SAM ring at Yen Bai. (Our confidence in the F-105 terrain avoidance radar system was at best skeptical.) Hopefully, our strike would cause enough confusion to allow another "Raider" crew to hit another target in the same area about five minutes later. Captains Chuck Horner (later Lt. Gen, AFCC, Desert Storm) and Dino Ragagli had planed their target approach from the same direction. A little touchy, but we figured we could get away with it if the timing was right on the button.

After a 2240 (10:40PM for you civilians) takeoff, a radar calibration run north of Korat, and a ticklish air refueling in the inevitable nightly rainstorm, we threaded our path through the karsts to find ourselves at the planned IP, on time. The run was uneventful until I activated the TBC from the back seat with a sure conviction that I was on target. About five seconds after I had "frozen" the problem on the radar, a blinding light emanating from Yen Bai locked on our aircraft. It was later revealed through intelligence that a Chinese AAA training detachment had a school at Yen Bai with about 25 old WWII radar tracking high intensity searchlights synchronized with 37/57 MM guns.

Jim started breathing hard as I tried to shield the intense light from the radarscope. Heavy flak was observed slightly above our altitude and on our course. As a novice and this being my first exposure to the "world's most heavily defended area since WWII", it looked like red rain on a Fourth of July evening to me. Our surprise and confusion lasted through the bomb run as we tried to concentrate on a constant airspeed and altitude. Jim reversed course to the left as I glanced at my map and discovered we were heading for high terrain. As I called for Jim to climb I noted a SAM signal on my radar homing and warning (RHAW) system with a launch caution light flickering. In the time tested fighter pilot tradition I was concerned, but not scared, and hopelessly lost. I knew we had to get back below 1000 feet where the SAM was thought to be less effective. The searchlights made it virtually impossible to see the scope well enough to find a pass in the mountains west of the Red River where I thought we would be safe. Suddenly the red launch light on my RHAW gear came on steady. I called for Jim to "Take It Down". His reply was "I'm going down you dip——" as he hit the jettison button to drop the external tanks. At the same time we could see the flak following our flight path. At the moment the searchlights went dark allowing me to direct our withdrawal by radar to an area that we could climb with safety from the SAM.

By now we were bingo fuel so we could not reflect on our good fortune. The SAC tanker crew, bless 'em, came north to meet us, passed gas, which allowed us to make a rather shaky landing after midnight at Korat. During debriefing we learned that Chuck Horner and Dino Ragagli elected to make a slight deviation from their bomb run to strafe the pretty lights at Yen Bai.

Jim and I made a full report to the awards and decorations guy about Chuck and Dino's exploits. As an interim measure we made our own award of a loving cup that I temporarily borrowed from a display case in the club. I was personally a little upset when Chuck refused to allow me to kiss him behind the ear.

Jim and I returned to Yen Bai several times and managed to knock out one of those searchlights with an AIM-9 one dark and lonely night along with some help from another "Raider" crew, the notables Major Larry Friedman and Captain Tracy Rumsey.

Of the five original "Weasel" crews that served as "part-time help" with General Ryan's Raiders, two crews finished "100" in November 1967, and one crew was lost during a night raid at Phu Tho, North Vietnam on 04 October 1967. Jim Mirehouse, Colonel retired, lives in North Dakota as a

Story by Billy Sparks WW # 330

The Guy That Landed With 7 Ounces of Shrapnel in His Left Lung Cavity

Major Bruce D. Stocks

Maj. Bruce D. Stocks, WW # 341, pilot, was the guy that landed with 7 ounces of shrapnel in his left lung cavity. He and Frank N. Moyer, WW # 338, EWO, caught a SAM just south of downtown Hanoi that exploded between 2 Weasel Fs. Russ Brownlee, WW # 359, Bear and Gus Gustafson, WW # 355, pilot, were in the other bird. Stocks lost his radio, among other things and was severely wounded. He chased Russ and Gus out until they bailed out over Channel 97 (a TACAN) on a karst in WAY north Laos) and then started for home. Moyer, his EWO, could transmit on guard only and set up a rescue. Bruce headed for Udorn and found a humungous thunderstorm over Udorn when they got there. He flew another 175 NM to Takhli and landed. He went to dearm and Dr. Smith came up the ladder and made him shut the bird down and evacuated him to the Hospital for emergency surgery. Bruce was flown to Clark and recovered OK. Bruce made Lt. Col early and was on the F-111 test team. He disappeared on a flight to Mobile and was found, still in the seat, in a swamp in Louisiana about 3 weeks later. The seat malfunctioned and killed both guys. He was a hell of a good driver and a better man. One of the strange facts surrounding his fatal F-111 accident was that Bruce's reputation was questioned in the press coverage of the disappearance of the F-111 since the aircraft had range sufficient to fly to Cuba. During the time it took to find the wreckage with the bodies, the press had a field day with a myth that he had defected to Cuba. Bruce was an Air Force Cross recipient. I am still appalled with that bit of Bull S*** from the media.

Bruce was one of the smartest and best people I ever met. He was a hell of a Wild Weasel and a warrior. He had a Masters in Aero and a PhD in EE. He was about as good as they get. Moyer lives in Albuquerque.

Billy W. Sparks, WW # 330

Story by Edward T. Rock WW # 185

Wild Weasel III-2 Memories

Wild Weasel Assignment

It was early spring 1966, Nellis, Air Force Base, Nevada; I was an F-105 instructor pilot, a newly assigned gunnery instructor. An old friend, who had just returned from Thailand where he was flying combat mission in the F-105D against North Vietnam told me about a mission he was on where the target was a Surface-to-Air Missile (SAM) site located northwest of Hanoi, the capital of North Vietnam.

The plan was for a low level approach to the target to avoid radar detection and when in the vicinity of the target the flight would "pop up" to bombing altitude, about 12,000 feet, locate the target visually, dive bomb to deliver their weapons and depart toward home, at very high speed and very low altitude. The mission went as planned except that when they popped up there was no SAM site to be found, or perhaps it was heavily camouflaged and it could not be located in the limited time available. The mission was unsuccessful. It turned out that this was typical of most North Vietnamese missile site attacks up to that time. In areas where SAM sites were easy to find, US forces were prohibited, by rules of engagement, from attaching them. In other areas the sites moved before they could be attacked, were dummy sites, or were so well camouflaged that they could not be found and attacked by strike forces in a timely and accurate manner.

Shortly after this I received orders for the Wild Weasel "anti-SAM" program and was to be a member of the second group of F-105 pilots and Electronics Warfare Officers (EWOs) assigned to this new mission. The program was still classified and we were told to report to a motel in or near Long Beach, California and our training would began in some old hangers located on the grounds of Long Beach International airport.

Training

I thought the training we were given was adequate. I just didn't know any better, no one did. We did the best we could under the circumstances, considering that there was almost a complete lack of robust tactical planning, tactics development, training and weapons development against the SAM threat. In retrospect I think it was awful, deficient in almost every respect. Low-level operations were then the accepted answer to almost every threat!

Training in Long Beach consisted primarily of some classroom lectures by retired, or at least former, Strategic Air Command (SAC) Electronic Warfare Officers (EWOs) and "flying" a simulator, which had Radar Homing and Warning (RHAW) equipment and a signal analysis receiver installed in what was probably supposed to be a replica of an F-100 cockpit left over from F-100 Wild Weasel training. The main thing I recall from the lectures was the capabilities and limitations of the Soviet Union SA-2 SAM system. The Radar Homing and Warning receiver displays were located in the front cockpit for use by the pilot and a signal analysis receiver and radar warning receiver and displays were located in the rear cockpit for the EWO. The "threat" radar signal would be displayed in direction by an azimuth strobe. When the strobe was located at the 12 o'clock position, that indicated the threat was straight ahead. If the azimuth strobe pointed to the left then the threat was to the left and so forth. The length of the strobe gave some indication of signal strength and threat range because a threat that was relatively close had a strong signal and a long strobe and a far away threat had a weak signal and a short strobe. The azimuth display was a small 3-inch circular display with rings etched on the surface. The outermost ring was called the "Ah Shit", "Oh Shit", or just plain "Shit" ring and when the strobe reached this ring it gave a good indication that you were the target and the SAM was about ready to shoot. However, a threat could still be close and the strobe short if the radar was pointed at some target other than you and the received signal was relatively weak. Generally you had to be in the main beam of the threat radar to have a long, strong strobe. An exact range to the threat could not be determined from the displays under any circumstances but an educated guess was possible. A "Dr. Pepper" was strobes at 10, 2, and 4 o'clock and indicated that there were three sites targeting you from three different directions.

In the flight simulator at Long Beach, CA we were instructed to put the azimuth strobe at the 9 or 3 o'clock position, fly straight and level, maintain a constant airspeed, and time the rate of change of the azimuth strobe to get an estimate of range to the emitter. For example, if you were flying at 540 knots and the angle changed 10 degrees in 60 seconds, you had traveled 9 miles and the angle change was 10 degrees. It could then be calculated, using trigonometry, that you were 51.8 miles from the emitter. This may have been a viable tactic for SAC reconnaissance but it was sheer madness for flying in a real combat environment where the enemy was shooting real bullets and real missiles.

It was stated that the SAM fire control radar could not track a target if the target was below an altitude of 3,000 feet above the ground. The reason given was that the target would be lost in the radar ground clutter and therefore it would be impossible to track an aircraft at "low" altitude. No statement was ever more wrong. In spite of numerous testimonials by combat pilots, both Wild Weasel and strike, Air Force and Navy, a realistic estimate of the low altitude target tracking capability of the SA-2 was never, and has never been, as far as I know, given by the Intelligence community.

We were paired with our EWO at Long Beach by some mysterious act or intuition of the folks running the training program. I was crewed with Capt. Curt Hartzell, an ex-SAC B-52 EWO. I was a bit concerned that Curt might not easily adjust to fighter aircraft considering the relatively highly maneuverable and high-speed fighter environment compared to the hulking, lumbering B-52. I shouldn't have had a moment's concern because he never complained or reacted poorly to any aspect of fighter aircraft flying in training or combat. The only thing was he often referred to me as "Pilot" which was a carryover from SAC standard terminology. Since I had been flying single seat fighters for many years, except when I was a flight/gunnery instructor, I definitely wasn't used to being referred as "Pilot" by another crewmember but instead by my name.

Flight training was at Nellis AFB, Nevada. A review of my flying record (Air Force Form 5) indicates that I had a maximum of 10 Wild Weasel training flights at Nellis before departing for SEA on 19 June 66. Training consisted primarily of flying against radars of opportunity since there were no SA-2 radars or replicas available in the Nellis area. We did use some simulated radars at two SAC Radar Bomb Scoring (RBS) sites but they were poor physical substitutes for the real thing. Most important is that they were not transportable or mobile and never moved, were not camouflaged, didn't shoot back, and were very unrealistic in appearance compared to enemy SAM sites. They were simply radar simulators located in the desert and easily observed as a few buildings at a remote location and could be seen for many, many miles.

I was provided with one or two AGM-45, Shrike, Anti-Radiation Missiles (ARMs), which I fired at a small, low powered and expendable simulated radar emitter located on a dry late bed in the desert on the Nellis gunnery range. Others in our class also were allocated AGM-45s to fire. Unfortunately the missiles did not perform well and most missed their target. Years later Dave Mount, who was then a Capt. in Air Force Headquarters (USAF/AFRDQ) in the Pentagon, told me that in those days missile-firing reports were being sent to the President. When President Johnson read that most of our missiles had not functioned properly, he sent a Presidential Inquiry to the Air Force requesting an explanation. Dave told me that the Air Force reaction was to remove the President from the address list of those who would receive future missile failure reports. I have tried to verify this story regarding the reaction of President Johnson but have been unable to do so.

The AGM-45 Shrike was developed by the Navy at China Lake, California. The preferred concept of employment assumed that the target was in a known location and was cooperating by being active, that is emitting its radar signals. The range of the AGM-45 Anti-radiation missile varied with the altitude and speed of the release aircraft and the angle of release. For the longest range a high speed, high altitude and high release angle was required. In the preferred concept, indicated in the Navy weapons manual, a route of flight was planned so that the target was approached at low level to avoid radar detection and at some convenient position an Initial Point (IP) was selected, the range and azimuth from the IP to the target was measured, and the time and distance from IP to weapon release was calculated based on the pre-determined weapon range under the given release conditions. If all went as intended after launch, the missile flew its planned range, nosed over, picked up the radar signal, homed on the radar and exploded when the proximity fuse was activated damaging or destroying the radar antenna and perhaps the radar van. Unfortunately NVN was not cooperative; we almost never knew the exact location of the transportable SA-2, and they were not going to emit radar signals for convenient attack. The Shrike was not a robust anti-SAM weapon. Its major shortcomings were a relative short range and the fact that it went ballistic if the target radar shut down after launch. Its nominal range was approximately 5-7 miles while the major intended target, the SA-2, had a range of about 20 nautical miles. Thus the release aircraft was always well within lethal range of the target when in range to launch the AGM-45.

There were a few members of the combat experienced F-100 Wild Weasel (WW-I) crews around the training squadron but most or perhaps all, were not checked out in the F-105 and frankly, as far as I can remember, were not much help. So training for WW III-2 was more or less the blind leading the blind. The two most important things that were never, or seldom, mentioned was (1) the extensive and very creative and successful use of camouflage by the North Vietnamese in helping to prevent the accurate and timely location and strike of targets, especially SAM sites; and (2) the lack of successful and effective counter-tactics.

The members of my class, Wild Weasel III-2, included eight two-man aircrews, sixteen airmen in all. They were: (Pilots/EWO Crews), Major Joe Brand/Major Don Singer; Major Glen Davis/Capt. Bob Marts; Capt. Ed Larson/Capt. Mike Gilroy; Capt. Bobby Martin/Capt. Norb Maier; Major Gene Pemberton/Capt. Ben Newsom; Capt. Buddy Reinbold/Capt. George Metcalf, Major Ed Rock/Capt. Curt Hartzell, Capt. Bob Sanvick/ Capt. Tom Pyle, Major Joe Brand was the senior officer.

Standing left to right: Capt. Tom Pyle (POW), Capt. Bob Marts, Capt. Norb Maier (shot Down on 2nd combat tour in 1972, recovered), Capt. Mike Gilroy (Shot down Aug 66, recovered, returned to action), Capt. Bobby Martin, Capt. Ed Larson (Shot Down Aug 66 - never flew again), Maj. Gene Pemberton (KIA), Capt. Buddy Reinbold (Wounded and returned to US). Kneeling left to right: Capt. Bob Sandvick (POW), Maj. Curt Hartzell, Maj. Ed Rock, Maj. Joe Brand (KIA), Capt. Ben Newsom (KIA), Maj. Glen Davis and George Metcalf (Transferred to EB-66). Missing, Major Don Singer (KIA). Photo courtesy Ed Rock

Combat

Six of these crews were selected by Major Brand to fly six F-105Fs Wild Weasel configured aircraft from Nellis AFB, Nevada to the 388th Tactical Fighter Wing (TFW), Korat Royal Thailand Air Base (RTAFB). Two crews, I, my EWO, Curt Hartzell and Bobby Martin and Norb Maier were sent on ahead by military transport. Our orders directed us to report to Snake School (Jungle Survival) in the Philippians enroute to Korat, but due to the urgent requirement for F-105 Wild Weasels, we instead were sent directly to Korat. After arriving at Korat in late June 1966 we were told that our group (WW III-2) would be going directly to the 355th TFW, Takhli RTFB instead of remaining at Korat as originally planned! Korat was generally known as the garden spot, or country club, of combat bases in Southeast Asia while Takhli was regarded as more like ghetto housing. I was not pleased by this turn of events. We departed Korat for Takhli on the earliest available military transport aircraft, a C-130 affectionately referred to as "The Klong". The six aircraft and crews arrived at Takhli on 4 July 66 and we started flying combat missions shortly thereafter.

The 355th Wing Commander was Col. William H. Holt, known as "Chrome Dome Holt" and/or Mr. Clean ("cleans your whole house and everything that's in it") because he was completely bald and had a very shiny head. One of our first assignments was to attend a meeting with the Wing Commander in which he greeted us and said a few words about the 355th Wing, our mission and our coming combat tour. The most memorable thing about the meeting was that Holt exploded in a temper tantrum and delivered a tirade directed at Buddy Reinbold when Buddy appeared to doze off during his remarks. Holt also told us that we had a 100% chance of being shot down and a 50% chance of being rescued. He was very nearly right as far as our group was concerned. I never heard from Col. Holt again, or any other wing commander at Takhli.

The Wing Deputy Commander for Operations was Col. Aaron J. Bowman, affectionately known as "Bo". I had worked directly for Bowman when I was assigned to the 35th Tactical Fighter Squadron, Itazuke Air Base, Japan. He had flown fighters in the Korean War and was kind of an old warhorse brought in to help the newer guys get into the war with confidence, and success. Unfortunately it didn't happen quite that way. Bo had a reputation, deserved or not, for not being able to find the target and was referred to by some as "Mr. McGoo", the humorous, blind and bumbling, but often extremely lucky cartoon character. However, it wasn't very funny, and you sure didn't feel lucky if you were drilling around in a high treat area with a mission commander who couldn't find the target while you were getting your ass shot off.

Some targets were just simply extremely hard to find regardless of who you were or what your level of experience. Large bridges, airfields, railroad marshaling yards and so forth were easy to find while others were extremely difficult to locate and identify. Two come to mind: one was a small petroleum, oil and lubricant (POL) barrel factory located near the northeast end of "Thud Ridge" about 30 miles west north west of Hanoi. The intelligence photos were so poor and the plant so small that the factory could not be found on the first attempt to attack and destroy the target. Another particularly difficult to find target in the Hanoi area was a small number of POL barrels in a trench and in a very high threat environment. You may be able to imagine trying to find and hit a bunch of barrels in a slit trench and risking 24 F-105s in the effort. Even if successful the return on destroying a few barrels of petroleum at the risk of losing even one multi-million aircraft somehow escaped me.

I was initially assigned to the 354th Tactical Fighter Squadron as a Wild Weasel Flight Commander. The Squadron Commander was Lt. Col. Don Asire. I only saw him once that I recall; however, I probably saw him on other occasions that I simply can't remember after nearly 40 years. Lt. Col. Asire was shot down over North Vietnam on 8 December 1966. He was flying as number three in a flight of four F-105Ds. The original mission was a strike against the railway and POL storage area at Phuc Yen. However, weather precluded the planned attack and the strike force was diverted to its secondary target. There are many confliction reports on just what happened to Don Asire. One source indicates that the flight was somewhere in the vicinity of Thai Nguyen when it was engaged by several enemy aircraft and that Asire was last seen as he dove into a cloud layer with a MiG-17 or MiG-21 enemy aircraft in hot pursuit. In this account it is alleged that USSR Sr. Lt. Vadim Petrovich Shchbakov, who is credited with six kills during 1966, probably downed Don Asire. It is known that Soviet pilots were used as "advisors" to the North Vietnamese and authorized to engage American aircraft during training or as replacements for North Vietnamese pilots who had been wounded or killed. In another account Don was shot down by AAA. The most authoritative source I have been able to find is from a member of his squadron at the time and he indicated that: "The common consensus at the time was that Asire was flying at a very high airspeed (which he really believed in) and became disoriented from the haze and glare off the rice paddies and crashed accidentally. Apparently Don Asire didn't make any radio calls that he had problems, had been hit, was evading MiGs, etc. before he crashed." Regardless, there was no reported chute or beeper. His remains were supposedly suddenly discovered by the NVN (a likely story) and returned to US control on 29 June 1989.

The 354th squadron Operations Officer was Major James H. Kasler. Kasler was a Korean War "Ace" (credited with six victories) flying the F-86, Saber Jet. During WWII he had been a B-29 tail gunner in the Pacific Theater. In the 354th he was respected by all, nearly worshiped by a few and mistrusted by some of the squadron pilots. I was concerned that he appeared reckless, probably trying to repeat as an Ace in this war as in Korea. Kasler was shot down by the North Vietnamese on his 91st mission on 8 August 1966 and spent the next nearly seven years as a Prisoner of War. AAA hit his aircraft while he was participating in the attempted rescue of another F-105 pilot downed near Yen Bai. When he was hit, the aircraft burst into flames almost immediately. He turned to the west but was forced to eject nearly right away, and was soon captured by the North Vietnamese. As a POW he endured years of torture and pressure and was a true American hero

The squadrons had signs throughout operations saying "Do Not Fly Below 4,500 Feet" which meant that you should keep your speed and altitude up and keep the aircraft moving in a high threat area to survive. I attended briefings in which flight leaders and mission commanders advocated low level tactics in direct contradiction to accepted survival operations of flying above 4,500 feet. They were by no means alone and many advocated low altitude penetration primarily to avoid SAM detection and attack. However, at low altitude you were within range of every threat imaginable, especially automatic weapons, anti-aircraft-artillery, missiles and aircraft not to mention sticks and stones. At medium altitude or above you simply were out of effective range of most of these threats. The SAM threat drove many to low altitudes where they were most vulnerable to most threats.

One of the things about the war over North Vietnam that has always exasperated me was that; in some respects, we were not a well disciplined force to the extent that such rules as "don't fly below 4,500 feet", "don't press the weather", "don't press the bingos", "don't make multiple on-axis strafing passes", "don't fly in trail", etc., etc. were regularly violated. Those "rules" were known by all, and briefed almost religiously, then violated time after time by flight leads who demonstrably knew better, with consequences that were predictable.

Our first combat missions were not Wild Weasel missions but strike missions! The 355th Wing decided that we should have some strike experience so that we would be better able to understand the local procedures and the strike pilots wants and needs before we proceeded on our own.

Despite the urgent need for Wild Weasels, my first Combat mission was in a single seat F-105D strike mission on 11 July 66 and the target was a large concrete highway bridge located northwest of Hanoi, North Vietnam. I think I was flying number two in a flight of four F-105Ds and our aircraft were configured with two 3,000 pound bombs each.

The mission was unremarkable except it was the first time I had seen the Radar Homing and Warning gear light up like a Christmas tree from all of the radars trying to track and destroy us with real bullets and real missiles. In addition each radar made its own peculiar sound. The SAM radar had a very distinct aural signature that sounded like a rattlesnake about to strike. The lights and noise were enough to scare the hell out of you regardless if the enemy was shooting or not. Soon enough we penetrated enemy air space, crossed the Red River and headed down the south side of Thud Ridge toward Hanoi and the target area. When we reached the end of the ridge and just about the time we went out into the flat land around Hanoi the mission commander called the whole thing off due to weather over the target. We diverted to our alternate, a road reconnaissance mission in Route Package I (RP1), the southern area of North Vietnam closest to the Demilitarized Zone (DMZ). Somewhere about the middle of the pack, the flight leader found a relatively small wooden bridge and we blew it to smithereens with our 3000 pound bombs. In reviewing my Form 5 (my Air Force flying record), I note that the next mission I flew was a Wild Weasel mission but out of the next several there would be three more strike missions in F-105Ds before all remaining missions would be Wild Weasel missions. On that first mission I didn't see a shot fired. That doesn't mean there weren't any; it just means that I was so busy hanging on that I just missed half of the fun.

In addition to the strike missions, two F-105F Wild Weasel crews from the 388th Tactical Fighter Wing at Korat were placed on temporary duty at Takhli to help us rapidly and successfully adapt to Wild Weasel combat operations. One was of the pilots was Rick Westcott but I have forgotten the names of the other(s). This also proved to be of little or no help. The weather in the high threat areas around Hanoi was not cooperating and most of the missions were weather cancellations or weather aborts at this time. Thus what few missions were flown were often in the lower areas on North Vietnam just above the DMZ and referred to as Route Package 1 or RP1. The main problem was that at this time there were no SAM radars located in RP1. In spite of this, we were declared combat-ready by our Korat helpers and sent on our way after about two weeks. I cannot recall ever flying any mission with the boys from Korat. In addition it should be mentioned that the 388th "experts" had been in SEA for only about four weeks longer than us "new guys".

In July 1966 there were 19 F-105s lost to enemy action and in August there were 19 more F-105 combat losses. July and August 1966 were the high water mark for F-105 combat losses during the Vietnam War. Wild Weasels made their contribution to these losses. During August 5 Wild Weasel aircraft were lost from Takhli and one from Korat including one Takhli bird that was so badly damaged that it was boxed up and sent to depot for repair. This left only one of the original six Takhli Wild Weasel configured F-105Fs and two of the original aircrews remaining at Takhli after mid-August 1966.

Due to the very limited number of Wild Weasel aircraft we were rightly considered a high value limited asset. During this time period we were always scheduled only for missions planned to attack targets in the Hanoi area. If for any reason the mission to Hanoi was cancelled, then the Wild Weasels were also cancelled. Thus, at this time, we normally flew on only the most dangerous missions and in the area where the threat was the very highest. I flew my first mission on 11 July and was scheduled to fly on every single day for the remainder of the month. However, I flew only nine times out of 17 scheduled. All missions on which I did not fly were cancelled for adverse weather in the primary target areas and the Wild Weasel flights were cancelled while the strike force went on alternate missions. I never aborted a mission for any reason. Flying only half the missions scheduled seemed to indicate that it would take twice as long as the regular F-105 strike pilot to complete the traditional 100 mission combat tour if in fact you made it through the full 100 without getting shot down. This turned out to be correct.

The Air Force was responsible for an area around Hanoi, which was referred to as Route Package VIA and was the most heavily defended area of North Vietnam. SAMs were first deployed in a 30 – 40 mile radius around Hanoi. Soon extensions of this air defense system were established along the northeast railroad and somewhat along the northwest rail line. These defenses continued to grow in number and spread throughout the time I was there. Eventually the NVN moved SAMs into the area just above the DMZ and at times could be found almost anywhere from North of Hanoi to the borders of South Vietnam. Mostly the North Vietnamese with Russian advisors operated these SAM sites.

The first 355th TFW Wild Weasel III-2 loss occurred on 23 July 1966, nineteen days after arrival of our Wild Weasel configured aircraft at Takhli. As usual the target was in the Hanoi area. The flight call sign was Drill, the Wild Weasel flight leader, Drill 1, was Major Gene Pemberton, pilot and Major Benjamin Byrd Newsom was the Electronic Warfare Officer (EWO). They were flying F-105F tail number 63-8338. Drill 2, F-105D tail number 58-1151 was piloted by Capt. Buddy Reinbold. Reinbold was one of the Wild Weasel III-2 pilots flying number two on the wing of the flight leader in a single seat F-105D as a strike pilot to help gain combat experience. Should a SAM site be found he would deliver his six general-purpose bombs on the target identified by the flight leader, Drill 1. His EWO, Capt George Metcalf, remained on the ground waiting for his pilot to return. Drill 3, was Capt Paul H. Dwyer from the 333 TFS, Drill 4, was 1Lt Jerry C. Smith also from the 333rd TFS, both were flying single seat F-105Ds configured with six 750 pound bombs each. Flying in limited visibility, in the Hanoi area, at altitude, the flight ran into a barrage of SAM missiles. The F-105F with Pemberton and Newsom on board was hit and went down almost immediately. Both Pemberton and Newsome ejected. During the ensuing scramble, Reinbold's aircraft (58-1151) was exposed to a SAM blast and he was hit by shrapnel from a proximity burst close to the left side of his fuselage. His aircraft received a total of 87 holes in the side of the fuselage. The blast was so severe and close that it blew off the ventral fin, engine gang drain, and the top of the fin and rudder. Buddy sustained injuries to his left hand and leg. After egress from the target area, he was able to rendezvous with a KC-135 tanker and in-flight refuel. Later, he was able to rejoin with his flight and flew to Udorn RTAFB where he made an emergency landing. Touchdown was normal except that vapor completely shrouded the left side of the fuselage, making it impossible to tell what type of aircraft was on the landing roll. The vapor was fuel emanating from holes in the damaged fuel cells. The aircraft would be repaired in Taiwan. After the repair was completed in Taiwan, Buddy's aircraft was returned to Korat where it was shot down on

26 April 67 by a MiG-21 and its pilot, Capt Franklin Angel Caras from the 44th TFS, was killed.

Pilots in Pemberton's flight from the 333 TFS, "Capt Paul H. Dwyer ("Drill 3") and 1st Lt Jerry C. Smith ("Drill 4"), ... showed outstanding judgment and dedication in this tragic situation. Following attempts to locate some evidence of the missing plane (63-8338), they were instrumental in effecting a rendezvous with the tanker." (355 TFW History, Jul - Dec1966, USAF microfilm NO462.)

As a result of his wounds Capt. Buddy Reinbold was returned to the US for further treatment and eventual recovery. I don't believe he ever returned to combat flying in Southeast Asia.

This one mission resulted in the loss of two Wild Weasel crews. Pemberton and Newsom were shot down and died in captivity or were KIA. Without a pilot, Capt Metcalf could not complete his Wild Weasel tour and he was transferred to the EB-66 Squadron at Takhli where he finished his combat tour as an EB-66 Electronic Warfare Officer. There were now six of the original eight crews remaining.

On 7 Aug 66 two more F-105F Wild Weasel aircraft were shot down over North Vietnam. Both were supporting the same mission, a strike against a railway bridge/marshalling yard on the Northeast rail line that led from Hanoi into China and was the main railway supply link with China and the Soviet Union. Capt. Bob Sandvick and Capt. Tom Pyle were flying F-105F tail number 63-8361 when an SA-2 SAM or 85mm AAA shot them down near Kep airfield. Both Sandvick and Pyle ejected safely and were captured by the North Vietnamese and spent the almost seven years as POWs. Sandvick and Pyle were assigned to my flight. I was the summary courts officer for Sandvick, and had his personal effects packed up and sent to his wife. Curt Hartzell, my EWO was the summary courts officer for Tom Pyle.

On the same day and supporting the same mission, and at nearly the same time, Capt. Ed Larson and Capt. Mike Gilroy were the crew of F-105F tail number 63-8356 that was hit by an SA-2 SAM. The cockpit was badly damaged when the aircraft caught fire and the 20mm gun ammunition drum exploded. They were able to make it to the Gulf of Tonkin where they bailed out not far from shore. The both made it into their life rafts and were being fired upon by mortars when they were picked up by an SA-16 Albatross flying boat in a very dramatic rescue. Ed Larson hurt his back in the bailout and never flew again. After a brief recovery period Mike Gilroy returned to combat flying and flew with various pilots to successfully complete his combat tour. (See "First In…Wrong Way Out" by Mike Gilroy in this book.)

There were now two of the original six Takhli F-105F aircraft remaining. The next F-105F Wild Weasel from Takhli that was lost was hit by AAA just behind the rear cockpit and caught fire. However, the pilot, Maj. Glen Davis was able to successfully land the badly damage aircraft at Udorn. The aircraft was so seriously damaged that it could not be repaired in country and was boxed up and transported to Taiwan for depot repair. I don't know if it ever flew again or not. There was now only one Wild Weasel- configured aircraft remaining at Takhli.

One of the replacement pilots Mike Gilroy flew with was then Capt. Merlyn Dethlefsen and on 10 March 1967 Merle and Mike were one of a flight of F-105 aircraft on a Wild Weasel SAM destruction and/or suppression mission. They were supporting the strike force attacking the major North Vietnamese Steel Mill and industrial complex (Thai Nguyen Steel Mill). Despite being damaged by AAA their actions resulted in rendering ineffective the enemy defensive SAM and antiaircraft artillery sites in the target area and enabled the ensuing fighter-bombers to strike successfully the important industrial target without loss or damage to their aircraft. Merle was awarded the Medal of Honor and Mike the Air Force Cross.

After about 45 days at Takhli only 25% of the crews (Rock/Hartzell and Martin/Maier) and one or zero Wild Weasel configured aircraft were still available for duty. I say one or zero aircraft because as I remember it we had lost all six of the original F-105F Wild Weasel configured aircraft. However, a review records indicates only five were lost and we must have flown the last one to Korat when we transferred there on temporary duty (TDY). Regardless, the remnants of WW III-2 were sent to Korat to continue flying Wild Weasel missions with the Wild Weasel III-1 group of about seven Wild Weasel crews then assigned to the 388th Tactical Fighter Wing (TFW), 13 Tactical Fighter Squadron (TFS). A review of my records indicates that we departed for Korat RTAFB on 23 August 66 and returned to Takhli on 24 October 66.

I remained at Korat for about 60 days, flying Wild Weasel missions out of the 13th TFS until new Wild Weasel-Configured F-105F aircraft were delivered to Takhli along with replacement aircrews. The replacement crews included pilots Leo Thoresness and Merle Dethlefeson, both subsequent Medal of Honor recipients and Jerry Hoblit subsequent recipient of the Air Force Cross (AFC). Jerry got his AFC 36 years late, but that's another story.

When I first arrived in theater and started to fly Wild Weasel mission the aircraft armament usually consisted of two pods of 19 each 2.75 rockets and the 20MM cannon with about 1000 rounds of ammunition. When and if I found a SAM site I was supposed to mark the target with the rockets and follow on attacks would be made by other F-105Ds usually configured with six 750-pound bombs each. The rockets would make a nice splash but would disperse in such a fashion that you could salvo all 38 rockets at the target and still not hit anything except the ground. Before long we received the AGM-45 Shrike anti-radiation missile. However, they were always in short supply and if you fired them in the morning there just might not be any available for the afternoon mission!

Surface to Air Missile (SAM) Site Attack

It has been about 38 years since the summer of 1966 and I simply can't remember most missions in great detail. However, some SAM engagements still are etched in memory. One SAM engagement that I remember vividly occurred when we were, as usual, flying down the south side of Thud Ridge toward Hanoi and about the time we reached the southern end, a SAM launch occurred. Three SAMs were launched, one after another at a spacing of about six seconds. I was the flight leader and I appeared to be the intended target. Our initial altitude was about 9,000 feet and when the missile launch occurred we ignited the afterburner and dove for lower altitude, put the SAM strobe at about the 2 o'clock position, and watched the SAM arch over and follow our descent to lower altitude. The first SAM exploded prematurely shortly after it arched over and was on the way down at a range of about 2,500 feet from our aircraft. The second SAM was following behind the first and arching down from above as we speed over the ground at very high speed and very low altitude, about 200 feet above the ground. I wasn't watching the airspeed indicator but we had to be going about Mach 1 or faster. The third missile was coming at us straight and level over the ground and going at a speed in excess of Mach 2 or more than 1300 knots. I had never seen anything move at that speed and that close to the ground. One missile was coming down from above and the other was level with my aircraft just above ground level. It appeared that both missiles were going to arrive at my aircraft at about the same time and I began to wonder just what maneuver I could make to avoid taking a bad, bad, hit. To find out if the low altitude missile was really tracking me I moved the aircraft up and down a few feet and watched the missile move absolutely in synchronization with my movements. You will recall that the SA-2 was not supposed to be effective against aircraft flying below 3,000 feet but here I was at about 200 feet (or less) and I was being tracked absolutely perfectly. The second missile fired and coming down from above exploded at a range of about 1,200 feet but the low altitude missile just keep coming until it ran into a small hill located in the flat land rice paddies that we were flying over. The small hill just stuck up in the middle of a flat field and could not have been more than 200 feet high at the most. The missile impact and explosion was really spectacular, it threw dirt and debris for a long distance, and just took the top of the hill completely off. I estimate that the missile hit the hill at about 10-20 yards from the top of the mound. I can still see the explosion in my mind even today. It was a miracle that the geometry worked out to put the hill in the flight path of the SAM at a critical moment.

MiG Engagement

I had several MiG engagements. Mostly the MiGs would make one pass and haul ass, but not always. That is, they would strike under ground control attacking from above at very high speed firing missiles and/or guns as they went through or approached their target(s) and just keep going down and away as fast as their planes would go. Defending against this tactic it was often necessary to light the afterburner, jettison your ordnance, turn into the MiGs, and attempt to get them to overshoot. If you jettisoned your ordnance, then the MiGs had largely completed their mission because you were no longer effective and you would be unable to complete your primary mission. If you had been through this type of engagement several times you began to realize that you could normally keep your ordnance and just turn into the attackers attempting to get them to overshoot and go on about your business because they would not stand and fight unless they thought they had a significant tactical advantage.

On one occasion my wingman and I were attacked by a flight of four MiG-19s when outbound from the target, which was located in the vicinity of Kep Airfield and near the northeast railroad. We had no warning and did not sight the MiGs until they were nearly in firing position. The next thing I remember is that my wingman, a very young Lieutenant and probably on his first mission to the Hanoi area, is screaming, "They're firing at you, they're firing at you!" I thought, "What the hell would you like me to do that I am not already doing." We had broken into the attacking fighters, jettisoned our external 450-gallon fuel tanks and had attempted to light the afterburner. Our externally carried weapons had already been expended. I didn't think the afterburner would light at first and I tried to accelerate as best I could at full military power and continue to dive and turn as tight as I could into the attackers. All of this was to little avail. When the MiG-19 and an F-105F are going approximately the same speed and in a turning engagement, the MiG-19 will win every time. The MiG was turning right with me and firing his cannon as he gradually closed the range with my aircraft and me. My wingman continued to scream warnings and my frustrations were growing. Eventually the MiG pulls up line abreast and is just off my right wing maybe 10 feet between his wing tip and mine. I can see the pilot in the cockpit just as clear as you can possibly imagine. We look at one another. I think of giving him the finger but instead I unload the aircraft completely, the afterburner finally lights and I accelerate away. I also was thinking of a last ditch maneuver which would put me behind the MiG in a firing position. I gave up on that idea when I thought of the three other MiGs in his flight. I knew I could get behind that MiG but at the same time I knew I would be putting myself in great jeopardy from the other three aircraft in the enemy flight. The MiG can out-turn the F-105 at low altitude but he sure can't outrun or out-accelerate an F-105 in full afterburner. The last thing I see of the MiG pilot, he is just gradually turning away to the right as I accelerate down and away. But it isn't over by a long shot. The next thing I hear is my wingman yelling again and this time that he is under attack by the same flight of MiGs. I look back and sure enough I can see one MiG in a diving attack just like he is in a gunnery pattern and my wingman is the target. All four MiGs are apparently taking turns firing at him one at a time. I immediately make a 180-degree turn still in full afterburner and head for my wingman and the flight of four MiGs. For whatever reason about the time I get turned around and begin to close on the action, they break off the attack and apparently head home, probably to Kep airfield. I rejoin with my wingman and we proceed east, feet wet, and to our outbound refueling rendezvous over the Gulf of Tonkin. Those MiG pilots must have been the poorest shots in the North Vietnamese Air Force and we were the luckiest pilots in the USAF.

There were many MiG attacks on the Wild Weasels as they preceded the strike force into the target area, or exited behind the strike aircraft. There were probably more MiG attacks against Wild Weasels than any other single group in the summer of 1966. Therefore, 7th Air Force decided to provide the Wild Weasel flight with close escort—a flight of fighter aircraft to help ward off the MiGs and perhaps have a few successful MiG engagements. 7th Air Force selected the Lockheed F-104 interceptor as the escort aircraft. The F-104 was originally conceived and designed as an interceptor against high altitude penetrating enemy bombers and was really not designed as a dog fighter or medium to low altitude fighter escort aircraft. I was the flight leader on the first mission where F-104s were assigned as close escort fighters. One major problem was that the F-104s were not configured with Radar Warning receivers and therefore had to rely on the Wild Weasels for any and all SAM warnings. The flight was uneventful through refueling, rendezvous with four F-104s from the 435th TFS, Udorn RTAFB, and crossing of the Red River heading southeast toward the Hanoi area. Curt Hartzell my EWO began to call out Ground Control Intercept (GCI) Radars, Whiff and Fire Can Anti Aircraft Artillery (AAA) fire control radars and also a SAM threat radar at about the 1 o'clock position. We alerted the other members of our flight and our escort to the threat radars.

The SAM radar was first detected shortly after crossing the Red River and before reaching the top of Thud Ridge. They would be on the air for a few seconds and then go off for a short period and then come back on, probably trying to detect our flight and wait until we were in the heart of the SAM threat envelope before firing. As we flew southeast the threat signal became stronger, but still had not reached the "Ah Shit" ring. However, I thought that they were getting ready to shoot and I called the flight and escort fighters to "Take it down!" which meant to dive to lower altitude and try to use terrain masking to shield the flight from the SAM threat. Very shortly after my "Take it down!" call, one of the F-104s was hit right behind the cockpit with a SAM. I never had an electronic indication of missile launch nor saw the SAM in flight. If more than one SAM was fired no one reported it. There was no chute and no beeper. It appeared that the

F-104 had suffered catastrophic damage and the pilot had no chance to eject.

The next mission, in the afternoon of the same day and in the same general area, resulted in essentially the same scenario and the loss of another F-104. That was the end of close escorts for the Wild Weasels. Probably the main cause of the loss of both aircraft on the same day and in the same area was the failure to have the F-104 configured with their own Radar Warning equipment. Trying to rely on another aircraft to provide timely and accurate SAM threat warning simply wasn't good enough and did not work.

Bolo Fighter Sweep

Bolo I, conceived by Robin Olds, the 8th TFW commander, is a well-known aerial battle over North Vietnam that resulted in the destruction of several MiG aircraft. However, Bolo II is never mentioned, and for good reason. I was one of the Wild Weasel Flight Leaders on Bolo II, but I did not participate directly in Bolo I. First, you need to understand the situation at the time, and the results of the first Bolo Mission then you will better appreciate the results of Bolo II.

During my first SEA combat tour in 1966/67 North Vietnamese enemy MiG-17, MiG-21 and occasionally MiG-19 aircraft were nearly a constant threat whenever flying in the Hanoi/Haiphong area. In 1966 the rules of engagement prohibited attacking enemy airfields. All enemy fighters were "Made in Russia" or "Made in China" so there were no industrial plants or centers that could be attacked to reduce the enemy fighter threat at the source. In addition, new or repaired enemy fighter aircraft could be flown in from safe sanctuary bases in China and returned to these sanctuaries nearly at will. Therefore, the only practical solution to deal with this threat was a well designed and executed fighter sweep that would result in an air-to-air engagement of considerable numbers of enemy MiG and American F-4 fighters. With a bit of luck the engagement would result in a large aerial battle and the destruction of a considerable number of MiG fighters causing a huge reduction in the MiG threat.

Past experience indicated that the US government would institute a bombing halt of North Vietnam during the Christmas and New Year's holidays. The North Vietnamese Air Force and their communist supporters would use this opportunity to increase their in-commission rate, reinforce their flying units, increase their training and improve their tactics and techniques with little fear of attack or other interference. This would result in a substantial number of MiG aircraft and well-trained crews ready for battle during the initial phase of any renewed bombing of North Vietnam (NVN). This would set the stage for a large air battle and the code name of the operation was "Bolo."

In late 1966 a typical bombing mission against NVN consisted of a strike force with 16 to 24 F-105D strike aircraft escorted by 8 F-105F Wild Weasel SAM destruction/suppression aircraft, and 8 F-4 Fighter escorts. The F-105Ds were the bombers and were typically configured with six 750 pound bombs on the centerline, two 450 gallon wing fuel tanks and one or two ALQ-71/QRC-160-1, electronic countermeasures pods on the outboard wing stations. The F-4s were there to help protect the strike and Wild Weasel aircraft from MiG attack.

Ordinarily there would be a total of about 40 strike and support aircraft in one strike package. The Bolo plan was designed so that it would appear to be a normal F-105 strike mission with normal fighter escorts. However, the entire force, except for the Wild Weasel aircraft, would by composed of only F-4 air superiority fighters. The F-4 would be configured with the ECM pods normally used by the F-105Ds so that they would appear to be F-105s, not F-4s, on enemy radarscopes. If the plan appeared to be successful and the MiGs were taking the bait, a code word would be broadcast over the normal strike radio frequency and the "fighter sweep" mission would proceed as planned. If the MiGs did not react as anticipated, if they did not respond by launching significant numbers of aircraft to intercept our strike force, then a different code word would be broadcast and the mission would be aborted at the discretion of the mission commander, in this case, Col. Robin Olds, commander 8th TFW.

In the original plan, the mission was to consist of 20 flights (80 aircraft) of F-4 air superiority fighters and F-105F Wild Weasel defense suppression aircraft. On the morning of 2 January 67, the weather over North Vietnam was marginal. However, it still appeared good enough to launch the mission. Aircraft were planned to penetrate North Vietnam simultaneously from Laos on the West and the Gulf of Tonkin on the East. Approximately half the force or about 32 F-4s each would penetrate from the east and the west. The plan was to form a pincer to close off any MiGs attempting to recover at Chinese bases. F-4s were assigned specific areas to sweep; areas where intelligence sources indicated MiG fighters usually orbited to intercept inbound strike forces.

A few aircrews at Ubon were assigned specific talks including Everett T. "Razz" Raspberry, WW # 89, who was tasked to train the aircrews in air combat maneuvering, a subject which very few had a clue as to even what it was! Razz decided that the easiest maneuver to master was the "roll to the outside" so that's what he concentrated on. As it turned out, all seven kills on 2 Jan 67 were attributed to the "roll to the outside".

It is particularly interesting to note that just a short time before this, I had been sent to Hq. 7th Air Force as an "F-105 advisor" for approximately two weeks and worked in the operations plans office that was responsible for planning all strikes against North Vietnam. I also attended the 7th Air Force Commanders daily briefing and at one such briefing I was asked to leave the room before intelligence information was provided indicating where MiGs most regularly orbited to intercept inbound forces. Now, as part of Bolo, this information was being provided to a wide range of interested parties. When I was asked to leave the room I thought to myself "Who the hell has more need to know this information than me. I am the only one here required to face the enemy MiG threat regularly but still I have no need to know and will not be told!!! I was never told for that matter, not then, and not later, not even when I was a flight leader on the Bolo II mission!

Bolo was the first time the F-4s had ever flown with ECM pods. They were flown into the F-4 bases by C-130 the night before and installed without a word from anyone. The aircrews were just told to turn on a specific switch and maintain 1500' separation. The electrons would take care of all the evil things that could happen. I guess they did.

On ingress they would use Thud terminology such as "Green 'em up," and tried to maintain Thud airspeeds — which was not easy for the F-4.

Not long after the fighters launched from their bases, the weather over the Hanoi/Haiphong area became worse than expected. The fighters entering from Laos were able to sweep their assigned areas but the aircraft entering from the Gulf of Tonkin had to turn back after several attempts to penetrate to their designated areas.

The MiGs reacted exactly as anticipated. There was a low overcast over their main base. They took off in elements of two and popped through the overcast to attack what initially appeared to be a normal F-105 strike force. MiG pilots were completely surprised. They had expected to encounter heavily laden fighter-bombers but instead they found primarily F-4s loaded with only air-to-air missiles and configured with the M-61 cannon, no bombs. The F-4s were ready for a fight and after only a few minutes they had shot down and destroyed seven MiGs without a single F-4 or F-105F Wild Weasel loss. The first operation Bolo gave the US the largest single MiG battle of the war and the greatest number of MiGs destroyed on any one day over North Vietnam.

As I indicated I was not a participant in the first "Bolo" operation but I was in the second on 23 January 1967. The initial MiG sweep worked so well that it was decided to attempt to implement essentially the same operation again. This mission was not led by Robin Olds, the 8th Tactical Fighter Wing commander but instead by another 8th Wing full colonel. I don't know which one.

Everything went very much like the first operation Bolo including the marginal weather in the Hanoi/Haiphong area at takeoff. Mission air-to-air refueling and ingress were essentially as planned except that the weather was much, much worse for the forces going in from Laos. The clouds were in layers from the ground up with individual thunderclouds popping up from layer to layer so that it was difficult or impossible to maintain visual contact between flights of aircraft and even between aircraft within the same flight. Even so the mission commander pressed on.

During the first operation Bolo, the North Vietnamese relied primarily on the MiGs for defense against our penetrating fighters and fighter-bombers because they did not want to shoot down any of their own aircraft with surface-to-air (SAM) missiles as had happened in the past. Therefore, only MiGs or surface-to-air missiles would be committed to the defense of one area at the same time. This time, as the F-4s and F-105Fs passed the Red River Northeast of Hanoi the code word was passed indicating that the MiGs had not taken off from their bases and apparently were not going to react to the American attack. However, the mission leader continued to penetration of enemy airspace. My EWO, Curt Hartzell was identifying AAA and SAM radar threats and I was broadcasting warnings that the enemy SAM radars were on the air and apparently getting ready to fire on the inbound forces. The enemy SAMs appeared to be too far away for us to launch an attack on their radars with our AGM-45 Shrike anti-radiation missiles. However, we were reaching the point where we would be within their range and they would almost surely begin launching missiles soon. This was ideal SAM operating conditions because clouds prevented visual acquisition of the missiles, the target aircraft was sometimes unaware that it was under attack until it was too late to take evasive action. Successful evasive action was all but impossible in weather and the firing site was safe from conventional attack because it could not be seen through the weather.

I was trying to keep my Wild Weasel aircraft between the enemy SAM threat and our fighters. However, due to the weather and trying to keep in a relatively clear area between layers of clouds where we would have some chance if fired upon, I was not always able to do so. All at once I looked up to my right and about 3,000 feet away I saw a single F-4 silhouetted against a thundercloud. Unexpectedly a SAM burst out of the cloud to his right, the F-4 received a direct hit and disintegrated in a ball of fire. I felt certain that the pilot had no warning and he could not have taken any evasive action between the time that the missile popped out of the clouds and the aircraft was hit. There were no chutes and no beepers. There was absolutely no chance that the aircrew could have survived, or so I thought until today! In researching this mission I found that then 1/lt. Barry Burton Bridger, pilot and 1/Lt. David Fletcher Gray, Pilot-Systems Officer (PSO), in fact survived the SAM hit! Their plane was completely engulfed in the SAM burst, erupted into flames immediately and fell in pieces beneath the cloud layers. As I said, no parachutes were seen nor were beeper signals heard, so Barry and David were carried in a missing in action (MIA) status. It wasn't until early 1970 that Hanoi acknowledged their prisoner of war status! Barry's family received their first letter from him in May 1970. They were released by NVN on 4 March 1973.

I had a terrible feeling of frustration, anger and regret that another aircraft and crew had been lost on a mission that should have been aborted when the MiGs failed to react and the weather was so bad that our pilots had little chance to respond properly to any attack. I also wondered if there was not more that I could or should have done to help prevent the loss. It was another day in a long war much like any other!

Shortly after the loss of the F-4, the mission commander did give the order to abort the mission and return to base or proceed onto the secondary mission. Tomorrow would be another day and another mission in the enemy heartland but there would never be another Bolo, at least not during my combat tours.

SAM Kill

On 12 October 1966 my EWO Curt Hartzell and I were assigned to an early morning mission to Route Package I (RP-I). We were still assigned, temporarily, to the 388th TFW, 13th TFS at Korat. We were a flight of one F-105F Wild Weasel aircraft. Flying one Wild Weasel aircraft by itself and no wingman or other supporting aircraft over North Vietnam on a combat mission was almost unprecedented but that's what was called for on that day. It was especially risky since there would be no one to report if we were shot down or had other problems that might require a rescue effort if necessary. Sending a Wild Weasel configured aircraft to RP-I was also very unusual because there normally weren't any SAMs deployed that far south and since the Wild Weasel was a very limited resource they were only sent on the missions that went to areas where there was a known SAM threat present.

Missions to Route Package I, the area of North Vietnam (NVN) closest to the South Vietnamese border, were generally considered to be less hazardous than those in other areas of NVN. However, the fact is that we lost just as many fighter aircraft in RP-I as we did in the higher threat areas around Hanoi, maybe even more. Pilots would have a sense of well being that wasn't really justified and would take chances that would never be considered in and around the Hanoi area. I knew one pilot who was shot down in RP-I and rescued who told me that I just wouldn't believe the barrage of anti-aircraft fire that was being directed at aircraft when they were flying in RP-I unless I was on the ground and saw and heard the tremendous amount of shooting taking place. In and around Hanoi you were normally fired at by 37mm, 57mm, 85mm and 100mm anti-aircraft artillery and it was readily apparent by the telltale gray or black smoke at the point of artillery shell explosion. In the lower route packages you were more apt to be fired at with small arms and automatic weapons and although these could be very deadly, they were not as easy to see as the larger caliber weapons when they were firing.

The evening before the mission Jim O'Neal (my Operations Officer in the 17th WWS in 1972) came up to me and said he had seen that I was on the schedule the next day for a mission to RP-I. He told me that he had the same type mission assigned that very after noon and an EB-66 electronic reconnaissance aircraft had reported detecting an SA-2 SAM signal coming from somewhere in RP-I. He had been sent over to try and locate the threat. He indicated that they had detected a few SAM signals but that the radar never remained on the air long enough to get a good location and that therefore, they had not been able to locate the site.

The next morning we took off and completed aerial refueling as scheduled so as to arrive in RP-I at first light. Sure enough shortly after arrival about the center of the pack Curt began to pick up intermittent SA-2 SAM signals! I could also hear the telltale SAM rattlesnake sound coming through the AGM-45 Shrike missile system. The signal was weak and did not register on the RHAW cathode ray tube except as a very weak, very short strobe or dot at the center of the scope. Curt would attempt to give me directional information on the signal and I would observe the AGM-45 Shrike anti-radiation missile azimuth and elevation indicator (normally the ILS needles) on the attitude indicator. These azimuth and elevation needles would respond to any signal detected by the Shrike by moving to give an indication of where the SAM signal was coming from in azimuth and elevation. When you were headed directly at the SAM the needles would be centered on the display just like they were when making an ILS approach if you were on centerline and on elevation. To help determine if you were within firing range we had a series of small, home-made cards that would help us determine the range to the emitter. For example, if you were flying at 9,000 feet and you had to put the nose down in a 10 degree to center the needles you were approximately 8.5NM from the emitter and probably out of Shrike range. If you were able to drive in toward the emitter until the nose went down 15 degrees with the azimuth and elevation needles centered, you would be at a range of about 5.7NM or within Shrike range to the emitter and you could fire the weapon. If the signal remained on the air, then you had a high probability that the missile would home in on the signal and at the very least destroy the antenna or at best destroy the missile fire control radar van and kill the operators.

By this time I had fired more than a few AGM-45s. Normally when you fired you noted the time and if the signal went off the air at a time equal to the time of flight of the missile, you probably had a kill. Usually you simply fired the missile, watched it as best you could, but lost it in the haze or when the motor burned out or it simply disappeared in the ground clutter. On one of the visits of Gen. Momyer, the 7th Air Force commander, I had recommended that they configure each AGM-45 with a flare that would burn brightly and enable the pilot to follow the missile to impact. This concept was used on the Bullpup missile with success. Momyer had made a note and shortly thereafter a program had been established to do just that. Instead of a flare, which supposedly made the missile unstable, the missiles were configured with white phosphorous warheads, which would cause a large cloud of white smoke or vapor when the missile exploded. During tests of this concept in the desert around China Lake, CA, the smoke could be seen for miles. In the jungles of SEA I don't think I ever saw even one target successfully marked with a white phosphorous warhead configured Shrike!

Today the signal came on and off for short periods and as it did we could gradually narrow the area where it was to be found but could not get a visual identification on the site location even though we had a good idea of the general area where it was located.

Finally when I was going in a direction away from the site, it came up and was located at out about seven o'clock position, and the signal was rather strong. I was able to turn quickly toward the site, get a quick check of estimated range, about five miles, and pull up and launch the missile. I was able to follow the flight of the missile but finally lost it just about the time it appeared that it would impact the ground at a very low angle. However, all of a sudden I saw the missile explode! When it exploded a very expertly camouflaged SAM site just popped out of the clutter and we could now see plainly what we had been looking for. The missile detonated right on the radar van and the signal went off the air simultaneously with the explosion. It was a very definite kill with an AGM-45. About this time the area exploded with automatic weapons and AAA fire. There were at least three batteries of anti-aircraft weapons firing at us from cleverly camouflaged positions.

We climbed to an altitude of about 12,000 feet and orbited the area keeping the site in view. Simultaneously I called the Airborne Command post and requested additional fighters be diverted to attack our SAM site to help insure complete destruction of the remnants before they could be moved to a more secure location. For this mission our aircraft had been configured with only the AGM-45 and the 20MM cannon. This was rather unusual as we nearly always carried the AGM-45 and two GBU-24 cluster bombs. However, these bombs were in extremely short supply at the time and this may have been the reason we were not configured with any other weapons.

Soon the Airborne Command post came back and said that they were diverting two F-104s for additional attack of the SAM site. These aircraft were configured with two 750-pound bombs each. The F-104 was never intended to be an air-to-ground weapons delivery aircraft but rather a high altitude interceptor. Nonetheless a small number had been configured with a depressible sight that could be used for delivery of air to ground ordnance. When the 104s arrived in the area I strafed the site with my 20MM cannon in a high angle-strafing pass starting at about 12,000 feet. As soon as we went into our dive the AAA opened up again with great vigor, but to no avail. My bullets hit in the target area and on pull off one of the SA-2 missiles on a launcher exploded. The F-104s proceeded to make their attack. I watched in disbelief at their bombs hit at least a mile from the target. I had heard of so called "dip bombing" but this was the first time I thought I might have actually seen it. Dip bombing is when the pilot simply dips his nose toward the ground and lets his bomb go with little or no attempt to actually aim at and hit the target. It was safe but not effective. I believed that with even a half-hearted attempt they could have come closer to the target than they did.

We had now reached Bingo fuel and we informed the Airborne Command post of our need to refuel or return to our base. They released us to return home. Upon arrival at our home base four F-105D strike aircraft were on alert and ready to go with pilots in the cockpit awaiting us to provide target coordinates and a better description of the location of the heavily camouflaged SAM target. After shutting down my aircraft I ran over to the alert aircraft and climbed up the ladder of the lead aircraft, showed him the location of the site on his map and gave him a description of the target, which I knew would be hard to find. The flight taxied out and preceded to RP-I and attempted to find the target to no avail. In the meantime 7th Air Force had dispatched a photoreconnaissance aircraft to the area to take photos of the reported SAM site. A review of the photos revealed not one but three SA-2 SAM sites in the same general area. The sites were located so that they could provide overlapping coverage of each other for mutual protection and they were all three protected by heavy concentrations of AAA sites. The North Vietnamese had made a major effort to infiltrate the southernmost area of North Vietnam with the SA-2 and gain air superiority.

The next day, 13 October 66, 7th Air Force cancelled the entire effort planned for strikes in the Hanoi area and diverted all fighter-bombers to Route Package I in an effort to strike and eliminate the SAM threat in that area. Because the sites were so well camouflaged, a fast-FAC (Forward Air Controller) was assigned to the area to coordinate and direct the strikes. The area was marked off into grids, the areas where bombs need to be dropped were marked by the FAC and the strike aircraft delivered their ordnance on the marked location. This procedure was intended to simply obliterate the entire area and insure that even expertly camouflaged SAM sites and AAA emplacements would be destroyed. However, post-strike photos revealed that the only SAM target destroyed was the one originally struck by me on 12 October!

As a result of my finding the enemy SAM site, I was put on standby to go to Headquarters 7th Air Force in Saigon to brief Secretary of Defense Robert Strange McNamara about the Wild Weasel and its capabilities. McNamara was visiting Saigon at the time. However, the next day the planned visit and briefing was cancelled with no reason given. I guess the Secretary was busy with more important things.

Ed Rock, WW # 185

Story by Bill Sparks, WW # 330

A Typical Takhli Mission In '67

Scheduling, planning, and even some Tactical considerations were different between Korat and Takhli because Takhli chose to assign the Wild Weasel crews to each squadron. Korat, instead, kept all of the Wild Weasels in one squadron. There are strengths and weaknesses in both systems; however, I am partial to the Takhli assignment and plan. That is based on my observations from 15 May 67 until 2 Dec 67 as a Wild Weasel and as a Strike pilot in the 357TFS. The reason for my preference is that I was able to fly with the same Force Commanders more often. Since the Force Commander was selected from each squadron, I was able to really get to understand those from my squadron and to help them understand how the Wild Weasels could best support them. The familiarity with the Mission Boss paid great dividends. Each squadron in the 355TFW had five flights instead of the normal four. E-Flight was the Wild Weasel Flight in each squadron of the wing. The E-Flight Commander was normally the ranking Wild Weasel and was also, normally, the Route Pack 6 (RP-6) Wild Weasel Flight lead for his squadron. I was E-Flight commander in the 357TFS as a captain and usually had at least one pilot and always had an EWO who out-ranked me. I did have the most combat and total Fighter time. This seemed to be enough for the 357TFS/CC to name me as his Wild Weasel Flight Commander. I kept the job until Carlo went to Saigon with Col White in Oct and I was assigned D-Flight. I scheduled my folks to fly on a daily basis by giving an updated list to my Operations Officer each day for the next day's flights. I led almost all of the RP-6 Wild Weasel missions given to the 357th. In addition to the crews directly assigned to each squadron, all Wing Staff Pilots were attached to a squadron for flying duties. My squadron, 357TFS, had Col Bob White, 355TFW/DO, assigned as well as two very good folk from Standardization and the Wing Weapons shop. Everyone was needed and everyone was used. We always seemed to be short-handed. We periodically were short of RP-6 qualified Wild Weasel Leaders in the wing. We would often be asked to furnish a flight lead, an element lead, or a wingman. This happened quite often early in my tour and I flew with all three squadron and almost every Wild Weasel in the wing. We did not fly with other EWOs. I would rather share my toothbrush than share Carlo. We flew as designated crews unless we were short of two-seat aircraft and had to fill in with F-105Ds. We later had some very experienced strike pilots volunteer to fill in when we were short-handed and had to use F-105Ds in the Wild Weasel flight. It worked extremely well.

Takhli and Korat both were scheduled for two Alpha Strikes each day. Alpha Strikes were those flown into RP-6. An Alpha package normally consisted of sixteen F-105D, single seat aircraft, loaded with bombs and four F-105F, two-seat aircraft, for the Wild Weasel support part of the mission. Each Alpha package also had four F-4C, two-seat aircraft from the 8TFW at Ubon or the 366TFW at Da Nang. Although there were variations of this scheme, over 90% consisted of sixteen F-105D strike aircraft, four F-105F Wild Weasels, and four F-4C MiGCAP. The targets, ordnance, refueling tracks, times, special instructions, and a Partridge In A Pear tree were all sent out daily in what was called the FRAG.

The FRAG, or Fragmentary Order, was a huge thing that arrived each day electronically to the Communications van sometime in the afternoon. If we were lucky, it would get it by about 1500 and if not, we were stuck with a late session planning for the early morning launch. It took about an hour for the CRYPTO folk (code breakers) to "Break" the Frag apart and hand the portion that applied to us to our Operations staff. On a normal day we would get a call that the FRAG was in and ready by about 1630. The responsibility for each Alpha Strike rotated through each of the squadrons in the wing. The squadron responsible for furnishing the Strike Commander also, normally, furnished two flights of four F-105Ds strike pilots and one flight of four F-105F Wild Weasel crews PLUS one spare for each flight. Each of the other squadrons furnished one flight of four F-105D strike pilots and a spare. That worked out so that any given squadron had two days with responsibility for an Alpha Strike in a row, and then had to furnish only one flight for each Alpha Strike on the third day. Of course, there were also missions assigned each squadron every day for Laos and the lower parts of North Vietnam. Maintenance would assign aircraft, including spares for each mission, as soon as they could figure out how many flyable aircraft were available in each squadron. They did an absolutely wonderful job and all of the ground personnel worked incredible hours to keep us in the air. You were usually were able to fly your assigned aircraft or, at least, a bird from your own squadron. When we had been hurt badly, we were assigned what was available from any squadron.

The planning for an Alpha Strike started as soon as possible after notification. The Force Commander would take those folks he thought he needed, or wanted, down to the Wing Operations Center and look at what was on tap for the next day. The first mission was usually a very early launch. Mission briefing for the crews was seldom later than 0400 and normally earlier with a takeoff time of 0530 or so. In order to be ready for the 0330 briefing, the dawn patrol was planned the day before. The Mission Boss—the Force Commander—would look at the target and the included instructions and ask for comments from his picked guys. The planners almost always included the Wild Weasel Flight lead and at least the Deputy Force Commander. Each Mission Boss had his individual way of planning and of obtaining advice. The good ones always asked for advice, especially contrary positions. The key to any mission was the quality of the planning. The best way to have the loss rate climb was to assume that anything was easy and that we could repeat what had been done before. We kept a BIG book that held a debriefing of each mission, stressing what was good and what was not for the mission flown. Smart folks really paid attention to the book. Once the Mission Boss had decided his plan for the next day, the Worker Bees with him would draw up a map, fill in the mission cards with the pertinent information, and hand them to the super staff in the Ops Center. They would prepare all of the materials for each member of each flight and have it all filed in slots for the 0-dark-30 briefing. The planning could take from one hour to several hours depending on the target, the thoughts of the Mission Boss, and the phase of the moon. Each mission consisted of a Primary Target, a Secondary Target, and a Tertiary, or dump, target. All were planned for each mission. When planning was over, the planners could go to the Officers Club and relax.

Carlo and I had a ritual that we went through for every trip to RP-6. We would walk the walls in the Ops Center. The walls of the planning area were lined with very detailed maps and photography. Several very detailed maps of the Hanoi area were kept updated daily ranging down to 1 to 20,000 scale. The photography was updated as often as possible and was to similar scale. If you walked slowly about six to eight feet from the walls, it was like looking at the ground from 4,000 to 10,000 feet altitude.

We would walk along our projected route of flight and visualize the actual ground. We would check for any markers that would lead to suspected SAM sites, locate the most numerous gun pits, and try to memorize what we would be seeing the next day. This would continue for at least an hour every time we planned a mission. Even if I had not been scheduled to lead, Carlo and I would walk the walls. I was not nearly as senile as I am now and could remember what I had visualized. We had points to hit in order to loft Shrikes at each site, references to find each SAM site, offsets in order to roll in the flight and bomb a given site, and, lastly, not be surprised if every thing turned dark brown. When you play 'You Bet Your Rear,' there is never too much preparation.

When the evening stroll was completed, we would repair to the Takhli Club for attitude adjustment. The Club was our home. If I had ever acted the way I acted at my lovely Lady's abode, I would have been shot. The CRUB was home there and it was a fairly rowdy place. Mostly it did allow us to let off what passed for steam and forget what was on tap for the next day.

My alarm would wail at about 0230 or so and I would be out of the trailer I shared with Carlo and walk the fifty feet to the back door of the Club. Breakfast was quick and we would be at the Ops Center in a very short time. The morning briefing always started with a time hack and a word from our favorite weather guesser. Stormy would pull out his crystal ball and give us his very best guess for the target area. INTEL would follow Stormy and then the Mission Boss would start his brief on the Targets. If we were lucky, the WORD would come in telling us which target we were going after. If not, the Mission Boss would brief all three. The Ops Center would deliver the WORDS. Each target had a designator word with an assigned code word for success, a code for SAMs, a code word for MiGs, etc. These designators were the WORDS. Every activity has its own silliness and that was ours. The Mission Briefing took maybe thirty minutes. Once we were committed, i.e. sent to a target, the Mission Boss would finish his pitch, and then each flight, including the spares, would head for their own squadron and conduct a flight briefing. The flight brief covered procedures, bombing tips, MiG look-out, RHAW (Radar Homing and Warning) items and/or what the flight commander wanted to cover. Most briefings were brief. The average briefing lasted thirty minutes or so. If you had an NEWBIE (New Guy), the brief could push the walk time.

Once the briefings were over, each crewmember tried to have a few seconds alone before donning his flight gear. When the flight was suited up, the squadron Pie Van would drive you to your aircraft. By the time you had put on your G-suit, helmet, survival vest, guns, knives, parachute, survival radios, lucky charms, several baby-bottles full of water, etc, you had added about ninety pounds to your weight. The Crew Chief would meet you with the aircraft forms and hold your flashlight so you could read them and sign the release. Preflight was normal given the darkness and it was very normal to have a flight line supervisor show up and follow you around. This was their way of showing you and the Crew Chief that they cared about each pilot. I have never seen better maintained aircraft anytime, anywhere. I can't say enough about our wrench-benders. They worked incredible hours and gave all of their effort to the aircraft. Start-engine time was when the pace really started to increase. We used a big shotgun shell-like charge about the size of a gallon jug to start the big bird. Black smoke would roll and the engine would wind up in about thirty seconds. All checks followed in sequence and about 95% of the time, all five in a flight would be ready to taxi in sequence. The Alpha Launches were called Elephant Walks by the folk. The flight line would go from silence to bedlam in less than a minute. The first aircraft to taxi were the five or six KC-135 Tankers (Boeing 707 full of gas) for a takeoff about 20 minutes before the fighters. The last two flights in the Strike Force would taxi first, followed by the Wild Weasels, and then the Force Commander and the #2 flight. We would have all twenty-five F-105's following each other like a circus parade out to the arming area at the takeoff end of the runway. Weapons were armed and the four primary birds for each flight would take the runway together. Run-up was followed by single ship takeoffs at 10-second intervals. The burner plumes of each Thud lighted the night as it accelerated to takeoff speed. As soon as one flight took off, the spare for that flight taxied to the far end and sat in the de-arming area until released by his flight leader. The next flight would pull into the arming area and the cycle would continue.

After all the Force was launched, we would head to the Refueling assembly point. The refueling tracks were named for colors. The one used most often for trips to Hanoi was Green Anchor. Green track ran from about 180 miles north of Takhli into northern Laos. The Anchors were the ends of the tracks. The KC-135s would join up with the low cell of three leading them at about 17,000 feet altitude. Each aircraft in the cell was stacked up 500'. The high cell took off first and was based at 19,000. The low tanker cell refueled the Wild Weasels on the lead tanker, the Force Commander's flight next, second flight next. The high cell was only about 5 miles in trail and refueled the third flight, forth flight, and the MiGCAP. Each flight joined with its tanker and initially took only about 1,000 lbs. of gas just to check the system. Occasionally we would take two or four spares along to the end of the track where, if no one needed a spare, they were released to a mission in Laos. About forty minutes prior to our drop point, I would start the refueling cycle. We always refueled Lead, #3, #2, and #4, in that order. It takes five or ten minutes to fill up from the airborne gas station and the order cited insures that the wingman have the most fuel at drop-off. Wingmen always use more fuel than the leader or #3 since they have to maneuver more to stay in formation. After #4 finished, I would jump back on and top off, followed by #3, #2, and #4. We would continue this dance at shorter and shorter intervals until we were only taking about 100 to 200 lbs. We could hook up, sip a bit, unhook and have the next guy on the boom at less than 30-second intervals. When we hit the drop point, Barracuda always had maximum fuel in every bird. There is no such thing as too much fuel.

When we dropped off the KC-135, the Mission really started. Up until then, there was always a chance that you could be recalled or diverted. After drop-off, you were committed to go Downtown. The Wild Weasels were supposed to be "First in and Last out" on every mission and we were, with few exceptions, since it was best for the Force to have us out in front and sniffing for SAMs. The MiGCAP worked best when they trailed the Strike Force by five to ten miles. The distance that the Wild Weasels would be in front depended on several factors. How many MiGs were we to expect? What was the weather? How obstreperous were the SAMs going to be? How good were the Wild Weasel Crews? What did the Mission Boss want? All of these things had been thrashed out in the planning phase, and the agreed distance had been decided. The sixteen-ship Strike would form up in a gaggle of four separate flights that actually were a single jamming package. Each flight flew with all of the aircraft about 750' apart (no less than 500' and no more than 1000'). This allowed the jammers to overlap each other and create a huge blob of jamming coverage on the enemy radar screens. The Force Commander would fly as smoothly as possible since all four flights were cueing from him. The #2 flight would move into position about 1500' out and almost line abreast from his lead. His wingmen would fly the same formation as the lead flight. #3 flight would fly in trail about 2000' from lead and the #4 flight would fly behind the second flight. We called it The Gaggle and even though it worked and cut down tremendously on SAM losses, we still hated The Gaggle. It was very hard to maneuver and really cut down on our ability to look around for attacking enemy fighters. The clumsiness of the formation caused us to fly in straight paths more than anyone liked. Since there is really no free lunch, we did the best we could and flew the Gaggle since it did keep down the losses from SAM missiles. The Wild Weasels didn't carry any jammers because they would jam our receivers and we would be blind to the threats. Think of it as having a very sensitive listening device that can hear whisper at 80 miles and then having a Rock Band start to play ten feet away. We only existed to protect the Strike force and couldn't do it if we used the jamming pods. The Strike package would be joined up in the briefed formation with the Wild Weasels in front and the MiGCAP in trail and head for the Barrel.

As we crossed into North Vietnam we would "Green 'em up, Music on." When the gunnery switches were ALL set to dispense ordnance, the station buttons would light up Green i.e. "Green 'em up." The jammers were a kind of music and we always wanted to be to be escorted into the Barrel by a band. The normal distance for the Wild Weasel Flight was five to ten minutes ahead of the force. This allowed us to root around and stir up the SAMs. Once we got them on the air, we could play games with them and place ourselves in position to best cover the Strike package. We needed to be between the Force and the main SAM threat when the Force broke formation and started their dive bomb runs. They were very vulnerable at this time since a single jammer didn't help against the SA-2 system. They needed all the help they could get until they were able to get back into overlapping jammer formation. Another trick the bad guys tried was to fire missiles, especially from behind the Force, and try to get them to break formation. By being several minutes in front, the Wild Weasels could also give a weather report to the Force Commander. An accurate weather report would allow him to change the direction of attack, change altitude, or even abort the mission if the weather was really foul, before getting into the nest of SAMs that lived in the Hanoi area. The real high threats started at the Red River. Once past the Red River, the SAMs and guns multiplied at a great rate. The area around Hanoi, the Barrel, had over 10,000 37MM and larger guns, up to eighteen SAM sites, and two MiG Bases. This was in an area about thirty miles in diameter, about the size of the Las Vegas valley. It was a bit like being in hell with your back broken. As we approached the pool table flat ground near Hanoi, the Wild Weasels would double back and set up a much closer coverage of the Force. The MiGCAP would move out of trail and cover from a flanking position. The radio would get very noisy if we weren't careful and radio discipline was always a problem. One of the jobs for the Wild Weasels was to "Call Threats." The EWOs in each Wild Weasel would keep a running commentary about the electronic threats around us and discriminate valid missile launches from spurious ones. They could tell if the indication was valid, where it was coming from, and who was being fired at with a fair degree of accuracy. Calls of "Shark Force, disregard the Launch Light; Barracuda, heads up, it's at us" were common and helped the Strike Force when they were at their most vulnerable. The Wild Weasels would try to have at least two Shrike Anti-Radiation-Missiles launched at the SAM sites that were the worst threat to the Force during their dive bomb run. The Shrike homed in on the Radar energy from the SAM Radar. If the SAM driver kept emitting in order to guide his missile, the Shrike would hit his antenna. To stop the Shrike from hitting him, he had to shut off all power to his radar and abandon the missiles in flight. Very seldom did the SAM site stay on the air and risk both their radar and their own rears. If we could find a SAM visually and if the situation allowed us, the Wild Weasels would dive-bomb it using our cluster bombs. It took only one of the eight CBU's we carried to total the site. They did not want that to happen, so they were very cautious. The whole idea was to make the SAM drivers nervous and shaky. When the Strike Force rejoined and started out, the MiGCAP would fall in a staggered trail to cover them and the Wild Weasels would trail every one out of the barrel. Happiness was re-crossing the Red River.

The trip home was much easier since we were almost impossible to chase down from behind and the Wild Weasels were in position to hammer any SAM stupid enough fire at the Force. The tankers would be waiting at Green Anchor Extend in Laos with fuel for anyone who needed it. We would climb to a good cruising altitude of about 30'000' where we used much less fuel and it was cold. When we were in RP-6, we normally kept the air conditioning system shut down to inhibit fire and smoke if case of a hit. The cockpit temperature would be well over 120°. We were expending energy at a great rate, drenched with sweat, and everyone had a mouth full of cotton as we crossed the Red River. Happiness was the cold water behind the headrest of the ejection seat. The 450 miles to Takhli was very easy and allowed time to determine what had happened that was good and what could be done better the next day.

The entire Force of twenty F-105s would arrive at home base at nearly the same time. The ground crew all would stop and count the birds as we came down initial and broke for landing. If they counted all of us, they were very happy; if we were shy of that number, the faces that came up the ladder were very grim. The ground crew took every loss as a personal affront. We were always marshaled into out of and into the revetments with a salute and a big grin. The Crew Chief would hook the ladder onto the cockpit and almost run up to hand us a cold washcloth and a very welcome cold beer. They would bring up our Aussie Outback hat and take the helmet. Their first question was about the mission and the next was, "Can I turn her around?" We would go to maintenance to debrief the aircraft for any discrepancies and then head for the squadron and rack our flying gear. As soon as possible we went to the INTEL shop at Wing Ops and sat through a detailed briefing. The Force Commander would normally have the Strike Flight leaders and the Wild Weasel lead meet him for a very quick debrief and then we would "Put It In The Book" for the next planning session. A debriefing at the squadron followed for each flight to determine how we could do better and to ensure that anyone who had messed up learned not to do THAT again. After this last debriefing, the Mission was over and we could go to the bar. The Mission really lasted about a day for the Force Commander and the planners. It was a short ten hours for the line jock that flew #4. No hill for a stepper.

The next day, we would do it all over again. In June of '67, I flew 24 Wild Weasel combat sorties and was scheduled every day. Six missions were canceled for weather and I led on 22 of the 24 that went. I had 18 sorties in RP-6 of which I led 16. In my spare time, I flew 7 test hops. I logged 107.5 hours that month. I had never previously gotten over 40 hours in a single month in my life. The typical Thud Driver at Takhli was tired and needed rest. To quote Tom Kirk, Commander of the 357TFS, "All you have to do is hurl your butt at the ground 100 times, and then you can go home and peck crap with the chickens." That summed it up as well as anything.

Bill Sparks Once known As Barracuda

Story by Clearance Dick, ECM Technician

Training, Working, Living Conditions, Snakes, RATS, Inventions

August 1966 with orders in hand and gamma globulin (GG) shot, I moved down the hall at Keesler, AFB, Mississippi from an office to the room where a class of fifteen men attended a five-day crash course on the IR-133 signal analysis receiver and the AN/APR-25/26, Radar Homing and Warning (RHAW) Wild Weasel equipment. The assignment was Takhli Royal Thai Air Base, Thailand, arriving on 13 December 1966. The aircraft parking area was being widened and lengthened. The small circular wagon wheel type parking arrangement left over from the old Japanese base in World War II was being filled in with concrete. The administration offices, dispensary, post office, Airman's chow hall were all located in one large building #1.

The NCO Club was the NCOs' source of meals since they were not allowed to eat in the Airman's Dining Hall. The choice of food left a lot to be desired. The No Hab (no have) menu was the usual fare. It was not unusual for the little Thai waitresses to repeat "no hab, no hab" several times when ordering. In addition to the No Hab, we had to use plastic silverware, which would not work for me when eating meat. In the village of Takhli was an Air Force approved eating-place called Charnes's restaurant. Twice a week several of us would dine there eating steak smothered in onions and peppers, cooked over charcoal. It was good even if it was water buffalo, and they had real silverware!

Before leaving the states I had been paid a clothing allowance for Jungle fatigues and combat boots. When clearing through finance the clerk wanted to pay me for a clothing allowance. I informed him I had received it. He was sort of indignant and insisted on going by the record so I was paid again. A week or so passed when supply notified our section that some of us were due a jungle issue....... so the acronym SNAFU (Situation Normal, All F—— Up) held true to military tradition.

The Takhli Armament and Electronic (A&E) maintenance shops were along the flight line and were of the temporary kind with boardwalks everywhere. One in particular was elevated leading to building one.

Several months later there was no question why they were elevated. The Monsoon season started in mid-April. The hooch was screened in with fixed louvered shutters to prevent the direct sunlight, but was of little help when the monsoon rain came. An old Sergeant told me when you see those black clouds building at about a sixty-degree angle from where you stand, go to the hooch and wrap your bed in plastic because it will rain through the hooch. I had been watching the clouds build for several days until they were as he said. I used the pickup to hurriedly go to the hooch and wrap my bed. That night when I had finished my shift I found my bed dry but the interior of the hooch was filthy. All the dust that had accumulated was washed down upon our beds and floor. There were four of us to a hooch; my bed was the only dry one. Monsoon winds drive the rain horizontally at a fierce rate. It rains so hard and fast that the water because of the flat terrain does not drain away. The temporary boardwalks sometimes floated away. The permanently built walkway from near the flight line to building one, Officers' Club and the NCO Club were elevated in places to two feet above ground level. The standard issue was a flashlight with a swivel holster. After the rain, the snakes would crawl to high ground; this is where the flashlights came in handy.

When the rains came it was like clockwork. A minute or so later each evening, all work would cease on the flight line for the duration of the storm that would last for about an hour. When the rain stopped, it would be abrupt and work would resume. Small silver fish would be stranded on the flight line by the hundreds. It rained every night for several weeks. Each evening the fish would be everywhere on the flight line.

One other notable aspect was the constant noise of the Diesel generators each shop had for electricity. The Thais did not have the ability to handle the required power demand and did well to supply the living quarters; even then one-half the hooch would at times be with out electricity. I thought this was strange until I noticed it was 220 volts and one leg was wired to each side. Several months later a power plant was built and underground transmission lines were buried. One night a large stretch of cable disappeared out of an uncovered trench. From then on the trench was covered as the cable was laid and if the trench had to remain uncovered, an auxiliary light was borrowed from Ground Power and guarded.

Getting acquainted with the operation and responsibilities was normal, but somewhat different and of course there are those that are always fond of pets, mostly the unusual kind. The screen door to the rear entrance of the shop had a boardwalk and along side were the "fly away kits" (kits, on wheel and in aluminum bins, of parts used to maintain the aircraft armament and electronic systems). On my way to check their contents I heard a rattle and then something jumped on my back. It startled me for a moment. When I got back to the shop I asked whose monkey it was and of course the owner had left it to the shop when he shipped out. In looking around there was a cage near A&E where a large Python was kept. A few days later someone had placed one of those black Thai chickens (which looked more like a crow than chicken) in the cage and the thing was hysterical. A few days later I was to pass the cage when I noticed the chicken peacefully sitting on the snake's back. Among the various shops was a Central Latrine. This particular Latrine should have been placed in the Air Force Museum at Wright Patterson Air Force Base. There was hardly a vacant spot on the walls where names, addresses and, of course, some very enlightening poems were written.

Having cleared in, the Non-Commissioned Officer in Charge (NCOIC) of Electronic Countermeasures (ECM) first assigned me to the night shift. The Sergeant I was replacing took me for a tour of the flight line. The first thing I saw was two GIs carrying a large Python. It must have been ten or twelve feet long. We toured the flight line and I saw it as a very busy place, as a beehive of activity. In my rounds I met the Line Chief and I asked him if there were any problems with ECM that I could help improve or resolve. His concern was with the time it took to load ECM pods and the sharing of the MJ1 weapons loaders or "Jammers" with the armament personnel. As a result, pod cradles were built that required no tools for the changeover, requiring only ten seconds to install on the jammer. [Editor's note: The MJI jammer had a lift platform or table that the various adapters were bolted to. The adapter Clarence designed eliminated the use of bolts and it was locked into position by hand quickly. Before, tools were required and were time consuming. It could be put on the lift table in 10 seconds.]

Each night I would eat at the NCO club and on the way I would go through a storage area that a Thai guarded. The first time coming back from the club this Thai guard was saying a distasteful word. I could not figure out why. I told the men at the shop what he said. I never heard such laughter to learn it was a F. you lizard.

The Quick Reaction Capability QRC-160 ECM pod had been in use since October. Every mission three to five pods failed. The RAT (Ram Air Turbine) that was turned by a propeller and located on the pod nose produced the electricity for the ECM transmitters. Although the rpm of the generator was controlled by an rpm governor clutch, the bearing would still seize up. My opinion is these were never designed to be used on a fast airplane like the F-105. The RAT was a depot item, restricted to remove-and-replace only. We were always short on pods and had to use all the ingenuity we could muster in order to provide the needed amount. In order to expedite the turn-around time, an ECM man would meet the plane beyond the de-arming and taxi area where the pilot would give a thumbs up/down. The pod would be tagged with a red flag to identify it as a malfunction. At the shop those flagged pods would be given immediate attention. Before the pods could be returned to the aircraft, each had to be thoroughly gone over and output frequencies settings checked or changed to fit the mission requirement. Supply had a parts expediter assigned to the POD shop. He had a direct line to the depot where the parts were sent to Takhli via the fastest means available. When an F-105 had to land at another base, a C-47 cargo aircraft assigned to Takhli would go after the pod.

In January of '67, Robin Olds had a plan, which required borrowing pods from Takhli. We were required to send a pod trailer of ten pods and two men to Da Nang. They canceled because of weather and our pods and men returned that evening.

The ECM pod reliability situation would not improve and at best we were treading water so it was decided to make a study to see if aircraft power could supply the pod. Our ECM technicians with the help of the Electric shop were permitted to modify one aircraft. The RAT propeller was removed and replaced with aircraft power and a combat test mission was successful. A second aircraft was modified and the RAT removed to check the Center of Gravity (CG). No appreciable negative effects were determined. A radome was made to cover the front of the pod. Later on, after the modifications were proven successful, a Depot team arrived and began modifying the F-105s. ECM continued to modify planes and even assisted the Depot Team for a short time. At the start we as well as the pilots were hampered by the lack of sufficient pods. As time progressed, so did the supply of improved pods.

For the maintenance technician, the APR25/26 RHAW gear was very reliable with infrequent Cathode Ray Tube (CRT) azimuth warning display replacement. Occasionally attention was required when failure occurred from flying too close to SAMs, other radars, or picking up stray aerial Foreign Object Damage (FOD).

Receiving multiple signals on the APR25/26 made it difficult to identify valid SAM launches. "Bear" Tom Wilson visited the shop and talked with Welden Bauman. Working together, Bauman devised a circuit which would show only the strobe associated with the true launch signal. Bauman's improvement was well received by the pilots and Bears. (Note "Bear" was a term of endearment for the Wild Weasel Electronic Warfare Officer!)

In the early months of '67, someone decided to try an experiment with a chaff bomb. ECM loaded up chaff in a leaflet bomb and it went north. We were told it was dropped by tossing it. This experiment was the first and last with unknown results to ECM, other than we got their attention. [Editor's note: Chaff bombs were used again in 1972 along with pod dispensed chaff. The chaff bomb was used to provide a vertical chaff column in conjunction with the horizontal chaff corridor from the ALE-38 chaff dispenser.]

The on-board dual track Combat Event Recorder was the most interesting of the equipment we maintained. It was the technician's chance to hitch a ride with the "Wild Weasel crew." One tape I listened to I shall never forget. A pilot had been shot down and was on a hillside in North Vietnam. For some reason his rescue had been denied. It was an afternoon mission; possibly it was too late to mount a rescue. The downed pilot could see the Vietnamese looking for him and he was frantically asking to be rescued. There must have been several planes in the area and brief words of encouragement were being spoken to him. His last words were "It is too late; they are here now." I never learned his name or if he was released from the "Hanoi Hilton." To know he came home would be gratifying to me. Some tapes were a little amusing such as the one from a "Wild Weasel" when I heard "Do you see all those tracers on our left, must be a million"...Reply... "Have you looked to your right?"

We would remove the tape to the shop where it was saved and degaussed if not called for. We were doing our job and minds seldom dwelled on the

Story By Paul Chesley WW # 154 and Weldon Bauman WW # 819

The BAUMAN MOD

Paul Chesley Writes:

The quest for better weaponry is constant and many seek solutions people from many walks of life. On one occasion, a bit of genius by an obscure low level electronics warfare maintaince technician gains him instant fame and his "solution" is incorporated in all applicable weapons systems. The Bauman modification to the APR-25/26 Radar Warning System installed on Air Force fighter aircraft in 1967 saved many lives and these features are still used in all Threat Warning Systems currently employed on all US combat aircraft.

The early Radar Warning Systems were cobbled together using available technology under Quick Reaction Capability (QRC) management techniques. QRC programs are authorized for acquisition of hardware for countering new enemy threats where there is no current capability. QRC is used almost exclusively in electronic warfare and reconnaissance arenas. The chief advantage is fielding a system rapidly; the chief disadvantage is that the device is usually barely good enough but it can be improved at some future time.

The APR 25/26 met both descriptions. One of the most frustrating things was its lack of capability to adequately highlight the specific surface-to-air-missile (SAM) site that was firing at an intended victim aircraft in a multiple radar threat environment. When a SAM site launched a missile, it started to emit guidance signals to guide the missiles toward the target. When these signals were received and analyzed, a red "launch light" was illuminated. When in a high threat environment each target aircraft could have between four to eight threat signals displayed on a 3-inch round television tube. The signals were coded into lines of dots, dashes, or solid lines radiating from the center to a direction indicating its relative position, i.e., straight up indicating the threat was directly ahead of the aircraft. Each signal was a different length, the longer the line, and the closer the threat radar. It was commonplace for three or four radars to "track" a victim aircraft simultaneously. When a red launch light illuminated the problem of identifying the shooter among all the portrayed signals became critical. Missiles can be out-maneuvered under ideal conditions, but visual contact with the missile is mandatory. The pilot would have to scan around toward each indicated direction looking for missiles on the way. The last thing a pilot wants to do, who is flying in close formation at barely subsonic speeds, loaded wall-to-wall with bombs and rockets, is have to stare at a 3-inch scope with a psychedelic appearing presentation of waving, blinking lines that constantly change positions. When the red launch light illuminates, the sensory overload almost defeats the system's primary purpose.

The aircrew members grumbled and wondered how to make the system function better, but they did not know the methods to communicate with the weapon designers so no action was taken.

Cool Bear became a Wild Weasel because he was the Wing Penetrations Aids Officer at Loring AFB, Maine, and his experience caused him to be handpicked for the Wild Weasel job. Cool Bear spent many hours in the B-52 Electronic Warfare shops working with the enlisted technicians trying to improve an already very high, but not perfect, operational ready rate. At Takhli, Cool Bear, time permitting, would go to the ECM shops and continue his efforts to improve capability. He was deeply involved in several improvements.

One day in March 1967, Airman 2C Weldon Bauman told Cool Bear that he had an idea to connect the launch light to the intensity circuit controlling the brightness of the 3-inch display. When the launch light was illuminated, his modification would diminish the brightness of all signals except the one firing the missiles. He then demonstrated this on a workbench, and the display was stunning in its clarity of the true threat signal among all the other confusing strobes. Airman Bauman had originated the idea, proved it electronically, researched the application to determine if it could be installed, and designed the modification for installation. However, he was discouraged from pursuing this effort by his superiors. Cool Bear recognized the idea for what it was, a truly life-saving idea, and was very enthusiastic to have it incorporated in the fleet. Cool Bear went to the maintenance officer, Major Herman L. Hawkins, and asked to have it installed on a trial basis in F-l05F 63-8349, Cool Bear's assigned aircraft.

The next day, in a trial-by-fire, the utility of the modification was proven. The F-105F Wild Weasel crewed by Captains Arnold Dolejsi and Paul Chesley (Cool Bear) was shot at by SAMs in a multi-radar tracking environment. The display immediately highlighted the direction of the threat SAM and evasive techniques were successful. During mission debriefing, the efficacy of this modification was outlined; and by the direction of the maintenance officer, the modification was to be repeated on another F-105F Wild Weasel aircraft at Takhli for further testing. The tests were successful. Within several days, after several more F-105F and F-105D aircraft were modified, the clamor for additional use by the aircrews resulted in formalizing the modification for use in all applicable Air Force tactical fighters. Many aircrews were saved to fly and fight another day. Airman Bauman was encouraged by Cool Bear to submit his idea for an award in the Air Force BIG R Program.

Captain Chesley, after finishing his tour at Takhli on July 4, 1967, was reassigned to Hill AFB, Utah. He was initially assigned to the Plans Division at Headquarters then was assigned to the F-4 Systems Management Division. For flying time he flew back seat in all series of the F-4 during functional check flights for the modified F-4s. After 2 years at Hill AFB, Cool Bear was recognized for his participation in several high-visibility modifications to the F-4. His records were forwarded to Headquarters Personnel, USAF, to see if he could be replicated in the form of a lieutenant colonel with a masters degree in electrical engineering and with Cool Bear's experience. There was no LtCol with his experience. Cool Bear, a brand new Major was pulled up to the Pentagon to serve 5 years in the Requirements Division of the General Purpose Forces, AF/RDQRT.

A few years into Major Chesley's Pentagon tour, a civilian from the Air Force BIG R Suggestion Program came to see him. He had an Air Force BIG R recommendation for award that he was impressed with because of the high level of approval by all screeners. There was one major problem: his signature was the last one required for approval of the $10,000 award and it was written in electronic jargon. He couldn't begin to understand the plot. He had hunted down Major Chesley hoping to receive clarification. On the first page of this folder was the name of the intended recipient: WELDON BAUMAN. Major Chesley explained the modification in plain English and introduced him to several other former F-105 combat pilots in the division. They all agreed that on at least one mission, this modification was crucial to their survival.

The final approving agent, with the flourish of John Hancock, signed the approval form and left the office with a broad smile.

Weldon Bauman Writes:

It was March 1967 and the quantity and concentration of ground radar threats, both Anti-Aircraft-Artillery (AAA) and Surface-to-Air Missile (SAM), had grown considerably since the first of the year. The many bombing halts or restrictions coupled with poor weather conditions had provided North Vietnam time to significantly increase their air defenses over key target areas. As the weather cleared and US bombing restrictions were lifted or modified to include more high value targets, it became common for a pilot or Wild Weasel backseater (EWO) returning from a mission to report that the APR-25/26 Radar Warning Receiver (RWR) scope was displaying so many threat signals that it was difficult to tell which of the SAM tracking radar signals was associated with a SAM launch warning. The March 1967 time frame was somewhat of a turning point as the EWO threat density reports changed from "difficult" to "impossible" to tell by looking at the RWR scope which direction to look for a missile launch.

I was an enlisted Airman EW technician working in the Vector Shop; a radar-proof screen room (roughly 10' X 15') tucked away in the corner of the much larger QRC-160 pod ECM shop at Takhli RTAFB. The Vector Shop technicians were responsible for Radar Homing and Warning systems maintenance on the single seat F-105D and two seat F-105F Wild Weasel aircraft as well as the post flight servicing of the two-track tape recorder installed in the rear cockpit of the F-105F. The tape recorder was a simple voice recorder intended to provide a record of communications between the pilot and EWO and any air-to-air or air-to-ground communications while in the vicinity of the target area. Since all cockpit audio was recorded, including the RWR audio signals, one could easily discern the buzz of the AAA radar signals and the very distinctive rattlesnake-like sound the SAM tracking radar made as the mission tapes were played back. Quite often we would get a "heads up" from the crew returning from a particularly tough mission that we should listen to their tape ASAP. Before the tape had finished, the Vector Shop would be packed with bystanders, all glued to every sound and word. Sometimes the communication and radar sounds on the recording played back at an almost comical higher pitch and speed due to the recorders inability to record accurately during the high G forces of combat maneuvering. The excited but terse communications between aircraft, or pilot and EWO during a SAM launch or dogfight, the AAA buzz and SAM rattlesnake sounds occasionally accompanied by the wail of a downed flyers beacon, coupled with the pitch and speed change of the recording, gave the listener an audio based emotional experience that few, if any, Hollywood productions have ever been able to create using both audio and visual inputs! I didn't need access to daily threat briefings or current ELINT information to know that the EWO threat density reports were accurate!

It was obvious that we had a Radar Warning system problem that needed to be solved. At that time, I wished that we had an electronics lab full of test/simulation equipment and a team of design engineers at our disposal. The reality was that all we had were the Vector Shop test and alignment signal generators and a few extra repair components. However, I did have a great tool; the mission tapes from the two-track tape recorder. With a little modification to the recorder output, I fed several mission recordings of raw SAM and AAA audio pulses directly into the APR-25 processor to determine where the processing "choke point" was. It was clear that the APR-25 display was unable to present a meaningful display of high quality inputs from our bench test equipment while simultaneously processing the recorded AAA and SAM pulses. After a couple of days of trial and error, I designed and bench tested a simple APR-25 circuit card modification that significantly reduced the density of non-threat or low-threat pulses at the "choke point" and changed the display from unreadable to readable. When Capt. Chesley saw my bench demonstration he said that he wanted to test it ASAP. Several weeks later, Gen. Ken Dempster and Col. Pierre Levy stopped by the Vector Shop and asked for a demonstration of the modification. At the conclusion of the demonstration, Gen. Dempster turned to Col. Levy and commented, "Now that we have this solution, we don't need to put the QRC-317 (SEE SAM) into production". I didn't learn until several years later the impact of that decision!

We installed a modified RWR (APR-25/26) system in Capt. Chesley's plane sometime in March, 1967. Shortly after his first flight with the modification we modified the rest of the Weasel planes at Takhli RTAFB. I don't remember if the F105D's were modified at that time but I do recall that local base approval was sufficient for installation of the modification as long as the aircraft was assigned to Takhli. Just before I finished my one year tour at Takhli in Oct.1967, my shop chief informed me that I must submit a Form 1000 "Suggestion" which, when approved, would serve as the authorizing vehicle for modification use by other wings. I didn't give the modification another thought until I was notified in 1968, April I think, that I was being awarded $1200 for the suggestion. At that time I was repairing APR-25/26 Radar Warning systems on the B-52's at Anderson AFB, Guam.

In Oct of 1968, I finished my AF enlistment and went to work for Applied Technology (ATI), the manufacture of the APR-25/26 system. Once again, the modification was but a distant memory when one day in November, 1970, I received a phone call from Hq. PACAF advising me that they were sending me a suggestion award check for $800 and asked me to fly, at Air Force expense, to Hickam AFB, Hawaii to receive the next $3000 part of the suggestion award. They then added that the final $5000 (for a total of $10,000, the largest award in Air Force history) should be approved by the time I arrived at Hickam AFB and that Pacific Air Force Commander, General Nazzarro would make the award presentation on 10 Dec. 70. WOW, talk about speechless! It took a bit of convincing that the call wasn't a prank as I had a hard time believing that the Air Force would continue the suggestion award process even though the recipient was a civilian.

As it turned out, Gen. Nazzarro had to be in Washington DC on Dec. 10 and so Lt.Gen. Lavelle, PACAF vice Commander in Chief, made the presentation at a PACAF Generals briefing. Prior to that presentation, the award had only meant "reward for an idea that saved some money" to me. During the award presentation I listened to Gen. Lavelle and came to realize for the first time that the mod represented not only a savings of munitions and planes but also most of all, lives. At the conclusion, each of the Generals in the "General only" audience shook my hand and gave me a very sincere "thank you" as they filed past me. Believe me, I walked tall that day!

My Air Force tour consisted of enlistment in March of 1965, six weeks of basic training at Lackland AFB followed by electronics and EW equipment repair training at Keesler AFB. From Jan through Sept 1966, I was assigned to a new RF4C wing (67th TRW) at Mt. Home AFB.

My next assignment starting Oct 1966 was quite a change; there were 60 plus F-105's (355th TFW) at Takhli RTAFB flying combat missions, many of which needed Radar Warning system attention each day. My next assignment, which I thought would be my last prior to discharge, was to the 5th Bomb Wing, ECM shop at Travis AFB in Oct of 1967. As luck would have it, I was the only one there with Radar Warning experience and was sent TDY to Guam (Anderson AFB) a couple of days after the Pueblo was captured in Feb 1968. Even though my assistance was never needed in support of the Pueblo, the B52 ECM shop kept me busy repairing, guess what, the APR-25/26's for the next 6 months! I returned to Travis in August 1968 to a Bomb Wing (the 5th) that had been deactivated. At that time, my career field was saturated and I was offered an "early out" which I accepted in Oct. 1968.

In Oct. 1968 I joined Applied Technology (ATI) in the engineering department and worked on the development of the APR-36/37 and subsequent radar warning system updates. In 1971 I transferred to the marketing department at ATI and held various product and service related (i.e. Air Force, Navy) marketing, marketing management and business planning positions. In July of 1982, I resigned my position at ATI to pursue my long held dream of running my own business. That same month, my wife, Sandy (also an ex-ATI'r) and I purchased an appliance store (major appliance retail sales and service) in Paradise, Ca., a small town 90 miles North of Sacramento in the Sierra foothills. Here we are 22 years later, still enjoying being small business owners. I also enjoy being active in our local community as a Director of the Chamber of Commerce and as a member of the Paradise Economic Development Commission. Of course, we have expanded the business to include support staff so that we can get away to an occasional Wild Weasel function!

Paul Chesley and Weldon Bauman

Story by Robert W. King, Wild Weasel # 484

The Day Roy Brenner and I Became Honorary Negroes

In April 1972, the North Vietnamese unleashed a long planned and carefully prepared military offensive against South Vietnam. The USAF responded by hurrying a number of units from the land of the big BX to Southeast Asia. It was called Operation Constant Guard. Among the very first units to get the order to go was my outfit, the 561st Tactical Fighter Squadron, based at McConnell AFB, Wichita, Kansas. I got a phone call about 0200 in the morning of 7 Apr 1972. As I had so often practiced, I threw my gear in the car and headed for the squadron. Within the hour we had been briefed that this was no drill. We were going back to the war. I say "back to the war" because the 561st TFS was unique. We were the only Wild Weasel squadron in the continental US and all the officers, without exception, were combat veterans of the war against North Vietnam. The first loads of cargo and personnel departed about sun-up followed a couple of hours later by the Thuds. I drew the short straw and wound up making the trip in the belly of C-141. I spent most of the trip rolled in a blanket on the aluminum floor of the cargo compartment under a J-75 engine on a dolly that kept me entertained by occasionally dropping a drop of frigid hydraulic fluid on me. Every time I would manage to drop off for a snooze, that cold drip would startle me back to wakefulness. With stops for fuel, the trip to Korat RTAFB in Thailand took about 27 flying hours spread over two days. We arrived, dropped our gear at the BOQ, and spent a few hours sleeping, eating, and recovering from the trip. Some clever troop visited a Thai embroidery shop and placed an order for some patches for us. Then we briefed the first sorties. I am immensely proud of the fact that in just over three days, the 561st had flown literally halfway round the world and then launched their first combat sorties against the North Vietnamese in what was named Operation Constant Guard. We were needed. Among the other preparations the North Vietnamese had made for their assault was to build up an enormous stockpile of SA-2 Guideline SAM missiles. They fired more SAMs in April 1972 than they had fired in the entire war until then. When it came to weaseling, there was simply far too much work for the 17th WWS, the sole Wild Weasel squadron in SEA prior to our arrival.

SAMs weren't the only air defenses the North Vietnamese had stockpiled. They had also built up their stocks of anti-aircraft artillery. Both SAMs and AAA batteries had been moved south to support their assault across the DMZ into South Vietnam. That meant that Route Package I, the southern-most portion of North Vietnam was no longer the relatively safe backwater compared to the defenses around Hanoi and Haiphong that it once had been. Previously, you rarely saw any flak larger than occasional 37mm gun. But in April 1972, it had become a very hot area — with many more and larger AAA guns — as I found out on 28 April 1972.

That day, Maj. Roy Brenner and I took F-105G 63-8296 and using the call sign Swanny 2, we went to Route Package I to support the many strike aircraft that were working over the North Vietnamese convoys and equipment headed for the DMZ. We were hit over Fingers Lake. We GIs had named many landmarks in Southeast Asia to suit ourselves because we didn't know or couldn't pronounce the Vietnamese names. We usually named them for their shape. This lake was shaped like a hand with the fingers outstretched. Hence "Fingers Lake."

Our leader had called for a channel change in preparation to leaving the area and heading to the tanker for more gas. So we were not on the same frequency at the moment when the 85mm anti-aircraft round went off just off our left wing tip. I found out later that our leader, Swanny 1, had seen a series of flak bursts advancing towards us from our deep six o'clock but couldn't tell us about it because we were not on the same frequency.

When the round went off, I heard it — both as a 'bang' and as a burst of static on the Wild Weasel receivers. I researched that occurrence later on. It turns out that ANY explosion creates a momentary cloud of plasma or ionized gas. The creation and decay of plasma generate an electromagnetic noise pulse or EMP. The larger and hotter the explosion, the stronger the electromagnetic noise pulse. When you get to nuclear weapons, a major portion of the energy generated by the explosion may go into producing the EMP. This EMP is like any other radio wave. It decreases in amplitude as the square of the distance from the origin. So for most chemical explosions, no one hears the EMP. You would simply have to be so close to the explosion that you will probably be blown away. So when I say I heard it, there was no doubt in my mind — it was too damn close!

What happened next was that the nose of the airplane pitched down and we rolled into a hard bank to the left for a second or so and then continued to roll so that we were turning to the right. Understandably, I wanted to know whether this was all according to some plan of Roy's or if the airplane was doing all this maneuvering on its own. Roy reassured me that he was just jinking and conducting a controllability check. So I decided to stay with him and await further developments. After all, we were over Route Package I and I didn't fancy my changes of walking home. A scan of the instrument panel showed nothing exceptional. A look out the window wasn't so satisfactory.

On the outboard pylon on the left wing, where our AGM-45 Shrike missile had hung, about half of it was gone. Specifically, the back end with the rocket engine was no longer there. What we had left was the front end containing the guidance package, the fusing package and more importantly, the one hundred forty-five pound warhead. Think of the latter as a hand grenade on steroids. It had an explosive charge surrounded by a metal casing that was designed to break into cubes. When the charge went off, the cubes were supposed to penetrate any radar antennas, radar sets or radar set operators that happened to be in the vicinity. At the moment, I was in the vicinity and I didn't much like the idea. We had no idea at all whether the damn thing was going to blow up or not at any moment.

And there wasn't a thing we could do about it. The outboard pylon on an F-105 could not be jettisoned. Oh, you could jettison whatever was hung on the pylon, but the pylon itself was going with you until it was removed on the ground. And the jettison arrangements for the AGM-45 left something to be desired as well. The missile was carried on the pylon by two short rails. The aft rail can be described a metal plate about eight inches long and eight inches wide. The missile gripped the edges of the plate by a couple of lugs that slid along the edges when the missile was launched. The front mount has two metal plates with a single missile lug (like a large bolt head) that slid in the slot between them. Then there is a metal bracket that stuck down behind the aft end of the missile to prevent it sliding backwards off the rails. This bracket had a pyrotechnic charge that moved it out of the way when you wanted to jettison the missile. The drag of the air (you are presumed to be flying when you do this) simply pushes the missile backwards a couple of inches. It clears the aft end of the front and rear rails and drops away. This seems rather a passive jettison system compared to the more positive systems used on the other ordnance stations.

By the way, we found out later from our leader that when the back half of the missile ignited, it burned itself in two and the aft end fell away still burning. He thought momentarily that it was a SAM coming up at us. However, we were STILL not on his radio frequency, so we didn't hear his warning call. This was probably just as well. We already had plenty on our plate for the moment.

Having convinced ourselves that we weren't going to blow up immediately and that the airplane was likely to fly for a little bit, and having traveled a few miles away from Fingers Lake in a generally southerly direction, we finally got the radio switched to new radio frequency. We invited our leader to come look us over. He reported that he could see no holes in our airplane, nothing was leaking out and other than that piece of a Shrike missile hanging on the pylon, and everything looked normal. By now, we were getting close to the DMZ area and we had to make a decision. Should we take the airplane home to Korat or look for some place closer. Since we didn't really know whether the airplane was undamaged and there was that missile hanging around out on the wing — conceivably making up its mind to explode – some place closer such as Da Nang AB seemed like a logical choice.

Then there was the matter of getting there. Instead of heading south directly toward Da Nang, we immediately headed east to get "feet wet." That is, we flew out over the Tonkin Gulf. There was a reason for this. If the airplane quit on us or any other untoward event took place, that might mean we would have to step over the side and make a nylon letdown. Tramping around in the brush amidst a collection of hostile people with guns didn't seem like the best of plans. Whether you encountered North Vietnamese or South Vietnamese wouldn't have mattered much. In that kind of situation, grunts in all armies tended to shoot first and sort out the players on the field later. It was much better to go "feet wet"' and let the Tonkin Gulf yacht club (more popularly known as the U. S. Navy) collect us in the event of unscheduled happenings.

Once over water, we contacted Da Nang Tower, told them who we were and where we were, and declared an emergency with battle damage. He instantly told us to hold until he cleared us to the approach, and informed us that we were "number three in the emergency pattern." It seems that other folks were having troubles right about then as well. They landed uneventfully ahead of us and then it was our turn.

We made a straight in approach from the north and landed on the right or west runway. Once we were established on the approach, our leader, Swanny 1 broke off and went in search of a tanker. He still had a war to fight.

Generally, when a Thud touches down, there's a pretty authoritative thump when the main gear touches the runway and another when the nose gear is lowered. Not that day! Roy's landing was so smooth that I couldn't tell just when the main gear touched. He held the nose off for a bit to get the aerodynamic braking effect and then lowered the nose to the runway. He delayed a second or so on the drag chute to allow another few knots to bleed off so the deceleration tug from the chute wouldn't be quite as great. It would have done no good at all to have made the best landing of his life if he decelerated too fast and caused the missile to slide forward off the rail, hit the ground beside us and then do whatever missiles with overheated warheads and damaged electronics do.

The drag chute tug was gentle enough and the missile stayed put although it did some heart stopping waggling up and down. About this time I noticed that every fire truck based at Da Nang was chasing us on the parallel taxiways. I was glad to see them although I wasn't too sure what they could do for us.

Roy gently started applying the brakes and we continued to slow down. Before we got to the end, we were slowed down to normal taxi speeds. Tower called us and instructed us to turn to the right away from the inhabited part of the base when we got to the end. We turned off on the taxiway and stopped. The fire trucks quickly formed a circle around us.

The fire chief stuck his head out of his truck window and studied us for a moment. Then he slid back inside and grabbed his radio microphone. I don't know what he said, but all the fire trucks departed. It seems that if we decided to blow up, we would have to do it unaccompanied.

We called the tower ground controller and asked where we were to go. The controller told us to just stay put and that we would have assistance in a minute. He was as good as his word. The Transient Alert folks showed up, looked us over and then decided it was safe to pin our gear, chock the wheels and let us shut down. We stop-cocked the engine, shucked our parachutes and used the ladder they provided to climb down. Then we all wandered off two or three hundred yards at a brisk pace and then settled down in a ditch to consider the situation.

About that time, a grizzled black Master Sergeant showed up driving a truck that said EOD (Explosive Ordnance Disposal) on the side and had a couple of airmen and some gear in the back. He drove right past us to the airplane, climbed out and looked it over. Then he got in his truck and drove back to where we were catching our breath. He told us that it would take him about 45 minutes to get the missile off the bird and dispose of it, and that we might as well go on to Base Ops in the meantime. He'd come by when he was finished.

So we bummed a ride to Base Ops with the Transient Alert folks to get a Coke and call home. We needed to tell them we were on the ground at Da Nang AB. The EOD sergeant showed up a little after we got off the phone to tell us that the Shrike had been removed and hauled away to be exploded in a safe area. Then he told us that he was intimately familiar with Shrikes. In his younger days, he had been in the Navy and had been stationed at China Lake NAS in the California desert where he had been on the team that developed them.

Then he grinned and handed pink cards to both Roy and me. He told us that we may have had a bad day, but perhaps this might help make up for it. Obviously not professionally printed, the cards stated that we were now Honorary Negroes!

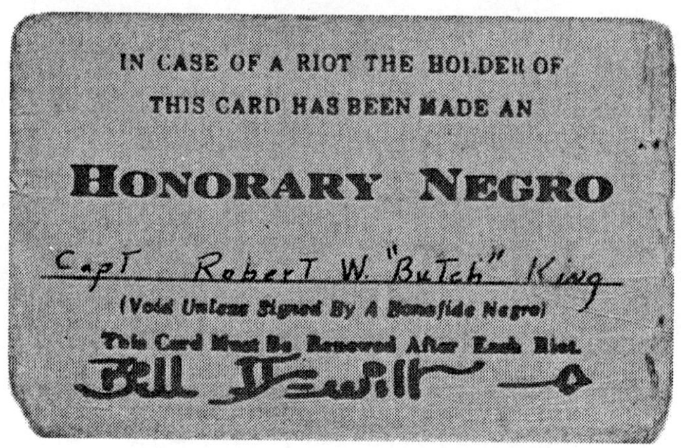
IN CASE OF A RIOT THE HOLDER OF
THIS CARD HAS BEEN MADE AN

HONORARY NEGRO

Capt Robert W. "Butch" King

(Void Unless Signed By A Bonafide Negro)

This Card Must Be Renewed After Each Riot.

Card courtesy of Bob King

Then the discussion turned to the time of day. During that period of the war, you told time at Da Nang by whether it was before or after the afternoon rocket attack. It was determined that it was 'before.' For some reason, Roy wasn't anxious to stay and watch it. I didn't feel like arguing the point. So we got a ride from the Transient Alert folks back out to the airplane, and installed the packed Thud drag chute that they had thoughtfully brought along. At least we didn't have to break out the manual and repack the chute we had used on landing before installing it. Jumping up and down on that drag chute door trying to get it to latch while hanging on to the hand-hold cutout in the rudder is not my idea of fun, but we managed.

Then we did a walk-around preflight inspection of the bird. You may understand me when I say that I have seldom inspected a bird so carefully. Astonishing as it may sound, there were NO holes in the airplane that hadn't been put there by the foundry and there were no leaks dripping on the ground. So we climbed up the ladder, strapped in and cranked the engine. We checked in with Da Nang ground control, had the chief pull the chocks and taxied north a mile or so.

Then we stopped by a collection of large fuel bladders. Each large rubber bag lay in its own little revetment and they were connected by an assortment of hoses. The Transient Alert folks had followed us in their pickup. They chocked our wheels, connected some grounding wires and then for the first and only time in my experience, our Thud was hot refueled. That is, the bird was refueled with the engine running. Considering that it was now about one in the afternoon and the rocket attacks generally took place between one and three o'clock, this much quicker method of refueling seemed like a splendid idea.

Take-off and return to our home base at Korat was uneventful — just what our frazzled nerves needed at that stage.

Robert W. King, Wild Weasel # 484

Story by Phil (Quack Bear) Steeves, WW # 1174

From The Doc's Perspective

When flight surgeons were transferred to Southeast Asia, they were assigned first to a specific base, and only then assigned to a particular squadron. Thus when I arrived at Korat, hoping for an assignment to a fighter squadron, I was regretfully informed that the three F-4 squadrons already had their assigned flight surgeons. The only other fighter squadron was the Wild Weasel squadron, which had a perennial problem of getting its own flight surgeon because no doc wanted to fly with them, given their famously hazardous mission, which meant that they flew exclusively in North Vietnam where the SAMs were. While the F-4 squadrons also flew at times to North Vietnam, they also had many missions to South Vietnam, Laos and Cambodia, which the flight docs could fly to fulfill their flight requirements.

Those flight requirements were, as the official orders stated, to fly "regularly and frequently." Although over the years, some flight surgeons assigned to combat squadrons have satisfied this requirement by flying relatively safe missions with squadrons other than their own, such as tankers and transport aircraft, it was clear that the flight doc who could make the most useful medical contribution to the mission, making the best judgments of when a pilot was medically fit or unfit for the mission in question, was the one who knew his pilots best by living with them—eating, drinking, sleeping, playing and, of course, flying with them. This allowed the doc the best information both about the specific pilot and also about the demands of the squadron's unique aircraft on any particular mission.

Since it was my goal to have this kind of aeromedical experience, and to make this useful contribution to the war effort, I immediately accepted the assignment to the Wild Weasels when offered it. I presented myself to the squadron commander, Lt Col Rock, and I recall that he looked at me kind of funny at first. He must have been wondering what kind of nut would want to do this. But he also seemed appreciative about the prospect of having a flight doc dedicated to his squadron instead of playing catch-as-catch-can to get medical support. The squadron had just lost a plane with both crewmembers unaccounted for, and Col Rock was concerned that there could have been aeromedical issues like fatigue involved.

There was an occasional FCF that I could hitch a ride on to get used to the plane, and to adapt to the equipment in the back seat. I already had a commercial pilot's license, and having flown with MAC for a year in C-141's, I didn't have much trouble understanding the nav and comm radios in the Thud. The only problem was getting up to some degree of speed with the ECM stuff that was all magic to me. I was most fortunate to have two experts on the Wild Weasel gear available to tutor me—Mike O'Brien (Panic Bear) and Bill Barbery, the Applied Technology Incorporated (ATI) tech rep. They spent hours with me one-on-one giving me enough basics that, we hoped, would get me to the point that I could access and interpret the info in the back of the Thud, enough at least that maybe, with a very, very experienced pilot, it might not be unreasonable for me to go on an actual mission or two. These two seemed to take it as a personal challenge to see if they could teach a Doc anything. I didn't have to master tactics, just "flip the shiny switches" to get the essential gear in the back seat on line. Somehow, eventually, we convinced Col Rock that we had arrived at that point, and I'm eternally grateful that he was willing to make the command decision that the Doc could go up North. In the long-established tradition, I started in Pack-1, eventually working up to Thanh Hoa in Pack-4 where I became night-SAM qualified. Col Rock had declared Pack-6 to be definitely off-limits to the Doc—a limitation that made a lot of sense to me at the time…and still does!

You never forget your first 01-B, the first mission to North Vietnam. The briefing was scheduled for 0-dark-hunderd, of course, and it was all very exciting. They paired me up with Lt Col George Bowling, the squadron XO, one of the old hands at Weaseling, and one who didn't have a regular Bear. We had just suited up, still before dawn, getting ready to step, when a 2- or 3-striper grabbed me and said, "Capt Steeves, your number came up on today's Operation Golden Flow list, so you gotta provide us with a urine sample before you do anything else—highest priority!" Of course, I had already emptied my bladder anticipating a long mission in a cramped ejection seat. But the ROE's of Operation Golden Flow (the program of random urine spot-checks for illicit drugs) stated that whenever one's number came up, be he the lowliest airman or the base commander, that person had to drop everything else and provide a specimen before resuming any duties.

I quickly guzzled some coffee, and then some more coffee, and somehow was able to produce the requisite few drops of urine before jumping into the crew van. Then we were off to Pack-1, and it turned out to be a 4-banger mission (meaning 4 individual forays into hostile territory separated by in-flight refuelings over Laos.) Some time during the 2nd or 3rd IFR, that guzzled coffee began making its presence very well known. By the time we RTB'd, my bladder was ready to burst. To top it off, Col Bowling decided that successfully flying the Doc into combat deserved a victory roll in the pattern, which was the final push on my bladder. I confess a few drops may have leaked out on downwind, and the rest came gushing out on the ramp as soon as I alighted from the ladder!

I figured I could make my first aeromedical contribution to the mission by suggesting we take piddle packs with us, but I was quickly embarrassed to be informed that there was a relief tube already built in to the Thud which somehow everyone had neglected to inform me about. Of course the relief tube didn't do much for the occasional brown stains on the seats of the flight suits; there were a lot of diarrhea-causing bugs over in the jungle, don't you know! And in fact, as a flight doc, I did treat a lot of traveler's diarrhea over there. Naturally, those stains were never from a hairy mission.

It was also George Bowling as my FUF on the mission to Thanh Hoa when I had the unforgettable opportunity to watch a SAM fire up at night, accompanied by both the ML (Missile Launch) and the AS (Acquisition Sector) panel lights which clearly annunciated that our bird was the target of that particular SAM. Of course, Col Bowling expertly avoided the missile with a last-second break, and we had a chance to respond with an AGM-45, which also makes a neat fireworks show at night.

Southeast Asia was a primary source of illicit drugs for the world. However, I never had any aircrew with a positive drug test; that was a problem only for the ground-pounders. This is not to say that aircrew were immune to the local temptations, however. We had worked out an arrangement with the local Thai public health officials who kept weekly track of which girls at the downtown Rub & Scrub (literally a Holiday Inn) tested positive for a social disease. I would then post that list on the door of my hooch, calling it the BP list (i.e., Bad Pussy). Folks could look at the list each week, and either breathe a sigh of relief, or else track me down ASAP as indicated by the girl's numbers, assuming they'd had the presence of mind to mark down the number while availing themselves of her services.

Other medical duties included monitoring the food supply. On one occasion the Wild Weasels had a pig roast, the whole beast rotating on a spit for hours over coals. Since it was a local animal with who knows what exposure to trichinosis, I made sure it was well cooked. And nobody got sick from it. Attempts at moderating alcohol intake in an environment of nickel-a-bottle beer during happy hour, by fighter pilots who literally may get shot down tomorrow, met with limited success. Smoking in those days did not have the social disfavor it now has. On the other hand, no one seemed to have a weight problem in that environment. Flying combat sweats off a lot of calories. I might add that keeping the Wild Weasels fit to fly occasionally involved some psychological counseling, as there were plenty of stresses including exhaustion, career issues, and family crises 12,000 miles away. Finally, the flight surgeon together with the veterinarian assigned to the base bore the awesome responsibility to keep Roscoe—the prognosticating mascot whose demeanor at briefings supposedly predicted the hairiness of the upcoming mission—healthy, which included periodic de-worming.

After returning to CONUS, I resumed my specialty training in Radiology. I went completely inactive as a Reservist for years, getting established in a civilian practice. But after about 15 years, I felt the urge to get back into fighters. I joined the Air National Guard unit in my state flying in F-15s. It was a nostalgic thrill flying in fighters once again. And I enjoyed the camaraderie of that unique group of highly skilled, aggressive and patriotic Americans called Fighter Pilots. But the intensity of living and flying 24/7 with a fighter squadron, one that was flying regularly in combat and suffering occasional losses, would never be equaled in peacetime. The lifelong bonds that were forged by my tour with the Wild Weasels were unparalleled. Being able to fly with the Wild Weasels is the proudest achievement of my life. It was a tremendous experience to have been associated with such outstanding men. As the squadron doc, I can most accurately say, No, I wasn't a hero; but I was sure privileged care for, and occasionally to fly with, men who were.

Stories by Don Henry WW # 927

Biography

Don Henry, a former Air Force Colonel, has extensive experience flying fighter aircraft as well as commanding a nuclear tasked F-111 squadron. He flew 129 combat missions in F-105s over Laos and North Vietnam. His combat decorations include the Silver Star and three Distinguished Flying Crosses. His novel, *THUNDERCHIEF* (Pelican Pub.) is the story of a young F-105 pilot on his first combat tour. He and his wife, Dixie, live in Laguna Beach, California. He was a flight commander and instructor in the 17th Wild Weasel Squadron at Korat RTAFB, Thailand.

RETRIBUTION

Overview: On 22 November 1972, Wire, a flight of four F-105Gs, supported three cells of B-52's. The bombers' target near Vinh, North Vietnam, brought them within range of four surface to air missile (SAM) sites and numerous anti-aircraft (AAA) batteries. Fighter aircraft had operated around Vinh since 1965 and the B-52s had been operating there for about seven months. Over time, Vinh defenses had grown increasingly dense and sophisticated. A SAM launched out of a Vinh site severely damaged a B-52 on the night of 22 November making it the first Stratofortress lost to direct enemy action over North Vietnam. As an F-105G Wild Weasel escorted it south, the B-52 caught fire. All of the crew abandoned the aircraft safely before it crashed in Thailand.

Captain Don Henry, pilot, and Captain Tony Radko, electronic warfare officer (EWO), were in an F-105G operating with the call sign Wire 03. After accessing the enemy's successful attack on the B-52, Wire 03 neutralized a SAM attack by enticing the site to launch on their aircraft instead of the remaining B-52 strike force, then achieved a probable kill on the site that had hit the Stratofortress minutes earlier.

Narrative: We positioned our aircraft in front of the first B-52 cell so we could intercept signals that might threaten the bombers from 12 o'clock. After we passed abeam of the target, two SA-2 missiles launched from our six o'clock position. Two other members of Wire flight initiated missile attacks, but the enemy's excellent use of radar emission control negated these attacks, and we could only watch as one SAM climbed to altitude and exploded in the vicinity of the strike force. I thought I saw the outline of a B-52 in the flash of the SAM detonation but the explosion temporarily destroyed my night vision and I wasn't sure. Soon we learned a B-52 suffered battle damage and was turning south.

The launch site was in our six o'clock position so we maneuvered to make a rough visual identification of the launch area through the patchy clouds and haze. Tony used our onboard electronics to analyze the attack and determine the radar emission control procedures the site used to make its successful attack. With the second bomber cell due on target in a few minutes, we set up an attack based on the site location and the enemy radar emission procedures just observed. As we maneuvered into firing position, the site launched another SAM. I followed the missile visually while Tony confirmed electronically that we were the intended target of the missile. An evasive maneuver would have been a good choice but Tony and I both knew the aggressive SAM site could easily transfer its attack to the bomber force behind us. We had a very short conversation.

"Let's do it," I said.

"Get 'em," Tony replied.

We felt vulnerable as we maneuvered to launch a Shrike since this maneuver practically solved the attacking SAM site's tracking problem. After launching a Shrike anti-radiation missile at the SAM radar, we began a high G evasive maneuver. Now a second SAM launched and Tony electronically confirmed we were still the intended target. Nothing gets the adrenaline rushing like a persistent enemy.

The first SAM streaked pass us and detonated, but the second missile continued to guide. While diving to evade the second missile, which was now closing at roughly twice the speed of sound, we saw the Shrike impact. Immediately enemy radar emissions ceased, the airborne missile stopped tracking then passed dangerously close to our right wing and detonated. Then, immediately, we observed a fire in the SAM complex.

We had silenced the aggressive SAM site but had to hustle into position to protect a third bomber cell from the same threat. For the rest of the mission, the site did not come up and the remaining B-52 force was unopposed. The fire continued to burn and we watched it for miles as we left the target area and headed back to Korat.

We would lament the loss of the B-52 later, when the mission was over, and we were safely on the ground. There was nothing else we could do or should have done, but that was my head talking; later I would hear from my heart. Things happen fast flying at 500 knots in the dark. We made choices, and the enemy made choices. There is nothing in reason or revelation that explains the arbitrage of risk that occurs in combat. We had a measure of satisfaction knowing we "got" the SAM site, but it was impossible to know how much our attack diminished enemy capability, or even if it did. But we were hoping.

FIRST NIGHT OF LINEBACKER II

Overview: On 18 December 1972, the first night of Linebacker II, 129 B-52s attacked in the Hanoi area in three separate waves. The targets were MiG airfields, a railway yard, a storage area, and Hanoi radio station. Surface-to-air missiles (SAMs) hit three B-52s. Two of the bombers crashed in North Vietnam (seven crewmembers became prisoners of war (POW), the other five crew were killed in action (KIA). The third bomber had two engines blown off and was streaming fire but made it to Thailand before the crew had to abandon the aircraft. Helicopters rescued all seven crewmembers. Also, an F-111 was lost, both crewmembers KIA. Wild Weasel forces supported all B-52 operations. Missions were conducted entirely at night, which required Wild Weasel aircraft to patrol their assigned areas single ship and operate independently. B-52s operated at altitudes of 34,000 to 38,000 feet. F-105 Wild Weasels, various altitudes up to 28,000 feet; and F-111s, 500 to 2,000 feet. Precise timing and navigation were important for Wild Weasels and other planes operating below the B-52s as they dropped tons of bombs on numerous targets. SAM activity estimates for the first night of Linebacker II range from 160 to more than 200 launches.

Suntan Flight: On 18 December 1972, four F-105G aircraft, call sign "Suntan," made up one of the flights providing SAM suppression for the second wave of B-52's ever to enter the Hanoi area. Suntan 02, crewed by Captain Don Henry, pilot, and Major Bob Webb, electronic warfare officer (EWO), flew into the target area several minutes before the second wave. No intelligence data was available from the first wave attack, except for the knowledge that the element of surprise was gone. With surprise lost, and enemy defenses fully alerted, the second wave encountered extremely heavy defenses. The ensuing air battle has been called the greatest electronic engagement in the history of aerial warfare. I was there and I believe it

The bombers' flight path required Suntan 02 to operate within the lethal range of at least 12 SAM sites and numerous gun positions of every caliber of AAA. There were many SAMs and countless rounds of AAA in the air constantly during this 24-minute engagement. Intense radar- directed medium altitude AAA fire was coordinated with SAM launches. The AAA, largely ineffective against the high-altitude bombers, was directed almost entirely against the Wild Weasel forces. Each member of Suntan flight had total responsibility to suppress threats in his operating area since the in-depth enemy defenses did not allow overlapping coverage. Timing, positioning, and area of responsibility were based on the assumption that each Wild Weasel aircrew would flawlessly execute his portion of the overall plan.

During this engagement Bob Webb and I neutralized three SAM attacks by firing a Standard Arm and two Shrike anti-radiation missiles, and scored a possible and a probable kill. After expending our missiles we conducted five feint attacks to intimidate enemy radars into silence. The feint attacks turned out to be surprisingly effective, so much so that when our support requirements were complete, we returned to the target area to reinforce the efforts of other Wild Weasel flights supporting additional bomber sells. Our mission was not unusual; it was typical of the actions of all the Wild Weasels during the target-rich battles of Linebacker II.

Narrative: Making our way into the target area we encountered numerous SAM site radar signals and associated launch indications. In the target area, it quickly became apparent that the enemy was practicing excellent radar emission control; further we saw concentrated barrages of AAA associated with SAM launch and guidance radar signals, which we assessed as a sophisticated flak trap.

Two minutes prior to the first bomber strike, we were carefully picking our way through dense AAA near Phuc Yen airfield. We had seen several missile launches on the way in and, as two SAMs passed abeam of our left wing, we detected another strong SAM radar signal. The signal correlated to an area adjacent to Hanoi, from which most of the missiles had been launched. Bob Webb programmed our AGM-78 Standard Arm and we fired it to suppress the SAM site during the first bomber cells attack. The SAM site's radar signal fell silent at the Standard Arm impact and did not come up again.

Then we saw a salvo launch of three SAM's, which illuminated the night sky and were heading directly at our aircraft. Since we had positioned ourselves between the bomber cell and two active SAM sites, we thought the bombers were the likely targets. We had "Weaseled" our way into position to attack the site. This was a classic tactic, but now the airborne SAMs were going to fly right through our position. If the enemy was aiming at us instead of the bombers, this would be a big problem. There was no way to find out—except by waiting. But hey—we're Wild Weasels—we're supposed to be in the cone of attack. The downside was the proximity fuse envelope of the SAM; that could be a problem. The upside: we could roll into a Shrike delivery for a point-blank attack. The SAMs were closing fast and Bob confirmed we were in the lethal cone. We dove into the attacking SAMs realizing that if we were the target, we had solved the SAM site's tracking problem. We met the Shrike delivery parameters and fired. The Shrike left the launcher and passed the oncoming SAM missiles. Immediately three blinding flashes illuminated the cockpit as the flight of missiles streaked dangerously close to our aircraft. Within seconds, the threat signal went down confirming neutralization of the attack, and the SAMs detonated aft of us and short of the bombers.

Bob Webb then detected an intermittent SAM signal, and while we maneuvered toward it, radar control guns locked onto our aircraft. We pursued an attack against the SAM radar and, just as a signal went down, our aircraft was engulfed in AAA. We noted the flak trap, and at once observed a salvo launch of three missiles at our 10 o'clock. While we maneuvered to attack the SAM site, the gun-laying radar continued tracking our aircraft. A few seconds before reaching our Shrike missile-firing parameters, the threat radar signal went down. We didn't fire our weapon but continued to press the attack to keep the enemy site down, and then we maneuvered to evade the heavy AAA, which was going off all around us.

We repositioned to protect the next bomber cell and started receiving strong threat signals from a SAM site that had previously led us into a flak trap. The signal couldn't be discounted as a threat to the bombers so we set up another attack. Again we were led into a barrage of flak. Then, as the next bomber cell began its attack, this aggressive SAM site reappeared as a steady threat signal looking at the bombers. We maneuvered to set up an attack, while still being dogged by the persistent radar directed AAA. We rolled in and fired a Shrike as the site launched the first of three SAMs. The site fell silent at Strike impact and the SAMs detonated harmlessly away from the bomber force. We then escorted the last bombers along their egress route.

We were out of ordnance but still had some gas so we returned to the target area to reinforce the suppression efforts of another Wild Weasel flight, which was covering additional bombers. SAM and AAA fire continued to be heavy. There was enough enemy activity for everyone so we picked out a SAM site and made feint attacks, keeping it occupied until the bombers finished. Running a tad below bingo fuel, we departed the target area, found our refueling tanker and took on enough fuel to recover uneventfully at Korat.

Long Road to Complete a Tour

On a clear day in September 1972, I was droning across the Pacific in a C5 cargo airplane, sitting at a table, enjoying a hot lunch, riding in the crew quarters just behind the cockpit or whatever they call that place where the pilot and copilot in that huge aircraft reside. I'd been to squadron parties in smaller apartments. Nice crew quarters those. I could relax in bed, walk around, fix something in the kitchen, listen to music, or languish in the Jacuzzi. Just kidding—but only about the Jacuzzi. The accommodations were great, sort of like a motor home with wings. I was working hard at relaxing. I was a Wild Weasel pilot headed for Korat. It was going to be a tough year.

I was returning to Thailand to fly combat for the third time. Before you reach in that box to hand me another medal, let me explain. I wasn't flying my third combat tour. I was on my third attempt to complete my first combat tour. At least the only tour that meant anything to me —one hundred missions over North Vietnam. But Air Force needs had modified the way tours were counted and it was beginning to get more complicated. This time I wasn't going to combat in TDY (temporary duty) status but as a full-fledged permanent party member of a unit. I had flown over 70 combat missions and had made it back into combat before the war ended only because the Air Force needed F-105 Wild Weasel pilots and I was a volunteer. To get back into combat, I signed up for a full PCS (permanent tour) of a year—not just to fly the 30 counter missions left to complete my 100. But what the hell, some guys had flown 200 counters. A lot of others, of course, had completed one more takeoff than landing.

I had started out six years earlier as a lieutenant F-105 pilot assigned to the 67th Squadron on Okinawa. By spring 1966, F-105s had taken a lot of combat losses and needed pilots to fill in until permanent replacements arrived. And they needed them quickly. Summer help they called us. I volunteered and the next day flew an F-105D from Okinawa to Takhli, Thailand.

There were two types of pilots flying F-105s in the mid 1960s: the old heads with years, often decades of experience and the new kids like me with few hours in the airplane and no combat time at all. Early in the conflict, the F-105 force flew combat exclusively in the daytime—the Air Force had very little night capability. It was a great place for a new kid, like me, to learn how to fly combat. And we had great combat leaders: Risner, Kasler, Hutto, Alder, Black Matt and many others. Several had flown combat in Korea and a few in the big war, WWII. But as they were quick to explain, the big war is the one you are currently fighting. They had "been there" and loved to teach the lessons they had learned through hard experience. It was the best school for combat flying one could imagine.

I was assigned to a flight and we did everything together. We had flight integrity—even on Rest and Relaxation (R&R), at the Princess Hotel or the Siam Intercontinental four days a month in Bangkok. It was good duty. After a few sorties, I felt fairly confident, even proficient flying combat. But as soon as I got proficient, permanent party replacements pilots began to arrive from the States and the view toward TDY pilots changed. We were looked on as soaking up sorties, which lengthened the tour of PCS pilots. No one said anything but we could read the signals. TDY guys were scheduled for fewer and fewer counters. It was no surprise when the wing commander called us in and said what we knew was coming. We weren't needed in combat as much as we were needed on the island of Okinawa for nuclear alert duty. (Today we often forget that the F-105 remained on 24-hour-a-day nuclear alert in Germany and on Okinawa throughout the Vietnam conflict.). I protested not being able to finish a combat tour on the spot; however, the "needs of the Air Force" prevailed and reluctantly I returned to Okinawa. My combat sorties were over, at least for 1966.

It had been an amazing summer. I had survived 37 combat missions and learned valuable lessons about how to stay alive. Another important lesson was reinforced; lieutenants have no priority anywhere at anytime. But after surviving combat, I gained a new view on life. Now when things got tough, I could keep perspective by remembering: I once had a job where people shot real bullets at me.

So it was that I spent the rest of 1966 on Okinawa flying the F-105 and sitting nuclear alert. By December, the prospects of getting back into combat looked okay for many F-105 guys, if one had enough rank, but pretty grim for a lieutenant. In December, an assignment to F-4 stateside training with a follow-on combat tour became available. I got the nod, and in January 1967, loaded my household goods and car on a boat for shipment back to the states. As I waved goodbye to the boat, my assignment was canceled. It would be a year before I would see my car and stuff again, and during that year I would spend two or more months at each of the following places: Kadena AFB, Okinawa; Yakota AFB, Japan; Korat RTAFB, Thailand; the Pentagon; Nellis AFB, Las Vegas.

My F-4 assignment had been canceled because General Ryan wanted to improve night bombing capability and was going to use the F-105 to do it. Ryan's Raiders we called it. The F-105 wing at Okinawa provided four front seat pilots with combat experience. I got the nod—first cadre. Yakota provided another four. Eight pilots fresh out of stateside F-105 school were assigned as radar operators in the back seats. They had been diverted from their single-seat F-105 assignments and were not happy campers. Missions were to be flown exclusively at night. We were sent to Yakota to practice for a few weeks. Several two-seat F-105s destined for the Wild Weasels at Korat were assigned to the Raiders. We had co-opted some of their aircraft and the Wild Weasels weren't happy. We deployed from our training base at Yakota to Korat where we began flying combat. The Raiders had early combat losses and were revaluated and restructured and the mission became an additional task for Wild Weasels. Raider's backseat pilots were PCS so they were assimilated into single seat F-105s, which they were happy to do. Since I was TDY and there was no shortage of pilots, I had to return to Okinawa after only four months of combat flying. Another summer, another combat assignment as summer help.

After a short stay on Okinawa, I was assigned to Nellis AFB, Nevada, as a Wild Weasel instructor pilot with an intermediate stop for ninety days at the Pentagon. No one, especially me, had any idea what I was to do in Washington. After finding my way in the warren that is the basement of the Pentagon, I was instructed to write a first hand account, a "Lieutenant's eye view," of the war and especially the Air Force night capability, or as I wrote, lack of it. "Tell us what you really think," they said. No restrictions. And I did. I wrote for a month and a half, copies were distributed, and, for the next month, I met with staff and answered questions. This was heady stuff. Until then, I didn't know the Air Force cared a whit what any lieutenant thought.

I returned to Nellis as a student in the Wild Weasel school. I had flown Wild Weasel aircraft in Ryan's Raiders but never on a Wild Weasel mission. Then a big change: I was reassigned as an F-111 instructor and made available as a follow-on replacement pilot for Harvest Reaper—the first cadre of F-111s sent into combat. At least I was headed back to the war. But, Harvest Reaper didn't fulfill expectations and there was no follow-on. My next reassigned was to fly F-111 Operational Test and Evaluation. Great job but it didn't get me back into combat. In my first year at Nellis, I had been in four different squadrons in two different wings flying two different planes. I had been a Wild Weasel, as well as an F-111 student, instructor, then OT&E pilot. However, my chances of getting back in combat were fading and the conflict wouldn't last.

But the conflict did last. In 1972, as a Captain, I was again assigned to Wild Weasels. Since attending Wild Weasel school the first time a lot had changed. So I went again, to get recurrent in the F-105G and updated on the Standard Arm weapon. I'm not positive, but I may be the only two-time attendee. I reported to Korat in September 1972 trained and ready. At school, I had crewed up with a permanent sidekick, my Electronic Warfare Officer, Major Robert A. "Bob" Webb. Bob had flown on the B-52, B-58, and now F-105Gs. He had flown higher, faster, farther, and longer than all except a handful of people on earth. There wasn't anything I could do in an airplane that would amaze or even impress Bob in the least. He had done it all. We trained hard and became a well-rehearsed team. If I were concentrating on an airborne surface-to-air missile, I could feel secure that Bob would be looking out the other side of the cockpit, scanning the rest of the world for MiGs, missiles or other previously unseen threats. We both understood the greatest threat is the one you don't see until it is too late. We worked well together and were seldom surprised. We flew challenging combat missions at an interesting time: September 1972, through Linebacker II in December and then until the POWs were returned in April 1973.

The following paragraph from the novel *THUNDERCHIEF* by Don Henry (Pelican Publications) talks about what it was like to be stationed in Thailand during the Vietnam conflict.

"A word about technology and the times. [It]...was before the digital economy, the cruise missile culture, sensitivity training, and female fighter pilots...before personal computers, the Internet, and email. Aviators in combat had very little contact with loved ones and news from the outside world in general. A telephone call from Thailand to the States was time consuming to initiate and so expensive it could only be justified for emergencies. A stamped letter was the primary communication tool but most [aircrew] activities were classified and what wasn't seemed too dull to record. Typically, a box of homemade chocolate chip cookies, lovingly baked and carefully wrapped, arrived crushed so badly we ate them with a spoon. Not much represented home which was probably why pinups were so popular. As Bob Hope reminded us every Christmas, it was nice to see what we were fighting for."

I have come to understand the jumble of assignments and reassignments—the start and stops in my attempt to finish a combat tour—are more the nature of war playing out than something unusual. Of course it would have been nice if things had gone faster and smoother. But they didn't. War interrupts lives. The history of war is the history of things going wrong and adjusting for them. War always evolves as a series of crises.

One of the questions anyone faces when going into combat is how will I react? Do I have what it takes? Will I be afraid? Can I face an enemy and not embarrass my buddies, my squadron, my country or myself? Finally the day comes and one faces the enemy. Soon you are gripped by a single transcendent emotion as you experience something that you encounter nowhere else in life. It becomes clear that a hostile military force is making every effort to kill you. And that one fact focuses your efforts and changes everything.

The Wild Weasels I knew and flew with were exceptional warriors. I sometimes have to remind myself that they were not superhuman; they were only flesh and blood, which in many ways made their achievements even more remarkable.

Colonel Don Henry, USAF Ret., WW # 927

Story by Steve Victor, F-105 Crew Chief

An Evening with My Thud

Editor's note: Story written by Steve Victor, an F-105 Crew Chief at Takhli RTAFB. Although not a regular Wild Weasel aircraft Crew Chief, his experience is typical of all F-105 Crew Chiefs.

Note: Steve Wrote: "I never had a Wild Weasel model assigned to me but I have fixed and launched quite a few, as we all helped each other out. When I was a Takhli we had Wild Weasel birds 316 and 320 assigned to the 333rd TFS (1968-69) and I have worked on both of them."

Photo courtesy of Steve Victor
Steve closing the canopy to keep out the rain and the rice bugs.

My Thud, 59-1734, has returned home to its resting place for the night in front of revetment A-3. I signal the pilot, Capt. Dewitt to hold his brakes. I chock the wheels and then give him the signal to cut the throttle.

He sits in the cockpit for a moment as the engines spins down, but then takes off his helmet and starts to unstrap. I hang the ladder on the left side of the cockpit and then run up it to make sure the shoulder straps are clear from his parachute before he stands up. He hands me his helmet bag and I back down the ladder as he climbs out of the cockpit. When Capt. Dewitt reaches the ground, he takes a moment to tell me that 734 had a nav problem in flight. I nod, hand him his helmet bag and the 781 forms as he climbs into the Step-van for the ride to debriefing.

I check the oil quantity while the engine was still hot and get a sample for the lab guys. The ML-1 demineralized water cart gets towed in behind my bird. I start the engine that powers the pump; grab the hose and refill 734's water tank. I replace the filler cap, close the access panel, and then shut down the water cart engine. It gets towed away for the next customer. Then the tug shows up. I hook the tow bar the Thud's nose wheel, grab a couple guys from the revetment next door for wing-walkers and we get 734 pushed back into my revetment.

The night is typical for Takhli. It's hot and humid, and filled with the sounds of rice bugs flitting around the NF-2 light carts and generally being pests. An occasional bat flutters by chasing a rice bug. The fuel truck I called for shows up and it is waiting to refuel the plane. I hook up the grounding wires and then insert the single-point refueling nozzle into its receptacle. The fuel truck engine surges for a few minutes while the JP-4 is pumped into my bird. When it's full, the pump stops. I remove the nozzle and the hose is reeled onto the truck's reel. I unhook all the grounding wires, and the driver heads on to his next stop. I grab a packed drag chute from the flight chief's pickup and wrestle the awkward bulky thing into its compartment over the tail. I use my Phillips screwdriver to hold the pilot chute bungee cord in place and then jump up and down on the door while hanging onto the handhold cutout in the rudder until the latch engages. I retrieve my screwdriver and hop down to the slab and on down to the ground. The line truck swings by to drop off the 781 forms. I take a moment and add my entries about the servicing I've completed so far.

By now the bird has cooled down enough for me to put on my bunny suit and crawl the inlets to check for FOD or damage. I can turn the engine turbine by hand. The blades give off a tinkling sound as they move. After I finish with that I also check the tail pipe. Everything looks good. Even though here at Takhli, the pilots are running them much harder than in peacetime training, the J-75 engines are very reliable. 734 had a nav problem, so of course an electronic box had to be changed. In order to get at the box, the air conditioning duct had to be pulled to get it out of the way. We called the duct the Iron Maiden and it is located in a belly compartment (Hell Hole) just aft of the nose gear. Pulling the Iron Maiden is a job which every Crew Chief would like to let one of the new guys do because it is such an unpleasant job. But not tonight!!! I squeeze up into the hellhole, stretch my arms up over my head to get at the top clamp and release it. Now I can pull the Iron Maiden out.

The Doppler shop guys swap out their black boxes. When they finish, I re-install the Iron Maiden. One good thing was that 734 was in standard configuration and is not set up with a 650-gallon centerline tank. If she'd had a 650, it would have to be pulled to get into the Hell Hole and then re-installed afterwards. But 734 has flown the last several sorties in the same configuration: a jamming pod on the right outboard wing station, an AIM-9 Sidewinder missile on the left outboard, 450 gallon fuel tanks on both the inboards, and a center-line MER (multiple ejector rack) for bombs. The Thud has an internal bomb bay but it has a 390-gallon fuel tank loaded in it. So the bomb-bay doors are closed and there are bellybands supporting the centerline station for the MER. If 734 had been scheduled for a sortie in southern Laos or Route Package I, the Sidewinder might have been downloaded and pod of folding fin rockets loaded instead.

A tug drops off a bomb cart loaded with six 750-pound bombs in front of my revetment. The load crew arrives with their jammers and makes short work of loading the six bombs on the MER. A couple of the bombs at the front of the MER have three-foot long extenders for 'daisy cutter' fuses installed on them. The load crew installs the fuses and the arm-safe wires. Then they run a quick check on the AIM-9 Sidewinder missile on the left outboard station. The missile tracker head inside its glass 'eye' moves and points at the flashlight used as a heat source regardless of how it was moved. Good missile. The tug driver collects the empty bomb cart as the load crew finishes and hurries on to the next revetment.

The gun 'plumbers' show up with their gear, hook it to the bird and quickly crank new 20-millimeter rounds into the ammunition drum of the Vulcan cannon. The same equipment simultaneously removes the empty brass from the previous mission. They button up the hatches they'd opened, and move on to the next bird they need to re-arm. It was getting close to time for an 'o'dark-thirty' start-up. Now I've got a lot of little jobs that have to be performed to get the plane ready for its next mission. I fill the cockpit thermos bottle with ice crushed by a screwdriver handle along with ice-cold water. Thud pilots think very highly of that thermos bottle of cold water mounted behind the ejection seat. They drink from a rubber hose that clips onto the side of the ejection seat headrest. While I'm in the cockpit, I position the lap belt and shoulder straps so they will be out of the pilot's way when he climbs in. I clean the canopy so the pilot won't see a bug speck and think he sees a MiG. The chief next door finishes servicing his bird and then pushes the green painted liquid oxygen cart into my revetment. I put on my cotton overalls, the face shield and the heavy insulated gloves before I hook the hose connector from the cart to the Thud and put liquid oxygen into LOX system for the pilot to breathe in flight. You service the system by filling it up with liquid oxygen until it comes out of the overflow tube. I don't have to service the LOX system every flight. The Thud holds ten liters of LOX, but rarely uses more than one or two liters during a single flight. When it hits the overflow pan, liquid oxygen has a deep blue color that I will never forget.

I plug in my headset so I will be able to talk to the pilot after engine start. I make one last walk around, trying not to catch the climb/dive vent in my back as I pass under the tail. I bang on all the panels with the heel of my hand as I go and listen for the rattle of a loose Dzus fastener. Then I wait for the TAC trained airplane driver to arrive. The pie wagon pulls up and Maj. Jim Howerton gets out. I salute him. He asks about 734. She's his assigned plane and has his wife's name "Mona B II" painted in bright red outlined in white on the side of the intakes and his name on the left canopy rail. My name is on the right canopy rail. He looks over the forms and I answer his questions. We make the pre-flight walk around. Then he goes to the back of the revetment for a few quiet moments. He then climbs up into the cockpit, I help him strap in.

While this is going on, one of Crew Chiefs helping me opens the coffee can that contains a starter cartridge. He's careful because it's easy to cut yourself on the sharp edges of the can. The starter cartridge is a cylinder a little larger than my head made of solid rocket fuel by the Thiokol Company. He bends up the tabs slightly and spits on them to insure a good contact, puts the cartridge in the breach and locks it in the belly of my Thud. Now the cart just needs a minute electrical spark from 734's battery to unleash its power. I keep a spare cart stashed in the corner of my revetment in case the one he just installed doesn't fire or the engine doesn't start.

Once Maj. Howerton is strapped in, I take the ladder down, put on my headset and wait for him to switch on the battery. When he flips on the battery switch, the interphone comes alive with its high-pitched whine. Then Maj. Howerton hits the start cartridge switch and the igniter plugs start firing. The J-75 engine begins turning. When the rpm gets high enough, he opens the throttle. The igniter plugs ignite the fuel and the Thud comes alive. On the ground, I can hardly see thru the foul smelling smoke from starter cartridge. My helper secures the start cart panel.

The smoke dissipates and I make the walk-around checks while talking to Maj. Howerton on the headset. Everything is working and there are no leaks. I wish him Godspeed and unplug the headset. I go to the right front of the Thud making sure that he sees me. He gives me the 'remove chocks' signal. I pass the same signal to my helpers. I marshal the Thud forward. Shortly after it begins moving, Maj. Howerton taps the brakes to check if the stab aug (stability augmentation system) is working. I continue to marshal him forward until he reaches the taxiway guideline, then I signal him to turn. As he rounds the turn to taxi away, I salute him and give him thumbs up.

Now the wait begins until takeoff. I help get other planes launched while Maj. Howerton taxis my Thud among the others down to the arming area at the end of the runway. There the 'last chance' crew will check for leaks, cut tires and so forth. If everything is OK, they pull the landing gear safety pins and arm the bombs.

Then the other Crew Chiefs and I go out to the picnic table to watch the takeoff. The sun is just coming over the mountain to the east of the base. My Thud taxis onto the runway half a mile away and stops momentarily. The canopy comes down. I can see the nose wheel strut compress as Maj. Howerton runs up the engine. Then the nose suddenly comes up again when he releases the brakes. The afterburner flame shoots out twenty feet or more. The Thud is rolling well now. Maj. Howerton switches on the water injection. You can tell if the water injection is working by the rings coming out of the tailpipe. About this time, the boom of the afterburner lighting off reaches us. Mona B lifts off.... The gear retracts. My Thud is off to work.

Steve Victor, F-105 Crew Chief

Story by Charles D. "Dave" Mount WW # 248

Recollections of the T-39 Wild Weasel Training Aircraft Program

Between mid-1966 and mid-1969, I was an Action Officer and a Captain in AF/RDQRT, Tactical Division in the Directorate of Operational Requirements. My office was the focal point for initiating modification requirements (MRs) to operational aircraft for special missions. One of the major MRs that went through my office was the conversion of the F-105F into the Wild Weasel III. The basic conversion MR had occurred prior to my assignment. I worked on various MRs to improve the WW III war bird, such as adding SEE SAMS, COMBAT Spider (mini-VHF jammers), the "famous" WW III video tape recorder, and the ALQ-105 blister jammer. During this time, I worked closely with Capt Jack Donovan at the Nellis school house. Jack was always a font of interesting ideas to improve the F-105F's capabilities. During this time, my office was also deeply involved with "birthing" the F-4C and F-4D versions of the Wild Weasel. The infamous APS-107 RHAW was another EW system that our office managed for use with the F-4s. Since the number of Weasel students grew to support the war and the F-4C was trying to reach some degree of operational readiness, the teaching tasks at the Nellis school became rather busy. Out of this exponential growth of students came the "far out" idea to convert a small quantity of T-39As as Wild Weasel trainers.

I recall the first time I heard Jack attempt to sell this idea to me over the telephone. After listening to him expound on the greatness of this idea, I started thing of how this idea would float among the key players on the Air Staff that had to buy in if the project was to go. I got Jack to make a visit to the Pentagon so his idea could be fed to others. Jack had done some homework and had some preliminary sketches and costs to modify the aircraft. We floated the idea to the Dempster Committee (MG K.C. Dempster, AF/RDQ; Maj Dick Haggren, AF/RDQRT; myself; Lt Col Pierre Levy, AF/RDRE (our chief "scientist"), Lt Col Marty Selmanovitz, AF/SME (EW Loggy rep), Maj Tom Stedman, AF/SPDQ (QRC money); and Col Joe Wack, AF/XOOPE (I think)(EW chief in Ops). The consensus was to go ahead. I had the job of taking the MR package around the Air Staff to collect signatures from all the offices required for approval. Since I knew I was in for some flack over the use of a T-39 as a Wild Weasel, I had to prepare a short but attention-grabbing means to get into the various O-6s that had to sign off on the MR. I devised a cover sheet with big red letters that announced "This IS really HOT, a Wild Weasel Project!". Generally, anything with a Wild Weasel label on it got priority attention. This got me in the door. When the individual (who generally wasn't familiar with the trainer effort) read the details, the smoke rose, I was called a fraud, but I was eyeball to eyeball with the O-6 and had a chance to make my case. Logic prevailed and I get the needed signatures and the program became a reality. Jack told me later how impressed he was that I could float this concept through in such a short time and get the needed funds. I think the time span from brain fart to approval was in the area of 3-4 months.

The idea was to modify the T-39 passenger compartment with 3 stations. One station mirrored the F-4C Weasel with the APS-107, the second was a copy of the F-105F rear cockpit, and the third station was the instructor station. Once the MR was approved, the task of conversion was the job of the Nellis gang, North American Aviation and the T-39 depot (Sacramento?). By this time, I had left the Air Staff for other challenges and never got a chance to see the finished product.

Dave Mount, WW # 248

Sacramento Air Material Area (SMAMA) Meeting and Merriment

I recall another event that took place in the early days of WW III. This story is about an evening of merriment during one of the periodic Wild Weasel III program reviews, held at Sacramento Air Material Area (SMAMA). At he end of the meeting a large group of us headed out for dinner and drinks. I can't recall all of the gang in the group but it did include a senior officer, who was assigned to AF/RDQRT at the time, and myself. I also recall Tony Eithier from ATI being involved. Before dinner, we hit a strip bar to "unwind" from the day's meeting. Most of us immediately got into Beefeater martinis while we heckled the Master of Ceremonies (MC), a short fat guy who told bad jokes. The place was arranged so that the bar was right up against the stage and was curved so as to make an "S" curve. We all sat up at the bar in a group that was strung out for maximum harassment of the MC. After about an hour of this merriment, someone decided it was time to go eat steaks at a place across the street. We began to stagger out and head for the steak joint. The AF/RDQRT senior officer was either the last out or close but didn't meet up with us until the rest of us had ordered our food. He still had his drink from the club since it was unfinished. By this time, he was feeling no pain at all and ordered steak and lobster. Since he ordered late, his food arrived just as the rest of us finished. The plan was to go back to the strip club for more "merriment" after dinner. He decided that, since his meal was late in arriving, he didn't want to hold us up so he put the steak in one pocket of his new suit coat and the lobster tail in the other pocket. He then took his latest drink of gin and off we went. As we arrived back into the strip club, the MC saw us and started to crack jokes about us leaving earlier for dinner, and how did we enjoy it etc. Mr. AF/RDQRT promptly sat down at the edge of the stage, pulled out his steak and lobster and began to chomp on it. The MC went ballistic at this and we all had a good laugh. The only one not amused was his wife after he got home with the steak and lobster grease inside his new suit!

Dave Mount, WW # 248

Story by Robert W. "Bob" King, WW # 484

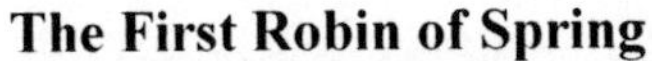

The First Robin of Spring

'Betty Lou' belonged to the Wing Commander of the 388th TFW from Korat and visited Takhli for the Dec 1968 River Rats Practice Reunion. In addition to the red enamel decorations, note the King Cobra stencils on the inlet ramp and the front canopy rail. Our hosts, the 4th Wing, Royal Thai Air Force, had left their mark.
Photo courtesy of Jim Howerton

In conjunction with the December 1968 Red River Valley Fighter Pilots Tactics Conference and Practice Reunion, the 388 Tactical Fighter Wing (the 'Avis' wing) Commander, Col. MacDonald, flew over to join the festivities. However for a colonel commanding a wing whose principal striking arm was three Thud squadrons, he made the unfortunate decision to arrive in a multi-engined mini-BUF or F-4. This occasioned some less than complimentary remarks among the Thud drivers at Takhli. These feelings coupled with a desire to make the practice reunion a memorable occasion (and if the truth be told, probably too much consumption of intoxicating spirits) led to that F-4 being redecorated overnight with a substantial quantity of bright red enamel. Since the statute of limitations has long since run out, I now have no compunction in naming the culprits. Many years afterwards, I learned from his son that Maj. Jim Howerton was the original instigator of this dastardly plot and that his paint crew consisted of 1Lt Pete Lindsley, 1LT Cecil Snell and 1Lt Gary Confer.

What follows only took me thirty-four years to figure out. I was looking at the two photos of 'Betty Lou' that appear on this page when it struck me. It appears that one of the reasons the Takhli folks took offense (and the paint brush) at 'Betty Lou's' original paint scheme was that she sported a set of shark teeth under her nose. There is some history involved here. So far as I can find out, the first aircraft to sport the toothy shark's grin were the P-40 Warhawks of the American Volunteer Group of the Chinese Air Force commanded by General Claire Chenault prior to the United States engagement in World War II. In addition to the teeth, they usually had painted eyes on each side of nose following the Chinese custom of painting eyes on the prow of their ships so that the ships could 'see where they were going.

After the US had been attacked by Japan and joined the war, the AVG was transferred to the US Army Air Force and became the 23rd Fighter Group. That lineage had been passed down to the 23rd Tactical Fighter Wing which was stationed at McConnell AFB, Kansas at the beginning of the Vietnamese War. When some of their squadrons were sent TDY to Takhli with their F-105s, their Thuds were wearing a set of grinning teeth and eyes to see where they were going. You can see a photo of their appearance in the September 1965 issue of National Geographic. At Takhli, the Flying Tigers were once again in the same skies where they had won their fame. Maj. Howerton knew his military history and the unit lineages involved. So when this F-4 showed up at Takhli in December 1968 sporting a set of shark's teeth, he resented it, and he decided to do something about it.

Maj. Howerton's paint crew was willing, but not too careful (those intoxicating beverages again?). They did take particular care to insure that they had painted over the eyes and shark teeth on the nose of the bird. Then they applied the remaining paint wherever the spirit moved them. When they had finished, not only the F-4 had acquired a lot of red paint. There was a good deal of it that had dripped onto the ramp so that there was a F-4 shaped silhouette outlined in red spatters on the concrete.

Some members of the Royal Thai Air Force 4th Wing got into the act and stenciled their cobra emblem on both splitter plates. (By the way, the 4th Wing guys were good with their stencils and spray paint. There were very few aircraft that stopped in at Takhli that didn't acquire a cobra on it somewhere. That includes the U-2's and SR-71's when they made their occasional visits and parked in the super secret secured hanger that was fenced off from the rest of the base.)

Col. MacDonald was not pleased with the new trim job on his airplane. He expressed himself loudly and profanely on the subject the next morning when he strode up to his bird to return to Korat. He said unkind things to Col. Horgan and the other Takhli colonels who had come to see him off. It probably didn't help in the least that some of them giggled while he was holding forth. There was also an audience of folks from a variety of other bases, and even some Navy folks watching the proceedings from nearby on the ramp while they were preflighting their own birds for their return to their various places of duty.

When Col. MacDonald took off, he simply left the afterburners cooking rather than trying to conserve fuel. He remained low for a bit to pick up speed and then did an Immelman to come back over Takhli enroute for Korat. He left the burners on as long as he could in an attempt to try to burn or peel that enamel off his airplane. It didn't work.

After Col. MacDonald's dramatic departure, there was an effort that afternoon to find out who had painted that F-4. For some reason, suspicion fell on the pilots of the 333rd TFS. Of course, that might have had something to do with the squadron color being bright red. There were nasty rumors of summary courts-martial swirling around. A number of our junior lieutenant type Thud drivers suddenly decided they should try to look inconspicuous for a while.

Now let Lt. Col. Dick Heyman, the commander of the 333rd TFS, pick up the story in an email message to me:

When Col. Horgan saw the F4 sitting on the ramp after the big party and it had that horrible paint job on it, he called me at my hootch and said "get down here" no ID or location, he just hung up.

I waited and about 10 minutes later he called again and this time I had a chance to ask where, "base ops" was the reply. He told me to find out who had done that job, I said our squadron wouldn't have used red paint, that would be a dead give-away. He didn't buy that at all. Said get those responsible and get them to Korat to repaint it. I said I would take care of it. I then called all available crews together and told them I didn't ever want to know who had done it. Next day I got two professional painters out of FMS and you were selected by the crews to go with me, I inquired to be sure you had had nothing to do with it, everyone said no so away we went. As we were finishing up a Sgt. I knew came asked if we needed anything, We needed stencils for numbers and names, I asked for my name and yours and a big [333]. We then - it was getting dusk - painted 333 on tail and our names on the rails. We went to the CO's hootch and had a drink and he said good job. Next day when he found those names on the rails he told a painter to get them changed and as he was doing it, it started raining so he closed the canopy and a can of paint was caught with the normal results. Yes I heard that somebody wrote a letter and McDonald called me but said don't worry. Weren't you in the crowd that we took the rear end of the papier-mâché to Korat and gave it to the squadron? Called it the horse's ass of the month award.

Colonel Horgan sent for Lt. Col Dick Heyman, the 333rd commander. When he reported, Col. Horgan told him to collect the culprits and take them to Korat as a working party to clean up that F-4. Our boss said that he wouldn't ask any of his troops to put themselves in the position of either lying to him or confessing to an offense for which they could be severely punished. When our boss got back to the squadron, I suggested that I go along. I had a couple of motives for volunteering. I had never seen Korat and I wanted to take a look at their operation. Second, I had an ironclad alibi for my whereabouts at the time the red paint was being spread around. I had been at the party the night before. In addition to numerous witnesses, I also had the photos in my camera to show that I was there from beginning to end. The boss agreed and I was told to meet him at Base Ops in the morning.

Col. Heyman and I traveled over to Korat in the base C-47 gooney bird the next morning. When we arrived about 0930, we noted that there seemed to be fire truck escorting the gooney bird to its parking spot. Considering that sufficient warning, we gave our billfolds and paperwork

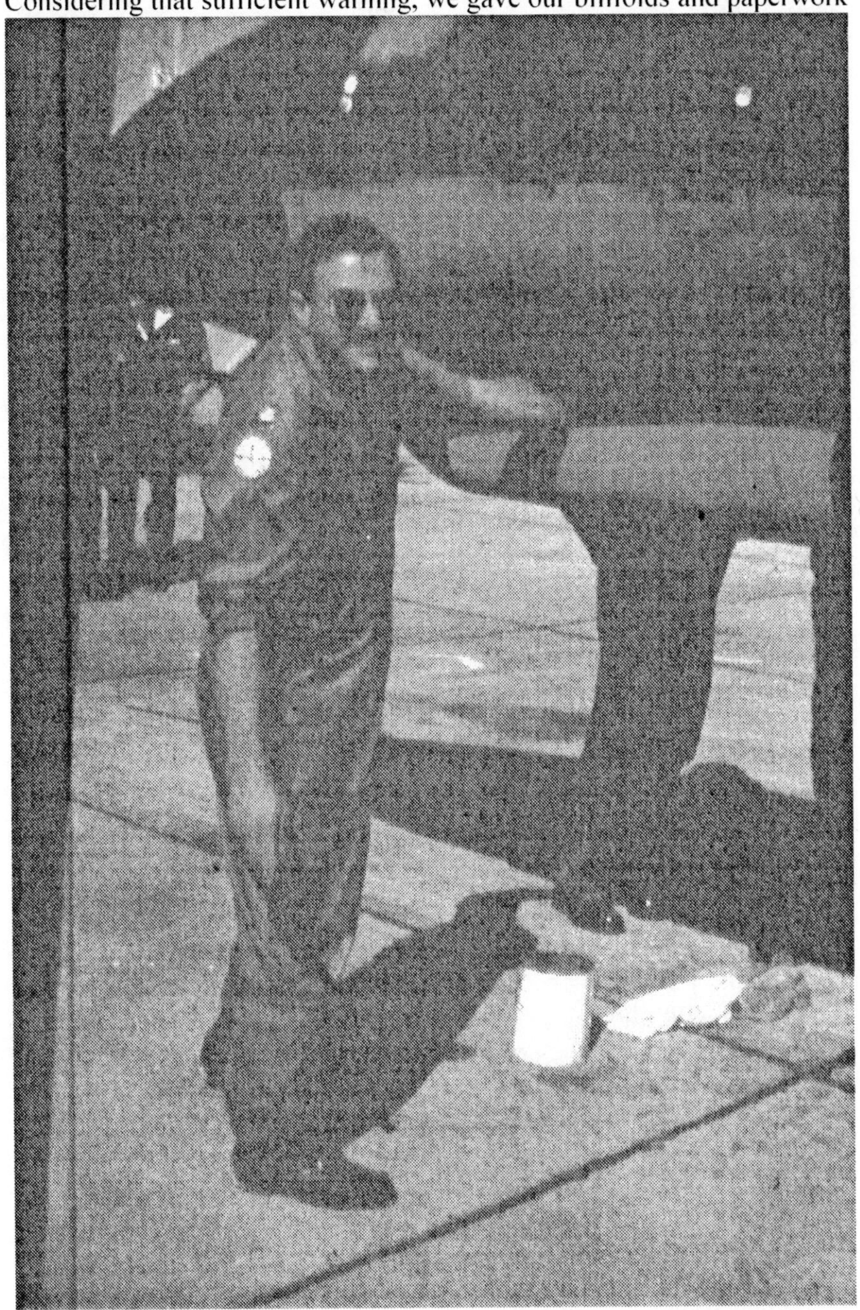

Lt. Col Heyman Removing Paint from "First Robin of Spring"
Photo courtesy of Bob King

After we were well soaked, we reclaimed our stuff and caught a ride to the airplane wash rack where the airplane was parked. We consulted with the Korat paint shop boss and were provided with rags and paint thinner. Then we set to work.

The Korat wash rack was between hangers and adjacent to the road that ran along the back of the ramp and hanger area. That seemed to be a very busy road that day. There were remarkable numbers of folks who had to come along and critique our efforts or photograph us. On several occasions, Korat pilots dropped by with six packs of beer which were very welcome in the heat.

We worked on that bird until the sun went down with only a brief break for lunch. Truth to tell, we weren't all that effective getting that red paint off. The solvents we tried just didn't do much to it. Apparently, the 388th Wing Commander's high-speed flight to 'burn' the paint off had the unfortunate effect of baking it on instead. Since the underlying surface was aircraft aluminum, we couldn't use something like steel wool that would cause all sorts problems later on.

After we had gotten the bulk of the enamel off the bird, we needed to replace some of the other paint that had come off as we scrubbed. They were minor items really—the tail number and the names of the pilot and backseater on the canopy rails. With the assistance of some folks from the Korat paint shop and some quick stencil cutting, we put our names on the canopy rails and big 333 on the tail as the aircraft number. Then we went to Col. MacDonald's hootch to report we had finished. We had done the best we could by hand and he seemed satisfied that we had shown a good faith effort. Of course, that was before he had a look at his bird. At any rate, we were allowed to return to Takhli that evening. And I never got a chance to look around Korat that trip. That had wait for a couple of years.

Now this tidbit is hearsay evidence. I didn't recall this at all. But I have been assured that it's true. One of the displays made up for the Takhli tactics conference had been a papier-mâché horse. I have been told that horse was cut in half and the rear part was taken to Korat and given to one of the squadrons there. One version of the tale has the horse's rear being painted red. But the story goes that this horse's patoot wound up atop Col. MacDonald's hootch.

I heard a few days later that the professionals in the Korat paint shop had to use a sandblasting technique with ground up walnut shells or something similar to get the rest of that red enamel off.

I had occasion to visit U-Tapao RTAFB for another 'tactics conference' a couple of months later. While there, I noticed 'Betty Lou' parked on the ramp wearing her newly refurbished paint job—sans red trim. The tail number had been restored to its original value and Col. MacDonald's name was once more on the canopy rail. And she once again had eyes and shark teeth under her snout.

Concerning that letter mentioned in Lt. Col. Heyman's email message. That was a reference to a letter supposedly written to his Congressman by one of the troops in the Korat paint shop who was unhappy about having to repaint the airplane. The Congressman fired off a letter of inquiry to the Secretary of the Air Force along the lines of "what's going on." I presume Col. MacDonald and his staff fielded the Congressional query when it trickled down from the exalted levels of the Puzzle Palace to the working Air Force. At any rate, I never heard of any consequences coming out of it.

Robert W. King, WW # 484

Story by Mike O'Brien, WW # 847

DOWNTOWN – FINALLY!

Six years earlier I'd seen the terror of the Thuds going "Downtown" when, for six months, I was a GCI radar controller at "Brigham" in Udorn, Thailand. Then, I'd listened in on Strike Primary, hearing the real time radio calls of the action underway. At first, it was the business of marshalling the Force after tanker drop-off (the refueling tanker joinups I'd "controlled" a fraction of an hour before), then the buildup of Anti-Aircraft Artillery calls, the Surface-to Air Missile and Bull's-eye MiG engagement calls, "target in sight", flight maneuvering and position calls, etc., etc. It was an overwhelming picture of warriors at work that imagination couldn't add to; and, back then, we lost an average of an F-105 a day.

On this day, 29 July 1972, finally it was my turn to see if I'd measure up to that "Downtown" challenge. Ed Cleveland, already a distinguished veteran of 100 missions over North Vietnam in F-105s, was my pilot. I was his "Bear", in the backseat of #4 on an F-105 Wild Weasel escort mission to suppress the AAA and SAMs that threatened the Strike force… just as I had witnessed years earlier. The target that day was about ten miles Northeast of Hanoi, just East of the Northeast Railroad that went into China.

The real day began with the flight briefing where you went over all the essential details of the upcoming mission: target description and location, target area and refueling weather forecasts, "step" and takeoff times, air refueling "anchor" and refueling times, tanker drop-off and Time Over Target times, Strike force enroute and recovery plans, Intelligence assessment of the threats to the Strike force, etc. These were the details that defined our challenge.

In this flight briefing, Lead outlined our planned response: we'd fly two minutes ahead of the Strike force, a few miles South of their intended route, elements split to maneuver "out of phase" but within sight of each other. We'd feint towards any AAA or, especially, SAM site that was active, unless the site was a definite threat to the inbound Strike force. We needed to conserve our missiles until we approached the immediate target area where the Strike force would be most vulnerable; with an AGM-78 missile and a pair of AGM-45 Shrikes on each Thud, we'd have ample opportunity to go "Winchester". It would be a busy day.

After takeoff and flight join up, Ed let me fly formation to the tanker. He knew how nervous I was...almost puked on the way up the ladder to strap in...so "keeping busy" by flying formation was a great way to keep my mind off what I knew lay ahead. After Brigham joined the flight onto our Red Anchor tanker...been there, done that...we dropped off, heading East/Northeast towards Thud Ridge.

It was time to go to work so I was now too busy to be nervous... equipment on and checked, AGM-78 warming up, out of the cockpit most of the time to keep the rest of the flight in sight, looking for MiGs and SAMs and AAA . The flight is constantly maneuvering, almost like a "dance". As we head towards the Black River, the Barlock GCI radars are already up. AGM-78 off...don't want it to overheat. A Firecan AAA radar...too far off to acknowledge with a turn...then a SAM missile launch signal for 5 seconds. Not much later, we get a weak Fan Song SAM radar...AGM-78 coming back on...but the radar goes down. Another Fan Song, so weak that it's probably South of Hanoi, too far away to be a real threat. It's down...A lot going on and yet we haven't even crossed the Black yet. MiG CAP in sight, very high...

There's the River; making a slight turn towards the target area. We're in the flats now, but the SAM radars are eerily quiet and there are only a few Firecans in an otherwise dense radar environment. There's the Red River, Hanoi...Strike force already in sight. Centerline tank's empty.

STRONG Fan Song up...down before I can lock up the –78. Another strong Fan Song...looks like it's right by the bend in the Red, a little East of Hanoi. Then another strong Fan Song, just as I lock the –78 on the first Fan Song and Ed fires it. Good shot...The second Fan Song goes down; heavy AAA coming our way...I get distracted by the AAA and forget to follow the –78 to see if it puts the SAM radar down. We're maneuvering heavy now, constantly turning and reversing, jinking, staying with our element lead, slightly East of the target area looking towards where the Strike force is; they should be "rolling in" about now. Another Fan Song at 2 o'clock, a second new one on the nose...Ed pulls up and fires a Shrike...a third Fan Song...the ALR-31 says we have a valid launch on us; looks like the one Ed just fired at. SAM on the way; Ed maneuvers to put it at 2 o'clock, pulls...then, the #2 SAM...pulls...they only fired two. Heavy AAA again, seems like it's from everywhere...another Fan Song up, another valid launch...don't see any SAMs; he's down.

It's gotten so busy and we're maneuvering so much I now have no idea where we are. I'm just calling out Fan Songs, valid launches, AAA, keeping other aircraft in sight, looking for MiGs...but I have no idea where we are. I'm doing the best I can, but it's confusing.

Lead calls "bingo". Our element has enough gas for another pass or two in the target area to cover the Strike force egress, until we have to fight our way across Haiphong to go "feet wet" for our egress.

AAA continues everywhere; mostly 37mm, some 23mm and 57mm, occasional 85mm. Another Fan Song, at 11 o'clock; again, a Fan Song on the nose. Valid launch from the Fan Song on the nose; maneuver; visual on the SAM now at 3 o'clock, low; pull...repeat...again...New Fan Song at 2 o'clock...hard right...he's down. New Fan Song at 9 o'clock...hard left...Ed pulls and fires the last Shrike. Ed calls "bingo" fuel, but I can see we're already heading towards the South China Sea and will pass just North of Haiphong...getting the picture back of where we are for the first time in a long time. A launch tone, a new Fan Song, the previous Fan Song goes down; no SAMs in-flight. There's five fires on the ground, just East of that bend in the Red towards where I thought our –78 was headed...

It starts to get quiet as we get "feet wet"; no Fan Songs stay up for more than a few seconds, only a few brief launch tones and Firecans. We feel "safe" now, as everyone knows the MiGs don't fly over water...maybe they don't have rafts and life preservers.

All is well. We're together as an element of the original F-105 four-ship; we check each other over and everything looks good; #3 still has an AGM-78 remaining, on the right inboard. We did our job and no one got hit. We're on our way home.

We're in the haze, at least a few hundred feet below the top of the haze layer ... it's that time of the year when they're burning the rice fields there. But I can see a long ways in that clear, beautiful blue sky above the haze. Then, I see a dot in the distance... about our 4 o'clock, probably over 5 miles away. I tell Ed; he tells me to keep it in sight. It stays in the same relative position for a while, though it's getting closer. I can make it out as an airplane, then I can see it appear to "rock" its wings, paralleling our course, but getting closer; I call it again. At about 2 miles out, it slides towards our 5 o'clock; it looks to me like a MiG-21. But, there's some question as to whether it's a MiG-21 or a friendly Navy F-8. Then, the… MiG-21 fires a missile at us. I see the burst of smoke as the rocket motor lights off…and I call the missile shot. Ed calls the "Atoll" shot on the radio and for #3 to break left; #3 unloads his airplane, jettisons his external stores and breaks left. Meanwhile, as we're in a right break, I see the MiG-21 turn back towards land. The missile passes between us.

But now we have problems. When #3 jettisoned his stores, unloaded, the centerline tank came off and wrapped itself around the leading edge of the right wing and around the AGM-78 pylon on the right inboard… shorting out the wiring in the pylon, which fired off the AGM-78. This is not good for many reasons, but the immediate reason is that we now have a very capable anti-radiation missile on its way towards many radiating radars…which happen to be on our own Navy ships in the Gulf of Tonkin. I admittedly violated crew discipline and made a call on Guard channel, telling the Navy they had an AGM-78 coming their way and that they should shut their radars off. Sure enough, my APR-35 receiver went almost completely quiet.

First problem taken care of. However, with the centerline tank wrapped around the right wing leading edge, #3 has so much drag he can't get the Thud over 250 knots without using the afterburner…and we're already getting low on gas. He tries to shake the tank loose, but to no avail. Ed slows down and "S" turns around him to stay with him, so we're using more gas than planned, too.

We go over to GCI frequency…though we're still quite a ways North…tell them about our situation and asks them to turn the nearest tanker towards us (I've done that before…) and to give us his refueling frequency. We contact the tanker, who's near the DMZ heading North as we requested…but he wants to stay high, initially about 30,000 feet… probably so he can avoid threats from North Vietnam. We can't get much higher than 10,000 feet without using afterburner, but it can work. And, it does. We get a visual on the tanker, plug in the afterburners, struggle up to his altitude while we have him turning South, and #3 gets on the boom with mostly fumes in his tanks. He has to refuel in afterburner, using most of the gas he's taking on, or he doesn't have enough power (with all that drag) to stay on the boom…so, it takes a while for him to get enough gas in his tanks before he can drop off long enough for us to get gas. We are now very low on gas also, but it doesn't take us too long to get a partial load since Ed only has to cycle the afterburner now and then to stay on the boom. Both airplanes cycle on and off the tanker as he refuels us and drags us almost all the way to Da Nang.

Second problem taken care of. We made it back to friendly territory with a nice, long runway waiting to receive us. But, we have a final problem. When #3 attempts to lower the landing gear for landing, the right main landing gear hits the centerline tank that's wrapped around the right wing and inboard pylon…it won't come all the way down and lock in place. He tries everything he can think of…violently rocking the airplane, with and without rudder to try and shake it loose; same for rapid acceleration with burner/rapid deceleration with speed brakes, etc. etc. After about half an hour of fruitless attempts, it's obvious the right main landing gear isn't going to come down and locked. You can't land the airplane unless both main landing gear are down and locked, so the only other option is to eject from an otherwise perfectly good F-105 for a parachute letdown. So, #3 flies high over Da Nang harbor, points the Thud towards the South China Sea, trims it for level flight and punches out. #3 pilot and Bear are picked up uneventfully. We land at Da Nang for an exciting evening in Rocket City.

So ended my first mission Downtown. Ed Cleveland, my pilot, carried me through it all; I'm eternally grateful. I was absolutely terrified most of the time, but I did the best I could; I think I got the job done. However, we lost an F-105.

Did I measure up to the challenge that I'd known and pursued for six years? I leave that judgment to you.

Mike O'Brien, WW# 847

Story by Kenneth D. Thaete, WW# 923

My Second Shoot Down in Vietnam

Editor's Note: Ken was first shot down by anti-aircraft artillery (AAA) on 1 September 1968 while flying F-105D 60-0512 on a mission over Laos. He was then assigned to the 34 TFS, 388th TFW, Korat RTAFB and was successfully rescued but was injured. Major Norb Maier the EWO in this story is deceased. Norb was on his second tour as a Wild Weasel EWO when this shoot down occurred. On his initial tour in 1966/67 he was the very first Wild Weasel EWO to successfully complete 100 Wild Weasel combat missions while assigned to the 355th TFW, Takhli RTAFB. **This was the very last F-105 shot down during the Vietnam War!**

On 16 November 1972 I was scheduled to fly as the pilot on an F-105G Wild Weasel mission in North Vietnam along with Major Norb Maier, my Electronic Warfare Officer (EWO) in by back seat. The mission that night was to support B-52s, which were scheduled to bomb targets near Vinh, North Vietnam. I was assigned to the 561st Tactical Fighter Squadron, 23rd TFW, McConnell AFB, KS on temporary duty assigned to the 388th TFW, Korat RTAFB and we were flying out of the 17th Wild Weasel Squadron. We were scheduled to take off about 7:30 PM but had a problem with the first aircraft. We had to abort so we got into another aircraft, F-105G tail number 63-8359, and got airborne a little later than the rest of our flight that had already taken off. We got airborne, headed for the tanker, a KC-135, completed the rendezvous, filled up with fuel and headed into the target area. I knew which direction the B-52s we were scheduled to come from so I positioned myself in front of the bombers and cruised in just ahead of them toward the target area. The weather was broken to undecast clouds and the enemy radars were very active. Norb said that there were quite a large number of radars up that night, so we were looking for a good target to attack with our AGM-78 Standard Arm missile. (The AGM-78 is a big missile.)

We were cruising in toward the objective and about 15-20 miles out from the target. All of a sudden, a SAM radar came up and was locked onto our aircraft. Norb set up the AGM-78 to home on the radar emissions and said "FIRE". I fired the missile and normally when an AGM-78 comes off the wing it goes straight ahead for a little while and then climbs. It climbs so that it will reach higher altitude where the air resistance is less and the missile range will be greatest. For a shot where the target is relatively close the missile does not climb but instead noses over and heads down right away toward the target. Our AGM-78 headed down IMMEDIATELY. I engaged the afterburner for maximum power and made a hard turn to the left. As I was about to pull out of the turn, I remember seeing a big orange glow and that is all I remember at that time. Normally you have about 20 seconds from the time the SAM starts receiving guidance commands to when the missile gets to you, but this was not a normal situation.

We were flying at about 18,000-19,000 feet with a few clouds under us at about 15,000 feet and apparently they shot the missile in our general direction based on where they predicted we would be and did not guide it except for the terminal engagement. They aimed their radar where they thought we would be and lo and behold that's where I was when they turned their radar on and started to provide guidance commands to the SAM. Normally you could expect at least 20 seconds of missile guidance time before the missile would reach you, but in my case there was only about 6 seconds of guiding time and I did not have time to attempt to evade the missile. To evade the missile, you normally put the SAM on your wing tip and then when the missile gets fairly close to you, you start to out-pull and out-turn the missile so it won't hit you and will miss far enough that you wont be significantly damaged if the proximity fuse detonates the weapon. I was just getting ready to roll out to pull maximum G's when the SAM hit our aircraft and was still belly up to the missile when it went off.

Apparently Norb and I were both unconscious in the aircraft, because later on we found out that from where we got hit to where we ejected and landed on the ground was about 21 miles! That meant that we were unconscious in the aircraft for at least 2 minutes. Only the Good Lord kept that airplane flying.

When I did come to, I remember there was a big hole in the side and I felt like my right foot was outside the aircraft. I remember pulling my right foot inside and getting ready to eject. Fire was coming up between the console into my face. I remember seeing that all the caution and fire warning lights were on. So immediately I knew I was in bad trouble so I just squeezed the ejection triggers.

After departing the aircraft I faintly remember checking the chute as I was coming down. You have to remember it was dark outside. There was a moon shining but I don't remember too much of that part of it, but I faintly remember checking the chute. The next think I really remember consciously was that I was standing and looking around; I had already taken off my parachute harness but I don't remember doing it. I saw a few little lights around and was trying to get my bearings to help determine where I was. As it turns out, to the southwest there were some low hills and I was sort of on a high spot down in the valley. The lights were to my north mostly and to the east. I knew I had to get myself a hiding place for the night. I gathered up my parachute and all the things I had with me and started walking across what I thought was a cow pasture. It had short grass in it and was fairly easy walking. So I headed for the hills.

I apparently landed on my seat survival kit and damaged it, but as I was gathering all the stuff up and walking across the cow pasture, all of a sudden I heard a loud hiss that almost scared me to death – it was my life raft inflating! As I was walking across the cow pasture, it took me a few seconds to get my breath and calm down again. And so I took out my knife and punctured a hole in my life raft so it wouldn't be so big and heavy and I started up the hill.

As soon as I got to the base of the hills I started up and the going got a lot tougher. The brush was getting taller and the elephant grass was getting taller and it was tough going up the side of the hill. I got maybe, 100-200 yards up the side of the hill and the brush and stuff was getting up to my waist so I decided I would get rid of my parachute, my life raft, and everything I didn't need to make my journey up that hill a little lighter.

At that time I decided I'd better check my radio. Over there if you didn't have a radio you weren't going to get out. So I had one radio in my seat pack. I also carried two others, so I had three radios and two extra batteries sewn in my G-suit.

I got out my radio and turned it on and I heard my backseater, Norb, on the radio hollering for somebody to help him. He was trying to get anybody to answer him on the radio. So I finally broke in and said, "Norb, is that you?" He said "Yeah, who is this?" He said, "Oh God, I thought I was up here by myself!" I said, "No, I'm with you." I said, "Where are you?" and he said, "Oh, I'm kind of on a hill." I told him, "No use using our radios tonight, there probably won't be anybody around until in the morning so just get off the radio so they don't find out where we are." So we both decided to get off the radio and we would talk to each other in the morning.

I kept climbing up that hill all night until daybreak. It got tougher and tougher, the grass got higher and higher, and that elephant grass was like a knife, and it had real sharp blades on it. I lost my gloves during the ejection, so my hands got all cut up, like little paper cuts. About that time the sun was coming up and I decided I had better get a good place to lie down and hide. I was on the side of the hill and had real good cover so I made a little spot to lie down and I would end up lying there all day long. I was thirsty so I drank one can of water that I had in my seat kit. Now I only had one can of water left to save until later.

When it was getting light, close to 6:30 or 7:00 o'clock in the morning, I heard the sound of a jet flying somewhere over the valley. I turned on my radio and just listened, and sure enough it was a Fast FAC (Forward Air Controller). He was looking for us. I saw him coming down from north to south, headed down to pretty close to where we were and he was only about 1500 feet off the ground. I gave him a call that we were down here and I had him in sight. He asked, "What is your position?" So when he got fairly close to me I told him "I'm about one mile at your 2 o'clock now." And was off the radio again. I didn't want to make my transmissions very long so that the North Vietnamese could not DF (directional finding) where we were.

So he had a pretty good idea of our location, and he said, "Where's your backseater?" And Norb came on the radio and told him that he thought he was not more that about 400-500 yards to the southwest of where I was. The Fast FAC said, "Well, we're going to try to get some equipment in here today to get you guys out." So all we had to do is lay there and wait, wait, wait, and wait some more.

About noon I heard some more chatter on the radio, and it was the Fast FAC coming in again and they were flying around the area. The clouds were fairly low and as I remember about 2 o'clock in the afternoon, they decided to call things off. They wanted to get a good indication about where we were and about what they wanted to do. So Fast FAC called off the search and rescue mission for the day. I also noticed a photo reconnaissance airplane, an RF-101, come over and take pictures of the area, so I assumed they would get ready the next day to get us out of there.

Just before evening as the sun was beginning to set, the Fast FAC came in again. He wanted us to move from our present positions. He gave me directions. His instructions were to take a line from the squadron operations building at McConnell Air Force Base, Kansas, to my house, and go the distance from my house to Norb's house, about 200 yards, and then take a line from my house to Lake Cheney and go from my house to Squadron operations, about 400 yards, which is all around Wichita, KS and McConnell AFB. He gave directions to Norb the same way using our house, squadron operations, and Lake Cheney as points in the directions. We knew approximately the directions and distances that we were to move. So that was our assignment for the night.

As soon as it got dark I picked up the rest of my stuff, what little I had, didn't have a whole lot with me, little pieces of candy, etc. and drank my other, and last, can of water. Then I started up the hill. I worked and worked, it was hard going, the vines and elephant grass were very thick and heavy, now about 8-12 feet high in most places. But, I kept wiggling my way through it. Got to the top of the ridge, which I thought was about where I was supposed to turn directions. I turned directions and went a little ways and kept watching my clock and about 2:00 to 3:00 in the morning I crossed a washout that was coming down the hill where water had washed out and there was a little ditch. So I crossed it and went into the elephant grass and vines again. They were about 10 feet tall. I went in about 15 feet from that trail.

I thought I'd rest for a little but. My watch was under my flight suit and when I would pull up my sleeve I could see my watch, which was luminescent. I would sit there and rest a little bit and then kind of wake up with a start because I thought I had fallen asleep. I looked at my watch and as far as I could tell only a couple of seconds had gone by. I had to keep awake so I had to make sure I wouldn't let myself fall asleep.

About an hour later, as I was resting, I wanted to move about 50 –100 feet, but I heard what sounded like a dog barking. I lay very still and the sound of the barking kept getting closer. Apparently down this washout the enemy was hunting for me and was truing to make me move. But he screwed up the bark real bad; he was trying to sound like a dog. And I knew it was just a person with no dog. I knew he probably was coming down that washout so he would be real close to me; probably about 10-15 feet away. So I remained very still and I was hoping I hadn't torn up the vines enough for him to see where I was going. He got real close to me and he would bark like a dog and then stand and listen. Then he would move down the hill a little bit more. I had my right hand on my .38 revolver in case I needed it, but I wasn't moving a muscle. He moved on down the hill further and further away. When he was far enough away that I thought it was safe to move, I moved about another 50-70 yards across the side of the hill and sat there and waited until morning. Now it was the second morning. I figured I was about in the right spot where they wanted me to be.

As it turned out Norb and I were across a little horseshoe valley from each other. He was on one side of the little hill and I was on the other side of the hill. I was about 150 yards from the crest of the hill. When morning came we could hear dogs barking down below and we knew the enemy was out looking for us in that general area. They didn't know exactly where we were because we had come down at night. Then we just had to wait.

I turned on the radio and listened to the SAR (Search and Rescue) effort that was getting ready to come and attempt to pick us up. We had sort of an overcast, it was broken in places and some sun was shinning through here and there. We heard a SAM (Surface to Air Missile) launch and the Wild Weasels were shooting back at them but nobody got shot down. We were listening to them on the radio, and we could even hear some of the tankers that were about 200 miles away from us refueling aircraft that were supporting the SAR mission.

We were lucky in that 7th Air Force had recently received a new commander; General John W. Vogt, and he had recently told his people that the morale of the pilots was getting low because the air rescue was not getting anybody picked up. So he decided that when the next plane went down there would be an all out effort to pick up the crew. Norb and I happened to be the next airplane that went down. What we had learned later is that they had stopped the whole war and just concentrated on rescuing us.

So anyway, the SAR effort was underway and we were listening to it. They were coming in; it was the first time the A-7s were flying cover for the choppers. Before it had always been the A-1E prop driven aircraft. Well, if it hadn't been for the A-7s they wouldn't have even come to get us because we were about 60 miles south of Hanoi and near the Than Hoa Bridge where a lot of F-105s had been shot down earlier in the war.

The Navy said they couldn't come in and get us because we were too far inland and they couldn't come across that much open terrain to get us. The foothills were about 15-18 miles from the coast. So the Air Force had to come in by the way of the mountains in the back.

That second morning I was very thirsty. And it was sprinkling a little bit. So I took out my waterproof cloth map, which was about three feet by three feet, and I laid it in the grass so it would catch rainwater. All that morning I must have got a whole glass of water and drank it. I made a little funnel with the map and poured the rainwater into my last empty water can which I had kept.

We listened on the radio and the lead A-7, call sign "Sandy," came in and dropped down using his instruments to get down below the clouds in between the mountains and was circling in our general area. He DF'd the chopper to his position and the chopper would let down on radar altimeter. The first chopper almost hit the mountain which scared him to death, and he said he couldn't do it and he headed out. So they got the spare chopper to come in. He got underneath the clouds and started to head in and then he called for the A-7 and said, "I don't have enough fuel to complete the mission. "I've got to turn back." About that time the lead Sandy (A-7) was getting awful upset and he said, "Everyone, and I mean everyone, return to the tankers." So everybody headed to the tankers.

Meanwhile, all this time they were still dropping bombs on targets all the way around us. There must have been 60-70 airplanes in that area all morning, dropping bombs, hitting targets, shooting missiles at SAM sites and trying to keep everybody's head down so they could get in and pick us up. So everyone went back to the tanker, everybody filled up with fuel and lead Sandy said "Chopper #3, are you ready?" So he was getting another chopper. And that was the spare for the spare, and Chopper #3 replied, "Yes, I'm ready to roll." And the A-7 left the tanker, he got down below the clouds and DF'd the chopper in on top of him and we heard that the A-7 and the chopper were inbound.

Then the Sandys turned their attention to the machine gun nest that was on top of the hill just above Norb and they started firing rockets and dropped a couple of bombs on top of there. Most of it was rockets so they could be pretty accurate. About that time I saw the Helicopter and one of the A-7s hollered at the helicopter that he was supposed to stay back, but he didn't stay back. He was coming in to get us.

They told Norb to pop his smoke and the A-7 said to the helicopter, "We're flying right over the top of you." The chopper said, "I know, I'm in the clear, just keep their heads down." Norb popped his smoke and I hid across the hill a little over a quarter of a mile from me. They picked up Norb in the helicopter.

About that time the helicopter guy said "Alpha, (Alpha is the term used to indicate the front seater in two place fighters and Bravo is the backseater) pop your smoke." I grabbed my smoke grenade and I pulled the trigger and I thought, "Naw, I'm going to throw it down the hill about 30 feet." So I threw it down the hill a little ways and was hiding in the brush, and then the smoke started boiling up out of there, bullets started whizzing everywhere. The enemy was a long ways from me, but the bullets were still whizzing around, and here came the chopper.

When the chopper got to me it was a little bit too high so I couldn't jump in the door. So they had to use the cable and tree penetrator. I was just climbing on the tree penetrator when I heard a machine gun open up on the hill behind me. Quickly the door gunner opened up with his mini gun and they had about a five second duel and the door gunner won.

The P.J. (Para-rescue jumpers) that rode on the Jolly Green helicopters for rescuing downed aircrews, operates the tree penetrator and machine gun threw me in the copter, swung the door shut, and swung his gun around to defend the aircraft. The crew were all in harnesses so that they were hooked up to the aircraft so they couldn't fall out of the chopper or couldn't go up or down too much. With his gun in position, he started shooting, and the helicopter turned on its side to the left, starting down the hill just almost like a ski run, got some speed up, and went over the next hill as I was trying to get buckled in. I had my seat strap in my right hand and was just getting ready to sit down when he topped the hill. Well, he put negative G's on the helicopter. Everybody else was strapped in but I wasn't. All of a sudden, there I was holding on to that strap and my feet were on the ceiling and I said, "Oh boy, I'm going to hit hard when he comes to positive Gs." He put the positive Gs on fairly slowly and I came down but not very hard and I got strapped in. The door gunners were shooting the whole time. They also had a gunner on the tail on the flap door of the helicopter and he was sitting there just shooting away.

We were headed out just as fast as we could go. Two A-7s were circling us as we were heading out and it took quite a while before we got into the mountains far enough to where they thought it was safe to come up into the clouds. So we started up into the clouds and broke out on top and I looked out the side and there were two Wild Weasel aircraft (part of my squadron) coming up along side. They were flying real slowly with the helicopter and we were headed to the C-130 tanker as the helicopter had to get some fuel. So the helicopter plugged into the tanker and we were taking on fuel and then some A-7s joined us. Then everybody was heading home. So the other choppers were there and the 105s were there too.

When we got to Nakon Phanom, (NKP) RTAFB, we had one heck of an air parade. All of the helicopters were popping smoke out the rear because this was the first successful rescue they had done in quite a while. The whole base had turned out on the flight ramp to see us come in so we had to make a fly by—the C-130s, the helicopters, the 105s, the A-7s—all of us making a fly by. Everyone was having great fun. Needless to say I was very, very happy to get down.

After the fly by we turned around and got on the ground we then learned a lot of other things. My good friend, Tony Shine, was right there to meet us. Had coordinated the whole thing. Of course, the flight surgeons and everybody came and got us and took us to the base hospital. There we were checked out by the flight surgeons. I had some burns on my face and cuts and bruises and got them all patched up. We were informed that they were having a big party at the Non Commissioned Officers (NCO) Club and that we were invited to go over there. Everybody was having a party, that's for sure, as we were one of the first guys they had picked up in three or four months.

We stayed at NKP RTAFB that night, and the next day we were transferred to our home base, Korat RTAFB, and met the rest of the squadron. It was getting close to Thanksgiving. Since, as a crew, Norb and I had been shot down twice, they were sending us home. Norb was shot down this time and he also had to get out of a B-66. This was considered being shot down twice.

During the debriefing at Korat we learned that two of the A-7 Sandy's were hit by enemy fire but, thank goodness, they did not go down. The pilot of the helicopter that rescued us was certainly a gung ho pilot. We probably wouldn't have gotten out if it weren't for his being so courageous and aggressive. So I really credit his courage, strength and forcefulness for getting us out. The helicopter had several holes in it. The copilot told me that the Vietnamese were taught to lead aircraft like you lead a duck in hunting; otherwise you couldn't hit the target. So he was shooting with his machine gun right across the front of the nose of the helicopter when the door gunner got him.

The tankers had been very active that morning. A lot of the tankers made three missions to reload with fuel and take off again. They carried gas up over Laos, went back twice to fill up and come back to refuel all the fighter aircraft that were airborne. There were almost 300 aircraft missions flown that morning and afternoon. Also, we heard word from the B-52 that we were supporting, that night, that they were sure glad we were there because the jamming equipment of the lead B-52 was not working quite right, and they were sure they would have most probably gotten hit with the missile that hit Norb and me.

We got home in time for Thanksgiving and had a big reception at the Wichita airport for us when we arrived.

Kenneth D. Thaete, WW# 923

Wild Weasel I Team. Aircrews Front Row in flight suites. Left to Right: Walt Lifsey, Shep Kerr, Ed Sandelius, Ed White, Garry Willard, Jack Donovan, Allen Lamb, John Pitchford, Maurice Fricke, Bob Schwartz. Not Pictured Aircrews: Les Lindenmuth, Don Madden, and Bob Trier. Photo courtesy of John Revack

VN-162, hit by Bobbin flight on 18 December 1967, lead by WW-3 F-105F crew -pilot Major Unangst and his EWO Capt. Carter.
Photo Courtesy Joe Telford

WW III-1, Front Row Left to Right: Herb Friesen, Rick Westcott, Bob Brinkman, Vince Scungio, Marion Angel, Standing Left to Right: Clyde Hayman, Jim O'Neal, John Hill, John Buick, Bob Tondreau, Ed Rock (WW III-2), George Kennedy, Ken Ryckman. Missing: Bill Robinson and Pete Tsouprake, Shot down and MIA/KIA before photo was taken: Roosevelt Hestle and Charles Morgan. Photo courtesy of John Revack

WW Class III-5 Front Row Left to Right: Rich McDowell, John Geiger, Fred Bell, Paul Chesley, Tom Wilson. Standing: Left to Right: Arnie Dolejsi, Howard White, Bob Johnston, Charlie Hanson, Ron Strack, Jerry Hoblit. Not Pictured : Marty Chrone. Photo courtesy of John Revack

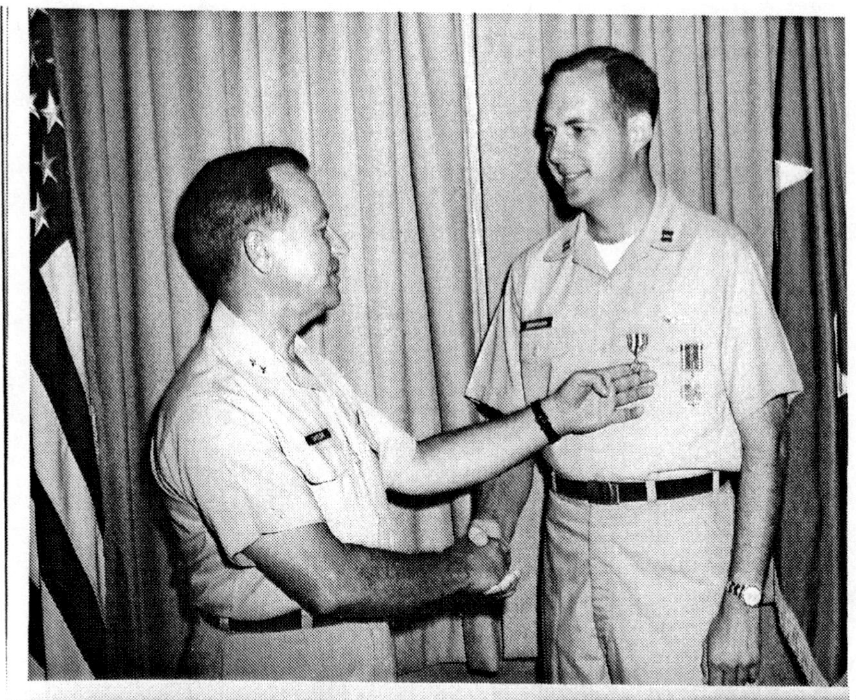

Bob Dorrough being presented Silver Star and Distinguished Flying Cross
by Maj. General Taylor, Nellis AFB, NV. 1968.
Photo Courtesy of Robert E. (Bob) Dorrough

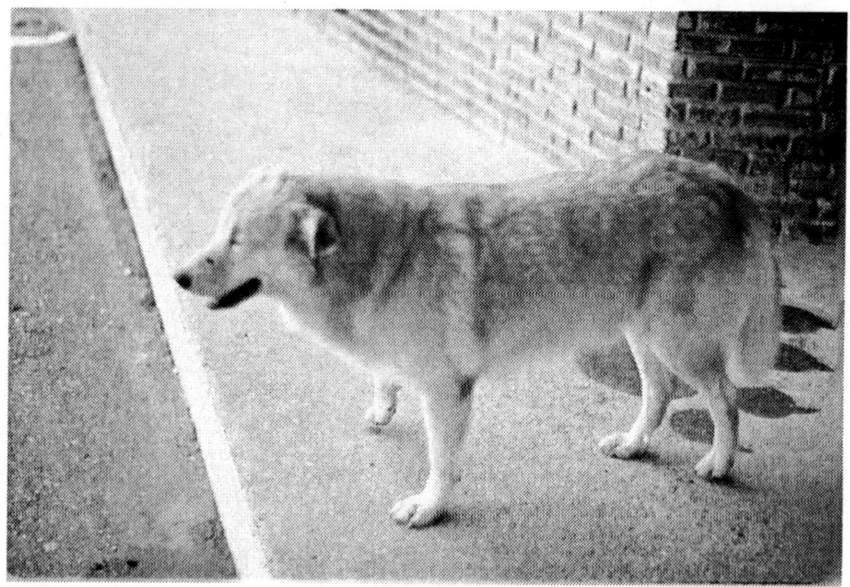

ROSCOE

Roscoe was everyone's pet at Korat RTAFB, especially the F-105 pilots and EWOs. He originally belonged to Merrill Raymond (Ray) Lewis, an F-105 pilot who was shot down while bombing a railway bridge on the northeast railroad on 20 July 1966. Ray was assigned to the 34th TFS and was flying F-105D 62-4308 when he was shot down. When I got to Korat in June 66 it was rumored that Roscoe had been brought to Korat in the cockpit of Ray's F-105 when he and his squadron were transferred to Korat RTAFB from Yokota AB, Japan. Some claimed that Roscoe was really flown to Korat in a C-130 transport piloted by a friend of Ray's. Personally I liked the F-105 cockpit story and that is the account that was accepted when I arrived at Korat. After Ray was shot down, Roscoe became the pet of all the aircrews and the mascot of all the squadrons at Korat. Roscoe lived in the aircrew hooch area and traveled to and from the various squadrons on the crew buses with the crews. He attended mission briefings, went to the officers club for his meals, and was looked after by more than sixty aircrews. The Flight Surgeon and the base Vet were responsible for his health. Eventually it was said that he developed heartworms but was kept in reasonably good health by his personal doctors and his many masters. He was still there when I came back from my second tour in 1972/73. Some said that the war would not end until Roscoe passed away. That was very nearly the way it was, as Roscoe lived until September 1975. He was surely the most famous and beloved dog in the 388th TFW.

F-105 below and SA-2 Guideline SAM above. above. USAF Photo Courtesy of Robert E. (Bob) Dorrough And Mike Gilroy

F-105G Wild Weasels refueling over Laos at Dusk 1972.
Photo Courtesy of Phil Steeves

Ed Cleveland at the Conclusion of his End of Tour Parade, 17th WWS Korat RTAFB 1972. Tony German, then on his second tour threw flour all over Ed Cleveland. The person in the back seat and only partially visible is Tom Coady. Photo Courtesy of Phil Steeves

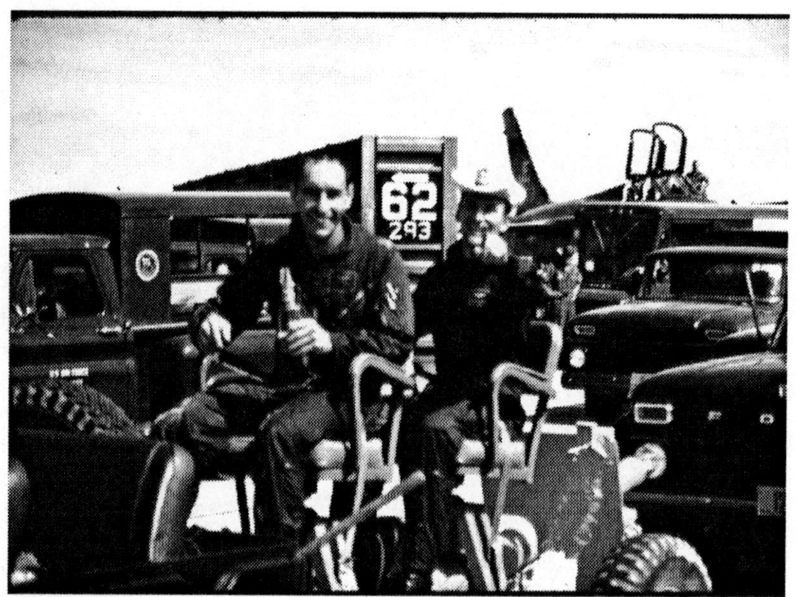

Capts. Dick Arnold (Pilot) and Jim Bartsch (EWO) ride the cannon in their 100 mission parade.Photo Courtesy of Robert E. (Bob) Dorrough

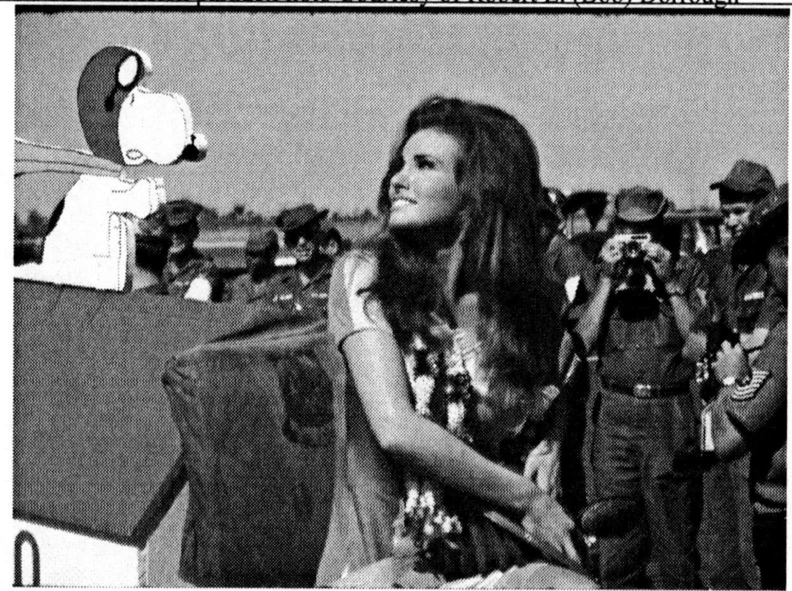

Snoopy and Miss World, 27 December 67, Korat RTAFB. Photo Courtesy of Robert E. (Bob) Dorrough

Bob Hope, Barbara McNair, Eileen Dunn and Miss World Dec. 27 1967, Korat RTAFB. Photo Courtesy of Robert E. (Bob) Dorrough

Tom Edge End of Tour Photo. Note Dual Shrike Launcher On F-105G left Wing. Photo Courtesy of Phil Steeves

WWW III 68-21

Wild Weasel School Class 68-HWW:

Photo courtesy of John Revak, Text by Bob King.

"The following named officers attached to the 4537th Ftr Wpns Sq, are entered into Class 68-HWW, USAF Fighter Special Training Course (F-105). Crs Nr 111506G, commenced training 28 Mar 68 and will graduate 13 May 68. TDY from permanent duty station as indicated. Officers cleared for access to classified material up to and including TOP SECRET. Upon completion of this course, duration six (6) weeks, officers organization, stn and command indicated, will acquire a one (1) year active duty commitment from date of completion. Authority: APR 36-51."

Front Row - EWOs - left-to-right: 1Lt. Ralph M. Reed, Capt. James Rossetto, 1Lt. Robert W.King, Maj. Russell Tagliareni, Maj. Howard H. Smith

Back row - pilots - left-to-right: Maj. Ralph D. Waddell, Maj. Raymond M. Viscarra, Maj. Albert Villaret, Maj. Robert J. Beck, Maj. Russell Youngblood, Capt. Clifford Fieszell

We posed ourselves so that each bear is kneeling in front of the pilot he was crewed with. As Maj. Bill Sparks, one of our instructors, once said, we were "joined at the hip for one hundred missions or until death do you part, whichever comes first." Capt. Fieszell and Maj. Smith were lost on 30 Sep 1968 in Route Pack I. They remain listed as MIA today. In April 1969, Mike Reed and Ray Viscarra had to jump out of a Thud in northeastern Thailand when they were returning from a mission to Laos. They lost the oil pump and their engine seized. Mike Reed completed his combat tour at Takhli, but died in 7 Dec 1969 in a crash on Okinawa. And I don't even know what happened to the four guys that went to Korat for their combat tour. So this little group would lose three Thuds and have three of its members killed within eighteen months of this photo. The Wild Weasel line of work was not for the faint of heart.

Above: SA-2 SAM going after a Thud, Center: Red River, Below: Kep Air Base. Photo Courtesy of Robert E. (Bob) Dorrough

Left to Right: Capts. Phil Drew, Joe Howard, Jim Bartsch and Dick Arnold, Clark Air Base 1968. Photo Courtesy of Robert E. (Bob) Dorrough

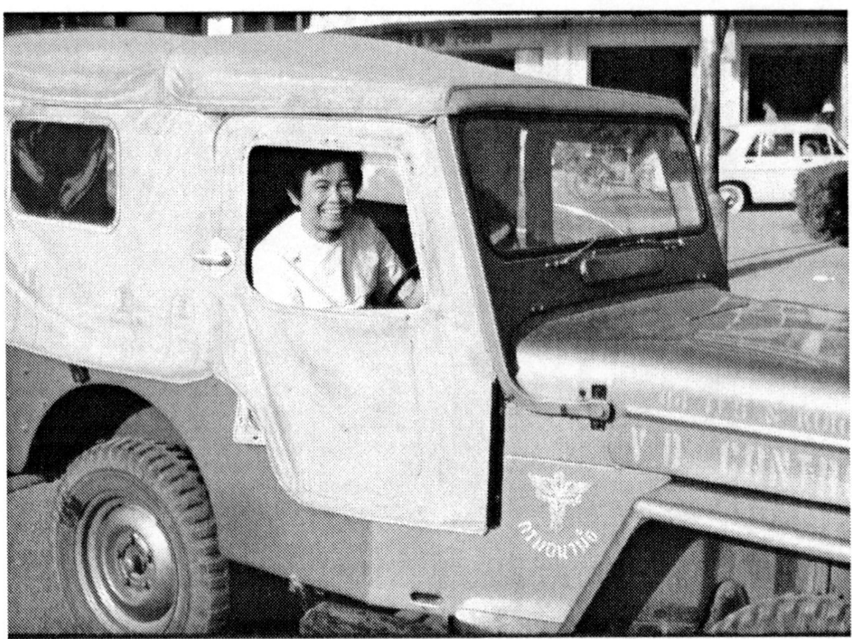

Roxy, Wild Weasel Mascot and VD Control Officer Korat RTAFB 1967/68.
Photo Courtesy of Robert E. (Bob) Dorrough

North Vietnamese SAM Operators at their morning pep rally. USAF photo.
Courtesy of Mike Gilroy

1967 Society of Wild Weasels Board of Directors: L to R: Lt. Col. Ron Johnson 4537FWS/CC, Capt. Mike Gilroy, Mr. Bill Hickey ATI, Capt. Chuck Horner. Courtesy of Mike Gilroy

CBUs exploding on SAM Site. USAF Photo. Courtesy of Mike Gilroy

Dr. John Grisby, President Applied Technology Incorporated.

Robinson and Tsouprake 100th Mission Celebration
Photo Courtesy of Joe Telford

L to R: Merle Dethlefsen and Mike Gilroy receiving Wild Weasel Crew of The Year 1967. Society of Wild Weasels. USAF Photo Courtesy of Mike Gilroy

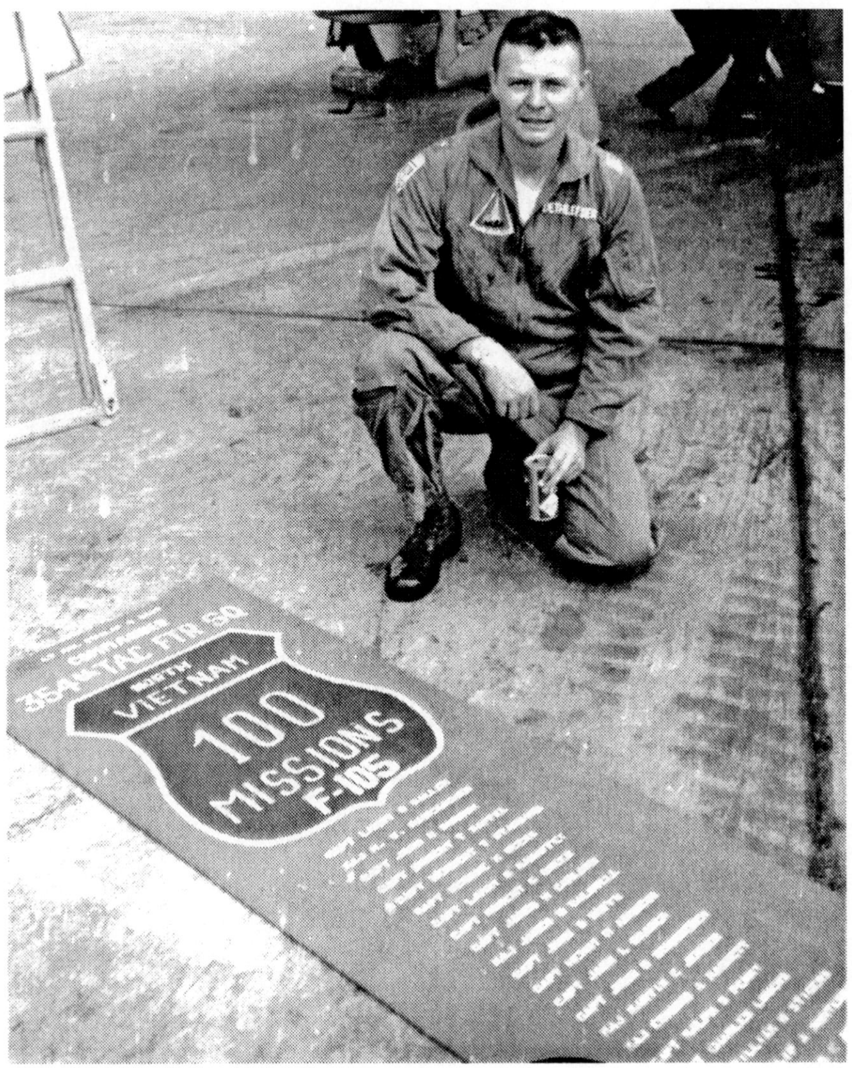

Merle Dethlefsen, Medal of Honor recipient 100 Mission Photo Courtesy of Mike Gilroy

44 TFS, L to R Kneeling: Capt Simanski, Capt Ferrel, Capt Metzler, Capt Stetson, Capt Viloette, Capt Grimaud, L/C Evens, Maj Unangst, Maj Beresik, Sapt Radko, Capt Balut, Capt Carter. L to R Standing: Maj Walsh, Capt Bohr, Maj Steere, Capt Gainer, Maj Telford, Capt Ferguson, Maj Braden, Capt Gross, Maj Muskat, Dr. Schwartz, Maj Ott, Baj Beale, Capt McGuire, Capt Hager, Capt White, Capt Stouder, Maj Tobin

F-105 Air-to-Air refueling from KC-135 Tanker. Note Mekong River in background. USAF Photo. Courtesy of Stan Goldstein

PRIVATE AND CONFIDENTIAL

MAR 26 1968

DEPARTMENT OF THE AIR FORCE
HEADQUARTERS THIRTEENTH AIR FORCE (PACAF)
APO SAN FRANCISCO 96274

21 March 1968

Dr. William Ayer
Applied Technology Incorporated
3410 Hillview Avenue
Stanford Industrial Park
Palo Alto, California 94304

Dear Bill:

First, I would like to thank you very much for your consideration in forwarding me the periodic status letters which Tony Ethier has been preparing. I received the latest one dated 15 March and this served as a reminder that I hadn't responded to your most kind letter announcing this program. I think it is a great idea and we are and will obtain useful information to initiate any action where we think foot-dragging has occurred Secondly, this will keep us up to date on the status of other items in our area of responsibility.

Since arriving here I have been closely watching the status of the radar homing and warning systems. In this respect it has been pleasant to know that the 25/26s have been maintaining an operational ready rate of between 97 and 99.6 percent. Conversely, the 107s have been running consistently low and seldom exceeding 52 percent. As a result, an exchange of correspondence was undertaken with Goldsworthy, ASD, Wright Field, and my successor in which I reiterated my previous position on the systems. I have received a letter back from both these people indicating that they were taking action to place the 25/26 in the A-7s, and I believe you have been given the word on this subject. I believe they are also taking a very serious look at what they can do in the F-4E area. Unfortunately, the die is pretty well cast for the present as far as the F-4Ds are concerned.

With reference to the ECPs, we are starting action to prod a little and get this off dead center. I hope by the time this letter arrives or shortly thereafter a little more activity will be noticed. With reference to the special Eglin project, Jim Odom passed through here on the twentieth with ten of the twelve boards. He had further indicated that an additional ninety-some were to be procured based upon successful testing that had been accomplished at Eglin. I think with any degree of success in the operations here added impetus will be applied to this requirement.

One of the things that is probably the most pressing requirement in the follow-on radar homing and warning systems is the ability to determine range to the SAM sites. I know I have talked to George Deskin and Dr. Grigsby in

PRIVATE AND CONFIDENTIAL

Letter from M/G K. C. Dempster to Bill Ayer
President ATI. Courtesy of Dr. John Grigsby

PRIVATE AND CONFIDENTIAL

the past; however, if this can be achieved and demonstrated I think there would be a wide-open market in all military aircraft for such a system and I would strongly recommend that considerable emphasis be placed upon this by ATI. It also appears that we are moving ahead with F-4D Wild Weasels using the 25/26 142 accommodation which I was glad to hear about.

I have been keeping in fairly close touch with Wally Storm, and he is managing to cover the entire Pacific theater fairly routinely. I have seen one or two of the tech reps on my visits to the various bases, and I plan to touch base with each one of them on succeeding visits. I am managing to cover all of our bases in Taiwan, Thailand, and the Philippines at least once every forty-five days. The only problem out here is there is an awful lot of water between point A and point B, so I am getting to see a lot of blue Pacific.

We are finishing up with the quarterly Electronic Warfare Conference today, and an awful lot of the old faces which you people have been working with are doing an outstanding and exceptional job in the field. I hope that if any of your people have an opportunity to come out this way you will give me some advance warning so I can adjust my schedule to be here and to sit down and wine and dine them.

Not much else for the present. I hope you and the family are in the best of health. Helyn sends her best to Mary, and I send my best through you to all the old hands at ATI. I remain,

As ever,

K. C. DEMPSTER
Major General, USAF
Vice Commander

P.S. Bill, I realize some of the information may be in the preferential category so please treat it as such.

KCD

2.

PRIVATE AND CONFIDENTIAL

Letter from M/G K. C. Dempster to Bill Ayer
President ATI. Courtesy of Dr. John Grigsby

17 Wild Weasel Squadron Photo 27 Jan. 73.

1st Row (sitting) Maj. Jerry Moss, Maj. Bob Webb, Capt. Bob Coffman, Capt. "Doc" Phil Steeves (Flight Surgeon), Capt. Bill Kennedy, Capt. Bill Dobbs, Maj. Tom Coady, Capt. Mike O'Brien, A1C Neal Polsky, L/C Ed Rock (Squadron Commander), Capt. "Bear" Gleason, L/C George Bowling (Operations Officer), 1/Lt. Cornell Varsogea, Capt Fred Schleik, 1/Lt. Rick Puseman, Maj. Hal Kurz, Capt. Jack Stone,

2nd Row (keeling). Capt. Chris Chrisman, Capt. Howie Tout, Capt. Jim Fake, Capt. George Connolly, Capt. John Baker, Capt. Don Henry, Maj. Dean Leverenz, Maj. Tom Edge, Capt. Bob Englebrecht, Capt. Ted Powers, Capt. Dan Breckenridge, Maj. Rex Lawson, Capt Kerry Killebrew, Capt. Dan Polis, 1/Lt. Doug Julsen, Capt. Roger Strantz, Capt. Paul Metz, Maj. Ed Cleveland (scheduling).

3rd Row (standing). Capt. Jimmy Boyd, Capt. Dave Roen, Capt. Rick Silz, Capt. Tom Skripps, Capt. Denny Haynes, Capt. Chuck Chattam, Maj. Fred Covington, 1/Lt. Tom Easley, Capt. Jim Terry, Capt. Dan Pearson, Capt. Jim Winzell, Maj. Boris Baird, Capt. Bob Pettit, Capt. Wayne Fisher, 1/Lt. Steve Marlowe, 1/Lt. Bill Lucas. Notice AGM-78 and dual Shrike Adapter on aircraft left wing.

Absent: Maj. Bruce Race, 1/Lt. Steve Fishman, L/C Harry Mathews (Asst. Ops. Officer), Capt. Larry Funk, Capt. Jim Pieczko, Capt. Gary Porter, Maj. John Brenner (Executive Officer) Maj. Duncan Wilmore. Photo courtesy of Ed Rock

AN/APR-25 3" Cathode Ray Tube With Simulated "Ah Shit" SAM Radar Strobe at About 1 O'clock. Photo courtesy of John Grigsbsy

Wild Weasel III-1 Pilots and EWOs at McClellan AFB, Sacramento, CA, May 66. Military Personnel left to right: Co.l J. T. Johnson, Maj. Bob Brinkman (Senior Officer WW III-1/KIA), Capt John Buick, Capt. Bob Tondreau, Maj. Rick Westcott, Capt. Vince Scungio (KIA), Capt. John Hill, Capt. George Kennedy, Maj. Jim O'Neil (POW), Major Ken Ryckman, Capt. Mack Angel (Air Force Thunderbird pilot). (WW III-1 aircrews are all in flight suits.) Missing: Maj. William Robinson, Maj. Peter Tsouprake, Maj. Roosevelt Hestle (KIA) and Capt. Charles Morgan(KIA) Photo Courtesy of John Grigsby

17th WWS Elephant April 73, Korat RTAFB.
Lt. Col. Ed Rock and Thai children on elephant ride.
Photo Courtesy Ed Rock

13th TFS Home of the Wild Weasels, Korat RTAFB Circa 1967. L/C Jim McInerney Commander. Photo Courtesy of Robert E. (Bob) Dorrough

Air Force Cross Recipient Pete Tsouprake
With his Steely Eyed Look
Photo Courtesy of Joe Telford

Story by George Acree, Colonel USAF (Retired) Wild Weasel # 289

Something better than the Shrike

AGM-78 Standard Arm Test Team, 7 Sept 67

"Something better than the Shrike (AGM-45)......." was the charge by the South East Asia Operational Requirement #52 (SEAOR-52) that started 13 challenging months of intensive development and the deployment of the AGM-78 Standard Anti-Radiation Missile. This is my story about the Standard ARM Wild Weasel initial combat employment over Hanoi, North Viet Nam at dawn on 10 March 1968. As best I can, I will share our emotions as we prepared the missile and Wild Weasel warriors for mortal combat with the intense anti-aircraft defenses of Hanoi. My story is based on personal experience, cockpit recordings, my diaries and 36-year-old recollections. It has been a long time, but the Society of Wild Weasels has kept my memory fresh and honest, I hope. I thank those "Barracudas" who helped me write our story.

But first, I must salute my Electronic Warfare Officer (EWO) "BEAR" Lieutenant Colonel Charles Francis "Frank" O'Donnell, USAF (Retired) "Barracuda 2B" now deceased of natural causes. I remember well Frank's Georgia drawl, good humor, stalwart courage, determined perseverance and exceptional intelligence displayed as we worked together on the Standard ARM program and he rode 32 inches behind me in the back seat of our sleek fighter, the F-105G Wild Weasel. I'll mention Frank throughout this story because he was the "brains" of the AGM-78 F-105F/G Wild Weasel development program and the following F-4G Wild Weasel program. Frank flew 53 Wild Weasel combat missions with the first Wild Weasels in the F-100F Super Sabre in 1965 and 38 Wild Weasel combat missions with me. I dedicate this story to the memory of Frank O'Donnell, Wild Weasel number 119, a great Wild Weasel warrior and pioneer, brilliant engineer, and my close friend. Listening to those mission tapes again, I was touched to hear Frank's confident and friendly voice. That brought back many memories. Rest In Peace, Frank. We will rejoin some day.

Why did we need something better than the Shrike? Fundamentally, to defeat the radar guided Soviet "Guideline" (SA-2) surface to air missile (SAM) system. That SAM was developed from Nazi Germany technology for Soviet Air defenses and deployed by the Soviet Union to improve the surface anti-aircraft weapons defending North Vietnam. From July 1965 through February 1968, the Air Force and Navy strike forces lost 116 fixed wing aircraft shot down by the SA-2 SAM. We lost one bird every eight days and many comrades. Of those, 23 were Wild Weasels and Iron Hands. Heavy, bitter losses!

Many attempts to defeat the SAMs were tried. Air Force and Navy air forces tried many tactics using bombs, bullets, rockets, napalm, electronic jammers and Shrikes. All proved lacking as the SAM success rate increased. We were "on the short end of the stick" (losing). The Shrike was the only Anti-Radar (radiation) Missile (ARM) available to the US Navy and US Air Force to counter radar guided SAMs. The U.S. Navy started developing the Shrike in 1958 to attack coastal surveillance radars and radar-directed shore artillery in defense of our fleet. When Major Gary Powers' U-2 was shot down by an SA-2 over the Soviet Union on 1 May 1960, Shrike's development quickly focused intensely on the SA-2 SAM system.

The Shrike evolved from the World War II unguided 5-inch High Velocity Aerial Rocket. The Shrike was a simple, ten-foot long, 390-pound, Mach 2.0 guided missile with a maximum effective range of about 10 miles. A fixed antenna radar receiver tuned to the Fan Song frequency and a "bang-bang" guidance system guided it. The SA-2's range was more than 20 miles, double the Shrike's. When attacking the Fan Song with the Shrike, the pilot aligned the missile with the target radar by centering azimuth and elevation indicators, noted the dive (dip) angle and altitude, calculated the loft angle from a small chart, then pulled the aircraft up to launch the Shrike at that angle. This maneuver is very hazardous because you are belly up to the threat. The 35-foot, 5,000 pound, Mach 3.5 SA-2 outgunned the Shrike's short range and challenging launch parameters. We were "Fighting a long sword with a pen knife in an Elephant stampede" observed Jack "King Bear" Donovan, Wild Weasel #15. It was not "fair". We needed something better than the Shrike to defeat the SA-2.

On 10 January 1967, Department of Defense joint project #304A began a high priority program to rapidly develop the AGM-78 Standard ARM. That day, I attended the AGM-78 "kick-off" conference at the Naval Ordnance Laboratory, Pomona, California. Leading was the US Navy in cooperation with the US Air Force. The China Lake Naval Weapons Center, California and the USAF Fighter Weapons Center, Nellis AFB, Nevada through the General Dynamics-Pomona Corporation, California, implemented the program. After a mandatory, but rapid planning, programming, and budgeting cycle, an intense test program began on 21 August 1967 at Holloman AFB, White Sands Missile Range, Alamagordo, New Mexico. Frank and I, Major Harlan "Harley" Wyman, Instructor Fighter Pilot and Captain Ron "Laughing Bear" Davenport, Electronic Warfare Officer from the USAF Fighter Weapons School, Nellis AFB, Nevada joined the AF Missile Development Center project team and proceeded to test the missile over the next six months. After 13 test firings produced a 28% a success rate, while not completely satisfied, we knew that we had something better than the Shrike. The Standard ARM would definitely improve Wild Weasel tactics and success against the SAMs.

The Standard ARM was a big, probably to big, missile compared to the Shrike and most other tactical missiles: 15 feet long, weighing 1350 pounds. It was based on the Navy's "Standard" surface to air missile, RIM-66. The F-105G Wild Weasel could carry two, one on each inboard pylon.

The Standard ARM, in conjunction with the APR-35 Radar Homing and Warning system operated by a skilled Wild Weasel "Bear" (EWO), could accurately locate radiating radar targets at long ranges through a gimbaled antenna feeding a broadband tunable receiver which directed an analog proportional guidance system. The missile could go more than 35 miles at Mach 2.5 and could be launched against targets up to 170 degrees off the nose. It was dropped from an inboard wing station and activated by an arming lanyard. When the rocket motor ignited, the Standard ARM could turn, climb, calculate and remember its own range to target radar ahead OR behind the attacking aircraft. It struck the Fan Song radar with a potent airburst of the 150# directional blast fragmentation warhead. Now, we could safely launch our weapon outside the SA-2 range and pick them off when they threatened the strike force. Finally, we had a long sword instead of a penknife.

At the end of the tests, the Department of Defense decided to take the Standard ARM to war. To carry the news and knowledge, Frank and I made our hopscotch journey across the Pacific briefing every interested commander and staff, high and low. We were encouraged and exhorted to "Do good and have good luck" by General Momyer, Seventh Air Force Commander, Saigon. While in Saigon, we were conscripted to "defend Saigon" during the "Tet 68" North Vietnamese, army attacks. We knew we were back in the fray when we were issued helmets, M-16s and 100 rounds of ammunition. We watched the rockets' red glare, saw the bombs bursting in air over Saigon for a few nights. Exciting, but we were happy to leave without firing a shot.

Frank and I arrived at Takhli RTAB at 0900 2 February 1968. We were met by our friends, Harley Wyman and Ron Davenport of the 357th TFS who had preceded us after completing their Wild Weasel training at Nellis. Over those next five weeks, the 355th TFW prepared for the Air Force employment of the Standard ARM while prosecuting the air war. We had excellent support by the Wing led by the "Big Kahuna" Colonel John "Big Kahuna" Giurardo. The Leaders, Pilots, Bears, Staff folk and especially the Troops pitched in and made it happen. Our spirits were high despite long, difficult hours of teaching, testing and fixing, and a no-notice Operational Readiness Inspection. Eight Wild Weasel crews were trained on the AGM-78/APR-35 systems, six F-105Fs were converted to F-105Gs and 17 Standard ARM missiles were in place. We were ready to go! HOWEVER, hurry up and wait! Over the next eight days, we were ordered to launch five times but were cancelled due to bad weather over Hanoi. That caused lots of frustration and tension. Compounding my frustration, on 6 March I was notified by Lt. Col. Donald Swedberg, pentagon Action officer, that Navy A-6Bs from the USS Kitty Hawk, VA-75, had launched six STARMS on 6 March with results similar to our test experience. I called 7th Air Force, Saigon and verified that report with our liaison officer, Lt. Howard Wendt, USN. So, the Navy Iron Hands had beaten the Wild Weasels to the punch. We were dejected, because we thought we had agreed to coordinate our attacks: Iron hands from the East and Wild Weasels from the West simultaneously. The coordination had broken down ant headquarters in Saigon and the Navy launched four fays before us. I suppose it was the "fog of war". Ce la guerre!

The first Standard ARM Wild Weasel attack against Hanoi Air Defenses was the culmination of over 13 months of hard, dangerous and successful work of the planning and development team. Superbly supporting that team were the USAF Fighter Weapons School and the 4537th Wild Weasel Training Squadron at Nellis AFB, Nevada, the technical cooperation between the Armed Services and the industry of our United States. We thought we were taking a pretty good weapon to war. Now we would find out.

Sunday 10 March 1968, Takhli Royal Thai Air Base, Thailand, South East Asia.

0100: Up and dressing in our neat four-man air-conditioned trailer. A solid four hours of sack time. Breakfast at the "O" Club with the usual "No hab." (No have) for most of the menu. I settled for white rice, fish and coffee. With the dim light of a flashlight, Frank and I rapidly stumbled down the pitch black mud path to the 357th TFS hoping no Cobras were interested in combat that early on that humid morning.

0200: briefing in the 357th Tactical Fighter Squadron. All eight members of that first Wild Weasel AGM-78 mission had a plan, good intelligence, lots of coffee, cigarettes, and a few macabre jokes. The air was confident but tense. Target weather was not favorable – visibility less than two miles below clouds layered from 800 to 13,000 feet above the ground. The strike force of 16 F-4Ds was tasked to strike the Hadong Army Barracks four miles west of Hanoi at 0600. Major Harlan "Harley" Wyman, and

Captain Ron "Laughing Bear" Davenport, would lead "Barracuda" flight to protect the strike force from SAMs during their attack. Frank and I were Barracuda 2. Barracuda 3 was Major Gene Goodwin and Captain Roger Elmer. Number 4 was Captain Warren Kerzon and Captain "Scotty" McIntire (KIA 10 December 1971). Harley asked me if I wanted to lead. What a gracious gentleman to offer Frank and me the honor of leading that first Standard ARM mission. I replied, "No, thank you, because you are the designated lead and have more recent Wild Weasel experience. Besides, you and Ron are one of the world's greatest Wild Weasel crews." So with a chuckle, Harley said, "Well George, you take the first shot." I said "OK!"

0335: Preflight: Configuration: two AGM-78As on the inboard stations, one 650 gallon fuel tank, centerline, one QRC160-8, left outboard: 1,028 rounds of 20 millimeter ammunition for the M-61 "Vulcan" Gatling gun. Good cartridge starts. Lots of smoke in the cockpit, smelled good! All systems checked OK, Taxi, Arm. Some delay in arming our left missile. We'd find out why, later.

0420: launch, DARK! Four good Barracudas and eight Standard ARMs airborne, no need for the spare. My join-up was slow because I kept losing Harley in the soup while trying to join with the intermittent planet Venus. With Frank's help, I finally joined Harley and we refueled smoothly.

0515: Crossed the Mekong river enroute to Hanoi at 13,000' 480 knots ground speed, between cloud layers. Greened (armed) systems. Standard ARMs checked OK. Harley called for "music" (jammer pod on). Frank asked me to turn it on. I couldn't find the red knob pod control, which was not in the usual place. I asked Frank if he had the pod control back there. He replied negative. We both agreed we did not have a control for the pod and we really didn't need it anyway. This would lead to a running dialogue that had a funny ending.

0530: Starting to get SAM radar "Fan Song" songs (transmissions) at 100 miles out. Mostly Low Blow and Barlock long distance radar signals. They knew we were coming and were tracking us. We were ready for them.

0545: Checked in with F-4 strike flights Cheetah, Cactus, Waco and Falcon. Weather was bad, layered 10-12,000. We were just above the cloud tops. The sun peeked through the murk starting to illuminate the sky with rosy red and gold light. Beautiful. Frank and I felt good about the mission. We said a little prayer. We had about 30 signals up now with four confirmed SAM Fan Songs singing their high pitched rattlesnake- sounding deadly chorus. They were looking us over. Twenty-five miles from the target we lit the burners and accelerated up to 540 knots, climbing to 16,000'. Harley smoothly led us on and up. We were ready to show those SAM shooters something better than the Shrike. We were "First In…" again.

0600: Strike flights were in low on target. Weather was not good, two flights aborted for weather and broken jammers, but eight F-4Ds pressed on. We Barracudas setting up a racetrack cover pattern at 16,000' 20 to 25 miles from the target. Standard ARMs rechecked and armed. More Fan Songs singing. Our breathing rate increased. Pulse was up. Chatter minimized. No more jokes. We were peaked! The SAMs and AAA opened fire. We counted six valid SAM launches. We thought they were aimed at the strike force since we did not see them. The 85 and 100 mm guns opened up their black flak. Our radar detection receivers and Standard ARMs saw the Fan Songs. Frank and I had a green missile acquisition lock light on the left missile. We were in range. We were in a "target rich environment," just what we had hoped for. NOW was the time!

0601. <u>Barracuda 2:</u> Cleared for the first shot as briefed, I called "Barracuda Two-Otter" and mashed the red "pickle" missile firing button. THUMP! The missile dropped away cleanly and kept dropping. Harley called "NO LIGHT UP–NO ROCKET MOTOR IGNITION!" The missile dropped into the murk. I was sad and mad. Frank said "Well, we've got another missile and lots of targets." I said "Hmmmm." (When we returned to Takhli we found the cause–human error.) Zero for one, seven to go.

0601+: <u>Barracuda Lead:</u> Quickly, Harley and Ron Ottered (fired) their left ARM. GOOD MOTOR! Beauty! It flew a perfect trajectory pushed by a stream of red-hot exhaust turning white, up, over and then streaking down into the murk headed for a Fan Song. Ron timed the target signal against the missile time of flight. That Fan Song went down at the end of missile flight time. A HIT! We saw two SAMS coming our way and appeared to be unguided. No threat. Frank said, "Maybe lead got their radar". One for two, six to go.

0604: Barracuda 3: Sorting out four Fan Songs and locking on the closest, Gene and Ron Ottered their first missile. It fired OK, then pulled up and exploded two miles in front of us. Harley called, BREAK UP THREE-BAD MISSILE." I was really torqued. (We had seen that type explosion three times during the 13-missile test. Fortunately, none damaged our aircraft due to safe separation from the explosions. We found later that some rocket motors were cracked and they exploded when stressed as the missile started its five-G pull-up two miles from the launcher. All missiles were x-rayed and passed before delivery from the factory. They may have cracked in transit. Procedures were implemented to x-ray the motors AFTER delivery to the field. That worked. We wished we had thought of that before today!) One for three, five to go.

0604+: Barracuda 4: Immediately, Warren and Scottie Ottered their missile. Good launch, good rocket, but it was descending, then pulled up going into a beautiful up and over trajectory enroute to its singing Fan Song. Two for four, four to go. AGAIN, it pitched up and exploded about three miles ahead. Another bad one. One out of four. I was really torqued. More SAMs coming up through the undercast. More black blossoms of flak from 85/100 mm guns. They were getting hostile!

0608: Barracuda 2: With a good lock, Frank and I Ottered our right missile. Good launch, good rocket, good trajectory. Frank tracked the signal and missile time. The signal went down at the end of missile flight. A HIT! We were elated! Several Sierra Hotels! Two for five, three to go. Lots of targets.

0611: Barracuda Lead: After completing their turn on the back of the racetrack, Harley and Ron fired their last missile and it went well. Looked like another hit. We all felt better. Three for six, two to go. The pace slowed as we flew the back leg of our racetrack. Then, two more SAMs popped through the clouds and even more flak burst in front of us. They were stirred up, but ineffective.

0616: Barracuda 3: Gene and Roger locked and fired their last missile. It looked good! Another probable hit. Four for seven, one to go. There was very little radio chatter the Strike aircraft had left.

0620: Barracuda 4: Two more SAMS came at us from the haze. Warren and Scottie Ottered their last missile at the SAM site firing at us. Another good launch! A probable hit. The SAMs went out of control, no threat. Warren told Scottie, "We shoved that one right down their throat!" Five for eight: three definite hits, two probable hits and three failures. The Sam and AAA activity had ceased.

0625: We were "...Last Out" of the target area. Ron chuckled to Harley, "Just as we were starting to get the hang of it we ran out of missile, but, we had enough to hurt those SAM sites". We were headed home. Mask off and a long drink of water. Pulse back to normal. Satisfaction.

0630: As we approached our refueling track, Frank asked again, "Where is the jammer control?" I muttered a few expletives asking why? Frank said he wanted write it up as missing in action. I looked and looked everywhere as did Frank. No sight of the red pod knob.

0635: On the tanker taking 3,500 pounds of fuel and heading back to Takhli with a feeling of satisfaction. Frank and I discussed the mission and the background of this effort. As Frank said in his Georgia drawl: "We considered carrying only four missiles, BUT it's a good thing we had eight." During the Standard ARM tests at White Sands our failure rate was running 28% including all missile failures like we had just seen. This first mission failure rate was a disappointing 37% (3 for 8). Later, we found a human error that caused one failure resulting in 27%, very close to the test results. Now we could stay out of SAM range and pick off the Fan Songs as they threatened. We folded our penknife and finally had a long sword. We did have something better than the Shrike, the Standard ARM.

0705: Smooth recovery and landing back at Takhli. Good chute! It felt good to get home. Once more Frank asked for the pod knob. I said "no hab." Then, as I swung out of my sweaty seat, I saw that cowardly red pod knob which had hidden under my right elbow during the entire 2 hour 45 minute mission. I was embarrassed as I showed it to Frank. He chuckled, "I knew it! and look at the pencil lead you saved me." I found Frank a case of cold beer later.

0730: Post-flight inspection explained why our first missile did not ignite. The woven steel arming lanyard was not there. It was to be retained by a pin in the missile launch adapter. The pin was there but no lanyard, hence no rocket motor ignition! The lanyard that would have pulled the switch to arm and ignite the rocket motor stayed with the missile. The right lanyard was still on the launcher. I found the armament Sergeant who had armed me and asked him about it. He immediately admitted that he had screwed up. In the darkness and excitement of that first Standard Arm mission launch, he had forgotten to put the pin through the lanyard loop. He got the right missile but missed the left. He didn't realize that until after we had taken off. I said, "Well, that cost us $100,000, but we sure relearned another lesson: sometimes stuff happens."

0800: Our debriefing went though the entire mission as we compared our memories and tape recordings. Colonel John Giurardo, "The Big Kahuna" 355th Tactical Fighter Wing Commander and staff listened intently. We mutually decided that we had definitely killed three Fan Songs with two others probable. That gave us an estimated success rate of 37% (3 kills by 8 missiles). Three times better than the Shrike!

After debriefing, that brave armament Sergeant sheepishly apologized while offering a case of cold beer and a carton of Salem cigarettes. I thanked the Sergeant, gave Frank the beer and passed around the Salems. Then we told the Sergeant about the mission as the Barracudas shared Frank's beer. It was a big day.

Major General K. C. Dempster (Wild Weasel number ONE, RIP) dropped by Takhli on 12 March to say hello and get a first hand report. General Momyer sent a message of congratulations and dropped by on 21 March. We were honored, but we still had a lot to do. Debrief all the Wing Wild Weasel crews and maintenance troops. Prepare the report and finish our missions at Takhli. Frank and I left Takhli on 10 April to return to Nellis and continue the tests of the next version: F-105G/APR-35/AGM-78B. We helped train new Wild Weasels coming through the Wild Weasel College of SAM destruction knowledge. Frank went on to define and produce the F-4G/APR-38 "Geasel" advanced Wild Weasel that established Air Superiority during Iraqi Freedom in 1990. I salute those many good men and their loyal, loving families that helped us through the initial Standard ARM program and followed on to develop and employ better Standard ARMS and kill more SAMs. I left Nellis and the Standard ARM program on 7 April 1970 for the Tactical Air Warfare Center and the Thunderstick II program at Eglin, AFB, Florida. It was an intense and successful two years that produced a new level of Wild Weasel combat operations...and something better than the Shrike.

The Shrike was modified at least ten times with marginal effectiveness improvement. But, as General Garry Willard (Wild Weasel number Five and first Squadron Commander) said, "It DID keep their heads down". Shrike retired in 1978. The Standard ARM was modified extensively resulting in more capability but plagued by a low reliability rate. It's cumulative success rate stayed above 20% throughout its life. Not too good when compared to today's precision weapons, but better than the Shrike. It retired in 1980 and was replaced by the AGM-88 High Speed Anti-Radiation Missile (HARM) in 1980. The HARM was developed and deployed by the Navy and Air Force from knowledge gained from the Shrike and Standard ARM experiences. The HARM is now the only anti-radiation missile in the inventory. The HARM is carried by the Air Force F-16CJ Wild Weasel, the Navy F-14, F/A-18 Hornet and EA-6B Prowler. The HARM has established air superiority over radar directed air defense systems throughout the world. What is left of the SAM operators has learned to respect the Wild Weasel's motto "Cave Putorium!" (Beware the Wild Weasel).

Notes:

Before I was lucky enough to find my way into the Wild Weasel den, I flew F-100 "Super Sabres" and F-105D "Thunderchiefs" with the 67th TFS "Fighting Cocks" of Okinawa, Japan. From 8 December 1965 through 21 June 1966 I flew 126 combat strike missions over North Vietnam in the F-105D from Takhli RTAB, Thailand with the 333rd Tactical fighter Squadron "Lancers". Then two years as the Air Force Program Manager for the Standard ARM described below, flying 38 Wild Weasel missions over North Vietnam again with the 333rd TFS. In 1973, I commanded the 555th TFS "Triple Nickel" at Udorn RTAB flying F-4Es. Then I flew F-15s as ADO of the 36 TFW at Bitburg AB, Germany. I endured several staff jobs, retiring with 28 years of service on 30 June 1985, totaling 3,450 flying hours and 2,013 successful landings. A rewarding, exciting career that has allowed me to serve my beloved United States of America honorably with stalwart warriors and loyal comrades, to have so many wonderful friends, and enjoy my deep love of my fantastic wife, Margie and my happy family. I have been blessed.

I have elected not to footnote this story because it is from my own memory, perceptions and records. I you are interested a deeper discussion of Standard ARM development and employment, I recommend: Iron Hand,

Story by W. J. "Sonny" Lane Jr., WW # 784

Was Your Airplane Bugged?

Once upon a time, when I was stationed out at Nellis, I got a request for help from Jerry Potter, an old SAC buddy of mine. Jerry was assigned up at that most secret and least understood agency of all, NSA. Now when I say "least understood," I really mean that a lot of the folks who work there don't understand it. Jerry had been asked to give a briefing to some NSA new hires on the Military/Air Force and how we use all that good information that he hoped they would collect and disseminate, and he wanted an attention-getting device to open with. I know that sounds like a really cheap trick, but that's the kind of a guy Jerry is. Jerry's real claim to fame is that way back when he was a two-striper in Berlin, Johnny Cash was his roommate. I sincerely hope that everybody reading this has a claim to fame: and if you don't its not too late to make one up.

Jerry knew exactly what he wanted. He asked me to get him a copy of the very best Wild Weasel combat aircrew tape I could find. I probably need to explain exactly what it is I am talking about. I used a surplus of jargon and shortcuts in one of my previous accounts and then discovered that it was sent outside the Wild Weasel community and perhaps outside our military family. And that is absolutely OK with me. Many of the guys carried their own personal tape recorders and recorded their missions. The radio shop would make you a 'Y' cord. You plugged the straight end into your recorder and the "Y" or two-wire end into the aircraft communications cord and your helmet. So, everything that the aircrew hears would be recorded. That includes all the interphone chatter, the radio, and all those wonderful radar receivers we had back in the Bear Throne. When it got busy during the mission, you could most certainly hear it later on the ground.

I asked around and previewed some tapes. This was just after Linebacker II, and I found several to choose from. I finally picked it, duped it, and mailed it. Later on I saw Jerry and asked what his folks thought of the tape. He told me that they became absolutely galvanized in place when he played it. Some of them even stayed in the classroom during their break so they could hear it again.

By this time, I just know that my feeble attempt to build suspense is working and you are just dying to know whose tape I sent Jerry. I won't keep you in suspense any longer so you can finish this and get on with your lives. It was none other than Ed Cleveland and Mike O'Brien.

I have thought about how much of their actual dialogue I remember, probably not much, but I do remember the tone and type of comments.

Ed mostly said things like: "SWEET JESUS! LOOK AT THAT SON-OF BITCH, HERE IT COMES! THAT DAMN THING NEARLY HIT US! HERE COMES THE OTHER ONE!"

OB mostly said things like: "3 rings at 4 o'clock, launch at 2 o'clock."

They both said: Uggggh, hard breathing, grunts, groans.

[The recorder appeared to slow down when they pulled Gs]

Explanation: During these hectic moments of combat, the pilot would be maneuvering the plane trying to get a Shrike off and then trying to spot the missiles after they were launched. The Bear would mostly stay on his equipment and try to pass the "electronic" or threat situation to the pilot. Like when OB says "Launch at 3 o'clock," that's where Ed would look cause that's where missiles are coming up.

AUDIO: Overwhelming. Every receiver on that plane including the Shrikes were going crazy. I know that some of you know that the Shrike is a missile and are now a little confused as I seemingly attempt to transform it into a receiver. It did, in fact, have an excellent radar receiver in the nose which we could monitor.

But the icing on de cake was during egress. Egres, for some of you folks' benefit, is a French word which means "I am so damn glad to be getting out of here alive."

Ed was singing during egress.

The song was "Tiptoeing Through the Sam Sites", I think.

Sonny Lane WW # 784

Story by Richard Moore, WW # 913

Bastard Bears

In August 1970 six USAF EWO's reported for combat training at Nellis AFB with orders enroute to the F-105G WW squadron at Takhli RTAFB. No pilot was crewed with any of them and the six quickly became known as the Bastard Bears:

Robert G. (Bob) Crawford, Maj. #910 History Professor, USAF Academy

Edward C (Ed) Kennedy, Maj #911 former SAC RB-47H EWO

Orville L (Mac) McPherson, Maj. #912 HQ/SAC, former B-52 EWO

Richard W. (Dick) Moore, Maj. #913 AFIT graduate, former B-58 EWO

Edwin A. (Ed) Thomas, Lt. #917 USAF Academy graduate

Samuel S. (Sam) White, 2Lt #918 EWO Course graduate

Upon arrival at Bangkok's Don Mong Airport the six were informed that Takhli had closed and the Wild Weasels moved to Korat RTAFB as the 6010th WWS commanded by Lt. Col. Gus Sonderman. This new combat support squadron had 12 F-105G's from Takhli and some crew support from Kadena AB, Okinawa. The designation helped reduce the official count of combat units in the Southeast Asia Theater. Making their way to Korat, the Bastard Bears were informed that verbal administrative instructions indicated that they would be transferred to fly observation in the O-2—no requirement existed for more EWO's at the 6010th. Forcefully unwilling to give up the chance to be a Wild Weasel, the Bears protested and within a couple of days the 7th Air Force personnel office confirmed the six Bears to the 6010th.

The six Bears commenced squadron training and had a familiarization flight with borrowed pilots. All looked forward to their first mission. The 6010th WWS had high morale and the new bears felt very welcome and eager to take part. In less than a week their first missions appeared on the schedule. Bombing was halted in other than Route Packs I and II. Wild Weasels missions were flights of two F-105's escorting Arc Light B-52's carpet-bombing at either Ban Karai or Mu Ghia passes on the Ho Chi Minh Trail. The Wild Weasels carried two Shrike anti-radiation missiles and the nose cannon.

Each new Bear flew in number two aircraft with a regular crew in the lead. My (Dick Moore's) first mission was scheduled for the early evening flight but while getting the intelligence briefing just prior to going to the flight line, the squadron commander apologetically cancelled the mission to give the aircraft to another special classified mission. It was the Son Tay raid. Experienced crews flew that mission and received the Silver Star for first-in last-out combat support. The third SAM of a full SA-2 salvo damaged one aircraft. The aircraft was losing fuel but no fire occurred from the hit. The crew bee-lined to Laos and made it across the border before fuel ran out. The pilot and bear ejected successfully but spent the night hanging in the forest canopy until first light. Flashlights moving below in the forest scared them for a while until they figured they were seeing fireflies, not people trying to capture them.

After the Son Tay raid, routine operations resumed. The 6010th was dedicated full time to the Arc Light escort role. Around-the-clock missions found the crews scheduled for takeoff every 20 hours. The missions were four hours in duration with a refueling and escort of two Arc Light drops. Crews from Kadena helped sustain the schedule and the Bastard Bears were handy in absorbing the load. The Bastard Bears were awaiting an assigned pilot to crew with. Regular pilots were enroute to arrive by February 1971.

New Year's night of 1971, two SA-2s were fired at B-52s bombing Mu Ghia and the lead Wild Weasel (Leo Flaherty and Dick Moore) fired two Shrikes at the launch site. The SAMs tracked toward the B-52s but the launch site went off the air. The SAMs burst at the end of flight without hitting any aircraft. A few days later another Fansong came on the air and the lead Wild Weasel (Flaherty and Moore) fired the first AGM-78A launch from an aircraft in SEA. The AGM rocket took the missile straight out in front of the aircraft a half-mile then went nose up and exploded. No SAM was launched. These engagements were a surprise to 7th AF since SA-2s were thought to be only in the northern Route Packs, particularly around Hanoi. B-52 raids were halted. Conjecture that triangulation of USAF aircraft using various ground radars enabled the SA-2's to be launched manually, if inaccurately, led to the Flaherty and Moore briefing the 7th AF commander Lucius B. Clay and him justifying the resumption of B-52 raids. Present at the briefing to Gen. Clay was Admiral Cooper, Carrier Task Force commander, who then invited the crew to visit the USS Ranger and brief the naval aircrews.

Major Bob Belli arrived with the pilot class to match up with the Bastard Bears. Lt. Col. Ken McCarn became the 6010 WWS commander. Belli was the squadron operations officer. In the spring a flight of two with Ed Thomas and Sam White as the Bears tangled with SA-2s and both aircraft were hit but made it home. The only damage was scrapes on the nose radomes. In the spring of 1971, MacPherson and his pilot ejected on short final at Nakhon Phenom in an emergency landing attempt due to flight control failure. Both ejected safely.

Dick Moore

Story by Charles R. "Doc" Dougherty, P-38 Pilot

Sky Spot

A Tribute to Bill Baechle WW # 410

Bill Baechle in rear seat of jeep getting set for 100 Mission parade.
Photo Courtesy of Ed White

Editor's Note: Doc Dougherty has been my friend, sometime boss and neighbor and great flyer for almost 50 years. He was a P-38 pilot in WW II, shot down on his very first combat mission as a P-38 pilot. If you want a good read I recommend, "Return to Combat" by William Spore. ***Return to Combat*** is the story of Lieutenant Charles R. Dougherty, whose P-38 fighter aircraft was shot down by antiaircraft fire while on a mission over

Villach, Austria, on 30 January 1945. Doc was located and rescued by the Partisans, hidden from the Germans, fed, protected, and finally escorted across the country to a British evacuation airstrip. **Doc writes this article in memory of our, now deceased, friend Bill Baechle, WW # 410.**

Doc's Story about Bill Baechle

I have nothing but good words for the Wild Weasel guys. Although I wasn't one, they did shepherd me around RP VI on many an occasion. "First In, Last Out" is also my recollection of their mission.

I was stationed at Ubon RTAFB flying F-4 C/Ds, in '67 as Ops of the 433rd and in '68 as Commander of the 555th (Triple Nickel).

I have a short story of one of the many missions with these Wild Weasels leading the way (reminding me of the stage coach chap riding shot gun) for the strike force. This particular day the Wild Weasel force of eight was being led by an old and dear friend of many years as we grew in TAC fighters, Major Bill Baechle. It was a "Sky Spot", alias Splat, with the target being Phuc Yen airfield. What a silly-ass mission, especially during typhoon days with multiple cloud levels. The so called "force" consisted of my four F-4s armed with a load of "daisy cutter" 500# bombs with nose extenders and center lined CBU-24s. Our MiG support was 8 F-4Ds also from Ubon.

Our route was landside, hitting the tankers before reaching Channel 97 (Channel 97 was a TACAN station located on a hill top in Northern Laos). As we approached the Black River the weather was closing in; a lower stratus now concealed ground contact and an upper thin stratus appeared to thicken as we crossed the Black. Our clever route was to up-date our Inertial Navigation System at Yen Bai, our turning point, then to proceed to the top of Thud Ridge (flak at Yen Bai didn't disappoint us).

For those not acquainted with a Sky Spot delivery, it is a radar drop initiated by the lead aircraft's WSO (weapon system operator). The mission commander would give his flight a countdown to the bomb release (pickle call). This particular mission was called an harassing strike, because we had not gone north with a sizeable force for days due to the typhoon weather in the Hanoi area. We also knew as soon as this storm passed it would be clear for a time. So I guess we were just letting them know we were still around. To this day, in my opinion, a highly questionable reason to expend these resources.

Whenever I was the lead force commander, I would brief with the supporting aircraft flight commanders. This is how I found Bill Baechle was leading these Wild Weasels that day. Since we were such a piddling flight of four, Bill was going to have his team of eight straddle us as we turned inbound to Phuc Yen. I wanted him to call all valid launches and I would keep my flight off the air as we started our run. I told Bill I would try and keep my flight above the undercast to allow maneuvering room for any SAMs heading in our direction.

As we turned at the north end of the ridge the RHAW gear started serious noise. As we started up Thud Ridge, the tops of the undercast started to climb and the overcast above became solid. I was being squeezed between the cloud layers. Half way up the ridge, to our target the flak joined in and the fragments started to tinkle off our aircraft. The guys in my flight were maintaining excellent pod formation. I had numbers 3 and 4 on my right side because we were going to break left and down after we released our ordnance. I guess they were motivated with all of the RHAW visual and sound effects.

The second Wild Weasel flight started calling SAM launches. I could see SAMs off to our left, coming up through the undercast. No calls from Baechle. When my WSO called, "One Minute," I called my flight to arm their weapons and prepare for our release. Our RHAW gear was full of long radar warning strobes and piercing warning noise, but still no calls from Bill! I couldn't stand it any more. I had to look and I racked her up to the right to look beneath the flight. THERE WERE TWO SAMS JUST COMING THROUGH THE UNDERCAST...and not moving on my canopy...THEY WERE HEADED RIGHT FOR ME AND MY FLIGHT. It was too late to act with purpose. I didn't say a word, my WSO started the count down to weapon release when a SAM exploded by my number four man and we pickled just as another SAM went by, trailing on my left between me and my wingman 1000 feet out. This SAM proceeded on its hellish way exploding out of harm's way above us. The last I saw of my number four he was in an orange fire ball, and had been flipped vertical on his right side. I called the "pickle" and the break down to the left. No call from Bill.

I couldn't wait to get back to base, use the scramble line to talk to Bill. As we were regressing, I heard a call from Bill's Bear, saying that lead had lost his transmission capability!

Upon recovery at Ubon I found out that my number four did not buy the farm. The force of the SAM explosion had placed the max gross weight F-4 out of control and into the overcast. That aircraft commander, Rick Bennett, was a damn good stick. He recovered, after he jettisoned his heavy load and went home alone. His backseater was Dick Jonas, who soon afterwards wrote a song, that most of us have heard often entitled "I've Been Everywhere." Editor's Note: Dick Jonas also wrote "Will There Be a Tomorrow," one of my favorites.

I hounded Bill Baechle for years to send me a copy of his mission tape. He finally did in October 1970. He was then working in the basement of the Pentagon as the F-105 Project Officer of USAFWC (DRR). I have listened to that tape recording many times, just to hear his voice and that of a cool calm Bear (I never knew his name.). A few years later, Bill surprisingly passed away from a melanoma tumor. What a great friend! I wanted to tell this story to help honor his memory.

Charles R. "Doc" Dougherty, P-38 Pilot
In Honor of Bill Beachle, WW # 410

Story by Stan Goldstein, WW# 415

99th O1B and Counting

Stan Goldstein, 1968. USAF photo courtesy of Stan.

Editor's Note: O1B was "a counter," the mission symbol logged in the Aircraft Form 781 to indicate the type of mission flown—in this case a combat mission flown over North Vietnam. It would subsequently be entered into the aircrew's Form 5 or flight record. 100 missions flown over North Vietnam ("counters") was the standard to complete a combat tour for most F-105 aircrews prior to the bombing halt instituted by President Johnson in 1968. O1A was the symbol logged for a combat mission that was not flown over North Vietnam. After the 1968 bombing halt, a one-year tour was the normal standard for a tour in Southeast Asia regardless of the number of missions flown or where they might be flown.

How We Did It

Major John Revak, my Wild Weasel front-seater (and World's greatest fighter pilot, or so he told me) and I may have been the last Wild Weasel crew of the Rolling Thunder era to fly 100 missions over North Vietnam. Here is our story of how we did it.

Let's start on Thursday, 31 October 1968, when we prepared to fly mission 98. As an aircrew begins to fly those last few sorties, he gets to be a little more cautious. No one wants to be killed or shot down any day, but even less as the goal is in sight. Our tour was somewhat less demanding than those Wild Weasel crews who were being chewed up in the time prior to the start of our tour with the 44 TFS at Korat that began in April 1968. Friends and comrades were still being lost, but, thankfully, in fewer numbers. We were more attuned to our survival gear, checking the emergency radios, making sure we had our baby bottles full of water. Flight planning took on an even more focused portion of our preflight as we prepared to support the other Thuds that would be dropping on this day's targets. Bud Young and his back-seater would lead the flight and we were number two. This was going to be Bud's 100th and he was fairly excited. Tomorrow or the next day was going to be ours. Was our call sign Cadillac or Buick that day? I can't recall, and I wish we still had all our mission cards as some others still do. All went as briefed and we covered for the F-105Ds that were flying their interdiction mission. After supporting the strike fighters, Bud called for us to "Green 'em up" (have bombs and guns ready), and he started trolling the highway that ran up to Dong Hoi hoping to wake up some of the more recalcitrant NV gunners and get them to "come out and play." But this all went for naught and we finally expended our ordnance on a road intersection, doing our small bit to impede the flow of supplies "down the trail." So, with that done, we left the Pack and rendezvoused with the return KC-135 tanker for enough fuel to get us comfortably back to Korat Royal Thai Airbase, logging 2.4 hours of daylight and our 98th O1B. Bud landed shortly after we did making his 100-mission pass straight down the runway.

For those of you who may not recall what an O1B is, let me digress. Every USAF military aviator has an Individual Flight Record, commonly referred to as a Form-5. It documents every airborne event of the aviator's career, from his first military flight to his last. It records the date, type of aircraft, mission symbol, duty position, total length of flight and how many hours flown during the day or at night. To many aviators, the mission symbol "O1B" was the most coveted mission type. It indicated a combat mission over North Vietnam. During our tour in SEA, the combat policy was that when a crewmember amassed ONE HUNDRED O1Bs, he got to go home. To John and me, our 98th meant that we were almost home. Back in the land of the Big PX (as the States were referred to), an aircrew member wearing a 100 Mission patch (usually also indicating the aircraft type he flew) was looked on with admiration and envy by those still waiting or preparing to go to SEA.

On 1 November 1968, John and I logged our 99th O1B flying our assigned aircraft, F-105F 62-4424, that had our names stenciled on the canopy rails and carried the name "*Crown Seven*" on its fuselage. I have no significant memory of whether we were the flight lead on this date, or what the assigned frag/mission was. It must have been ops normal or routine. Upon landing it was back to the PE (personal equipment) shop to hang up our parachutes and helmets and take off the G-suits. We then proceeded to the maintenance debrief which was rather quick as we had no aircraft write-ups. Also quickly resolved was the debrief with the Intelligence shop, recounting our non- encounter with hostile fire and how we had disposed of our ordnance. Then it was off to the KABOOM (Korat Air Base Officers Open Mess) for a bite of lunch.

At first it went as usual, sitting at the 44th Squadron table with its red Klaxon light in a prominent place. The cute Thai waitresses gave us the menu and told us what was "No-hab" that day (those items listed on the menu but, not available as usual).

Then one of the other Aircrews came in with a "that day's" copy of the Bangkok Post, our primary "real world" source of information other than the "Stars and Stripes," a military organ primarily good for keeping up with delayed sports news and the comics. The Paper spoke of LBJ's intention to halt the bombing on Friday. The following quote from President Johnson's speech can be found on a Google search of the phrase, "LBJ and the October bombing halt": *"I have now ordered that all air, naval, and artillery bombardment of North Vietnam cease as of 8 a.m., Washington time, Friday morning."* NOTE: The President recorded the address on 30 October 30 1968, in the Family Theater at the White House for broadcast over nationwide radio and television at 8 p.m. on 31 October.

Further search shows that 31 October 1968 is a Thursday. Also my Form Five shows our 99th combat mission was flown on 1 November, but that must be because of all times appear to be listed in Zulu (Greenwich Mean Time or GMT) time in the forms. Also you have to remember that we were seven hours ahead of GMT (Zulu+7), which is eleven hours ahead of DC time. Regardless of what the calendar says, we return to this saga as we learn that President Johnson according to the Bangkok paper is going to halt the bombing of NVN the very next day.

We dropped our food and hastened (drove like crazy) to the Squadron Operations building and asked our 44th Commander, Guy "Jack" Sherrill, to schedule us again that day (a rather unusual event to fly two sorties in one 24 hour period). To my last day I will never forget his words. In his best imitation of Julius Caesar, Guy said, "I do not schedule based upon the front page of the Bangkok Post."

With that decree ringing in our ears, we proceeded to plan B. Plan B was to run over to the Form 5 section where the NCOs who document all our flying kept the holy of holies—our flight records. We went through the records with a fine-tooth comb, looking for some error that would allow us to arrive at 100 O1B missions versus the 99 missions that we continually kept counting. "What about this mission that was four plus hours long?" we asked. The obvious implication was that to have flown that long, we had to have exited North Vietnam and hit a tanker to return and carry out a SAR (Search and Rescue mission) we had been working. No soap!!! Our 99 missions remained 99.

Crestfallen, John and I return to the KABOOM to await the arrival of a 100 Mission parade of a fellow Wild Weasel crew who had the good fortune to get their 100th O1B on this, the last day of the Rolling Thunder bombing campaign. After the lucky fliers had descended from their carriage, an old WWII Japanese cannon and been thrown in the pool as custom dictates, a sorrowful flier can be seen sitting on the steps of the O'club bemoaning his fate. That was me, and somewhere in someone's shoe box there is a picture of this sad scene.

The Bombing Halt and now 01A's

With the announcement of the 1 November bombing halt, many changes in daily life take place at Korat and at the other fighter bases in Thailand. The change begins with a Squadron briefing of the new ROE's, or rules of engagement, that direct what can and cannot be done in the flights we will be conducting. The ROE's and other restrictions are sometimes referred to as the "be-no's" (stated as "there will be no more of ____...." and you can fill in the blank with anything you can think of). Most importantly, **there will be no unauthorized over flight over North Vietnam**. All flights will now be conducted at least 20 miles west of the NVN border, nominally demarked by the Mekong River. Thus, all missions will be coded 01A's (non-counting combat missions flown outside of NVN in Laos). We will be assigned hard altitudes to fly. The latter becomes the scary part, as numerous aircraft of all types are all jammed into the same airspace separated only by two to four thousand feet in altitude. We sure hoped everybody had a good altimeter read-out. There were BATCATS (EC-121's), Command and Control C-130's such as Cricket and other assorted pieces of aluminum that could be dangerous if they strayed from their assigned altitudes. Our task as Wild Weasels would be to, somehow, protect the recce forces that were authorized to fly into NVN to record activities there. But for the first time we would not be allowed to tactically place ourselves between the suspected Surface to Air Missile (SAM) sites and the RF-4's we were tasked to cover. We were armed with AGM-45's and a full load of 20 mm cannon shells (some one thousand rounds). We would fly in race-track patterns as close as we could get to the North Vietnam (NVN) border offset abeam the Recce's flight's target, normally the Mu Gia pass down which most of the NVN supply trails ran into South Vietnam (SVN).

Meanwhile back on the ground at the base, things are no longer quite the same. In fact, we no longer take on the air of a combat wing. The Wing Weenies lead by the Wing Commander start to institute all the little annoyances that are found at a stateside Fighter wing with no real combat mission. The Air Police are now authorized to write up Aircrews who are walking around with their flight-suit zippers not fully closed. Mustaches and haircuts go under closer scrutiny. No longer is it cool to wear your 100 Mission counter hat—the Jungle Jim hat on which you mark, with a felt tip pen, each and every O1B mission. So we now don Ball Caps or the AF Blue flight cap. This is especially true around the Base Exchange and Movie Theater which start to see increased utilization as the flying quiets down. There is a general malaise as the Fighter crews now see their hundred-mission tours change to at least one year on base, an increase of four to five months. Additional duties, those other jobs that we all have been assigned, take on a larger role. As the Squadron Executive Officer, I now have more time to get all the Officer Efficiency Reports (OER's) processed. John, as Wing Flying Safety Officer, prepares for the visit of the 7th AF Safety Inspection Team (always a fun event). Grumbling and drinking in the O'Club become a little more strained. (It's noteworthy to discuss the different strata that exist within the makeup of the club clientele. At the top of the pecking order are the Strike and Wild Weasel aircrews; next come the "other fliers," mainly the EC-121 Bat Cat and College Eye crews; followed by the ground-pounders or support types such as maintenance and personnel, though the Thud-maintainers hold their heads a little higher than those who keep the Connies (EC-121's) flying. Oops! I forgot to include the Chaplains, all who are seen as good to great guys, one of our special favorites being Chaplain/Father Frank Daley. You can always count on one of the "God Squad" being out in the arming area giving us a hearty wave as we got ready to take the "active" runway. God bless 'em!

As cancellation of the Rolling Thunder campaign continues to impact all the aircrews, John and I wonder what we can do to change our luck. In today's society you would put on your rally cap or turn around your ball cap to get things going. We reverted to what had seemed to work for us in escaping our earlier stint at Osan AB, Korea, in support (or non-support as it may have been) of the Pueblo crisis—to start growing mustaches in revolt. All the aircrews knew of our plight and we were becoming rather infamous for possessing 99 missions and a hold. Some suggested that if we wound up our tour without the 100th, we could have a patch made with "99 missions" and a screw sewn on it. In fact, at that time we came up with two patches. One was in yellow and had "0 (zero) mission North Korea" on it to represent our time at Osan. Another patch, to ridicule our River Rat heritage, showed some mice on a river which we dubbed the Mekong Mice patch. (Don't ask for one as there are only a limited number of these patches in existence.) Even the Brass was aware of our "sad situation." Gen. Chairsell, former 338Th TFW Cmdr visiting Korat for some reason, came up to me at the KABOOM and said,. "Stan, if you can't get your 100 in the Thud, study the RF-4C check list and I will send you up North in a Recce bird." I thanked him and did give it some consideration, but figured John would kill me if I left him there on his own.

While fighter pilots from Korat couldn't fly over North Vietnam, unarmed reconnaissance pilots from Udorn could. They were finding that North Vietnam was still a dangerous place. On 23 November, North Vietnamese guns shot down an RF-4C flying a photoreconnaissance mission over the lower panhandle. The pilot, Capt Bradley Gene Cuthbert from the 14 TRS at Udorn, died while missing, and his back-seater, Capt Mark J. Ruhling, became a POW. Two days later, on the 25th, the North Vietnamese blasted another Udorn plane, this time F-4D 66-7523 from the 555 TFS, flying armed escort for an RF-4C over the same area of North Vietnam. The "Triple Nickel" crew ejected and rescue forces were called to recover the two men.

As it happened, John and I were flying a Wild Weasel mission in Laos near the border of North Vietnam. Our F-105F was 63-8306, call sign "Ozark Two" in "Ozark" flight led by Maj. Floyd Dadisman, Jr., a fellow pilot from the 44 TFS, and his EWO, Capt. Richard L. Thompson. On Memorial Day 2004, I replayed the audiotape of this mission. After all these years, the adrenalin still starts to flow as I hear all the communication chatter indicating that an Aircrew has taken a hit and is forced to eject. We can hear the Search & Rescue (SAR) forces launch. The Sandys are airborne and they switch to their private channel. Meanwhile there are Misty FAC's in the area offering their assistance. John calls out an O-2 low and some B-52's high. Crown and Invert advise all that the crash scene is at 300° and 61 miles off of Channel 109 (Dong ha). There are intermittent Firecan signals at nine o'clock on my gear, but nothing steady.

Shortly after the F-4D goes down, "Ozark Lead" calls Invert and offers our Iron Hand services to the RESCAP force. After being cleared into the area, we start to fly into North Vietnam looking for radar signals that would warn of a SAM or AAA threat while the rescue force tries to locate the F-4D crew. John and I have not said anything, but we both realize that this crossing into NVN will result in our 100th O1B. Trolling in the crash area, we find no more threats to the airborne forces. Unfortunately, this is not true for the downed pilots who parachute safely, but land close to an NVA jungle encampment. Maj. Joseph Castleman Morrison and his WSO, 1Lt. San Dewayne Francisco, will survive this; but, due to bad weather that precludes rescue, will be captured and killed on the 26th. Their personal effects will later be displayed in the museum of the North Vietnam's 280th Air Defense Regiment.

With our fuel starting to run low, Invert clears us back to the RTB Tanker. So it is with mixed emotions that we leave the airspace of NVN for our last time. We are saddened as to the unknown fate (at that time) of our shot-down comrades. We, of course, are happy for ourselves that we have flown the 100th O1B and will get to go home and wear the 100-mission patch, and not have to remain a full year in Thailand.

On the way back, Ozark one calls Apache, the 388th command post, and alerts them that a 100-mission flight is inbound. Until the bombing halt, at least several times a week, a crew or crews would fly their 100th mission, have a parade, and then "buy the bar" for one and all. This one was different in that there had been no such celebration for the past twenty-five days. John came up on the interphone and said, "Guess who we are going to buy a case of champagne for?" Being fairly astute on occasion, I replied, "How about Ozark One"? Once again I came up with the correct answer, hooray!!!

Setting Channel 125 in the TACAN, we smoke back to Korat. Back at the ranch, preparations are being made to greet us. All the 44th crew trucks and those of the other Squadrons that are alerted assemble in the parking area. They are headed up by the Wing DO, Bill "Machman" Craig, one super guy, who has riding shotgun with him, Keith Ferris, aviation artist nonpareil (that's erudite, not fighter pilot, talk for the best darn aviation painter I know) who will take photos of the entire proceedings. Fire trucks and hoses are readied to wet us down once we alight from our trusty steed...but first we will make a high speed pass down the runway. John agrees to give me the stick and let me make the flyby from the back-seat. He mulls over letting me pull it up and make an aileron roll, but on second thought cancels this wild idea. He recalls that a previous Flying Safety Officer had dinged a bird on final and thinks this might not be a good way to end the tour. At any rate, we safely complete the circuit and touch down, deploy the chute, and extend the refueling probe, a symbol of completing 100 BIG ONES.

As we taxi into the de-arming area, we can see the crew trucks filled with cheering squadron mates and those from the other units eagerly waiting to lead us in a parade to our revetment parking area. We insert the pins and for once don't descend the ladder with chutes on. Some other crews in times past, knowing that this would be there final mission, have prepared for that glorious day by wearing their party suits beneath their normal goat skins, but this is not the way we will deplane. Greeting us were all available members of the 44 TFS and some newly arrived F-4E crews from the 469 TFS who are seeing their first 100 Mission parade. These 469th crews had arrived at Korat on November 17th delivering the first F-4E's in SEA to replace that squadron's F-105D's and their pilots. (The E model was distinguished by being the first F-4 to have an internal gun, a weapon that the Thud Drivers had from the beginning.)

With the canopy raised, we can be seen smiling with shit-eating grins and giving two thumbs up. With help from the Crew Chief we unbuckle and descend the longest ladder in NATO. Today climbing down is like descending from a heavenly experience. Yes, scores of others had made this trip down the ladder on completion of their 100th mission. But this one was ours and we had never anticipated it happening today. At that moment we had no other thoughts except for being glad we had made it and would finally get to wear the most desired patch of all—the red, white and blue one that reads **"North Vietnam, 100 Missions, F-105."** I can't recall if there was champagne or not, but after many handshakes, there was the traditional hosing down, almost as a baptismal event. In retrospect, I guess it was. Then John and I, as the script usually called for, wrested the hose away from our gleeful comrades and turned it on all who were in range, causing a great scattering of all. Guy Sherrill, Dick Haggren, even the ever-present Flight Surgeon, Jerry Swartz, and the duty God Squad Chaplain broke for cover.

Phase Two of the 100 Mission Parade commenced with John and me mounting the Japanese WWII cannon normally shackled at the Ft. Apache Compound. Floyd Dadisman, Ozark lead, covered our Intel and maintenance debrief requirements as we had no Form 781 write-ups. So, with Dick Haggren driving the 44th TFS commander's jeep and with Larry (Bearly Larry) LeMieux riding as safety observer and as the new cannoneer (having replaced the recently departed Frosty Sheridan), we took off for the grand tour of the flight line and base. Our ultimate destination was the KABOOM for more water survival training. But prior to reaching that wet conclusion, with John in the front seat and me in the rear one, cigar in mouth, we led the grand procession of other crew vehicles. Cruising down the flight line hangars and maintenance shops we were greeted with cheers, water hoses and ignited smoke canisters.

I could not have felt better than Caesar riding his chariot into the Rome Forum. After we arrived at the entrance to the KABOOM , with the help of our comrades, we did not have to walk, but were carried and dragged to the pool and ceremoniously launched into the water. It is best not to fight the inevitable and certainly safer as you did not want those throwing you in to slip in their performance of this time-honored ritual. Our comrades and hooch girls then joined us—not all willingly in this instance. My soggy cigar still in my mouth, John and I climbed out of the pool and headed into the longest bar in SEA and rang the Bell signifying that we would buy the bar not only for one round, but for as long as we could stand it. We ordered the bartenders to take every bottle of cognac they had and mix it with suitable quantities of champagne and place the brew known as "French 75" in the largest soup container they had.

We drained the club of all its cognac, and consumed a copious amount ourselves. We had someone drive us to the NCO club where we could share our good fortune with those guys who made it possible every day for us to safely aviate the skies in our steeds. It always amazed me how the maintainers could work those long hours, especially through the night to prepare and arm the Thuds we would take north. It still sticks in my mind on those rainy, monsoon afternoons as we walked to our assigned bird, with ponchos on to keep our parachutes dry, that many of them would have to stand in the swirling, windy rain as we preflighted and then climbed the ladder to our relatively dry cockpit. (One such afternoon as we strapped in, they placed us on a fifteen-minute hold as a local thunderstorm passed over the Air base. We were a bit warm in our closed cockpit with only an iced "Sawadee Towel" around our neck to help cool us off. But out on the ramp, as the troops took what little cover they could find, one lad climbed into an empty engine canister just as a great gust of wind sent him for a scary and unintended ride rolling down the ramp. Yes, they were there for us every day, strapping us in, wishing us good luck and buttoning us up. So, we wanted to share our good fortune and honor them at the same time. How long we stood and toasted them and they us, I do not know, but after becoming fairly well lubricated we were some how escorted back to our hooch. I don't know about John, but I fell asleep immediately. I was always a sleepy drunk anyway. After a few hours, I managed to get out of my goatskin, shower, don some shorts and a shirt and return to the fray at the O'Club to continue to celebrate this 25 November 1968, a day I will never forget.

The pressure was off now. It was time to prepare for going home: getting rid of those additional duties and cleaning up unfinished business. John and I would fly one more O1A in December to fill the square for combat pay, flying pay, etc,. I don't recall a thing about that sortie, but I guess we lived, because we were able to attend our private 44th TFS going-away party. We got our plaques and our mugs and wore our blue party suits one more time, but this time with the coveted 100-Mission Patch sewn firmly on the left shoulder. It is always sobering to leave a great flying organization and good people. For a little over eight months we had called Korat and the Wild Weasels of the 44th TFS our home and comrades in arms, but now it was time for us to go. We had done our duty and played our part in the game of "stopping the dominoes from rolling over the rest of SEA". We would have no direct involvement in what would happen afterwards. However, fate would smile on us one more time as my follow-on assignment changed and I found out that I would be going to the 479 TFW, George AFB, CA to be their first Wing EWO, the same Wing where John was going to become an F-4 Instructor. On 7 December 1968, I departed Bangkok for the CONUS on a MATS chartered flight drinking my way home sitting next to a Colonel Firecan Dan Walsh.

Notes:

Keith Ferris, who took the pictures of John's and my 100-mission parade, deserves more praise then I can adequately give him. He flew and painted his way across the Pacific in the back of Major Paul Leming's brand new F-4E and he arrived at Korat to observe operations there and get ready for his follow on adventures. As a freelance aviation artist he has given of his time and skills painting and donating artwork to the US military. His work can be found at the Smithsonian and the WPAFB Museum.

I spoke to Keith in the days after his observing and photographing our 100th mission and asked him if he was ever to paint a Thud Wild Weasel, would he consider painting Crown Seven, 62-4424, the bird assigned to John and me. He did create such a painting as a tribute to all Wild Weasels, titling it "Big Brass Ones." This was just the start of a long and ongoing friendship with Keith, his gracious wife Pegg, and the Wild Weasels, that continues till today.

Big Brass Ones.
More about Keith and Big Brass Ones can be found at
http://www.keithferrisart.com/

Final Aircraft dispositions (Courtesy of W. Howard Plunkett, F-105 Historian)

F-105F AF 63-8306 (our 100th 01B) was converted to a G model and flew as one of the five Firebird Wild Weasels on the Son Tay Raid on 20 November 1970 almost exactly two years after our 100th mission. In 1983, it was used as a ground target for Army munitions testing at Aberdeen Proving Grounds, Md.

F-105F AF 62-4424 (Crown Seven) was converted to a G model and shot down by a MiG's Atoll missile on 11 May 1972. The crew, Major Bill Talley and EWO Major Jim Padgettt became POW's. Both Talley and Padgett survived captivity and were returned to the US in early 1973.

For those who may be interested, following is a look at our November and December Form 5 with amplifying remarks provided by John:

Date	Pilot	EWO	A/C	MSN	#	TT	Day	Nite	Remarks
1-Nov-68	Revak	Goldstein	F105F	O1B	99	1.9	1.9		8 PM Bombing Halt Begins
4-Nov-68	Revak	Goldstein	F105F	O1A		2.3	2.3		
5-Nov-68	Revak	Goldstein	F105F	O1A		2.3		2.3	
10-Nov-68	Revak	Goldstein	F105F	O1A		2.5	1.3	1.2	
11-Nov-68	Revak		F105D	O1A		1.6	0.3	1.3	
12-Nov-68	Revak		F105D	O1A		1.7		1.7	
13-Nov-68	Revak	Goldstein							R&R Bangkok - Florida Hotel
17-Nov-68									F4E's Arrive - Keith Ferris
19-Nov-68		Goldstein							Stan flunks tine test - later is OK
21-Nov-68	Revak	Goldstein	F105F	O1A		2.7	2.7		
22-Nov-68	Revak								SAFETY INSPECTION TEAM
23-Nov-68	Revak								7th AF Safety Inspection Team Departs
24-Nov-68	Revak	Goldstein	F105F	O1A		2.7	2.7		
25-Nov-68	Revak	Goldstein	F105F	O1B	100	2.7	2.7		100 MISSION PARTY
27-Nov-68		Goldstein							Stan gets George AFB assignment
2-Dec-68	Revak	Goldstein	F105F	O1A	2.6	2.6	2.6		Last Flight - Vietnam Tour Complete
4-Dec-68	Revak	Goldstein							SQUADRON GOING AWAY PARTY
6-Dec-68		Goldstein							Stan departs for Bangkok
9-Dec-68		Goldstein							Stan departs for States
12-Dec-68	Revak								Dept Korat for Takhli
13-Dec-68	Revak								7th River Rat Tactical Conf @ Takhli
14-Dec-68	Revak								River Rat Conf continues
15-Dec-68	Revak								FLT F2T4 to Yakota
15-Dec-68	Revak								to Travis arr 1300 US time

Stan Goldstein (WW# 415)

Story by William H. Talley WW # 554

Some Days Are Better Staying in Bed

Editor's Note: Bill Talley deployed to Korat RTAFB in April 1972 at part of Constant Guard 1 in response to the North Vietnamese "Easter Offensive" and the resumption of bombing of North Vietnam. Upon arrival at Hickham AFB, Hawaii I discovered that my aircraft had an oil leak and required an engine replacement. Since I was the Squadron Commander I took Bill's aircraft and pressed on to Korat and left him to lounge on the beach at Waikiki until a new engine could be flown to Hawaii, installed in the aircraft, flight-tested and tankers were available for deployment to Korat. It was to be a well-deserved vacation, but we didn't know just how well deserved at the time.

In the spring of 1972, I was stationed at McConnell AFB, KS in the 561st TFS, the only F-105 Wild Weasel Operational Squadron Stateside. Even though the Vietnam War had not ended, I did not expect to be sent there because I had completed a tour of duty and a temporary tour of duty there. I had been selected for a promotion, and on Good Friday I received verbal confirmation of an assignment that I intended to be my last in the Air Force. I would retire from the Air Force and build a home on an acreage that my wife and I bought in 1964. However, God has the final approval of all our plans.

Shortly after midnight on Easter Sunday the alert siren sounded announcing a recall to the base. After a review of plans a decision was made to deploy our entire squadron of twenty plus F-105s to Korat AB, Thailand. The Commanding Officer of McConnell sent word to our squadron for me to deploy and as soon as orders could be cut for my new assignment, the base would send a message for me to return home. A couple of days later, we left McConnell flying to Korat via Hickam AFB Hawaii, and Guam. I flew 12 combat missions and received a message for me to return to McConnell. The system was working. After a couple of days taking care of some paper work, I was in the barber shop about an hour before reporting to the departure area for my flight home when one of my squadron buddies came in saying that he had been looking for me because another message had come to operations. The message told me to remain at Korat. I asked to be put back on the flying schedule while I was there and was put on a flight with a dawn takeoff the next morning.

We began flight planning about 0200 hours to support a large strike in the Hanoi, North Vietnam area. The weather forecaster told us that the weather in the Hanoi area would be bad until noon, but the weather for our alternate target on the coast would be good at takeoff time. We expected a target change even as we preflighted our airplanes, but never got one. About fifteen minutes after take off; we got a recall to return to the base and land. I had flown 181 combat missions and had never been recalled to land right after take off nor had I ever heard of any one else who had been recalled like that. Once airborne there was always somewhere to go. Our alternate target would have been open.

We landed as soon as we burned some of our fuel, and while we were shutting down the engines, the Commanding Officer of Korat was walking very briskly toward our airplanes. He told us to turn our planes around as quickly as possible because at the moment, the Vice President of the US was speaking live on television announcing the resumption of bombing in Hanoi.

We were airborne again about noon and after in-flight refueling arrived in the Hanoi area at about 15,000 feet. There were Surface to Air Missiles (SAMs) and antiaircraft explosions in the air, but none close to my airplane. We felt a jolt and the engine rpm began dropping along with warning lights for hydraulic pressure, oil pressure, and engine fire. I jettisoned all external fuel and ordnance and turned southwest toward Thailand. I also made a comment about another bearing failure. About ten days earlier we had experienced a similar condition on a mission just North of the DMZ in North Vietnam. We were gliding toward the Gulf of Tonkin hoping to get over water before we bailed out. At 5,000 feet the engine rpm increased enough for us to turn toward South Vietnam and make a straight in landing at Da Nang AB. After turning off the runway, I shut down the engine and got out of the airplane. Oil covered the bottom of the airplane. We got a ride back to Korat and learned that the airplane had a bearing failure in the engine. Now, gliding away from Hanoi, I thought the same thing had happened again.

We were approaching mountains that were about 1,000 feet high that I thought we would not be able to clear, so I asked my backseater if he was ready to eject. He said that we were right over a village. I rolled the airplane, saw the village, saw the mountains ahead and raised my feet to clear them. We did and while in a valley between mountains we ejected about 1,000 feet above ground. I had slowed the F-105 to about 350K, and we were making a controlled bailout. Still the windblast surprised me, and I could not determine whether I was upside down or right side up. I could feel the windblast peeling the glove off my right hand and even though I clenched my fist, the glove came off. I swung once in the parachute, heard an explosion, looked to my side and saw a large ball of fire which had been our airplane. Then I looked down to where I was going to land and saw a steep slope with a very large boulder with no hope of avoiding it. All the techniques we learned in training about parachute landing falls was of no value as I smashed into the boulder. I turned on my emergency radio and heard someone asking for a short count. A fast jet flew low overhead and told me he had a good fix on my location. My parachute was hung in the tree limbs so I abandoned it, and started climbing to the top of the mountain, which took about thirty minutes. The zippers on the pockets for my emergency radios on my survival vest came apart and the radios were falling to the ground. I put one radio in my helmet and carried the other in my hand, which made climbing up the steep slope more difficult. At the top of the mountain I found a place to sit down and took out the two water bottles in the bottom pockets of my flying suit. Both had been ruptured and the water was gone. Then I looked at my knees; which had received the blunt of the landing. One had a gash about three inches long. The other just scraped. I opened my first aid kit but could not find either antiseptic or bandages. Then I saw a large rock on a slope about 15 feet below the crest of the mountain. There was a hole under the rock large enough that I could squeeze through. Once there, I waited for rescue, but the only sound that I heard was Vietnamese voices getting closer. After dark I could hear people walking near by.

At first light the next morning, I crawled out from the rock, turned on my radio and listened. Within a few minutes, I heard someone asking for me by my call sign. After establishing radio contact I got under my rock and waited. About noon I heard rifle shots and shouting around my rock. My hiding place had been discovered. As I crawled out from under the rock I could see about 25 or 30 people surrounding the rock and that many more running toward me. One man was holding a bolt-action rifle and firing shots to alert others. Just as I raised my arms to surrender, I could hear the sound of an A-1 Sandy flying overhead. In the mid 1990s the number two Sandy pilot got in touch with me and told me about the attempt to rescue my backseater, which failed. He had put a recording of the rescue attempt on a website. Sandy Lead had trouble with an oil sump pump warning light, and two times they had to leave the area because of MiGs.

Four or five Vietnamese tackled me and began taking off my boots and flying suit. I believe they might not have been familiar with zippers because they kept tugging at my flying suit as if they expected to pop open buttons. I also had zippers on the sides of my flying boots and they had difficulty removing them. I was not cooperating either. I locked my ankles stiff to prevent them from removing my boots, but they did succeed. One of them put his knee on my chest and the world's largest machete on my throat. Then they stood me up and tied my arms above my elbows and behind my back with one end of the rope held by one of the guards. We started walking down the mountain. I wear boxer type shorts and evidently the fly was popping open as we walked. The guard in front of me stopped, produced a safety pin, pointed to the fly of my underwear and gave me the pin. He expected me to pin my shorts with my arms tied behind my back. The scene would have been funny if it were not so serious. These people who were unfamiliar with zippers were now "clothes critics" about how I was dressed. With some difficulty I pinned my shorts, and we continued to walk down the mountain then along rice paddies and flat land. A small storm passed over producing some pea size hail. I bent over a couple of times as we walked and got some of the hail off the ground and put them in my mouth. I had not had any water for about 30 hours. Once or twice the guards stopped walking and drank from their canteens. One of the guards filled the plastic canteen lid from his canteen and gave that to me to drink.

We walked until after dark and stopped in an area of about four or five very small huts and went inside one of them. Three or four elderly men were inside eating. The guards began eating from a bowl and one of them gave me a rice ball about the size of a baseball to eat. After about thirty minutes we left and walked another two hours before stopping in a larger village for the night.

The next morning we began walking south about sunrise. Midmorning one of the guards fired his rifle about three feet behind my back, which really startled me. When I turned to look, a guard walking to the side of our trail stopped and picked up a monkey that he had shot. I did not see what they did with the monkey.

My knee was hurting and walking was difficult, but I was not about to let these little people out-walk me. After all, American Pride was at stake. The young man holding the end of the rope to which I was tied was about 5' 5" tall. I felt like a trained bear. All that day we walked from one small village to another. We stopped at each village for the people to hear about the capture of the ugly American. Then they would vent their anger on me with sticks, stones, fists, and spit in my face before we went to the next village. We waded streams that were hip high, but I did not dare drink from them.

We stopped before dark the second day in a village with 20 or 30 huts. There was one large hut about 30' x 60' that was probably a community hall which we and about 100 other people entered. We went to the far end of the building and the people crowded up next to us. There was an imaginary semicircle around me and when anyone got inside the semicircle the guard would order him back. Because I was very tired I lay down. I noticed an older man sitting in front of me when he began measuring me with a stick that was about one foot long. After the measurement he stood up and announced the results to the people. There was a great deal of commotion, so he measured me again. I am 6' 3" tall, so the results may have been difficult for the people to believe. I got a banana to eat but nothing to drink.

The next day was like the last two days, however; I would not be able to live up to my American Pride. I stumbled and fell often. About noon I was laying face down in the dirt when one of the guards lifted my head and pointed toward an ox drawn two-wheel wagon. With their help I got on the wagon, which had large sacks of some kind of grain. We rode on the wagon an hour or so, then transferred to a large stake-bed truck with uniformed soldiers and AK-47s. The truck was moving east and about sundown we entered a large city with paved streets. The truck stopped next to a vendor on the sidewalk and the soldiers got what looked like popsicles. About ten minutes later a crowd began surrounding the truck. People tried climbing up the sides of the truck and the soldiers hit them with the butt of their rifles. The driver started the engine and began moving forward very slowly parting the crowd When the truck was through the crowd the driver accelerated. The people chased the truck on foot and bicycles about a block.

Well after dark I could see the Big Dipper and North Star. We were driving South. The war has ended, and we were going to the DMZ for release of prisoners. Wishful thinking. We entered a gated area and stopped. A woman appeared wearing a white lab coat and looked at my knee. Then I was helped off the truck and to a shed. An older man in uniform entered and began asking questions. Even though his English was not very good, I could understand him. I pretended that I could not understand him and kept repeating my name, rank, service number and date of birth. After about 20 or 30 minutes I was helped back on to the truck and told that I would be taken to a hospital. Now the truck was driving north and I could smell beach and ocean water. We had gone from the west side of North Vietnam to the east side. We entered another large city and the soldiers covered me with a tarp. Later the soldiers removed the tarp and I could see that we were climbing some more mountains. Now, we are surely driving into China and no one will ever hear from me again.

Late in the afternoon the soldiers covered me with the tarp and we entered another large city. The truck stopped in town. I was blindfolded and led into a room about 10' x 12". I lay on the floor in the corner of the room. Soldiers came and went and people asked me questions, but I was not fully aware of what was happening. Probably the next day I was given water to drink. I knew that I should drink slowly and thought that I did. However, about 15 minutes after drinking, I knew that I was going to lose everything. Not knowing when I would get water again, I vomited in a pan. The liquid was clear because I had nothing to eat for several days. When my stomach felt better, I drank the water again. It was a little warmer the second time, but I kept it down.

The interrogators warned me to cooperate or I would not receive any treatment for my infected knee. The knee was black about six inches above and below and red down to my feet and up to my hip. Cooperation was writing anti-war letters and making statements to the press. I was not being macho; I was in too much of a stupor to care so I refused.

One interrogation was heart-warming for me. There was a table in the room and a short-leg stool, like a stool I used when I milked cows years earlier. The interrogator brought in an electric oscillating fan, plugged it in to the wall and set it on the table pointing toward him. I was sitting on my stool, head below his and not paying a great deal of attention to his ranting and raving. A few minutes into the interrogation he told me in a loud voice to move back and made motions with his hand for me to move away. I moved my stool back about a foot and the interrogation continued. I was very weak, tired and uninterested in his comments. To rest, I leaned over, and then I realized why the guard had ordered me to back away. There was a very foul smelling yellow pus oozing from the wound on my knee. I had not bathed in a week and my 24-hour underarm deodorant had failed. I could even smell myself, that was how filthy I was. So, I straightened up on my stool and then began a rocking motion. Each time that I leaned forward I would slide my stool toward the interrogator's table. After a few minutes, I was closer to the table than when he ordered me back. At that point, he unplugged the fan, picked it up and left the room. I don't know why he did not bop me in the face, but he didn't, and I had a moral victory.

One night I was blindfolded and told that I was going to a hospital. I was put on a table for an X-Ray and after the machine whirred, I was blindfolded and returned to my room. The next day an interrogator told me that without medical treatment my knee would be permanently stiff and that likely my leg would have to be amputated. I really did not think so, but I also did not care at that point. A day later a guard came into the room wearing a white lab coat. He put some yellow powder on my knee and gave me a shot in each arm. The next five or six days someone would come into my room and give me a shot in each arm, and the knee began healing.

One night I was blindfolded and taken to a room that was about 6 ½' x 6 ½'. A couple of weeks later I heard someone calling for the guy in the end room to stand on the bed and look over the door. Carefully, I did and saw a POW smiling back at me. Over the next few days he taught me the tap code, hand code, and gave me "The Plums", some supplemental rules to the Code of Conduct. I also finally learned where I was…in the Heartbreak Hotel area of the Hanoi Hilton. The first room I had been in was called "New Guy Village." We were about 30 miles southwest of Hanoi when we bailed out. I walked for three days, rode in a truck for over 30 hours just to get to Hanoi. There was no extra charge for the scenic tour.

I was taken out of the room every night for interrogations. I was not asked for military information, which surprised me, but for propaganda statements and press conferences. I did not receive the severe torture that the earlier NAM-POW received, so I was able to refuse all their demands. The small room in Heartbreak was unventilated and became very hot. I developed a heat rash that was as uncomfortable as poison ivy. Also, a dozen or more festering sores appeared on my body. Each day a guard would bring a quart size teapot into my room for my drinking water. I would pour about half of the contents on my back to cool and would lean in a pushup position against the wall to keep from scratching. I wore only the shorts that were issued; however, before interrogations a guard would come to my door, and tell me to put on "Long Clothes." That meant the pajama-like prison clothes that were issued. During the time I waited for the guard to return and take me to the interrogation, I would pray for strength and wisdom. Miraculously, the itching would stop and not bother me until after the interrogation, and I was returned to my room. After two months in Heartbreak, I was moved to a larger room with 12 other POW. Life was better with someone to talk to in a part of the Hanoi Hilton we called "Camp Unity." I was still taken out of the room about once a month for interrogation.

We were allowed outside of our rooms for about 15 minutes each day to bathe and wash our clothes. A concrete tank about 7' x 3' x 3' held our bath water. We used a bucket made from a tire caisson to dip water out of the tank and pour it over our bodies. Each POW was given one bar a month of homemade lye soap for bathing, washing our clothes, and shaving. The weather in Hanoi was hot about nine or ten months of the year, and bathing was a pleasure. During the winter the temperature was in the 40s or 50s during the day, and the cold-water baths were not as pleasant, but I always took a bath when given an opportunity.

We were allowed to shave about once a week. During bath time the guard would give one of the POWs a safety razor. The double edge razor blades were of less quality than the old Gillette razor blades we had in the U.S. in the 1940s that we would throw away after each shave before we got titanium blades. The Vietnamese sharpened the razor blades on a flint stone like one used to sharpen a pocketknife. The razor blades were not very sharp and three men were expected to shave using one blade. The first POW would shave using only one edge of the blade. Then he would clean the blade, give it to the next POW pointing to the edge of the blade he had used. The second POW would shave using the other edge of the blade, clean the blade and give it to the third POW who could use both edges of the blade. The lye soap and cold water did not produce much lather, and the dull blades were terrible. I often scraped the same area on my face several times and still could not cut whiskers that had grown for a week.

About once or twice a week our room would be escorted to an area next to the kitchen to make "Coal Balls." There was a large pile of coal granules similar to sugar granules on the ground. We would add water to the coal and form them like a snowball. We stacked the coal balls along the wall to dry before they were used in the kitchen stoves. Because our hands got very black, we were allowed to wash them before returning to our rooms. Each POW was given one bar of lye soap a month for personal use, but because our room made coal balls, our room was given two extra bars of soap a month for the entire room.

The large courtyard in the Camp Unity area was cordoned with bamboo curtains and only one room at a time was let outside to bathe. This was an attempt to prevent contact with other POWs. Our room of New Guys was isolated in the corner of Camp Unity. Other rooms in Camp Unity adjoined and the Old Guys could communicate with each room using the tap code or other techniques.

We were fed a bowl of soup twice a day. We got pumpkin soup in the summer and cabbage soup in the winter. We also got a side dish occasionally and often did not recognize what we got. For a short period of time in the 1980s, Vietnamese Pot Bellied Pigs were popular in the States as pets. Those were the kind of pigs that were in Hanoi. We saw them occasionally in the prison area. The pigs were skinned and the meat was given to the guards. The skin was diced into pieces about one square inch. The skin had a layer of fat on the inside and hair on the outside. These pieces of "Pig Fat" were put into our soup. Maybe one or two POWs would find a piece in his soup about once a week. Some of the POWs did not want to eat "Pig Fat" and would give it away. It had some protein and calories and was not wasted.

The Vietnamese did all they could to prevent our "Chain of Command" from functioning. The junior ranking officer in our room was the point of contact for prison activities. Some of the POWs in our rooms smoked cigarettes. They were given a ration of three cigarettes a day. Each day a guard would bring all the ration of cigarettes to the junior ranking officer who would then distribute the cigarettes to the smokers. Some of the POWs were allowed to receive boxes from home. A guard would enter the room, call out the POW who had received a package, tell him to put on his "Long Clothes" and escort him outside the room The POW would be allowed to look inside the box at the few remaining items that had not been pilfered, then return to his room, but not allowed to take anything from the box with him. The junior ranking officer in the room would be allowed to go outside to where the box was and take items from the box to the room. The boxes from the States usually contained a bottle of vitamin pills. The Vietnamese were suspicious of U.S. technology and to make sure that an escape kit was not hidden in a vitamin pill, a guard would cut each vitamin pill in half with his dirty pocketknife. Only then was the junior ranking officer allowed to take ½ a vitamin pill to each of the POWs in the room. Other items received in a box from home were shared the same way.

When a POW received a letter from home, he was escorted outside the room wearing his "Long Clothes" to a table where he was allowed to read the letter, but could not keep it. After reading the letter, he was escorted back to the room.

Our room had acquired a homemade pencil. On one occasion, when a POW was taken to a table outside our room to write a letter, he stole a piece of lead from the guard's mechanical pencil. Then he put the lead between two pieces of bamboo and tied the bamboo with a piece of string pulled from his blanket. The pencil was a treasured item and kept hidden. The pencil was used to write messages that were secretly moved from our room to the room of the "Senior Ranking Officers" in the prison. We wrote our messages on the toilet paper, which were 4" x 4" sheets of brown paper about the consistency of a grocery bag.

The Senior Ranking Officer in our room asked me to be the Chaplain and conduct a religious service every Sunday. We had absolutely no religious materials in the room. We did not have any kind of materials in the room. The first Sunday we gathered at the far end of the room, turned our back to the door and began. I suggested a song that I thought most people would know, led the song, gave a brief lesson, then closed with a prayer and another song. We had our beginning.

The next week I got the pencil when it was not in use and some sheets of toilet paper. Then from memory, I wrote the Apostles' Creed, a prayer, and a verse from a couple of songs. This was our "Worship Book", and I made three or four copies to distribute to roommates. The next Sunday we used them. Can you imagine the hypocrisy of what I was doing? Making worship books on toilet paper with a stolen pencil!! About once a month, the guards would come into our room and order everyone outside. They would pat us down as we walked out. Most of the year, we wore only shorts, so we could not hide anything in our clothes anyway. Then the guards would thoroughly search the room. They always found the Worship Books, but I would make new ones the following week.

During the summer of 1972 the population of our room grew as more planes were shot down. When there were only about 15 in a room the guard would come into the room for a head count and leave quickly. By the end of the summer there were 25 or more POWs in our room. One day the guard came into our room and ordered every POW to sit. We thought that he was being arrogant and while some of the POW sat down, others refused to do so. The guard then began yelling and screaming at us. When the guard left the room, we huddled for a conference. We decided that we would completely ignore the guard and pretend that he was invisible, and we did that the next time he came in the room. Of course he was threatening, yelling and his face turned red with anger as we walked around the room as though nothing unusual was happening. Shortly after, several guards came into the room and escorted our senior ranking officer out of the room. He did not return for several weeks. We held another conference among ourselves. The second in command was reluctant to continue our stand for fear that he would be taken away too. I was the third ranking officer in the room, but was willing to risk our stand for the principle so we continued. We sent messages to the "Senior Ranking Officers" in the Hilton explaining what had happened. We got word back from the senior officers that we should sit down when the guard came into the room for a head count, and we complied. Another guard replaced the guard for our room and everything returned to normal.

In the fall of 1972, negotiations in Paris to end the war must have appeared promising for the Vietnamese. They told us that "Peace was at Hand" and even moved about 20 Old POW into a room that was across the hall from our room. We immediately began communicating. The Old guys wanted to know what had happened at home in the last four years during the bombing pause in North Vietnam. We told them about clothing styles, short skirts on girls and long hair on boys, movies, sports, politics, and even pay scales. Then the Vietnamese began letting both rooms out at the same time to bathe. There was still a bamboo fence dividing our bath area, but a couple of us would stand by the fence and pretend we were talking to each other. A couple of the Old Guys would be on their side of the fence pretending the same thing, but the conversation was between them and us. We exchanged names and other valuable information. Eventually, the Vietnamese took down the bamboo fences and let us out at the same time. Now, we could see the faces of those we had talked to for a month. The Old Guys wanted us to know the history of the Vietnam POWs and each day would tell some part of that history to a couple of people from our room. After lockup those POWs would tell the story to the others in our room. The Old Guys said that if only one POW returns home, they wanted him to be able to tell the rest of the world what had happened.

Our room received a message from the senior ranking officers that there might be a big movement of POW within the prison. That night guards came into our room, called out the names of about ten of us and told us to put on our "Long Clothes." About thirty minutes later several guards came into our room and called us outside the room. We were blindfolded, led to a truck, put in the back and told to be quiet. We thought that we were being moved to another camp. After a thirty-minute ride we were taken off the truck and escorted inside a building. When the blindfolds were removed, we saw that we were in a room about 15' x 20' with a large table in the middle of the room. We were told to set at the table and when a guard brought a plate full of cookies, we knew that there would be an attempt for propaganda. I began talking quietly to one of the POWs sitting next to me. We knew that we should do something but did not know what. Then two guards escorted one of the POW to the next room. He made an initial refusal before leaving the room, which gave me an idea. The guards took the second POW out of the room. I was next, and instead of standing up, I slid to the floor and grabbed the table legs. Several guards pulled my arms away from the table and began dragging me across the concrete floor. When we got to the doorway, I grabbed the doorjamb, which prevented the guards from pulling me farther. The guards were able to pull one of my arms from the doorjamb and bend it behind my back while shoving my face into the concrete floor. At that time the senior ranking officer in our group came to me and told me to quit resisting and enter the room. He also told everyone else to leave the table and come into the room before anyone was hurt. We were in the "War Crimes Museum" and the Vietnamese wanted to show us parts of US planes that had been shot down over North Vietnam. If one of the POWs refused to look, a guard would grab his hair and force his head up. Then the POW would close his eyes. After about twenty minutes of this activity we were blindfolded, escorted back to the trucks and returned to the Hilton and our rooms. We had been tricked. I was asked to brief the rest of our roommates about the events of the trip, and we retired for the night. We later learned that some of the Old POWs had been tricked also.

Late in the fall there was a bombing halt in North Vietnam like the one that went into effect in 1968. We carried on our daily routine not knowing what was happening in Paris. In December the guards gave each POW a pair of army green socks and a sweater. The two winter months in North Vietnam were not tropical. The cold wind from China swept over Hanoi and the concrete floors and walls never were warm. There was nothing covering the iron bars of the windows either and the few calories that we received did not keep us warm.

One night, a week before Christmas, another POW in the room and I were tying some of the newly given green socks end to end to make a Christmas Wreath. Then we, and everyone in the room, heard a loud rumbling in the distance that slowly moved closer. I had no idea what was making the noise, and I don't believe anyone else in the room did either at that time. Then we heard air raid sirens and the sound of AAA and saw a bright yellow glow of a fire in the distant sky. The bombing had resumed. The next day the POW were busy talking back and forth between rooms. One of the Old Guys said, "Pack your bags, boys, the B-52s are coming." Bombing continued around the clock and sometimes the explosions were close enough to rattle the walls. The guards were frightened and were even making shelters inside the prison. We were told to lie on our beds during attacks. I was on my bed during one attack when a two square foot piece of ceiling plaster fell on my feet. The F-111s came low level at night. We would hear them roar overhead at a very high speed and drop bombs and depart the area before we heard the sirens and AAA.

There was no bombing on Christmas Day. The Vietnamese made a big show out of feeding us a Christmas dinner that day. We had only one meal and did not get it until afternoon. As I recall, we had a very small egg roll, a tablespoon of rice, a cigarette and a small glass of wine that tasted like gasoline to me.

Bombing resumed the day after Christmas and ended within the week. We did not know what was happening or what to expect. Our group was moved into another room with POWs who had been shot down later than we had. We stayed together for a couple of weeks, then during daylight, and not blindfolded, all of us were moved to the New Guy Village area of the Hilton. These rooms were smaller with only three or four people to a room. There were two B-52 crewmembers in New Guy Village who were semi-conscious. They both had very bad bedsores just below their spine.

One afternoon we were ordered out of our rooms and told to assemble in formation. This was extremely unusual because the Vietnamese did not want us to do anything in a military manner. While we were assembled, several guards and the camp commander entered the area. Using an interpreter, the camp commander read the short peace treaty that had been signed ending the war. There was a statement that all POWs had to be released in 60 days. The camp commander and his entourage walked out and left us standing. We were action-less for a minute not knowing if this was another of their tricks. Then we broke ranks and began smiling and hugging one another.

Long before us new guys were shot down, the old guys had planned that there would be no early releases and that everyone would go home in the order in which they were shot down. The Vietnamese knew of that plan and honored it. Within a few days the Vietnamese began moving POWs around in preparation for the release. The Hanoi Hilton was to be the prison where the first POW would be released. After dark one night, all of us new guys were blindfolded, put in trucks and moved to another prison in the Hanoi area that we called "The Zoo." There were about 120 of us there who were shot down in the last year of the war.

Up until this time we were given two meals a day...pumpkin soup in the summer and cabbage soup in the winter. We occasionally had side dishes of some foods that we did not recognize. Now, we were given vegetable soup and not limited to one bowl. We were also given a banana or some type of fruit each day. Often we were given a small can of Russian sardines or some kind of fish that tasted very good. The guards brought in bowls of sugar to put on our bread. In spite of this fattening process, when I returned to the Philippines I had loss over 40 pounds since my shoot down.

A week or so before we were released, each POW was escorted into a room to try on Western clothes for size. I stood with each one of my feet on a piece of paper. A guard drew an outline of each foot on the paper. From that, the Vietnamese made a pair of lace up black shoes for me. The morning that we came home we were escorted to a room, entered one door, took off all our clothes and walked to the other side. A guard gave us the Western style clothes, which included a pair of underwear, shirt, trousers with buttons, not a zipper, a jacket with zipper, belt, and the shoes, which fit very well. We were given a small bag, which contained a washcloth, towel, a bar of their good Vietnamese soap, toothbrush, toothpaste, and a package of their good cigarettes. We were escorted to a bus and without blindfolds rode through Hanoi to the airport. We could see the results of the heavy bombing as we traveled to the airport. When we got to the airport we were escorted to a covered pavilion and given a cookie and some tea. Then we formed and marched around a hanger to the waiting personnel for our release. I remember a smiling Air Force Colonel, and as our names were read, we reported to him and were escorted to the waiting C-141.

When the C-141 broke ground, we yelled and did again when the pilot announced that the plane was out of Vietnam and over international water. We flew to Clark AB, Philippines and were greeted by hundreds or thousands of cheering people. There was a red carpet to the waiting buses and a trip to the hospital. We showered, were given clean pajamas and a bathrobe. The Hospital Commander told us that we would be at Clark about three days, then flown to the States. He said that unless there were any questions, the dining hall was ready. The cook had steaks on the grill and asked me how I wanted mine cooked. I told him any way he wanted.

One of my cellmates was flying a F-4 and shot down about 15 minutes after I was. He was leading a MiG-CAP and said that he was right behind me and that there were no MiGs behind me. So, all during the time that I was a POW, when I was asked what shot me down I said that that our plane had a bearing failure. Not until we came home and our squadron had a welcome home party for us did I find out from another pilot in my formation that a pair of MiG-21s flew right over our F-105 formation and another ATOL missile went between the other F-105s after I was hit and turned toward Thailand.

On my first tour in Korat, my wife and two children went to her hometown to live. When I returned, she said that if I had to go back to Korat, she would not live in her hometown again. We were living in base housing at McConnell when the squadron deployed to Korat. After I was shot down, I knew that my family would have to move out of base housing, but I did not know where they would live. I was allowed only one letter while I was in prison. At Christmas the guards allowed me to read but not keep a letter from my wife. When I finished reading the letter, my roommates asked me where my family had moved. I smiled and said, "To my wife's hometown."

William H. Talley, WW # 554

Stories by Paul L Chesley WW # 154

SOAP, Pink Towels, Toothpicks and Salt Tablets

SOAP

In 1967 the Spectrographic Oil Analysis Program was a new program that did not have much credibility because it was relatively unknown. The Air Force maintenance types knew of it and slowly expanded its use without fanfare.

Aircrews knew of it, but only as one of many obscure tests that were used to monitor jet engine health, but with little or no thought of it being a critical test.

Because Wild Weasels had to be the first to arrive in the target area, they started first, met the tankers first, and then proceeded to the target so as to arrive about three minutes ahead of the strike force. Timing for each step of aircraft launch was timed to the second and very little leeway was allowed. By the clock the aircrews ate, briefed, started up, arrived at their designated aircraft, performed the preflight inspection, started engines, and taxied to the run-up/arming area in the proper order. The Wild Weasel flight leader lined up first followed by numbers 2, 3, and 4. Then they were given a final preflight check by ground crews who removed a bundle of "remove before flight" safety and arming pins. The aircraft then waited with engines running until takeoff time, about ten minutes after the final pins were pulled.

While the pins were being removed, the aircrews put their elbows on the canopy sills with their hands up in the air so that the ground crew could be sure that no switches would be moved during this arming sequence. When all the pins were removed the Crew Chief stepped back, displayed the pins to the pilot, and gave a snappy salute indicating that all is ready and we were armed for combat or "cocked."

Because we would sit for a few minutes with engine in idle until takeoff time, the aircraft were parked with their noses pointed parallel to the runway, just one more safety measure, and nothing was allowed to be in front of the aircraft, and so we sat in the predawn darkness in an airplane that was wall-to-wall fuel, bombs and rockets, watching the clock tick down the last 4 minutes before takeoff time.

Then the impossible happened. A "bread truck," one of those square, light trucks that delivers people and parts on the flight line drove in front of three armed F-105F's, turned directly toward us, the lead aircraft of the whole formation, blinked his headlight to make sure we saw him and then parked about 30 feet in front with his headlights illuminating our plane. A sergeant hopped out, stood silhouetted in the headlights and signaled for us to cut the engine. We were stunned. Cap. Arnold "Arnie" Dolejsi, my pilot, changed radio frequency to the Command Post and told them about this idiot out front and asked what should be our response. The calm voice called back and said to shut down our aircraft, put the pins in our ejection seats, get down out of the aircraft and get in the bread truck and return to the Command Post. Our airplane had failed its SOAP test and we were cancelled. Arnie advised that all engine instruments indicated normal. Command Post advised No. 3 was now No. 1 and spare Wild Weasel would be No. 3. Arnie shut down the Thud; we got out and watched the ground crew insert the safety pins. The strike flight taxied around the inert Wild Weasel and took off on time.

At the Command Post we were advised that our engine had elevated levels of iron in its SOAP test, and that triggered the mandatory removal of the engine for further testing. The engine would be removed, put in an engine test cell and run up in a test to get accurate readings before being shipped back to the States for overhaul.

During the test cell run-up, the engine appeared normal until afterburner was selected. After 15 seconds in afterburner the engine blew up. A few days later we were invited to the Command Post to review what would have happened if we had not complied. After the start of a takeoff roll, we would have rolled about 2,000 feet in afterburner at about the time the engine would have blown up, disintegrating the F-105F from the wings aft. A huge fireball containing thousands of pounds of high explosives and fuel would have continued down the runway scattering parts of the airplane that would have closed the runway for all further flights for many hours. Our probability of survival was estimated as nil.

After this close call, the first question asked by all the pilots to the Crew Chief was, "has the engine passed its SOAP test?" Aircrews are fast learners.

PINK TOWELS

GI's travel a lot. It seems like with all the schools, TDY's and PCS's, portable toiletries are an art form. When in doubt, we carry a washcloth and a hand towel, which doubles as a bath towel in emergencies. When a PCS happens, we don't drag bath towels but buy them at the next duty station.

Upon arrival at Takhli, after a two-week stopover in the Philippines for snake school (jungle survival), our towels were ready for replacement. No problem, just go to the Base Exchange and buy new ones. The BX was an updated building that was built by the Japanese in WW II and was across the street from the Officers Club. The BX interior was bare bones, just things sitting on pallets, a lot like the "Big Box" stores of today. Considering that we were at the end of a long supply line, it worked real well, usually. However, it did have a chronic problem when demand exceeded supply. The capitalist system just didn't work in the boondocks. High demand didn't result in greater supply, just greater shortage. The normal ubiquitous towel is white, monotonous but normal. Odd-colored towels are shunned and some colors are considered hideous. Takhli had no white towels for sale but two pallets of bright, feminine pink towels. Utility was not even considered, neither the Thai nor the GI could envision themselves wrapped in pink. Further, the price of the pink towels was not reduced as an incentive to buy. Even worse, a constant pilfer rate reduced the available white towels available to the GI's. Frustration for new arrivals with minimum body-drying equipment was just another thing to be faced. This was a very minor problem in December 1966.

Fighter pilots have never been accused of being humble. In contrast, navigators have never been accused of being proud. Does anyone use the title of "the world's greatest navigator?" It doesn't have a good ring to it like "the world's greatest fighter pilot." Can you imagine the world's greatest fighter pilot toweling himself with a pink towel? Unimaginable. However, Wild Weasel "Bears" don't have to live up to being the world's greatest anything. They are navigators that have additional training to be electronic warfare officers, considered a further status downgrade. We have to include the word "officer" in our title to avoid confusion as to our place in the military hierarchy. Fighter pilots are not called officers—everyone knows they are officers. All things being considered, Cool Bear bought a complete set of pink towels and washcloths. No one "borrowed" them during his tour of duty. He took them home after the tour and used them for years afterward.

The BX buyers may have been confused on colors, but they knew quality.

TOOTHPICKS

Good business practices dictate that contracts are put out to bid and the lowest price bid for a specific product wins. Most products have long lists describing in great detail what the product is, what it does, and what kind of manufacturers support will be provided. Contract officers are punished if they do not follow this rule in all cases. Consider the lowly toothpick. Two types are available, both made of wood. One type is round with pointed ends. The other is flat with one end rounded; the other tapered but not sharpened. The flat toothpicks are cheaper and always win the competition. Among the flat toothpicks the competition for cheapness introduces another variable, the quality of the wood. The unintended consequences of a good business rule skew the choice toward the poorest wood. The result is that dental hygiene is the victim of toothpicks that break easily, splinter without effort and are not a full step above useless. To overcome the high probability of a toothpick's failure to perform, each person would take at least three toothpicks to ensure that the job could be done; the result was institutionalized frustration!

While contracting officers are prohibited from thinking outside the box, aircrews are not. The solution was elementary. Cool Bear saved the day; he requested that his wife send several boxes of high quality, round toothpicks. She did, and they were placed next to the salt tablets near the exit. How satisfying—one meal, one toothpick.

SALT TABLETS

Thailand is a beautiful country, lots of green, lots of jungle, lots of rice paddies, lots of water and lots of heat. We all would glow, perspire or sweat depending on one's dignity. This was a constant environmental curse to all unless they were in an air-conditioned building or airborne in an air-conditioned cockpit. Flying provided sweet relief even if the job was to shoot and be shot at.

The absolute worst sweating event was to be the "spare" during the afternoon mission. The spare filled in if and when anyone aborted on the ground before takeoff or airborne until refueling was complete. We were required to taxi out last and park just short of the runway, fully armed, and ready to go. The normal duration was about 40 minutes based on the time to take off, climb out, get refueled and catch up to your element. For the tough targets, flak suppression and Wild Weasel are "must fill" positions. Because Wild Weasel crews were so few, they were called on all too often. After pulling the "cocked" Thud into the next takeoff position, the engine was left running, the canopy left open, the radio was on the command pilot frequency and your hands remained elevated. The sun would beat down on your head, dripping off your nose and chin into the oxygen mask. Sweat would run down your back soaking everything down to your buttocks. The underarm perspiration circle would enlarge downward to below belt level. The back of the thighs would be soaked through. You just sat, cooked, watched the clock and waited to be launched or be released by the Command Post.

When you were launched, you poured the sweat from your oxygen mask, made it secure, put on your gloves, lowered and locked the canopy, taxied out and took off. During climb out, leaning forward in the seat would let cool dry air down your back and start the drying process. By alternately lifting each limb and squirming, most of the sweat was evaporated by the time you caught up with the formation. Then off to war in relative comfort.

If you are released, you put the safety pins in the seat, signaled the ground crew to safety all the weapons and landing gears, then taxied back to your parking position, slowly prying your wet carcass out of the seat, climb down the ladder, take off the parachute, get in the bread truck and return to the squadron parachute shop. Your oxygen mask would be thoroughly cleaned and dried, your survival vest hung up, the .38 cal. pistol oiled and secured, the G-suit hung up to dry, and your wallet returned. Then you walk back to your hooch where a clean dry flight suit, underwear, and socks waited for you. Then a long cool shower revived you. A short walk to the Officers Club for a bite to eat, with a tall cool glass of iced tea, then a practice nap before the next event.

Salt pills were a mandatory addition to your diet and were found in a dish near the exit of the dining hall part of the Officers Club. Two to three pills a day were recommended. You could gauge your lack of salt by the tone of your thigh muscles. If they ached after significant exercise, then you needed more salt. If your flight suit was over 40 percent white from salt stains, then you were overdosed. Quite simple, really.

WINGMAN PAR EXCELLENCE

Fighter tactics evolved from experience during WWI, barely a dozen years after Kitty Hawk. After WWI, many different tacticians worked to improve them. In WWII these improved tactics were tried in the crucible of combat where the winner survived and the losers died. The heart of fighter tactics is the element of two aircraft. One is the leader and the other his wingman. This duo is the absolute minimum quantity that allows fighters to be aggressive and still have a reasonable probability of survival. Lead is the sword; the wingman is the shield. The skills required to do each job are different, but the skill levels must be equally high for a team to perform the mission.

The Wild Weasel mission used the most experienced pilots and electronic warfare officers in the USAF. They were always the sword because their purpose was to be the most lethal counter to the enemy surface-to-air missile (SAM) threat. Their unique capabilities derived from two highly experienced aircrew members and the special electronic equipment onboard the F-105F. This mix was not for defensive purposes, but to be the most lethal weapons system that could be devised. When two F-105Fs were used as an element, the wingman was in training to be lead or he was simply there to be an airborne spare in case lead was disabled. The Wild Weasel mission was not the stock standard fighter mission of countering enemy aircraft to achieve air superiority nor of bombing tactical or strategic targets. The Wild Weasel was designed to kill SAM's. The average F-105D (single seat) fighter pilot was not trained to be a Wild Weasel.

The Wild Weasel mission did not exist until the SAM's were introduced in North Vietnam in 1965. Therefore, tactical experience dating back to WWI was of very little use. New tactics had to be developed during daily combat operations. Deliberately dueling with a 30-foot missile that could fly three times faster than you was considered suicidal, and the survival statistics supported this conclusion. Korat had its first Wild Weasel crew complete the required 100 missions in the fall of 1966 and Takhli in February 67. Stock, standard fighter pilots did not line up in droves to volunteer to be a Wild Weasel wingman; they were pragmatists. However, the Wild Weasels were almost always short of aircrews and aircraft, hence, F105D single seat fighters were used As Wild Weasel Wingmen. Over time, a small cadre of select F-105D pilots came into being that would volunteer for the Wild Weasel mission. Nobody asked why.

The most common way to complete a combat tour was to fly 100 missions over North Vietnam. An exception to this requirement was for Wing staff officers who had to be in theater for one year. An early accumulation of missions would not get them an early return, yet they had to fly for time. Several pilots in the command post, all majors, flew regular combat missions with the goal of getting their 100 mission patches before the year was up. However, one Major joined the select cadre to be a Wild Weasel wingman. Initially the Wild Weasel pilots and EWOs were not enthused. Most headquarters pilots were promoted out of the cockpit to desk duty and inexorably lost their superb flying shills that got them promoted. Most Wild Weasel crews preferred Captains as wingmen. However, this pilot proved to be the ideal wingman. He was always tactically correct in his flying duties. He anticipated our aggressive maneuvers and always placed himself in the right position. When he spoke he had something to say, otherwise no chatter.

Most people resent being hollered at. However, when your wingman hollered out, "Lead there is a SAM at your six – take it down, Down, DOWN – Pull up, PULL UP", these imperative words were welcomed. When during the high G pull-up, a loud thump from the SAM's exploding warhead was heard and the F-105F escaped damage; a very strong trust was formed with our wingman.

We flew with this major about six times. We didn't know his background, but he was clearly a "good stick". Major Chesley saw him later as a colonel in the halls of the pentagon in the early 1970s. Alonzo L. Ferguson, "Lonnie," was awarded a Silver Star something before retiring in 1982 as a Brigadier General. He was one of those guys that we were privileged to fly combat missions with, and we remember his as one of he best!

Paul L Chesley WW # 154

Story by Joe Telford, WW # 256

More Memories of Interesting Events During My Association with the Testing and training of Wild Weasels

Jim Odom and Joe Telford In F-105F Wild Weasel Korat 1966.
Courtesy of Joe Telford

WILD WEASEL III (F-105F) OT&E AND TRAINING

The Wild Weasel-III OT&E and Training was conducted from about January thru May of 1966. For this OT&E the TAWC TPO was changed from Maj. Odom to a Capt. Robert Lavo, and I continued as APGC's TPO. In the area of writing the necessary documentation for the conduct of this OT&E by TAWC and APGC, the responsibilities and relationships for the different documents remained the same as they were for Wild Weasel-I. Also, for this OT&E there was more time in which to write the necessary test documentation. While there was certainly a sense of urgency associated with the conduct of Wild Weasel-III OT&E and training of the first crews, there was not the panic element that was experienced in Wild Weasel-I.

One thing that made a big difference between Wild Weasel-I and Wild Weasel-III OT&Es and training was, these two objectives (testing and training) were conducted in a more independent situation of each other during Wild Weasel-III. In addition to the Weasel F-105F aircraft the first crews trained with and deployed with to the 388th TFW at Korat RTAB, TAC supplied a dedicated test F-105F for the conduct of the OT&E. Having a dedicated OT&E aircraft allowed testing not to unduly interfere in the training schedule of the crews, and vice versa. As both OT&E and training progressed there was a constant cross feed of information between each other.

Also, the learning curve for everyone involved on base with the conduct and support of a Wild Weasel OT&E and training also made a significant positive difference. More along this line, during the conduct of all the different Wild Weasel OT&Es, and radar warning equipment tests on other types of TAC aircraft, such as the RF-101, I experienced an outstanding attitude and effort by everyone on Eglin. Especially was this true during Wild Weasel-I when everyday of the week was a workday, and they were all long workdays. On several occasions I called civil service personnel or other types of government employees at home, on a week end, or after normal work day hours, and asked them to come out to the base and perform some kind of task that needed to be accomplished right then for Wild Weasel support. I cannot remember a time anyone talked or acted in a non-cooperative manner. It was truly amazing.

There was also a dedicated Wild Weasel-III OT&E TAC pilot who was here TDY, a Maj. James P. Randall. Before Randall's arrival at Eglin he had recently been shot down while flying an F-105D and successfully rescued in the far north of North Vietnam. In fact, at the time of his rescue it was the most northern successful rescue conducted. And, Capt. Art Oken, in TAWC, was pretty much my dedicated EWO for this OT&E. Oken later completed 100 Weasel missions at Korat in the back seat of an F-105F. Having the same dedicated crew for the OT&E also made for a much smoother and efficient operation.

An interesting note for the Wild Weasel-III OT&E concerns Maj. Pete Tsouprake, who was Maj. William "Robby" P. Robinson's EWO. Pete was probably at least 6' 3" tall and much of his height was due to a long waist, which meant he sat tall in the F-105F seat. If my memory is correct, the flight surgeon told Pete due to his long waist situation it could be the cause of several different types of problems for him in the cockpit and he did not have to take this Wild Weasel-III assignment if he did not want it. Pete's answer was, he would take the Weasel assignment.

TESTING OF THE APR-26

The APR-26, a SAM missile launch warning device, a relative new piece of ATI equipment at this time, was not really tested much during the Wild Weasel-I OT&E due to the unavailability of a proper threat radar at Eglin to exercise it. When the Weasel F-100Fs deployed to Korat, TAWC had a serious problem in learning what was happening with the effort in Southeast Asia. One of the pieces of information that "dribbled back" was that the APR-26 did not seem to be working correctly, but that was about all that was known. One of the many problems with this new and unique Weasel effort was the lack of anyone attached to the Weasels, or the 388th TFW at Korat, who was suppose to, or could, spend the time to keep TAWC informed of what was happening and what were the successes and problems in the Weasel operations. This was probably one of the prime impetuses for the implementation of TAWC's Anti-Sam Combat Assistance Team (ASCAT) program.

It was not until April of 1966, toward the end of the Wild Weasel-III (F-105F) OT&E that I was able to completely, after a fashion, "exercise" the APR-26, and indeed, observed the APR-26 did have some problems.

During the first week of April Mr. Howard L. Dimmig, the Technical Advisor for the Deputy for Effectiveness Test, called me into his office and informed me he had located a Fan Song SA-2 threat surrogate radar that would "exercise" the APR-26, and he had received permission for me to go to where it was located and conduct tests. This threat radar was a "home made" radar constructed under a Navy contract and was located at the Sanders Associates plant in Nashua, New Hampshire, or maybe more accurately, at their Merrimack Test facility. I think its name was the "Flintstone." I was told it had been built by one of the Sanders engineers in a "sunk works" environment and the engineer thought of the radar as his baby, a living and breathing thing. I believe it attempted to duplicate the complete Fan Song SA-2 radar, but for sure, it attempted to duplicate the

Russian radar that transmitted guidance and command signals to the SA-2 Guideline missile while in flight, and the APR-26 keyed, so to speak, on these signals, and other characteristics. It was also determined at this time in some aspects this replica of the threat system was not always accurate, which caused some testing problems.

I was told by some of the Sander's personnel that the engineer who was responsible for the major design and building of this threat radar left Sander's employment sometime after the radar's construction. However, the engineer remained so interested and concerned about his "baby" that he would call almost everyday to find out how it was functioning. After some time had passed someone suggested to him that he really should come back and work for Sanders again, which I guess he did.

So, from the 6th to the 14th of April 1966 I was TDY to the Sanders Associate plant, conducing a test of the APR-26. In order to conduct this test I had to base and fly the Wild Weasel-III F-105F OT&E aircraft out of Pease AFB, New Hampshire, approximately 80 miles from the Sanders plant in Nashua.

Sanders was on contract with the Navy for a number of electronic warfare equipments and systems and the Navy was pretty much in control of the situation at this location. I had to check in with the senior Navy officer, a commander, and he let me know about this situation, and instructed me not to do anything to upset their relationship with Sanders Associates. It was also obvious by his conversation he did not at this time hold the AF Wild Weasel program in high regard. I thought about this Navy commander about ten months later when Maj. Odom and myself were on our first TDY tour to the 388th TFW at Korat as the members of TAWC's first ASCAT Team. The then, Captain Julian Lake, USN (later Adm. Lake and known as the Navy's Mr. Electronic Warfare) came ashore from, I think, the USS Roosevelt and visited the wing and the Weasels. He made statements to the effect that he wondered how the Air Force had jumped out ahead of the Navy in the ability to counter the SAM, seeing how the Navy had a head start on the Air Force in programs to counter the SAMs? My guess is that Adm. Lake had in mind the numerous jammers, such as the ALQ-41 and ALQ-51, already under contract and in production for the Navy by Sanders Associates.

At the Sanders plant, near the threat radar and the bubble that covered it, was a control van complex with radar control scopes and consoles, and an x-band radar used to track the target aircraft. A Navy Lt. Commander controller was in charge of this complex. Right from the start, the first day I visited, the Navy controller informed me who ever was using the facility, and was not Navy, and had an aircraft flying – they controlled their own aircraft – not him.

I was there by myself and I was not a controller. I had never even tried to control an aircraft. However, having had a tour at a USAF Air Defense Command early warning and control radar site as its Electronic Counter-Countermeasures Officer, and its Radar Operations Officer, I was not totally unaware of what was required – I had just never performed the controlling task myself, nor attended the controller's school. There was a range area near the Sanders plant where test aircraft flew that were associated with Sanders testing, but I did not believe it was as dedicated as the ranges were at Eglin, which was my main, and safety, concern.

Due to communications security reasons, in order to fly a mission I would have to drive from Nashua to Pease AFB, brief my test crew, drive back to Nashua to conduct the mission, drive back to Pease AFB to debrief the crew and hopefully also brief them for the next mission, or else make another round trip. The camouflaged Wild Weasel F-105F was certainly a sight on the SAC Pease AFB with all of its B-47 bombers, and the F-105F attracted more than it share of attention.

The first test mission was flown fairly early in the morning. After Maj. Randall and Oken were air born and approaching the test range, Randall came up on the Navy's control frequency and checked in. I responded by saying something like, "This is Capt. Telford, and I will be your controller for this mission." Randall replied by saying, "Acknowledged, and I think I am in trouble!" However, in a way Randall was better off with me controlling the mission than most other people. The reason was, I knew about his shoulder being injured when he was shot down and ejecting over North Vietnam. Randall was keeping this injury close hold and had not told the AF, or for that matter, few people at all for fear he would be grounded. When he was flying and had to make a turn into the injured shoulder it would hurt severely. I have forgotten now which shoulder was hurt, but for a turn into the injured shoulder's direction he always desired more time and air space than normal, if possible.

Oken and I had a set of code words worked out which he could call out when I asked him what he was seeing on the APR-26, and in turn, I had code words by which I could tell him what the threat radar was doing. Right from the start of testing we both realized there were major problems. Before the crew had landed at Pease AFB, while I was still in the control van, I was on the phone to APGC and then to Capt. Robert Lavo, my TAWC TPO counterpart for the Wild Weasel-III OT&E.

After I hung up the TAWC people were immediately on the phone to ATI. John Arnold, the APR-26 hardware circuit and box designer, must have caught a plane for Boston immediately after the TAWC phone call was completed because early the next morning, when we flew the next test mission, he was sitting in the control van right by my side. As Oken transmitted the APR-26's response codes as the threat radar was cycled through its functions, John Arnold literally pulled out a used envelop from his coat pocket and commenced drawing draft circuit changes on the back of it. During my career I had always heard the phase, "it was designed on the back of an envelop" when someone wanted to indicate the design was quick. Well, I saw the fix for the APR-26 start off like that, but I am sure there were many more hours put in on this redesign after John Arnold returned to ATI.

Bill Doyle, who was the ATI systems engineer who came up with the idea for the APR-26 may have accompanied John Arnold on this trip to Sanders. However, I only remember one ATI person, but I could be wrong.

I don't remember that I ever heard just how much time it took for the redesign package to get to the field, but I am sure it was not long at the rate everything else was happening.

I want to relate one humorous incident of interest concerning the Sanders threat radar and the pressurized bubble it was housed in. During the testing at Sanders, on this one occasion, I was standing outside between the threat radar and the control van. I was talking to the engineer who had built the threat radar and thought of it as his "baby." We were at least 40 yards from his "baby" when someone yelled for him to look at the bubble. The bubble was losing pressure, very rapidly, and was starting to collapse from the top down. The engineer was not tall and had short legs. When he looked up and saw his "baby" getting into serious trouble he made those short legs fly – and his speed saved the day.

BACK TO SANDERS AS JUST AS AN OBSERVER FOR TESTS OF OTHER EQUIPMENTTS

On 17 April 1966 Mr. Howard L. Dimmig again called me into his office. He stated, "Joe, I know this is short notice but I want you to go back to Sanders again, tomorrow, and this time just be in the control van and observe the testing of several other radar warning equipments with the Sanders threat radar. I don't trust the TPOs for these systems. I think some of them may be so involved, and identify so much, with their systems that they are to the point they can no longer be objective about test results. I want you to observe, take notes, and report back to me. I have you a seat on a T-39 tomorrow that will depart Base Operations at 1000 hours and take you as far as Andrews AFB, and from DC you can fly commercial to Boston. Can you be ready?" I told him I would be ready.

My orders read I would be TDY to observe the testing of two APGC projects: 0435Y and 0420Y. Actually, I was TDY from 18 to 29 April 1966 and I observed the testing of more than just two systems. The only system I now have clear memories of was the Bendix APS-107. I believe all these systems were undergoing engineering testing at APGC by the Electronic Systems Test Directorate (PGOY) of the Deputy of Test Operations.

Just as the ATI APR-26 had experienced problems with the Sanders threat radar, so also did all these other equipments. Some problems were due to the threat radar and some were due to the equipment being tested. However, in my opinion, the TPO for the APS-107 equipment seemed to try to minimize or ignore the problems this system was experiencing, and on my return to Eglin I so briefed this opinion to Mr. Demmig.

I have no idea why Demmig, of the Deputy for Effectivness Test, had an interest in the Sanders testing of equipments that were undergoing engineering tests at APGC by the Deputy for Test Operations. It may have been that someway Gen. Dempster or Lt. Col. Levy was behind this involvement, which was what I suspected.

Also, someone with influence must have said something to the Navy Lt. Commander controller at Sanders between the time I tested there, when I had to control my test aircraft, and these tests that I observed later. The

Navy Lt. Commander did control these later Air Force missions. However, I may have unnerved the Lt. Commander so much when I performed the controlling function that he believed it would be in his best interest to just go ahead and control the Air Force missions too.

OT&E OF THE FIRST INSTALLATION OF AN APR-25 ON A TAC RF-101

Soon after I was through with Wild Weasel-III OT&E test, about the June 1966 time frame, two TAC RF-101s arrived with APR-25s installed. This was also a quick and dirty test of how accurate the various threat strobes (C, S, and X) were in 360 degrees around the aircraft, and homing too. To the best of my knowledge these two RF-101 aircraft were the first F-101s to have an APR-25 installed.

Again I piggybacked this testing on the Wild Weasel-I OT&E test documentation, but used a lesser priority. I know there was some type of a report but I can no longer remember it. Most likely it was just a message report. Also, I do not think TAWC was involved in any way, except maybe to coordinate on the message.

Two enlisted ground maintenance personnel accompanied the two RF-101s and the two pilots. Both pilots had already had at least one tour in the Southeast Asian War, and I believe one pilot had several TDY tours. He had not seen his family very much in the last couple of years and he made a vacation out of this TDY. The C band signal source he flew against was located on Oakloosa Island. Whenever the pilot would fly a homing sortie against it, his ground path would take him right over the campground and the tent his family was living in, and his children would be on the beach waving to him.

I asked this pilot how he navigated when flying reconnaissance missions over North Vietnam and he answered, "Entirely by compass heading, speed, and a stop watch, and I sat as low as I could in the cockpit so as not to see what was going on." I guess he was telling me the truth.

By keeping one of these RF-101s on the ground and using it for spare parts we were able to keep the other one in the air and complete the test in the allotted time. Early on in the test, probably the first flight for the aircraft, after it landed the pilot tried to raise the canopy and it blew off, up and away. This was then became our spare parts aircraft.

Shortly after the RF-101s arrived Hill AFB sent me a package of rubber like antenna coverings for the APR-25 antennas. A phone call from the package sender at Hill explained how he had been instructed to send these several different types of coverings to me to be installed on the RF-101s and to be tested when flying in the rain. I guess the Weasel-I birds, and now the newly arrived Weasel-III birds, were having problems with the heavy rains in Southeast Asia peeling off the APR-25 antenna coverings. So, in addition to flying against radars, I now tried to find rainstorms to fly in.

Toward the very end of the test, I think late June, it looked like a Gulf of Mexico tropical storm heading in our general direction was going to turn into a minimum hurricane shortly before it reached Eglin. This was the first hurricane of the season. The APGC colonel who was the chief of maintenance was getting an early start in having all the flyable aircraft to depart the base for safe locations. As such, a maintenance major called me and stated something like, "Well, it is obvious your RF-101 with the broken canopy will have to stay at Eglin in a hanger, but fly the other one out of here as soon as possible." I replied something like, "I only need one more mission to complete my test, and besides, I have been requested to fly this aircraft in rain to test some antenna coverings. I think I can fly the mission and then launch the bird for a safe base before the weather conditions become too bad to depart." Well, he did not like my answer but he did not have the time to argue with me, and he hung up.

The RF-101 launched and flew the mission. While all the other flyable aircraft were taking off for a safer place, my bird was flying a mission. It turned out the RF-101 did not encounter any bad weather, or rain, until it returned and was in the traffic pattern. The hurricane was turning and it by passed the Eglin area and went ashore on the southeast side of Panama City.

However, the rain in the traffic pattern was enough. I don't know if the rain was that hard or if the pilot had the airspeed up abnormally, but – the rain acted like a giant file and it just sawed off the front, black, Plexiglas glass like material of the nose of the RF-101, where the cameras would be located had they been carried. When the pilot shut down the engines and the ground crew checked it out, the aircraft was given a "Red X" in its maintenance files – meaning it was no longer flyable until repaired.

The RF-101 was pulled into a hanger to wait out the approaching hurricane, which nobody at this point in time knew it was not going to materialize. Back at my office, probably about 30 minutes after the RF-101 landed, my phone rang. It was the Eglin colonel chief of maintenance himself. He stated, "Well Captain Telford, you won this round (meaning he was now forced to put the bird in a hanger - he still thought I never really intended to fly the bird out to begin with) but you will not win the next round." I did not know if that was a serious threat, or what. Anyway, I never heard from him again.

This was all taking place at the end of the week and this aircraft was suppose to depart Eglin the next Monday. Since the hurricane did not materialize, some shop on Eglin that repaired problems such as the RF-101 had, worked on it all weekend and it was ready to fly when Monday came. Again, Eglin civilians came through in a tight situation.

I think Hill AFB, or ATI, or someone had to go back to the drawing boards and try again to come up APR-25 antennas that would withstand heavy rain.

WORLD WIDE RHAW/WILD WEASEL TASK GROUP MEETING AT ROBINS AFB

From 5 to 8 July 1966 I was TDY to attend this meeting. From the start of the Wild Weasel program the special Weasel electronic equipment (ATI's APR-25/26 and IR-133) were supported by the AMA at Robins AFB. Once again this was a situation were people were not concerned about working only a 40 hour workweek. These people worked overtime and on weekends, what ever it took to get the mission accomplished. I was involved with numerous people from the Robins AMA that provided the Weasel effort outstanding support, but I especially remember a Mr. Joe Black.

There were many people attending this meeting at Robins and the Sacramento AMA had a significant number of its people attending. I now can no longer remember how much of a support responsibility the Sacramento AMA had, or was picking up in addition, but it must have at least included the modifications on the F-105s for the Weasel equipment. What does stand out in my memory was the reaction of the Sacramento AMA people when the Robins AMA people recounted time, and time again, how they had flat out ignored regulations, partly or totally, in order to provide the necessary Weasel equipment support in a timely manner.

The Sacramento people openly expressed shock and disbelief. However, as the meeting progressed you could see the Sacramento people understanding and grasping the seriousness of the mission and the situation and their formulation of an attitude of, "If Robins could do it, then we can do it too!"

I believe one thing that helped to "charge up" the Sacramento people at the meeting was news of what had happened on 5 July 1966, the day before the meeting started. Word was received about the Wild Weasel mission, Eagle Flight, lead by Maj. Robinson and Maj. Pete Tsouprake where their flight of one F-105F and three, or four, F-105Ds had attacked four SAM sites and had numerous SAM missiles launched at them, with nobody getting hit. I later remember hearing the cockpit tape of this mission and as they were returning to Korat RTAB Pete was summarizing all the SAM sites attacked and the number of missiles launched at them and he ended it with the understatement of, "Its been a busy day!" For this mission both Robinson and Tsouprake were awarded the Air Force Cross.

THE FIRST TAWC ANTI-SAM COMBAT ASSISTANCE TEAM (ASCAT) AT THE 388TH TFW, KORAT RTAB

Colonel Ross L. Blachly was the TAWC Deputy Chief of Staff for Anti-SAM, and as such, he led TAWC's initial charge to counter the SA-2 by developing and deploying the Wild Weasels and providing tactical electronic countermeasures capabilities. In early September of 1966, Colonel Blachly was reassigned from TAWC to be the commander of the APGC Deputy of Test (PGO). As such, his new office in building 1 at Eglin was up front in the command section, and mine was down the hall. During the preceding year I had worked closely with Colonel Blachly and his TAWC staff on Wild Weasel-I, IA, III, and IVC OT&E programs. Actually during this period of time he had come to think of me as a TAWC asset, rather than an APGC asset, and now he was about to prove it. Shortly after he was assigned to APGC he saw me in the hall outside his office. He stopped me and stated, "Joe, I am loaning you to TAWC for a 120 day temporary duty (TDY) to Thailand. You and Jim Odom are going to the 8th TFW at Ubon RTAB to conduct a combat evaluation of the first Wild Weasel-IVC (F-4C), which will be flying out of Ubon.

Odom departed Eglin before me but when I arrived at Ubon on 16 October 1966, not only was Odom not there, neither were the Weasel F-4C aircraft and crews. The problems identified in the previous section had delayed the arrival of the crews, and the aircraft till an even much later date. However, in one sense, I was greatly relieved to have arrived at Ubon even if Odom and the Weasel F-4C crews were not there. I had hand carried a brief case full of secret documents, Test Plan for the Combat Evaluation of Wild Weasel-IV (F-4C), all the way from Eglin AFB. Even when I went to the bathroom or slept, this brief case was my constant companion, never out of my sight and possession. I signed those plans over to the 8th TFW Operations Office and that was the last I ever saw or knew about them.

After cooling my heels at the 8th TFW for three days I received a call form Odom who was at the 388th TFW at Korat TRAB. He stated TAWC had changed our mission with the demise of the Wild Weasel-IV (F-4C) combat evaluation effort and we were to be a pilot/electronic warfare officer (EWO) team at the 388th TFW, assisting the wing in matters of electronic warfare. Actually, we were the prototype of numerous future pilot/EWO teams that TAWC trained and deployed on a one-year duty status to every wing in Southeast Asia flying fighter and fighter type reconnaissance aircraft over the high threat areas of North Vietnam. The name of this TAWC effort was the Anti-SAM Combat Assistance Team (ASCAT), I believed established by TAC Operations Plan 105. TAWC assigned Lt. Col. Milton "Jim" E. Allen, Jr. the responsibility of starting up the ASCAT effort. TAWC would train the members and send them to Southeast Asia where 7th Air Force and the local wings would then have operational control of the teams. The time frame for the ASCAT effort, starting with Odom and myself, was from late 1966 to 1970 when they were phased out due to the start of the bombing pause of North Vietnam in late 1968.

After Odom's phone call to me at Ubon I caught a flight the next day to Korat, on 20 October. However, by the time I arrive Odom was off again to someplace. I did not yet understand just exactly what it was we were going to do, except to work with the crews. The first Wild Weasel F-105F crews, who trained at Eglin and who I had worked with during their OT&E and training, were now more than half way through with having flown their 100 combat missions. By this time they had also lost two crews, the only ones to be lost; the commander Maj. Robert "Bob" Brinckmann and his EWO Capt. Scungio, and pilot Maj. Roosevelt Hestle and his EWO Capt. Charles Elsy Morgan. Maj. William "Robby" P. Robinson was now the Weasel's commander, and his EWO was Maj. Pete Tsouprake.

So, the first couple of nights while Odom was off someplace, I slept in EWO Capt. Robert E. Tondreau's bed, who roomed with his pilot, Capt. Marion "Mac" M. Angel. After this I was bunked in the bed for two or three nights of one the F-105D pilots who had been shot down earlier that day. It was not a pleasant experience to lie in a man's bed and look at the pictures on his dresser of his wife and children who were maybe never going to see him again. I cannot describe what a lasting impression this made on me. In the days to come, when rest was short and work was long and frustrating, this experience would spur me on to do anything I could to help these crews to survive and come back from a mission. To this day, I can shut my eyes and still see that room and its contents. I continued to spend other nights in other rooms, under the same condition, like this last one until finally on 10 November Odom and I were assigned to a room of our own for the remainder of my TDY.

Odom and I were assigned an office in the 13th TFS building, which housed both strike pilots and all the Wild Weasel crews, and at this time was commanded by Lt. Col. Gerald F. Fitzgerald. Our office was far down the hall form the front door and all the normal operations activities. Someone did not just stumble onto us by accident; you had to want to see us to find us. Later, this turned out to be a blessing at times. Also at this time there were three other squadrons in the wing comprised of all F-105D strike pilots: the 34th, 421st, and the 469th.

So, our first task was to find out just how this war was conducted. We attended all the briefings for the new crews, and any other meetings or briefing we thought would educate us. In addition we attended all the different types of mission briefings and debriefings. Almost immediately we were asked by wing operations personnel to assist in briefing new F-105D strike pilots on the operation of the APS-25/26 equipment.

MISSION DEFINITION

There were normally two large missions each day, one flown early in the morning and the other flown early in the afternoon. Usually each of these missions would consist of four flights of strike F-105Ds, four aircraft to a flight, for a total of 16 strike aircraft. Normally the mission commander would be in the lead flight and the one to identify the target and "roll in" on it. Usually this lead flight of four aircraft would be carrying cluster bomb units (CBUs) to suppress the anti-aircraft guns normally located around a good target. The remaining three flights, 12 aircraft, would normally each carry 12 750-pound "dumb" general purpose bombs. In addition to these aircraft there would usually be two Wild Weasel flights. Most of the time a Weasel flight consisted of two Weasel aircraft, with each one having an F-105D strike aircraft as its wingman. And, in addition to these two main missions for the day there were always smaller special missions being flown, often during both day and night.

The normal method to deliver bombs on a target was for the mission commander in the lead flight to locate and identify the target at altitude, say 15,000 feet. Then one flight right after the preceding flight would roll in (dive) on the target, with aircraft in trail within each flight while in the dive, and each aircraft releasing their bombs when near the bottom of the dive. This was very similar to the way the same type of "dumb bombs" had been delivered during World War II.

The two Wild Weasel flights would normally be out ahead of the main strike force during its ingress route to the target. The Weasels would be searching for active SAM sites while maybe roaming from side to side of the ingress route to the target, launching Shrike AGM-45 radar homing missiles at active SA-2 radars. The Shrikes would usually make the SA-2 shut down for at least a short time, even if the Shrike missiles did not hit the SAM site. Or, the Weasels would roll in on the more aggressive SAM sites and attempt to kill them with CBUs, bombs, rockets, or guns.

After bombs had been dropped on the target, and the strike F-105Ds were attempting to form up again by flights and exit the area by the planned egress route, the Weasels would try to provide the same type of SAM protection for the strike force in reverse. The Weasel's mission required them to be the first aircraft of the mission into the target area and the last aircraft to exit it. Hence, the Weasel slogan or saying of, "First in and last out." This was a simple, short way, of saying the Weasel mission was the most dangerous.

Always complicating a mission's ingress and egress, and the Weasel mission, was the threat of a MiG attack. Normally MiG attacks occurred by just one or two MiGs. They usually attacked the mission force from behind, or from the side and somewhat to the rear, at a fast speed coming from a lower altitude and climbing to a higher altitude while launching one or two Atoll heat seeking air-to-air missiles per aircraft. They would continue their escape at a high speed in case any US aircraft should try to give chase. And, there was always the possibility that a MiG would attempt the same type of hit-and-run missile attack on a Weasel flight while it was searching for or trying to maneuver into position to attack a SAM site. There were some instances when the North Vietnamese SAM operators, with their Russian instructors, became confused and targeted and shot down one of their own MiG aircraft.

MISSIOIN PREPRIATION AND BRIEFINGS

Using the an early morning mission as an example, it was suppose to start with Headquarters 7th Air Force Operations at Tan Son Nhut AB, Saigon, South Vietnam, sending the wing, by secure teletype, the fragmentation order (frag order) by early evening the preceding day of the mission. This order would specify, among other things, the target or targets, the ingress and egress routes, and altitudes. By arriving early evening the day before the mission this allowed the mission commander, his flight commanders, and his lead Weasel crews time to formulate detail plans and tactics and draw their mission maps, with the location of known active SAM sites, that evening. They would then have enough time to have adequate sleep before being up very early in the morning and in the mission planning room with all the mission crews and instructing them on how to plan and draw up their mission maps.

The individual flights would have a brief meeting and then they all would attend the big overall mission briefing in the wing's large briefing room, which included a stage and all manor of visual briefing aids. Here, different wing support personnel would brief the crews on the targets, defenses around the target and those along the ingress and egress routes, other intelligence information, weather, tanker tracks and locations, MiG combat air parole (CAP) fighter support, search and rescue procedures, communications, and etc.

Then the crews would suit up in all their flying equipment and get a ride out to their assigned aircraft by small flight line vans. By the time everyone had gone through their checklists, started engines and run through more check lists, taxied out to the arming area, and had taken off by flights, the first signs of day light would be observed.

However, this was not the usual way a morning mission would start out. What normally happened was that the frag order did not arrive at the wing until very late at night or early in the morning the day of the mission. This meant the key people in the mission were up late, waiting around for the frag's arrival and then doing their overall planning and map making. This delay often forced these key men to receive only a few hours of sleep before a combat mission.

What was happening, President Johnston and his administration were micro managing the Southeast Asian War. They required their review and approval on target selections in North Vietnam before they were sent to 7th Air Force, and then on down to the operational wings for execution. The White House approval process was most often delayed – this was dereliction of duty and inexcusable!

Odom or I, or both of us, attended all of the big over all mission briefings and at times the mission planning activities.

MISSION DEBRIEFINGS

When a mission returned there were three different types of debriefings the pilots participated in. The debriefings were, in the order they occurred: the maintenance debrief (but not necessarily by all four pilots in the same flight at the same time); the intelligence debrief of each particular flight with all the pilots in that flight present; and the big overall mission debrief with all the pilots in attendance and conducted by the pilot that had been the mission force commander. The purpose of the big overall mission debriefing was to go back over the mission to find lessons learned; what to repeat and what to avoid in the future.

We sat in on all four of the separate strike flight debriefings by intelligence, and also the separate debriefing of the two Wild Weasel flights. We were listening for anything that would be of interest from an electronic warfare point. A short time later we were especially interested in the details of each SAM encounter, and anything that might indicate that the North Vietnam SA-2 operators, with the help of their Russian advisors, had added something new to their method of operations that would affect the radar warning equipment, and the QRC-160A-1 jamming pods. These pods which would soon be carried starting about late November 1966. Then we attended the big overall mission debriefing.

Attending these, and later, briefings was a 1/Lt. Karl W. Richter who became famous because of his skill and zeal in pursuing the air war over North Vietnam. His feats included, at the time of its occurrence, being the youngest pilot to shoot down a MiG. It was a MiG-17. Also, he completed 198 known combat missions, possibly the final count was well over 200 missions. Richter was later shot down in Route Package 1 and either died before being picked up or in the HH-3E Jolly Green Giant rescue helicopter that recovered him. Later, the wing's large briefing room was named "Richter Hall" in his honor.

Also attending nearly every mission briefing was Roscoe, the yellowish-sandy colored, shorthaired dog that was the mascot of the 388th TFW F-105 pilots. Roscoe had the run of the entire base from the officer's club to wing headquarters. The word was, if Roscoe slept through a mission briefing it was going to be an easy mission. However, if he remained awake and alert during the briefing – watch out! There was a flight surgeon, Capt. Joe Tricky from Dallas, Texas, on base that was the 13th TFS' surgeon, and also doubled as Roscoe's personal physician. The doctor and about 30 other people, most also from Korat, were killed in a C-47 crash on 26 November 1966 while the aircraft was taking off at night from Tan Son Nhut Air Base, South Vietnam.

DAILY ASCAT WING MESSAGE REPORTS

Odom and I repeated this routine morning and afternoon every day for the two normal big missions of the day, plus numerous other smaller special missions occurring all through the day and sometimes the night. At the end of the day we would write and send a message summarizing these mission with emphasis on electronic warfare matters. These messages went to a long list of addressees at a multitude of levels at different commands, including units involved in testing, intelligence, research and development, pod and radar warning equipment logistics support, and of course TAWC and other TAC units.

Also, when we arrived at the 388th there was little to no operational results feed back to the people that maintained the radar warning equipment. Since Odom and I heard all the mission results we started to appraise these maintenance troops of this type of information. It boosted their moral and interest in their work tremendously. A pilot or an EWO would at times make the statement if the equipment could only be modified to do such and such it would be a great improvement in capability and enhance the mission accomplishment. We would then pass these comments on to the maintenance troops and in a few days someone would come up with the modification. It was just amazing what the young maintenance troops could do with that antilog equipment, mainly at this time ATI's APR-25/26, when they were motivated.

QRC-160A-1 JAMMING POD BACKGROUND

General Electric developed and manufactured approximately 160 QRC-160A-1 pods in 1963 by a Quick Reaction Contract (QRC). Some of these pods had actually been introduced into the Southeast Asian combat theater around June 1965. They ahd been flown on RF-101 Voodoo aircraft based at Tan Son Nhut Air Base, South Vietnam, flying reconnaissance missions over North Vietnam. At that time neither Headquarters Pacific Air Force (PACAF), nor any unit in PACAF, wanted the pods. The pods had first been stored in the theater and neglected, producing a degraded condition. There was a poor to no theater maintenance capability available, and there was no organization in the theater that was their advocate or knew how to employ them to produce optimum effectiveness. So, after a short and dismal showing, the pods were sent back to the States.

Several efforts followed in the US to further improve and test the QRC-160A-1 pod. The major effort to test the pod on F-105 aircraft was conducted at Eglin AFB by the Electronic Systems Test Directorate (PGOY) of APGC/AFSC. The title of this test, begun in October 1965, was Problem Child. Mr. Ingwald "Inky" Haugen, (Lt. Col. USAF Ret.) was the Problem Child technical advisor while the TPO was Capt. David Zook. One very important feature of this test was to fly two pods on each F-105D aircraft in a flight of four, with 1,500 feet lateral and horizontal separation between the aircraft. This positioning of the jamming aircraft produced optimum jamming of the simulated Fan Song radar operator's scope. This formation was termed the "pod flight formation" and it was the brainchild of Inky Haugen. During this test 16 mm film was taken of the simulated Fan Song operator's jammed scope and it was very convincing.

After the completion of the Problem Child test, Captain Zook had to drop out of the final report writing effort since he was reassigned as an EWO crewmember to the 41st Tactical Reconnaissance Squadron flying EB-66 and RB-66 aircraft located at Takhli RTAB. At this time, Inky Haugen and Captain Zook were probably the two most knowledgeable people concerning the operational capability of the QRC-160A-1 jamming pod.

Capt. Zook's loss to the Problem Child test was a great gain for the 355th TFW. Around September 1966, the 355th TFW started receiving shipments of the QRC-160A-1 pods. I do not know how many pods they received at first but it appears they did receive enough to fly with two pods on each F-105D aircraft in a mission force of four flights, 16 aircraft. Of course, Capt. Zook's experience and expertise with the pods was put to good use at this time introducing the pods to the 355th F-105D strike pilots.

About early November 1966, APGC sent Inky Haugen to the 355th TFW with a copy of his Fan Song scope jamming film to assist Capt. Zook, and others, in the introduction and flying of the pod. The 355th commander, Col. Robert Scott, asked Inky if one pod per F-105D would still provide adequate jamming protection while a flight was flying the pod formation. Inky immediately made a phone call to APGC requesting test flights utilizing this type of pod configuration be flown in the pod flight formation.

Within two days APGC called back and confirmed that one pod per F-105D would still provide protection while flying the pod formation. When Col. Scott received this information he immediately transferred an estimated 8 to 15 of his pods to the 388th TFW at Korat RTAB to allow it to start carrying pods. Inky states that with this shipment of pods to the 388th, the 355th was now forced to also fly with only one pod per F-105D until it shortly received more pods.

I estimate it was in late November 1966 that Inky came to the 388th TFW for several days with his film of the simulated Fan Song operator's jammed radar scope. Capt. Zook visited the 388th for one day on 16 November 1966 to also give us the benefit of his expertise on the pod and its employment.

INTRODUCTION OF THE QRC-160A-1 JAMMING PODS TO THE F-105D STRIKE PILOTS OF THE 388TH TFW

Sometime in early November 1966 the wing commander, Col. William Chairsell, called Odom to his office. As Odom related to me, Col. Chairsell said something like, "The wing has just received from the 355th TFW some General Electric QRC-160A-1 jamming pods which were recently tested at your base, Eglin. Since you and your partner are form Eglin do you know anything about these pods?" Odom answered affirmatively. The colonel continues, "Good! I want you two guys to instruct my pilots on how to use these pods. Also, I want you to convince them to fly at a higher ingress and egress altitude in order to get above the low altitude anti-aircraft artillery (AAA) ground fire while having jamming protection at the higher altitudes from both the the radar-directed AAA and the Russian SA-2 SAM missiles." The Wing Director of Operations, Col. Howard "Scrappy" C. Johnson, was also an advocate of giving the jamming pods a try.

The reason I believe Col. Chairsell had such an immediate trust and confidence in Odom regarding matters of electronic warfare is because I think he had in just the recent past met Odom, and learned of his knowledge first hand, while Odom was on a Southeast Asian visit to various wings with Brigadier General Kenneth C. Dempster and Lt. Col. "Pierre" Irwin J. Levy. The names of these men were, and are, synonymous with the Wild Weasel program and electronic warfare.

I know the first delivery of the QRC-160A-1 pods to the 388th TFW, from the 355th TFW, was a small number because initially the wing received only enough pods to put one pod on each of the F-105Ds in two flights of a normal four flight mission force. The decision was made to put one pod on each aircraft of flights one and three, hoping that flights two and four would somehow receive some beneficial protection too. I do not remember briefing the 388th to fly the "pod flight formation" initially, especially for the first three missions that the pods were utilized. I am not sure at that point on time Odom and I even knew about the pod flight formation, until the later visit of Inky Haugen and Capt. Zook, which I have previously written about.

Immediately after Odom's visit with Col. Chairsell we started the preparation of the jamming pod briefing we were going to present to the 388th pilots at the next morning's big mission briefing, at about 4 o'clock in the morning. The target for this mission was going to be in Route Package 6 and there was sure to be some SA-2 missile action. The wing operation complex where the large briefing room was located was better known as Fort Apache.

Since Odom was a pilot, and it would be pilots we were trying to convince to carry the pod to enhance their survival chances, we decided Odom would be the one to explain the jamming action. Also, as I have already stated, Odom was one of the most convincing and persuasive briefers I had ever seen. He just radiated confidence and knowledge while briefing. He could very quickly and in broad terms explained how the jamming countered both the radar controlled AAA and the track-while-scan Fan Song radar of the SA-2.

I obtained a large piece of cardboard and drew, in detail, a picture of the pod's control head, which was located in the cockpit and explained the pod's switchology. The control head did not have just a simple on and off switch. On some of the control heads the switch could be moved through all settings by simply turning the switch. However, on others in order to move the switch from the "STBY" position to the "TXMIT" position there was a detent, and the switch had to be pressed in to allow it to move into the "TXMIT" position. All pod control heads looked alike from the exterior and a pilot would not be able to tell which type of control head he had in he cockpit by just looking at it.

We knew that in the heat and excitement of the mission some pilots were not going to remember the switchology, especially forgetting about the detent action, and assume the control switch was malfunctioning when it would not move in one continuous smooth motion. The pods could, and some did at first, malfunction in flight for various reasons and the pilots would have to recycle the control switch through its different positions to get the four transmitters back on line. The power for these early pods was routed through a switch or relay that was mounted on a bracket that was prone to malfunctioning, especially when the aircraft was pulling high Gs when coming off a target after dropping its bombs.

As a matter of fact, we found this power relay malfunction was so common at first that Odom sent a message to APGC asking that a test be conducted to determine the cause. We would receive an APGC message that would read something like, "Pulled three Gs and could not duplicate problem." Odom would send a short message back to APGC that simply read, "Reference your message – pull more Gs." The next APGC message would read something like, "Pulled four Gs and could not duplicate problem." Another short message would go back to APGC stating, "Pull more Gs." This type of exchange of correspondence went on until we finally received an APGC message, which in part stated, "Momentarily pulled 8 Gs, problem duplicated." Due to a fading memory I would not now swear that the APGC message stated 8 Gs, but if it was not that much, it was close.

The first big mission briefing that included our pod briefing, first, included all the normal briefers and their subjects that I have I have already written about. So, by the time Odom and I walked onto the stage the pilot's mental state and attitude was akin to a football team that had just received the pre-game pep talk by their coach. The mission briefings before our briefing were not exactly inspirational like a pre game pep talk, but like the football players, by the end of the normal briefings the pilots were eager to move on out to their assigned aircraft and get on with the mission. However, there was a factor the players never had to contend with which the pilots did have, and the pilots had to find a way to handle it. The football players knew they would not be shot at during their game, whereas the pilots knew they would be shot at during their mission. How each pilot handled this factor could enhance or detract from his focus during the mission briefings. We knew this was going to be the situation and that we were, in all probability, not going to have every pilot's undivided attention when our turn came to brief at the end of the usual scheduled briefing subjects.

We stepped onto the stage and Odom introduced us; so far so good. He began to briefly inform the pilots in flights one and three they would be carrying a jamming pod, how it jammed, and why it was to their advantage to be flying with one on their wing; and again, so far so good. Toward the end of his short briefing he stated, "... and the bombs on your wing station number (I have forgotten the exact number) have been down loaded and the pod uploaded at that wing point."

With the utterance of these words there was an immediate and very loud response of booing from the pilots in flights one and three! For the first time I witnessed Odom to seemingly "strike out" during one of his briefings. Probably some of the booing was also from pilots in the other two flights too. The availability of fewer dumb 750-pound iron bombs to be dropped on the target reduced the probability of success for the entire mission and in the long run negatively affected every pilot, since they might have to bomb the target again the next day.

Odom's portion of the briefing was completed and I started my show and tell briefing of the operation of the pod's control head. It was an understatement to say at this point I did not have the attention of the pilots in flights one and three. However, I quickly pressed on and finished what I had to say in short order. We also had 5 by 8 inch instruction cards titled "QRC-160A-1 Operation Instructions" that we handed out to the pilots in flights one and three, and in the future to every pilot in the wing. I still have one of these pod operating instruction cards and it shows evidence of having been folded often and worn from being stuffed into flying suit pockets.

At this point during the air war over North Vietnam the F-105D pilots were flying as low and fast as was possible, which was their usual reaction to ground threats, and their loss rate was accelerating. The younger pilots still thought this was the way to fly but the older and more experienced pilots of the 388th Tactics Committee had reached the point where they were willing to consider something new. I believe the timing of the older pilot's change in thinking, the arrival of the pods, and the results on the first three pod missions was providential.

The first pod-carrying mission was launched and flown as briefed, hitting a target in Route Package 6. The mission did encounter SAMs and there was the loss of at least one F-105D to AAA or SAMs. All pod carrying aircraft in flights one and three returned safely. I am sure this last fact did not go unnoticed by most of the strike pilots in the wing but at this time none of them said anything to Odom or myself.

After this mission, in addition to attending all the intelligence debriefings of the strike and Weasel flights, Odom and I also attended the maintenance debriefings for the pod carrying aircraft of flights one and three. We had a pod debriefing form titled "QRC Pod Debriefing" which we gave to all the maintenance debriefers to use, and I still have one of these forms today. The pilots' comments were pretty much what we had anticipated. Some of the pods worked without any type of a malfunction while others came off line but the pilots were able to recycle through the switching functions and restart most of them. Then there were a couple of cases where the pilots stated they could not get the pod to come back on line again after a malfunction, and we suspected the switch detent procedure.

This first pod mission probably occurred in early November 1966 and the weather in Route Package 6 at this time of the year was not consistently good. Consequently, it was another two or three days before the second Route Package 6 mission with pods was flown. This was a good training routine for the North Viennese SA-2 crews. They were not attacked both morning and afternoon every day and they would get experience jamming and then have two or three days for their Russian advisors to coach and teach them on what to do the next time. I am sure the 355th TFW was also experiencing the same flying conditions and schedule at this time.

The second mission with the pods was almost a duplicate of the first, including the loss of a non-pod carrying F-105D in either flights two or four and no aircraft losses in the pod-carrying flights of one and three. Again, I am sure this fact did not go unnoticed by most of the strike pilots for by now Odom and I were no longer being booed during our part of the big mission briefing.

Two or three days after the second pod-carrying mission the third pod-carrying mission was flown. I remember the target for this mission was located close to Hanoi. There was an overcast covering almost all of North Vietnam that mission with a large clear area right over Hanoi. The mission force ingress route was from out of the north to the south, right over Thud Ridge, and then on over the flat land to the edge of Hanoi. The force received no AAA or SAM firings on their ingress route even though they were flying above the overcast; however, the second they were in the area around Hanoi with clear visibility below them, all hell broke loose from the ground defenses. One of the four strike flight leaders was Maj. Alfred "Lash" J. Lagrou, Jr. He thought he heard someone call out "MiGs" just before reaching the roll-in point for his flight's dive on the target, so he gave the command for his flight to jettison heir bombs and make an evasive maneuver.

At this time President Johnson had a no bombing edict on downtown Hanoi and a number of other cites and airfields in North Vietnam. Lagrou was not sure where his flight's jettisoned bombs had landed. It was a visibly nervous and pale Lagrou that walked into the wing's debriefings after landing. Fortunately, for Lagrou, the bomb damage photo coverage of the area showed the bombs had not hit downtown Hanoi. As the last flight pulled off the target and very quickly climbed above the overcast, the firing of the AAA and SAMs stopped and the egress route was as non-eventful as the ingress had been.

It was believed the jamming had intimidated the SA-2 operators. When the operators could not observe the F-105Ds on their scopes, or only observe them poorly, and could not also physically observe them from the ground, they were afraid to keep their radar transmitters on, afraid an undetected Wild Weasel flight was going to roll in on them or fire an AGM-45 Shrike missile at them. However, the North Viennese SA-2 operators and their Russian instructors were rapidly learning. Such a situation did not intimidate them for long.

After this mission Odom and I had the strike pilot's undivided attention in our pod briefings before a mission. As I stated earlier, our office in the 13th TFS was hard to find, but now we had individual strike pilots coming to the 13th squadron and asking at the operations desk, "Where are those two guys form Eglin that know about the jamming pod? I want to talk to them!" At this time we also started to receive invitations form the three strike squadrons in the wing asking us to attend their squadron meetings, ". . . and by the way, tell us again, in more detail, just how do those pods work?"

Shortly after this third pod-carrying mission I had an unusual conversation with a strike pilot that was about to fly right after our briefing of a morning mission. I had walked back to the operations area where there were a number of people that kept track of various data concerning the pilots by name and the aircraft by tail number. This young captain waked up to me and he had a very serious demeanor. He was dressed in all of his flying gear, all ready to "step" – get on the crew van that would take him to the aircraft he had been assigned to fly. He looked me right in the eye and stated, "Your are trying to kill me." I did not recall having ever seen this pilot before, although I could recognize most of the pilots by now even if I did not know their names.

It appeared to me this pilot was dead serious. I replied, "What are you talking about? I don't even know who you are." He replied, "You have assigned me to a plane that will not be carrying a pod and I will be killed." At that instant several thoughts flashed though my mind. One was, "I never figured on pod success ever coming back around like this and hitting me from an angle I was not prepared for!" The best I could do was to say, "I am here to tell you how the pods work and how to use them. That man over there, at that desk, is wing permanent party and his job is to assign pilots to fly in aircraft by tail numbers. Go talk to him." To this day I am not sure if that pilot was "pulling my leg" or was serious. I don't ever remember seeing this pilot again after this incident.

Having obtained the attention and interest of the pilots, it was not long after this that Odom and I no longer needed to provide our pod briefing during the big overall mission briefings. However, we would instruct new pilots in our office concerning the operation and effects of the pod.

About this time there was an incident where an F-105D strike pilot was, or thought he was, being attacked by a MiG. In an effort to accelerate his movements to evade the MiG he, and possibly his wingman too, not only jettisoned their bombs but also the QRC-160A-1 jamming pod they were each carrying. After this incident Col. Chairsell issued the order to his maintenance people that the capability of the pilots to jettison the pods would be terminated. If a pilot returned, he returned with the pod.

Also, at this time one of the major subjects addressed each day in Col. Chairsell's wing standup briefing was the status of the jamming pods. For a few weeks a major concern was the number of pods the wing had received and their total number. A continually concern was the pods operational rate and maintenance status.

By the end of the first three weeks of November 1966 the 388th TFW had received enough pods to put two on each F-105D in a mission force of four flights. As I stated earlier, about this time frame Capt. Zook from the 355th visited for a day and provided us with his expertise on the pod. Also, Inky Haugen was with us for several days with his 16 mm movie film of how the jamming of the pod flight formation affected an SA-2 operator's scope. By this time the 355th strike pilots had accepted the pods and after seeing this convincing film they were more than willing to try the pod formation. Flying a steady 1,500 feet separation horizontally and laterally in a flight of four F-105Ds, by just eyeballing it, was not easy, especially at first. Also, the pod formation was not the best posture to defend against a possible MiG attack, or perform a roll in of a flight of four F-105Ds into a dive on a target. However, the drop in the F-105D loss rate after the introduction of the pods was a great incentive for the pilots to give the pod flight formation their best effort.

During this time a General Electric team of engineers and technicians arrived at the 388th TFW. This team worked in shifts, 24 hours a day, 7 days a week, while taking every pod apart and refurbishing it and accomplishing various actions that increased the pod's reliability, especially during a high G maneuver.

I know for certain that by 22 November 1966 the 388th TFW was carrying two pods per F-105D, and the General Electric team was still modifying the pods, because of what happened to Capt. Buddy L. Bowman on this date. Bowman was flying a mission that hit a target in Route Package 6. He was carrying two pods on his F-105D, tail number 58-1161. Right after releasing his bombs and pulling out of his dive something happened to Bowman's aircraft. He heard a loud noise and felt a strong jolt in the aircraft, to the aft of the cockpit. Immediately he lost all of his radios, the aircraft started losing power, and a grinding and vibrating noise started coming form the engine.

Bowman was number four in his flight, the last off the target, and the other flight members were rapidly out-climbing him and pulling away. Number three did look down and back and see flames coming out the aft of Bowman's aircraft and radioed Bowman to eject. Of course Bowman never heard this transmission and was not aware of the flames during the remainder of his flight. Instead, he pressed on southwest toward Thailand without any contact with the rest of the force. His aircraft's power and handling was rapidly decreasing as he flew back. Fortunately, when the aircraft did lose all power he had just crossed over into Thailand and he ejected. Bowman states he was not clear of the aircraft for more than two or three seconds before it exploded. Bowman made a safe chute landing near the remains of his aircraft. My guess is that a probable AAA "almost miss" was at the root of Bowman's aircraft problems, but the official records for the aircraft just stated its demise was due do to "engine failure/ malfunction."

The next day several members of the General Electric maintenance team at the 388th TFW accompanied other wing personnel to inspect the crash site. The General Electric people gathered up the remains of the two jamming pods that were on the aircraft and took them back to their work area at the 388th. From the remains of these two pods, and some new parts, they created a single pod. This pod was produced with tender loving care!

It was only a short time before this pod held the record for flying the most hours without a malfunction. Because of its durability and reliability it quickly earned the name of "Old Reliable." Col. Chairsell would not let his Director of Maintenance inform 7th Air Force of the existence of Old Reliable. It did not exist, it was not listed on any unit's asset records – so the wing had an extra pod for its F-105Ds. Of course, Col. Chairsell recognized the value of the jamming pods form the onset, but what better example to demonstrate the change of the tactical fighter pilot's attitude toward electronic warfare, and carrying jamming pods.

Joe Telford, WW # 256

Story by Robert E. (Bob) Dorrough WW# 349

Vegas Odds

Overview

If you flew fighters over North Vietnam, the magic number was 100. That was the number of missions you had to fly in order to complete your combat tour and return home. The crews flying over North Vietnam had one objective, and that was to complete 90 missions so you could become “golden”. When you became golden you did not have to make any more flights over Hanoi, and the odds were greatly increased that you would not be shot down during your last ten missions. The trick was completing that first 90, for as they say in Las Vegas, the odds will catch up with you sooner or later, especially if you were a Wild Weasel crew. The Wild Weasel’s responsibility was to precede the main strike-force of 16 single-seat F-105Ds (nick-named Thud) into the target area, entice enemy defenses to concentrate on attacking the Wild Weasel aircraft, and, if possible, the Wild Weasels would try to cripple as many surface-to-air (SA-2) missile sites as possible. Finally, we would trail the Ds as they left the target area, protecting their 6 o’clock from any missile site that tried to fire on them. For my EWO (electronic warfare officer), Major Bud Summers, and me, it was on mission number 83, December 19, 1967, that the odds almost caught up with us on a strike in the Doumer Bridge area, near Hanoi. One intelligence source estimated that there were over 2,000 anti-aircraft artillery (AAA) guns of various sizes and 40 SA-2 missile sites active around Hanoi. Each missile (SAM) site was equipped with one radar control van and six radar guided missiles ready to launch. The SA-2 had a speed of over three times the speed of sound (Mach 3), and looked like a fast telephone pole coming at us. Each missile site could only guide one SA-2 at a time, but around Hanoi, several sites would fire at us simultaneously. Fortunately, the USAF’s 2-seat F-105F, built by the Republic Aircraft Corporation, was a great Wild Weasel aircraft. It was fast and could take hits and keep going, as we would prove on this mission. The Wild Weasel aircraft were equipped with special electronics that could detect the SA-2 radar when it was turned on, and could also indicate when a missile was launched. However, our detection gear could not tell us how many sites were firing at us at the same time! At the time of this particular mission, our goal was to make it until December 27, because that was day the Bob Hope Christmas Show, featuring Raquel Welch, was going to be at our airfield, Korat Air Base, Thailand. The next nine days, especially this one, would prove most challenging.

Mission Planning

We were tasked to take the "water route" to our target, refueling over the Gulf of Tonkin before heading inland. If we entered North Vietnam from the Gulf, a lot of our ingress routes in the past to the Hanoi area had been down Little Thud Ridge. This was a good idea since you could get some terrain masking from enemy radar, and it was easier to evade capture if you were shot down. However, the enemy knew that, and a lot of AAA (37, 57, and 85mm), SA-2s, and MiGs (17s and 21s) would wait for us there. To cross them up we made two tactical changes for this mission. One, we deployed a second Wild Weasel flight, led by Major Mike Muskat and his EWO Capt. Kyle Stouder, as a decoy north of Little Thud. Second, rather than going down Little Thud Ridge, the main strike-force of 16 F-105Ds, 8 F-4D MiG CAP fighters, and my Wild Weasel flight went south of Little Thud, up the flat Red River delta. The bad news about going up the river delta was there no place to hide, but we had to do something to confuse the enemy defenses.

Flight Planning

After Mike and I had agreed on the ingress route with the strike-force commander, we met with our flights to discuss specific Wild Weasel plans. We did not have enough F-105F Wild Weasel crews at Korat to have four crews in the same flight. Therefore, the lead and number three were Wild Weasels and numbers two and four were single seat F-105Ds. For some reason most of the single seat strike pilots did not enjoy flying with the Wild Weasels!! I guess being first in and last out of the target area did not appeal to them. On this mission my number two wingman was Bill Scott, number three was Ezz Ott and his bear, Tom McGuire, and number four was Verne Ellis. Verne was in a spare aircraft that had not been loaded with Shrike missiles (which homed in on the SA-2 missile controlling Fan Song radar antenna), so that reduced our attack capability. The call sign assigned to my 4-ship was (I am not making this up) Vegas flight. The armament loads for the Wild Weasels were Shrikes on the two outboard wing stations. Inboard was a 450-gallon drop tank on each wing, and four CBUs (cluster bombs) on the centerline belly station. We did not mount a radar jamming pod because it would mess up our enemy radar detection gear in the cockpit and reduce the number of Shrikes we could carry. Note: The 16 strike-force aircraft did carry jamming pods. All F-105s had bomb bays, but we always carried an extra fuel tank in that space rather than any weapons during the Vietnam conflict. The two Ds in the Wild Weasel flight carried the same wing configuration as the Wild Weasels, but carried six 500-pound conventional bombs on their bellies. The Ds usually carried 750 pound bombs, or larger, plus heat seeking sidewinder missiles for the MiGs, but not when flying with the Wild Weasels. The 500 pounders worked fine against SAM sites, and the lighter bomb weight made the Ds more maneuverable when dodging SAMs.

The Mission

Take-off, join-up, and KC-135 tanker rendezvous at 14,000 feet over the Gulf of Tonkin were routine. Just before the tanker drop-off point, Vegas flight did a fuel top-off recycle, stowed any loose gear, cinched the harness up real tight, took one last drink of water, and dropped off the tanker to join up with the rest of the strike-force. The two Wild Weasel flights stayed just below the F-105D "bombers" to be masked from the enemy's radars by the D's jamming pods. The F-4s flew MiG cover above and behind the entire group. The F-4s always protected the main force, since the F-105Ds had to fly a level, bomber-type radar jamming formation to their target, then roll in one at a time. Of course, the MiGs knew the Wild Weasels were not protected, and I had several friends shot down by these very agile adversaries, but not today. Approaching the coast, we depressurized our cockpits to eliminate the effects of rapid decompression if we were hit. The force then accelerated to .9 Mach at 14,000 feet and armed our weapons. At the split-up point, Major Muskat's flight broke north and Vegas flight accelerated straight ahead, spreading into a wide, almost line-abreast, formation. We were no longer masked, and sitting ducks for all the enemy had to offer. We got two to three minutes in front of the main force, and radioed back that the sky was clear in the target area, but the visibility was only three to five miles with bad haze. This was not good for spotting MiGs or missiles coming at us, but this was the hand we were dealt. The Wild Weasels then went to a different radio frequency. This was important, because we could not take the chance of someone in the strike-force or MiG CAP making a transmission at the same time we were trying to call out an incoming MiG or missile. Since our primary job was to pull enemy fire away from the "bombers" (some say Wild Weasels were guinea pigs) we needed every advantage we could get. Twenty-two miles from Hanoi the first Fan Song radar started tracking us and the red "missile launch" light came on in my cockpit. As we turned toward it another site came up at 2 o'clock. We could not spot any missiles headed our way, so I instructed Vegas 3 to prepare a Shrike launch at the second site, while Vegas 2 and I fired at the first one. The haze was so bad that we never saw the two SA-2s that exploded beneath us as we began a climb to launch our missiles. Fortunately, the flying shrapnel hit no one. As the three Shrikes were fired, Major Summers called out three more SAM sites to the right that were tracking us, plus two to the left, and had multiple launch signals. I called out the new threats to the flight and broke to the right as two SA-2s went beneath Vegas 1 and 2, and two more between Vegas 2 and 3. The SAMs missed, and we took out two Fan Song radar vans with our Shrike attack. At the same time, Red Crown, our early warning aircraft flying over the Gulf, called "Bandits at Bulls-eye". That meant that MiGs were airborne, and near Hanoi. The good news was I knew that the MiGs would not bother us as long as we there were a lot of SAMs being launched. The reason? Rumor had it that a SAM had accidentally shot down a MiG a few weeks before! Wonder where that SAM crew was shipped? Bud kept saying, "Three rings" (our radar detector indication of a missile getting ready to fire), "3 o'clock, 6 o'clock, 9 o'clock, 12 o'clock. Launch, launch." Then I spotted four more "telephone poles" headed our way from seven to nine o'clock, first the glow of their red exhaust in the haze, and then the missiles themselves came into view, traveling faster than a .357 magnum bullet. As I called them out we made a hard diving turn into them, and they passed harmlessly overhead, exploding in huge orange fireballs at about 80,000 feet. The red "missile launch" light was on almost continuously. It felt like we were on a merry-go-round, and everywhere we turned, here came more SAMs. Pull it up, take it down, in afterburner, out of afterburner, the fight raged on. The missiles kept forcing us lower and lower, because the only way the big, beautiful, rugged, heavy F-105 could accelerate was to dive. This put us into lethal AAA fire, so dense it looked like a wall. One could only pray that the next shell was not our "golden BB". The flak missed, and, continuing to make hard jinks, we managed to gain altitude back to 12,000 feet. As we climbed, more SAMs homed in on us from northeast of Hanoi. Turning and diving toward them, we tried to decide which one was closest, so we could dodge it before the next one got there. There were at least five SA-2s in that salvo, and one got so close that I swear I heard the missile's rocket motor as it roared by. It's the one you do not see that gets you, so we kept turning and checking our 6 o'clock position to make sure one was not sneaking up on us. For sure I counted eighteen missiles we tangled with that day, and probably more I did not see. The strike-force was still over their target, so we jettisoned our empty external fuel tanks to reduce drag and give us better fuel economy.

We were unable to attack the SAM sites northeast of Hanoi since they were under a low cloud cover, so we swung back to the southeast, avoiding more 85mm bursts. Bud picked out the strongest Fan Song returns on his scope and pointed me in that direction. Another SA-2 came smoking by, so close I could have hit it with my 20mm Gatling gun. Then I realized if I blew it up, it would probably get Bud and me, too. No glory in shooting yourself down. Just as we crossed the Red River, Bud got a strong Fan Song signal at one o'clock. I spotted the missile launch smoke from a camouflaged SA-2 site, called it out to my flight and prepared to roll in. The AAA was not expecting us, and the flak was not too bad as I made my first bombing run. Unfortunately, there was a malfunction, and only one of my CBUs released from the bomb rack. Vegas 2 put his six bombs on target, but Vegas 3 and 4 had become separated from us while avoiding all the SA-2s. I was amazed that Vegas 2 was still with me! Determined to put that site out of business, I recycled the bomb switches and prepared for another pass. We really stirred up a hornet's nest after our first bombing run. A barrage of 37 and 57mm AAA poured into the sky as I started my dive. At the release point, I was relieved when my last three bombs dropped from the rack. Meanwhile, Vegas 2 had to abort his pass because the flak was bouncing him around real good, and he was hit in the tail of his Thud. The flak was all over me as I began the pullout from my attack, then there was an explosion and a large ball of smoke and fire engulfed the aircraft from a direct hit just in front of the cockpit. Recovering control, I continued to jink and climb to get out of the murderous onslaught. Vegas 3 and 4 found us after my second pass and each one made a good drop on the SAM site. Either I had knocked out some of the AAA with my second pass, or they had run out of shells, because the flak was not near as bad on 3 and 4's bombing runs. As we left our target, we could see it engulfed in smoke and fire.

The strike-force had hit their target and were outbound, so it was time to protect their rear and get out of dodge. We were getting low on fuel and had just turned toward the Gulf when we got a strong Fan Song signal from 6 o'clock. Wheeling back toward Hanoi, here came another SA-2, pointed right between Vegas 2 and 3. We split and dodged that one when another one came at us from the left. Diving toward it, more 57 and 85mm AAA opened up on us, but missed. Pulling up just before the missile arrived, it passed below us and we were safe again. Sure glad those SA-2s could not make 180-degree turns. This time Vegas 3 and 4 could not find us, and we did not see them again until back at Korat. Did not know it at the time, but we would really need their help before the day was over. Had to avoid two more barrages of 57/85mm AAA before reaching the coast, but after all we had been through, this was duck soup. While headed toward the Gulf, my adrenalin started going back to normal. Then I noticed that my left knee was sore, looked down and discovered I had been injured when we got hit! I guess in the heat of battle I was too busy to feel it. Fortunately it was minor, so the flight surgeon patched me up and we flew a mission north of Hanoi the next day. Had a dogfight with six MiGs, four -17s and two -21s, but that is another story for another day.

Remember me bragging on how rugged the Thud was? Well, when that shell hit just in front of the cockpit, the only damage it did to the aircraft was to knock out the air conditioning system and radio transmitter. I could receive fine, but could not talk to anyone. Bud tried to call from the back seat with the same results. Things could have been worse. My cockpit instruments, the LOX (liquid oxygen) bottle, 20mm cannon shells, radar, and nose gear hydraulics, were all undamaged. I'm thinking my guardian angel has really worked overtime on this mission. No problem with the radio malfunction, just turn the lead over to my wing-man, hit the tanker for some much needed fuel and head home. Not so fast, found out that number 2 had no radios at all. No radio meant no tanker rendezvous, and since we did not have enough fuel to make the closest base (Da Nang), that meant an ejection with a water landing. We would have to find a Navy ship in the Gulf of Tonkin, do a low flyby rocking our wings, pull-up, eject, and hope they see ejections from both planes and pick us up. Where was Vegas 3 and 4 when I needed them and their radios? It was a little frustrating to know my buddies were hooking up on tankers without me knowing how to find them. We continued to head south down the gulf, looking for a ship and making numerous radio calls in the blind. With no ships in sight and fifteen minutes of fuel left things did not look so good. I made another call to Red Crown and my guardian angel came through once more as my radio started working! Red Crown heard my transmission and wanted to know if I needed a tanker to head toward me. YES!! Red Crown vectored a KC-135 with the call sign of Brown Anchor toward me ASAP. We hooked up with about five minutes of fuel left for the Thud's thirsty engine, got enough JP-4 to make Korat and headed home, knowing we had beaten the odds once more. Like all fighter pilots who flew in Southeast Asia, I will be eternally grateful for the airmanship and courage of the tanker crews who saved us so many times. The best thing about this mission was that none of the strike-force was shot down. We had done our job. It's a great feeling to know that all your buddies made it back safe. Really did not think we would last until Bob Hope arrived on the 27th. Bud and I flew six more times before his show, five up North, plus one "non-counter" to Laos on Christmas day, but we made it. Bob Hope and Raquel Welch were great; God bless them for raising our spirits.

Epilogue

After completing 100 combat missions over North Vietnam, plus three to Laos, Captain Bob Dorrough and Major Bud Summers returned to the United States. Major Summers became a professor at the Air Force Academy, received his doctorate in electrical engineering from the University of Denver, and retired from active duty as a full colonel, commanding the 1957th Communications Group, PACAF, Hickam AFB, HI. At the present time, 2004, he is a senior engineer on the F-22 flight test program at Edwards AFB, CA. Captain Dorrough left active duty, but stayed in the Air Force Reserves, flying C-130s and A-10s. He retired as a full colonel attached to HQ SOCLANT (special forces), Norfolk, VA. After thirty years in the airline industry, he retired as a Captain with US Airways. Both Colonels Dorrough and Summers received three Silver Stars and Four DFC's during their tour at Korat. Their eight-crew Wild Weasel class from Nellis AFB had one crew shot down. Capt. Joe Howard and George Shamblee were shot down by a MiG 21, and were recovered in the Gulf of Tonkin but they were too seriously wounded to complete 100 missions. The other crew was hit by a SAM but still landed OK but the crew had been too badly injured to complete 100. All four were rescued, but injuries kept them from completing their 100 missions.

Robert E. (Bob) Dorrough WW# 349

Story by Edward T. Rock, WW# 185

Two Combat Losses

The worst job any commander has is telling the next of kin that the love of their life has been lost.

I was the commanding officer of the 561st Tactical Fighter Squadron, then based at McConnell AFB, KS. when it was ordered deployed to Korat RTAFB in April 1972 as part of operation Constant Guard. The 561st was the very first of several squadrons deployed at that time in response the North Vietnamese "Easter Offensive" when they invaded the South in yet another attempt to defeat the South Vietnamese and their American allies. In response to this aggression President Nixon ordered resumption of the bombing of all North Vietnam. During this deployment the 561st would be supporting this expansion of the bombing campaign against North Vietnam by flying Wild Weasel defense suppression/destruction missions.

Shortly after arrival at Korat, the Commander of the 388th Tactical Fighter Wing called me to his office and requested that I volunteer to take command of the 17th Wild Weasel Squadron. I said I would provided I could return to the US and relocate my family and then return to Korat. He agreed.

While clearing McConnell I was just finishing up and on my way home and I "rolled" through a stop sign. As luck would have it there was an Air Policeman right behind me and he immediately pulled me over and gave me a ticket for "Rolling through a stop sign." He handed me the ticket and said, "Here, sir, give this to your commander." I said, "I am the commander." He replied, "Then give it to the Wing Commander." I duly sent it to the Wing Commander and forgot about it. Col. Harry W. Schurr was the acting Wing Commander at the time. Months later I saw Col. Schurr again and he said, "Do you remember that ticket you got just before you departed for Korat again?" I replied, "I sure do, Colonel." He said, "I always wondered what the Air Police thought when they got that ticket back. On the back of the ticket in the space where I was required to show the corrective action, I wrote, "Col. Rock relieved of command and sent to Southeast Asia!" I wondered what they thought too.

The same day Col. Schurr called me at home and told me Maj. Bill Talley and Capt. Jim Padget had been shot down by a MiG-21 on 11 May 72 and that their fate was unknown at that time. They were flying F-105G tail number 62-4424 which was assigned to the 17th Wild Weasel Squadron, Korat RTAFB. Bill was assigned to the 561st TFS and was flying an aircraft from the 17th WWS because that was the aircraft available at the time. Col. Schurr wanted me to tell Mrs. Talley about the loss. I absolutely hated to have to perform this duty but could think of no alternative since I was the commander and the job went with the territory, so I agreed. He asked me to report to personnel and get a briefing on what was known and then I would proceed to the Talley home and give the bad news to Bill's wife. As part of this briefing they gave me a copy of the official notification from the Air Force to Mrs. Talley. It read as follows:

"To Mrs. Talley: It is with deep personal concern that I officially inform you that your husband, Maj William H. Talley, is missing in action in SEA, 11 May 72. He was the pilot officer of an F105 aircraft that is presently missing. No details are known at this time; however, I will furnish them to you as soon as possible. Search and rescue efforts are in progress. Please be assured new information received will be furnished you immediately. If you have any questions, you may contact my personal representative, toal free, by dialing 1-800......... Please accept my sincere sympathy during this period of anxiety." Brig Gen K. L. Tallman, Commander, AF Military Personnel Center. I have kept that message for more than 32 years.

When I arrived at the Talley home, some of the squadron wives were already there! Supposedly word of the loss had not been released but somehow the information had already begun to spread though the officers' wives grapevine. They had not told Mrs. Talley anything regarding the situation but were there to provide moral support when the official notification took place.

When I arrived at the home Mrs. Talley answered the door. She must have suspected it wasn't good news when the commander arrives at her door in his blue uniform and wants to talk with her. Nonetheless she remained composed and we went into the living room where we both sat on the couch, I took her hand, and gave her the news she must have expected. Thanks goodness there was still hope and I did not have to report the death of her husband.

The good news is that Bill and his EWO, Jim Padget, survived their captivity and were repatriated along with many of the others released by the North Vietnamese in 1973.

It is particularly interesting to note that Bill thought his engine had experienced a bearing failure and was unaware that he had been shot down by a MiG-21 until months later.

Not all instances have such a happy ending.

On 17 September 1972 an enemy SAM shot down Lt. Tom Zorn and Lt. Mike Turose. They were flying F-105G 63-8360 assigned to the 17th Wild Weasel Squadron, 388th Tactical Fighter Wing, Korat RTAFB. They were able to make it to the Gulf of Tonkin before severe damage to the aircraft forced them to eject. The ejection appeared to be successful and US naval rescue forces were near by and able to get to the downed crew shortly after ejection. However, something apparently went terribly wrong during the bailout. When the rescue force arrived on the scene, the crews were in the water and appeared unconscious. When Para-rescue divers reached the crew they were still in their parachute harnesses, appeared lifeless, and the circumstances forced the Para-rescue personnel to abandon the remains because they were being pulled down deeper and deeper by the weight of the lifeless bodies, parachute and seat kit and could not release the bodies from their parachute harness in a safe and timely manner. The bodies were never recovered.

On 20 September 1972, I wrote the following letter to Tom Zorn's parents.

"Dear Mr. and Mrs. Zorn,

I know that you do not know me but I have been Tom's Commanding Officer in the 17th Wild Weasel Squadron since June of this year. I was also stationed at McConnell AFB, Kansas and was Commander of the 561st TFS while Tom was in the 562nd. I knew Tom at McConnell but I really got to know, and respect and love him here at Korat. I will always remember his laughter, his vitality, his love of life and his bravery. I know you are proud of Tom as we all are. I can only hope that my own boys grow up to be as fine as Tom in every way.

I had just signed Tom's leave request the day before he was shot down. He was really looking forward to going home again on leave. Most of his young friends from McConnell were trying to talk him into getting married to his girl Cindy while he was back in the states. However, Tom wanted to wait because he thought that was the right thing to do and that Cindy should have a regular church wedding with all the trimmings, not just a hurry up affair during an all too short two week leave. I only mention this so that you will know that Tom always did what was right, even if it was unpopular or hard. That's the type of young man he is. His is a super pilot and an outstanding officer in every respect. For that reason I had selected him for some of the most responsible jobs in the squadron well ahead of many older and more experienced pilots. He never let me down.

I know this war is very unpopular and that this may make his loss seem doubly hard. However, I think this was one of those hard and unpopular things that Tom knew had to be fought, even if it is viewed unfavorably by most. For myself, I fight because I owe it to all those that are still captured or missing. All of us have a responsibility to see that we get every man home again as soon as possible and that those that died did not die in vain.

Tom's main job here was to see that our planes and crews got safely to their target and back out. He was shot down while trying to insure that other men might get home safely and he was an expert at this job. While in the 17th, Tom was a pilot's pilot. I shall miss his youthful vigor and quiet presence around the squadron.

I know that others have written or talked with you regarding the details of the shoot down so I will not go over those here. However, if I can be of any service please let me know. If I were ever near Waycross I would consider it an honor to meet Tom's parents if you would have me.

I know I speak for every man in the squadron when I say that we are all deeply grieved at his loss and that he is remembered in our prayers.

Sincerely,

Edward T. Rock"

I think it is very hard to fully accept the loss of a loved one especially when the body is not recovered and never will be. Tom's parents did visit me after I returned to the states. I wish I could have been more help.

It was great to be a fighter squadron commander in peace and war but many responsibilities that went with the job were unwelcome

Ed Rock, WW # 185

Story by Ch. Col. Thomas A. Heffernan (Ret.)

A Chaplains Story

Editors Note: In Mike Gilroy's story "First In, Wrong Way Out" he mentions the Chaplain that was often found in the arming area and gave a "blessing" to each aircraft just before they took the runway. Billy Sparks mentions the Chaplain that ran up the ladder to give him a blessing/ absolution just before take on on Iron Hand One. I too appreciated the presence of the Chaplain at the end of the runway and his blessing just before take off. All of us, regardless of religious affiliation, could have used whatever help was to be found in the summer of 66 at Takhli RTAFB. When going on a mission to the Hanoi area we were almost sure to loose at least one aircraft and, in fact, we lost as many as seven on one mission. I thought it would be interesting to see if I could find the Chaplain who stood there, day after day, and gave us a blessing or absolution and perhaps he could share a little story about the Wild Weasels. I wrote to the Director of Office of Chaplain Personnel in Washington, DC to find out whom that Chaplain was. I knew it was the Catholic Chaplain but I could not recall his name. The folks at Chaplain Personnel had no record of exactly who was stationed at Takhli in July 66 but they provided me with the names of a few Chaplains that were stationed in Thailand at the time. Further investigation led to the conclusion that some had already died but I ended up making contact with Father Thomas Heffernan who is now assigned to the Pastoral Care Department, St. Francis Hospital and Health Centers, Poughkeepsie, NY. The following is his response to my request.

"Dear Ed,

I finally received your letter of 14 June, yesterday, and was pleased to receive it. Yes, I remember well the Wild Weasel Program since my previous assignment before UBON Thailand during the 66-67 period was McConnell AFB, Wichita, Kansas. I even had a ride in the F-105 during my year and a half in Kansas. I remember Major Joe Brand, who was killed in Vietnam, and his wonderful family and the many great men for whom we held services. (**Editors Note:** Joe was the senior officer in WW III-2, the first Wild Weasels assigned to Takhli in July 66. He was shot down and KIA on 17 Aug. 66)

I can't remember the name of the Takhli padre you might be thinking of who blessed the aircraft at Takhli.

I was at UBON with the F-4s who often flew cover for the F-105s in combat, Robin Olds and Chappie James Inc in command.

I have a story you might find interesting. One night we got word that we lost a plane from the squadron for whom I was Chaplain. Capt. Doug Peterson and Lt. Ron Tally were shot down. When I went down to the 433rd Squadron and was told the names of the pilot; and "GIB", I cried. I knew them both well. I wrote a letter to Doug's wife and Ron's mom and dad. I received a letter (a fabulous letter) from Dong's widow which the Squadron Commander placed on the Squadron Bulletin Board.

Shortly afterwards the Officer of the Day, Capt. Frank Markey, became very conversant with me at the club, etc., and took me for a check ride in the F-4 where we did Mach II and became friends.

It wasn't until my farewell party that Frank (after a few drinks) told me he wanted to get to know me because he was the Officer of the day when I found out Peterson and Talley were shot down. He saw how I felt and he wanted someone to feel that way about him if "he got his".

We all need to be loved—And I loved those tough warriors who did a great job and I was honored to be their Chaplain.

Hope the book sells a million.

Peace,

Ch. Col. Thomas A Heffernan (retired)"

Editors Note: Both Peterson and Talley became POWs and were released in March 73. Both went into politics after retiring from the Air Force. Peterson became the first US Ambassador to Vietnam in 1997.

Story by H Lee Griffin, WW # 2510

From A Grunts Perspective

War Story One – Welcome to Korat

This story requires a preface: It is written from a "Grunt" perspective. I was the Line Loading Officer for the 44th TFS at Korat (and Takhli) RTAFB's from 08 Nov 1968 through 11 Nov 1969. I was a brand new Second Lieutenant straight out of Tech School. This was my first "real Air Force" assignment. What a way to start!

My trip to Thailand was quite an ordeal. The contract flight on World Airlines was about eighteen hours late dispatching out of Travis AFB, CA. We had a 'broke' DC-8. At this point in my 'ridership', I was unable to sleep on airliners. I was way too interested in what was going on with the aircraft. I was a post solo, Student Pilot at the time and REALLY liked airplanes. My journey had initiated from Memphis, Tennessee where I had spent four weeks with my folks after graduating from the Munitions Officer Course at Lowry. I think that the trip consumed something over 26 hours. Upon arrival at Don Muang International Airport in Bangkok, I was a 'pooped puppy'.

A short stop in Bangkok included the obligatory trip to the 'local tourist trap' Thailand In Miniature. The C-130 ride to Korat was my first in that workhorse of an airplane.

Upon arrival, with baggage in hand, and dressed in my best 1505's. I found a niche to stash the baggage in and inquired as to the location of the 44th TF Squadron Orderly Room. I was told, "Fort Apache". Of course, I had not the slightest idea where this famous Fort was; in fact, I was somewhat perplexed as to what-in-the-heck a Fort was doing on an Air Force Base???

After a little wandering around, wide eyed at all the marvelous aircraft on the flight line, I wandered to "Fort Apache". Still lost and confused, I finally found the 44th. I went in, marveled at the fact it was air-conditioned, and told the Airman there that I was 2nd Lt. Griffin reporting. He looked at me like I had just appeared in a Martian costume. Of course, at the time, I was about 98 pounds 'soaking wet' and looked for all the world like I was about 16 years of age.

Well, I had duty to do. So, once the Airman sufficiently recovered his composure, I was ushered into the Commander's (Lt. Col. Guy Sherrill) office. Again, I got the Martian costume look. In my best attempt at Air Force tradition, I 'popped to', rendered my snappiest salute, and proclaimed, "Lt Griffin reporting, Sir". It seemed that Lt. Col. Sherrill was in shock. He informed me that he had no Second Lieutenants in the 44th Tactical Fighter Squadron and that he really didn't want any. He fortunately suggested that I find myself a home in the 388th Munitions Maintenance Squadron where the Line Loading Officers 'hung out'. I was hurt! Here was my first assignment and I had already 'blew it'.

I was both embarrassed and crushed. I wandered back to where I had stashed my baggage and inquired as to how to get to the billeting office. I hitched a ride and in-processed with billeting. I was pleasantly surprised with the nice concrete block 'hootches' (although I didn't know that term yet). They were not air conditioned, but that was not too much of a problem until much later on when I was working the 'night shift'.

It was somewhat obvious which of the two bunks in the room was occupied, so I threw my meager stuff on the other one. I walked back to the flightline. This was truly 'hog heaven' for I guy who has been obsessed with airplanes since he was four. I just wandered around and gawked. There were F-105 D's and F's and way off in the distance were C-121's and EC-121's. There was a general hubbub of activity. There were REAL bombs!

After I sufficiently recovered, I asked one of the troops where the 44th TFS was located and which line expediter truck belonged to that Squadron. He pointed me in the general direction and told me to look for the "Muzzle 3" truck for the 'loading guys'.

I slowly worked my way in the proper direction and started actually looking for the 'bread truck' with a 'Muzzle 3' sign on front. I was still in shock! There were real airplanes, and great big, beautiful ones at that, real bombs and missiles all over the place. It was going to be OK. After awhile, I saw the "Muzzle 3" bread truck heading in my general direction and flagged it down. Inside was a very harassed and tired-looking, tall, black, NCO dressed only in jungle fatigue pants and a white 't' shirt. I introduced myself as his new Line Loading Officer. I still got that 'Martian outfit' look!

Well, the first words out of TSgt Smith's mouth were, "God, that's all I need a fu@*&#in' Second Lieutenant! Lieutenant, get in the back of the truck. I don't want to hear a peep out of you for at least two weeks!"

Welcome to Korat!

Epilog: TSgt Smith and I got along famously! He was the consummate professional. I followed his admonition to the letter (almost). There was one of those small sized, gray metal, desks bolted into the back of 'Muzzle 3' that was my home for the duration. I finally got properly in-processed and through coordination with the 388th MMS attempted to make myself useful.

H Lee Griffin

War Story Two – My Backseat Ride

I was obsessed with airplanes. I have been an 'airplane nut' since age four. I broke my first 'piggy bank' for a ride in an Aeronca Champ in 1950, before I started the first grade.

As soon as I arrived at Korat, I wanted a back seat ride in those marvelous F-105F's. I worked the flightline 14 hours per day, seven days per week and 'drooled' every time engine start, taxi-out, and takeoff occurred. I spent quite a bit of time in the arm/dearm areas close to the action.

After I got all settled in and learned my way around, I made an effort to go and see Lt. Col Guy Sherrill, the 44th TFS Squadron Commander. I requested at the earliest opportunity I get a back seat ride. I didn't see any difficulty with this request, since the 44th possessed all of the F models in the 388th TFW. Remember, I'm only a 'butter-bar'.

Well, after a few nanoseconds of contemplation, Lt. Col. Sherrill informed me that that it was impossible. The Squadron only flew combat missions and FCF's (Functional Check Flights). Back seat rides were prohibited in both instances.

Months went quickly by. The 469th Squadron converted from F-105D's to F-4E's. We deployed the two remaining F-105 Squadrons to Takhli while the Engineers rebuilt Korat's runway. Soon after we returned to Korat, we had a change-of-command in the 44th. The new Commander was Lt. Col. Herbert Sherrill (no relation). Go figure the odds!

Meanwhile, Republic 'Locomotive Works' had developed a flight control modification for the 'Thud' that would provide some redundancy in the event of battle damage. This was a field modification and the mod center was set up at Takhli.

Being eternally devious, and aware of the principle of 'ask the other parent', I inquired of Lt. Col. Herbert Sherrill as to the possibility of a back seat ride. I acknowledged that I knew of the prohibition of rides on combat sorties and FCF's. But, I pointed out that we were ferrying aircraft to Takhli for the flight control mod.

He took several seconds of contemplation, and sadly informed me that my lack of an 'altitude chamber card' (and documentation of the required training) would preclude me from getting a back seat ride. I reached in my thin billfold, fumbled through it as casually as I could under the circumstances and tossed my 'altitude chamber card' on his desk.

(At the completion of the Munitions Officer Course at Lowry and while awaiting assignments, several of my classmates and I signed up for Physiological Training and the chamber 'ride'. Since Lowry had no flying activities by the late sixties, its altitude chamber was somewhat underutilized. We spent three days going through the course, and took the 'ride'. Best time I ever invested.)

I got my back seat ride shortly thereafter. It was a cross country to Takhli. The aircraft was "Crown Seven". The pilot was Lt. Col. "Black Jack" Gaudian. The aircraft was 'clean'; no external bomb racks or pylons. Lt. Col. Gaudian flew a very crooked path to Takhli. He did loops, rolls, split-esses and a few gyrations that I knew no name for. I managed to keep my breakfast in the proper location. I regret that we never went supersonic.

I did incur some physical deterioration as a result. I had sore face muscles for a week following. I grinned A LOT!!!

H Lee Griffin

War Story Three – Hung Mk-84

I was now a seasoned Second Lieutenant and had spent many long hours on the Korat flightline.

As the 388th TFW transitioned from F-105's to F-4E's, the Wing changed. "Doc" Blanchard departed as Wing Commander and an F-4 driver took command. I think that his name was McDonald. Things generally deteriorated and the light-hearted, 'let's-get-it-done' camaraderie that was the hallmark of the "Thud" folks became a scarce commodity.

About this time we got a new DCM (Deputy Commander for Maintenance). I think that he came out of SAC. I had already resolved to move to Takhli when the 44th TFS moved out. Since I was technically an asset of the 44th this was not a real problem. In actuality, I had already shipped 'hold baggage' to my next assignment at Eielson AFB, Alaska and was a 'short timer'. Anyway, I got tasked to show the 'new' DCM around the flightline and indoctrinate him to the 'fighter' world. I started out with the "Thuds" and explained the "Wild Weasel' mission, AGM 45 'Shrike' missiles, bomb bays, belly bands, MER's, M-61 gun systems and our 'cannon plug in the barrels trick'.

The F-105 had an exceptional weapons release effectiveness rate and gunfire out rate (not counting the 6,000 rounds per minute). This is starkly contrasted with the F-4E; it had significant 'teething' problems with it's new gun system and lotsa 'hung bombs'.

Anyway, as I was in the middle of my 'tour' for the "FNG", we got a radio call from "Job Control" of an IFE (In Flight Emergency) an F-4 had a hung MK-84 (2,000 #). I preceded to the edge of the taxiway adjacent to the runway in my 'trusty/rusty' 1966 Dodge 6-pack (that had been resurrected from the 'junkyard'). I always kept a old set of binoculars in the front seat along with my 'brick' radio. I still had the Colonel in tow. I kept the binoculars and instructed him to watch carefully. I no sooner got parked in a prime location to observe the 'show' (this was a relatively routine occurrence) than two F-4's approached in formation. The guy with the problem had his wingman alongside to assist and observe.

The IFE aircraft made the usual F-4 'controlled crash' onto the runway and as soon as it touched down, the MK 84 came off of the inboard pylon (MHU 12C bomb rack) and skipped out in front of the drag-chute-deployed aircraft. Upon seeing the bomb come off the F-4, the chase helicopter (H-43B 'Huskie') 'peeled off' and made space.

There was a Thai guard alongside the runway. He had a 'fox' hole several yards further away from him in the opposite direction than this bomb skipping happily down the runway. He made several running steps towards his 'foxhole', calculated that it was too far away, then abruptly stopped, squatted in the local fashion, and put his fingers in his ears!! I thought that this was the funniest thing that I had seen during my entire tour. I rolled out of the Dodge (since I already had the door open for a little added ventilation) in a fit of laughter and had tears rolling down both cheeks.

The new Colonel did not think that it was funny at all. I knew that it was time to go to Takhli........

Epilog: Within a few days I PCS'd along with the 44th to Takhli. Hung bombs were routine. They seldom went off. I was more than the required safety distance from any blast. I did not expose the Colonel to any undue risk. I **still** think it was funny.......

H Lee Griffin.

Story by Edward T. Rock WW# 185

561st Tactical Fighter Squadron Assignment

I was walking down the hall at Headquarters Tactical Air Command (TAC) one day in the early winter 1970 when I saw the Director of Fighter Requirements, Colonel Claude G. Horne, coming toward me with a piece of paper in his right hand. It was obvious that he was coming to talk to me and when we finally came together he handed me the paper and said "They gave me this at the morning staff meeting." I took the paper and read it. It was from Headquarters 12th Air Force and it said, "What is the availability of Lt. Col. Edward T. Rock to become the commander of the 561st Tactical Fighter squadron, McConnell AFB, Kansas?" I was more than surprised; I was shocked, thrilled, elated and overjoyed all at the same time. When I was first assigned to TAC Headquarters in early 1967 the TAC Commander, then General Gabriel P. Disosway, met with all new officers assigned to his headquarters staff. There were probably five men at the meeting I attended, mostly Majors, and one of the things he told us is that we would, more than likely, never return to a flying again as an operational pilot or crew member. Well, I had just defied the odds and was on my way back to an operational unit as a Squadron Commander. It was really awesome. I believed it was a real honor to be picked to command a flying unit, especially to be picked out of a staff job and sent back to fighter unit.

My family and I left for McConnell in early January 1971. We had four children, two boys and two girls, a Basset Hound named Sam, and my wife was eight months pregnant. We went in two cars—a Chevrolet station wagon, which I drove and Volkswagen Carmon Gia, which my wife drove. It was a surprisingly good trip considering the facts that we had several children, a dog, and a very pregnant wife.

When we arrived at McConnell, the house I had been assigned was still occupied by a person who was being separated from the service. Commanders had to live on base and we had to wait for base housing until the current occupant of what were to be our quarters moved out. The wing commander had given him a special dispensation in allowing him extra time to remain in base housing until he could complete arrangements for his move to civilian life. In the meantime we were assigned the base VIP quarters as our home. Since I had a fairly large family we were actually assigned two VIP suites, one across the hall from the other. Each one had a very small kitchen, two bedrooms and a sitting room. It was livable but not really appropriate or suitable for a family of six, including four young children, soon to be a family of seven, including a newborn. Sure enough my wife delivered our new daughter while we were still in the VIP quarters and we ended up using a dresser drawer as a bed for our new daughter. We were not delighted with the arrangements.

Eventually we moved into base housing, a three-bedroom ranch, located across the road from the main base. We visited the base in 2003 and stayed in the VIP quarters again, only it was a completely new building and a completely different VIP quarters. We went to look at the old location of our house and it had been replaced by a two-story duplex. We went to look at the base hospital where our daughter had been born and it also had been replaced by a completely new medical facility. The area where the squadron barracks had been located was now completely vacant. Much of the base had been severely damaged by a tornado and the only thing that remained that I was intimately associated with was the squadron operations and maintenance complex on the flight line.

Soon after our arrival, the Wing Commander had the formal change of command for the 561st. It took place during a "Commander's Call" and it was notable for the number in attendance. Commander's Calls were generally boring and if you could think of a reason to stay away you probably did. This day I think everyone wanted to get a look at the new guy; the room was packed with standing room only. In those days a Tactical Air Command (TAC) fighter squadron had about 600 men assigned including administration, maintenance, operations, medical, supply, food service, motor pool and other support staff. The idea was that the unit had to be able to deploy as a cohesive, self-contained combat unit that could operate on its own if necessary.

The very first night I assumed command, the phone rang while I was in bed asleep. It was the Wing Command Post and they said. "A member of your squadron has been killed in an auto accident and the wing commander wants you to go to the scene now. It is located at ...." and they gave the location. I had absolutely no idea where the spot was. I was not familiar with the area. I just hadn't been there long enough to get to know my way around the local community. I got out of bed, got dressed, and drove out to where I thought the location was. Just about the time I was arriving on the scene, the ambulance was pulling away with the remains of the young airman that had died in the accident. The next morning I found out that the airman was not really assigned to my squadron but had recently been transferred to another fighter squadron on base and therefore I was off the hook as far as this accident was concerned. It was just the first of many late night calls from the Command Post or the Wing Commander whenever anyone assigned to my unit had a problem of any kind. A few days later the family of the dead airman came to the base and met with the Commander of his unit. I was especially thankful it wasn't me.

Every day at 0720 hours the Wing Commander held a staff meeting with all of his direct reports, which included all of the fighter squadron commanders, the Director of Operations, and The Director of Maintenance, the Hospital Commander, and the Base Commander. The meeting included a daily weather briefing, a briefing on the planned flying schedule, a review of the previous day's flying schedule, any maintenance inspections that had been performed by Quality Control, and any other items of note. There were always a fairly large number of hangers-on who came to see who was going to get their ass chewed today. The airplanes had to take off with no more than five minutes difference from the scheduled time or the Squadron Commander had to explain the deviation from the schedule. The aircraft maintenance inspections by Quality Control always resulted in a least a few discrepancies and the squadron commander had to explain what action he was going to take to help insure those discrepancies never occurred again. If there were any serious discrepancies there would be hell to pay. It was management by objective. There was a standard for everything. On the aircraft inspections there was a standard for a very limited number of discrepancies and if that number was frequently or regularly exceeded, you could expect that heads would roll. The same numbers were reported to 12th Air Force Headquarters who had the same standards and if the standards were not met, then the Wing Commander had to explain what action he was taking to insure his unit would meet the objectives in the future. If you didn't measure up you would lose your job. The same was true for the flying schedule; if everything didn't happen in a safe, efficient and timely manner you had to explain why not and what was being done to get back on track.

Ordinarily a fighter squadron commander was picked form among the pilots within the wing. First the candidate had to be on the "Squadron Commanders' List" which was a list maintained at major command (Hq. TAC) headquarters and was determined by a board of senior officers from among potentially eligible individuals.

If you were on the list then you at least had a chance for an assignment as a fighter squadron commander; if not, then you were just never going to command a flying unit. There were always a lot more candidates than there were squadrons to go around. In 1970 the policy was that you had the chance for one command for a two-year period; then you were replaced by someone else form the list. The experience was key to most future promotions for line officers. In my case I would end up commanding three squadrons, including two at one time. A very unique experience and as far as I know never repeated.

Ed Rock WW # 185

Story by Clarence T. "Ted" Lowry WW # 848

Thuds at Son Tay

Our participation on the Son Tay raid was an apparent afterthought on the part of the Joint Task Force Leadership. On a normal day in mid-November 1970, after we returned from a mission over the North, our Squadron Commander Lt. Colonel Gus Sonderman called 10 of us from his squadron into his office individually and asked us if we would be willing to volunteer for "a special mission." It turned out this was two days before the raid, and all of us said we would go on the mission. Even when we took off from Korat, we did not know the purpose of the mission. All we knew was that we would be supporting American soldiers and airmen in a very dangerous mission very near to Hanoi, North Vietnam. Again, looking back, we had intelligence photos of the Son Tay prison camp in our crew briefing area at the base, but I'm not sure any of the eight guys who had not been in on the planning put the POW camp and where we were going together. That came the next day.

For the Wild Weasels, the Raid was only unusual in where we went. We used essentially the same tactics we used on every other mission. The only real difference was in the number of F-105s involved; once we got into the target area we did what we always did. Our tactics were to set up two opposing orbits with altitude separation for four aircraft. This allowed us to have at least one aircraft pointing toward known threats at all times. This was a fairly effective tactic although it deprived us of the mutual support most fighter crews preferred with a wingman formation. Our ingress was along the same route that the ground part and support aircraft took, and our planned egress was to retrace that route. Our flight lead, Lt. Col. Bob Kronebush selected it for us.

Major Don Kilgus was the pilot and I was the EWO on this mission. We were flying F-105F tail number 62-4436, assigned to the 6010th Wild Weasel Squadron, Korat RTAFB and we were originally assigned as an airborne spare aircraft for this operation. This was my first combat tour of duty but this was the third for Kilgus. Don had previous tours in Southeast Asia in O-1s and F-100s as a "Misty" fast FAC and shot down a MiG-17 on 4 April 1965 although this kill has not been officially confirmed.

I think the mission was the first time any of the Wild Weasel crews actually saw SA-2s. 1970 was a pretty light year in terms of missiles coming off the ground although we had gotten into a few engagements when the SAM sites would start to track us or someone in a flight we were supporting. I was crewed with Don Kilgus, and we had flown close to a hundred missions together so far that year. In fact, Don and I had gotten into one of the few engagements our wing had experienced back in March. Before that in 1970, the 355th Fighter Wing's only SAM engagements had been the one in which Dick Mallon and Bob Panek had been shot down over Route Package 1. But even those engagements were not common that year.

We arrived in the target area near Hanoi shortly before the strike force got there. Our job was to suppress air defenses that posed a threat to the lower and slower flying helicopters and C-130s. That meant SAMs; the helicopters and C-130s would have been sitting ducks for them, so it was our task to divert their attention and hopefully put a few of their sites off the air while our guys were doing their job on the ground.

Shortly after we got there, the SAM sites started tracking us and in fairly short order they started shooting. I think the first SAM that came off the ground detonated very close to the number three aircraft in the flight, flown by Lt. Colonel Bill Starkey and his Bear, Major Ev Fansler. Kilgus and I were out to the west of the target area watching the fight. Our job was to replace the first airplane we lost. When that SAM blew up it apparently put hot shrapnel into the number three Wild Weasel aircraft, causing it to look like it blew up. Flames shot up around the airplane as if it were just one ball of fire. Starkey called a Mayday saying he was on fire, but then just as quickly as the explosion occurred, the fire went out. Then we heard him say they were okay, the fire was out. He stayed in the area a short time, although at the time it seemed like several minutes, and then headed back to a recovery base in Thailand. He made it safely back to Udorn, and Kilgus and I moved up to take his place.

We almost immediately got one of the SAM sites off our nose and attacked it with a Shrike anti-radiation missile just about the same time he fired at us. I think we were going about 325 knots when the Shrike came off the rail, and Don rolled the aircraft to get the SAM in a position where he could build some airspeed and evade it. Kilgus was probably one of the best pilots I've ever known, and he easily made the SAM miss, and the next one that followed the first. The sky was alive with missiles, but about all we could see when one was airborne was a big fireball oscillating upward as it guided toward its target. The scary part was when the fireball only got bigger; we knew we were the target. Don made three SAMS miss, but in the third actual engagement, the fourth missile, he wasn't so fortunate. We thought we were clear of the missile, but it blew up pretty close to our aircraft. There is no fireworks display that can match the brightness and noise of that 450-pound warhead going off in your ear and throwing your aircraft around like a toy. Don never had a problem controlling the airplane, and after he sorted out what had happened, and I had indicated my desire that we leave the area, he told me the airplane was still flying and "we still have guys on the ground down there so we're staying." In fact the airplane did fly well even with a damaged stability augmentation system. Shortly after being hit, we engaged another SAM site and fired our second and last Shrike at it. In a very few minutes we realized the SAM had blown some holes in our fuel tanks because we were losing fuel faster than we were burning it. Don told me that we didn't have enough gas to make it back to Udorn, and we needed to start setting up to find a place to bail out as close to our own people as we could. He chose to take the airplane back the way we had come, over Western North Vietnam and across Laos to get into the heaviest mountains we could find. So we headed west and ended up jumping out of the airplane about 100 miles north of Udorn RTAFB.

Don Kilgus was a truly remarkable man and a great warrior. While we were engaged at Hanoi, he was so totally focused on protecting the other slower aircraft and our people on the ground he did not mention our SAM problem to the other members of the flight. Only when he realized that we could not get home did he ask for help. As soon as he made the call that we had been hit and needed a tanker fast, a KC-135 started north. That crew who I've never met came well up into hostile airspace to try to get us home, and if we had had only 3 more minutes of gas they would have succeeded. We flamed out at 32,000 feet and glided west for another 20 miles till we got down to about 12,000 feet which was 4,000 feet above the average terrain there before we had to eject. As we were gliding to a manageable ejection altitude, the controller at Udorn, Capt. Jim Startin was trying his best to get the tanker to us, but by the time it got close to us we had already flamed out. Once, Jim told us the tanker was at 12 o'clock 8 miles ahead and Don replied, "even if I could get to him we probably don't have enough hydraulic power to open the (refueling) door." He was probably calmer at that moment than most people are in their daily lives. But Jim Startin kept trying; one more time he told us the tanker was dead ahead at 24,000 feet and Don told him that about the only way they could help us was "if they open the(ir) door and these seats can take us up to them." All Startin could do was apologize again. About that time Kilgus told me it was time for me to leave.

An aircraft ejection is quite an experience. I pulled my seat handles up and squeezed the triggers. I remember seeing two little white puffs of smoke on either side of my canopy and seeing the canopy start to lift off the aircraft. About the same time, I felt the seat start up the rails, and the next thing I knew was I was in my parachute somewhere over northern Laos. My first thought was my crotch hurts, and then I looked down and saw some lights at what looked like a runway. We didn't know exactly who owned that part of Laos but I knew I did not want to land in a lighted field. Then I felt the wind and thought "great, this wind's going to blow me back to North Vietnam." But I really knew better. It didn't take long till I hit the ground. Amazingly, I didn't fall down and have to do the parachute-landing fall that we had spent so many hours practicing in flight school and survival school. One of the things they teach you in survival school is that when something like this happens you're going to be in shock, so the first thing to do is gather yourself and take a drink of water to calm yourself down. The lesson must have taken because that's what I did, but only after I had to cut myself out of the parachute because the quick release mechanism on the left side of my chute didn't want to open. Then I couldn't find my knife scabbard and ended up losing my knife. The survival instructors also tell you to keep on the "military crest" of a hill when you are moving away from where you landed. I knew I was on the side of a mountain even though it was really dark that early in the morning (about 2:00 AM) so I moved along what I thought was the military crest and tried to find a place to hide. About then I was wishing I had paid more attention to the jungle survival school instructors. I finally found a bamboo thicket which was about the densest part of the jungle there and got my survival radio out to let our people above know I was all right. Almost immediately, an American airplane answered and let me know that Don was down safely and was okay.

Then a short while later, our guys came back and told me they were going to try to pick me up that night. I thought that was a great idea because I could hear dogs barking, and I didn't know whether they were friendly dogs or bad guy dogs. I did know that if they were bad guys, I would not have a very long or prosperous life if they got to me first. The helicopter came in pretty shortly after that, and told me to light a flare so he could get to me. I did what he asked, and he turned his spotlight on me, and for some reason that I still don't know he just left. At that moment, I was scared more than I can say. I remember saying "where are you going?" but nobody answered. I don't know whether they could talk to me because I was babbling or my radio quit. Anyway, a couple of minutes later I got my second survival radio out and heard the Sandy (A-1) leader tell me they knew where I was and would be back at first light. I said "thank you" and almost immediately felt completely at ease and all my fear went away. I lay back on the ground and went to sleep, and the next thing I knew I heard a rooster and woke up. Years later, the first time I spoke of this in public, a major's wife told me that I must have had an army of angels guarding me. She must be right because there is no other explanation for why the bad guys did not get near me; they were in control of the area and were all around I'm sure. When the sun came up, I got my radio out and heard the Sandys call me. I answered and they told me there was a fog bank building and would I like for them to pick me up first or get Don first. I told them "I'll go first, thank you" so they told me I would have to fac (guide) them in. I heard the helicopters, and saw them behind me. I stood up and told them "I'm at your 11 o'clock." Within a minute they were hovering about 40 yards from me at the top of the hill and I ran to the jungle penetrator and they pulled me up. Another thing they tell you in survival school is to let the rescue crew take you off the jungle penetrator. I'm not sure why they think they have to tell you that, because in my case, there was no way I was going to turn loose of that thing until they pried me off of it. I remember looking up and seeing that HH-53 and the PJ standing in the door over his minigun and feeling completely safe. Wayne Fisk, who was the PJ and I became great friends several years later, and he remains one of my favorite people to this day.

Once I got on the helicopter I felt like I had been run over by a truck. Up until that time, I had felt no pain or any discomfort at all. It's amazing how your body masks pain as long as stress is high. Anyway, by this time I hurt in places I didn't know I had.

Also while all of this was going on, the other helicopter went over and picked up Don. He had gotten about three miles farther west than I did and had spent his night in a tree. He told me he had been on a pretty big limb and managed to be fairly comfortable all night. The trip back to Udorn was a pretty happy ride for all of us. We still hadn't been told what the mission was for.

The next day, we read in the Stars and Stripes that there had been a raid on a North Vietnamese prisoner of war camp but no prisoners were there. Then we knew what had happened.

There were eight SAM sites in the general vicinity of the mission objective that night and they fired 18 SAMs. The only damage was to Wild Weasel aircraft. The Wild Weasels were successful in protecting the Son Tay task force.

Being able to participate in a mission that is intended only to help your fellow airman or soldier may be one of the best things that a combat aviator can do. The Son Tay raid was probably the single most important night of my 30 years in the United States Air Force.

Ted Lowry WW # 848

Story by Jim McInerney WW # 295

Wild Weasel

Late in the fall of 1966, while serving as an F-4 Phantom pilot at Bitburg, Germany, I received a phone call from Washington giving me the good news that I was to be reassigned to Southeast Asia in the F-105 program. Don't read me wrong. There was nothing wrong with the F-4, and I am proud of the fact that as one of the first Air Force pilots to have flown the Phantom (a pair of F-4B's borrowed from the Navy and designated as F-110's), I was honored to have made some small contribution to developments which led to the F-4C/D/E. It was simply that F-4 units in that time were distributed among the in-country war (South Vietnam) and the out-country war (North Vietnam). And, I wanted to be sure I got a piece of the action in the latter.

As so often happens, good news is accompanied by bad. I was to go through the *"Wild Weasel"* training program at Nellis AFB prior to reporting to the Korat AB, Thailand. In those days, and I am persuaded a lot has changed since then, there was not a lot of information given to the flying crews about high tech intelligence information. But, thanks to the camaraderie that exists among those who do the work, I knew that Wild Weasel was

1. A project designed to counter the Surface-to-Air Missile.

2. A project which had its roots in WWII and Korea in seeking out hostile electronic warfare sites under a wide range of ambitious code names.

3. A project which did not give a comfortable reassurance that I would complete 100 missions alive or even return as a POW.

Having made a deal with the devil there was only one way to go. Thanks to the generosity of Colonel John Giraudo, Commander of the 49th Tac Ftr Wing at nearby Spangdahlem Air Base, I was able to get recurrent in the "THUD" prior to leaving Germany and returning to the States. Did family things with folks in New York, reported to Nellis, and re-established ourselves with friends in Las Vegas from previous duty tours.

The training program run by the Lt Col Garry Willard and other survivors of previous Wild Weasel programs was thorough and good. One of the principal challenges was forming a pilot-EWO (electronic warfare officer) team to carry us through the training program and hopefully through 100 missions. As the senior officer in the class, I had the pick of the litter. Captain Fred Shannon was a long time SAC EWO but he thought like a fighter pilot. It was to be a relationship that served us both well.

Following eight weeks of training I installed my small but growing family in Fairfield, California near Travis AFB where flights from Southeast Asia recovered and I could get back to during breaks in the action.

I reported to McClellan AFB, California with 3 other brand new Wild Weasel crews to pick up newly modified F-105F aircraft especially fitted out for the Wild Weasel mission. The “F” was originally acquired as an instrument trainer to get F-105 crews ready for the challenging low-level all-weather nuclear weapons delivery mission. For the Wild Weasel mission, the EWO occupied the back seat and was equipped with sophisticated RHAW (radar homing and warning) gear. With the capability to fire the AGM-45 SHRIKE missile it was to prove a barely adequate weapon against the Soviet-supplied SA-2 system in North Vietnam. However, we were not sure of that at the time.

The log book shows we left McClellan on 8 March 1967 destination Korat AB, Thailand with intermediate stops at Hickam AFB, Hawaii and Anderson AFB, Guam. Approaching the coast of South Vietnam, our accompanying KC-135 tankers broke off sharply to the south and the safety of the big SAC base at U-Tapao. I still have vivid reflections of cruising over the Bon Son Plain at 25,000 feet wondering how in the world there could be a war going on in such beautiful, peaceful countryside. I was to get my answer in two days.

We were well received on arrival at Korat and escorted to the Officers Club that was to provide so much substance and entertainment over the next nine months. A flying tackle from behind reintroduced me to Group Captain Na We, the Thai Base Commander who had been a good friend in T-6 days at Goodfellow AFB. We have kept up that friendship unto this day as Na We rose to 3-star rank as Deputy Commander of the Royal Thai Air Force.

My wonderment about the beauty of the Bon Son Plain came full cycle when the man I was to relieve as Commander of the 13th Tac Str Sqdn, Lt Col Jerry Fitzgerald, called me in two days after arrival to notify me that my youngest brother, Captain Dick McInerney, 1st Cavalry Division, had been killed on the Bon Son Plain within minutes of the time we transited. Went back to the States for the burial at West Point while my wife, Mary Catherine, minded his two children in California. A helluva way to start a combat tour.

The first order of business was to figure out how to relate what we had learned in training to what was going on in theatre. Fortunately, the spring monsoon which so dominates Southeast Asia weather kept the sortie rate low but unfortunately the tactics were pretty much what we had been taught at Nellis—and I really didn't like them. The Wild Weasels would go in with the strike force (typically 16 F-105D aircraft) and "troll" using big figure eight patterns to get the SAM sites excited into firing missiles which the Wild Weasels would hope to dodge while pressing his own attack based on information received by the RHAW gear. Not the kind of odds this fighter pilot liked.

So, we huddled both the old crews who had a number of missions and the new guys who had come with me. At first the problem appeared devastating. The North Vietnamese had over 400 SAM sites spread over the country. And they had some 35 firing batteries that they moved around in an endless shell game. But the more we studied the problem, the less daunting it became. From intelligence we determined that some sites were occupied more often than others. We could establish a gambler's estimate on that likelihood. As the weather cleared and we started going "North" more frequently I could see a major problem - our Wild Weasel crews were viewing a SAM site as a source of electronic emissions rather than using traditional fighter pilot tools ("up by the crossroads near the bend in the river") to locate and attack them, so I established a SAM library of site photographs. Since the typical target recognition features were influenced by the fast changing seasonal foliage of North Vietnam, we established some rules on the currency of the required photographs.

We were starting to get our hands on the problem. How to execute? Taking a page out of the World War II history book and observing the results of freeing up the escort fighters from the B-17/B-24 force—*as long as the security of the bomber force remained the primary mission of the fighters*—I talked to our wing DO, Colonel "Scrappy" Johnson and the Commander, Colonel Bill Chairsell about our new tactic. Their combined answer was as good as any subordinate is ever going to get, "It's up to you, Jim. You are the head Wild Weasel. Do what you think is best. We won't second guess you as long as we don't lose airplanes".

With that we devised our tactics. Coming off the tankers a few minutes ahead of the strike force, the IRON HAND flight (two Wild Weasels with special armament and two F-105D aircraft with six 500-pound bombs) would enter the target area some 30-40 miles ahead of the strike force. Our purpose was to determine which of the SAM sites *of potential threat to the strike force* were occupied. It was a cat-and-mouse game including speed, deception and maneuver. Once we knew what we wanted to know, it was a diving turn out of the target area (the old THUD was built to move out on the deck and we took advantage of that fact) and a chandelle up behind that strike force. The strike force was most vulnerable when it rolled in on the dive bomb run and we were in position to take on any SAM site that tried to take advantage of that fact. If it was a long ways out, a SHRIKE would be lofted; if it was in close a direct shot was in order. If the site practiced emission control (EMCON) and turned his radar off, the SHRIKE would miss but the SA-2 site had lost his chance—and another USAF fighter was saved. If the site commander was a "hero" and stayed transmitting, we would usually be able to wipe him out before his missile was effective. After the strike force had safely egressed the area the IRON HAND flight would police up the other SAM sites observed to be occupied as long as our munitions held up - giving rise to the Wild Weasel slogan, *"First in—Last out"*.

Sounds simple but it required a great deal of discipline and courage on the part of the crews.

The Wild Weasels of the time were highly experienced THUD drivers who had earned their spurs by displaying the highest qualities of airmanship over an extended period of time. It was a year to be proud of many things but I am proudest of the fact that all the guys I brought over with me came back despite the fact that the air war in the North reached an intensity not to be seen for 5 more years and none of them had lost a plane they were escorting to a surface-to-air missile.

Jim McInerney WW # 295

Ryan's Raiders

One of the significant contributions to the neutralizing of the Soviet-supplied SA-2 air-defense system was made by a very special group of F-105 crews known as RYAN'S RAIDERS. The story of RYAN'S RAIDERS, named after the then Commander-in-Chief Pacific Air Forces (PACAF), and later Chief-of-Staff of the United States Air Force, General John D. Ryan offers an interesting insight into the courage, flexibility and adaptability of our United States Air Force tactical fighter crews.

As I was to find out later in a subsequent assignment to PACAF headquarters, in 1967 there was a spirited competition between the Air Force and the Navy at the Pacific Command Headquarters at Oahu as to who was making the most significant contribution to the air war over North Vietnam. Particularly galling to the Air Force was the great reported success of the Navy's A-6 attack plane operating around the clock in the Hanoi/Haiphong area. The Air Force really didn't have anything in PACAF at the time that could compete. Although the F-105 was designed with an all-weather weapon delivery capability, that design CEP (circular error probable) of twelve hundred feet realistically limited that capability to delivery of nuclear weapons—and no one was thinking seriously of that during the Southeast Asia air war.

I was to find out later in reading Lt Gen Gordon Graham's book, "Down For Double," that 7th Air Force headquarters in Ton Son Nhut Air Base took a very dim view of the PACAF suggestions that the F-105 be used to conduct night all-weather operations in the sectors assigned to the Air Force (one of the significant advances in tactical air operations in the Persian Gulf War was the elimination of service sectors which had inhibited our air operations in both the Korean and the Vietnam Wars). The 7th Air Force headquarters opposition notwithstanding, early in April 1967, twelve specially modified F-105F aircraft and aircrews showed up at Korat as part of PROJECT NORTH SCOPE. The Wing Commander, Brigadier General Bill Chairsell, assigned them to the 34th Tactical Fighter

Squadron commanded by my trailer-mate, Lt Col Fritz Treyz. I took an immediate interest in both the airplanes and the aircrews.

First, the airplanes. Upon close inspection it turned out they had several modifications designed to improve their bombing accuracy and make it more compatible with the conventional bombs they were to carry. I recognized them immediately as modifications I had personally recommended several years earlier as Director of the F-105D Category III test conducted at Nellis Air Force Base in 1962 and 1963. Unfortunately, funding for these simple mods simply was not forthcoming for the F-105 force but I assure you it was very gratifying to me to see a radar altimeter, as well as fast-scan and sector scan on the R-14A radar, installed in these high priority aircraft.

My pleasure in viewing the modifications to the airplanes was more than offset by my displeasure at the selection of the aircrews. In explaining that displeasure, let me back up by pointing out that at that time PACAF had four F-105 wings. In addition to our sister-wing (355th) at Takhli, Thailand, the 18th Tactical Fighter Wing at Kadena Air Base, and the 347th TFW at Yokota Air Base Japan rounded out the force. It turned out that the crews selected to be RYAN'S RAIDERS were relatively inexperienced F-105 pilots who had been sent back from Thailand in late 1966 to bases in Japan for further training. Half were selected to be front-seat aircraft commanders and half as back-seat weapons system operators. The individuals, all volunteers to enter the F-105 program with the understanding they would participate in the ROLLING THUNDER campaign in the single-seat F-105D, showed their "enthusiasm" for the program with their self-designed patch, an F-105 with a large carpenter's screw through it, and the slogan *"Peace Was Our Profession,"* a snide reference to the fact that many of them had come from the Strategic Air Command.

Now, you must understand that night, all-weather, low-level navigation is one of the most challenging tasks imposed on combat aircrews whether they are flying fighters or bombers. While significant advancements in technology in the last thirty years such as automatic terrain-following radar, LANTIRN, GPS, and moving map displays have made the task easier, let me assure one and all that in 1967, it was not a task to be assigned to relatively inexperienced aircrews.

My notes show that on the night of 26 April, the first NORTH SCOPE operations were launched with Major Bob Johnson, flying the WILD WEASEL SAM-suppression mission. Night operations were nothing special for the WILD WEASEL force since we already flew in support of the B-52 Arc Light missions against targets in the lower route packages and the early RYAN RAIDER missions were targeted against similar low-threat target areas. The tasking was to generate four sorties per night. That was not difficult for twelve dedicated aircraft even with their hi-tech (for the time) modifications. Both Fritz Treyz and I were worried about the relative inexperience of the aircrews. As in any tactical fighter organization, we were competitors as squadron commanders. But, as a result of several past tours together at Bitburg and Nellis—respectful competitors. Fritz, as the squadron commander, had very definite concern in addition to his worries over the deadly missions of his eighteen strike fighters going North against targets in what was then the most heavily defended target area in history. My concerns were somewhat different. Perhaps ones of guilt, for my Wild Weasel pilots had some ten to twenty and, in some cases, thirty times the hours in the Thud that the newly minted RYAN RAIDER crews had.

Our concerns meshed and became one as we quickly lost two Raider crews on the nights of 12 May and 15 May. In typical Air Force fashion we grounded the mission while management attempted to come to grips with the problem. From the very first day when the Raiders appeared I had been trying to figure out a way to apply the extensive F-105 experience my Wild Weasels had to the solution of the problem. While it was clear to me that the Wild Weasel pilots could have done the mission by themselves, as they had for years in Europe and the Pacific, it was not clear how the Electronic Warfare Officers (EWO's) would fit into the scheme. In an effort to find out, I tested my own EWO, Fred Shannon, to the limits. After the final post-strike refueling coming back from an IRON HAND mission, I would turn the flight over to number three, the element leader, and go off on our own to put Fred through the drill of working the terrain avoidance and contour mapping modes of the R-14-A radar. While the Wild Weasel birds did not have the RYAN RAIDER mods I previously described, it was clear to me that stepping up to the plate would be no problem once the general principles were understood. After a couple of missions, aided and abetted by the fact that the F-105F was built as a trainer and that enabled me to coach Fred through the motions in a way that could not be done in other tandem-seated aircraft such as the F-4, I was able to formulate a plan which would enable us to simultaneously apply the experience of the Wild Weasel crew to the enormity of the task at hand and the very low morale of the Raider crews.

And, that was simply to suggest, in a properly orchestrated way, that operation NORTH SCOPE could be taken over by the WILD WEASEL aircrews. I emphasize properly orchestrated for I can not tell you how many great ideas I have seen in the course of the last forty years which have been derailed because all the right bases had not been touched. Absent the benefit of that knowledge, I started with my own Wild Weasel crews simply saying, "if Shannon can do it, you can." "You bet," came the cry in response. Next was the 388th Wing staff. Fortunately, General Chairsell had personal knowledge of many of my Wild Weasel pilots in his previous roles as Commander, 49th Tactical Fighter Wing at Spangdahlem, Germany, and his enthusiastic support swayed the Wing staff.

Had I known of General Graham's reservations earlier described, I might not have been so aggressive at talking the proposal to 7th Air Force headquarters at Ton Son Nhut Air Base near Saigon. But, fools tread where angels fear, and my log book shows that I briefed the 7th Air Force Staff including the Commander, General William Wallace (Spike) Momyer, on Thursday, 4 May, with "unexpected results" which surprised many of his staff. Perhaps it was helpful that I had served under General Momyer in the waning days of the Korean War when he commanded the 8th Tactical Fighter Wing. Also, instrumental to that favorable decision was the presence at the briefing of then L/Col Garry Willard, Commander of the Wild Weasel training program at Nellis AFB who assured one and all that the Wild Weasel training program at Nellis could be adjusted to insure that all graduating crews were fully capable of performing around the clock all-weather bombing missions upon arrival in theater.

Without further ado the program was changed. At Korat the Wild Weasel crews started picking up the NORTH SCOPE mission. The Raider crews joyfully moved into the front seat of the F-105 in other squadrons—with special glee on the part of those who thought RYAN RAIDERS meant consignment to the back seat of a THUD for 100 missions. Wild Weasel crews from Nellis started arriving with the full understanding that their first fifteen to twenty missions would be night-all weather strikes into the heartland of the North Vietnam air defense systems. And, that was very helpful to them being able to see, under relatively favorable conditions, the cockpit displays of potentially dangerous threats.

The RYAN RAIDERS program continued through the end of 1967 when it was supplanted by the first combat deployment of the F-111A in Project Harvest Reaper. Despite the two early losses with the original crews only one RYAN RAIDER aircraft was lost during the remainder of the program.

But, the payoff, which many of us failed to realize at the time, was tremendous. For four sorties a night—a relatively small investment considering the size of our deployed forces in Vietnam and Thailand, we were forcing the North Vietnamese air defense system to work around the clock. From air defense radars burning precious reserves of diesel fuel in their generators to the big 85 and 100 mm guns to the ominous SA-2 to the MiG-17s and -21s, it was a tremendous strain on their system. It was particularly dangerous for the MiGS and I still have vivid memories of a MiG flying over me as we were flying at very low level down the Red River and watching him explode on contact with "THUD RIDGE". They simply were not designed for night operations while we in the F-105 were operating in our design envelope.

My days of Ryan Raider operations come to a sudden halt on the night of 7 September when the engine on F-105F S/N #63-8260 blew just as we were closing on the tanker. I shut it down and tried an air-start but when I saw the tailpipe temperature going through the red line while the RPM was doing down, I know it was not going to work. I shut the engine down again and ordered Fred Shannon to bail out. Unfortunately, Fred broke his leg in the bailout ending his brilliant combat career. I ended up tangled with my parachute in a tree and hung upside down for three hours until a chopper from Korat got me out. I was able to pick up a replacement EWO Captain Cal Miller who did a superb job filling in for Fred Shannon on the IRON HAND missions but never had the need to upgrade him to RYAN RAIDER status given the fresh supply of new crews arriving from Nellis. I don't think anyone who has ever seen a SAM fired at him at night will ever forget it. And, as the days of summer turned in the fall and winter, those of us who were responsible for testing the North Vietnam air defense system could tell we were winning. One of the ways in which the RYAN RAIDERS closely complemented the WILD WEASELS was in providing last minute up-to-date information on the SA-2 site activity. The

North Vietnamese were very capable of moving their 35 SAM batteries around some four hundred prepared sites and the Raider crews coming in from their night missions could tell the IRON HAND crews exactly which they would be facing when escorting the strike forces going up in the day time. That information vastly increased the effectiveness of the WILD WEASELS and allowed them to significantly de-grade the surface to air missile threat. No doubt they regrouped after President Johnson declared the bombing halt in January 1968, and wrecked havoc on the B-52 force when the latter group was committed to the Hanoi/Haiphong area in the Linebacker operations, but that's another story to be told by another person. Gordon Graham was clearly correct in his assessment of the F-105's capability to destroy point targets at night—as you would expect from a man who himself had commanded the first tactical fighter wing equipped with the remarkable aircraft. What he failed to predict was the impact OPERATION NORTH SCOPE would have on other aspects of the air war.

Jim McInerney WW # 295

Story by Tom "Bear" Wilson WW # 160

An Air Force Cross 36 Years Late

During my USAF career as an electronic warfare officer I flew in various roles in several different aircraft, yet to this day, many years after climbing up the ladder of the enormous F-105 for the last time, I identify myself as a Thud Wild Weasel. I think too often of it, and when engaged in conversation, I tend to talk too much of it. I am not unique. There is a brotherhood of those who ventured into the terrible Hanoi defenses, or over the northeast railroad where there was absolutely nowhere to hide, or into the bloody cauldron of Thai Nguyen. There, in April of 1967, the North Vietnamese massed their defenses to protect their proudest symbol of modern industry developed under communism, the Thai Nguyen Iron and Steel Works, which had been threatened since February 1967. When the American strike forces arrived (no surprise), the New Peoples Army (NPA) threw everything at them, filling the skies with light and medium and heavy flak, launching dozens of MiG-17's, MiG-19's and MiG-21s, and scores of big Mach 3 SA-2 SAM's. Our commanders, many of whom had fought in the skies of Germany and North Korea, had seen nothing like it.

Col. (later B/G) Robin Olds, commander of the F-4 Phantom Wing at Ubon (who flew a year tour over Germany in WW-II), said of Thai Nguyen: "The flak. Oh God, the flak! … I have seen flak at high altitude and at low level over Berlin, the Ruhr, Magdeburg, Stuttgart, Merseberg, Schweinfurt, Wurzburg and Tarnewitz. I have seen it come up to darken the sky in flame and smoke. … But I have never seen the absolute sheets of fire that erupted over Thai Nguyen. A nearly solid wall of orange fire blazed in front of and all around us. …"

Lt Col (later Col) Bobby Wayne, a squadron commander (another West Pointer who had been graduated early to see combat in WW-II), called it the worst he'd ever seen — "the heaviest defenses in the history of air warfare." Ever instructive, he would add that there is always a way to survive and accomplish the mission. He urged us to "fly smart."

But that was then, and as the years passed, many of the individual combat missions I'd participated in blended together, and specific actions became forgotten. There were exceptions, the hairiest memories and the funniest ones remained vivid. For instance, I recalled very well the mission where our Wild Weasel flight commander deservedly won the Medal of Honor. Also, in my prioritized memory, was a big mission to protect the force as they struck Thai Nguyen — as we had been doing daily for weeks — which had ended up in a wild yet productive mission.

The 357th squadron was leading the morning "go." Capt. Charlie Hanson and his EWO, Capt. John Geiger, were flight lead, and Lt. Gordy Jenkins, number two. We (Jerry Hoblit, my front-seater, and I) took off as number three. Another experienced Wild Weasel crew, Maj. Ben Fuller and Capt. Norm Frith, from the 354th squadron, were number four.

Since there were a god-awful number of active SAM sites in range of the target, as we crossed the Red River we split into two two-ship elements (each acting independently), so we could have two attacking Wild Weasel elements. "Surrounding the poor bastards," as one pilot joked.

We flew on toward Thai Nguyen, flying medium high, and Charlie angled north, using terrain masking and hugging Thud Ridge while he positioned for attack. We found and struck a site near downtown Thai Nguyen, releasing our four CBU's, and Maj. Ben Fuller followed us in and did the same. As we pulled off target, number two announced that our flight leader, Charlie Hanson, had been hit by a SAM that had torn off part of his tail. We immediately turned north to find and preoccupy the site while flight lead and his wingman egressed.

The SAM operator fired again, that time at us. I called the launch and Jerry had no great trouble acquiring it visually. Our wingman pulled back some to watch the duel. Jerry said the missile was glued in place, that his SAM-dodging techniques weren't working. He pulled one way then the other, but the missile made minor adjustments and continued to track. Finally, at what seemed far too late, Jerry yanked so hard into the missile that the g-meter had to be pegged. The missile over-corrected, slid past, and detonated.

Jerry then continued his climb, positioned, and dove on the well-camouflaged site in a high-angle strafe. While we never claimed credit for a site kill, I hope to hell the operator soiled his pants, because I came close.

Jerry assumed control of the flight and, as we followed the strike force out of the pack (with no losses), received word that an RF-4C (Chicago) had been shot down and we were closest. Jerry assigned Maj. Fuller and Capt. Frith (our number four) to escort Hanson/Geiger's badly damaged Thunderchief to safety. Lt. Jenkins fell back on our wing and we turned back to locate the downed RF-4. My recollection is that Jerry saw the glint of a survival mirror from one of the downed crewmembers and then I saw it and confirmed the position. After transferring responsibility for the RESCAP to another flight (with more fuel remaining in their tanks) Jerry proceeded toward the tanker, anxious to refuel.

We were very low on fuel, as was our wingman. When the tanker was diverted to accompany Capt. Hanson, who was missing more than three feet of his vertical stabilizer, to Takhli, Jerry asked for vectors for a straight-in approach to Udorn AB, which was closest. Except for the facts that we landed on fumes, and the transient Crew Chief found small arms punctures in our bird, the remainder was uneventful. After a thorough inspection we were cleared for a one-time flight and returned to base at Takhli (as did flight lead, who was missing).

* * *

A few months later, at my new assignment to an F-4D unit in Germany, I received a letter from the wing awards and decorations officer at Takhli explaining that Jerry and I had been put in for a number of medals for various missions we'd flown. Among those were two Air Force Crosses, one for the mission on April 23rd. I recall thinking that while it had been a pretty good mission for me, it had been a great one for Jerry and, in that instance he was the more deserving one. When I was awarded a Silver Star for the mission, I felt it was justified.

* * *

Then all of those years passed. While Jerry and I remained in close contact (and still do; there are no closer comrades than those whose lives have depended upon one another), we never got down to comparing medals received.

In 2000, I received a phone call asking if I would participate in an interview for the History Channel's "Suicide Missions – the Wild Weasels." I agreed. It was sometime about then that I discovered that Jerry had received one less Silver Star medal than I had. When I compared orders numbers, I also found that it had been for the mission of 23 April 1967.

I set out then to learn more about what had happened to the medal and to round up some help. Most helpful were the facts that Col (Ret.) Gordy Jenkins had a flight log of the mission in question, detailing times and certain specifics; and our squadron commander at the time, Col (Ret.) Ben Murph, had kept specific information regarding the missions in which battle damage had been incurred, including our mission that day, and wrote it all down in a letter. Another Takhli commander was not as helpful, misunderstanding and thinking I was asking for a medal higher than my pilot had received, never realizing I was asking for the opposite. I suppose he would have had a cow if I'd told him that at my base in Germany I'd turned down a fifth Silver Star medal that I'd felt was not deserved.

Finally, I wrote a letter to the only person I knew who could set me on a proper next path. He was also the highest ranking officer I knew. The Vice Chief of Staff of the Air Force (General Richard Myers, another superb Wild Weasel pilot) wrote back that I should contact the office of the Chief of Personnel of the Air Force. Before I responded, a letter arrived from a Chief Master Sergeant there, outlining the required steps to make the medal happen. Write it up (which I'd already done) and, for sure consideration, gain the support of a congressman.

Again, I wrote down the chain of events in a letter that required only a signature, and (since my own congressman was of the wrong persuasion) took it to Jerry's congressman. A helpful assistant retyped my missive on Congressional stationery and trotted it in for a signature. Before leaving I asked that if it happened, would the assistant make sure the medal was sent to me and not Jerry, and he agreed.

A year later, in May 2003, I was given a call by the congressman's office. "*Someone* at the Pentagon," said the assistant, "had made it happen." I still do not know who. Honest.

In June of 2003, Jerry "Hognose" Hoblit received a phone call from a Captain in the 357th Fighter Squadron at Davis Monthan AFB asking if he (and I) would appear for a speech to the squadron discussing fighter tactics. Jerry cajoled me into going along.

Two weeks later, when Jerry went into the "briefing room" in the Officer's club, a hundred fighter pilots and several general officers were on hand. So was Col. (Ret.) Leo K. Thorsness, Medal of Honor (MOH), who spoke eloquently about his assistant flight commander and pinned on the well-deserved Air Force Cross. Jerry's close friends, such as Billy R. Sparks, Wild Weasel extraordinaire (and best man at Jerry's wedding) were there as well.

Jerry tried to get me to say some words, but I refused. "This one's all for you."

Tom "Bear" Wilson WW # 160

Story by Billy R. Sparks (AKA Barracuda) WW # 330

Something All Fighter Pilots Would Like To Do!

Having been a totally unreconstructed Fighter Pilot for 21 years, all of which were in Tactical Fighters, I have a very biased view of SAC. TAC crews pulled about twice the TDY load that SAC crews did and got $1.00 per diem. We went for 4 month stretches while SAC went for less than 1 month and got R & R each tour. Enough bitching!

I delivered an F-105D to the 355TFW in '68 and was asked to ferry an F105D - (818) back to the States (Takhli to McClelland) for NDI (Non-Destructive Investigations) tests since, I think, the bird had the most combat time of any THUD in the inventory. 818 deployed with the 563TFS in '65 and stayed in SEA until it took a large round through the left wing spar in '68. The jock got the bird into Da Nang and a RAM (Rear Area Maintaince) team put a big reinforcement around the spar that was guaranteed to get the bird back to the States for testing. It made a big ugly bulge in the left wing just outboard of the strut. I was handy from a delivery to the 355th; so, Col Girado, the 355th Wing Commander asked me to fly it back. Anything is better than a ride on a Military Airlift Command (MAC) aircraft, so, I said, "Yes, sir". The bird was limited to takeoffs with only internal fuel and a max of 2"G" in flight. All of the avionics were in perfect shape. It looked shitty—worked well. I flew to Clark Air Base in the Philippines with two refuelings and picked up a KC-135 air refueling tanker that would take me to California via Guam and Hickam. We ran into a Typhoon as we left the Philippines (PI). We were in solid weather and turbulence for over 3 hours as they flew me south of the core of the storm. I saw 4 degrees North latitude on the Doppler at the farthest south part of the trip. The tanker crew did a wonderful job of keeping me out of the worst part of the turbulence and we never had more than 2 "Gs" for the whole trip. I left them 1,000 nautical miles (NM) out of Guam and met them with a case of beer when they landed. I took the Officers to the Guam Club for booze berries and we were enjoying ourselves when some Jerk of a Strategic Air Command (SAC) Lt. Col. Aircraft Commander (AC) came over and told us to leave since the COMBAT CREWS were coming in. I had just made Major, had also completed my 2nd combat tour at Takhli, and was wearing my 100 Mission Patch; so, I told him to attempt a solo sexual act and threw a drink in his face. He left. The tanker crew was a little nervous and decided to leave and as they were going, the same idiot brought a second Lt. Col. Aircraft Commander (AC) over to tell me to leave. I doused both SAC pukes and escorted them back to a table where both of their crews were sitting. I offered to take them out and teach them some manners and had zero takers.

During this time, the Colorado Air National Guard came into the Bar. They were on their way home from a year in South Vietnam and were not charmed with anything. Their Boss decided that we should chase all of the SAC candy asses out of the bar and we did. The Air Cops were called, a small altercation occurred, and the bar was closed. We, me and the (Colorado Air National Guard) CANG, repaired to the grass in front of the club with several jugs of booze and made rather nasty remarks about the folk that were going into the Club for a Dining Out. We finally ran out of booze and went to bed about 2400 hours. I was awakened at 0400 and given a written order to leave the base signed by the 3-Star Guam Boss. I went down to Base Ops and met the tankers and we flew to Hickham and then to McClellan. I made it back to Nellis several days after the letter of reprimand landed on the desk of my boss, Grady Morris (Wing DO). He had a yard of my butt and took me to see Buckshot White, Fighter Weapons Wing Commander (FWW/CC), who also dined on my posterior. They both escorted me to the Tactical Fighter Weapons Center Commander (TFWC/CC), Maj. Gen. Zack Taylor, for his comments. He asked me if I had done all those things and I said "YES, SIR". He asked why and I had no real answer except that I was probably crazy. He told me that I was obviously nuts and said that since I had so angered the 3-Star (Lt. General) in Guam, I was prohibited from going back there for a year. He then had me hold out my hand and smacked me on the wrist—case closed. Col. Grady Morris, my Boss- AKA the Alligator- took me off base to the old 25 Club at about 0830 local and bought me several Martinis and congratulated me on doing something that "ALL FIGHTER PILOTS WOULD LIKE TO DO". That was the end of it. Can you imagine what would happen in today's Air Force? That may let some of you know how much most Fighter Pilots liked SAC..

Billy Sparks WW # 330

Story by Robert W. King, W W # 484

Pre-emptive Shrike Launches

In the 561st TFS, flying from Korat RTAFB in 1972, we lofted pre-emptive Shrikes on a fairly regular basis on "force goes" to high threat areas. We also briefed this tactic to the non-Wild Weasel guys because we had a couple of incidents where the MiGCAP or the strike guys saw the Shrike in flight, yelled "SAM", and called for a break. Calling a SAM launch when only a Shrike had been fired was particularly bad when supporting B-52 operations. The B-52s were spring loaded to the "all tensed up" position and reacted to almost every Anti-Radiation Missile (ARM) launch with great alarm.

I vaguely recall it being discussed as a possible tactic among the Wild Weasel crews as early as my tour with the 333rd at Takhli in 1968, but I don't recall ever actually deliberately launching in that mode on that tour. Of course, there was the day that Bob Beck pre-empted a Shrike from level flight on a "patrol the border" mission over Laos after the bombing pause was ordered by the President in November 68. (Bob was Major Robert J. Beck, Command Bar-Stooler and highly experienced Thud driver previously stationed at Spangdahlem AB. He was a Sierra Hotel dive-bomber.) It was a couple of months later when that happened. My memory says it was in Feb 1969, but I'm too lazy to dig out my logbook. It was mid-morning. We were cruising at altitude southbound over Laos a few miles west of the west end of the DMZ. I had my head down in the cockpit updating the Doppler when, from the corner of my eye, I saw the Shrike come off the outboard station!

Being the Wild Weasel Bear of our little crew and in charge of listening for enemy radar signals (There were none.), and being an all-around alert chap, I said, "What the hell was that?" and then asked Bob what he was shooting at. He mumbled a bit and then said "We'll talk about it at the debrief." So I held my water until we got on the ground. In the step-van on the way in from the flight line to debrief, I got the whole story. As you know, there aren't a lot of suitable locations to stash loose items such as checklists, maps, and whatnot in the cockpit of the Thud. Bob's solution for map storage, when it was not in use, was to stick it under his left thigh.

In the course of stretching, he had shifted his weight on the seat and the map had slid off the seat to the very small and narrow area between the seat and the left console. He then tried to reach the map with his fingertips. So, in an effort to force his left hand a bit farther into the narrow space between the seat and the console and to recapture the map, he moved his right hand from its normal position on the stick and re-gripped it with his right wrist rotated so that the thumb was pointed down instead of up. In that unfamiliar configuration, while fishing for a map near the cockpit floor with his left hand, his right pinkie came in contact with the pickle button on the stick. The Shrike, ever obedient to its electrical signals, launched on an independent search and destroy mission over southern Laos.

It was astonishing how much attention we garnered after landing back at Takhli without that AGM-45 hanging on the outboard. With the bombing halt still in progress, the Wild Weasels hadn't expended a Shrike in months. As Bob put it later that night at the bar, "I've been on this base nine months, but I had to debrief to guys whom I'd never seen or heard of before this afternoon."

Robert W. King, Weasel # 484

Story by Clyde "Bear" Hayman WW # 82

Early Wild Weasel Training?

When the Wild Weasel started, they were F-100Fs. This was quickly changed to F-105Fs. The F-100 Wild Weasels (WW) were all TDY (Temporary Duty) which meant that they were Wild Weasels for six month, or less, and then scheduled to return to their home unit. The F-105 Wild Weasels were PCS (Permanent Change of Station) to SEA which meant that we were to be in the Wild Weasels for over 6 months and then reassigned to some unit most likely not our old unit.

The training we got as the first F-105 Wild Weasel was scant. The pilots, of course, were all flight-lead qualified, which meant that they had considerable flight time in the bird. The EWOs were from everywhere but tactical aviation. We were from B-52s (SAC), B-57s (ADC), and T-29s (ATC). Our training in the F-105F consisted of ejection seat training (about two hours) and whatever your pilot wanted you to know. Since the F-105F was in essence two single seat fighter cockpits in a single airplane, the pilot had all the systems, as did the back seat. He was in the habit of doing everything himself, and so we, the EWOs, weren't expected to do anything but to operate the Electronic Equipment which he knew nothing about. We had been given a couple days of briefings, on its operation by the engineers who had designed the electronic equipment, and how they thought it was to be employed: i.e., homing down the beam or making a triangulation maneuver. (We never did these things in combat that I know about) We had learned to use the equipment in a crude simulator put together by North American Aviation at Long Beach airport in California. After about 15 hours of flying on the Eglin AFB test range against a very cooperative SA-2, we were deemed ready for combat.

An interesting side note as to how unprepared the program was: our orders included a list of flight equipment we were supposed to have when we got to Elgin. In this list was a G-suit; and, being in B-52s, I, of course, did not have one. When I went to our supply, i.e. the SAC wing supply, they told me they didn't have any G-suits. They suggested that I go to the other side of the base to the Air Material Supply and see if they had any.

When I got there, the Airman said he didn't have any, but an old sergeant said "Wait a minute" and led me to the back of the warehouse and found a box of six G-suits that were not on the inventory lists. He told me that in the five years he had been at the base I was the first to ask for a G-suit and that I could have all six. If I had known anything about fighters, I would have thanked him and taken only one, since a G-suit never wears out or breaks. But not knowing S— about fighters and G-suits I said, "OK" and took all six.

When I got to Eglin with my six G-suits, I discovered that the other EWOs had had less luck than I and had not been able to get a suit at their original bases. Furthermore, Eglin's personal equipment supply didn't have enough G-suits for us. In other words no one had done any more planning than to make a list of what we needed. Fortunately, because of my dumb-ass ignorance, we all got a G-suit, and no delays in training were incurred.

When our combat tour was over, almost all the Wild Weasel III-1 (as we were later called: Wild Weasel III being the F-105 Weasel and -1 being the class number) the pilots Ken Rickman, Rick Westcott, John Hill, and Jim O'Neil; and EWOs John Buick, Pete Tsouprake, George Kennedy and I were assigned to Nellis AFB and to the Wild Weasel School.

When we got to Nellis, the Wild Weasel school was up and running. Gary Willard was in charge, and he had had most of the F-100F (WW1) EWOs reassigned from their home bases to Nellis. There was Jack Donovan, Rick Morgan, Marsh Goldberg, John Mojica, Walt Lifsey, and Frank O'Donnell. Only four of the F-100 pilots other than Willard were there: Allen Lamb, Shep Kerr, Ed White, and Maury Frick. Lamb was assigned to the Fighter Weapons School and the F-4C test program. There were three F-105D single seat pilots in the school, Gordy Lewis, Gordy Walcott, and Jack Carson. They had been assigned to the Fighter Weapons School F-105 section; but, because the F-105 was being rapidly phased out of the inventory by attrition and was to be replaced with the F-111, the F-105 Weapons School had been stopped.

These guys were doing a great job of training the new Wild Weasel crews. They had everything well in hand and had set up great academic classes. In fact I would sit in on Jack Donavan's lectures every time I got a chanc, which was quite often. I never tired of Jack's presentation. You may observe that there wasn't much need for us new EWOs, except to fly in the back seat on training missions. The pilots were needed as they had the actual Wild Weasel combat experience that the F-105D pilots didn't.

The toughest part about the job was on one flight for each class, the "student" pilot flew with a Wild Weasel EWO who had been in combat as a Wild Weasel, and the student EWO with a seasoned Wild Weasel Pilot. A fact of life was that when you take EWOs from slow moving non-maneuvering B-52s and put them in a fighter, some of them at first are going to get air sick. I was one. Everyone would joke with these guys and after a few flights they would lose their nervousness and be OK. This was why at times the job of flying with "student" Wild Weasels was tough. Some of the "student" pilots would intentionally try to get the EWO instructors sick. They never did, but one came damn close to getting me when he ran the cockpit temperature up high and then put the aircraft through its maneuvers.

The Wild Weasel school had been assigned the F-4C Wild Weasel planes that had not been deployed to combat because of massive equipment problems. Most of the EWOs and a few of our F-105 pilots, along with most of the F-100 pilot, were assigned to the F-4C flight. We had no real job except to fly. Since the F-4C at that time was a crew of two pilots, I was again put in the back seat with no training and had to learn everything on my own. It was fun, because all we did was fly out on the gunnery ranges and try to bounce other fighters. I learned to use the radar in a tactical situation, but not how to run intercepts in the way the system was designed to do. I never did any radar bombing, as at that time, all tactical fighters in the AF were bombing in combat only by visual means.

I was assigned to give a class to teach "Sam Site Recognition." This was a class that had been put in the course by someone of rather limited knowledge of North Viet Nam, and no one wanted to teach the course. I got some slides made of all the equipment that was in a SA-2 battery, a lot of slides of SA-2 sites, and presented a lecture that boiled down to that SA-2s were extremely well camouflaged and you mostly likely wouldn't recognize it until it shot a missile at you.

To establish that I wasn't a complete idiot, I offered an unofficial briefing about Thailand and the people. When at Korat, I had become good friends with three Royal Thai Officers and spent most of my free time with them. I spent my R&Rs in their homes and almost every night would eat and drink with them. On the day of my 100th mission, every F-105 flight that landed at Korat had a Thai AF T-6 V formation greet it. They were flying it for me, but I could not tell them my takeoff or landing time as it was top secret. In thinking back, I should have told them to look on the Officers Club bulletin board where the flying schedule, which was Top Secret but not marked as such, was posted.

In my ramblings, you may have detected that I knew more about the Thais than the average GI. Unlike the bullshit Site Recognition class, I enjoyed describing the Thai culture and cuisine. I enjoyed pointing out things such as if you by chance go to a Thai movie, never sit on the main floor; go up to the more expensive balcony seats. The reason was that the Thais eat fruit at movies instead of pop corn and take great pleasure in throwing the peels over the rail onto the heads of those below. This lecture wasn't going to make anyone a better Wild Weasel and would only save someone's life by preventing them from slipping on a banana peel. So much for my contribution to the Wild Weasel school.

Actually, we contributed a great deal because of one person: Bill Hickey. Unlike most other Air Force units, we had a Technical Representative from the equipment designer company. This was Bill. Bill was the outstanding man for this job. He, in many ways, was one of us, even though he was a civilian. He was always at the bar with us and always had a drink in his hand; however, unlike most of us, I never saw Hickey drunk.

Since Wild Weasels were by then a success, follow-on designs were coming. Bill sought out our ideas, needs and suggestions, and with the Wisdom of Solomon, he sorted out the wheat from the chaff. We provided lots of information and became unofficial consultants to Bill's company and, for that matter, any other company that was interested. Because of Bill's eagerness to seek out our ideas, his company was producing the equipment that the Air Force later bought. It was a win-win situation, but if it hadn't been for Bill, and his personality, it would have never happened. It is interesting that so many people, each making his contribution big or small, made things happen. Without these inputs and Bill passing them on in 1967 and 68, the F-4G Wild Weasel may not have been a success and saved so many lives in Desert Storm. (Bill also for many years kept the Wild Weasel Society alive by running it almost single handedly.)

Unfortunately, or fortunately, depending on how you look at it, this situation ended, and the flying club was shifted into other jobs. Several of us were shifted to positions in the Fighter Weapons Center as there had been no Electronic Warfare Officers at the center before 1967. I was assigned to the F-111 Test Force. This was another two seat aircraft that the Air Force was going to man with two pilots, and I again flew in this aircraft without any formal training.

The Wild Weasel program was, at first, a rapidly drawn together event; rules and regulations meant nothing. Since no one had ever done it before there was no one to train us. The concept was go out and kill SAM sites. Discover how, and come back and tell us. This is how the Wild Weasel training started. However, I strongly believe that the follow-on crews got great training at Nellis because of the program set up by Gary Willard, Jack Donovan, and others. The school saved lives. The first Wild Weasels took a heavy toll, but, with the good training and changes in weapons and tactics, the loss rate dropped dramatically in later years.

Clyde "Bear" Hayman WW # 82

Story by Jim Winzell, WW # 1098

Linebacker-II: The Eleven Days of Christmas

I came to the Wild Weasel mission via the Air Force Academy. I had been determined to be a fighter pilot, but I received a major disappointment when I took my senior physical and failed the eye test. Since I still wanted to fly, I decided to become a navigator. After Nav school, we had to decide what specialty to enter. The choices were straight Nav, Radar Nav (Bombardier) or Electronic Warfare Officer (EWO). I picked EWO only because the recruiting team had the best pitch. After graduation from EWO school, it was now time to pick an operational assignment. Actually, "pick" was not really accurate. We had 90% of our assignment pool as SAC, B-52 crewmembers. And I was one of them, which led to B-52 initial upgrade training at Castle AFB, Merced, California.

I spent this initial formative time either flying, pulling ground alert, pulling airborne alert or going TDY for Arc Light (SEA) tours. Let me explain each of these challenges. Flying was spent preparing for nuclear warfare by navigating low level (500') routes, usually at night, in weather and popping up to drop a simulated bomb (I remember one particularly rough mission where the gunner, flying in the tail, came back with a cracked helmet and a broken arm due to the turbulence). Ground alert consisted of living in a concrete bunker under the ground and being prepared to dash to your fully loaded B-52 and to take off within 15 minutes any time of day or day of the week. We were usually on rotations where you pulled alert 5 days and were off 3—flying on your off days. Airborne alert had the same effect except you were flying the fully loaded B-52 for 24 hours along the Northern border of Russia instead of sitting on the ground. There were some interesting aspects to this mission. First, since you were flying in the Arctic, compasses were of little use. Because we did not have precision navigation equipment like GPS, we had to use a less sophisticated means of navigation—three star fixes using a sextant! In addition, we would get our "go code" over HF radio that was filled with static due to the Aurora Borealis. Think about it—here is a crew of twenty-something's flying a B-52 loaded with up to four thermonuclear, "city-buster" bombs, navigating along the border of Russia using 18th Century techniques and waiting for the go-ahead on a system that was almost unreadable. 'Tis a wonder the world survived!

In 1966, the decision was made to commit the B-52 to the war in South East Asia (SEA). We were selected to be part of the initial cadre to begin operating from Guam, a part of the Micronesian Islands, in the South Pacific. That first three month tour proved how little we really knew about "tactical" bombing from an eight-engine strategic bomber. We initially tried formation flying on the bomb run in a three ship "finger tip" formation with wings "overlapping." It made for a tight three ship bomb pattern but was extremely difficult because of the aerodynamic interaction of these fast moving, giant aircraft. This fact of nature—the interaction of two large bodies in flight—was dramatically, and fatally, demonstrated when two B-52s collided on the way to their target in SEA due to the "sucking action" created when they attempted to change position while in formation flight. I was painfully aware of this incident because my crew was to fly the lead aircraft. We were substituted at the last minute by a sister crew—good friends who lost their lives developing tactics for a strange war in a strange land. And those tactics changed as a result of the accident. Instead of formation "finger tip" bomb runs we would fly three ships in trail with one mile spacing, all dropping based on the leader's bombs using the gunners fire control radar for spacing and the Nav's stop watch for timing. This tactics change would come back to haunt SAC and the B-52 crews.

My second tour was six months on Guam flying 12 hour combat sorties to South Vietnam. Six hours inbound, with refueling over the Philippines, ten minutes over land, bomb release and six hours back to the island. This routine was repeated every third day with little to show other than an occasional secondary in a "suspected truck park", I can not begin to describe the drain this had on us—until we were called in to help out at a skirmish occurring at a Marine outpost called Khe Sahn. Suddenly and decisively this power we had built over the years came in to play—big time. We were the Marines' "Close Air Support" dropping within yards of their lines, night after night without an errant bomb. We had a mission and it worked!

My third and last Arc Light Tour was spent flying out of Okinawa and Thailand. We were now venturing further North in the B-52 and found ourselves in harm's way. My stock as an EWO increased as the threat increased. We found ourselves on missions to bomb the Mu Gia Pass—a particularly vulnerable piece of the Ho Chi Min Trail. I remember one mission on a very dark and foreboding night into North Vietnam. We were lead in a three ship. At the IP, the Radar Nav declared the release point was in the middle of a massive thunderhead. You have to have experienced a SEA thunderstorm to realize why this put the hair on the back of our heads on end. There is nothing that compares to the power of these thunder boomers—rising to over 50,000 feet and crackling with lightening bolts, tornado clouds and encased in blackness like a bottomless ink well. Well, this target had been classified as POR—which meant Press On Regardless. So that is what we did—into the jaws of death. I can remember not being able to read any of my instruments due to the vibration but not caring because I knew no radar could find us in this mess. But what I most remember is the copilot gasping as we eggressed from the target that he had seen our bombs going past his windscreen—GOING UP! I'm not sure that really happened—but it could have. The target must have been important because the crew got the Distinguished Flying Cross for the mission.

At the end of this tour I got an opportunity that changed my career and my view of where I wanted to go in life. I had had enough of flying 12 hour sorties that ended up with making toothpicks out of jungle trees. So in 1970 I accepted an offer by the Air Force to send me back to school to get my Master's Degree. What a deal this was. In addition to the Air Force paying all school expenses, I continued to received full pay and benefits—unlike most of my classmates who were working to support their families. I guess this was a partial payback for the long separation my family had endured. Having milked the system by squeezing a 12 month curriculum into 18 months, I graduated with an MS in Ops Research and most of my PhD course work completed.

Part of the deal that came with this opportunity to get a graduate degree was the stipulation that I would have to "volunteer" for another SEA tour. That was the bad news. The good news was I would get to pick the aircraft I would fly. I had my fill of flying the heavies and wanted to finally fulfill that dream of flying fighters—maybe not as a pilot but at least to experience what it meant to be in the business. So I made the fateful decision to become a Wild Weasel "Bear" (the nickname given to the Wild Weasel backseater—which has dubious origins).

So in the summer of 1972, we sold everything, bought a motor home and began a 5,000 mile circuit of the U.S. that would end up at Nellis AFB, Las Vegas with my introduction to the F-105G Wild Weasel. Flying a two-seat fighter was everything I had anticipated and more. The more in this case was the Wild Weasel mission. Our responsibility was to protect the force from a new threat called SAM or Surface to Air Missile. The SA-2 was designed by the Russians to take out high flying bombers like the B-52 and, in fact, had its first success shooting down Gary Powers' U-2. The Russians had provided them to the North Vietnamese who built an integrated air defense system around Hanoi that, at that time, was the densest concentration of antiaircraft systems in the world. Our fighters flying in NVN were getting hammered by the SAMs so the Air Force created a quick reaction capability that armed a two seat F-100 with special electronic equipment that could located the SA-2 radar and anti-radiation missiles, like the Shrike, that would home in on the radar signals. The F-100 was soon followed by the F-105 which allowed the Wild Weasel to keep up with the F-105 strike aircraft it was protecting.

The basic Wild Weasel tactics were to enter the target area ahead of the strike force and set up a pattern to "troll for SAMs." The idea was to get the SAM site to turn on his radar so you could locate the site and fire your Shrike at him before his missile reached your airplane. Once his missile was in-flight guiding on you, we had developed an evasive maneuver which would, hopefully, cause the missile to miss your aircraft. The maneuver was basically a split S where you rolled on your back, pulled the nose toward the ground and then reversed the maneuver by rolling and pulling the nose up. In theory, this put the missile in a square corner where it didn't have the ability to pull enough g's to follow your pull up. Success was based on timing; you had to know when to begin the maneuver and when to pull. Too early and he got you when you ran out of airspeed; too late and he got you before you built up the g's. All of this became painfully clear when I confronted my first SAM shot.

I arrived at Korat Royal Thai AB, Thailand in the Fall of 1972. Things were heating up after an extended bombing pause that had led nowhere at the "Peace Table." We were beginning to go North again and the B-52s where targeted for areas like Vihn just North of the DMZ. We had been briefed on potential SAM activity around Vihn so we were especially alert on this particular night's BUFF attack that we were supporting with a flight of three Wild Weasels. We had set up three individual orbits that would hopefully put one of us between the SAMs and the BUFFs if they decided to dance tonight. The weather was typical for that time of year—a low undercast at about 5000 feet with a high overcast at about 15,000 feet. This left 10,000 feet open for our orbit altitude which is where we preferred to operate.

As we approached the target area, I began picking up early warning signals that indicated we might be in for an interesting evening. After we had established our orbit and before the BUFFs arrived, I picked up a sound that made the hair on the back of my neck stand up—it was the distinctive warning of the SA-2 track-while-scan radar that sounds just like a rattlesnake. I announce this to Howie, my front seat nose gunner "SAM 8 O'clock, three rings" (noting the strength). Howie announces it to the flight. Shortly, the big red AS or Azimuth Sector light (sometimes called Aw Shit) comes on which tells me we are in his radar cross-hairs. Now I'm looking outside to get a visual. Sure enough a flash of light goes off under the clouds below and a glowing ball bounces along on the cloud surface, becoming smaller and more intense until...out pops the SAM trailing a wicked stream of fire. I announce this discovery only to feel the airplane vibrate for some seconds. Not having time to investigate this, I chose to ignore the anomaly. (I found out later, after talking this over with Howie, that he had initiated the vibration by rapidly moving the stick forward and aft—duplicating what he thought we had learned in training—to porpoise the airplane so that we could see if the missile was tracking us. Needless to say, the execution of this maneuver needed some work!)

As the missile approached, I am calling out visual contacts: "SAM going to 9 o'clock—bring it to the nose" (we were supposed to put the missile just to the left or right of the nose). "Two more launches at 8 o'clock!" (not good—now we had to deal with three of these monsters). We were approaching that critical time for rolling and executing the evasive maneuver. The intensity was extreme as the pitch and loudness of our cockpit exchanges can be attested to from the cockpit tapes I still replay periodically. The SA-2 missile was referred to as a "telephone pole" because it was about that size and structure—it was a big missile—and getting bigger. "Pull now! Pull now!" We had rolled and began a high "g" inverted split S. I'm disoriented and can't find the number two and three missiles. Howie is "flying" the first one preparing to pull up when...the world turns totally black!

We had inadvertently flown into a cloud bank! This was definitely not good. Just then there was an explosion and a concussion that shook the airplane. Number one missed! We started climbing in afterburner after we figured out which way was up and—flash, bang!—another miss. As we popped out of the clouds, two sets of eyeballs were as big as saucers looking for number three. No tally—apparently it did not guide or arm. Holy moly! We cheated death—but certainly not because of any great skill or cunning on our part. After we got back to altitude and stabilized ourselves—in pulse rate and verbal expressions of awe and wonder. It was time to do lessons learned over the experience.

There is a saying that if you can survive your first 10 combat missions you have a good chance to finish your tour. I am a testament to that adage. We should not have survived that first encounter with SAM but we lucked out—and learned a lot. It was enough to get us to Linebacker II's Eleven Days of Christmas.

As the Fall of 1972 moved toward Winter, the intensity of our activity increased until, in December, President Nixon decided to send a message to the NVN government. He authorized the B-52s to strike Hanoi and the Navy to mine Haiphong harbor. Prior to this, there had been periodic B-52 sorties into NVN (note my discussion about Mu Gia Pass and Vihn) but nothing this far North nor this strategic. In the end, the raids accomplished their objective and the NVN came to the peace table and we got our POWs back. But the path to success was littered with airplanes and crews—in many cases, in my opinion, unnecessary loses. But I'm getting ahead of my story.

The Wild Weasels' job was to protect the BUFFs. To do this we examined their ingress routes, bomb release points and egress routes. We overlaid these routes on our charts that contained the latest information on the threat. From this information, we tried to come up with orbits that would put us between the SAM sites and the B-52s which was a three dimensional problem because of our different operating altitudes (B-52s at 40,000+ feet, Wild Weasels at 10,000+ feet). These orbits were necessarily offset from the bomb release point so we could avoid getting hit by the BUFF bombs. The first three nights were very upsetting in their outcome.

Sitting in orbit on the outskirts of Hanoi, we peered into this black hole that contained the world's densest air defense system knowing they knew the BUFFs were coming and where they were coming from (this was due to their Early Warning radar system and the jamming from the BUFFs). As the countdown began, we could mark the progress of the lead BUFFs as they came down Thud Ridge by the triple-A tracking, firing and exploding along a bomber stream that stretched all the way back to Thailand. When the countdown reached bomb release time, I watched a phalanx of SA-2 missile arc through the black night and one of them bury itself in the bomb bay of a very unlucky B-52. The airplane exploded and as I watched pieces of burning wings and fuselage spinning toward the ground, I realized with a sinking heart that those five men were most likely friends of mine from a former life. But the most frustrating aspect was—we never picked up any SA-2 radar signals and thus had to sit and watch the BUFFs getting hammered without being able to knock out those SAMs—which was our job. As it turns out, there were reasons for this lack of success.

Earlier in this story, I discussed the change in B-52 tactics that created the three ship in-trail approach of having the lead BUFF set up the bomb run, ID the target and drop his bombs to, hopefully, impact in a stream of 106 500-pound bombs down the center of the target box. Using station-keeping methods (the B-52 radar was used to provide separation distances and azimuth corrections) and timing (the Nav's stop watch), number two would attempt to pickle his bombs precisely at the same point in the sky as number one. Number three would follow and perform the same procedure. The objective was to increase the accuracy and density of the bombing results. Another part of the tactic was a throwback to the nuclear bombing missions we trained for in the States. At bomb release, each airplane pulled into a high "g" (for a BUFF) turn away from the target. This maneuver was necessary to avoid the blast from a nuclear explosion but for some reason became standard procedure in SEA.

All of this worked fine in the non-threat environment in the South but was a catastrophe over Hanoi. The NVA knew the BUFF tactics and they also determined another, critical weakness—the setup of the antennas for the jamming equipment on the aircraft. The system was designed to transmit jamming signals to the sides, forward and aft of the aircraft while it was flying at low level during a nuclear mission. As a result there was a "hole" under the aircraft with no jamming. So when the BUFF turned after bomb release, he presented his belly to the SAM and the radar was unjammed. This presented the enemy with all the information he needed. He now had the point of bomb release and he knew precisely when the next B-52 would arrive at that point. You can visualize this by remembering the elephant walk you saw in the circus as a kid. They would lumber in one behind the other, trunk holding the tail of the elephant in front. Where the lead elephant turned, they each turned in the same spot. So take a bead on the first elephant, close your eyes, count "one potato, two potato, three potato" and squeeze—one dead elephant!

Losses in the first three nights were devastating and our leaders considered pulling the BUFFs out of Hanoi—but cooler heads prevailed. Those cooler heads were the veteran fighter crews which included the Wild Weasels. They recommended instead of coming in from a single direction and altitude, the BUFFs should approach from ALL DIRECTIONS at differing altitudes. Instead of approaching in a long string of three ship cells, they should all hit bomb release AT THE SAME TIME. Instead of a hard turn at bomb release they should egress either straight ahead or after a gentle turn. The down side would be the total chaos after bomb release and the real danger of collision over Hanoi. It was considered worth the risk—and the fight was on!

The next night was very tense. A lot rode on this switch in tactics—not only lives but also the potential outcome of the war. We once again set up our orbit points but had to pull back even further due to the multiple ingress routes. Sitting on that perch that night provided quite a show. As the time to bomb impact ticked down to zero, we stared into the black abyss that was Hanoi. Suddenly a ring of explosions encircled the entire city (there were no military targets "downtown"). SAMS had been fired just prior to bomb impact but ended up going unguided prior to impacting the BUFFs (another tactic change was to have the B-52s target the actual SAM sites). The results were remarkable: all targets hit and no BUFFs lost due to collisions. Losses due to SAMS were way down. We had a winner!

But one thing remained. We still were not picking up the amount of radar signals we expected and we were pretty ineffective in suppressing the ones we did shoot at. On the night we were flight lead, I decided to try something very different. Rather than sit in orbit prior to bomb impact, let's fly across downtown Hanoi and see if we can pick up the SAM signals from that position. Of course this put us in the kill envelope for all the sites located around the city but our frustration level was high enough we agreed to give it a try.

The timing was critical. We needed to be in position in the city to monitor any activity as the BUFFs ingressed but we needed to be clear before the bombs rained down. We also needed to provide each other mutual support so as one of us "trolled" downtown; the others would be in position to cover in case SAM came up. As lead, we would be first across the abyss.

As we got our Mach up and entered the threat area, I was amazed at how quiet it was—kinda like the eye of a hurricane. No signals, no AAA, no SAMs. Then all hell broke loose. "T" Scrips was number two and yelled "Lead, SAM at your six!". I pulled myself around to look over our tail and sure enough there was the fireball attached to a telephone pole. My Nose Gunner said "No threat—press on". Let me pause here and explain. I didn't have my regular pilot, Howie, on this mission. I was, instead, teamed up with Tom Cody—one of the more experienced front-seaters in the business. So when Tom said no threat I relaxed a bit and started breathing again. Tom started a gradual turn to the right and basically kept the missile "pinned at our six o'clock." I think Tom felt he had enough lead that the missile would pass to the rear of us. So as the rest of the flight was engaging the SAMs, I was riveted on the one following us. As it got closer, I kept probing Tom and I continued to get "No threat—press on". Tom tightened the turn and the missile got really big and then—BAM, it went off right on our tail. I do not know to this day why we were not cut in half. "T" said later in debrief, he thought we were a goner. The explosion engulfed our plane and then seconds later we motored out of the fireball as if we were out for a Sunday drive. Tom's comment in debrief was "Didn't I say no threat?" Whatever—that mission got me my second DFC and we finally picked up some signals.

The last few days of Linebacker II were thankfully anticlimactic. Between our change of tactics and the enemy apparently running out of missiles, we had almost no activity and the B-52s bombed with impunity. The bombing was halted and the NVN signed the accords. We got our POWs back and it was time for me to go home in the Spring of 1973.

Jim Winzell

Story By Dave Brog WW # 420

The Black SAM

I remember a time, in 1972, when there appeared in the skies of North Vietnam a Black SAM.

No one had ever seen or heard of the Black SAM, but everyone had a suspicion of what it was. A Wild Weasel crew, Tom Coady and Sam Peacock, flying in the F-105G saw it close up and personal. Most folks did not think that it was the SA-2. The prevailing suspicion was that it was an SA-4. Many did not think that it was the SA-4, either, but that "many" could not prove that it was not. That "many" included a group of politically incorrect USAF majors who worked in the Pentagon. These majors, three of whom had already completed a combat tour in the Wild Weasels, were non-PC, because they were all above the rank any of them ever expected to be and were very mission oriented. The Wild Weasels were Lou Chesley from R&D and Jack Donovan and myself from Ops. The others were Bob Klimek also from R&D and Jim Thompson and Leon Hoffman from LG.

We all recognized the limitations of the AN/APR-36/37 RWRs, which were hardwired and could not be changed with the threat. We had already seen the SA-3s used in the Middle East and the growth of SAM threats in the Warsaw Pact. We had no RWR in USAFE, or anywhere, that could see the newer threats. We did, however, have a system in R&D, nicknamed Mongoose, which was a digital RWR processor built by a west-coast company called Dalmo Victor (DV). Unfortunately, we were moving very slowly in development and testing.

"Aha," said the Majors. This new Black SAM might be bullshit, but it could be the horse to ride to get the digital reprogrammable RWR that we knew we needed for the future. So we caucused in the basement of the Pentagon, near the Purple Water Fountain, and agreed that we would push to the limit to get the digital RWR into the inventory.

The first step was to get with the Warner Robins Air Logistic Center and its Ace EW software engineer, Joe Black, to find out what it would take to get DV to speed up its effort. He told us the amount of money and time that we would need and what had to be done. This was March 1972, and if everything went right we could have the first operational install into the F-105G in January 1973. The F-4Es would follow. We then had to find the money. So Klimek and Thompson started to root around for the dollars. The R&D dollars were easier to find. Jim Thompson had the hard job, finding Class-5 mod money for the installs. He finally found the dollars by robbing the usual sitting pots, T-38 windscreen mods and F-4 smokeless-engine mods, which almost always sat number one and two on the Class-5 mod list priorities but never got funded. It was a wonderful petty cash fund.

Once we got the funding lined up, we decided to find out what kind of priority we could get to move the program. Fortunately, we had a colonel named Howard Leaf (bless his good heart) heading up the special SEA/ Mid-East emergency requirement effort. We went to him, and he said to go to a certain colonel and ask him to give you a "DX Brickbat" priority - the highest priority in DOD. We got it and drafted the message that we intended for General Jack Ryan, then CSAF, to sign out to get the this program going. Within a week we had 19 general officers across the Air Staff coordinate.

There were some staff officers who did not want to concur - not the generals, but the colonels and below. We would not, however, accept a simple non-concurrence. We said that if they did not agree with the message, they should write a letter of non-concurrence explaining their reasons, and we would take their letter with us to the next level of coordination. Interestingly enough, all the non-concurrers backed off. Ryan signed the message, and we were on our way.

The next step was to get some flight-testing once we had the system ready. We knew that using the system in Europe would be a hit/miss proposition. We didn't know if the Warsaw Pact would cooperate and turn on the threats when we flew by the border. We did know that the Israeli Air Force was seeing the SA-2C (the G-band version) and the SA-3 on a daily basis. I decided to ask the IAF if they would be willing to flight test the new digital RWR, now called the AN/ALR-46, against the threat along the Suez Canal and in Egypt. Their response was "Yes, but." I asked what is the "but?" They replied, "We want it, too." I very shortly got the Air Staff and powers that be to agree that in return for flight testing, the IAF would be allowed to get the ALR-46 for their F-4Es.

In August 1972, we put a team together consisting of DV engineers and Warner Robins engineers, led by John Lavecchia. In three weeks they installed the ALR-46 and flew enough flights to determine that the ALR-46 worked as advertised. We started the procurement and had the first ALR-46 in an F-105G in SEA in January 1973. Again, the Wild Weasels were First In. And the rest, as they say, is history.

Dave Brog, a retired USAF colonel, flew F-105F Wild Weasels during the Vietnam War. He later served on the Air Staff and at USAFE, where he was responsible for tactical-fighter EW and Wild-Weasel operations. He is president and CEO of I.R.D., Inc., an international defense consulting firm in the Washington-DC area.

Dave Brog

Story by Joe Telford WW # 258

AN IGLOO WHITE STRIKE MISSION ON THE HO CHI MINH TRAIL BY WILD WEASEL F-105F PILOT MAJOR MIKE MUSCAT AND ELECTRONIC WARFARE OFFICER (EWO) CAPTAIN KYLE STOUDER

BACKGROUND

The subject mission occurred while I was on my second temporary duty (TDY) assignment to the 388th Tactical Fighter Wing (TFW) at Korat Royal Thai Air Base (RTAB), Thailand. I was the USAF Tactical Air Warfare Center (TAWC) Anti-SAM Combat Assistant Team (ASCAT) leader from 25 October 1967 to 17 April 1968. Specifically, the subject mission occurred on the night of 24 December 1967, Christmas Eve, on the Ho Chi Minh Trail in Laos.

IGLOO WHITE PROGRAM

Igloo White was the name for a US surveillance system along the Ho Chi Minh Trail that was primarily located in the countries of Laos and Cambodia. The Ho Chi Minh Trail was the route Communist North Vietnam military trucks traveled in order to supply their war effort to drive the US Military out of South Vietnam. The trail was a network of crude unimproved roads through some of the most inhospitable jungle and mountainous terrain in the world. The Igloo White surveillance system sought to collect, interpret, and rapidly act upon enemy infiltration information gathered from electronic sensors implanted along the trail.

At this time the majority of the sensors were either seismic or acoustic. That is, they reacted to vibrations caused by such things as moving vehicles or troops, or guns firing; or noise caused by vehicle engines, guns firing, or human voice.

These sensors were two to three feet in length and were painted a camouflaged scheme to look like jungle plants or small limbs, or even animal droppings. If need be these sensors could receive, record, and store their information, and then transmit it upon request. The sensors were usually dropped by aircraft in strings of 4 to 12 sensors, and their location identified. The sensors were battery powered.

At Nakhom Phanom (NKP) RTAB, Thailand was located the highly classified US Igloo White Infiltration Surveillance Center (ISC), also know as "Task Force Alpha." At this time the ISC was housed in the largest single air conditioned building in Southeast Asia and consisted of computers, plotting boards, radios, and many other electronic devices; and of course the people to make all of this work.

For at least the first two years of the Igloo White Program the sensor information was up-linked, by ultra-high frequency (UHF) transmitters in the sensors, to orbiting Lockheed Super Constellation EC-121R aircraft, and then relayed from the EC-121R, by very high frequency (VHF) transmitters, to the ISC. The EC-121R also used high frequency (HF) radios to transmit data for long distances. At any one time there were usually at least five different active orbits of these EC-121R aircraft covering the Ho Chi Minh Trail.

From the information provided by the known location of the sensors, the computers at the ISC could, among other things: determine how many trucks were in a convoy traveling down the trail, where they were located as they passed a string of sensors, the speed of the trucks, and where the trucks would probably be located on the trail by the time strike aircraft could be called in to drop their ordnance on the trucks. A real bonus in all this would be if a truck park could be identified and located where there would maybe be scores of heavily loaded trucks. Of course truck traffic was most active at night in order to make their detection and location more difficult for the US strike aircrews.

EC-121R AIRCRAFT

The EC-121R "Batcat" aircraft was probably the most expensive US aircraft to operate per flying hour of all the aircraft flying at this time in Southeast Asia. These aircraft belonged to the 553rd Reconnaissance Wing (RW) that arrived at Korat RTAB in October 1967 and commenced its combat missions on 25 November 1967. The wing had two flying squadrons and approximately 30 aircraft.

The crew for a Batcat aircraft normally consisted of 17 to 18 people and its on station orbit flying time was usually about 8 hours. The reason for all the additional crew members was to enable the Batcat to perform the function of the ICS should the ICS be out of commission for whatever reason, or loss of communications between the Batcat and the ICS. Of course, if this occurred the sensor information readout, interpretation, and the resulting targeting information would be on a manual level and at a much slower speed than had it been accomplished at the ICS, but nevertheless it could be accomplished, after a fashion. Also, the Batcat had all the necessary communications and people to interface with the strike flights and any forward air controllers (FAC) that might be working with the strike flights.

On every Batcat crew was at least one EWO who operated Applied Technology Incorporated's (ATI) APR-25/26 radar warning equipment and at least one jammer, if necessary. The two biggest threat worries of the Batcat crews were: for a MiG to sneak down from North Vietnam and launch a heat seeking missile; and for a North Viennese SA-2 Surface-to-Air Missile (SAM) unit to be moved, unobserved, into Laos and sited along the trail. The Batcat aircraft usually flew its orbit between 15,000 to 19,000 feet, well above most of the anti-aircraft artillery (AAA) that were located in Laos. I believe the wing EWO was a Captain Moran and not long after the Batcats started flying he asked myself, and my other ASCAT member, Major Keith Barker, if we would fly some Batcat missions and assist in the training of their EWOs on the operation of the APR-25/26. The two of us normally worked with the 388th TFW F-105D strike pilots and the F-105F Wild Weasel crews concerning electronic warfare and other matters.

CHRISTMAS EVE, 24 DECEMBER 1967, OVER THE HO CHI MINH TRAIL IN LAOS

So, in an effort to assist in the training of some Batcat EWOs was how I happened to be flying on this particular, and special, night.

After a couple of hours just about everything possible, in that electronic environment, had been covered with the two Batcat EWOs that were aboard. This included a few seconds of severe consternation on one occasion with the sudden illumination of the airborne interceptor radar warning light and its loud warning audio, plus a long strobe pointing to the rear, as a flight of our own F-4s checked us out as they quickly and without any warning over took us, and passed, from our rear and on out in front of us.

After awhile I sat down next to a window and turned my attention to the ground war taking place below us on the trail. The US had initiated a unilateral Christmas day halt of its war efforts in South Vietnam, but this halt did not apply to its conduct of the war along the trail in Laos. And of course, the Communist had not halted their war effort on this particular night at any location. If anything, they had increased their efforts. As I looked out into the inky blackness of the night it was continuously interrupted by bursts and flashes of exploding bombs and resulting fires, and the muzzle flashes of ground AAA guns firing and their exploding shells in the air. The situation looked more like a celebration of the Fourth of July than, "Silent night, holy night, All is calm."

After a few minutes of looking out the window I walked up front to the flight deck to observe the pilots and the navigator. All of a sudden the navigator let a wild yell of, "The TACAN, the TACAN, it has gone crazy!" When I looked at the TACAN instrument, the needle was spinning around and around at a very rapid rate. I don't know about the other Batcat orbits, but for this particular orbit in southern Laos, the primary navigational aid the navigator used to keep the EC-121R on the correct course was a TACAN located in the town of, I believe, Saravan. At this instance the aircraft was pretty much right over the town and it could not be seen from the flight deck. The aircraft commander stated, "Let me roll the airplane over a bit and lets take a look down at the town." As he rolled the aircraft up on a wing we all looked down. We could not begin to see details but it looked as if the entire small town was on fire!

For the preceding week before this flight I had been reading in an English edition of a Bangkok newspaper how the Communist Pathet Lao forces were encircling this small town of Saravan, and that their obvious intentions were to attack it once they believed they were strong enough to take it. Well, this night was the time the Pathet Lao believed they had become strong enough to take the town – and they did. I was told the next day that a Central Intelligence Agency (CIA) (Air America) helicopter had been sent to the town to look for the five Air Force enlisted personnel that operated the TACAN equipment. I was told the CIA could find no trace of the men.

After this I went back to looking out a window, seated at the vacant position of one of the intelligence officers aboard. In a few minutes a young lieutenant told me to "hook up" to two particular frequencies on the console at this position. He stated that on one frequency we would be listening to a FAC who was about to be handed off a flight of fighters to bomb a truck park that was on the starboard (right) side of our aircraft, and we would be able to hear and see all the action when the flight dropped its ordnance. He also told me on the other frequency there was a AAA battery located right by the truck park and that there was obviously one of our acoustical sensors right by the battery and the voices of the gun crews could be clearly heard, and of course the firing of the guns. In fact, the lieutenant helped me to locate the muzzle flashes of this particular AAA battery when it fired, and I could clearly hear the commands of its commander as he directed its firing.

As I was listening in on the FAC's frequency the leader of the strike flight reported in to him. Immediately I recognized the voice of Mike Muscat! Even on Air Force air-to-air radios, Mike Muscat's voice was unmistakable. It was bold and authoritarian, just like Mike. Mike was a little taller than average and a powerfully built person, and I thought, with somewhat of an out of character cherub looking face. Mike was one of the most aggressive Wild Weasel pilots I had observed in all my associations with the Weasel program. At this time, all three of the following major Weasel pilots, Mike Muscat, Bob Beal, and the operations officer of the 44th TFS, did not want to fly a mission unless it was in Route Package 6. And since this trio included the squadron operations officer, Route Package 6 missions were what they usually flew.

Mike was the epitome of the military axiom, "Know thy enemy." Nearly every F-105D and F crewmember carried a mini recorder on their missions that was plugged into the audio of their radios and the cockpit intercom. At mission debriefings these tapes of the mission radio conversations were often invaluable in sorting out just what had occurred during the heat of the battle. On two different mission debriefings I listened to a recording where Mike make a radio call to an F-105D pilot he was observing, and on which a MiG was making an unobserved high speed missile pass from the rear, and Mike told the victim F-105D pilot to break hard on Mike's command. Both times the F-105D pilots listened and complied with Mike's instructions, and they were able to out turn the Russian heat-seeking missile that was launched at them.

Now, I can no longer remember why Mike was flying a mission at night, but he was. I assume he was in a Weasel F-105F with his EWO, Kyle Stouder. Kyle had come to the Weasel program from the crew position of an EWO on a Strategic Air Command (SAC) B-58 Hustler. Mike and Kyle made a good team, for Kyle seemed up to and was enthusiastic for anything Mike wanted to attempt during a mission.

Mike and the FAC had the usual conversation which included what type of ordnance the strike flight was carrying, the FAC providing information on the target and its defenses, and suggesting the particulars of the target approach and egress. During this conversation I continued to listen to the commands of the AAA battery commander and watch its guns muzzle flashes as it fired. During all this time I had no idea where the FAC and Mike's flight were located due to no lights showing on any friendly aircraft.

Mike finished his conversation with the FAC, gave a few brief instructions to his flight members, and started the fight's run into the target. Somehow the AAA battery knew they were about to be attacked, for the voice commands were now coming even more fast and furious and louder, along with the firing.

I could hear Mike tell his flight he had released his bombs and could hear in his voice the strain of pulling Gs as he climbed after the release of bombs. At this point the commander of the AAA battery was going wild with his commands.

The bombs struck the truck park and the night lit up. Just for a second, at first, I could hear screams from the AAA battery, and then the sensor frequency went dead, and there were no more gun muzzle flashes.

Joe W. Telford

Chapter Four

Wild Weasel F-4C

Story by Joe Telford, WW # 256

F-4C TESTING

OT&E OF THE FIRST INSTALLATION OF THE APR-25 ON A TAC F-4C

Soon after Wild Weasel-IA testing at Eglin, still in December 1965, I conducted a quick and dirty test of what I believe was the first installation of the APR-25 on a TAC F-4C. This test was approximately six months prior to the start of the Wild Weasel-IV (F-4C) OT&E at Eglin. And, unlike the Wild Weasel-IV OT&E, I do not remember having any major problems with the APR-25 installation on this early, single, F-4C. Again I piggybacked this test on the Wild Weasel-I documentation, but with a reduced priority. And again, I do not remember the report but there must have been at least a message report, with TAWC's coordination on it. This was the same type of quick and dirty 360 degree accuracy and homing test I later conducted on a TAC RF-101.

For this test there was only one TAC F-4C, and the usual two pilots, and they were TDY from Shaw AFB, South Carolina. They were two young, sharp, captains who had a "can do" attitude.

Fairly early in the test I had a personal request from a 1/Lt. Tom Churan, also in my organization, to help him in a test he was trying to conduct. The name of Tom's test was, Track Alert Warning Receiver Evaluation. His test required some radiation time from the SADS-I radar at Site A-7 and his test had such a low priority it would probably never be scheduled. The test item was a small Singer or Sanger, but I think Singer, radar receiver that only provided an audio sound of the threat SAM radar as the beam would illuminate the receiver. This receiver provided no indication to the crew as to which direction the threat was located from them. In other words, about the only thing this device would do for the crew was to just increase their already high "pucker factor" in a SAM environment. Churan just wanted a crew's confirmation that the receiver did work.

The receiver was so small; you could hold it in the palm of your hand. The receiver had two rubber suction cups on it that you moistened and stuck to the inside of the canopy. There was a wire running from the receiver with a male plug on the end that was plugged into one of the audio ports on a pilot's helmet, thereby allowing the receiver's audio to be heard at all times by that pilot.

I wanted to try and help Tom with his test but I told him it was up to the pilots if they wanted to participate. Also in the back of my mind I was thinking, no APGC paper work on this effort, don't know if this is really legal. If something should go wrong what kind of problems would arise because of no test plan, PD, safety officer's approval, and etc.? The front seat pilot stated he would accommodate Tom and so I thought nothing more about any problems that might occur.

On this particular mission when the Singer receiver was flown, I was, as I often did, located myself at Hanger 68 on the second floor in an office usually not occupied by anyone. The office had a desk and a telephone and I could view the north end of the northeast to southwest runway where most of the time my test aircraft would take the active runway. First, they would stop to run up the engine, or engines, and then start their takeoff roll to the southwest. About half way through their takeoff roll a portion of Hanger 68 that protruded to the west would block the view of the last half of the takeoff roll. However, you could still hear the aircraft as it continued. For some forgotten reason now, I had been talking to the tower about some matter concerning this mission just before the crew took off, so the tower knew where to locate me by phone.

As the F-4C picked up speed on its take off roll my thoughts returned to the Singer receiver and the fact that there was no official sanction or approval of this test item. Then I thought, "Aw, nothing is going to happen, I am really worrying needlessly for such a small deal." The aircraft hurdled down the runway and out of my field of view, but I could still hear the roar of its engines as it obviously took off, flew over the base road that went around the southwest end of the runway, and flew on out over the large cleared field known as Cobb's Overrun.

I took the time to write a short note before I started to leave the office. I had almost finished my note writing when the phone rang – it was the tower, wanting to talk to Capt. Telford. I replied I was Capt. Telford. The person in the tower stated, "Sir, your test aircraft has just declared an emergency. Just as it was over the end of the runway the pilot hit the gear up switch and his canopy blew off and it has landed in Cobb's Overrun." I think I said something like, "Is the pilot still alive, is his head still on his shoulders?" The tower replied, "Oh yes sir, he is alright and is coming around to make a landing right now." What a relief, I could just envision the canopy laying on the ground with the wire from the Singer receiver still attached to the pilot's helmet, with his head in the helmet.

Later, I asked the pilot if he felt anything when his canopy blew off and he stated he did not feel a thing. The wire broke, of course, and the Singer receiver must have remained attached to the canopy by the suction cups. I can no longer remember, but I guess Tom Churan retrieved the Singer receiver from the canopy. Nobody asked me any questions concerning this incident, and I certainly did not ask any questions or volunteer any information. And you thought the phrase, "Don't ask, don't tell" originated in the 1990s. Churan did not ask me again if I would fly his receiver on one of my missions.

Toward the end of the test it started to look like we would be testing until shortly after Christmas. The two pilots started to press me to complete the test in time for them to return home and celebrate Christmas at home.

At this time the only missions we still had to conduct were low level homing runs on the SADS-I at Site A-7 on the island. I showed the young pilots how many homing runs we still required, which was a significant number. I told them if they could "put the throttle to the wall," and hustle, and complete the required number of runs, and collect the data too, they would be home for Christmas.

It turned out I under estimated these young pilots ability and endurance to pull G's in a turn. These two guys were inspired! So much so, that it almost got me into trouble.

Just north of Site A-7, across the sound and on the north shore by US Highway 98, just a little to the side of the F-4C's ground path centerline, was the Howard Johnston Motel. And, just about a mile north of Howard Johnston, was the city of Fort Walton Beach's only commercial AM radio station at that time.

I observed this first mission of increased speed and effort at Site A-7, and picked up the radar tracking plots to take back to my office. And, I was impressed as to how many more homing runs these two captains accomplished than was the normal situation. On the return to my office I first drove to Hanger 68 where the crew parked the F-4C and I was going to pick up their mission data. About the time I drove into the parking lot the crew had just shut down the engines and were climbing out of the aircraft. As I hurriedly walked out to the aircraft I noticed to my left the Base Operations Officer, a major, was also hurriedly walking out to the F-4C, with a stern look and a firm jaw.

The major beat me to the aircraft by a few seconds and asked the crew who was their TPO, to which they stated he was the approaching the captain. The Base Operations Officer turned to me and stated, "Follow me to my office, you are in big trouble!" All the way to his office I keep wondering what could be wrong? I was at the control site for the entire mission and there was no indication there was any problem during the mission, and, the crew did land safely, and they were not "invited" to go to the major's office?

When we got to the office, and settled, the major stated, "When your crew flew across both the island and the sound and then started their turn back south they were making so much engine noise that the owner of the Howard Johnson Motel called the base and complained profusely! Also, during each of their turns they continuously knocked the needle off the record that was being played on the turntable at the radio station, and they have called and complained too! Let me see your mission profile for this mission."

What the Base Operations Officer thought he would find was I did not have a profile for the flight path my crew had just flown, or the profile lacked his signature (coordination), or at the least, my crew had badly deviated from the approved profile. As luck would have it, I had a copy of the approved profile, with all the signatures, in my briefcase and I pulled it out and handed it to the major – and sat back. He studied the profile for a short time and wrinkled up his forehead. He looked up at me and with the hint of a little crooked simile on his face, he stated, "You are one lucky PTO! I did approve and I did sign this profile, and your crew did fly it as approved."

On future homing flights on A-7 the F-4C crew reduced their engine noise during their turns over Fort Walton Beach, and the two pilots did celebrate Christmas at home at Shaw AFB.

WILD WEASEL-IVC (F-4C) OT&E AND TRAINING

The Wild Weasel-IV (F-4C) OT&E and training was again a joint effort between TAWC and APGC, with the same relationships and responsibilities continuing as in Wild Weasel-I and Wild Weasel-III. Again I was the APGC PTO but for the life of me, I can no longer remember who was the new TAWC TPO. This effort took place at Eglin from about June to September 1966.

My notes indicate the following men were involved as the first Weasel-IVC crews:

A/C Maj. Richard Merkling Commander
P 1/Lt. Dan Lafferty

A/C Maj. Karl Park Operations
P 1/Lt. Joe Mulligan

A/C Capt. Everett Raspberry Weapons (Also test crew
P 1/Lt. Frank Gullick at Eglin – see note)

A/C Capt. Dick Pascoe
P 1/Lt. Norman Wells Tape recorder; A & E maint.

A/C Capt. Earl Friesel
P 1/Lt. Frank Barrett

A/C Capt. Wlat Radeker Aircraft maint.
P 1/Lt Jim Murray KA-71
EWO Capt. Eddie Adcock Also test crew at Eglin
EWO Capt. Roger Peden Also test crew at Eglin

Capt. Allen Lamb TAWC Representative

As the above information indicates, most of my contact with these individuals during this OT&E was with the identified test personnel.

The same atmosphere and degree of effort as experienced with the previous Wild Weasel-III (F-105F) OT&E was also experienced with this OT&E. That is, there was not the sense of panic as with Wild Weasel-I

OT&E, but the effort was expedited. Also, because this was the third full-blown Weasel OT&E the learning curve for all the support organizations, and concerned people in general, was higher and made the test conduct smoother.

But, there was a big compatibility and accuracy problem with the F-4C aircraft and the ATI APR-25 equipment. As best as I remember now it was mainly caused by stray, or random, voltage on the airframe. The question is begged, why was this not encountered on the "quick and dirty" test with the Shaw AFB F-4C back in December 1965? My answer – I don't know, don't remember if I ever knew, now. I know the answer was absolutely not discovered, if ever, at Eglin.

By this time the crews involved in the early Wild Weasel-I and III efforts had returned and a new organization and effort, using some of these experienced crews, was spinning up at Nellis AFB to test and train future Weasel aircraft and crews. There was a designated date for the deployment of the Wild Weasel-IVC aircraft and crews, but the new Nellis Weasel organization wanted to put the finishing touch to this effort before they deployed, and time was running out.

TAWC did not want the Weasel-IVC aircraft and crews to go to Nellis before the problem(s) were found and resolved at Eglin. However, Nellis prevailed and the aircraft and crews flew to Nellis. At Nellis more testing, and more testing, and etc., was conducted. Eventually the Air Force sent the Weasel-IVC crews, including the two EWOs, to the 8th TFW at Ubon RTB to fly their 100 combat missions as straight strike F-4C crews. However, Capts. Adcock and Pedon, the EWOs, did not fare as well or quickly as the pilots did in obtaining their 100 combat missions. I don't know if I ever heard all the details but they were, so to speak, pushed around from "pillar to post", before they finally completed their 100 combat missions. I am sure Eddie Adcock will go into this situation in detail in his written comments.

The Wild Weasel-IVC aircraft and crews departed Eglin and flew to Nellis AFB, and the test report writing commenced between TAWC and APGC. Just as the report effort started I was "loaned" to TAWC at their request, and I departed Eglin for a four month TDY to the Korat RTAB. This TDY will be discussed in detail in another section. With my sudden departure my organization, Deputy of Effectiveness Test, and TAWC, assigned Mr. Lawrence "Larry" R. Bentley to take my place in the report writing effort. Larry had been a member of my APGC organization until just about the start of the Wild Weasel-IV (F-4C) OT&E, when he was assigned to the TAWC OA (Operational Analysis) shop.

Joe Telford, WW # 256

Story by Everett T Raspberry WW # 89

F-4C Wild Weasel (The Early Days)

The time was the early to mid-sixties and the place was Nellis AFB NV. I was assigned as an instructor to the USAF Fighter Weapons School in 1962 and a couple of years later moved over to the R&D Section to do all the fun stuff. Then Major Dick Merklin was the head of R&D, and that's how I got involved with the F-4C Wild Weasel program.

Apparently, some work had been done on re-packaging the Wild Weasel gear into a pod that would fit onto the left inboard pylon (later the Weasel gear was installed in the left forward Missile well) of a F-4C and connect with antennas mounted around the forward and rear fuselage. Signals were supposed to be detected by the antennas, transmitted to the pod, processed by the electronic stuff in the pod, and displayed on an APS (could have been APN)-something-or-other (APR-25/26) in the rear cockpit. In the front we had another display (APR-25 cathode ray tube), which was round and had concentric strength/range rings. The guy in the back (GIB), however, could interpret the signals displayed on his signal analysis receiver and figure out what and where something was looking at us with their radar.

I was assigned as Project Manager/Pilot to the F-4C Wild Weasel project. I had no real combat experience; but I think, because of my training, I had some appreciation for the real world requirements to support this mission. In the Spring of 1965 I went to George AFB for an F-4 checkout and, later in the year, along with eleven other pilots and/or EWO's, went to Los Angeles for Wild Weasel systems training. The plan was to have four F-4C aircraft and six aircrews deployed to SEA by the summer of 1966. This didn't quite happen.

In the past, I was of the opinion that no matter what kind of crap the development community could devise, we as operational guys could overcome their lack of technical expertise by training and applying appropriate 'bugger factors.' For what was then an advanced electronic system, I must admit that the Wild Weasel stuff worked real good cruising around at medium altitude below 400 knots. As part of the test program, we deployed to China Lake NAS and did some pretty good work firing Shrikes at simulated SAMs. We even went to Navy Fallon and interpreted their more complicated signals to the amazement of everyone involved. Everything worked great until we started operating at speeds and altitudes that would probably be required to survive in RP-VI. Of course, the development community wanted to know why we were operating at those speeds at low altitude. The obvious answer was, "Cause it won't go no faster!" I don't think McDonnell-Douglas could ever be accused of trying to combine power and aerodynamics all in the same airplane.

Anybody that ever wanted to add any capability to the F-4 always wanted to use the left forward Sparrow well. That's OK, except there is a lot of turbulence in that area and anything but very robust, solid state components couldn't have survived. Apparently that was not in the cards in the middle sixties. They tried using rubber shock mounts and any other thing that came to mind. I went to Eglin AFB in the summer of '66 to fly the equipment against simulated sites in an environment where all the parameters were a little more documented. The system didn't work there either.

After a lot of soul searching by the powers that be, it was decided that the six original crews should be transferred to Ubon RTAFB and await the arrival of the new and improved F-4C Wild Weasel aircraft. The development community was really sure they had the answer. Right!

We arrived in Thailand on Thanksgiving Day of 1966. By year's end I had at least 40 trips to RP-VI as did most of the other F-4C Wild Weasel guys. Then word came that we should not be flying so much because the arrival of the new and improved F-4C Wild Weasel aircraft was just about to happen and there would be no trained crews. Right! As it turns out they never showed up.

I was taken off the no-fly roster long enough to participate in Bolo 1 and I was fortunate enough to clobber one MiG-21. Being on the no-fly list really meant you couldn't be on a mission that was a "counter," but you could be an airborne spare. It was then that I made an amazing discovery, if a guy could be a spare in Chappie James' flight, you were guaranteed a trip to RP-VI. I was always amazed how one person could have so many drop tanks that didn't feed or missiles that didn't check out, but who am I to complain?

Story by Eddie Adcock WW # 100

Wild Weasel Eddie Adcock Memories

This is a tale of woe for the first two Electronic Warfare Officers (EWOs) assigned to the first cadre of the start-up of the F-4C Wild Weasel. For historical purposes, following is the list of the initial personnel:

Editor's Note: "a/c" is Aircraft Commander and "p" is for pilot. During this period pilots, not navigators or weapons systems operators, were filling all rear cockpit positions in the F-4.

a/c Maj. Richard Merkling Commander
p 1/Lt. Dan Lafferty

a/c Maj. Karl Park Operations Officer
p 1/Lt. Joe Milligan

a/c Capt. Everett Raspberry weapons (test crew Eglin)
p 1/Lt. Frank Gullick

a/c Capt. Dick Pascoe
p 1/ Lt. Norman Wells tape recorder& A&E maint.

a/c Capt. Earl Friesel
p 1/Lt. Frank Barrett

a/c Capt. Walt Radeker aircraft maint.
p 1/Lt. Jim Murray KA-71

EWO Capt. Eddie (Ed) Adcock Wild Weasel
EWO Capt. Roger Peden Wild Weasel maint.

At Ubon RTAB

ATI Rep. Mr. Larry Lipsom USAFTFWC Rep.
Capt. Allen Lamb (test crew, representing USAFTFWC)

Capt. Davis	7th AF PLGR (ECM Plans)
Col. Frank Witry	7th AF DoD

Ubon Maint.
L/C Potter, Maint. Control Officer, 8 TFW
Capt. Caputo, A&E Maint. Sup.
Lt Flash, Comm. Nav Sup
M/Sgt Silvery, Comm Nav Sup.
S/Sgt Hartfield

April 1966, I was notified to report to Nellis AFB as soon as possible. End assignment was classified. After settling the family matters, off I go.

Turns out, like a lot of other efforts in those days, it was all hurry up and wait. Nothing was in place except the people. The first F-4C to be modified was still in the hangar at McDonnell-Douglas.

Raz Raspberry and I flew the first modified F-4C from St. Louis to Eglin some time in May. It was a lousy installation. Sunlight washed out the displays in the rear cockpit, auto DF was off most of the time, on-board radar put a continuous strobe on the APR-25, etc.

May, June, and July passed with everyone test flying the bird and trying to work out the problems.

I don't know how it came about, but it was determined that the Roger and I and Allen Lamb should leave Nellis and head to Ubon as the "Advance Party". This was in the Aug. 1966 time period and never should have happened. But it did.

Arrived at Ubon and waited and waited and waited. Here we were, two EWO's assigned to an F-4 wing with nothing to fly. Air Force manning was 2 pilots to each F-4. How the heck were we going to get our missions (counters) so we could rotate back to the States.

Meanwhile, back at Nellis the aircraft modification fell apart. So we were stuck at Ubon for about 45 days simply lollygagging around. I did manage to get one counter (night Sky Spot) out of Ubon.

We got transferred to Korat in the hopes to crew up with someone in the F-105F Wild Weasel squadron. We spent about another 30 days at Korat doing absolutely nothing. Everyone was crewed up, so no chance of any missions.

Finally, personnel figured we were misfits and transferred us to Takhli. I had never seen a B-66, but it was a way home and I certainly was appreciative of them taking us in. Finished my hundred counters and got to return back to the family in June or July 1967.

The 6 front seaters and 6 back seaters were assigned to Ubon and completed their tours as line crews.

To recap. I was exhilarated, thrilled, that I was assigned to fighters and the Wild Weasel program. But alas, it cost me 14 months away from my family and 14 months of frustration from not being able to accomplish the F-4C Wild Weasel assignment. However, 5 years later, I completed 74 missions over NVN in the F-105G.

Eddie Adcock, WW # 100

Story By Joe Snoy WW # 2067

Early F4C Wild Weasel Operations In PACAF

These are my recollections of the evolution of the F4C Wild Weasel mission in PACAF during 1968 through early 1972. I was fortunate to be in the first F4C class in 1968 and performed the "additional duty" of squadron historian during assignments to the 35th, 67th, and 80th Fighter Squadrons. This narrative attempts to provide additional detail to the history of the Wild Weasel mission as chronicled by Larry Davis in his book Wild Weasel – the SAM Suppression Story. - Joe Snoy, Major (ret) USAF

Initial F4C Wild Weasel Training at Nellis circa 1968.

The F4C Wild Weasel program finally got off the ground at Nellis during the summer of 1968 (See page 50, Larry Davis' book - Wild Weasel - the SAM Suppression Story for a description of the problems with the initial F4C Wild Weasel aircraft modification). My class began in August and I graduated in October with all crews reporting to their respective PACAF or USAFE fighter squadrons. The training syllabus consisted of both classroom and flying activities. The 17 flying missions including air-to-air, air-to-ground and Wild Weasel missions plus APR 25/26 and ER-142) for the EWOs. For those of us EWOs who had no previous fighter experience the flying training was extremely demanding – we learned the fighter business by the seat of pants. . I remember returning to Nellis with a full barf bag in hand on 11 of 17 sorties. I was told that later EWOs were sent to F4 RTU before Wild Weasel training at Nellis.

The initial PACAF crews formed at Nellis were; Captains Klaus Klause/Joe Snoy, Nick Kemp/JimViolette, Billy Gough/Bob Emerson and Jerry Timm/John Fraser. All the F4 aircraft commanders were experienced Vietnam F4 pilots while EWOs Jim Violette (F105F), John Fraser (F105F), Bob Emerson (EB-66) and myself (Joe Snoy EB-66) had just completed combat tours in Vietnam. The Nellis F4C Wild Weasel instructors that I remember were; Jim Hill (IP), Norm Wells (IP), Tony Paytek (EWO) and Marsh Goldberg (EWO). Two non-Wild Weasel instructors of note were Tom Swalm (later M/G and TAWC CC) and Chris Patarakis (later

Thunderbird lead). I remember Jim Hill asking me if I had ever been supersonic and I truthfully said "No". So he said "There is a brand new F4E on the ramp with no tanks or pylons that needs a flight control test - lets go!" To make a long story short we took off, got permission from LA center to enter the Nellis supersonic track and accelerated to Mach 2. After reaching Mach 2 Jim said, "I wonder how high this plane can climb?" Passing 55k on the altimeter he said, "We need to nose this baby over". I can vouch for the sky being very dark at 58,000 feet!

In 1968 the Nellis electronic combat training ranges were primitive by later standards. Caliente Range (located on BLM property east of the Nellis bombing ranges) was the closest range and had a single AAA signal (no live bombing and limited low level tactics possible). At that time an EWO by the name of Dick Syzmanski was running around the range in a truck/ camper trying to modify/install surplus WWII AAA radars as a surrogate threats for training. A little farther from Nellis was the St. George, UT radar bomb scoring site (RBS) that had a Fansong signal (no live bombing or low level tactics possible). The most sophisticated site/range was Fallon NAS in northern Nevada that provided Fansong, and AAA signal plus an adjacent live-bombing range. The Wild Weasel sorties to Fallon provided the best combination of threat signals and tactical weapons delivery but time on the range was short because we were operating at the maximum range of the F4 with two wing tanks – only two short simulated attacks were possible before we were "bingo fuel" for Nellis.

The 347th TFW struggles to understand the Wild Weasel mission

After completing training at Nellis in October, PACAF's first F4C Wild Weasel aircrews were assigned to the 80TFS at Yokota AB, Japan (347 TFW) despite the fact the only three F4C Wild Weasel aircraft in existence were assigned to the Wild Weasel School at Nellis. The 347th was in sad organizational shape and was still recovering from the aftermath of the USS Pueblo debacle of early 1968. The Pueblo crisis caught PACAF's two fighter equipped bases in Japan (Yokota and Misawa)) in a transition from F-105s to F4Cs. Neither base had the resources to provide a conventional response to the North Korean atrocity. As a result, starting in mid 1968, PACAF populated Yokota and Misawa with old F4Cs from Cam Rahn Bay and inexperienced F4 aircrews from the US. Few F4C aircraft commanders had many hours in the F4 and the backseat was totally filled with Pilot Weapons System Operators (PWSOs) mostly First Lieutenants. The 347th senior leadership had little fighter experience (many had transitioned from B-47s or B-52, etc). When the first F4C Wild Weasel crews arrived they were met with questions; "What is a Wild Weasel?", "What 's an EWO?" or better yet "What do you mean you're not a pilot?". Thus began the 347TFW's painful adjustment to the new AF policy of replacing the F4 backseat pilots with navigators and a small number of EWOs. Bob Hipps ("the Hippogator") was especially glad to see the Wild Weasel crews because he had just arrived at Yokota from his Vietnam tour as a Nite Owl FAC backseater and was the only non-pilot backseater at that time. Although equipped with fighter aircraft, the primary mission of the 347 TFW (Yokota) and the 475 TFW (Misawa) was nuclear weapon delivery in support of the Single Integrated Operations Plan (SIOP) from forward operating bases in Korea (i.e., Osan and Kunsan). A secondary mission was air defense of Japan. The first challenge faced by the new F4C Wild Weasel crews in late 1968 and early 1969 was to become "combat ready". My first "tac check" was dropping a Mk106 on a shear rock island somewhere in the ocean south of Tokyo after flying a low level to the simulated target +/- 2 minutes. (I passed that check ride and everyone thereafter for the next nine years). During this time period the Yokota Wild Weasels lost their first aircrew (Capt John Wadsworth/Maj Burt Fontenot) recently graduated from the second Nellis F4C Wild Weasel class in a night aircraft ferry accident to Korea. The crew apparently suffered a major electrical failure on takeoff at Yokota and hit some power lines while trying to land the aircraft under a low overcast. Finally in April 1969, the first two modified F4C Wild Weasel aircraft arrived at Yokota – the TAC ferry crews were surprised to be met with champagne was they deplaned the aircraft much to the joy of Wild Weasel crews who were waiting for them. These were the first of seven Wild Weasel modified F4C aircraft (Misawa received eight). Although the Yokota Wild Weasel crews were assigned to one flight in the 80th TFS, the Wild Weasel aircraft were distributed throughout the 347th's aircraft pool at Yokota or Osan without regard to its special electronic equipment. The Wild Weasel aircraft were not liked by the non-Wild Weasel backset pilots or backseat IPs because the cockpit visibility was restricted by the ER-142 display and this hampered formation flying or landing from the backseat.

In June 1968, much to the dismay of the Wild Weasel crews, the 347 TFW Wild Weasel crews were reassigned throughout the squadrons (35th, 36th and 80th). The struggle to raise the importance of the Wild Weasel mission continued through 1969 and 1970 despite the increasing number or Wild Weasel aircraft and Wild Weasel crews. Also the replacement of PWSOs by young navigators right out of nav school by way of F4 RTU continued. I remember having to take my first annual navigator written exam based on C-130 navigation problems. Also at that time our F4 stan-eval written test was heavily based on pilot skills or equipment located in the F4 front seat. I had little interest in understanding what the minimum startup hydraulic pressure should be if he gauges are only visible in the front seat. The navs and Wild Weasel crews complained loudly that the stan-eval tests never asked questions focused on the back seat equipment (e.g., radar, INS, radio, etc). I vividly remember my frontseater, Klaus, asking me to get the letdown book out for a weather approach at Yokota and my answer – "What's a letdown book?" after I had been flying F4s for months! Eventually it took a directive from PACAF to force changes to the stan-eval and annual flight exams for EWOs and navs. Instrument School replaced the annual refresher nav school/exam – what a smart decision for us non-pilots flying fighters.

The Wild Weasel Mission is Recognized - Training Improvements

Slowly the importance of the Wild Weasel mission in support of the Korean theatre became recognized within 347th as more senior Vietnam experienced personnel replaced the early Wing leadership. Despite the early lack of embrace for the Wild Weasel mission at the Wing level, the Wild Weasel crews were able to practice Wild Weasel tactics in 2-4 ship formations while deployed to Osan, Korea. The addition of an AAA radar at the Koon-ni bombing range added more realism to the practice weapons training missions in Korea. Also captive Shrikes were installed on Wild Weasel aircraft. As more Vietnam experienced crews populated the three F4 squadrons more and more advanced training events were conducted including "shooting the dart", air-to-air combat maneuvering, live AIM-9 and AIM -7 firings at drones. Wild Weasel crews were rotated back to Nellis for short refresher courses and advanced tactics missions against the greatly upgraded electronic-threat ranges at Nellis. Consolidation of PACAF's F4C Wild Weasel Resources

In 1970 PACAF HQ directed the consolidation of all F4C Wild Weasel crews and aircraft at Yokota. Shortly thereafter the Wild Weasel crews and aircraft from Misawa were transferred to Yokota and all Wild Weasels crews from both Yokota and Misawa were assigned to the 80th TFS. With only a few exceptions the squadron was composed entirely of Vietnam-experienced veterans - the aircraft commanders all had over 1000 hrs F4 time and the EWOs either had a tour in F-105s or EB-66s. Late in 1970 or early 1971 Captain "Dickey Duck" Myers was assigned to the 80th (Dick was later to become the Chairman of the JCS during Gulf War II).

The 67th TFS becomes PACAF's F4C Wild Weasel Squadron

In late 1970 the long standing rumor that PACAF was about to reorganize the fighter forces in Japan and Korea became reality as the fighter squadrons in all of Southeast Asia were reorganized more closely to historical unit lineage. The 80th was included in the reorganization and in Feb 1971 all 80th Wild Weasel crews were reassigned to the 35th then on or about 15 Mar 1971 the entire squadron of Wild Weasel crews and aircraft flew to Kadena, Okinawa and become the 67 TFS (the squadron designation having been reassigned from Misawa). The 35th, 36th and 80thk squadron designations were reassigned to Korea along will all Yokota and Misawa aircrew personnel who had not completed a combat tour in Vietnam as of that time.

On Okinawa, home of the 18 TFW, the 67th joined the 12th TFS (F-105s) and 15th TRS (RF4Cs). In early 1971 Lt Col David Oakes, former 80th and current 67th CC, was promoted to Colonel and Lt Col Don Parkhurst, former 35th and current 67th Operations Officer become the new 67th Wild Weasel squadron commander. During 1971 and 1972 new Wild Weasel pilots and EWOs joined the 67th as the initial cadre of F4C Wild Weasel crews from the 1968-1970 Yokota and Misawa era began to rotate to the US after 3 years or longer in PACAF.

Joe Snoy WW # 2067

Story by Clyde Hayman, WW # 82

An F-4C Wild Weasel Story

In 1969 after having been in the Wild Weasel (WW) Program for three years, I was assigned to the F-4C WW in Japan. This was a jump from a war-orientated F-105 Wild Weasel program to peacetime weaseling. As I have mentioned in my early writings, I had flown in three different aircraft (actually four but that is another tale) without having any formal training.

When I was assigned to the F-4C WW School at Nellis AFB, I was finally in a formal Air Force program. I was crewed with a pilot, Frank Plescha, who was already stationed at Yokota AB, Japan. Frank and I went to the school together. Since I had over 600 hours in the F-105, F-4C and the F-111; and the school was designed for brand new Wild Weasels, the school was old hat to me. I knew all three of the EWO instructors (Tony Radko, Rog Hermeling and Don 'Ski' Simanski), as I had been an instructor in the 105 when they went through the school. They were doing a great job; the problem with the school was the instructor pilots. They were F-4 pilots who had never flow a combat Wild Weasel mission. Two of them knew their deficiencies and were content to let the EWOs run the show. The third was much more involved and wanted the deference that students usually give teachers. I am afraid that I often corrected him, and Frank didn't think much of his flying skills. We were not, to say, the most cooperative students he had had in the classroom or the mission debriefing room. After we graduated, we went to Yokota where we assumed the job of being a regular F-4C crew. Seldom did we fly a F-4C WW bird.

In about a year and some odd months Frank finished up his tour and went back to the states; I was sent back to F-4C Wild Weasel School to the same instructors. This time I went through the school with Jerry "Killer" Hoff. Jerry was the best pilot I had ever had. He was one of the greatest stick I ever flew with and I had flown with some greats. On the ground, he was the first pilot who made me look good because he got into more trouble at the bar than I did. I had been barred from drinking at the club at Korat. This is no easy chore. Jerry had had similar problems at Da Nang.

We were the senior majors in the squadron and often joked that if we crashed and burned, all the Air Force would lose was a tired old F-4C.

In the last week of Wild Weasel school we got a message from our wing that since we were already at Nellis, we were to be the PACAF representative at a Wild Weasel Symposium. Of course this was in some ways an honor as there were Wild Weasels from everywhere Europe, Southeast Asia and Iron Hand people from the Navy.

One of the things we were asked to do was write a paper on how the Wild Weasel would be deployed in Northeast Asia. Jerry took to this like a fish to water. He jumped into writing a plan applying all his newly gained Wild Weasel skills without asking me anything. His version of the story is that I was off talking with old Wild Weasel friends and left the chore to him. After he had spent a couple of hours writing, he handed me what he consider a finished masterpiece. I read an excellent paper and handed it back to him.

He asked expecting approval, "What do you think?"

I replied, "It lacks creditability"

Hoff almost screamed defensively, "What do you mean it lacks creditability?"

I replied, "You have misspelled 'Weasel'. It's el not le"

Hoff and I both bust out laughing and then he said that is what they got when they send someone who had not graduated from Wild Weasel School yet to a symposium. They should know that the Wild Weasel School didn't teach you how to spell "Weasel" until the last day.

Clyde Hayman

Hanoi in conjunction with a coordinated SAM attack on the high altitude F-4 chaff flight. Lariet was warned by the mission-controlling agency that the MiGs were on the 254 radial of Hanoi, at 53 miles, and headed south toward Lariet. At that time, Lariet was on the 240 radial, 58 miles from Hanoi, so the flight split to further complicate the tracking solution for the MiGs and the enemy Ground Control Intercept (GCI) operators. Flying in a blacked-out (no exterior lighting) configuration, Lariet successfully negated the MIG attack and assumed their Hunter-Killer role.

Once in their operating area, Lariet flight was within the launch range of thirteen confirmed SAM sites. Lariet 02, the F-4E loaded with CBU ordnance, was placed in an optimum position over the highest threat SAM site to bomb the site once it had been pinpointed by Lariet 01. The F-4C, loaded with ARMs, was in a tight orbit around the SAM site complex. From their vantage point, Lariet 01 was in prime position to detect an active site, attack it with an ARM and then protect the crew of Lariet 02 against a SAM launch as they rolled in to bomb the identified site. The degree of difficulty involved in maintaining this posture was extreme. The aircrews of both aircraft were forced to compromise their personal safety time and again in an effort to entice the SAM site operators into tracking their aircraft so that an ARM shot could be made. As the B-52 cell made it's final turn for the first target, Lariet 01 detected a strong SAM Fan Song radar at their 11 o'clock position and the deadly duel began. The crew of Lariat 01 immediately acquired the signal, obtained launch parameters for their ARM and fired at the threatening site. As the ARM left the aircraft, two SAMs punched through the clouds at their 12 o'clock position guiding on Lariet 01. Seconds later, another two missiles appeared from the same position and guided on the B-52 cell, which was, then in a turn over target. During this time frame, the airborne AGM-45 ARM continued to guide on the launching site. At the ARM projected impact time the Fan Song signal shut down, abruptly and all four SAMs went into ballistic flight. Lariat 02, acting on the visual cue of the exploring ARM, rolled in for a CBU ordnance delivery on the identified site. In spite or intense AAA fire and the dense undercast, Lariat 02 successfully struck their target and swung back out to cover subsequent launches. As the battle progressed, a second SAM site locked onto the bomber force and launched three SAMs in rapid succession. Lariat flight was nearly on top of the launching sites between the missiles and the B-52 force. Without hesitation, Lariet 01 turned head on with the rapidly closing missiles and made a down the throat shot with their remaining ARM. With the SAMs narrowly missing their aircraft, Lariat 01 pressed home the attack until site suppression was assured. As they pulled up from the ARM launch, AAA fire erupted around them on all sides. Determined to silence the SAM site, Lariat 01 maintained visual contact on the site location using moonlit cloud layer contours and directed Lariet 02 to the area for a strike. Braving intense AAA fire and subsequent SAM launches while working just above the undercoat, Lariet 02 methodically placed their ordnance on target to complete site destruction. The site remained off the air and did not launch for the remainder of the night. Although both Lariet aircraft were out of ordnance and ARMs after the last B-52 cell TOT (Time-over-Target), they continued to make feint attacks on launching SAM sites at close range in an effort to draw fire away from the vulnerable bombers then on target area egress. Disregarding their own personal safety, Lariet 01 and 02 succeeded in forcing the SAM operators to operate in a degraded mode to avoid detection and destruction. Due to Lariet Flight's aggressive attacks, the SAM radar operators could track their targets for only short periods of time, greatly reducing their accuracy. With this limited system capability, many missiles were detonated prematurely and still others fell back to earth shortly after launch. Throughout the time they remained on station, Lariet 01 and 02 evaded an estimated 50 SAMs and tremendous amounts of AAA fire of all calibers.

As a result of these actions, the enemy was denied the full use of his target area defenses thus enabling the B-52 bomber force to successfully complete their mission.

Joseph Snoy WW # 2067

HAMMER FLIGHT – HANOI, 18 DEC 1972

BELLES/KELLY HAMMER 01
BREMER/BERGMANN HAMMER 02
FLOYD/PALMER HAMMER 03
TIDWELL/HANEY HAMMER 04

During this mission Hammer flight provided SAM suppression for a B-52 bomber force attacking targets in the immediate vicinity of Hanoi. Hammer flight provided coverage of all threat radar emitters in the western half of the target area. They succeeded in continually harassing the active SAM sites in the western half of this area, easing the entrance and exit of the B-52 cells flying over their area of coverage. Their aggressive and sustained attacks resulted in four probable kills of Fan Song emitter radars and suppression of five other sites numerous times. These efforts were dramatically illustrated on the following night, when the noticeable lack of all but rare, Fan Song signals was observed. Further, only twenty SAMs were fired the second night, compared to sixty the first. And all SAMs fired the second night were ineffective, resulting in no damage to any strike or escort aircraft.

Hammer flight drove to a point northwest of the target area and split, each aircraft working as an individual entity. Working separately gives the threat radar operators more targets to keep track of, and allows better coverage of defensive installations by these electronically equipped aircraft. Each F-4C, armed with AGM-45 anti-radiation missiles then established a working pattern within firing distance of their assigned radar emitters, and were usually within range of at least six SAM sites at all times.

Hammer 01, immediately upon reaching their area of responsibility, acquired six SAMs visually, and noted SAMs continuously airborne during their entire time on station. Due to the location needed to optimize the number of sites they could shoot at, they found themselves initially hampered by extensive AAA firings. At this time one of the SAM sites in Hammer 0l's area of coverage began tracking them. Each time they turned into the site to fire, the radar emitter would cease emitting. Hammer 01 fired an ARM at the location of this site during one of their runs. They then broke from the site. The site once again came on to track them on their outbound leg. Disregarding the danger of placing this emitter at their 6 o'clock position, Hammer 01 continued outbound from the site to allow their ARM sufficient time to reach the victim radar. This SAM site's emitter went off the air, and did not reappear. Finding another site active, they fired their remaining ARM resulting in a probable kill. Although out of armament, they continued operating in their assigned area to further confuse and frustrate the remaining active SAM, AAA and GCI sites.

Hammer 02, after splitting with 01, entered their working area just to the west of 01. Maneuvering of the aircraft to effect an optimum signal intercept and firing position was constantly hampered by heavy and accurate AAA. Because of the AAA, Hammer 02 was forced into an awkward position for working their two primary sites and maintain a safe position on the AAA. However, Hammer 02 soon realized that one site was not active and they altered their position to provide maximum suppression of the second site and then continued maneuvering until the site began tracking and subsequently launched four SAMs at them. Hammer 02 fired an ARM at this site as they began their evasive maneuver. At the correct time for the ARM to impact, the radar signal ceased, and the missiles went ballistic. Realizing this site was no longer a threat, Hammer 02 began to work the other site of their concern, that was not active. After receiving the correct electronic indications, Hammer 02 fired their remaining ARM at this site. The site shut down almost immediately, causing two of the missiles it had just launched to loop over and impact the ground.

Hammer 03, noting the AAA that separated their sector from Hammer 02's, continually repositioned themselves to intercept radars emitting from one of the sites they were covering. Receiving strong electronic indications from one of these sites, Hammer 03 fired an ARM. Almost simultaneously the site fired three SAMs at one of the bomber cells Hammer flight was providing coverage for. But then the site shut down, and the missiles proceeded on only a ballistic course with no threat to either the strike or strike protection forces. The site once again came on the air, this time looking directly at Hammer 03. Hammer 03 continued on a course to permit this site to track them, to allow their ARM to work. At the correct time, electronic indications from this site ceased. Maneuvering to achieve optimum position to fire at another SAM site, Hammer 03 received strong electronic indications that a AAA site was near. This was confirmed shortly, when they found themselves surrounded by accurate and heavy, large caliber AAA. Performing evasive maneuvers they broke themselves loose from this radar emitter, and thereby evaded further accurate AAA. They fired their remaining ARM at another Fan Song that went down immediately after launching the AGM-45.

Hammer 04 experienced electronic equipment cooling problems that required that both engines be held to 95% or less to prevent equipment damage due to overheating. Noting that by working at a lower altitude they could maintain sufficient maneuvering energy to perform effectively, Hammer 04 elected to continue on their assigned mission. Hammer 04 worked the sector southwest of the target area. Having established their initial working pattern, Hammer 04 noted electronic indications form a

AAA site at their one o'clock position. They continued to line up for an optimum shot at a SAM site known to be in the path of an entering bomber cell. By this time, the AAA site had full threat indications for Hammer 04, at their five o'clock position. A different AAA site appeared at their ten o'clock position, and Hammer 04 noted AAA bursting off their right wing. At this time, the SAM site came up electronically. The site then fired three SAMs at the bomber cell. Lining up on the site, Hammer 04 fired an ARM, then broke hard left to avoid the more accurate AAA coming from their right side. The SAM site stayed on the air long enough for the ARM to impact, then went down. Hammer 04 then began to work a SAM site that had been intermittently tracking them, to the southeast of their position. They fired an ARM at that site with a signal present, then immediately turned outbound to lure the site to stay on the air. The site maintained intermittent surveillance for thirty seconds, then shut down.

Hazardous conditions encountered by Hammer flight included all defenses available to the opposing force, weather, and possible mid-air collisions. MIG aircraft were airborne in the earliest part of the mission. When the MiGs landed, SAMs were abundant and AAA was profuse. The 8000-foot undercast forced Hammer flight to maintain higher than normal altitudes, limiting their maneuverability. With hundreds of support aircraft in the area, and thousands of bombs descending from above, chances of a mid-air were tremendously increased. The persistent and aggressive actions by the members of Hammer flight, under these very hazardous conditions, contributed significantly to the effectiveness and success of this first and largest bombing activity in this war. With this mission, Hammer flight brought the first electronically configured F-4C aircraft into this most highly defended area.

Joseph Snoy WW # 2067

ROMEO FLIGHT – HANOI, 26 DEC 1972

FLOYD/PALMER ROMEO 01
PARKHURST/TAYLOR ROMEO 02
MCLEOD/LAVIGNE ROMEO 03
GRAHAM/WILLIAMS DOODAD 01

On this night, Romeo flight was a 4 ship flight of electronically equipped and armed F-4C Aircraft tasked with the mission of SAM suppression for the B-52 bomber force striking targets in the vicinity of Hanoi, North Vietnam. To accomplish this demanding mission Romeo and Doodad challenged all conventional tactics and procedures by devising a daring new approach to cover simultaneous TOT's by the bomber force striking targets on both the north and south sides of Hanoi. The F-4C aircraft of Romeo and Doodad were to position themselves among the SAM sites to the north and west of Hanoi so they could be in position to attack those sites during bomber ingress and egress. To do this meant exposing the flight to continuous SAM and AAA fire in order to detect SAM launches in time to react with an AGM-45 anti-radiation missile (ARM) and kill the threatening sites before they could guide their missiles on the B-52s. In essence, these electronically configured F-4Cs of Romeo and Doodad flights were to operate on a thin line, drawing fire from the SAM sites and yet retaining the capability to attack the sites when they launched missiles. After dropping off the pre-strike tanker, Romeo flight proceeded north to Hanoi and their individual working areas. Romeo 01 worked over Phuc Yen airfield, Romeo 02 orbited the south and of Thud Ridge and Romeo 03 covered an area south from the Red River to near Bach Mai airfield. Doodad 01's sector was to the south. Initial hostile contact was made 30 miles southwest of Hanoi as the flight ingressed the target areas. Enemy MIG aircraft were airborne to intercept Romeo and Doodad since they were the first support element into the area. Romeo and Doodad split, working as single ships at this point and successfully penetrated the MIG defenses to assume their positions over the SAM sites. It shortly became apparent that the enemy was using a two-pronged defense alternating MIG activity in certain quadrants of the city with SAM launches in the others. Thus, SAM activity was highly concentrated in the areas worked by Romeo and Doodad that night, with extensive MIG activity extending further outward to the north, west and southwest. Immediately assessing the change in enemy tactics, Romeo flight took advantage of the situation and methodically varied their positions to within 10 miles of the city of Hanoi proper to tighten their coverage of the SAM sites. Although this decision increased their exposure to heavy AAA, it put the F-4Cs in an optimum position from which to fire as SAM sites became active. The effect of Romeo and Doodad's aggressive challenge to target area defenses soon became apparent. Multiple SAM launches were directed at both Romeo and Doodad to break their hold on the SAM network. Seizing the

Story by Ray McNally WW # 1179

Wild Weasel F-4C Support for the Evacuation of Saigon — 1975

Background

The 67th Tactical Fighter Squadron, assigned to 18th Tactical Fighter Wing at Kadena AB, Okinawa was tasked with the Wild Weasel mission. The squadron was a 24 UE squadron manned at 1.1 aircrew to aircraft. The F-4Cs were a mix of wild weasel and strike aircraft. There were 16 F-4C wild weasel aircraft and 8 F-4C strike aircraft assigned to the squadron. The squadron manning was mix of wild weasel crews consisting of an aircraft commander (AC) and an Electronic Warfare Officer (EWO), and strike crews consisting of an aircraft commander and a navigator. The wild weasel crew training regimen included initial training at Nellis AFB, followed up by annual refresher training at Nellis. In addition, wild weasel and strike crews completed training as for the line F-4C aircrews. Training for Wild Weasel hunter/killer tactics were practiced and when possible, evaluated during the annual tactical evaluations. Aircraft and systems maintenance was performed by the 18th TFW Maintenance organizations.

In 1972, the 18th TFW tasking included support of Commando Domino, an air defense mission at CCK AB, Taiwan. Initial requirement was for two squadrons (both of the 18th TFW F-4C squadrons) on duty at CCK, then after about a year, one squadron from the 405th TFW, Clark AB PI and one squadron from the 18th TFW were tasked. Then, the 44th TFS and 67th TFS alternated crews every three weeks, until June 1975 when the Commando Domino tasking ended.

Chronology

Preparation of support for the evacuation of Saigon: (if it had an operation name, I don't remember it)

On 18 April, 1975, the 67th TFS was tasked to deploy ten F-4C Wild Weasel (WW) aircraft and twelve of the Wild Weasel aircrews to Korat RTAFB, Thailand. Most of the crews and aircraft were at CCK AB, Taiwan, but some of each were forwarded from Kadena to CCK, to assemble the necessary assets.

> Of the twelve aircraft commanders who deployed, ten had combat experience (Southeast Asia), and had an average of 982 F-4 hours. Of the twelve EWOs, five had combat experience (Southeast Asia), and had an average of 357 hours in the F-4 aircraft.
>
> The F-4 WW aircraft had lots of miles and hours and Gs on them.

On 19 April 1975, the 67th TFS deployed to Clark AFB, to remain overnight and join with tankers (buddy refueling) for deployment to Korat RTAFB, Thailand on the next day.

On 20 April 1975, the deployment to Korat AFB was accomplished, 9 aircraft deployed, with one ground abort. The crews were briefed on the situation and placed on 6 hour alert. Maintenance personnel and equipment, and extra aircrews were deployed by C-130 airlift.

On 21 April 1975, the tenth F-4C WW aircraft arrives. Detailed theater indoctrination, intelligence and mission planning were accomplished. Planning for each flight consisted of one F-4C WW, and one F-4D strike aircraft in a hunter killer Team. The 34th TFS of the 388th TFW at Korat RTAFB was assigned as wingman to team with the 67th WW flight leader. The 34th TFS provided experienced combat flight leaders to fly the wingman-killer part of the team. The F-4C WW aircraft were configured with two AGM-45s, two AIM-7s, one ALQ-87 pod, and two 370-gallon fuel tanks. F-4D aircraft were configured with CBU, AIM-7s, and fuel tanks. Team briefings and hot pre-flights were accomplished to complete preparations. At the end of the day, seven F-4C WW were combat ready, with three ECM/RHAW problems. The ECM shop did an outstanding job to get all ready.

The Rules of Engagement were complicated and restrictive, i.e., A changing Fan Song signal is not sufficient for attack, the only attack to be made is a defensive response to SA-2 missile firing. Mission is to protect the force, and provide warning to friendlies. Various F-5, A-37, and A-1 activities can be expected. Combat Air Patrol and Close Air Support missions as well as Search and Rescue missions and Navy activities can be expected as well.

Mission plan: Fly direct to Saigon, then refuel at Ash track (offshore, parallel to shore), then to Saigon patrol, three refuelings and three TOTs at the Saigon area. Then, RTB to Korat with alternate of Ubon RTAFB, Thailand. Hickory Air-to-Air Refueling (AAR) track in southern Thailand was available for refueling as necessary.

22 April – 27 April, the crews studied, planned, briefed, waited, flew seven F-4C WW total training sorties (with the 34th TFS wingman). Hot pre-flight and tire roll for all aircraft on standby.

Rules of Engagement (ROE) change: Now a threat SA-2 in high PRF can be attacked. Cricket also can clear attack.

The South Vietnam situation on the ground was very hectic, bases overrun and abandoned, aircraft flying to friendly countries, helicopters flying to offshore ships - landing, ditching, etc. There was a report of a single seat F-5 fighter pilot, loading his wife and children inside, and flying to Thailand, landing on a road.

There were a lot of uncertainties about who was in control of anything. Were friendly aircraft captured and would they be used to make attacks during the evacuation? Could anyone be sure of who was a friendly or enemy combatant, etc.? The order of battle appeared to be fluid, with no certainty about movement of equipment and forces, i.e., AAA, SAMs, etc.

Apparently, there was a political "understanding" that the evacuation of Saigon would be allowed without enemy combat action. Could anyone trust the understanding, and if so, did everyone "get the word"?

Monday, 28 April 0100 hours, crews were placed on one hour alert. Final briefings were conducted, cocking of aircraft were checked, and crew rest. At noon, we were placed on six hour alert. The operation didn't start on this day.

Tuesday, 29 April Evacuation of Saigon starts.

A total of eight two-ship flights of F-4C/F-4D aircraft were flown in this part of the operation. Two flights were launched as soon as possible about 1000 hours local Korat time. Others followed during the daylight hours of operation over Saigon. The evacuation continued during the night and was called "complete" before dawn on 30 April 1975. A brief summary of the missions follows:

Ramrod Flight had a 1030 take-off, had one period over the Saigon area, a Navy F-4 performed an attack pass over Saigon on Ramrod Flight. Red Crown must have been busy with evacuees, because they would not or could not provide information. Ramrod missed the Ash tanker due to weather, and started to divert to Ubon, refueled on the Hickory track and continued to RTB at Korat. No electronic activity.

Bucktail Flight had a 1040 take-off, the leader had mechanical problems and made an air abort. The spare joined on the tanker, and had two TOT periods over Saigon. Had fire can signals.

Miller Flight scrambled when Ramrod missed tanker. Take-off at 1120, worked three TOTs over Saigon. Had Line of Position (LOP) on fire can 3 miles West of Tan Son Nhut AB. On third Time on Target (TOT), had a fan song in high PRF, performed a LOP. Miller leader marked the site with a shrike, and wingman attacked with CBU. Defensive reaction to Fan Song to north of Bien Hoa. (Lead one)

Risky Flight had a take-off at 1130, had three TOTs over Saigon. Detected a fan song (Lead one) near Bien Hoa, and some flak. No attack made.

Sea Fox Flight had a take-off at 1345, had one TOT over Saigon, missed Ash tanker, low fuel state - wingman jettisoned stores, diverted to Ubon for turn-around and returned to Korat.

Sun Dog Flight had a take-off at 1430, had two TOTs near Saigon, weather deteriorating and orbit was moved South. No electronic activity.

Spoil Flight had a take-off at 1630, had one TOT, Lead one at Bien Hoa was active. Missed Ash tanker for weather, started RTB - had false join with Chestnut tanker and wingman jettisoned ordnance. After inflight refueling, the wingman was NORDO, and Spoil leader had no TACAN. Korat radar was also out. Completed night recovery OK.

Packer Flight had a 1700 take-off, and was recalled for weather and night after arriving in the target area.

On 2 May 1975, the ten F-4C WW aircraft departed by two ship formations at forty five minute intervals to join tankers for the return to Kadena AB, Okinawa. Four aircraft returned to Korat due to tanker problems. Six aircraft used buddy refueling and in about five hours returned to Kadena AB. One F-4C lost a canopy on descent to Okinawa. The other four F-4Cs that had aborted, returned to Kadena in the next few days.

67th TFS Commander: Lt Col Ray F. McNally

Wild Weasel crews:

Ramrod	McNally/Cruise
Bucktail	Miller/Anderson
Miller	Suggs/Dewey
Risky	Middleton/Farrell
Sea Fox	Moore/Grindle
Sun Dog	Lemon/Bunch
Spoil	Clason/Heidenreich
Packer	Hause/Andrews
	Leib/Jackson
	Larson/Monsell
	Chesson/Shamblee
	Buby/Reed

34th TFS Commander: Lt Col Phillip W. Offill

Ray McNally

Story by John Farrell, WW # 1263

Evacuation of Saigon

Bob Middleton and I were flying Wild Weasel cover over Saigon and the delta. There were two SA-2 sites active—one northwest of Saigon, and one in the direction of Ben Hoa. Neither was being particularly hostile early in the day, just letting us know they were there. Whenever we headed towards Ben Hoa, the AAA would let us know we were not welcome. Towards the end of our 5-hour watch, the helicopters became as thick as flies and the real evacuation got underway. The SAM site northwest of Saigon took exception to all this activity and the fixed wing action that accompanied it. It went into tracking mode. So we turned, asking permission all the while to fire (he hadn't fired yet which was our ROE). I had him lined up when the ALR-53 went dark. I told Bob what had happened. He immediately and wisely asked if we should withdraw. His EWO, possibly suffering from a bit too much adrenalin said, "No, continue, I can feel them!". We continued and the SAM site shut down. All was well. As we returned to our orbit I apologized to Bob saying that I had just done the stupidest thing I could imagine. He said "No, the stupidest thing was that I believed you!" And a young and foolish Bear got to live another day.

John Farrell, WW # 1263

Story by Jack R (Jay) Suggs, WW # 1142

The Last Bomb of the Viet Nam War
29 April 1975

In 1975, I was a Captain F-4C Wild Weasel pilot with the 67TFS at Kadena AB, Japan. As a relatively recent graduate of the USAF Fighter Weapons School, I was the squadron weapons and tactics officer. I had completed a South East Asia tour in 1971-1972, flying out of Ubon, Thailand, as an F-4D air-to-ground pilot. About 1 April 1975 we began hearing that the Viet Nam (VN) war was soon to come to an official end with the closing of the US embassy in Saigon. As PACAF's Wild Weasel unit, about mid April we were notified that our services would be needed in support of Operation Frequent Wind, the evacuation of the embassy. The 67th deployed 8-10 F-4C Wild Weasel aircraft and 10-12 crews to Korat AB, Thailand (please pardon me if I'm off by one or two aircraft or crew). We joined with the 34TFS, a squadron of F-4D's who were permanently stationed at Korat. The intent was to form Hunter-Killer (F-4CWW—F-4D) 2-ship flights as combat units. We did this and briefed details and tactics for a couple of days until we felt ready. Then, on a daily basis, we would gather for a mass intelligence situation briefing at 0500 hours each day. For nearly two weeks, the briefing ended with no orders and we adjourned to the Officer's Club pool. We were beginning to like this TDY.

29 April 75 started out normally with the intell briefing concluding in no action. Then, about one hour later, they hurried us all back to intell to announce "today is the day", and prepare to launch ASAP. My 2-ship was led by myself and EWO Captain John Dewey. We had two AGM-45 Shrike missiles for ordnance. The killer/F-4D aircraft commander was Major Bob Bolls. I cannot remember who was his (Weapons System Officer) WSO. They were armed with 4xCBU-52s on the centerline station. Two 2-ships would work together: one 2-ship in the "area" and the other on a tanker. Every half hour we would swap until we each had completed three periods of area work. Then we would (Return –to-Base) RTB and the next pair of 2-ships would relieve us. Now for a little tactical set-up and ROE's. There were many fighter/attack aircraft airborne that day from all services. They

were all assigned to holding patterns and told to stay there (sound like the rest of the VN war?) unless called into action by the C-130 command and control ship, call sign "Hillsborough". All of the fighter air power was there to suppress a potential North Vietnamese (NVA) air assault on Saigon. The NVA had MiG's and recently inherited F-5 and A-37 aircraft as the South Vietnamese (SVA) air force retreated in such haste that they left those aircraft ready for use. Our presence was to discourage their desire to use their air power. We were never expected to drop or fire a single weapon, although they did not tell us that. Wild Weasels, however, were exempt from the holding patterns. We were allowed to work an "area", and "rove in our allotted territory" within a 20NM radius of the Tan Son Nhut air base TACAN in Saigon. But we had been given some special Rules of Engagement (ROE), also. In a top-secret message sent directly from Joint Chiefs of Staff (JCS) to the 67TFS, we were instructed that we would "not fire solely upon electronic indications only". In other words, we had to be fired upon, and cleared by Hillsborough, before we could return fire (again, sound typical of the VN war?). The one exception was if we got ourselves in extreme danger, we could declare a "defensive reaction" and expend ordnance or do whatever necessary to get out safely.

My flight, call sign "Miller" took off from Korat fairly early that morning but definitely after sun up. Nearing Saigon, we entered the "area" and began the Weasel work of looking for SAM or Anti-Aircraft Artillery) AAA radars. We were flying a 2-ship "fluid-2" tactical formation back and forth around the northern part of our area. We detected FANSONG (SA-2) radar signals coming from somewhere slightly north of our area boundary. They just tickled us without firing anything. After a half hour we were relieved by our teammate 2-ship and we headed to the tanker. As we finished period 1 we told the other Wild Weasel about the FANSONG painting us. A half hour later we returned to the area to relieve our teammates. They said they did not encounter any enemy radar. However, soon after we began working the area, up came the FANSONG again. We tried to locate it. In the F-4CWW by either taking directions from the EWO interpreting his signal display scope, or centering the Shrike needles, the pilot could look through his 35 mil gun sight and theoretically have the target emitter under the pipper. This technique is called "homing-in" on a target emitter.

As a side note, while we were "trolling" around in period #2, I witnessed a very traumatic sight. Part of the area north of Saigon that we were working was the airspace over Bien Hoa (sp?) Air Base. I had landed at Bien Hoa many times during my 1971-1972 tour. We would land there for refueling and re-arming, and then depart on a second mission. We, at Ubon, called it the "Bien Hoa turn". What I saw under me was the old Bien Hoa AB under siege in real time. A wave of explosions was occurring slowly across the base as the NVA over-ran the base (or the South Vietnamese (SVA) retreated), burning everything as they went. I tell you, it brought tears to my eyes.

The rest of period 2 was interesting as we tried to better locate the FANSONG emitter, but rather uneventful. Again, our flights swapped out and we went to the tanker. We were about 2 hours and 15 minutes into the mission when we arrived back in the area for our third and last period. After this 30-minute period Miller flight would RTB, and another Hunter-Killer team would replace us. We exchanged Intel with the flight relieving us, as they headed for the tanker. They also had detected the SA-2 radar, but could not locate it.

Almost as soon as we began working the area, the FANSONG came up on us. This time it was not tickling us. It was tracking us in the center of its beam. However, there was no electronic launch signal, nor did we see a launch visually. But we were sure expecting one. I began centering the Shrike needles in earnest, and homing in on the site in hopes of either getting a visual on it or seeing the impending missile launch. Just then my wingman, Miller 2, called out "Move it around, lead, you're taking a lot of flack". I looked around and saw big black puffs of AAA explosions all around me. It looked like the old WW-II films of B-17's over Germany. I had made the classic mistake of getting "tunnel vision" and by homing in on the radar had made our aircraft very predictable. I started jinking and rolled the aircraft over almost inverted to see what was shooting at me. There, along a winding dirt road was several (8-10) 57mm AAA guns shooting at us. I knew they were 57mm from seeing many on my combat tour. They had a distinct photoflash muzzle flash, and no tracer. Then it dawned on me what was happening. Those wily NVN had used the FANSONG radar to draw us into a well-planned flack trap! With the AAA explosions all around us, I felt we needed to go offensive to get out alive. I announced to Hillsborough that we were executing a "Defensive

Reaction" (remember the ROEs?). I'll never forget the response from the Hillsborough controller as he nearly screamed, "Roger, you're cleared!" It was as if all the pent-up emotions of fighting a 15-year Viet Nam war with one hand tied behind you were expressed in that one radio transmission. Now I could see the guns shooting at us, but my wingman was the one with the bombs (CBUs). So I hurriedly asked him if he could see all the AAA sites shooting at us. He said he could not see a one. I had to get his eyes on at least one of the guns. Relying on that old fighter pilot axiom, "flexibility is the key to air power", I quickly announced, "well, I'm IN to mark". But all I had was two Shrikes. I instinctively reverted back to my combat tour where I was a nighttime "OWL" FAC. I had fired many Willie Pete marking rockets for fighters waiting above to get a "tally" on the target. So I rolled in to about only a 15-degree dive, aiming at one of the AAA sites about 2 miles away. Without time to adjust mils in my 35 mil gun sight, I guestimated at what would be about 45 mils (a typical rocket setting), and fired a totally unguided AGM-45. To my surprise the missile zinged right over the gun pit and hit only about 100 feet long. My instantaneous thought was that even though it didn't hit the pit, it must have scared the heck out of them. I pulled of the pass and asked my wingman if he saw the tall column of smoke and debris from the Shrike impact. He said he did. I said, "well, hit it!" He called IN from about 9,000 feet of altitude and 30 degrees of dive for a "one pass, haul ass" ripple of all four CBU-52s. CBUs make a circular footprint on the ground of about 500 feet in diameter. Designed to overlap, four CBUs rippled, clear a swath about 500 feet by 1,500 feet with softball sized incendiary hand grenades (a very mean weapon for lightly hardened targets).

As I watched his bombs hit, the first three hit short but the last one completely covered one of the gun pits. In addition to the gun pit blowing up we saw secondary explosions coming from several hundred feet short of the target where the first CBUs had hit. It was common for the NVA not to store all their shells in the pit with them, but to secure them a few hundred feet away (so if their ammo dump blew up it wouldn't kill those in the gun pit). As luck would have it, those first three short rounds walked right through their ammo dump.

I directed Miller 2 to come off his dive bomb pass headed west (towards home), and I joined on him in tactical spread formation. We all then noticed that the guns had stopped firing. It was again so typical of the whole VN war. It was as if they had read our daily Ops Order (now termed FRAG) and knew we were not supposed to expend any ordnance that day. But because we DID, they became confused and ceased firing across the whole region. The cease-fire allowed us to accelerate, climb and head out of the immediate threat safely. The strategy of turning offensive to save us defensively worked. Although our half hour period was not up, we were out of armament and had fired all our brain cells, so we RTBd.

Back at Korat, the after landing became interesting. My squadron commander, L/C Ray McNally, and the Korat wing commander met us at the aircraft. L/C McNally said, "Boy, I sure hope you have a good story. The 13th AF commander wants a full report". When I inquired as to why, he said "because you were the only two to drop anything all day". This is how I knew we had dropped the last bomb of the Viet Nam war. The Saigon embassy was evacuated this day, 29 April 1975, signifying the official end to the war.

So off I went to the Intell building where they verified that Miller flight was the only fighters to expend ordnance that day. They also asked me to write it all down so they could send it via classified fax to the awaiting 13th AF commanding general. I wrote 13 pages, all the time thinking that I might be drafting my own courts martial. Upon finishing, I adjourned to a well-needed drink at the O club bar. I was anxious to hear a response back from the general. Then, a couple of hours later, L/C McNally walked in with a smile on his face. I couldn't wait to ask of my fate. He said, "Well, the general read it..." Then he paused. The suspense was killing me. He then said, "The general said...I guess I would have done the same thing". Whew! I was off the hook.

The war was over and the detached 67TFS Wild Weasels returned to Kadena. Life returned to normal. About six months later, in a weekly Ops meeting, Capt. John Dewey and I were summoned to the front to receive an award. We were each presented with a plaque. It was a typical Thai-made wooden plaque formed in the shape of a shield. It simply said at the top, "To Miller Flight", and at the bottom, "From Hillsborough". In the middle was no writing but only a well carved and painted pair of Brass Balls. Today I still have this plaque on my wall. Coming from Hillsborough, I figured it was generated by the same guy that had so elaborately declared, "You're cleared!" He probably convinced his unit to sponsor an unofficial plaque commemorating the guts of two crews who legally challenged the ROE to actually finish the Viet Nam war with a bang instead of a whimper.

This would normally be the end to the story. But this one has an epilogue. Some twenty years afterwards I was a speaker at an aviation flight museum. I was telling the above story to an audience. Many in the audience were Viet Nam veterans. After I finished I asked for questions. From the audience Colonel Tom Halley (retired) stated that this talk had now put the pieces of a puzzle together for him. The story he told watered my eyes. As a little history, the Saigon evacuation of 29 April 1975 was not about fighters. It was about helicopters shuttling back and forth from the embassy to an aircraft carrier waiting offshore. The play, "Miss Saigon" was written about this day and the days that preceded it. Even if you're a young person reading this with no first hand knowledge of the Viet Nam war, you probably remember having seen newsreels of helicopters landing on the carrier in such large numbers that they were pushing them off the deck to make room for more.

The Colonel related that he had a friend that was one of those helicopter pilots that day. They took a lot of small arms fire as they shuttled in and out of the embassy. But, having mini-gun machine guns, they were able to cope with the small arms fire. But Anti-Aircraft Artillery was too big and powerful for a helicopter to deal with. As I had earlier stated, I watched from the air as the NVA swept across Bien Hoa AB, north of Saigon. What I didn't know was it didn't take them long to go right into Saigon. So this helicopter pilot began taking AAA gunfire on the flight towards the embassy, which was more than they could handle. He decided that he would have to turn back, and others in the convoy agreed. They did a 180-degree turn and began heading back to the carrier. With the AAA guns in place this would mean an early termination to the evacuation and many people left at the embassy that would have been evacuated. Just at this time Miller flight was about 15 miles north bombing one of the same AAA sites. As I previously said, after the bombing, all shooting by the AAA sites ceased. Apparently that cease-fire order went all the way into the AAA sites shooting at the helicopters in Saigon, and in their confusion, lasted for a long time. At any rate, the helicopter pilots noticed the cease-fire and chose to turn back towards the embassy and resume the evacuation. Thus, the dropping of the last bomb of the Viet Nam war had more impact (pardon the pun) than getting 2 fighter crews out of a tactical jam. It allowed many more souls to be evacuated to freedom instead of being left to the torture and death by the NVA. That's the part that watered my eyes.

Author's note. This "last bomb" story has been told in much shorter versions in at least three books:

1. The Air Force, by McCarthy and DeBerry, 2002, p.187.
2. Iron Hand, by Thornborough and Mormillo, 2002, p.147-148.
3. The Phantom Story, by Thornborough and Davies, 1994, 2000,p.254.

Jay Suggs

Story by Jim Winzell, WW # 1098

The F-4G Wild Weasel

What I went home to in 1973 was a joyful reunion with my family and an opportunity to take on a whole new career field in system acquisition. As a part of my Master's Degree deal, not only did I get to go back to SEA but when I returned, I went directly into a "Directed Duty Assignment" which was designed to use the education I had received in a related field. In this case, I was assigned as an engineer in a System Program Office (SPO) at Wright Patterson AFB in Dayton, Ohio. I elected to join the SPO that would eventually produce the EF-111A jamming platform. When I arrived, there were only a half dozen people in the organization and they had not even decided what platform would be used. In the 4 ½ years I spent in the SPO, I learned the entire procurement cycle from studying and selecting the platform to being a part of or running 6 major source selections to flying chase in an F-14 on the first flight of the prototype airplane. I started in engineering and was responsible for the EF-111A defensive systems and ended up on the production floor at Grumman Aircraft in Long Island responsible for managing the build-up of the prototype airplane. This experience would be invaluable throughout the rest of my career inside and outside the Air Force.

I also got to fly the F-14 with Chuck Sewell, the Grumman chief pilot and to get operational flights in the EA-6B and the A-6. A real treat was spending 5 days on the USS Independence in the Mediterranean getting three cat shots and two recoveries—which convinced me I'd picked the right service to fly in.

After pausing to attend Army Command and General Staff College in Fort Leavenworth, Kansas I was "invited" to return to the Wild Weasels This time it would be in a new airplane, the F-4G, which was built to replace the Thud that I flew in SEA. The home of the new Wild Weasel was George AFB in Victorville, California. So back to sunny California we went anticipating the challenges of establishing a home and getting our now older kids through school. There was another major challenge and that was bringing a new weapon system on line and making it operationally ready.

The F-4G was a modified McDonnell Douglas F-4E. The mod was done at Hill AFB by the government with help from MACAIR and the other suppliers that provided the APR-38, our first venture into digital avionics for a fighter. The APR-38 was cosmic...when it worked. It could provide reasonably accurate emitter location and, on a large display for the Bear, it could place that location in relationship to your airplane and the envelope of the missiles you were carrying. All of this information was only guessed at in the Thud—which accounted for our poor probability of kill.

The problem with the F-4G and APR-38s at George was they were delivered without working software, which was late in development. There were multiple teams at George working this problem when I arrived. We had people from three different test groups; we had teams out of the acquisition and support commands from Hill and Wright-Pat. We had the contractors and, of course, the local operational wing. It was taking an inordinate amount of time to code, load, fly and analyze each change to the software and the schedule kept slipping. Part of the reason for these delays was the length of the analysis chain for determining if a change to the code had worked. We would fly a mission in the morning, debrief, review the cockpit videos, wrap up the recorder tapes and hand carry them down the hill to Ontario airport where the package was given to the crew flying the next flight to St. Louis. We would alert the McDonald Douglas team and they would meet the aircraft, pick up the package and begin analyzing the results—which usually took several days. In the meantime we continued flying test sorties not knowing if the software was functioning properly. Something needed to be done to close this gap. We needed to consolidate the multiple teams into one, put someone in charge and get everyone pulling in one direction. We also needed to get the Wild Weasel Wing out of the testing business and turn the flight operation over to one of the professional test organizations. After considerable pushing and shoving, we came to an agreement as to the makeup of the team, who it would report to and who would be in charge. The in-charge person turned out to be me and, again, I got a chance to change directions in my career path.

What an experience. The F-4G Test Team was formed with hand-picked professionals. Crews were brought over from the operational Wild Weasel Wing, a full maintenance group was formed to support the three test coded Gs and an onsite engineering team was put together from the participating Air Force engineering groups. This core team reported into the Tactical Air Warfare Center at Eglin AFB, FL. The team also consisted of representatives from the Tactical Fighter Weapons Center at Nellis AFB, NV, the AF Operational Test and Evaluation Center at Kirtland AFB, NM and the acquisition and support centers of AF Systems Command and Material Command. It was the one of the first truly integrated product teams—before IPTs were in fashion.

Now that we were organized, we needed to focus on the physical elements of testing the G. We needed a facility and we needed onsite data reduction. Our initial home was an old bomb build-up facility that was not being used. The good news was we had our own facility. The bad news was it consisted of 12-inch thick reinforced concrete walls with no windows and no air conditioning. Everything had to be done in parallel if we had any chance to gain ground on the schedule so we began developing the data reduction software while we were modifying the facility for the data reduction computers. We had hired BDM to help do the software and combined their team with our existing engineering team. I will never forget the sight of rows of engineers at their computers wearing noise suppression headsets to keep out the jackhammer cacophony while hoping the concrete dust wouldn't freeze up their sensitive computers.

After weeks of difficult conditions and long hours we finally were up and running with a remarkable on-site data reduction facility and an integrated team for testing software, hardware and developing tactics for these new systems. We went from days to make software changes to hours. Instead of waiting up to a week to see if a change worked, we could turn it around overnight. As a result, we successfully completed and checked out the first operational software load and went on to the development testing and integration of the new systems such as the High Speed Anti-radiation missile (HARM) that replaced the Vietnam era ARMs. The combination of the F-4G, APR-38 and HARM was powerful. They were built on the lessons learned from Vietnam and proved themselves over the skies of Iraq in Desert Storm I.

This success was largely due to the Can Do attitude of the Wild Weasel community that was determined to make the F-4G a success. It started with the core group of Wild Weasel crews and then permeated out into anyone associated with the effort. One example of this occurred early in the program when the APR-38s that were delivered with the initial F-

4Gs began failing. We could not get replacement parts and the fleet was existing on cannibalized parts from the grounded Gs. Those replacement parts were supposed to come from AFLC at Warner Robbins, GA, but we could not seem to get their attention and the parts were just trickling in. So the Wing Commander and I flew one of the Gs to Warner Robbins where Col. Duke Terry, the Wing Commander, who used to play nose tackle for Texas A&M, put on quite a briefing, showing the AMC people what the Wild Weasel mission was all about. He then invited the people who process the parts orders out to our airplane to see what an F-4G looked like (most of them had never seen one). When they walked up the ramp and looked into the cockpit, there was a collective gasp for all they saw was a bunch of holes were there should have been displays and dials. Within days the supply line opened and we were back in business. The Warner Robbins bureaucrats had become Wild Weasels.

Another example of people becoming Wild Weasels was a young engineer assigned to us out of Warner Robbins named E F Hundley. We named him "E F" after the commercial running at that time whose tagline was "when E F Hutton speaks, everyone listens." And that is how we felt about E F—he was a phenomenal software engineer and the program relied on his understanding of what we were trying to accomplish. Sometimes, however, we had real problems trying to explain to E F what we wanted his system to do for us because his experience base was his laboratory and his coding abilities. To try to bridge that gap, we arranged to fly E F in an F-4G on a test mission. Wow, what an impact that had! He came back with saucer eyes exclaiming that he now understood how different the aircraft environment was compared to his lab. The communication gap was closed and we had another Wild Weasel for life.

The stories go on and on. From one generation to the next. The F-4G earned its spurs in the early 80s and proved itself over the skies of Iraq in the early 90s. We continue to bring in new and better systems and the mission evolves based on the threat. What remains constant are the people dedicated to the mission. Like the F-4G Test Team, success is based on the Wild Weasel crews and the Wild Weasel team—something we need to make sure continues into the foreseeable future.

Jim Winzell

Story by T. Bear Larson WW # 952

The F-4G/APR-38/HARM Evolves as a Weapons System

I came to George AFB, CA and the F-4G from six years of flying F-4C Wild Weasels in USAFE at Zweibrucken, Spangdahlem, and attached to the 81st TFS while assigned to HQ USAFE. Prior to that I flew F-105s at Korat. I stopped at Nellis on the way to George AFB to see some friends, and visited the F-4G Test Team there. Denny Haney took me to see the system and displays on the Integrated Test bench (I Bench), and I was immediately hooked on such a neat system! Astounding what 64K of software could do!! The fact that the computer could figure out the range to the emitter opened up whole new horizons in tactics and eliminated specific maneuvers and profiles that had bound Wild Weasel aircrews in the past. I was excited to get into the system and see what it could do in the air.

I checked into George AFB and immediately was assigned to F-4C instructor duties, and started "classes" in the APR-38 Advanced Wild Weasel system. The "classes" consisted of lots of time on the I Bench with previously trained APR-38 guys, and the contractor (McDonnell Douglas – or McAir as we called them) technical team assigned to support the system. This word of mouth training was required as the system was in testing, and no formal documentation existed for the aircrews yet. Two years later the APR-38 System Program Office (SPO) Program Manager, Lt Col Hank Keck of ASC/RWWW, sent his secretary to George AFB TDY for a month to help three of us originate the first TOs – the -34, -34-1-1, -34-1-2, and APR-38 handbook. We figured out that we better write it as the contractor and the Technical Order (TO) people couldn't get past first base with it, and the airplanes were starting to arrive!

My first sortie in the F-4G was a test flight – I guess the objective for Air Force Operational Test and Evaluation Center (AFOTEC) was to see if the "lowest common denominator" was capable of turning on the system and getting data. This was a challenge as part of the instrumentation was the CONRAC recorder built into the APR-38 (and extremely temperamental, so we had to make sure we had good video) and a video camera over each shoulder in the rear cockpit. They were state of the art at the time, but needed a sunshade over the entire rear cockpit to eliminate the glare from the APR-38 scopes and ruin the recording. This meant a lot of time for the test EWO in the dark, with his physical sensors "turned off" so he wouldn't get too airsick. Lots of hours for all of us under the bag rooting around at "three foot six" as Jerry Linn would say, or doing pop ups and tactical maneuvers. It became very confusing when the AGM-65 Imaging Infrared (IIR) Maverick was introduced, and the world outside the cockpit showed up on the radarscope in an orientation that was significantly different than what your brain anticipated!

We soon learned that we had to extract how the system software was programmed to work from the limited documentation available (we had to compare how we thought it worked, versus how it was programmed to work, versus how we really wanted it to work). We rapidly learned two things – the need to document the "shortfalls", and the high value of someone who could understand the McAir software, and extract the logic (or not) from that documentation. However the deals were struck, a young engineer named Mr. James Hundley (nicknamed EF) was assigned TDY from Warner Robins Air Logistics Center (ALC) support facility to support the test team. He extracted the actual flow charts from the hexadecimal, and walked us through the "logic" of the system whenever we had a question or were troubleshooting. We were all learning by doing! We worked with EF day in and day out to figure out how the system really worked, and educated him on why we wanted it to work that way. Early on we complained to him and McAir about how difficult it was to reach the buttons under G's because of the way the software displayed certain things. After a while we worked the approval "system?" and got him a range ride in the F-4G operating the APR-38 system. We had some flight test run cards and were trying to get him to work the system under Gs. Needless to say, we briefed "Goose" Gowell, the pilot for the flight, on certain things to emphasize and we had EF's number regarding making the system working under "Gs". Shortly there after the software changed to make the switches just how we wanted them!

This was my first exposure to the civilian aspect of the military, and I made the mistake of introducing him as a contractor to some of my friends at the Nellis stag bar the first night, and he ripped my lips off! However, I recovered, and as he had never heard fighter pilot songs, we ended up teaching him several that night (some of which got lost in the fog, but

"Sally in the Alley" still brings a smile to our faces some 25+ years later when we tip a few together). He stayed with us throughout test, and moved with us (still TDY in several week chunks of time) when we returned to George to start introducing the new aircrews to the newly modified jets.

The other aspect of software (all 64K!) was that it could always change, and would always have to be flight-tested. How would we control this – it was running away with us. The concept of block cycles evolved to get the critical ones fixed, and then bring more fixes on as the Warner Robins team became proficient in their understanding of the code, and their ability to program it progressed. The operational and test guys soon were intermingled with the software guys in understanding the system, and sorting out which problems to fix, and which ones to defer. This caused all of us to learn about software, new tactics, the hardware and the funding process to work on all of these issues.

By this time we had a lot of people involved – ASC/RWW as the developer, Ogden ALC as the mod facility and the System Program Manager, San Antonio ALC for test equipment, Air Force Test and Evaluation Center (AFTEC) (before it became AFOTEC in the early 80s) doing the Initial Operational Test and Evaluation (IOT&E) and Follow-on Operational Test and Evaluation (FOT&E) of the system and the new AGM-88 High Speed Anti-Radiation Missile (HARM), Tactical Air Warfare Center (TAWC) as the threat and software manager for HQ Tactical Air Command (TAC), Tactical Fighter Weapons Center (TFWC) as the Tactics Development and Evaluation agency, HQ TAC trying to work the requirements, fielding and management of the overall system, and finally, HQ Air Force Logistics Command (AFLC) and HQ Air Force Systems Command (AFSC), HQ United Stated Air Force (USAF) agencies that were sorting out the funding and Air Force level priorities. Plenty of oars in the water, and each area had its own funding chain and "color" of money. A vehicle was needed to tie these together via some form of structure for the management and test of the system. Several folks got together to hammer out a Memorandum Of Agreement (MOA) for the "Management Integration Panel" or MIP chaired by the System Program Manager (SPM) from Ogden, and a flight test detachment at George AFB lead by TAWC, with an AFOTEC operation location on site. This enabled a solid foundation to plan, integrate and fund programs coming onto the F-4G. This included the High Speed Anti-Radiation Missile (HARM), the

ARN-101 digital (Inertial Navigation System (INS), and a myriad of new tactics that exploited the vast new capabilities of the system.

A major challenge to the F-4G was the rapidly evolving threat. The bad guys had been quickly fielding new mobile SAM systems that stretched the hardware and software capability of the APR-38. This forced another subgroup to get together to address this. The first issue was to ensure the software guys at Warner Robins got the clearances to see the same data the operational guys and the threat guys at Eglin were seeing. Then they had to work out how to address the various new threat waveforms – via changes to processing algorithms in the basic Operational Flight program, or to the threat data provided by TAWC, or identifying a hardware deficiency. It was quickly apparent that the hardware needed more processing capability, and an upgraded receiver was needed to address the new double digit SAMs. The requirements guys at HQ TAC started a new Statement of Operational Need for the APR-38 Performance Update Program (PUP). It had two phases, the PUP I computer upgrade (to a whopping 512K!), and the PUP II new receiver. These were to be fielded in the late 80s.

Meanwhile, we had to field the new aircraft as they were delivered from the Hill AFB depot. The mod was to put a digital system into the old trusty analog F-4. Due to the nature of the APR-38 ranging system and its interfaces with the INS and other avionics on the platform, the mod could not be fully checked out on the ground. This drove the SPM to request some of the flight test EWOs to fly test sorties on an instrumented range before the mod was accepted. While waiting for the aircraft to get out of the mod line, we spent time training the Hill backseaters about the APR-38, so they could take up the slack. After the TAC crews accepted the first ten aircraft, the bugs were shaken out of the mod line, and Hill got an EWO assigned who went through the APR-38 school and took over the acceptance testing.

This took one job off the plate of the flight test EWOs. They were very busy. They were finishing the APR-38 FOT&E by documenting the test and the identified deficiencies, meeting with MacAir and Warner Robins to sort out priorities to resolve the shortfalls, flight testing some of the software fixes to the critical deficiencies, generating the draft TOs and hand books, as well as drafting the outline and slides for APR-38 system's ground school, platform instructing APR-38 basics, while flying as instructors to train new instructors! Soon there were enough teachers to take up some of the load, and the flight test guys could get on to testing the HARM missile.

The fielding of the aircraft was moving along, and some of the identified limitations that were acceptable for stateside use, needed to be fixed before the F-4G became operational in Europe, where the Fulda Gap mentality was alive and well. This drove to another OFP update and flight test validation. Time was not on the tester's side, and after the last sortie, the data tapes were hand carried by the test team to MacAir for analysis. As soon as it was validated that the system worked, the crews stayed and helped stack and sort the IBM computer cards containing the update so that a new OPF tape could be assembled. Fighter aircrews loading computers while MacAir and government software engineers "openly and frankly" discussed tactics and operational upgrades became the norm for the F-4G Test Team – we were starting to fully understand each other.

The APR-38 ranging opened up whole new capabilities, especially with the employment of missiles. Knowing the range enabled a faster, more accurate employment of the Viet Nam era Shrike without doing a "dip check", and guessing how high to pull up the nose to employ it. During the APR-38 FOT&E the test crews were exposed to the IIR Maverick, and an experimental launcher that enabled the Maverick seeker to be pointed by the APR-38. Wow! Stand off hard kill! We worked hard with the Maverick SPO and the F-4G SPM to procure the slaving launchers, and enable the EO Maverick to do the same thing. But the desires for longer stand off range lead us to really pursue the Navy's development of the HARM.

The testers had been working with the Navy program office to carry and launch the developmental AGM-88 HARM. The F-4G interfaces and control systems were starting to come together, but flight tests in the HARM basic modes identified a lot of the limitations driven by the radar warning system on the prime Navy aircraft, the A-7. Mean time the F-4G started really finding its feet. The basic ranging system only worked one signal at a time. This was upgraded by software changes to enable ranging on all the displayed signals. The crews started working out tactics to get good ranging in minimum time, and they were starting to trust the system to deliver. Several test EWOs and the AFOTEC analysis team was supporting a program review at Texas Instruments (TI) in Lewisville, TX. In an after hours meeting in a Lewisville honky tonk involving adult beverages, this group worked on the TI engineers and the HARM AF

System Program Office (SPO) representative and tried to figure out if the HARM could make use of the range the APR-38 provided. The TI engineers thought about it, and were wondering if the basic navigation hardware and software could support it. A few beers later, and numerous bar napkins of notes, they thought they may be able to integrate the rate gyros into something to guide a trajectory. This started an entire ground swell for "Equations of Motion" or EOM as the software subroutine became know. The AF SPO representative found a few dollars and enabled an engineering analysis followed by a three missile Development Test and Evaluation (DT&E) of the concept. We had to work with Warner Robins to quantify the statistical bounds of the APR-38 ranging to see if they matched the bounds of the HARM hardware capabilities. Fortunately the previous testing had generated a statistically representative database on the ranging algorithm to assist in the analysis. The TI six degree of freedom (6DOF) fly out model showed the APR-38's hand off accuracy was enough to make the concept work. The Navy wasn't really hot for the mod as they couldn't employ it with receivers they had, and funding was lost and then recovered several times on the way to the demonstration flights. The success of the demo shots was enough to split the IOT&E into two phases, delaying the second phase long enough to use the new EOM mode in the last part of the IOT&E.

The next challenge was trying to fit all of the HARM handoff and control software into the APR-38's 64K Operational Flight Program (OFP). The flight test version of the APR-38 OFP supporting HARM had several parts of the actual operational program missing to fit the HARM subroutine into the computer. EOM was an additional module in that subroutine, and we had to belly up to fit it in. Two things enabled the operational HARM module to get shoe horned in – Warner Robins software engineers and a whole team effort. The Robins engineers were starting to really scrub the code in the OFP to streamline it. The teaming of Mr. Hundley with the original test team was starting to pay dividends. He had gone back and cloned himself with a group of young engineers who took on a real operational attitude. (Once while at Warner Robins for a meeting, they asked if I was staying over to fly model aircraft with them the next day. Found out they would be out in a parking lot, flying their Wild Weasel profiles and dog fighting with model aircraft complete with WW tail flashes on the tails! Beer came out after the victory rolls – just like actual Weasels!). These guys cut the Shrike routine in half while adding two additional features, ensured the threat data base was sized right to handle the entire threat, and significantly streamlined Built In Test (BIT) and the display software size without impacting performance. In fact, in most cases the performance was improved. Not surprisingly, 20+ years later, these same guys are in several key management positions at Warner Robins generating their own clones. The second group was the team of engineers - MacAir, TI and government – as well as operators and testers that sat down together and literally counted the bits of each sub-routine. All sides traded things off, and the OFP fit with a small double-digit number of words left over! The OFP along with HARM could be fielded and give a significant new punch to the Weasels. Once the PUP I upgrade was in place, all of the "deferred" software could be reinstated.

Once again the testers took on the duties and responsibilities of writing the TOs and handbooks for HARM. To do that they "borrowed" the TI 6DOF to generate the footprint and P_k (Probability of Kill) tables on the Test Team computers. By the time IOT&E and FOT&E of HARM were completed, the 6DOF had been feed enough data to be trusted as a weapons and tactics tool. It was not uncommon to have numerous 6DOF runs cued up to run through the night or over the week end to get the data points needed for the Weapons and Tactics hand books or to validate the safety containment of a shot on the range at China Lake. The HARM was fielded and the aircrews started to understand how to use the extended range and other tactical advantages of the missile. The standard from Vietnam on was to call "Shotgun" on the Ultra High Frequency (UHF) radio to announce the launch of a Shrike from a Wild Weasel. This was to help ensure no one mistook a Shrike launch for an enemy missile. As the crews became comfortable with HARM, they began to differentiate the launch of a HARM by changing the call to "Magnum". Truly an accurate call sign! The Weasels had migrated from the "knife fight" and "Saturday night special" days of the F-100 and F-105 to a certified standoff kill capability.

By the mid 80s we were testing the PUP I computer. It was a challenge, as we had to integrate three digital systems (PUP I APR-38, HARM and the ARN-101 INS) on the analog F-4, and they all depended on each other, and were being developed by three different SPOs with three different contractors. Once again the management and test teams and Warner

Robins software engineers rose to the task, and the flight test of each was successful, and installations progressed.

By the start of Desert Storm all of the improvements were integrated into the system, there were HARMs out there in numbers. All those associated with the evolution of the weapon system were popping buttons with pride on the feedback of the performance of their "baby" during Desert Storm. By this time I was in the basement of the Pentagon, working on the Follow On Wild Weasel and new weapons to kill mobile SAM systems.

Years later I learned what a special relationship we in the F-4G management, development and test team had. This became apparent when Integrated Product Teams (IPTs) came into vogue, and the Air Force found out that they couldn't dictate cooperation. We had been a true Wild Weasel IPT in every aspect, and didn't even know it (and didn't care what they called it!).

T. Bear Larson

Story by Edward M "Victor" Ballanco, WW # 1774

Wild Weasel Planning for Desert Storm

I am currently employed by SAIC as a US Air Forces in Europe (USAFE) Warrior Preparation Center Senior Military Analyst; Author of the Air War Over Serbia Initial (Unclassified) Report; and Chief of the Society of Wild Weasels

In Aug 90, as a lieutenant colonel, I was assigned as Chief of the Weapons and Tactics Division, 52 Tactical Fighter Wing (TFW), Spangdahlem Air Base, Germany, and flew as a member of the 23 Tactical Fighter Squadron (TFS). The 52 TFW was a Defense Suppression wing, dedicated to support NATO in Central Europe. The wing consisted of three mixed squadrons, 12 F-4G and 12 F-16C each. In Wing Weapons we had two F-4G pilots, two F-4G Electronic Warfare Officers (EWO), and two F-16 pilots, most of whom were Fighter Weapons School graduates. Although I was not a Fighter Weapons School graduate, I had by that time eight years of fighter experience, six of which were in the F-4G. After my first tour at Spangdahlem, I had spent two years at the USAF Tactical Air Warfare Center (TAWC), Eglin AFB, as a Wild Weasel staff officer in the F-4G Program Management Office. While at TAWC, I was responsible for F-4G Operational Test and Evaluation of the F-4G digital navigation system (ARN-101) and the new AGM-88 High Speed Anti-Radiation Missile (HARM). I also was on the team responsible for integrating the HARM on the F-16C, and participated in reviewing Tactics Development and Evaluations (TD&E). This experience was invaluable for my role as a Desert Storm planner in 1990-91.

When I returned to Spangdahlem in early 1988, there had been several upgrades that improved the Wild Weasel mission. The first was a computer upgrade, the Wild Weasel Attack Signal Processor (WASP) to the F-4G's Radar Attack and Warning System that changed its designation to the APR-47. The APR-47 gave the F-4G a very rapid and accurate ranging capability, particularly at high altitude. There was also the AGM 88 HARM fielding, a significantly more capable anti-radiation missile than either the

AGM-45 Shrike or the AGM-78 Standard ARM. The F-4G and the F-16C, then being modified to carry the HARM, were a formidable Defense Suppression team. The F-16C with its superior air-to-air radar, gave the Wild Weasel Team an excellent capability against enemy fighters, while the F-4G provided a superior capability against enemy SAMs. Although nobody would say it officially, we believed that all of these upgrades gave the Wild Weasels an improvement in our kill capability using missiles rather than bombs. The Wild Weasels were also teamed with the EF-111 Raven and the EC-130 Compass Call establishing an Electronic Combat (EC) triad with both a jamming and a radar killing capability. The 65 Air Division (AD) was the parent headquarters for the EC Triad, responsible for the integrated EC Triad concept of operations, employment procedures, intelligence support, and training.

The Israelis had proven in the Bekaa Valley in 1982 that it was possible to mount a "Suppression of Enemy Air Defenses (SEAD) Campaign" against an Integrated Air Defense System (IADS) and to inflict significant damage to enemy SAMs. The Israelis put the Syrian SAMs out of business after the first day's operation, gained air superiority at high altitude and then proceeded to destroy the Syrian fighters with an 85-1 kill ratio. In studying the Israeli operation, we discovered that they did most of the damage to the SAMs using anti-radiation missiles. When they followed up the missile attacks with bomb attacks, they discovered that most of the sites were already destroyed. Using the HARM, we thought we could do as well or better.

Based on the Israeli experience and our confidence in the HARM capability, Wing Weapons developed a SEAD Campaign concept for Wild Weasel employment in NATO that analysis indicated could be very effective even against the full-up Soviet IADS we faced across the Iron Curtain. The 52 TFW wanted NATO to employ the Wild Weasels using a campaign approach not in a piecemeal fashion. Additionally, we required medium/high altitude airspace so that we could load the F-4G with one external fuel tank and four HARMs rather than the normal configuration of three fuel tanks and two HARMs. High altitude airspace for tactical aircraft was unheard of in Central Europe during the Cold War. Captain Mark Svestka was the primary briefer for the Wild Weasel SEAD Campaign briefing. He, along with Army Master Sergeants Mark Olin, our ground liaison officer, went on a road show, usually with the Wing Commander providing top cover.

Many of the briefings became very heated because not everyone thought the SEAD concept at medium altitude was sound. Our Wing Commanders stood behind us because they believed that we were right.

By 1990, we had made some progress "selling" the SEAD Campaign concept supported by several parallel but related efforts. NATO, in their Cold War standing air-tasking orders, tasked the Wild Weasels for campaign SEAD with a plan to exploit favorable conditions and roll back and roll down the defenses. They also changed the air route structure to give the EC Triad the high altitude airspace that we requested. As we practiced and studied the IADS further, our SEAD campaign ideas touched on what was then known as command and control warfare, because we saw the benefit to our mission of an orchestrated campaign against the command and control as well as the defense systems themselves. This approach used more than the EC Triad. As part of our targeting process we nominated IADS critical node targets that would be struck by NATO ground attack aircraft.

We worked closely with the 65th Air Division to develop a theater-training plan based on the SEAD campaign concept. First the EC Triad flew missions against EC ranges using structured scenarios and then we added different types of attack and support aircraft to join the training missions. The USAFE EC training program was accentuated by USAFE's participation in Green Flag in July 1990 with Lieutenant Colonel Tom Hanton, the 65 Air Division Director of Operations, as the project officer. During this exercise, the USAFE planning staff, with much resistance from the Red Flag Staff, tasked the missions at medium to high altitude and demonstrated a SEAD campaign. This concept of operations was not well received by all the participants, but two USAFE DOs, Major Generals John Corder and Jim Jamerson were strongly behind both the concept and training program. Many of these same leaders and USAFE people would be planning real missions in the following months based on many of the lessons they learned in Green Flag and the training program.

After Saddam Hussein invaded Kuwait in August 1990, I challenged the members of Weapons Shop to determine how the wing could get involved in what looked to be imminent military action. Major Kurt "2-Lips" Dittmer and Major Rich "Snooker" Snook seized the challenge immediately. The first thing we did was to obtain the Iraqi SAM and fighter orders of battle, and plot them. We then developed an option to deploy to Incirlik Air Base, Turkey and fight Iraq from there. We ran the flight plans and determined we could stage out of Incirlik and make it to Baghdad. We didn't think the 52 TFW would get involved in the main fight because the Wild Weasels from the 35 TFW at George AFB were already on their way to the desert, so we went about selling our "back door" option up the chain of command.

First we presented the plan to Colonel Rudi Peksens, our wing Commander, who took the briefing to the 65th Air Division and then in mid-August to Major General Jim Jamerson, the USAFE/DO. Soon the USAFE staff began further developing the plan with the US European Command, with Major 2-Lips Dittmer taking over the planning and coordination for the 52nd. In January 1991 the plan became Operation Proven Force with General Jamerson as the commander of the Joint Task Force, Lieutenant Colonel Tom Hanton as the J-3 Air supported by the USAFE Weapons Shop, and several other members of the 65 Air Division completing the staff.

As we were developing the Proven Force concept, the wing was alerted to develop a plan to deploy 12 F-4Gs to the desert to join the 35 TFW which was already in place with its 561 TFS. The plan was to send the F-4Gs from the 81 TFS, with some personnel from the 480 TFS. Because I was assigned to the Wing and flying with the 23 TFS, I did not expect to deploy; however, when we received the execution order, Colonel Peksens pointed to me and said, "Victor, you're going, I want you to make a SEAD campaign happen." All that we had been preaching was about to become reality; all we had to do was convince some people, and pray that we were right.

Late on the evening of 5 Sep 90, I arrived at Shaikh Isa Air Base, Bahrain. Shaikh Isa was a brand new air base at the southern end of the island of Bahrain. When we arrived, there were not only the aircraft from the 561st, but also a full wing of Marine aircraft. It was quite a sight to see over 100 fighters fully loaded with all types of live munitions parked wingtip-to-wingtip on the very small ramp.

My job was to work the mission planning, as a minimum for the 81 TFS, and eventually for the 35 TFW (Provisional). Fortunately, after being read into the Top Secret Desert Storm plan, I quickly saw there was no need to convince anyone in Air Force Component, Central Command (CENTAF) of the need for a SEAD campaign. It was already planned. A few days after arriving, I went to CENTAF headquarters in Riyadh, Saudi Arabia to meet the planners in the "black hole". Brigadier General Larry Henry was in charge of the SEAD planning. I knew him from my Wild Weasel recurrency training at George in 1987, where he was the wing commander. He was a real down to earth person and very easy to get along with. Brigadier General Glossen was in charge of the overall planning effort. He and Gen Henry appeared to get along well. Lieutenant Colonel Dave Deptula, from Headquarters Air Force Checkmate, was advising General Glosson on planning the air campaign.

The Desert Storm plan consisted of four phases:

1. Strategic Air Campaign
2. Air Supremacy in the Kuwait Theater of Operations (KTO)
3. Battlefield Preparation
4. Offensive Ground Campaign[1]

The command and control targets about which we were concerned were being hit early on in the campaign. From a doctrinal point of view, one could argue that the command and control bunkers were strategic targets (Phase1) as well as SEAD targets (Phase2). We really didn't care as long as they were taken out early in the campaign in the proper sequence to render the IADS ineffective.

Since the command and control aspects of the air campaign were well in-hand, we had to apply the proper SEAD to maximize our effect. The CENTAF planners had also studied the Israeli Bekaa Valley operation, and we more or less modeled the SEAD campaign on that. General Henry decided we needed drones to help stimulate the SAM radar environment, and made a few phone calls to find where in Saudi Arabia they were located. He was successful in finding and acquiring the drones, so this helped with part of the problem regarding how to stimulate the SAMs to turn on their radars for our anti-radiation missiles to home on and destroy.

---

[1] Conduct of the Persian Gulf War, Final Report to Congress, April 1992,page 74, Unclassified

Our preferred method was drones if available, and then EF-111 and Compass Call stand off jamming to force the SAMs to go autonomous. We expected these methods to work but as a last resort we could use our own aircraft flying within the threat envelope, and of course the attackers would be flying in the threat rings to deliver their ordnance to stimulate the IADS. We hoped to engage and kill the SAMs before the attackers entered the threat rings. If the threats did not cooperate, we would ensure we were positioned to protect them. This was the classic Wild Weasel "First In – Last Out" approach.

We planned two different types of Wild Weasel missions; SEAD only, and direct support. Our initial SEAD missions were in the Baghdad area with Navy EA-6B jammers and Navy HARM-shooters. In the KTO, we planned only direct support missions, but we built a targeting plan and flow that gave us a SEAD campaign in the area. We planned for quite a bit of joint SEAD. For example, Apache helicopters made some of the initial attacks on early warning radars, the Navy fired Tomahawk Land Attack Missiles (TLAM) against command and control targets, and there were USAF, Navy, and Marine HARM shooters, and British Tornadoes firing Air Launched Anti-Radiation Missiles (ALARM). Later in the war, the Army fired some Army Tactical Missile System (ATACMS) against SAM sites in the KTO. Some of the combinations of missions were interesting. During the initial attacks in the KTO, there were F-4Gs providing direct support to Marine F/A-18 HARM shooters who were supporting a Marine attack package in the Basrah area. The Marines requested F-4G support because of the mobile SA-6s positioned in the vicinity of the F/A-18's HARM launch points.

Because of the threat environment (approximately 300 radar guided SAMs, over 3000 IR guided SAMs, and over 6000 AAA pieces), the long distances we had to travel, the fact that our first missions were at night, and the possibility that the Iraqis could use chemical weapons, we determined that medium to high altitude employ would be best. Working at high altitude would also give our APR-47 optimum detection and ranging capabilities and the HARM had a longer employment range. The only drawback was that the minimum range of the HARM increased.

Most of the Desert Storm planning was done by a small number of planners because of the air campaign plan's sensitivity. This group was known as the "Secret Squirrels." It was a real challenge in training everyone for a plan we couldn't talk about, so we had tactics sessions where we would throw out a problem for people to discuss. Because Wild Weasels are not the most agreeable people there were many spirited discussions during these sessions.

When we first arrived, we began an around the clock flying training cycle, with aircrews normally flying day – day – night. Everybody got more night training than they had ever had before. We flew primarily as pilot and EWO crews and as dedicated four ships.

The biggest advantage we had was our previous training. Our specialized Wild Weasel training prepared us very well for the mission. We had also participated in Red Flag and Green Flag and that gave us a tremendous advantage. These large exercises raised everyone's situational awareness and gave us some idea what to expect in combat. We also participated in both day and night large composite force training with other units. Some of these missions were part of the deception plan to condition the Iraqi defenses. On almost every mission, we went to the tanker, and practiced running the flights through quick refueling communications out. We could do a final top-off of a four ship in only a few minutes, which was important for some of the longer missions.

The Secret defensive Air Tasking Order (ATO) called for the same target priorities as the Top Secret Desert Storm ATO, so this allowed us to have academic discussions on how best to target within the flights. There was no right answer, but all the aircrews were exposed to the thinking of various targeting options. In general, we targeted by geography first, and then by type. This meant that if there were multiple types of SAMs that threatened your target area, you went for the higher priority SAM first. Whereas if there were higher priority SAMs outside of the target area, you could wait until the attackers were out of the target area before going after them. Any launching SAM site became the highest priority.

In early January, 1991 all the flight leads were read into the Desert Storm plan, and took over planning the final details of their missions. The Wild Weasels were well prepared, well trained, and ready for the start of Desert Storm. Even when the weather turned sour and many of our flights flew into their target area in the clouds, we performed the mission because with the APR-47 and the HARM we didn't need to see the ground.

Our SEAD campaign was very effective. On Day One, after about 18 hours, we did not see a coherent SAM threat in the KTO. Major John "Stick" Ustick, one of our flight commanders, came in the first night and reported that his flight had flown up and down the area where the SAMs were positioned to protect the Republican Guards and did not see any radar activity. I know they were active at the beginning of the day, because I saw them on my first mission. In my estimation, our initial barrage of HARMs and other munitions must have hit many of their intended targets. The SAMs that survived just stayed off the air. We didn't hit the Baghdad area with SEAD quite as hard as we did the KTO, so there were some SAMs that remained up until the end of the war. But overall, the SAMs were largely ineffective, since they were not integrated and there were only a few of them active at any one time. These the Wild Weasels could easily handle. There were some losses to radar SAMs, but none while Wild Weasels were on station.

Despite pre-war predictions that Saddam Hussein would quit after four to six days of the air campaign, he did not. This meant that we had to plan for a little more than we had envisioned. After the initial day, we were tasked to fly almost all direct support missions. Unfortunately, by doing this, we couldn't cover all the missions who requested or required Wild Weasel support. In order to minimize the impact, we came up with an area support concept in the KTO that became known as "Wild Weasel Police," which was nothing more than a Wild Weasel Combat Air Patrol (CAP). By using the Wild Weasel Police tactic, we could protect a large number of attack missions over the KTO with a small number of Wild Weasels. This was only possible because of the limited SAM threat from the success of the initial SEAD campaign.

We encouraged CENTAF to develop an airspace de-confliction plan for the KTO, because aircraft were all over the sky, which at night was both dangerous and nerve- wracking—negatively impacting mission success. One night I completed a direct support mission and flew out of my target area to explore a nearby area where SAM activity was reported earlier in the day. Suddenly, bombs began exploding under me. Because it was dark, I didn't know if the aircraft dropping those bombs were below me, or above me. Needless to say, I turned and headed for home, not knowing who else was out in the area.

Story by Randy "Pyle" Comer, WW # 2521

Combat Sortie Number One

17 Jan 91 – We drive to work (23 TFS, Spangdahlem AB, Germany) listening to the reports of the Air War that had begun the night before worried that the war would be over before we got there – there being Incirlik AB, Turkey, which our squadron had just recently gotten orders to deploy to in order to open the northern front of Desert Storm. The flight to Incirlik was uneventful, although it was the first time I had heard of a term called "due regard," i.e., a way to tell the French air traffic controllers, we hear you that we may not have clearance to overfly your country, but we are going to anyway.

It was after dark, probably 1930 or 2000 when we landed at Incirlik and our ADVON team tells us to go get a couple hours rest, our brief for our first combat sortie begins at midnight–rest…yeah right. So as we're getting settled into our hooches we find out our midnight brief has been cancelled but our morning brief is at 0630. The brief is uneventful, but it was almost unanimous, the mission brief left quite a bit to be desired. And sure enough, the flight was a comedy of errors, crappy weather, numerous aborts, late takeoffs, and uncertainty as to if authority had been or would be granted for our package to exit Turkish airspace and open the northern front. After probably 2½ to 3 hours of this fiasco, our package became a mission abort and we all returned to Incirlik. Obviously we weren't the only ones who felt that the mission leadership left quite a bit to be desired. The package commander (an F-16 driver from Torrejon AB) didn't even come to the debrief; he was given a one way ticket home and we never saw him again.

With our fiasco for the day behind us, we returned to our hooches with an 0-dark- thirty brief planned for the next day. And again, as we watched the war reports on CNN, we were afraid the war would be over before we had a chance to play. But much to our relief, all the diplomatic hurdles were overcome quickly and our night flyers were part of the first raid into Iraq.

After a sleepless night it's finally time for our brief. This brief reaffirms our confidence in at least some of the F-16 drivers as package commanders and we're pretty confident as we walk out the door. The plan is for our eight Wild Weasels (two flights of four, each two ship a mixed element of one F-4G and one F-16) to follow an eight ship of F-15s who would be in the high block with the rest of the gorilla behind us and a four ship of Wild Weasels trailing the package.

So after a few hiccups necessitating a ten-minute rolex (postponement) to get almost everyone lined up, we're finally off on the first daylight combat sortie into northern Iraq. Well, the aforementioned "almost everyone" did not include our eight ship of air-to-air cover, the F-15s, so as we press into Iraq they are in about 20 mile trail – the Wild Weasels are truly the First In!!

The lead eight ship of Wild Weasels was led by our B-Flight Commander, Captain Dan "Book'em Dano" Williams with our squadron commander, Lt Col Dave "Mooman" Moody on his wing. We were in the lead of our four ship with the D-Flight's Captain Keith "Slot" Snyder my pilot with Captain Cal Tinkey on our wing. Our number three was Lt Col Carl Puels (squadron Ops Officer) with his bear, Major Keith "Beast" Trouborst and Lt John "Haze" McDevitt on their wing.

Eight Wild Weasels, leading the charge into northern Iraq, eight four ships of Vipers in trail and the Eagles trying desperately to catch up. By now we're well into Iraq, early warning and threat signals are starting to appear on our APR-47 scopes, and a quick scan of the radar shows two contacts, 25 degrees left, 40 miles, closing. The reply to my radio call is "Three same" from Beast. A squeeze of the APX-101 (identification friend or foe system) provides no warm fuzzies; it doesn't return any indications, friend or foe. "AWACS, contact 30 left, 25 miles, angels 25, request ID." AWACS replies with "negative contact that area." Thanks a lot! Well, now the bogies are at 18 miles, I'm breaking out a two ship, right echelon going to 50 degrees left and Beast confirms he's showing the same thing. Slot's got the AIM-7s tuned with CW (continuous wave signal for guiding the AIM-7) on as we close to 12 miles and start to cheat left so as to not gimbal the contacts off the radar scope and to stay within AIM-7 launch parameters. One last APX of the area prior to lock-on shows two friendlies at 50 degrees left and five miles, high, when we get a radio call that the F-15s are committed on these two bogies. The next radio call is a "blowing tanks," i.e., the F-15s are jettisoning their external fuel tanks so they can fire their AIM-7s. So as we watch our two bogies gimbal left at eight miles we're looking for air-to-air missile smoke trails and fireballs, but none appear. As we return to course the APR-47 shows several threat signals with sufficient quality and within HARM range and several "Magnum" calls are heard from the other Wild Weasels. A sudden "Break Right" call is heard from Mooman for his flight. HARM contrails fill the sky, we haven't seen any fireballs for the two bogies that the Eagles committed on and now Mooman has called a "Break Right." We're thinking, *&^$ Eagles, they've let the two bandits get through and now they're playing "plink the ducky" from down low. The SA-3 at Mosul is going strong, a quick wing rock to Cal and another HARM is on its way. Slot's yelling, "Shoot it, shoot it." I reply, "Give Cal's time of flight." "No, just shoot it" is his reply, so a quick target handoff followed by a squeeze of the pickle button and our HARM comes off the rail with a rumble and a swoosh. We continue monitoring but the signals disappear and as the strikers' vulnerability period ends we head north and start preparing for the flight back to Incirlik, livid that the Eagles let the bandits get through. So for the next hour all the way back to Incirlik, we're wondering how many aircraft we lost due to their ineptness.

In the crew van, "How many aircraft did we lose?" No one knows. Finally we pick up an Eagle driver, "Whadya mean?" is his reply. "Those two bogeys were EF-111s who didn't get the word on the ten minute rolex (postponement) and had executed per the original plan. They were just on their egress when you saw them."

"Well, thanks a helluva lot for telling us."

Combat sortie number one – COMPLETE!!

Bullets, Bombs and Brunch

Kudos to the planners of the Sunday morning missions in Operation Proven Force, the northern portion of Operation Desert Storm flying out of Incirlik AB, Turkey. The missions were always planned such that we could complete debrief before the O'Club Sunday Brunch closed. It was a tough life but someone had to do it. And the toughest part was coming back later that evening and watching the belly dancer get topless.

Chapter Five

Wild Weasels On The Vietnam Memorial

Story by Edward T. Rock WW # 185

Wild Weasels on the Wall

John 15:13 - Greater love has no man than this, that a man lay down his life for his friends.

Editor's Note: The following data was derived from my personal knowledge, U.S. Government agency sources, correspondence with POW/MIA families, published sources, and conversations with various sources including pilots, EWOs and others. In some cases conflicting data is available. If conflicts existed, I resolved them as best I could. Please note the many cases where the aircraft crewmember was known to be alive, and apparently well, on the ground after a successful ejection, but they are never heard from again.

ROOSEVELT HESTLE JR, WW # 83, Panel 08E - - Line 134
CHARLES E. MORGAN, WW # 71, Panel 09E - - Line 2

Roosevelt and Charles were the first F-105 Wild Weasel crew shot down. They were the crew of F-105F 63-8286 on 6 July 66 and they were assigned to the 388th TFW, 13th TFS, Korat RTAFB, Thailand. Both were thought to have been killed when their aircraft was hit by AAA and crashed without any parachute being seen or beeper being heard. However, his wife recognized Charles Morgan when he was shown on TV during a press conference recorded in Hanoi, North Vietnam. He was not repatriated with the other POWs in 1973 but his remains were returned July 1989. As a Wild Weasel EWO he was undoubtedly a very valuable asset to the North Vietnamese and their Soviet and Chinese supporters. The body of Roosevelt Hestle has never been recovered.

GENE THOMAS PEMBERTON, WW # 183, Panel 09E- -Line 64
BENJAMIN BYRD NEWSOM, WW # 184 Panel 09E- -Line 63

Gene Pemberton and Ben Newsome were the first F-105 Wild Weasel crew shot down from the 355th TFW, 354th TFS, Takhli RTAFB, Thailand. They were the crew of F-105F 63-8338 on 24 July 66 when they were hit by an SA-2 SAM. The aircraft crashed near Hoa Lac, North Vietnam. It is believed that they were both captured and died in captivity. Their remains were returned.

JOSEPH WILLIAM BRAND, WW # 123, Panel 10E- - Line 14
DONALD MAURICE SINGER, WW # 284, Panel 10E- - Line 15

Joe Brand and Don Singer were the crew of F-105F 63-8308 when they were shot down by AAA on 17 August 66. They were assigned to the 355th TFW, 354th TFS. Joe was the senior Wild Weasel officer at Takhli before his loss. The loss of this aircraft and crew represented the fifth loss of an F-105F Wild Weasel in combat since 6 July 66, just 42 days. This was particularly significant because there were only a total of 11 Wild Weasel configured aircraft in SEA and now nearly one-half had already been shot down. Joe Brand bailed out successfully and was heard on his survival radio on the ground after landing. Subsequent attempts to contact him by rescue forces were not successful. Don Singer apparently bailed out, but his parachute did not open properly before impact. Remains of both Joe and Don were returned in 1977.

ROBERT EDWIN BRINCKMANN, WW # 79, Panel 12E- -Line 18
VINCENT ANTHONY SCUNGIO, WW # 99, Panel 12E- - Line 25

Bob Brinckmann and Vince Scungio were the crew of F-105F 63-8273 when they were shot down by an SA-2 SAM on 4 November 66. Bob was the senior ranking Wild Weasel at Korat at the time he was shot down. They were assigned to the 388th TFW, 13 TFS. They were attacking a SAM site near Kep airfield when a SAM reportedly hit their aircraft. Neither Bob nor Vince was seen to bail out and they were declared Missing in Action. Remains eventually identified to be that of Bob Brinckman were returned in 1989. The remains of Vince Scungio have apparently never been found.

JOHN FRANCIS DUDASH, WW # 144, Panel 18E - - Line 92

John Dudash and Alton Meyer were flying F-105F 63-8277 on 26 April 67 when they were shot down by an SA-2 SAM in the general vicinity of Thai Nguyen, North Vietnam. They were assigned to the 355th TFW, 333rd

TFS, Takhli RTAFB, Thailand. Dudash was the pilot and Meyer was the EWO. The aircraft was hit by the third of three SA-2 missiles fired at their aircraft. Meyer ejected first, landed safely, and was captured almost immediately. After Meyer ejected, the aircraft continued in a southeasterly direction with Dudash apparently still at the controls. The aircraft continued to fly for a short period and was observed to explode in flight by Meyer. Dudash was declared MIA and his remains were returned in 1983. Meyer was repatriated in 1973.

MORRIS LAROSCO MC DANIEL JR, WW # 311, Panel 27E - - Line 49
WILLIAM ALLAN LILLUND, WW # 321, Panel 27E - - Line 49

Morris McDaniel and William Lillund were flying F-105F 63-8346 on 4/5 October 67 when they were apparently shot down by AAA about 40 miles northwest of Hanoi while on a Ryan's Raiders night bombing mission. They were assigned to the 13th TFS, 388 TFW, Korat RTAFB, Thailand. The last known contact with the aircraft was when they were refueling from a KC-135 tanker before they entered North Vietnam airspace. Their last known location was approximately 10 miles northwest of the city of Phu Tho in Vinh Phu Province, North Vietnam. They were not among the 591 Americans released by the Vietnamese in early 1973 and were apparently killed in action. Morris left a wife and three children.

CROSLEY JAMES FITTON JR, WW # 404, Panel 42E - - Line 5
CLEVELAND SCOTT HARRIS, WW # 405, Panel 42E - - Line 6

Crosley Fitton and Cleveland Harris were the crew of F-105F 63-8312 when an SA-2 SAM shot them down on 29 February 1968. Both crewmen appeared to have bailed out safely and turned their beepers off shortly after landing on the ground. However, they were never heard from again and they were not repatriated in early 1973 when the other 591 Americans returned from captivity in North Vietnam. Crosley Fitton's remains were returned in December 1975 and the remains of Cleveland Harris were returned in April 1985. The cause of their death is not known.

JAMES CUTHBERT HARTNEY, WW # 323, Panel 33E- -Line 48
SAMUEL FANTLE III, WW # 336, Panel 33E- -Line 47

Jim Hartney and Sam Fantle were the crew of F-105F 63-8356 on 5 January 68 when they were shot down by a MiG-17 near Kep Air Base, North Vietnam. They were assigned to the 357th TFS, 355th TFW, Takhli RTAFB, Thailand. They were on an Iron Hand defense suppression mission and had just fired a Shrike anti-radiation missile at an enemy SAM radar when they were attacked by a flight of MiG-17s. Their aircraft was hit in the left wing by MiG cannon fire and the aircraft caught fire and went out of control. Both crewmembers were observed to have bailed out and appeared to have landed successfully but no voice contact was ever made. Both men were married. The remains of Jim Hartney were returned in November 1989 and those of Sam Fantle in September 1977.

CLIFFORD WAYNE FIESZEL, WW # 482, Panel 42W- - Line 47
HOWARD HORTON SMITH, WW # 447, Panel 42W- - Line 51

Clifford Fieszel and Howard Smith were the crew of F-105F 63-8317 on 30 September 68 when they were hit by AAA and shot down while attacking an SA-2 SAM site near Dong Hoi, North Vietnam. They were assigned to the 333rd TFS, 355th TFW, Takhli RTAFB, Thailand. Fieszel was the pilot and Smith was the Electronic Warfare Office. Fieszel's wingman had just been hit and headed out to sea and did not see his flight leader's plane hit. Search and rescue (SAR) units heard beeper signals for about 24 hours after Fieszel's plane went down. However, they were unable to make voice contact with him or Smith. On the following day, Radio Hanoi announced that two F105's had been shot down in the Quang Khe province and the pilot of the second plane (presumably Fieszel) had been captured. On 7 October 68 a Hanoi newspaper repeated the story. It was thought that the Vietnamese believed the wingman's plane had also gone down since it was on fire when it headed out to sea. No mention was made of Smith in either report. Their remains have never been recovered and their fate remains unknown.

RICHARD JOSEPH MALLON, WW # 748, Panel 14W - - Line 76
ROBERT JOSEPH PANEK SR. WW # 751, Panel 14W - - Line 76

Robert Mallon and Joseph Panek were the crew of F-105G 63-8329 when AAA shot them down on 28 January 70. Mallon was the pilot and

Panek was the EWO. They were assigned to the 44th TFS, 388th TFW, Korat RTAFB, Thailand and were supporting an RF-4C photoreconnaissance mission over North Vietnam when they went down. They were fired upon by enemy AAA and returned fire by attacking the enemy AAA site that had fired on them. On the second pass their aircraft was hit by AAA and burst into flames. They immediately turned southwest and the aircraft crashed northeast of Mu Gia Pass. Both Mallon and Panek were seen to eject and land safely, and were observed alive on the ground. A rescue force was quickly assembled including rescue helicopters, a Crown HC-130 airborne rescue command post, a flight of A-1 "Sandy" aircraft, and air refueling support. MiG warnings were broadcast and an SA-2 SAM was fired at one of the Sandys during the attempted rescue. It was not realized how close the MiGs were and suddenly two MiG-21s attacked the SAR formation shooting down one of the rescue helicopters. The rescue force withdrew to the west. The entire crew of the HH-53 helicopter was killed. The F-105 crew was reportedly surrounded, captured and, according to one report, executed by NVN militia. The remains of the F-105 crew and the helicopter pilot were returned in December 1988.

SCOTT WINSTON MC INTIRE, WW # 434, Panel 02W- -Line 85

On 10 December 71 Bob Belli, pilot, and Scott McIntire, EWO, were the crew of F-105G 63-8326 when they were shot down by an SA-2 SAM. They were on a mission over the Mu Gia Pass in support of a B-52 strike. They expended two AGM-45 anti-radiation missiles against an enemy SA-2 Fan Song radar which had acquired their aircraft. Their aircraft was then hit by a surface to air missile; the explosion was of sufficient force that it rendered Belli initially unconscious. Belli ejected both himself and McIntire. Search and rescue aircraft soon rescued Belli, but McIntire could not be located. On the next day, 11 December 71, a search and rescue helicopter located McIntire hanging limp in his parachute in a tall tree. A flight surgeon on the aircraft stated McIntire appeared lifeless and stated that in his professional view, the conditions of weather and the position of the body after hanging suspended for 20 hours indicated McIntire would have died of hypothermia within six hours and was probably dead on 11 December. Heavy ground fire drove off the SAR aircraft before McIntire could be recovered. He was not reported alive in the North Vietnamese prison system and his remains have never been recovered. He was initially declared missing and in May 1972 was declared dead/body not recovered.

ROBERT DOUGLAS TRIER, WW # 107, Panel 04E - Line 032

Bob Trier, EWO, and John Pitchford, pilot, were flying a Wild Weasel configured F-100F when they were shot down by AAA on 20 December 1965. They were assigned to Korat RTAFB, Thailand, and were on their third Wild Weasel/Iron Hand mission over North Vietnam. They were members of Wild Weasel 1 and were the first Wild Weasel aircraft shot down in North Vietnam. Pitchford suffered a dislocated right shoulder on ejection as well as gunshot wounds in his upper right arm during capture. It is believed that Trier was killed by the North Vietnamese when he elected to fight rather than submit to capture.

Trier had detected an SA-2 radar southeast of Kep Airfield; they were able to home on and overfly the site. Pitchford pulled up, turned hard right, rolled the aircraft back left to level the wings, and then fired his marking rockets. The Wild Weasel then pulled off to the right and transmitted, "I am hit," having taken a 37MM shell in the afterburner of the aircraft while working the radar signal. Although an F-105 pilot saw only some small buildings and trees in the area marked by the Wild Weasel, he fired his rockets into the target area anyway. His wingman followed suit. A second element of F-105s that had been separated from the flight spotted the wounded F-100F and followed it. They observed pieces falling off the aircraft as it tracked toward the east-northeast. Then the canopy came off the aircraft, one parachute opened, and the F-100 pitched over into the clouds and disappeared. The pilot, John Pitchford, was to become the first Wild Weasel POW and was returned to the US after more than 7 years as a POW, coming home in 1973. The remains of Bob Trier were not returned until November 82.

CHARLES H. STONE, WW # 753, Panel 02W - - Line 103

Charles H. Stone was the pilot of F-105G 63-8347 when the aircraft experienced engine failure on takeoff and crashed on 2 February 72. He was assigned to the 17th Wild Weasel Squadron (WWS), 388th TTFW, Korat RTAFB, Thailand. Stone died in the accident.

ALAN PAUL MATEJA, WW # 1029, Panel 01W- - Line 1
ORVIN CLARENCE JONES JR, WW # 1028, Panel 01W- -Line 1

Alan Mateja, pilot, and Orvin Jones, EWO, were on an Iron Hand mission supporting TACAIR assets attacking targets in the Hanoi/Haiphong area of North Vietnam when they were shot down by an enemy SA-2 SAM on 16 April 72. This was the first time that the heartland of North Vietnam had been bombed since March 1968! Enemy reaction to the strikes were formidable, but largely ineffective even though more than 250 SAMs were launched and heavy anti-artillery fire was reported. One of two aircraft lost was the Wild Weasel configured F-105G flown by Mateja and Jones. They were hit by a SAM as they attacked a SAM support depot on the outskirts of Haiphong. The aircraft crashed near the harbor and neither of the crew was heard from again. However, the Air Force believed there was a possibility that both crewmen escaped the crippled aircraft and they were declared Missing in Action. Their remains have never been recovered.

THOMAS ONEAL ZORN JR, WW # 1049, Panel 01W- -Line 74
MICHAEL STEPHEN TUROSE, WW # 1045, Panel 01W- -Line 74

Tom Zorn, pilot, and Mike Turose, EWO, were flying F-105G 63-8360 on 17 September 72 when they were shot down by an SA-2 SAM. They were assigned to the 17th WWS, 388th TFW, Korat RTAFB, Thailand. They were on an Iron Hand defense suppression mission when they received electronic indications that they were being tracked and then fired upon by an SA-2 Fan Song radar about 20 miles north of Haiphong, North Vietnam. Their aircraft was subsequently severely damaged by one of the SAMs and they headed "feet wet" in an effort to get to the Gulf of Tonkin where USN rescue forces were on hand. They made it to the Gulf, the bailout appeared successful, and US Navy rescue forces were nearby when they exited the aircraft. However, when the Navy Para-rescue divers reached the crewmembers, they were both dead and still in their parachute harnesses. The weight of their parachutes, seat kits and other flight gear were pulling them down rapidly and the Navy men were unable to retrieve their bodies. Their remains have never been recovered.

MICHAEL JOSEPH BOSILJEVAC, WW # 1015, Panel 04W - - Line 69

James W. O'Neil was the pilot and Michael J. Bosiljevac the EWO of F105G 63-8302 a Wild Weasel fighter, which was shot down by a SA-2 SAM on 29 September 72. They were assigned to the 17th WWS, 388th TFW, Korat RTAFB, Thailand. Both Bosiljevac and O'Neil ejected successfully, and landed about 23 miles southwest of Hanoi. Radio Hanoi/Moscow/Cuba reported the capture of both "pilots" alive on 29 September 1972. O'Neil was subsequently transferred to the "Hanoi Hilton" and repatriated 29 March 1973. Upon his release, O'Neil stated that he had observed Bosiljevac in the parachute, and that Bosiljevac had manually cut the parachute risers for control and deployed his survival kit for landing. On about the fifth day of his confinement O'Neil asked an English-speaking guard about Bosiljevac. The guard later returned and said, "He is alive, well, uninjured, and luckier than you." Repeated US government, as well as family, inquiries met with little response from the North Vietnamese. In fact, the Socialist Republic of Vietnam (SRV) wrote to the family of Mike Bosiljevac and claimed to have "no knowledge of Mr. Michael Joseph Bosiljevac," and further stated, "They no longer hold prisoners within Vietnam." Yet, on 21 September 87, the government of Vietnam provided Bosiljevac's name, and his remains were returned to US control on 24 September 1987. The Central Identification Laboratory in Hawaii (CILHI) released the remains for a second opinion in January of 1988, and final identification occurred in January 1988. Bosiljevac's remains were returned to Omaha, Nebraska for burial on February 10, 1988. On 1 August 1989, Mike Bosiljevac's records were corrected to reflect that he died in captivity. While this correction does not define the total duration of his captivity, it stands as a matter of record. According to senior representative of the CILHI, Mike's body had "recently" been autopsied in a manner consistent with the way autopsies are performed in Eastern Europe. Mike was the last Wild Weasel casualty of the Vietnam War.

Where was Mike Bosiljevac between September 72 and September 87 when his remains were returned?

Editor's Note: I coordinated this writeup with Mike's widow, Kay, who originally provided much of the information above and wanted me to add the following:

"It is with the greatest of pride that Mike served with the 17th Wild Weasels. Over all the years of waiting, and working for his return, it was clear that those who worked with him, thought of him often, and tried so very hard to help. It was also clear, that the Communists were very annoyed by our persistence. Those who committed the war crime of continued incarceration and autopsy after his death should take no comfort from their actions.

Our family would like to thank the Wild Weasels, who are ever a touch of class, for truly being "First in, Last out". God Bless You All.

Kay

Ed Rock WW # 185

Chapter Six

What Happened To Them

1. Acree, George W., WW # 289 retired Colonel USAF, Chief Wild Weasel Emeritus Past President: Red River Valley Fighter Pilots Association (River Rats).
2. Adcock, Eddie, Lt. Col. USAF, (Ret.), WW # 100. Banker / Farmer In Kentucky.
3. Arnold, Richard W., WW # 348 got his law degree and practiced in Grand Junction, CO.
4. Ayer, Donald G. WW # 219, A.T.I. Engineering and Field Service. Owner The Capitol, Truckee, California. General Manager the Delta Saloon / Casino, Virginia City, Nevada. Retired Virginia City, Nevada.
5. Bagley, William P. "Bags" WW # 1855, F-4D/E/G, Maj, USAF (ret), current: Range Control Officer, 412 Test Wing, Edwards AFB, CA
6. Barnett, John R., WW # 570 ATI Retired and living in Yerington, Nevada. Member of "Nevada Wandering Wheels" MC.Currently riding a 2000 H-D FLSTC.
7. Bauman, Weldon W., WW # 819, Sgt. USAF, Applied Technology 1968-1982, now small business owner, Paradise, CA
8. Baxley, Brian "Basa" , WW # 2177, F-4E/G , F-15C, OSS Commander in Saudi for OIF, Retired and now a NASA Project Manager
9. Beaman, Richard C. Jr., (Dick AKA Beamer), WW#1691, Major USAFR (Ret), Bear, Currently an Imagery Analyst with the National Geospatial-Intelligence Agency (NGA), Washington, DC.
10. Bishop, Paul E. "Bish", WW # 1717, F-4E/G 81 TFS Spang, 563 TFS George, Det 5 USAFTAWC George, Lt. Col. USAF (ret), Currently Engineer for Avionics Test and Analysis Corp (ATAC) assigned to the 416 FLTS - USAF Viper testing.
11. Blackburn, Robert Earl, Jr. (Pinky), Capt (Separated), WW # 1911, F-4D/E/G, Electronic Warfare Officer, George AFB (1988-91), Operations Desert Shield / Desert Storm (1990-91) F-22 Operations Analysis, Lockheed Martin (1991-2002) Phantom Works Strategic Development & Analysis, Boeing (2002-Present)

12. Boyd, Jimmy, WW # 970, F-105G. Retired USAF Lt Col. in Paradise Island (PI), flying my Navion all over the Philippines.
13. Brand, A. B., WWI, WW # 110, LTC (Ret in '74), County of San Bernardino, CA, 1976-1999. Retired in Apple Valley, CA.
14. Brog, David, WW # 420, retired Colonel USAF, an independent consultant, National President of the Red River Valley Fighter Pilots Assoc.
15. Brown, Donald L. , Col USAF Ret, WW # 612, F-105F/G (44TFS, 561TFS), F- 4E/G, (39TFTS); Ret Dept Head Calspan Corp; Living in Bella Vista, AR.
16. Bryan, Bil, WW # 141, Bear; L. Col. USAF Ret; Northrop Acft. Div. Los Angeles Ret; — Curr: Project Manager, Policy & Procedure Development, Mariner Health Care, Inc. Atlanta, GA
17. Constant, Floyd, WW # 803, former AGM-78 techrep on F-105 and F4. Now retired and living at Sun City, Palm Desert, CA.
18. Cuttter, James D. (JD), WW # 993 Maj USAF (Retired), X-POW, F-105F/G Korat, F4E Ramstein (second ejection). Retired to Albuquerque, NM…Just moved To Coeur d'Alene, ID.
19. Davis, Samuel Jefferson, WW # 1012, retired, Cuyhoga Falls, OH
20. Domian, Brian C., WW# 1648, Director of Live Training Systems, Tec-Masters, Inc., Orlando, FL
21. Donovan, Jack, Charter WW # 15 Retired USAF Maj. Retired from Litton Corp . Now World Traveler Living in Tucson, Arizona.
22. Dorrough, Bob, WW # 349, Colonel USAF Retired, Capt. US Airways, retired. Clemmons, NC.
23. Doyle, Ed, WW # 683, Buff EWO - select crew - 2 years (asked to leave SAC), F4-C First Nellis Bear WW class to Europe via DM RO school, Woodridge changed to Hahn Instr./Stan Eval, Zweibrucken Instr/Stan Eval, Nellis twice as instructer and refresher training 3X, Nato 2TAF, Tac Hq twice, with 2 short SEA (Japan & Udorn) & 2 two long Europe tours (Hahn, Bitburg, Ramstein, Spangdahlem, and Rheindahlen,Flew till retired from Tac HQ in 89. Really miss it! WW-683 with 25 moves in 27 years. Retired as Bartender, Owned a Real Estate Company, and played/ worked with Radio Shack Toys for 2 years - until we built our dream house. Now, trying to stay healthy, sailing, going to friday Happy Hour, and visiting 8 grandkids…

24. Draper, Robert A. (Bob), WW # 979, F-4CWW at Zweibruecken and Spangdahlem, 71-75. Retired Lt Colonel, Universal City, TX (Randolph AFB). SATO Travel agent under US Navy contract.
25. Drew, Phil, WW # 347 B/Gen retired.
26. Duart, David H., F105 WW #143, Colonel, USAF (Ret), ex POW, died 10 Sep 03, Georgetown, TX
27. Edge, Thomas H. (Tom), WW # 1111, F-105G, 17th WWS (Korat), 66th Fighter Weapons Squadron (Weasel School at Nellis); Major (Ret.); Lockheed Missiles and Space, Austin Division (12 years). Now fully retired at 6704 La Concha Pass, Austin, Texas 78749, Ph (512)288-4047, edgetom@aol.com OR thudwildweasel@aol.com
28. Ekman, Leonard "Lucky" C., WW # 1013, Panama City, FL
29. Esters, Michael "Anwar", WW #1744, EWO, Lt Col (Ret), Living in the United Kingdom.
30. Figun, Steve, WW # 901, Major (ret), Residing in Marble Falls, Tx. Five years as a Beltway Bandit . High school science teacher for the past 11 years (currently teaching physics and chemistry at Burnet HS).
31. Finke, Thomas V. "Finkster", Lt Col, WW # 1754 F-4E/G EWO Spangdahlem 81 TFS & 23 TFS - 83-87, George 561 TFS- '87-92, DESERT STORM Shaik Isa, Bahrain Det 5, 79 TEG - F-4G Test Team - George AFB – 1992 , 422 TES, F-4G Test Team, Nellis AFB - 93-96 Commander - USAF Warrior Preparation School - Nellis AFB - 2001-03, Still active duty working at Space Warfare Center, Schriever AFB, CO Colorado Springs, CO
32. Freeman, Michael C., W W # 1325, Lt Col USAF (ret), F-4C/G's, Spangdahlem, GS-12 68 EWS (SEAD Flt) Eglin, AFB, Fl.
33. Geddes, Bruce D., WW # 1758, Lt Col USAF (ret), F-4C/E/G's at Torrejon, Keflavik NAS, and Spangdahlem, DESERT STORM, defense contractor currently with L-3 Communications Government Services Inc, living in Fairfax, VA.
34. Gelinas, Dan, Lt Col, USAF, WW # 2293, F-4G EWO at 190 FS/124 FG, currently Reconnaissance Programs Manager, Air National Guard Air Force Reserve Command Test Center, Tucson, Arizona.
35. Gilroy, Kevin A. "Mike", retired Colonel, WW # 174, Chief Electronic Warfare Research and Development, Pentagon; Chairman, NATO Electronic Warfare Advisory 13 Committee,

Brussels Belgium; Commander USAF Electronic Warfare Center; retired Mayor City of Gilroy, California.

36. Grigsby, Dr. John, WW # 231 retired, California.
37. Gummo, Thomas L. (Gummi Bear), WW # 1573, Major USAF Retired 1992, F-4G Instructor Pilot, Currently teaching Chemistry at Victor Valley Community College.
38. Goldstein, Stanley E., WW # 415, Lt Col USAF (Ret), General Secretary Red River Valley Association, Apopka Fl
39. Guzowski, Paul F., Col, USAF (ret) WW # 1882, F-4 C/D/Loran D/E/G at Spangdahlem, Ramstein, George, DESERT STORM. Currently Senior Military Analyst with Cubic Defense Applications Group, Inc. on station in Budapest, HU.
40. Hall, Mark S. "Monty" WW #1989, F-4E/G, F-15E, F-16CJ, Lt Col, SCANG, currently Wing EWO, 169FW and 157FS Swamp Foxes, McEntire ANGS, SC.
41. Hall, Robert W., Jr., WW # 941, Retired, LTC, USAF, Leesburg, VA., Staff Engineer, Air Line Pilots Association, Herndon, VA
42. Hartzell, Curtis L., WW # 175 Lt. Col. Retired, retired from Boeing Seattle, Concordia, KS.
43. Hayman, Clyde, AKA Clyde Bear WW # 82 Flew in first F105F weasels at Korat Major USAF Retired also retired Accountant presently living in Covington, LA
44. Heidenreich, Wes, WW # 1222, F-4 Bear; Col, USAF (Ret); Raytheon, Warner Robins,Georgia.
45. Henry, Donald D., WW # 927, Pilot, USAF Colonel retired; Senior Analyst, ANSER, Inc.; Consultant, Advanced Programs; Author-novelist; lives and writes in Laguna Beach, California.
46. Horner, Charles A. WW # 333 Commanded Air Forces during Desert Storm, Commander in Chief, Commander SPACECOM, retired.
47. Howard, Joe, WW # 351 Pilot, Killed in Thunderbird accident.
48. Huggins, Lawrence E., WW # 461, Brigadier General retired in Newton, NC
49. Handschumacher, James F. Jr.(Hands), # 727, F-4C Weasel EWO, 81st TFS '69 - '74. Retired Lt. Col., also retired from Northrop Grumman now living in Crestview, Florida.
50. Hale, James H. (Dick), WW # 1626, Lt. Col. (Ret) Spang—81st, 23rd, George—561, 562, 563 (OPS O), 20TH (GAF F4-E/F)CC, Former F-100F Pilot For Tracor/BAE Flight Systems Currently

flying for AirUSA Flying L-59 "Super Albatross" as 'Red Air' Aggressor Pilot in conjunction with US Gov't/Navy Contracts. Durango, CO. home base.

51. Idema, Thomas H., Capt. USMC, WW# 2497, A6A's (VMA (AW) 242), Living in Matthews, NC
52. James, Gobel D., WW # 416, Colonel, USAF, retired in Scottsdale, AZ.
53. Johnson, Ed "ET" "Nitnoi Bear", WW # 1014, F-105G, F4G (6010/17 WWS, 81 TFS). Current: Ball Aerospace & Technologies Corp, Supporting F-16 Wild Weasel/SEAD at Eglin AFB.
54. Jones, James G., WW # 517. Major General, USAF (Ret). WW "Bear" for 6 yrs. 11mos. (F-105 F/G, F-4C). 354 TFS, 66 FWS, 35 TFW DO/CV, Chief of Staff, Tactical Air Command. Retired in Tampa.
55. James, Curt, WW # 775, F-105F/G pilot, retired L/C. Shrike/ Standard ARM OT&E test manager, Air Staff HARM PEM, retired from Texas Instruments HARM program. Retired in AZ.
56. Jimenez, Daniel "Mitch" Callsign "LoRider", Lt Col (Ret) WW # 1730 F-111D 77-79 Cannon AFB NM, F-111F 79-82 RAF Lakenheath,UK. 81TFS 82-84 Spandahlem AB, 563TFS 86-89 George AFB, F-111E/F 94-96 Cannon AFB, Commander 27th OSS 95-96. Currently, Captain Southwest Airlines
57. Jondahl, Robert, WW # 386, killed in light aircraft crash.
58. Jowers, Wilbur E. "Will", WW # 1217, retired Major USAF, McDonnell Aircraft F/A-18 "Hornet" EW Chief, Lockheed Martin Int'l EW "Marketeer", currently Director w/ L-3 Communications, Security & Detection Systems.
59. Knotts, Jerry E. WW # 425, Colonel, USAF (Ret), independent financial consultant, eleemosynarian.
60. King, Robert W., WW # 484, ex-USAF Captain and Electronic Warfare Officer, presently employed as a consulting systems analyst, Winslow, AR.
61. Kilgus, Donald W. WW # 835 retired and killed in an auto accident on the Washington DC beltway.
62. Lamb, Allen T, Charter WW # 16 Retired USAF Lt/Col. Now President of the Lamb Group, LLC.A nation wide regulatory consultant firm specializing in Safety, Health and Environmental issues. Operating out of Lumberton, N.C.

63. Legan, Capt. Paul R., Capt. USAF, Wild Weasel I 1966 Korat, Aplied Technology 1967-1974. current retired, Riverside California.
64. LeMieux, Larry (Bearly Larry) # 453, former AF Captain, F-105 Bear, SoWW Historian and horse farmer.
65. Lemon, WW # 995, F-105 (354TFS,12TFS,66FWS), TAC/DRW (WW Requirements), F-15 (27TFS,94TFS,32TFS), HQ USAF/XOE, OSD, Col (Ret 87), Hughes Aircraft, Raytheon, Mammoth Lakes CA.
66. Lyles, J. David, ("Jd"), WW # 2373, F-4C,D,E,G /RF-4, ret. USAF Lt Col, Senior Analyst, OSD JCAS JT&E, SAIC, Nellis AFB NV.
67. Malebra, Lt. Col. Bill "Sky King", USAF Ret., 1965 USAF Academy graduate, WW # 1302. Flew F-105Gs (63-8332 was his bird) at George with the 561 TFS after completing 127 F-4 combat missions from Udorn. Helped transition the GAANG to F-105Gs. Retired in 1990 in Albuquerque with 25 years of service. Last worked at Intel. Died December 21, 1998, from a brain tumor.
68. Martin, Bobby, WW # 180, Colonel Retired Ft. Walton Beach, FL 32547.
69. Matthews, Harrison (Harry) W., Col, USAF, Ret, WW # 417, 44 TFS, 17 WWS, Fredericksburg, TX.
70. Matheson, Leslie P., WW #1492 F-4C,G/AC-130A/MC-130E EWO LtCol, USAF (ret) Geospatial Data Analyst, USSOCOM/SOFPREP.
71. McInerney, James E. Jr., WW # 295, Major General (Ret.) VP Membership & Chapters NDIA.
72. Merkling, Righard E., WW # 95 Lt. Gen., retired Albuquerque, NM.
73. Meyer, John C., (Jace), WW # 1402, F-105G, F-4G, F-16 blk50, ret. USAF Col, VP for Whitney, Bradley & Brown (DC defense consulting firm)
74. Meyer, Lyle H. Jr. (AKA Skip), WW # 402, AF EWO: B-66's(Shaw & Drab TRAB). Berlin for lunch bunch, F-105F, F-4C/D/E/G's. Retired in 1982 at Gerorge AFB. Now living in Las Vegas Nv.
75. Meyers, Richard B., WW # 1933 became Chairman Joint Chiefs of Staff.

76. Michael, A.L. "Mike" WW# 328, LtCol, Retired, Systems Engineer, Navigator, EWO, NKC 135, McDonnell Douglas, Retired Tulsa, Ok
77. Mojica, John, WW # 117, retired Las Vegas, Nevada
78. Moore, Richard W. (Dick), #913, EWO 6010 WWS Khorat, Lt Col, Air Staff PEM, Raytheon Principal Engineer, Retired, Fullerton, CA
79. Moser, Richard E. (Dick), WW # 914, Col. USAF, Retired, 2558 hours in the F-105D/G, Deceased, 4 June 2004, Dallas, Ga.
80. Mount, Charles D. (Dave), WW # 248, Lt Col Ret. EW engineer and program element manager at Hq USAF for WW III, WWIVC, WWIVD,and T-39 WW Trainer and numerous EW programs. Sr Research Engineer for Georgia Tech working as part of the EC support team at the ANG AGRC Test Center, Tucson AZ.
81. O'Brien, Michael B., WW # 847; retired Colonel, USAF; built and managed the Air Force Anechoic Facility @ Edwards AFB (Rockwell/Boeing); retired: Tucson, AZ, Yucca Valley, CA and Hua Hin, Thailand.
82. Odom, James R., WW # 259, pilot, tested first WW-1 (F-100Fs). Retired USAF Colonel in Fort Walton Beach, FL.
83. O'Donnell. Charles F. "Frank" Lt/Col, WW # 119 WW1 & 3 EWO, F-100F, F-105F/G, F-4G. Program Officer: AGM-78 and F-4G. Retired from Texas Istruments. Deceased 1/17/2002
84. Oehmann (Bear), Carl (Bad), Maj USAFR, OV-10 "Nail 215" at NKP, WW # 1298, F4E at Homestead (308th), F4C at Spang (81st), EWO instructor at Mather, assigned to AFEWC during DS, retired from reserves in '93, Systems Engineer at Raytheon (Formally E-Systems) in Garland, TX.
85. Oken, Arthur J., WW # 262, Lt Col USAF, Retired, Attorney at Law, retired and residing at Spanish Fort, Alabama.
86. O'Neal, Michael "Zap", WW # 2250, F4G EWO/EA6B ECMO, Lt Col, HQ ACC/DR, Langley
87. Peck, Frank E., Col, USAF (Ret), WW # 921, Thuds, Double-uglies, 'Lectric jets, Wart Hogs & few others. Buda, TX
88. Peden, Roger L., WW # 88, Col. USAF, Retired, F-4C, F-105G. Deceased, 1 Aug. 1999, Ennis, Texas
89. Porter, William E. Jr. "Bones" WW # 2369, Spangdahlem and Clark, retired Major USAF, F-4D/E/F/G, Pilot Delta Air Lines.

90. Reddoch, John H., WW # 312, retired Fort Walton Beach, FL 32547
91. Revak, John J., Lt Col USAF (Ret), WW # 419. 44TFS, Retired, Albuquerque, NM. WW History Committee.
92. Robinson, Dennis "Elvis", Lt Col (ret) WW # 1853, F4D WSO and F4G EWO. 31MSS/CC and 24AOS/CC, now private school headmaster in Deltona, FL.
93. Rock, Edward T., WW # 185 Colonel USAF Ret., became Manager Engineering, McAIR, McDonnell Douglas and later Boeing now retired, Chesterfield, MO
94. RUFFIN, Robert D. (Scruff), WW # 1804, Major (Ret), F-4C/E/G, F-5B/E/F (Royal Saudi Air Force), 34 Missions Desert Storm, 561FS (2 tours), 562TFTS, 563TFS. Ret. 20 FS (Luftwaffe Training Sq.) 1994. Flew the last F-4 off of George AFB. Currently, Captain with Southwest Airlines at Baltimore International.
95. Sherrill, Guy Jackson, Col USAF, Ret., Vampire 1, WW # 811(OJT), in golf heaven, Hot Springs Village AR
96. Sowell, Jerry, Registered Professional Engineer, WW # 578, Retired Supervisor EW Engineer USAF Civil Service. Presently working as Senior Staff Engineer with Northrop Grumman in Fort Walton Beach FL.
97. Spiers, Allen N. Major USAF (Ret) WW # 989 F-105G, F4CWW, F-GWW Northrop Grumman Test Operations. Retired in Paso Robles, CA
98. Steeves, Phil, WW # 1174 radiologist, retired Colonel MA Air National Guard
99. Stetson, Jack, Maj USAF (Ret), WW # 396. 44TFS, 354 TFS, 561TFS. Teacher/Administrator in Orlando FL
100. Summers, Clarence 'Bud', WW # 340, retired Colonel USAF and is Senior Avionics Test Engineer, F-22, Edwards AFB, California.
101. Stiles, Gerald J. (Jerry) WW # 616, Maj. (Ret) F-111A, AC-130E Spectre Gunship, 209 combat missions. Also, AFSC Systo for the F-4D Advanced Wild Weasel Program (later evolved to E's modded into F-4G's). Last, F-35 Systems Engineer, Northrop. Retired Sequim, WA.
102. Stocks, Bruce, WW # 341 Killed in F-111 Acident.
103. Shriber, Joe, WW # 1141, retired Col, working at Lockheed Martin Space Systems Co, Sunnyvale CA.

104. Sletten, John G., "Sleet" – WW # 1629, Major USAF (Ret), F-4C/D/E/G's at MacDill (61st RTU), Kadena (25th/67th), Nellis (430th), George (562nd RTU), Spangdahlem (81st/23rd), "Staff" - 57FWW, 7AF, USAFE, AMCOR. Currently Operations Analyst with General Dynamics at Wright-Patterson AFB, living in Beavercreek, OH.
105. Sparks, Billy R. WW # 330 Lt. Colonel USAF Retired. Commissioned '57, ROTC, Retired '77 of the effects of Foot in Mouth disease. Daedalian Life Member, Society of Wild Weasels, Red River Valley Fighter Pilots Association. Weasel School May '67, Instructed '68/'69. Crewed with Carlo Lombardo May '67 until mid Oct '67 in the 357TFS, 355TFW, Takhli, where we were credited with 5 SAM sites destroyed Photo Confirmed. Dell and I live in Henderson NV.
106. Smith, Douglas "Mongo" , WW # 1760, F4G EWO, Lt Col (ret), Senior Analyst for MTSI (Washington DC area)
107. Suggs, Jay, WW # 1142 S-80 Captain, American Airlines
108. Talley, William H., WW # 554 POW, retired Colonel USAF.
109. Taylor, Richard (Dick) D., WW # 1079 (Pretty Bear) F-4C WW Kadena, Korat, Nellis. Retired as Major from Nellis in 1980 and will reside in Georgetown (Sun City), Texas.
110. Telford, Joe W., WW # 258, EWO, tested first WW-I (F-100Fs), WW-III (F-105Fs), and WW-F-4Cs. Retired USAF Lt. Col. in Fort Walton Beach, FL.
111. Thompson, Robert M. (Tommy), WW # 151, retired LTC residing in Las Vegas, Nv.
112. Tondreau, Robert E., WW # 77, EWO, retired USAF Major. Fort Walton Beach, FL 32547
113. Tsouprake, Pete (aka soup), WW # 75, Colonel, USAF (Ret.) to Orleans, Cape Cod, MA
114. UKEN, James R (Uke), WW # 1657, Col (Ret), F-4C/D/E/G 1976-1996, Chief F-4G TD & E, 1985-8; Commander 561 FS, 1995-6, Currently, Director Barry M Goldwater Range (Luke AFB)
115. Van Buren, Conrad L., WW# 1950, Capt. USAF, (Ret.), F-4D/E/G's at Homestead 308 TFS, Moody 68 TFS, George 562 TFTS, Spangdahlem 23 TFS, F-15 Eglin wing EWO, Desert Storm with 33 TFW Nomads, 58 TFS Gorillas, defense contractor with Sverdrup Technology supporting F-15 & F-16 operational testing, living in Niceville, FL.

116. VAN GEFFEN, THEO W., WW # 2219, MEMBER HISTORY COMMITTEE FINANCIAL ADMINISTRATOR VET. FACULTY, UTRECHT UNIVERSITY, HOLLAND.
117. White, Larry, WW # 1716, Maj USAF (Ret), F-4G Spangdahlem 81 TFS, 23 TFS, EA-6B Whidbey Island VAQ-128, Staff - 65 AD, 17 AF, EUCOM, Incirlik, now a lawyer working with the Turkish-American Association, Ankara, Turkey
118. Willard, Garry A., WW # 5, Brigadier General retired in Florida
119. Willets, Gary W. "Hack!" #2199, F-4D/E/G, F-15E, Lt. Col, USAF, current: Chief, Advanced Programs Branch, HQ USAFE, Ramstein AB, Germany
120. Wilson, Tom, #160, Weasel EWO. Retired L/C, writer-novelist. Resides in big thicket country of East Texas.
121. Zorn, Thomas O., WW # 1049, KIA

Appendix A F-105 Wild Weasel Combat Losses SEA

F-105 Wild Weasel Combat Losses SEA

(Chronological Order)

NAME	WW #	DOWNED BY	RESCUED	POW	MIA/KIA
Hestle	83	Guns			X
Morgan	71	Guns			X
Pemberton	183	SAM			X
Newsom	184	SAM			X
Larson	176	SAM	X		
Gilroy	174	SAM	X		
Sandvick	186	Guns		X	
Pyle	182	Guns		X	
Brand	123	Guns			X
Singer	284	Guns			X
Brinkmann	79	SAM			X
Scungio	99	SAM			X
Biedger	165	Drop Tank			X
Silva	169	Drop Tank			X
Duart	143	SAM		X	
Kensen	145	SAM		X	
Everson	164	Guns		X	
Luna	163	Guns		X	
Madison	133	MiG-17		X	
Sterling	136	MiG-17		X	
Dudash	144	SAM			X
Meyer	146	SAM			X
Thorsness	173	MiG-21		X	
Johnson	167	MiG-21		X	
Davis	353	Hit Tree	X		
Walker	361	Hit Tree	X		
McDaniel	311	Guns			X
Lillund	321	Guns			X
Howard	350	MiG-21	X		
Shamblee	348	Mig-21	X		

Dutton	373	Guns		X	
Cobeil	377	Guns		X	
Gustafson	355	Eng. Failure	X		
Brownlee	359	Eng. Failure	X		
Fitton	404	SAM			X
Harris	405	SAM			X
Gustafson	355	SAM	X		
Brownlee	359	SAM	X		
Hartney	323	MiG-17			X
Fantle III	336	MiG-17			X
Fieszel	482	Guns			X
Smith	447	Guns			X
Mallon	748	Guns			X
Panek	751	Guns			X
Hurst	Unknown	Guns	X		
Bevan	699	Guns	X		
Kilgus	835	SAM	X		
Lowry	848	SAM	X		
McIntire	434	SAM			X
Belli	967	SAM			X
Stone	753	Eng. Failure			X
Cutter	993	SAM		X	
Fraser	994	SAM		X	
Mateja	1029	SAM			X
Jones	1028	SAM			X
Talley	554	MiG-21		X	
Padget	166	MiG-21		X	
Coady	969	Drop Tank	X		
Murphy	614	Drop Tank	X		
Zorn	1049	SAM			X
Turose	1045	SAM			X
O'Neil	72	SAM		X	
Bosiljevac	1015	SAM		X	X
Thaete	923	SAM	X		
Maier	177	SAM	X		

Appendix B
F-105 Losses 1965 – 1972

F-105 Losses 1965 - 1972

Year	F-105 Strike Combat Losses	Operational Losses	F-105 Wild Weasel Combat Losses	Total Losses
1965	60	8	0	68
1966	105	16	6	127
1967	77	15	10	102
1968	29	12	5	46
1969	14	5	0	19
1970	4	3	3	10
1971	0	-	1	1
1972	0	2 (F-105G)	7	9
Totals	289	61	32	382

Appendix C
Glossary

This section contains a glossary of terms found in this book and widely used by Wild Weasel pilots, EWOs, and other airmen during the Vietnam era but not limited to that time.

AAA – Anti Aircraft Artillery

ABCCC – Airborne Battlefield Command and Control Center

AB – Afterburner

Abort – Stop doing what you are doing.

AFSC – Air Force Specialty Code – letters and numbers that identify military jobs.

AGL - Above Ground Level, Altitude above the ground.

AGM-45 SHRIKE – a relatively small, passive air-to-ground missile whose mission is to home on and destroy or suppress radiating radar transmitters, directing both ground antiaircraft fire and surface-to-air missiles. Relatively short range weapon with relatively small warhead that could only be launched well inside the range of enemy SAM threats.

AGM-78 Standard ARM - a relatively large, passive air-to-ground missile whose mission is to home on and destroy or suppress radiating radar transmitters, directing both ground antiaircraft fire and surface-to-air missiles. Relatively long range with relatively large warhead and could be launched outside the range of many ground radar threats.

AGM-88 HARM – A follow-on ARM to the AGM-78 Standard ARM and used extensively in the Gulf War. The AGM-88 High-Speed Anti-radiation Missile (HARM) is an air-to-surface tactical missile designed to seek out and destroy enemy radar-equipped air defense systems.

Alpha Strike Packages – The package of Air Force fighters used to attack targets in the route package 6A area around Hanoi usually about 40 strike and supporting fighter aircraft. (24 Strike Aircraft, 8 Wild Weasels, 8 Interceptors)

Anchor – as in Red Anchor, Black Anchor and so forth. Refueling tracks flown by KC-135 refueling tankers flown over Thailand, Laos and the Gulf of Tonkin or anywhere.

AMMO – Ammunition

APR-25/26 – Military nomenclature for first generation Radar Warning Receiver (RWR) used in most aircraft during the Vietnam War

Arc Light – SAC B-52 operations in SEA prior to Linebacker II

ARM – Anti-Radiation Missile

Barlock – NATO code name for GCI radar found in many enemy countries

BDA – Bomb Damage Assessment

Bear – Wild Weasel Electronic Warfare Officer and/or Basic Electronic Analysis, Rearseat (BEAR)

Big Eye – USAF EC-121 airborne warning and control aircraft (later referred to as College Eye)

Bingo – Predetermined fuel level that warns the pilot to leave for refueling or home base.

Break – a very hard, high-G turn usually made to attempt to cause enemy fighters to overshoot or avoid other hazards

Brigham – Call Sign for Ground Control Intercept (GCI) radar located at Udorn, Thailand

CAP – Combat Air Patrol, also used when orbiting a location such as a downed aircrew.

CBUs – cluster bomb units – bomblets usually carried in bombs, each bomblet is about the size of a baseball and used primarily against personnel or light armor.

Chopper – a helicopter, Jolly Green Giant Rescue helicopter.

Chute – parachute

Cong – slang for Vietcong; enemy military

Crown – Airborne Rescue Command Post (later called King)

DCO – Deputy Commander for Operations, usually a full Colonel in charge of flying operations

DF – Direction Finding often used to help locate downed airmen and/or rendezvous with the refueling tanker or other aircraft.

Debrief – after action session with maintenance and intelligence reviewing aircraft status and mission results

Delta Sierra – substitute for vulgar term used by pilots and others to denote something is bad (Dog Shit). Like, the weather in the target area is Delta Sierra.

DMZ – Demilitarized Zone Dividing North and South Vietnam

Dragchute – a parachute deployed after landing to help the aircraft decelerate and reduce the landing roll.

Eagle – F-15

EGT – Exhaust Gas Temperature (observed by the aircrew on a gauge inn the cockpit.)

Eject – Bailing out of the aircraft by pulling the ejection handles and/or squeezing the ejection triggers.

FAC – Forward Air Controller, could be on the ground with the Army/ Marines or Airborne in light aircraft.

Fan Song – NATO Code name for the SA-2 SAM system

Fast FAC – FACs who flew jets. In Vietnam Fast FACs normally flew F-100s or A-7s

Feet Wet/Feet Dry – operating over water or over land.

Firecan – NATO code name for WW II vintage AAA fire control radar

Flak – smoke and shrapnel caused by anti-aircraft artillery shells exploding at pre-set times after firing. 37mm made gray smoke, larger shells made black smoke.

Frag – Fragmentary order. The daily tasking for Air Force operational units in combat. Each unit received only the fragment of the overall operational order that pertained to their tasking thus a small portion or fragment of the overall plan.

G/Gs/G Force(s) – the force of gravity exerted on a pilots body by turning the aircraft of puling back/pushing forward on the stick. If the pilot pulls 4 Cs he weighs four times his normal weight.

GIB – Guy in the back seat, refers to pilots, navigators, or others flying in the rear cockpit of fighters

Guideline Missile – The SA-2 system normally consisted of a radar van, six "Guideline" missiles on six missile launchers with the radar van located in the middle of a modified Star-of-David layout pattern. The SA-2B had a maximum range of approximately 20 nautical miles and a maximum speed of about Mach 3.5.

Haiphong – Major port of North Vietnam

Hanoi – Capital of North Vietnam

HARM or AGM-88 – High-Speed Anti-radiation Missile (HARM) Follow-on weapon to AGM-78 Standard ARM. Homes on and destroys enemy radar emitters.

Hilton/Hanoi Hilton – prison used to house Prisoners of War in Hanoi, North Vietnam.

Ho Chi Minh Trail – Network of roads and trails from North Vietnam through Laos and Cambodia to South Vietnam used by North Vietnam for infiltration and re-supply of Communist forces in South Vietnam

Hootch – living quarters

IFR – Instrument Flight Rules; or, in-flight refueling

Iron Hand – Code name for Wild Weasel Flights performing defense suppression/destruction missions.

Jink – rapid and unpredictable turns of the aircraft to confuse ground gunners and defeat the anti aircraft artillery or automatic weapons firing solution.

Jolly, Jolly Green, or Jolly Green Giant – Code name for HH-3 and HH-53 rescue helicopter.

Karst – Jagged limestone protrusions forming mountains common in North Vietnam, Laos, Thailand and China.

KIA – Killed in action.

King – Airborne rescue command post (earlier called Crown)

Knot or Knots – speed in nautical miles per hour. One nautical mile is 6080 feet.

KTO - Kuwaiti Theater of Operations.

Linebacker I – Air campaign against North Vietnam, April to November 1972

Linebacker II – Air campaign against North Vietnam, December, 1972

MAYDAY – international distress call.

MIA – Missing in action

MiG – Russian fighter aircraft from the Mikoyan design facility. For example the MiG-15 and so forth.

MiGCAP or MiG CAP – MiG Combat Air Patrol. An air superiority mission usually for protection of the strike force.

Misty – Radio call sign of Commando Sabre F-100F fast FAC aircraft.

O-Club – Officers' Club

PCS – Permanent change of station – a military move from one duty station to new duty station

PE – Personal Equipment – the flying clothing and other equipment worn by aircrews.

Pipper – the center of the gun sight used to aim the weapons.

PJ/PJs – Para-rescue jumpers that rode on the HH-53 Jolly Green Giant helicopters for rescuing downed aircrews

POL – Petroleum, oil and lubricant (anything from a barrel of oil to an oil/fuel tank storage farm)

POW – Prisoner of War

Punchout/Punch – eject/bailout from the aircraft

R & R – Rest and Recuperation – a vacation

Red Crown – USN early warning and control ship stationed in the Gulf of Tonkin.

RESCAP – flying over a downed aircrew or participation in an aircrew rescue operation

RHAW – Radar Homing and Warning - electronic equipment that warns the aircrew of electronic directed threats including surface to air missiles, anti aircraft artillery and interceptors.

ROE – Rules of Engagement

Route Package/Route Pack – North Vietnam was divided into six numbered geographical areas or Route Packages. Route Package I was closest to the DMZ and Route Package VI was the northern most and extended to the Chinese border. The Navy had primary responsibility in Route Packages II, III, IV and VI B. The Air Force had primary responsibility in Route Packages I, V, and VI A. Route Package VI was divided in half and the Air Force had the Western half (VI A) and the Navy the Eastern half (VI B).

Rolling Thunder – US air campaign against North Vietnam from March 1965 until October 1968.

RTB – Return to base

SA-2 – The SA-2 radar code name was "Fan Song". The system was the primary surface-to-air missile (SAM) threat employed by the North Vietnamese during the Vietnam War. The SA-2 system was designed, built, supplied to the North Vietnamese, and sometimes operated by the Russians. American reconnaissance aircraft detected the first signs of this weapon in North Vietnam during April 1965. On 24 July 65 a SAM site located Northwest of Hanoi fired on a flight of four F-4Cs, downing one and damaging the other three.

SAIC – Science Applications International Corporation. Commercial and government contractor.

Saigon – Capital of South Vietnam

SAM – Surface to Air Missile

Sandy – Radio call sign for A-1 and later A-7 rescue escort aircraft.

SAR – Search and Rescue Mission

SEA – Southeast Asia

SEAD – Suppression of Enemy Air Defenses

Sierra Hotel – substitute for vulgar term used by pilots to denote something good or hot. (Shit Hot)

Spad – Nickname for aircraft, usually A-1Es, used to escort Jolly Green rescue helicopters and coordinate rescue efforts of downed airmen

Strafing/Strafe – firing the 20mm cannon at a surface target

Tally/Tally Ho – I have you/it in sight.

Thud – F-105 Aircraft

Thud Ridge – mountain ridge located north west of Hanoi, North Vietnam and frequently used by pilots at the run in for targets in the Hanoi area.

Tango Uniform – substitute for vulgar term used by pilots (Tits Up) to indicate something is dead or inoperative. Such as "My radar is Tango Uniform."

Tanker – Airborne refueling station. Such as a KC-135 tanker

Viper – F-16

Wild Weasel – Specially trained and equipped aircraft and crew with the mission to destroy and/or suppress enemy air defenses, especially SAM sites.

Appendix - D

"First In ..." **a combat painting by** Keith Ferris
First Wild Weasel SAM kill, North Vietnam, 22 December 1965

Order Form

Please send me ___ (quantity) Limited Edition (#1 - 1,000) 20"x 31" Lithograph Print(s) of **"First In ..."** signed by **Keith Ferris** at **$150.00 each plus shipping:**

Artist note requested: ______________________________

____

____

Artist note requested: ______________________________

____

____

TOTAL PRINTS: ____ ***x $150.00 + Shipping ($10.00*** *US & APO*, ***$18.00*** *Overseas*)**= $ ______________** *. 00* **DUE:**

Check or Money Order) *to:* **Wild Weasel Foundation, LLC**. Ck. #______________ Date______________

Signature____

Name (Print please):

____

Shipping Address, (<u>No</u> P.O. Boxes, please) Street:

____

___________________________City_______________
State: ______________**Zip:** _________**Country:**_________

Phone: ( )____________E-Mail:__________@__________

Mail this with Check or M/O to: **Wild Weasel Foundation, PO Box 7637, Lumberton, North Carolina 28359**
Questions? Allen Lamb 910-739-3181 alamb@lambgroupllc.com or George Acree at 410-647-9511 acree5@comcast.net

Thank you for your order, The Wild Weasel Foundation **MO 032503V17**
CAVE PUTORIUM! (Beware The Weasel)

"First In...."

By Keith Ferris

Facing the heaviest defenses in the history of aerial warfare, American airmen encountered not only hostile MiG fighters and intense anti-aircraft artillery (AAA) over North Vietnam but, by July of 1965, took losses from Soviet supplied first line SA-2 Surface-to-Air Missile systems (SAM). This SAM threat was answered by the rapid development and deployment of the Wild Weasel "hunter-killer" force using dedicated Radar Homing and Warning (RHAW) signal analysis SAM locating systems installed in Wild Weasel F-100F fighter attack aircraft. Flown by teams consisting of a Fighter Pilot and Electronic Warfare Officer (EWO), the Wild Weasel crews would identify and locate SAMs by exposing their aircraft to the SAM radars. They evaded missile and gunfire to strike the sites with 20 mm guns and 2.75" rockets. To augment this firepower, the F-100F would be accompanied by a strike flight of four F-105D fighters also armed with 20 mm guns and rockets. Wild Weasel missions were among the most dangerous flown over North Vietnam. This painting depicts the first successful destruction of a SAM site by a Wild Weasel hunter-killer team.

Captain Allen Lamb, the Fighter Pilot, Wild Weasel No. 16 and Captain Jack Donovan, the EWO, Wild Weasel No. 15) in F-100F number 58-1226 (Spruce 5) flying from Korat RTAB, Thailand on 22 December 1965 are seen attacking the threatening SAM site near Phu Tho on the Red River northwest of Hanoi. The accompanying F-105Ds were manned by Spruce Flight Leader: Captain Don Langwell, Spruce 2: Captain Van Heywood, Spruce 3: Captain Bob Bush and Spruce 4: Captain Art Brattkus. This hard won success came after the Wild Weasels had been in action for twenty-two days after Captain John Pitchford and Captain Bob Trier became the first Wild Weasels lost to North Vietnamese surface to air defenses.

This painting, entitled *"First In...."* commemorates that first SAM kill, honor fallen Wild Weasels and remember the Wild Weasel motto: 'First in....Last Out" of the combat arena always protecting the strike force.

Internationally known aviation artist Keith Ferris specifically for The Wild Weasels Foundation, LLC, created the Painting "First In.". It is dedicated to those who developed the Wild Weasel concept, systems and tactics, and all who have flown and supported Wild Weasel combat missions ever since.

The painting has been reproduced in a signed and numbered limited edition of 1000 Fine Art Prints and in a signed and numbered limited edition of thirty Digital Giclee Canvas Prints.

The original painting has been presented to the U. S. Air Force Art Collection by the Wild Weasel Foundation for permanent display in the Wild Weasel exhibit at the Air Force Museum in Dayton, Ohio, USA.

The Wild Weasel Foundation, LLC, Post Office Box 7637 Lumberton, North Carolina 28359

About the Editor

Colonel Edward T. Rock retired from the United States Air Force in 1977 after nearly 27 years in uniform. He entered the United States Air Force in July 1950 at the age of 18 when he enlisted shortly after graduation from Dixon High School. He graduated from the United Stated Air Force Radio Mechanics course and the Radio Repairmen course and then was selected for pilot training in the spring of 1952. He became a fighter pilot and in March 1954 was sent to K-55, Osan, Korea where he was assigned to the 18th Fighter Bomber Wing, flying the F-86F. Subsequently he flew many different aircraft including the F-100, F-104, F-105, and F-4. He has combat missions in the F-105, F-4 and EB-66. He completed two combat tours in Southeast Asia flying mostly as an F-105 Wild Weasel pilot. He retired from the Air Force in 1977 and returned to his home town, Dixon, IL where he was the Director of the local Chamber of Commerce and later the Chief Pilot and Engineering Test Supervisor, Woods Division of Heston Corp. He then moved to St. Louis, MO where he was employed by McAir/McDonnell-Douglas/Boeing primarily as Manager Engineering. He retired from Boeing in 1997. He is the co-holder of two US Patents. His military awards and decorations include the two Silver Stars, the Legion of Merit, three Distinguished Flying Crosses, and seventeen Air Medals. He resides in Chesterfield, MO.

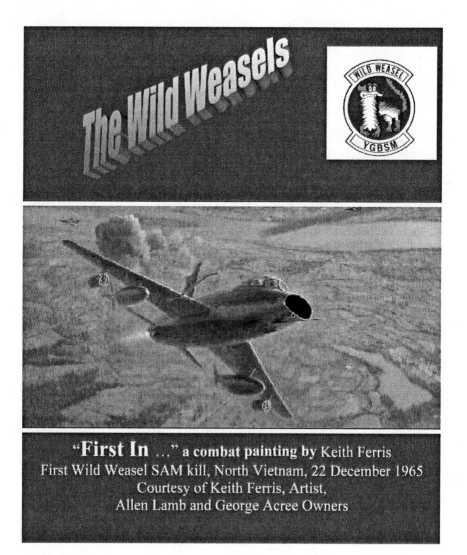

"First In ..." **a combat painting by** Keith Ferris
First Wild Weasel SAM kill, North Vietnam, 22 December 1965
Courtesy of Keith Ferris, Artist,
Allen Lamb and George Acree Owners

Printed in the United States
50713LVS00003B/1